The World's Most Notorious OUTLAWS, MOBSTERS and CROOKS

The World's
Most Notorious
OUTLAWS,
MOBSTERS
and CROOKS

AN IMPRINT OF THE GALE GROUP

DETROIT · SAN FRANCISCO · LONDON
BOSTON · WOODBRIDGE, CT

THE CRIME ENCYCLOPEDIA

by Marie J. MacNee

STAFF

Jane Hoehner, *U•X•L Senior Editor*
Carol DeKane Nagel, *U•X•L Managing Editor*
Thomas L. Romig, *U•X•L Publisher*

Rita Wimberley, *Senior Buyer*
Evi Seoud, *Assistant Production Manager*
Dorothy Maki, *Manufacturing Manager*

Jessica L. Ulrich, *Permissions Associate*
Margaret Chamberlain, *Permissions Specialist*

Michelle DiMercurio, *Art Director*
Tracey Rowens, *Senior Art Director*
Cynthia Baldwin, *Product Design Manager*
Barbara J. Yarrow, *Graphic Services Supervisor*

Marco Di Vita, Graphix Group, *Typesetting*

Contents

Reader's Guide

"History is nothing more than a tableau of crimes and misfortunes," wrote eighteenth-century French writer Voltaire. There certainly is more to history than criminal deeds, misdemeanors, and misfortunes, but these offenses do offer fascinating lessons in history. The life stories of outlaws provide a glimpse into other times and other places, as well as provocative insight into contemporary issues.

Who's Included

The first part of *The Crime Encyclopedia,* "Outlaws, Mobsters & Crooks," presents the life stories of seventy-three outlaws who lived (or committed crimes) in North America from the seventeenth century to the present day—from Blackbeard, the British-born pirate who terrorized the Carolina coast, to terrorist Timothy McVeigh.

Everyone's familiar with Bonnie and Clyde, Butch Cassidy, and Al Capone. But how many know the *whole* story: what their childhoods were like, what their first crime was, who worked with them—and against them—and how they ended up? *The Crime Encyclopedia* offers a thorough and provocative look at the people and events involved in these stories.

Familiar figures such as Jesse James and Billy the Kid are present, as are lesser-known outlaws whose careers reveal much about the times in which they lived. Cattle Kate, for instance, was little more than a cattle rustler, but her story provides insight into the cattle wars of nineteenth-century Nebraska and the tensions that led to the Lincoln County War. Also included are outlaws such as Calamity Jane, whose main crime was unconventionality, and lawmen who sometimes stood on the wrong side of the law. The many men and women who have been labeled outlaws over the course of three centuries cannot all be profiled in one volume.

But those whose stories are told in *The Crime Encyclopedia* include some of the best known, least known, weirdest, scariest, most despised, and least understood outlaws. In short, this work is intended as an overview of North American criminals—a jumping-off point for further inquiry.

LEGENDS, MYTHS, AND OUTRIGHT LIES

Many of the men and women profiled have been surrounded by legends that have grown to enormous proportions, making it very difficult to separate fact from fiction: Billy the Kid killed one man for every year of his life (he probably killed no more than six men); Jesse James lived to old age as a gentleman farmer (he was shot in the back of the head by Robert Ford at the age of thirty-four); Black Hand extortionists could bring bad luck to their victims simply by giving them "the evil eye" (they brought them bad luck, all right, but it was usually accomplished with a gun). In some cases, legends have fed on the published accounts of the criminals themselves—or the lawmen who pursued them. Some are accurate first-person accounts. Others are sensational exaggerations of true events—or wholesale fabrications. *The Crime Encyclopedia* attempts to present a fair and complete picture of what is known about the lives and activities of the seventy-three outlaws profiled. When appropriate, entries mention the myths, unconventional theories, and alternate versions of accepted history that surround a particular outlaw—without suggesting they are truthful or fact-based.

ARRANGEMENT AND PRESENTATION

The Crime Encyclopedia is arranged in a single volume. To enhance the usefulness of the volume, the seventy-three entries have been grouped into ten categories: Mobsters, Racketeers and Gamblers, Robbers, Computer Criminals, Spies, Swindlers, Terrorists, Bandits and Gunslingers, Bootleggers, and Pirates. Within each category, entries—which range from three to eleven pages in length—are arranged alphabetically by the outlaw's last name. The only exceptions to this arrangement are those outlaws who are listed by their "common" name, such as Billy the Kid or Black Bart; these entries are listed alphabetically by the first letter in that name. Aliases and birth names are presented when available. Each entry includes the birth and death dates of the subject (or the period during which he, she, or the gang was active). Part Two of *The Crime Encyclopedia,* "Murder Trials," brings to life 19 of history's most notable murder trials.

Entries are lively, easy to read, and written in a straightforward style that is geared to challenge—but not frustrate—readers. Difficult words are defined within the text; some words also include pronunciations. Technical words and legal terms are also explained within entries, enabling readers to learn the vocabulary appropriate to a particular subject without having to consult other sources for definitions.

WHAT'S INSIDE

A detailed look at what they did, why they did it, and how their stories ended. Entries focus on the entire picture—not just the headline news—to provide the following sorts of information:

- **Personal background:** interesting details about the subject's family, upbringing, and youth

- **Crimes and misdeeds:** an in-depth look at the subject's outlaw history

- **Aftermath:** from jail time, to legal and illegal executions, to mysterious disappearances, entries relate what happened after the dirty deeds were done

- **A look at the other side of the law:** Many entries also provide extensive information on the other side of the law, for example, the brilliant astronomer who tracked a West German hacker, the FBI agents who hounded John Dillinger and Al Capone, and the frontier judge who earned the nickname "the hanging judge."

ADDED FEATURES

The Crime Encyclopedia includes a number of additional features that help make the connection between people, places, and historic events.

- A timeline at the beginning of the volume provides a listing of outlaw landmarks and important international events.

- Sidebars provide fascinating supplemental information, such as sketches of criminal associates, profiles of law enforcement officials and agencies, and explanations of the political and social scenes of the era, for example, the anti-communist hysteria that consumed the United States at the time of the Rosenberg trial. Sidebars also offer a contemporary perspective of people and events through excerpts of letters written by the outlaw profiled, citations from newspapers and journals of the day, and much more.

- 139 photographs and illustrations bring the outlaws and trials to life.

- Suggestions for related books and movies—both fictional and fact-based—are liberally sprinkled throughout the entries.

- A list of sources for further reading at the end of each entry lists books, newspaper and magazine articles, and Internet addresses for additional and bibliographical information.

SPECIAL THANKS

The author would like to thank U•X•L Senior Editor Jane Hoehner, Permissions Associate Jessica L. Ulrich, and the research staff—particularly Maureen Richards—of Gale Research for their invaluable help and guidance. The author would also like to thank the staff of the Grosse Pointe Library for their gracious assistance.

Outlaws
Alphabetically

Timeline

Spring 1718: Edward Teach—also known as **Blackbeard**—and his crew of pirates blockade the city of Charleston, South Carolina.

November 1718: Thomas Spotswood, the governor of Virginia, issues a proclamation offering rewards for the capture—dead or alive—of **Blackbeard** and his shipmates.

November 22, 1718: A navy crew led by Lieutenant Robert Maynard attacks **Blackbeard**'s pirate ship near the Carolina coast. The severed head of Blackbeard is hung from the bowsprit of the navy ship.

1720: Captain Woodes Rogers, the governor of the Bahamas, issues a proclamation naming Calico Jack Rackam, **Anne Bonny,** and Mary Read as enemies of England.

May 9, 1800: Joseph Baker and two other pirates are hanged in a public execution in Philadelphia, Pennsylvania.

March 11, 1831: Charles Gibbs and Thomas G. Wansley are convicted of murder and piracy in New York.

March 19, 1831: An Englishman named Edward Smith commits the first bank heist in American history when he robs the City Bank in New York City.

April 22, 1831: Pirates **Charles Gibbs** and Thomas G. Wansley are hanged on Ellis Island in New York in front of thousands of onlookers.

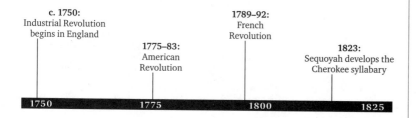

c. 1750:
Industrial Revolution
begins in England

1789–92:
French
Revolution

1775–83:
American
Revolution

1823:
Sequoyah develops the
Cherokee syllabary

1750   1775   1800   1825

July 11, 1859: Gold thief **Richard Barter** is shot and killed by Sheriff J. Boggs in the California foothills.

1861: Shortly after the Civil War breaks out, **Elizabeth Van Lew,** a Union sympathizer who lives inside the Confederacy, begins to send information about the Southern war effort to Northern officers.

February 13, 1866: Jesse James and the James-Younger Gang rob the Clay County Savings and Loan Bank in Liberty, Missouri.

April 5, 1866: Bill Miner enters San Quentin penitentiary after being convicted of armed robbery. He is released after serving a little more than four years of his sentence.

January 23, 1871: Bill Miner and two accomplices rob a California stagecoach using stolen guns. He returns to San Quentin the following June.

October 9, 1871: Swindler **Sophie Lyons** is convicted of grand larceny and sentenced to serve time in Sing Sing prison.

December 19, 1872: Sophie Lyons escapes from Sing Sing prison using a forged key.

1873: The James-Younger Gang commits its first train robbery.

1874: Gunslinger **Clay Allison** commits his first recorded killing.

July 26, 1875: Charles Boles—better known as **Black Bart**—commits the first in a series of stagecoach robberies near Copperopolis, California.

August 3, 1877: Black Bart robs his fourth stagecoach, leaving behind a poem signed "Black Bart, the PO 8 [poet]."

1878: Martha Jane Cannary—known as **Calamity Jane**—acts as a nurse during a smallpox epidemic in Deadwood, Dakota Territory.

1861–65:
American
Civil War

1868:
The Fourteenth
Amendment to the
Constitution of the
United States is adopted

| 1850 | 1855 | 1860 | 1865 |

Spring 1878: Sam Bass and his gang stage four train holdups around Dallas, Texas.

April 1, 1878: William Bonney—also known as **Billy the Kid**—participates in an ambush that kills Sheriff William Brady in Lincoln County, New Mexico.

July 15, 1878: Texas Rangers wound and capture robber **Sam Bass** in Round Rock, Texas.

1879: Bartholomew "Bat" Masterson is appointed deputy U.S. marshal.

October 7, 1879: The second James Gang robs a train near Glendale, Missouri, of $35,000.

December 1879: Wyatt Earp arrives in lawless Tombstone, Arizona, and is soon joined by brothers James, Morgan, Virgil, and Warren.

July 14, 1880: Bill Miner is released from San Quentin prison after serving nine years for stagecoach robbery. He returns to the California prison the following year.

April 11, 1881: Dallas Stoudenmire becomes marshal of El Paso, Texas.

May 13, 1881: Convicted of murder, **Billy the Kid** is sentenced to hang.

May 25, 1881: Livestock rustler **Curly Bill,** otherwise known as William Brocius, is shot in the mouth during an argument with lawman William Breakenridge.

July 14, 1881: Sheriff Pat Garrett shoots and kills **Billy the Kid.**

October 26, 1881: Wyatt Earp and brothers Morgan and Virgil, joined by Doc Holliday, confront the Clantons and McLauries at the O.K. Corral. The gunfight leaves three men dead.

1877:
Thomas Edison is awarded
the patent for the phonograph

1880:
The Metropolitan
Museum of Art opens in
New York City

| 1870 | 1873 | 1876 | 1879 |

April 3, 1882: **Jesse James** dies in St. Joseph, Missouri, after fellow outlaw Robert Ford shoots him in the back of the head.

June 1882: Pressured by city officials, **Dallas Stoudenmire** resigns from his post as marshal of El Paso.

September 18, 1882: **Dallas Stoudenmire** is shot and killed during a saloon brawl.

1883: **Belle Starr** is the first woman ever to be tried for a major crime in Judge Isaac Parker's infamous "court of the damned."

November 1883: **Black Bart** is captured in San Francisco, California. He pleads guilty to robbery and is sentenced to six years at San Quentin penitentiary.

October 6, 1885: Swindler **Ellen Peck** is convicted of forging a document to obtain $3,000 from the Mutual Life Insurance Company of New York. She is sentenced to four-and-a-half years in prison.

July 3, 1887: **Clay Allison** dies when he is run over by a freight wagon.

November 3, 1887: Robert Leroy Parker—better known as **Butch Cassidy**—and members of the McCarty Gang botch a robbery of the Denver and Rio Grande Express train in Colorado.

1889: Maverick calves stolen from the herds of Wyoming cattle barons find their way into the corral of **Cattle Kate**.

February 3, 1889: **Belle Starr** is ambushed and killed near her home in the Indian Territory by an unidentified gunman.

March 30, 1889: **Butch Cassidy** and other gang members rob the First National Bank of Denver of $20,000 in bank notes.

July 20, 1889: Cattle baron Albert J. Bothwell organizes a group to put an end to **Cattle Kate** and James Averill's cattle rustling. Watson and Averill are lynched.

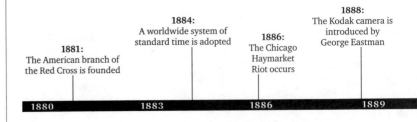

1881:
The American branch of the Red Cross is founded

1884:
A worldwide system of standard time is adopted

1886:
The Chicago Haymarket Riot occurs

1888:
The Kodak camera is introduced by George Eastman

1880   1883   1886   1889

1890s: Black Hand Society extortionists prey on Italian immigrants by threatening violence if their victims do not pay. The Black Hand reign of terror continues for approximately thirty years in Italian Harlem.

1890s: Swindler **Sophie Lyons** opens the New York Women's Banking and Investment Company with fellow con artist Carrie Morse. Before closing, the operation collects at least $50,000 from unsuspecting victims.

November 4, 1890: Marion Hedgepeth and other gangsters rob the Missouri Pacific train near Omaha, Nebraska. The following week they strike the Chicago, Milwaukee & St. Paul train just outside of Milwaukee, Wisconsin.

1892: After a long delay, **Marion Hedgepeth** is tried and convicted of train robbery. He is sentenced to serve twelve to twenty-five years in the state penitentiary.

1894: Posing as the wife of a Danish navy officer, **Ellen Peck** collects more than $50,000 from various banks.

July 4, 1894: Butch Cassidy is tried for cattle rustling. He is convicted and imprisoned.

July 28, 1895: Five young men, known as the **Buck Gang,** begin a murderous thirteen-day crime spree in the Indian Territory to the west of Arkansas.

August 10, 1895: All five members of the **Buck Gang** are captured and taken into custody.

1896: Calamity Jane works for an amusement company in Minneapolis, Minnesota, dressed as an army scout.

January 19, 1896: Butch Cassidy is released from the Wyoming State Penitentiary.

July 1, 1896: Rufus Buck and four other **Buck Gang** members are executed in a mass hanging at Fort Smith, Arkansas.

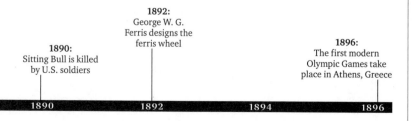

1890:
Sitting Bull is killed by U.S. soldiers

1892:
George W. G. Ferris designs the ferris wheel

1896:
The first modern Olympic Games take place in Athens, Greece

1890   1892   1894   1896

1897: Cassie Chadwick is released from prison after serving three years for fraud. She soon begins to swindle banks by claiming to be the illegitimate daughter of millionaire Andrew Carnegie.

1899: Pearl Hart and Joe Boot rob the Globe stage in the Arizona Territory—in what is recognized as the last American stagecoach robbery.

1900: When Mads Albert Sorenson dies in Chicago, his wife, **Belle Gunness,** is suspected of foul play.

May 1900: Found living in a brothel, **Calamity Jane** travels to Buffalo, New York, where she takes a job performing in a Western show at the Pan-American Exposition.

September 25, 1900: Union spy **Elizabeth Van Lew** dies in Richmond, Virginia, at the age of seventy-two.

July 3, 1901: Butch Cassidy and the Wild Bunch raid the Great Northern Flyer train near Wagner, Montana. It is the gang's final heist.

December 19, 1902: Pearl Hart leaves Yuma prison following an eighteen-month imprisonment.

August 1, 1903: Ravaged by alcoholism, **Calamity Jane** dies near Deadwood, Dakota Territory.

September 13, 1904: Bill Miner and others rob an express train outside of Vancouver, Canada.

December 7, 1904: Swindler **Cassie Chadwick** is arrested in New York. She is later convicted of six counts of fraud and sentenced to ten years in the Ohio State Penitentiary.

1905: Wealthy Brooklyn, New York, butcher Gaetano Costa refuses to pay a **Black Hand** extortionist and is shot to death in his shop.

1902:
Cuba achieves independence

1903:
The Hay-Bunau-Varilla Treaty is negotiated, giving the U.S. control of the Panama Canal

1898:
The Spanish-American War begins

| 1898 | 1900 | 1902 | 1904 |

1906: Cassie Chadwick dies at the age of forty-eight in the prison hospital at Ohio State Penitentiary.

1906: Belle Gunness begins to place personal ads in newspapers in Chicago and other cities in the Midwest to lure wealthy men to her Indiana farm.

1908: Joseph Weil works with Fred "the Deacon" Buckminster to trick clients into paying to have them paint buildings with a phony waterproofing substance. It is the first in a series of scams committed by Weil over the next twenty-five years.

April 28, 1908: After the farmhouse belonging to **Belle Gunness** burns to the ground, authorities discover the decapitated corpse of a woman in the ruins.

May 22, 1908: Ray Lamphere, **Belle Gunness**'s farmhand, is tried and acquitted of murder. Convicted of arson, he is sentenced to up to twenty years in prison.

1910: The six **Genna brothers**—later known as "the Terrible Gennas"—arrive in the United States from Marsala, Sicily.

January 1, 1910: Former train robber **Marion Hedgepeth** is killed by a policeman during an attempted saloon robbery.

February 22, 1911: Bill Miner commits his last train robbery at Sulfur Springs, Georgia, at the age of sixty-four.

1912: Mexican General Victoriano Huerta condemns soldier **Pancho Villa** to death. A stay of execution is later issued.

1912: The **Genna brothers** become involved in **Black Hand Society** activities in Chicago.

November 6, 1912: Eleven members of New York's Hudson Dusters Gang ambush rival gangster **Owney Madden** at a Manhattan dance hall. Left for dead, Madden lives.

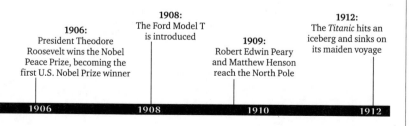

1906:
President Theodore Roosevelt wins the Nobel Peace Prize, becoming the first U.S. Nobel Prize winner

1908:
The Ford Model T is introduced

1909:
Robert Edwin Peary and Matthew Henson reach the North Pole

1912:
The *Titanic* hits an iceberg and sinks on its maiden voyage

| 1906 | 1908 | 1910 | 1912 |

1913: Forty-one-year-old **Diamond Joe Esposito** spends $65,000 to celebrate his marriage to sixteen-year old Carmela Marchese.

1913: *Why Crime Does Not Pay,* the autobiography of veteran swindler **Sophie Lyons,** is published.

September 2, 1913: Veteran stagecoach and train robber **Bill Miner** dies in a prison hospital in Georgia.

November 28, 1914: Owney Madden kills rival New York gangster Patsy Doyle. Sentenced to twenty years for the murder, he is released after serving nine years.

March 9, 1916: Pancho Villa and a gang of Villistas (followers of Villa) attack a small New Mexico border town and military camp, killing seventeen Americans.

1917: The obituary of stagecoach robber **Black Bart** appears in New York newspapers. Some people suspect that the death notice is a hoax engineered by the outlaw.

May 24, 1918: Bugs Moran is convicted of armed robbery and sentenced to serve time at Joliet State Prison in Illinois.

November 24, 1918: Bank robbers **Margie Dean** and husband Dale Jones are shot to death in their car by police near Los Angeles, California.

1919: Racketeer **Arnold Rothstein** masterminds the "Black Sox scandal"—the fixing of the 1919 World Series.

1919: Al Capone, a gunman for New York's notorious James Street Gang, moves to Chicago to escape arrest on a murder charge.

December 1919: Swindler **Charles Ponzi** launches an eight-month get-rich-quick scam using international postal reply coupons.

1914:
World War I begins

1917:
Russian Revolution

1918:
Kaiser Wilhelm II of Germany
abdicates the throne

1914   1916   1918   1920

1920: A grand jury meets in Chicago to investigate the 1919 Black Sox scandal.

1920: The **Genna brothers** turn Chicago's Little Italy into a vast moonshine operation.

May 8, 1924: Former swindler **Sophie Lyons** is attacked in her home. She dies later that evening in Grace Hospital in Detroit.

September 6, 1924: John Dillinger and Edgar Singleton rob an Indiana grocer, for which Dillinger is later sentenced to ten to twenty years in prison.

November 10, 1924: Chicago gangster Charles Dion O'Banion is assassinated in his North Side flower shop.

1925: Charles Ponzi is released from prison after serving four years in a Plymouth, Massachusetts, prison for mail fraud.

January 12, 1925: O'Banion gangsters attempt to ambush **Al Capone** by firing into the gangster's limousine. Capone is not injured.

January 24, 1925: Johnny Torrio, who rules Chicago's South Side bootlegging empire with **Al Capone,** is ambushed by rival gangsters.

June 13, 1925: A car filled with Genna gunmen ambushes **Bugs Moran** and Vincent "the Schemer" Drucci on Michigan Avenue in downtown Chicago. Both are wounded—but not killed.

September 20, 1926: Chicago gangster **Hymie Weiss** leads a squad of North Side gangsters in an attempt to ambush **Al Capone** at the Hawthorne Inn, the gangster's Cicero headquarters. Although more than one thousand bullets rip into the building, Capone escapes without injury.

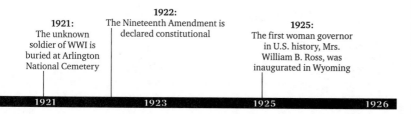

1921:
The unknown soldier of WWI is buried at Arlington National Cemetery

1922:
The Nineteenth Amendment is declared constitutional

1925:
The first woman governor in U.S. history, Mrs. William B. Ross, was inaugurated in Wyoming

1921   1923   1925   1926

1927: Wanted in connection with a robbery, **Ma Barker**'s boy, Herman, commits suicide during a battle with police in Wichita, Kansas.

1928: The **Purple Gang** trial ends the Cleaners and Dyers War in Detroit.

March 21, 1928: Joe Esposito dies near his Chicago home when machine-gunners fire on him from a car. Esposito is struck by fifty-eight bullets.

November 4, 1928: Racketeer **Arnold Rothstein** is shot at the Park Central Hotel in New York. He dies two days later.

1929: Twenty-year old **Irene Schroeder** abandons her husband to run away with Walter Glenn Dague. The couple soon rob a number of stores and small banks.

January 13, 1929: Former lawman **Wyatt Earp** dies in California at the age of eighty, having outlived his four brothers.

February 14, 1929: Members of **Al Capone**'s gang masquerade as policemen raiding a garage on North Clark Street in Chicago. The St. Valentine's Day Massacre leaves seven people dead.

June 13, 1929: Legs Diamond and his enforcer, Charles Entratta, kill two men at the Hotsy Totsy Club, a Manhattan speakeasy.

1930s: Meyer Lansky, Lucky Luciano, and others work together to help solidify a nationwide crime syndicate. Many former bootleggers and members of gangs such as Detroit's **Purple Gang** join the national syndicate.

November 17, 1930: Sam Battaglia robs Mrs. William Hale Thompson—the wife of the governor of Illinois—of more than $15,000 in jewels.

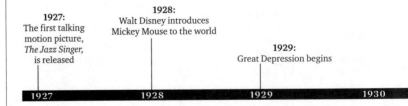

1927:
The first talking motion picture, *The Jazz Singer,* is released

1928:
Walt Disney introduces Mickey Mouse to the world

1929:
Great Depression begins

1927   1928   1929   1930

1931: Veteran gangster Joe "the Boss" Maseria is assassinated in a restaurant in Coney Island, New York. **Bugsy Siegel** is among the hitmen.

February 23, 1931: Irene Schroeder is executed at Rockview penitentiary in Pennsylvania. Her partner, Walter Glenn Dague, is executed a few days later.

April 1931: Legs Diamond is shot several times in a drive-by ambush. He survives.

June 1931: Federal officials charge Chicago gangster **Al Capone** with income tax evasion.

September 16, 1931: Three unarmed men are shot to death by **Purple Gang** mobsters. The incident is known as the Collingwood Manor Massacre.

October 1931: Al Capone is convicted of income tax evasion and sentenced to eleven years in prison.

December 17, 1931: Legs Diamond is shot dead by rival gangsters in his hotel room in Albany, New York.

1932: Gangster **Owney Madden** is released from Sing Sing prison. Later that year he is jailed again for parole violation. Released, he retires from the New York underworld.

February 2, 1932: Clyde Barrow is paroled from Eastham prison farm in Ohio—vowing that he will die before returning to prison. Barrow rejoins **Bonnie Parker** and the two embark on a two-year crime spree.

February 8, 1932: Dutch Schultz's gunmen murder Vincent Coll as Coll makes a call from a phone booth.

1931:
The *Star-Spangled Banner* becomes the national anthem of the United States

1932:
Amelia Earhart becomes the first woman to cross the Atlantic in a solo flight

1931

1932

1933: FBI agent Melvin Purvis arrests Chicago gangster **Roger Touhy** for the kidnapping of millionaire William A. Hamm, Jr. Touhy is cleared of the kidnapping, which was engineered by members of the Barker-Karpis Gang.

1933: Murder, Inc.—an enforcement division of the national crime syndicate—is formed under the leadership of **Louis Lepke.**

May 22, 1933: Thanks in part to a petition by friends and relatives, **John Dillinger** is released early from the Michigan City prison in Indiana.

July 22, 1933: Machine Gun Kelly and Albert Bates kidnap oil millionaire Charles F. Urschel from his Oklahoma City mansion.

September 26, 1933: Memphis, Tennessee, police detectives capture kidnappers **Machine Gun Kelly** and Albert Bates.

September 26, 1933: Using guns smuggled by **John Dillinger,** ten prisoners escape from the Michigan City penitentiary in Indiana. Bank robber Harry Pierpont is among the escaped convicts.

1934: Swindler **Charles Ponzi** is deported to Italy as an undesirable alien.

January 1934: The Dillinger Gang falls apart when police arrest **John Dillinger** and others in Tucson, Arizona. Dillinger is extradited to Indiana.

May 23, 1934: Bonnie and Clyde are killed by lawmen as they drive down a back road near Arcadia, Louisiana.

July 22, 1934: Tipped off by the "Lady in Red," FBI agents apprehend **John Dillinger** as he leaves Chicago's Biograph Theater. The gangster, who is recognized as Public Enemy Number One, is shot dead.

1933:
The Twenty-first
Amendment ends
Prohibition

1934:
American child
star Shirley
Temple makes
her first movie

1933   1934

1935: Two Gun Alterie is called as a government witness in the income tax evasion trial of Ralph "Bottles" Capone (brother of **Al Capone**).

1935: New York mayor Fiorello LaGuardia and district attorney Thomas E. Dewey join forces to destroy **Dutch Schultz**'s slot machine empire. Schultz later vows to kill Dewey.

1935: Ray Hamilton, a former associate of outlaws **Bonnie and Clyde,** is put to death in the electric chair.

January 8, 1935: Arthur "Doc" Barker, wanted for killing a night watchman, is captured in Chicago by FBI agent Melvin Purvis.

January 16, 1935: After a four-hour gun battle, **Ma Barker** and her son Fred are killed by lawmen near Lake Weir, Florida.

July 18, 1935: Former bootlegger **Two Gun Alterie** is killed in a machine-gun ambush.

October 23, 1935: Dutch Schultz, a member of the board of the national crime syndicate, is ambushed in a Newark, New Jersey, chophouse with three associates.

1936: Juliet Stuart Poyntz, an American communist and Soviet spy, is seen in Moscow in the company of fellow American and convicted spy George Mink.

May 1936: Alvin Karpis, a member of the Barker-Karpis Gang, is captured in New Orleans, Louisiana. FBI director J. Edgar Hoover personally places him under arrest.

1939: Gangster **Frank Costello** is tried in New Orleans, Louisiana, on charges of tax evasion. The government loses its case because of lack of evidence.

August 24, 1939: Racketeer **Louis Lepke** surrenders to the FBI through newspaper columnist Walter Winchell.

1935:
The Social Security Act is signed by President Franklin D. Roosevelt

1936:
Spanish Civil War begins

1939:
World War II begins

1935   1936   1937   1938

1940: Joseph Weil is sentenced to three years in prison for a mail-fraud charge involving phony oil leases. It is the veteran swindler's final conviction.

October 9, 1942: Roger Touhy and six other prisoners escape from Joliet penitentiary. The escaped convicts are soon placed on the FBI's Most Wanted list.

December 1942: FBI agents capture **Roger Touhy** at a boardinghouse in Chicago.

1943: American Communist Party member **Julius Rosenberg** is recruited by KGB agent Aleksander Feklisov to spy for the Soviet Union.

March 4, 1944: Murder, Inc., chief **Louis Lepke** is executed in the electric chair at Sing Sing prison.

1945: Meyer Lansky and **Bugsy Siegel** begin to establish a gambling hotel in a small western town called Las Vegas, Nevada.

June 1945: Julius Rosenberg arranges for his brother-in-law, David Greenglass, to provide a courier with classified information about the A-bomb.

December 1946: At a gangster summit in Havana, Cuba, **Bugsy Siegel** swears to fellow syndicate members that he has not stolen mob money through his Las Vegas gambling operation.

January 25, 1947: Retired gangster **Al Capone** dies at his mansion in Palm Island, Florida.

June 20, 1947: Bugsy Siegel is shot to death in the living room of **Virginia Hill**'s Beverly Hills mansion.

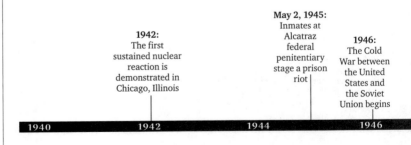

1942:
The first sustained nuclear reaction is demonstrated in Chicago, Illinois

May 2, 1945:
Inmates at Alcatraz federal penitentiary stage a prison riot

1946:
The Cold War between the United States and the Soviet Union begins

1940   1942   1944   1946

1949: Lloyd Barker, the only surviving member of the Barker Gang, is shot to death by his wife.

January 1949: Charles Ponzi dies in the charity ward of a Brazilian hospital at the age of sixty-six.

1950s: Working under **Sam Giancana, Sam Battaglia** becomes chief of the Chicago Outfit's narcotics operations.

May 10, 1950: The Senate Special Committee to Investigate Organized Crime in Interstate Commerce, spearheaded by Senator Estes Kefauver, subpoenas the testimony of numerous gangsters in a year-long attempt to piece together an accurate picture of organized crime in America.

June 15, 1950: Questioned by the FBI, David Greenglass implicates his sister, **Ethel Rosenberg,** and her husband, **Julius,** in espionage.

May 1951: "Queen of the Mob" **Virginia Hill** appears as a key witness before the Kefauver Committee and shocks committee members with her candid responses.

March 6, 1951: Ethel and Julius Rosenberg are tried for conspiracy to commit espionage.

June 19, 1953: In spite of worldwide pleas for clemency, **Ethel and Julius Rosenberg** are electrocuted at Sing Sing prison.

1954: Bank robber and kidnapper **Machine Gun Kelly** suffers a fatal heart attack in Leavenworth prison.

June 23, 1954: A federal grand jury charges **Virginia Hill** with income tax evasion.

1956: Retired swindler **Joseph Weil** is called to testify before a Senate subcommittee, led by Senator Estes Kefauver, investigating juvenile delinquency.

1950: Korean War begins

1953: The first atomic artillery shell is fired

1954: Racial segregation in public schools is declared unconstitutional

1948   1950   1952   1954

1957: Bugs Moran dies from cancer in Leavenworth penitentiary, where he is serving time for bank robbery.

October 25, 1957: Mobster Albert Anastasia is shot to death in the barber shop of the Park Sheraton Hotel in New York City. Rival gangsters **Carlo Gambino** and Vito Genovese are believed to be responsible for ordering the murder.

1959: FBI agents plant a microphone in the backroom of the Forest Park, Illinois, headquarters of mobster **Sam Giancana.**

November 25, 1959: Convicted kidnapper **Roger Touhy** is released from prison after the kidnapping he was found guilty of is revealed to have been a hoax.

December 17, 1959: Former bootlegger **Roger Touhy** is gunned down near his sister's Chicago home.

1960s: The U.S. government begins to subpoena gangster **Carlo Gambino** to appear before the grand jury to investigate his decades-long involvement in organized crime.

1965: After refusing to testify about the mob's activities before a federal grand jury in Chicago, mobster **Sam Giancana** is sentenced to one year in prison.

March 25, 1966: Virginia Hill dies from an overdose of sleeping pills near Salzburg, Austria.

December 1969: Diana Oughton, a former social activist, attends a secret meeting of the Weathermen, a terrorist organization, in Flint, Michigan.

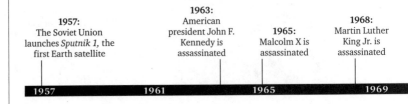

1957:
The Soviet Union launches *Sputnik 1,* the first Earth satellite

1963:
American president John F. Kennedy is assassinated

1965:
Malcolm X is assassinated

1968:
Martin Luther King Jr. is assassinated

| 1957 | 1961 | 1965 | 1969 |

1970: JoAnne Chesimard—also known as Assata Shakur—joins the Black Panther Party.

March 1970: Diana Oughton dies as a bomb explodes in a house in New York City. The house is a bomb factory for Weathermen terrorists.

March 23, 1971: Author **Clifford Irving** signs a contract with McGraw-Hill publishing company to write an authorized biography of billionaire Howard Hughes, who has not been interviewed by journalists since 1958.

November 1971: D. B. Cooper hijacks Northwest Airlines flight 305.

December 1971: Employees of **Jerry Schneider** inform officials at the Pacific Telephone & Telegraph company in Los Angeles, California, that their boss is using access to the phone company's computerized inventory system to order products illegally.

February 1972: Investigators for the Los Angeles District Attorney obtain a search warrant for the business of **Jerry Schneider.** Schneider is later charged with receiving stolen property and sentenced to two months in prison.

March 9, 1972: Author **Clifford Irving** is charged with federal conspiracy to defraud, forgery, and several other charges for writing the fake autobiography of Howard Hughes.

1973: Mobster **Sam Battaglia** dies in prison, having served six years of a fifteen-year sentence for extortion.

February 18, 1973: Retired mobster **Frank Costello** dies of natural causes at the age of eighty-two.

July 4, 1973: "To my people"—a speech in which **JoAnne Chesimard** describes herself as a black revolutionary—is publicly broadcast.

1972:
The Watergate affair—the burglary of Democratic headquarters in Washington, D.C., takes place

1973:
Skylab, the first U.S. space station, is launced

1970   1971   1972   1973

1974: JoAnne Chesimard and fellow Black Liberation Army member Fred Hilton are tried and acquitted of a 1972 bank robbery in New York.

February 4, 1974: Newspaper heiress **Patty Hearst** is kidnapped by members of the Symbionese Liberation Army (SLA).

April 5, 1974: Patty Hearst records a message to announce publicly that she has joined the SLA.

July 29, 1974: College dropout **Christopher Boyce** begins work at TRW Systems, an aerospace firm that works on many classified military programs. The following year Boyce and friend **Andrew Daulton Lee** devise a plan to provide Soviet agents with top-secret information.

June 2, 1975: John Gotti pleads guilty to attempted manslaughter in the second degree for the murder of James McBratney in Staten Island, New York.

September 18, 1975: Patty Hearst is captured with terrorist Wendy Yoshimura in an apartment in San Francisco.

October 15, 1975: Mobster **Carlo Gambino** dies of a heart attack at his home in Long Island, New York, at the age of seventy-three.

October 10, 1976: Convicted telephone thief **Jerry Schneider** appears on a *60 Minutes* television segment called "Dial E for Embezzlement."

1977: Gordon Kahl, a member of the conservative survivalist group called Posse Comitatus, is convicted of failing to file federal income tax returns. He is placed on probation.

March 25, 1977: JoAnne Chesimard is convicted of the murder of a New Jersey state trooper. She is sentenced to life in prison plus more than twenty-five years.

April 1977: Christopher Boyce and Andrew Daulton Lee— the Falcon and the Snowman—are tried for espionage. Both are convicted.

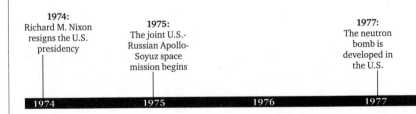

1974:
Richard M. Nixon resigns the U.S. presidency

1975:
The joint U.S.-Russian Apollo-Soyuz space mission begins

1977:
The neutron bomb is developed in the U.S.

1974   1975   1976   1977

November 5, 1978: FBI agents arrest computer thief **Stanley Rifkin** in Carlsbad, California.

January 1979: President Jimmy Carter commutes the prison sentence of convicted bank robber **Patty Hearst.**

February 13, 1979: Released on bail, computer thief **Stanley Rifkin** is arrested for initiating a wire fraud of the Union Bank of Los Angeles. A month later he is convicted of two counts of wire fraud and is sentenced to eight years in federal prison.

November 2, 1979: Convicted murderer **JoAnne Chesimard** escapes from the New Jersey Corrections Institute for women. She later flees to Cuba.

January 1980: Convicted spy **Christopher Boyce** escapes from a federal prison in Lompoc, California. Nineteen months later he is captured and returned to prison—with ninety years added to his original sentence.

April 1980: Two children discover a package containing several dozen $20 bills near Portland, Oregon. The serial numbers are traced to the ransom payment in the **D. B. Cooper** hijacking.

May 28, 1980: John Favara, the man responsible for the accidental killing of gangster **John Gotti**'s twelve-year-old son, disappears. He is never seen again.

January 15, 1983: **Meyer Lansky** dies of cancer in a New York hospital at the age of eighty-one.

February 13, 1983: Federal marshals attempt to serve tax evader **Gordon Kahl** with a warrant for violating parole. A shootout follows, in which two marshals are killed.

May 11, 1983: **Gordon Kahl** and two others are charged with the murders of two federal marshals.

June 4, 1983: **Gordon Kahl** dies in a shootout with federal marshals near Smithville, Arkansas.

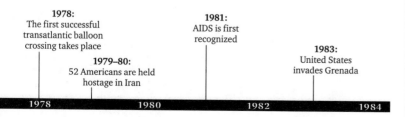

1978:
The first successful transatlantic balloon crossing takes place

1979–80:
52 Americans are held hostage in Iran

1981:
AIDS is first recognized

1983:
United States invades Grenada

1978   1980   1982   1984

April 1985: CIA agent **Aldrich Ames** begins to work as a Soviet spy.

June 2, 1986: San Francisco peace activist **Katya Komisaruk** destroys a government computer on the Vandenberg Air Force base as an anti-nuclear protest.

August 1986: Astronomer Clifford Stoll discovers a seventy-five cent shortfall in his computer system's accounting records. He later discovers that the shortfall is due to an unauthorized user who has broken into the system to access classified information without being traced.

March 13, 1987: Gangster **John Gotti** is tried on charges of racketeering. The "Teflon don" is acquitted.

November 1987: Katya Komisaruk is tried on one count of destruction of government property. During her trial, many supporters appear in court carrying white roses as a symbol of solidarity.

January 11, 1988: Convicted of destroying government property, **Katya Komisaruk** is sentenced to five years in federal prison.

March 2, 1989: Clifford Stoll's investigation of computer records leads to a spy ring of West German computer hackers. **Marcus Hess** and two others are arrested in Hanover, West Germany.

July 1989: Computer hacker **Kevin Mitnick** is sentenced to one year in federal prison at Lompoc, California, for breaking into telephone company computers and stealing long-distance access codes.

1992: John Gotti is tried and convicted of fourteen counts of racketeering and murder after being betrayed by former aide Salvatore "Sammy the Bull" Gravano.

May 12, 1993: The FBI begins a criminal investigation of **Aldrich Ames,** who is suspected of spying for the Soviets.

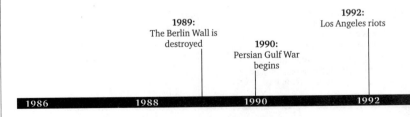

1989:
The Berlin Wall is destroyed

1990:
Persian Gulf War begins

1992:
Los Angeles riots

1986   1988   1990   1992

February 21, 1994: Soviet spy **Aldrich Ames** is arrested as he drives to work at CIA headquarters. He is later convicted of espionage and sentenced to life in prison.

December 24, 1994: Convicted hacker **Kevin Mitnick** steals data from the home computer of computer security expert Tsutomu Shimomura.

February 15, 1995: Federal agents arrest **Kevin Mitnick** in Raleigh, North Carolina, without a struggle.

April 19, 1995: A bomb explodes in front of the Alfred P. Murrah Federal Building in Oklahoma City, Oklahoma, killing 168 people. **Timothy McVeigh** is arrested a short time later.

November 21, 1996: Archaeologists find what they believe to be the long-lost flagship of **Blackbeard** the pirate.

April 1997: The trial of suspected terrorist **Timothy McVeigh** begins in Denver, Colorado.

June 2, 1997: **Timothy McVeigh** is convicted of all eleven charges against him involving the Oklahoma City bombing.

December 1997: A group of hackers break into an Internet site and leave behind a computerized ransom note threatening to release a computer virus if **Kevin Mitnick** is not set free.

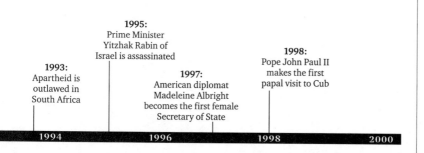

1993:
Apartheid is outlawed in South Africa

1995:
Prime Minister Yitzhak Rabin of Israel is assassinated

1997:
American diplomat Madeleine Albright becomes the first female Secretary of State

1998:
Pope John Paul II makes the first papal visit to Cub

1994   1996   1998   2000

Picture Credits

The photographs and illustrations appearing in *The Crime Encyclopedia* were received from the following sources:

AP/Wide World Photos, Inc. Reproduced by permission: pp. 3, 11, 18, 31, 35, 45, 50, 56, 67, 72, 80, 87, 100, 109, 110, 127, 139, 151, 156, 159, 178, 186, 190, 193, 207, 217, 220, 226, 227, 230, 241, 247, 262, 266, 269, 270, 283, 305, 310, 311, 313, 328, 336, 351, 373, 392, 394, 437, 440, 443, 451, 459, 462; **Archive Photos, Inc. Reproduced by permission:** pp. 13, 21, 89, 121, 235, 292, 378, 410, 450; **UPI/Corbis-Bettmann. Reproduced by permission:** pp. 16, 22, 28, 41, 47, 54, 55, 58, 75, 93, 96, 105, 144, 147, 164, 177, 205, 261, 278, 294, 297, 325, 430, 434, 448, 456, 465; **Photograph by Greta Pratt. New York Times Co./Archive Photos, Inc. Reproduced by permission:** p. 39; **The Granger Collection, New York. Reproduced by permission:** pp. 113, 333, 355, 367, 387, 397, 412, 419, 492; **Popperfoto/Archive Photos, Inc. Reproduced by permission:** p. 133; **Photograph by Tammy Lechner. Los Angeles Times Photo. Reproduced by permission:** p. 189; **Reuters/The News and Observer-Jim/Archive Photos, Inc. Reproduced by permission:** p. 197; **Reuters/Corbis-Bettmann. Reproduced by permission:** p. 221; **Wyoming Division of Cultural Resources. Reproduced by permission:** p. 253; **Reuters/Jim Bourg/Archive Photos. Reproduced by permission:** p. 315; **Photograph by Eric Draper. AP/Wide World Photos, Inc. Reproduced by permission:** p. 317; **American Stock/Archive Photos, Inc. Reproduced by permission:** pp. 341, 347, 368; **The Library of Congress:** p. 360; **Corbis-Bettmann. Reproduced by permission:** pp. 364, 384, 398, 486, 490; **Corbis. Reproduced by permission:** pp. 380, 477, 482.

Murder Trial photographs and illustrations: The Library of Congress, AP/Wide World Photos, Inc., Illinois State Historical Society, National Archives and Records Administration, Hulton-Deutsch Collection, United States Air Force, and the Georgia Department of Archives and History.

Mobsters

Extortion, election-fixing, and murder for hire. Gambling rackets and money laundering. Labor racketeering, narcotics trafficking, and prostitution. From the humble beginnings of pre-Prohibition era gangs to the latter-day nationally organized Mafia, mobsters of this century have transformed illegal opportunities into massive criminal operations.

In this section you'll be introduced to the Black Hand extortionists who preyed on Italian immigrants at the turn of the century, Al Capone's seemingly iron-clad criminal empire, the rise and fall of modern-day godfather John Gotti, and more. The mobsters' stories are filled with fierce loyalty and bitter betrayals, cunning schemes and brutal tactics—and few have happy endings.

1

Sam Battaglia

Born: 1908
Died: 1973

Sam "Teets" Battaglia rose from street crime to the top ranks of a criminal organization known as the Chicago Outfit before he received a prison sentence that ended his career. Over the course of forty years, he racked up more than two dozen arrests for assault, attempted murder, burglary, larceny, robbery, and extortion.

A STREET THUG ON THE RISE

Raised in Chicago, Illinois, Battaglia received very little education. He began a criminal record in 1924, at the age of sixteen, when he was arrested for burglary. During the late 1920s he joined the notorious 42 Gang, a loosely organized group of poor young street thugs. Among the 42 Gang's other members was **Sam Giancana** (see entry), who eventually rose to the top of the Mafia's Chicago Outfit.

Known as a crook with more brawn (muscle) than brains, Battaglia captured the attention of the general public—and other gangsters—when he pulled off a daring robbery on November 17, 1930. Using a gun, he robbed Mrs. William Hale Thompson—the governor's wife—of more than $15,000 in jewels. What's more, he pocketed the gun and badge of her chauffeur, who happened to be a Chicago policeman. Battaglia was arrested for the theft, but the case was eventually dropped. No witness was able to identify the gangster, who produced several witnesses to testify that they had seen him at the movies when the robbery was supposed to have taken place.

3

Forced to testify in court or before senate committees, mobsters often cited the Fifth Amendment. The Fifth Amendment allows an individual to avoid presenting testimony that may be incriminating (testimony that proves their involvement in a crime). When Battaglia appeared before the McClellan Committee he reportedly "took the Fifth" sixty times. Some people claimed that Battaglia had not done so to avoid revealing his role in the mob's activities. Rather, they said he took the Fifth simply to avoid having to speak in public. He was afraid that his poor speech would make him look unintelligent.

MURDER, FRAUD, AND DRUGS

The mobsters in **Al Capone**'s (see entry) Chicago Outfit were impressed with Battaglia's bold approach. Throughout the 1930s he rose through the ranks of the Chicago syndicate (association). Battaglia oversaw the bulk of the mob's loansharking (illegal lending business) which charged unreasonably high interest for loans and used violence as a method to ensure payment. Acting as a sort of judge, Battaglia determined the fate of those who failed to repay their loans. Clients who were late in making payments were brought to a back room at a place called the Casa Madrid by Battaglia's lieutenants. There Battaglia decided his victim's penalty. Some got off lightly with harsh beatings. Others were killed.

By the 1950s Battaglia was also involved in extortion (obtaining money through force or intimidation), fraud, and murder. Working under former 42 gangster Sam Giancana, he became chief of the Chicago Outfit's narcotics (drugs) operations. As the head of this profitable arm of the mob's activities, Battaglia was responsible for selecting the gangsters who were allowed to traffic (deliver) drugs. Having reached one of the highest positions in the Chicago underworld, Battaglia became a wealthy man—a multi-millionaire who owned a retreat in the Illinois countryside and a lavish horse-breeding farm.

GIANCANA STEPS DOWN

By the middle of the 1960s, the reign of Sam Giancana as a Mafia leader was about to end. Hounded by the Federal Bureau of Investigation (FBI), his every move shadowed, he began to draw too much attention to the mob's activities. Paul Ricca and Tony Accardo, Giancana's Mafia superiors, asked him to step down from the top mob position in Chicago. A number of Chicago gangsters wanted the position for themselves—including Battaglia.

Battaglia was, to all appearances, next in the Mafia's chain of command. Giancana wanted Battaglia as his replacement. As

Chicago's 42 Gang

Possibly the worst youth gang ever to arise in an American city, the 42 Gang provided Al Capone's Chicago mob with many young recruits. Founded in 1925, the gang included members as young as nine years old. One of the gang's original leaders was Paul Battaglia, Sam's older brother.

Most of the 42's original members came from an area known as "the Patch"—an Italian section on the city's West Side. At constant war with the Chicago police, gang members held up nightclubs, robbed cigar stores, stripped cars, and stole from peddlers. They also killed the horses that pulled peddlers' carts, and sold their hind legs to businesses that purchased horse meat. In an incident that received a great deal of newspaper coverage, three gang members were caught casing the St. Charles boys' reformatory—where many gang members were serving sentences. The boys admitted that they were looking for a way for machine gunners to enter the reformatory in order to free their fellow gang members. The situation sparked a debate about the sentencing of juvenile criminals. Many people argued that toughened criminals such as 42 Gang members—even if they were children—deserved tougher sentences. *The Chicago Tribune,* for instance, claimed that 42ers deserved one of two sentences: Joliet penitentiary (prison) or the electric chair.

Initially, Capone's gang avoided using 42ers because they were considered to be too violent and unpredictable. Sam Giancana was reportedly the first 42er to be accepted into Capone's gang. A rising star in the underworld, Giancana brought a number of other 42ers into the mob—including Sam Battaglia, Charles Nicoletti, Sam DeStefano, Fifi Buccieri, Frank Caruso, Charles Nicoletti, Rocco Petenza, Marshall Caifano, Milwaukee Phil Alderisio, and Willie Daddano. The old 42 Gang companions who accompanied Giancana into the mob became known as the "Youngbloods." By the 1950s, the Youngbloods had become the foundation of the Chicago Outfit. Although they continued to take orders from the Mafia's old guard—which included Tony Accardo and Paul Ricca—the Youngbloods remained in power until Giancana was assassinated in 1975.

a former 42 gangster and loyal follower, he would be sure to allow the former leader to keep his hand in mob affairs. But in spite of Giancana's wishes, Ricca and Accardo appointed Joey Aiuppa, the head of Chicago's Cicero activities, and Jackie "the Lackey" Cerone, as joint heads of the Chicago Outfit. Battaglia might eventually have mounted a successful bid for the position had it not been for a conviction that resulted in a long imprison-

"Teets" Battaglia

How Battaglia received his nickname—"Teets"—has been the subject of debate. Some say he was so named because he had a well-developed, muscular chest. Others say it derived from his poor speech, or diction. When challenged by other mobsters, he supposedly threatened them by saying, "Shaddup or I'll bust ya in da teets [teeth]!"

ment. Found guilty of extortion, he was sentenced to fifteen years in prison—a term that proved to be a life sentence. Battaglia died in prison in 1973, after serving only six years of his sentence. He was sixty-five years old.

Sources for Further Reading

Sifakis, Carl. *The Mafia Encyclopedia.* New York: Facts on File, 1982, p. 30.

Who's Who in the Mafia. [Online] Available http://home1.pacific.net.sg/~seowjean/Mafia/mafia.html

The Black Hand Society

Active: 1890-1920

The Black Hand Society, a loose collection of Sicilian and Italian gangsters and freelancers, targeted communities across the United States where large numbers of Italian immigrants settled, extorting money from some of the wealthier people by threatening violence if the victim did not pay a fee.

LA MANO NERA

Prior to 1903, extortionists (people who obtain money through force or intimidation) signed their threatening letters with the names of Old World criminal societies, such as the Mafia (which was based in Sicily, an island south of Italy) and the Camorra (based in Naples, Italy). But that year, a case in which an extortionist signed his letters "La Mano Nera" received a great deal of publicity. A sensational story appeared in the *New York Herald,* and other newspapers followed. Soon many extortionists began to sign their letters with the fear-inspiring signature of the Black Hand. Both the press and the criminals themselves helped to create the impression that the Black Hand was an organized society of criminals. Many people eventually used the label—incorrectly—to refer to any violent crime that occurred in Italian neighborhoods in American cities. Although the Black Hand became associated with Italian crime, other national groups operated under the symbol as well.

PAY OR DIE

The extortionist's method was simple. The victim—usually a prominent or wealthy member of the Italian or Sicilian American community—received a letter requesting that he pay a certain fee. The letter was "signed" by an imprint of a hand that had been dipped in black ink. The sender threatened violence if the victim did not pay. One Chicago Black Hander wrote:

> You got some cash. I need $1,000. You place the $100 bills in an envelope and place it underneath a board in the northeast corner of Sixty-ninth Street and Euclid Avenue at eleven o'clock tonight. If you place the money there, you will live. If you don't, you die. If you report this to the police, I'll kill you when I get out. They may save you the money, but they won't save you your life.

Most victims paid without question. Those who refused to pay were sometimes maimed (physically injured)—which gave them the chance to reconsider their refusal. Others were murdered, and sometimes entire families were killed. Black Hand victims were gunned down, knifed, poisoned, and hanged. Often, they were murdered in bomb explosions that killed innocent people in addition to the intended victims.

CHICAGO AND THE SHOTGUN MAN

The Black Hand business in Chicago began around 1890 and reached a peak around 1910 or 1911. Historians have estimated that about eighty unrelated gangs operated in the Black Hand business in Chicago at that time. Bombing was a common punishment for victims who refused to pay their extortionists. Officials estimated that during the thirty-year period from 1900 to 1930, eight hundred bombs had been targeted against Black Hand victims. Many of the bombings leveled entire buildings, killing the families of the intended victims as well as their neighbors. Among the Black Hand enforcers were Frank Campione, Sam Cardinelli, and a young man named Nicholas Viana, who was known as "The Choir Boy." The three, who had committed at least twenty bombings, were eventually hanged for murder.

Many Black Hand victims in Chicago were shot to death. And many were killed by the same hitman (person hired to kill). For several years during the peak of Black Hand activity in Chicago, between twelve and fifty victims were executed. One man, known simply as "the Shotgun Man," was reportedly responsible for one-third of those deaths. The hitman, whose identity was never discovered, was believed to have been a Sicilian who had operated as a Mafia assassin in his native country before settling in Chicago's Little Italy. In a seventy-two hour period in March of 1911, the Shotgun Man murdered four victims at the corner of Milton and Oak Streets—an intersection that became known as "Death Corner."

The Shotgun Man terrorized Chicago for about eight or nine years. Paid well for his services, he enjoyed the protection of clients who had political ties. Few citizens had the courage to identify a Black Hand killer—especially one whose political ties would probably keep him out of jail. The Shotgun Man eventually disappeared from Chicago's Little Italy. Nothing is known about where he went next, and his true identity remains a mystery.

BLACK HANDS IN THE BIG APPLE

Like Chicago, New York first encountered Black Hand activity around 1890. Within ten years, the extortion racket had

A tenor sings the blues

When Enrico Caruso, a famous opera tenor, received a Black Hand note demanding $2,000, he paid the fee. But when he received another threatening letter—asking for $15,000—he approached the police. After setting a trap, the police caught the thieves as they picked up the money from under the steps of a factory. The Black Handers were actually businessmen looking for easy money. (Many so-called Black Hand threats were actually made by businessmen who played on the public's fear of the mobsters.) Convicted of extortion, the two men were sentenced to prison.

Black Handers were rarely convicted and sent to prison. And Black Hand gangs wanted to keep it that way. Gangs often retaliated against victims who accused them. Because Caruso was responsible for the imprisonment of two extortionists, officials believed that his life was in danger. For the rest of his life, he was kept under police guard and private detective protection—both in the United States and in Europe.

Butcher in Brooklyn

In 1905 a wealthy Brooklyn butcher named Gaetano Costa received a Black Hand letter. It stated:

> You have more money than we have. We know of your wealth and that you are alone in this country. We want $1,000, which you are to put in a loaf of bread and hand to a man who comes in to buy meat and pulls out a red handkerchief.

Unlike most Black Hand targets, Costa refused to pay the fee. But his refusal did not go unpunished. Costa was shot to death behind the meat counter in his shop by Black Hand assassins. Although no one was ever charged with his murder, the hit men were known to work for "Lupo the Wolf," a Mafia gangster who terrorized Italian Harlem.

become a thriving business. In 1908 alone, 424 Black Hand cases were reported to the police. What's more, police estimated that for every case that was reported, another 250 were kept silent.

Ciro Terranova (who later became known as "the Artichoke King"), Johnny Torrio, and Frankie Uale (known as Yale) were among New York's Black Hand leaders. For thirty years, one of the most powerful Black Handers in the city was Ignazio Saietta—a man the newspapers called "Lupo the Wolf"—the leader of the Morellos, the most powerful Mafia crime family in New York at the turn of the century. The gang had ties to Palermo, Sicily, where it maintained contact with Mafia heads. The Morello family—which also had ties with gangs in Chicago and New Orleans—was involved in counterfeiting, kidnapping, murder, and extortion. As the leader of the gang, Saietta operated in the Italian Harlem district where many Sicilians lived. Although he openly practiced criminal activities, he managed to beat several indictments (charges of crimes), which earned him a reputation as an "untouchable"—someone who could not be touched by the law. He was feared by the Italian community—many of whom reportedly crossed themselves (asking God for protection) at the mention of his name.

It has been estimated that Saietta was responsible for about sixty Black Hand killings. Some were victims who refused to pay the extortion fee, while others were gangsters who threatened Saietta's territory. He was even responsible for the murder of a relative he suspected of having betrayed him. Many of the murders took place in a building at 323 East 107th Street in the heart of Italian Harlem. Victims were often tortured. Screams in the night were said to be commonplace at the site, which came to be known as the Murder Stable.

Eventually, police officials unearthed the remains of about sixty corpses on the grounds of Saietta's property.

Claiming that he was simply the building's landlord, Saietta insisted that he could not be held responsible for the killings that had taken place on the grounds. The supposed tenants were Italians whose names could not be traced. No one was ever convicted for the murders at the Murder Stable, and the site continued to be used for murder and torture until about 1917.

Black Hand threats spread throughout major cities in the East, South, and Midwest. Black Handers thrived in cities with large Italian and Sicilian American populations, such as Chicago, Illinois; Kansas City, Missouri; New Orleans, Louisiana; New York, New York; and St. Louis, Missouri.

Although Saietta was never convicted for his murderous activities in Italian Harlem, the Secret Service managed to peg him for operating a counterfeiting business in the Catskill Mountains in New York. Sentenced to thirty years in prison, he was paroled after ten years, in June of 1920.

NO WORK, SLIGHT RISK, VAST PAY

By 1920, Black Hand activity in the United States all but disappeared. The Saietta gang in New York had been broken up a decade earlier. Members of Chicago's Cardinella Black Hand gang were in prison or dead. And extortionists in Kansas City, Philadelphia, Pittsburgh, and San Francisco, were serving prison terms. Most were convicted of mail fraud—not of murder. Beginning in 1915, federal government officials began to enforce the laws that prohibit using the U.S. mail to defraud victims.

But successful prosecutions were only partly responsible for the decline of Black Hand activity. With the coming of Prohibition (when the Eighteenth Amendment outlawed the manufacture and sale of alcohol in the United States), many gangsters who had been involved in extortion turned to the much more profitable business of bootlegging. The illegal sale of liquor offered what writer Edward Dean Sullivan termed "No work—slight risk—vast remuneration [pay]." Soon the Black Hand—as a business and as a symbol—disappeared.

Sources for Further Reading

Nash, Jay Robert. *Bloodletters and Badmen.* New York: M. Evans, 1973, pp. 57–61.

Pitkin, Thomas. *The Black Hand: A Chapter in Ethnic Crime.* Lanham, MD: Rowman and Littlefield, 1977, pp. 1–14.

Sifakis, Carl. *The Mafia Encyclopedia.* New York: Facts on File, 1982, pp.l 36–38.

Al Capone

Born: 1899
Died: January 25, 1947
AKA: "Scarface"

Like many of his associates, Al Capone rose from the ranks of poor street thugs to the upper level of Chicago's underworld. As one of the nation's most powerful mobsters, he seemed untouchable—until the government charged him with tax fraud as a means to put him in prison.

SCARFACE

Born on January 17, 1899, Alphonse Capone was the fourth of nine children. His parents immigrated from Naples, Italy, and settled in New York. Raised in the tough Williamsburg section of Brooklyn, Capone left school after the sixth grade after becoming involved in a fight with one of his teachers. He never returned to school.

At a young age, Capone became involved with small-time street criminals operating in his neighborhood. As a member of the James Street Gang, he became close friends with the gang's leader, Johnny Torrio. The two remained lifelong friends, as did Capone and Lucky Luciano, who later became one of the most prominent criminals in the country.

Capone eventually graduated to the James Street mob's senior gang, the Five Points gang. Still in his teens, he worked as a gunman for the notorious New York gang. Torrio and his partner, Frankie Uale (known as Yale), employed Capone as a bouncer at a Brooklyn saloon. There Capone got into a brawl in which he was slashed on the cheek with a razor. The incident left the gangster with an unsightly scar—three jagged marks that remained pale and hairless—on his left cheek. The incident earned him the lifelong nickname of "Scarface."

BIG JIM AND THE WINDY CITY

In 1919, Capone moved to Chicago to escape arrest on a murder charge. Already settled in Chicago was Torrio, who had come to help his uncle, Big Jim Colosimo, run his far-reaching prostitution operations. Capone arrived in Chicago the same year the U.S. Congress declared the ratification (approval) of the Eighteenth Amendment, which outlawed the manufacture, sale, and transport of alcoholic beverages nationwide. Almost overnight, scores of Chicago gangsters turned their attention to the profitable business of bootlegging.

Working for Colosimo's organization, Capone started as a bouncer at one of the gangster's businesses. He later worked as a bagman (collecting payments) and enforcer, for which he was handsomely paid. In 1920, Colosimo was assassinated in what is considered to be Chicago's first gangland hit. Many assumed that Capone and Torrio had planned the murder in order to take over the mobster's rackets. Both had alibis—proof that they were elsewhere when the crime was committed.

AN EMPIRE SOUTH OF MADISON

With Colosimo out of the way, Torrio took control of one of the largest crime empires in America. An intelligent businessman, Torrio turned the organization's bootlegging activities into a multi-million dollar operation. Through a series of efficient murders, Capone became Torrio's top lieutenant. The Torrio-Capone gang expanded its influence throughout much of the city, taking over less powerful mobs and waging war with rival organizations.

Madison Street, in downtown Chicago, provided the dividing line between the city's two most powerful gangs. It separat-

Eliot Ness and the Untouchables

In 1928, when he was placed in charge of a Prohibition enforcement team created to bring down Capone, Eliot Ness (1902–1957) was just twenty-six years old. Ness examined hundreds of files of Prohibition agents before he selected the nine men who would make up his squad. He selected the agents for their clean records and loyalty to the cause. In time the agents became known as the Untouchables—because they could not be touched by bribery or threats of violence. Ness's agents—all of whom were in their twenties—were specialists in various activities, including the use of weapons and wiretapping.

Ness and his team of Untouchables attempted to ruin Capone by conducting regular raids of the gangster's illegal stills (apperatuses used to make alcohol) and other bootlegging operations. While these efforts hurt Capone financially, they did not succeed in dismantling his criminal empire. As Ness's team harassed Capone's organization, other federal agents focused on gathering evidence of tax evasion—evidence that would finally remove Capone from Chicago's underworld operations.

Although Ness is best recognized for his work with the Untouchables in Chicago, his career extended far beyond the Prohibition era. In 1935, he was hired by the reform mayor of Cleveland to investigate the racketeers who had placed a stronghold on the city's commercial activity. Ness introduced a program to reform the police force, attacking bribery and graft (to gain money by dishonest means) in the department and reducing crime by an estimated 25 percent. During the next three years a combination of surveillance and undercover work resulted in the destruction of Cleveland's Mayfield Road Mob, a violent gang of Italian and Jewish criminals.

Ness left his position in Cleveland to serve as the federal director of the Division of Social Protection for the Office of Defense during World War II (1939–1945). In peacetime, he became a private businessman. He died in 1957, at the age of fifty-seven.

ed the Capone-Torrio South Side territory from Charles Dion O'Banion's North Side empire. For the most part, the two rival organizations respected the territorial boundary—although Capone was eager to establish prostitution in the brothel-free North Side.

SCARFACE TAKES OVER

Three Capone gunmen walked into O'Banion's North Side flower shop on November 8, 1924, under the pretense of buying

Eliot Ness.

flowers for a funeral. As one shook O'Banion's hand, the two others shot him dead.

It was not long before O'Banion gangsters struck back. On January 24, 1925, Torrio was ambushed by mobsters from the North Side gang. He was shot several times in the stomach, chest, arm, and jaw. Next, **Bugs Moran** (see entry) put a gun to his head. The gun jammed and the would-be assassins fled. Critically wounded, Torrio was near death for days. Released from the hospital the following month, Torrio announced his decision to leave Chicago's rackets. Just twenty-six years old at the time, Capone stepped in to take his place.

Voter persuasion

Although other bootleggers operated in Chicago during the 1920s, Capone was more ruthless, greedy, shrewd, and systematic than the rest. He was suspected of being behind nearly two hundred killings in Chicago during the decade. To carry out his assassinations, he employed such notorious gunmen as Frank "the Enforcer" Nitti, August "Augie Dogs" Pisano, and Louis "Luigi" Morganno. He also managed to achieve working relationships with various powerful Chicago politicians, particularly Mayor William "Big Bill" Thompson.

Capone often bragged that he "owned" Chicago. To ensure that the politicians who were friendly to his organization remained in power, Capone controlled the outcome of many local elections. He sent gangs of thugs to the election polls (a place where votes are cast or recorded). Brandishing guns and other weapons, Capone's gangsters bullied voters into casting their ballot for the Capone candidate. Those who did not cooperate were often beaten, kidnapped, or shot dead.

A near-death experience at the Hawthorne Inn

Capone's role as a top player in the Chicago underworld was not without risks. He was constantly pursued by would-be assas-

The Saint Valentine's Day massacre

By early 1929, Capone had neutralized most of his major underworld enemies in Chicago. But one gang operating on the North Side, led by Bugs Moran, continued to challenge him. Capone decided to do away with the gang's leadership—and Moran, in particular. Through informants, Capone knew that Moran's gang gathered regularly in a garage on North Clark Street to await the arrival of their liquor-truck convoys. And he knew that one such shipment was due to arrive at 10:30 A.M. on February 14, 1929—St. Valentine's Day. Capone ordered his main enforcer, Fred "Killer" Burke, to prepare a surprise for Moran and company.

sins—one of whom attempted to poison his soup. One of the most notorious attempts on Capone's life occurred in 1926. The North Side O'Banion gang—which had been responsible for the attempt on Torrio's life—staged a massive ambush at Capone's headquarters at the Hawthorne Inn, on the West Side of the city.

On September 20, in broad daylight, several cars stopped in front of the Capone headquarters. North Side gunmen fired into the first floor of the hotel and surrounding shops—all of which were owned by Capone's organization. Capone's headquarters was riddled with bullet holes from shotgun, revolver, and machine-gun fire. Capone—who had been thrown to the floor by his bodyguard, Frank Rio—was unharmed.

A BLOODBATH, BRIBERY, AND LIFE BEHIND BARS

In the months and years following the Hawthorne Inn shootout, a number of Capone's rivals disappeared. **Hymie Weiss** (see entry), who had taken part in the shooting, was gunned down in front of O'Banion's North Side flower shop by Capone hitmen, Albert Anselmi and John Scalise. Vincent "the Schemer" Drucci, another North Sider who participated in the ambush, died at the hands of a policeman. **Two Gun Alterie** (see entry) left town, leaving Moran as the head of what remained of the North Side O'Banion gang. In February 1929, in an attempt to kill Moran, Capone ordered an ambush. The shooting, known as the "Saint Valentine's Day

Massacre," killed seven O'Banion gangsters. But Moran was not among them.

It was decided that three gunmen would gain access to the garage by disguising themselves as Chicago police officers conducting a routine raid. Through cash payoffs, Capone laid hold of a police car and several police uniforms. Since the intended victims already knew most of the Capone mob, members of the **Purple Gang** (see entry) from Detroit, Michigan, were hired to pose as the policemen.

When the disguised men entered the garage, they encountered seven men: Pete and Frank Gusenberg (Moran's most dangerous gunmen), Adam Heyer (reputed to be the bookkeeper for the gang), Albert Kashellek (Moran's brother-in-law), John

May and Reinhart Schwimmer (both minor gang figures), and Albert Weinshank (a speakeasy operator who bore a striking physical resemblance to Moran).

Mistaking Weinshank for Moran, who was having coffee in a diner three blocks away, the phony policemen ordered all seven to raise their hands and stand facing the back wall. At that point, Burke and a companion quietly entered the garage, and the hit team opened fire on the men with three machine guns, a shotgun, and a revolver. Within thirty seconds the seven lay dead on the floor. Two innocent bystanders were also killed. Leaving the floor strewn with two hundred spent cartridges, the killers drove away in the police car. None of the guilty parties were ever prosecuted for their role in the "Saint Valentine's Day Massacre." Capone, who was in Florida at the time, had an airtight alibi (proof that he was elsewhere).

Law officers were never able to prove that Capone was directly involved in any of the murders he planned—including the bloody Saint Valentine's Day massacre. But the previous year, after extensive investigation, U.S. Treasury agents uncovered evidence that Capone had never filed income tax returns on his vast earnings. In June of 1931, the gangster was formally charged with income tax evasion. Although he reportedly offered authorities a $4 million bribe, he was tried in October of that year. Before the trial ended, the original jury had to be replaced; Capone had bribed them.

Convicted in October 1931, Capone was sentenced to eleven years imprisonment at hard labor, which he served at a federal penitentiary in Atlanta, Georgia, and at Alcatraz (also known as "the Rock"), located in San Francisco Bay, California. During this long period in prison he lost all his power within American organized crime. Released on parole November 19, 1939, Capone suffered from paresis of the brain. (Paresis is a form of paralysis. It was probably brought on by untreated syphilis, a sexually transmitted disease he had contracted as a young man.) He retired to his mansion in Palm Island, Florida, where he died on January 25, 1947.

Savage Al

Capone refused to tolerate betrayal. On May 7, 1929, he threw a banquet in honor of three of his top gunmen, Albert Anselmi, Joseph "Hop Toad" Giunta, and John Scalise. The three killers attended, unaware that Capone had discovered they were plotting against him. Before the evening was over, Capone clubbed the three men to death in front of his horrified dinner guests.

Sources for Further Reading

Nash, Jay Robert. *Bloodletters and Badmen.* New York: M. Evans, 1973, pp. 97–105.

Sifakis, Carl. *The Mafia Encyclopedia.* New York: Facts on File, 1982, pp. 60–62.

Vandome, Nick. *Crimes and Criminals.* New York: Chambers, 1992, pp. 54–56.

Carlo Gambino

Born: September 1, 1902
Died: October 15, 1975

Carlo Gambino ruled the most powerful Mafia family in the United States. Unlike the majority of other Mafia bosses, whose careers were cut short by rivals and law enforcement officials, Gambino seemed to be unthreatened by his enemies—and by the government that attempted to curtail the Mafia's activities.

THE ROAD TO *SOTOCAPO*

Carlo Gambino was born in Palermo, Sicily, in a section that was so thoroughly controlled by the Mafia that police reportedly would not visit the area. As a teenager he traveled to America as a stowaway on a ship called the S.S. *Vincenzo Florila*. After arriving in Newport, Virginia, on December 23, 1921, Gambino made his way to Brooklyn, New York, where a number of close relatives lived. Living in a small apartment on Navy Street, he went to work for a small trucking company owned by his uncle. Gambino married Kathryn Castellano, his first cousin.

Together with his two brothers-in-law—Paul and Peter Castellano—and Thomas Masotto, a first cousin, Gambino joined New York's Mafia organization. At the time of his initiation into the family, Gambino worked for Joseph Masseria—known as "Joe the Boss." Soon after, Masseria was assassinated on the orders of a rival Mafia chief Salvatore Maranzano. The bloody ambush was carried out by Nick Capuzzi, Joe Profaci, Joe Valachi, and a Chicago gunman known simply as "Buster."

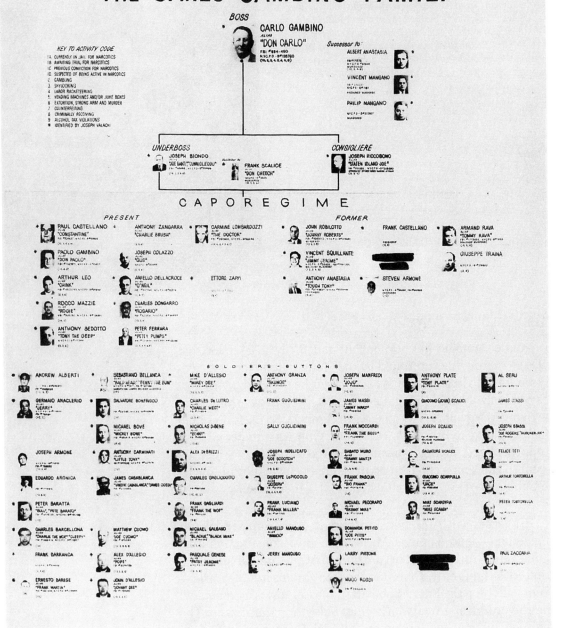

THE CARLO GAMBINO FAMILY

With Masseria dead, Gambino shifted his loyalty to Maranzano. But Maranzano's time as a Mafia boss was short-lived: he was killed in 1931 by associates of Lucky Luciano.

After Luciano divided the New York Mafia into five "families," Gambino and his cousins joined forces with the family of Vincent Mangano. The Mangano family ran a number of rackets in Brooklyn, including horse betting, the numbers (another form of betting), and the Italian lottery. The Manganos' reign lasted until 1951, when Phil Mangano was murdered by hitmen under Albert Anastasia. At about the same time, Vincent Mangano disappeared. His body was never found. Anastasia took over as the head of the family, making Gambino—who reportedly played a role in the Mangano affair—his *sotocapo,* or underboss.

A grave situation

At one point, Gambino was on the hit list of fellow New York Mafia boss Joe Bonanno. A treacherous gangster, Bonanno plotted to kill at least three other Mafia bosses before Gambino convinced him to leave New York in exchange for control of the rackets in California.

Bonanno has been given credit for an unusual solution to an age-old Mafia problem: the disposal of the corpses of murdered victims. He is said to have invented the split-level coffin. The victim's body was taken to a Brooklyn funeral home where it was placed in the lower compartment of a coffin. The top compartment contained another body. The two corpses were buried together in a legitimate (lawful) ceremony. Buried in someone else's grave, the victims were safely beyond the reach of inquisitive detectives and police.

ANASTASIA

Anastasia expanded the organization to include new rackets, such as loan-sharking, gambling, and narcotics trafficking. But Gambino was not content to remain an underboss in the Mafia. On October 25, 1957, Anastasia was shot to death as he sat in a barber's chair in Manhattan's Park-Sheraton Hotel. The assassins struck when Anastasia's face was wrapped in hot towels—after his bodyguards had mysteriously disappeared. Historians believe that Gambino and another gangster, Vito Genovese, were responsible for arranging the murder. According to Joe Valachi, a mem-

Opposite page: The Carlo Gambino "family" chart, shown at a Senate crime inquiry on October 8, 1963, during the testimony of Mafia informant Joe Valachi.

Gambino—who provided much of the material for Mario Puzo's novel *The Godfather*—was a traditional Mafioso (member of the Mafia). He followed the Mafia's many rules of etiquette (rules of conduct or procedure). For instance, when he shook hands with someone, he turned his palm *under* to indicate that he was simply going through the motions of courtesy. When he shook hands by putting his palm *on top* of the other's, he meant to show that the gesture was genuine.

ber of the Mafia who later became an informant, Gambino had arranged the hit with the approval of other Mafia bosses. "He had a good excuse," Valachi told officials. "Albert was losing at the track [betting on horses], he was there every day, and was abusing people more than ever on account of that."

With Anastasia out of the way, and other Mafia bosses on his side, Gambino set his sights on ruling the family. Together with Luciano and two other bosses—**Frank Costello** (see entry) and **Meyer Lansky** (see entry)—he plotted Genovese's downfall. Genovese had helped arrange Anastasia's murder in hopes of taking over his position. But before he was able to stake a claim to the business, Gambino and his three associates set him up to be convicted in a narcotics case. Captured by federal agents, Genovese was tried and sentenced to fifteen years in prison. He died in prison before the end of his term.

Carlo and the Little Lamb

The position Gambino assumed was that of the strongest family boss in New York. But his right to the position was not undisputed. Aniello Dellacroce, who had been a loyal supporter of Anastasia, wanted a piece of the business for himself. A smart leader, Gambino managed to win Dellacroce over. Before discussions began, Dellacroce's closest associate, Armand Rava, disappeared. Then Gambino invited Dellacroce to a meeting, where he offered to make him the family's *sotocapo*. Dellacroce accepted.

Gambino assigned the violent portion of his business to Dellacroce. Loan-sharking and extortion both relied on violence, or the threat of violence—something that Dellacroce excelled at. As Gambino's underboss, he earned a ruthless reputation even among Mafia hitmen. Dellacroce—whose full name translates as "Little Lamb of the Cross"—apparently enjoyed violence. A federal official once said of him, "He likes to peer into a victim's face, like some kind of dark angel, at the moment of death."

With Dellacroce in charge of the dirty work, Gambino was able to concentrate on other more profitable areas of business. He devoted his efforts to illegal rackets—such as fixing the price of construction bids, setting up dishonest connections in the labor unions, and creating a monopoly (exclusive control) in garbage collection. He also participated in gambling, hijacking, and narcotics ventures, and became involved in legal businesses that drew on Mafia manpower to threaten competitors. Made up of about one thousand men, Gambino's family had operations that extended from western Massachusetts to the far reaches of Philadelphia, Pennsylvania.

THE BOSS OF BOSSES

At the height of his power, Gambino headed what law enforcement officials described as the largest, richest, and strongest Mafia family in the United States. During his reign as Mafia chieftain, a number of other Mafia bosses toppled from their positions. Joseph Bonanno, the boss of another New York family, was forced into retirement after a failed challenge to Gambino's power. Joseph Colombo, another New York family boss, was shot at a rally after he angered Gambino with behavior that brought too much public attention to Mafia activities. Colombo's murderer was killed at the scene by an unknown shooter. Gambino also exercised a great deal of power over the four other New York Mafia families, and he played a key role in the national commission that determined the guidelines for all Mafia families in the United States. The single most powerful boss in New York's underworld, Gambino became known as the *capo di tutti capi*—the boss of bosses.

A soft-spoken man, Gambino had what has been described as a courtly (elegant and polite) manner. Joseph Catalupo, a government informer, described him as "very even-tempered, very polite, very much the gentleman in the presence of others." A strong family man, he lived on the upper floor of a two-family home in Brooklyn with his wife and children. He eventually bought a modest waterfront home in Massapequa, on Long Island, New York. An exceptionally wealthy man, he never attracted attention by assuming the lifestyle of the rich and famous. He dressed simply and was driven around New York in an inexpensive car.

POOR HEALTH

By the middle of the 1960s, Gambino received a constant flurry of legal summonses called subpoenas (pronounced suh-PEE-nas) to appear before the grand jury. He managed to avoid appearing in court thanks to lawyers who filed medical documents proving that his health was poor. Gambino's poor health also helped him avoid deportation (a forced return to his native country). Having entered the country as a stowaway, Gambino was considered to be an illegal alien. In 1970, the U.S. Supreme Court upheld an earlier order of deportation. When government officials attempted to carry out the order, Gambino was taken to the hospital. His family announced that the Mafia leader had suffered a heart attack—just in time to avoid deportation. Although the attack looked suspicious, government doctors determined that Gambino had, in fact, suffered a serious heart attack.

Gambino died of a heart attack five years later in his home on Long Island. Following his death, rumors circulated that another Mafia boss—Carmine Galente, whose nickname was "the Cigar"—had ordered his spies to convince Gambino to take a swine-flu shot. Such a shot could have endangered the health of a weak, elderly man with a bad heart. According to federal officials, Gambino received a flu shot shortly before he died. Gambino's role of mob boss was taken over by his brother-in-law, Paul Castellano.

Sources for Further Reading

"After the Don: A Donnybrook?" *Time* (November 1, 1976), p. 39.

"Carlo Gambino." *The New York Times Obituaries* (October 16, 1975), p. 26.

Jackson, Kenneth T., ed. *Dictionary of American Biography.* Supplement 10. New York: Simon & Schuster Macmillan, 1976-1980, pp. 268–270.

Sifakis, Carl. *The Mafia Encyclopedia.* New York: Facts on File, 1982, pp. 131–132.

Sam Giancana

Born: May 24, 1908
Died: June 19, 1975

Sam Giancana is believed to have been responsible for hundreds of mob-related murders. He entered the Mafia as a Youngblood—a new breed of young criminals who started out in Chicago's notorious 42 Gang—and worked his way up to head the mob's Chicago Outfit.

A TOUGH YOUNG THUG

Gilormo Giancana was born on the West side of Chicago in 1908. Baptized Momo Salvatore Giancana, he was known as "Sam." He lived with his parents—Antonino Giancana, a Sicilian immigrant grocer, and Antonia DiSimone—in a tenement (a housing structure for the poor) on South Aberdeen Street in a neighborhood referred to as "The Patch." A grade-school dropout, Giancana became involved in a violent gang of youths called "the 42s." One of the worst juvenile gangs in Chicago in the 1920s, the 42 Gang was often employed by more older, more powerful gangsters to carry out beatings, getaways, and other gang-related activities. By his late teens, Giancana was the head of the 42s and had become a well-respected "wheelman," or driver, for more established gangsters. He soon graduated to the position of "triggerman"—a role that called for a ruthless willingness to kill.

Giancana was first arrested and convicted at the age of eighteen for auto theft. He was also indicted (formally charged) for murder at the age of eighteen, although he was never tried. The key witness for the prosecution was killed before the matter went to trial. By the time Giancana was twenty he had been arrested as the prime suspect in three murder investigations. One of the murder victims was an African American man who had been running for committeeman in the Twentieth Ward—an area that was predominantly Italian.

MOVING UP

Giancana first worked for the "Chicago Outfit"—the Chicago arm of the Mafia—as a chauffeur and getaway driver for Paul "The Waiter" Ricca. As Ricca's protégé (someone who is trained by a person with more experience), he quickly moved up through the ranks of the Chicago Mafia. On September 26, 1933, he married Angeline DeTolve; they had three daughters together.

Convicted of moonshining (manufacturing alcohol illegally) in 1939, Giancana was sentenced to four years in prison. There he met Edward Jones, who ruled the South Side's numbers racket (illegal gambling). Giancana learned all that he could about the illegal lottery gambling operation. When he was released from prison, he set out with other former members of the 42 Gang to take over the numbers operations in Chicago's African American neighborhoods. Following a series of beatings, kidnappings, and murders, he won control of the numbers racket, which increased the income of the Chicago Outfit by millions of dollars each year.

Friends in high places

Giancana was at one time a friend to singer Frank Sinatra. The subject of nonstop surveillance by the FBI, Giancana asked him for help. Frank Sinatra, a popular singer and actor, was at one time a good friend of both the mobster and President John Kennedy. Giancana hoped that Sinatra would be able to use his friendship with the president to influence the Justice Department. One of Giancana's associates reported to him (in a wiretap intercepted by the FBI in December 1961):

I had a chance to quiz [Sinatra]. He says, "Johnny, I took Sam's name and wrote it down and told Bobby Kennedy [the president's brother, who, as the attorney general, had declared war on the mob] this is my buddy. This is my buddy, this is what I want you to know, Bob."

But Sinatra was not successful. Giancana later complained that Sinatra could not "get change for a quarter" from the Kennedys. He was so angry, in fact, that later wiretaps revealed that he discussed whether to "hit" Sinatra and some of his friends for failing to act on his behalf.

During World War II, Giancana avoided serving in the military by telling the truth. Asked what he did for a living, he replied "I steal." He was declared 4F (unfit for service) after a Selective Service officer (person who drafts people for military service) concluded that he was a "constitutional psychopath [someone with an aggressive personality disorder] with an inadequate personality manifested by strong antisocial trends." Giancana spent the war years operating a number of illegal rackets, including forging rationing stamps. (Rationing stamps were used during the war to distribute limited items such as sugar.) When Ricca went to prison in 1944, Giancana became the driver for Anthony "Tough Tony" Accardo, the next gangster in the mob's line of command. By 1945 Giancana had moved with his family to the wealthy Chicago suburb of Oak Park.

THE NEW MAFIA

By the 1950s, Anthony Accardo began to back away from heading the Chicago Outfit's operations. Many members of the old guard—mobsters who had worked for **Al Capone** (see entry)—were old, retired, imprisoned, or dead. With Accardo and Ricca's backing, Giancana became the head of the mob's Chicago operations. He took with him many of his former 42 Gang associates, who became known as the Mafia's Young Turks or Youngbloods.

By 1955 Giancana presided over 1,500 Mafiosi (members of the Mafia) in three states. He oversaw operations that included gambling, prostitution, loan sharking, narcotics trafficking, and other illegal activities. As a prominent figure in the "New Mafia," he took part in the corruption of labor unions and had interests in gambling casinos and legitimate businesses. Branching into new operations, the Chicago Outfit relied increasingly on dishonest police and corrupt politicians. Under Giancana's supervision, the Chicago Mafia evolved from a relatively small-time neighborhood racket into a large-scale criminal organization.

A BUG IN THE BACKROOM

Giancana's position at the head of the Chicago Outfit was short lived. In 1959 his career took a downturn after FBI agents planted a microphone in the backroom of the Armory Lounge in the suburb of Forest Park—the headquarters of Giancana's operation. With the listening device hidden among cans of olive oil and tomato paste, federal agents eavesdropped on the mobsters' conversations for six years. The bugging provided the FBI with intimate knowledge of the mob's activities in Chicago and elsewhere.

In 1965—after he refused to testify about the Mob's activities before a federal grand jury in Chicago—Giancana was sentenced to one year in prison. When he was released he left the

Sam Giancana's home in Oak Park, Illinois. Giancana was found shot to death in the basement on June 20, 1975.

31

Talk, talk

One of the seven bullets that had been pumped into Giancana's head and face had struck the gangster in the mouth. Mafia members who "talked too much"—by testifying in front of a grand jury, for example—were frequently shot through the mouth as a symbol that they should have kept their mouths closed.

United States to avoid further questioning. Living in an estate near Cuernavaca, Mexico, he avoided U.S. federal authorities until 1974—when the Mexican government forced him to leave the country, giving him no explanation for the expulsion.

When Giancana returned to Chicago, he was no longer a major player in the Mafia. Forced out of the boss's position, he was replaced by Joey Aiuppa—a situation that thoroughly displeased him. Granted immunity (protection) from further prosecution, Giancana appeared four times before the federal grand jury. During his final appearance, in February of 1975, he was questioned about mob activities in Latin America. He reportedly said little to shed light on the Mafia's activities. Giancana was next scheduled to testify in Washington before a Senate committee that was investigating the Mafia's involvement in a Central Intelligence Agency (CIA) plot to assassinate Cuban leader Fidel Castro.

THE LAST SUPPER

On June 19, 1975—having recently returned from Houston, Texas, where he underwent a gall bladder operation—Giancana invited a number of trusted friends to his Oak Park home to celebrate his homecoming. He invited only his closest friends and family, including one of his daughters and her husband, his driver, Dominick "Butch" Blazi, and Charles "Chuckie" English, a partner in many of his mob activities. The party—which took place days before Giancana was to appear in Washington—was watched by FBI agents who were interested in seeing who the mobster's associates were.

Sometime after his guests had left, Giancana went into a basement kitchen to cook Italian sausages and spinach for himself—and possibly someone else. But the meal went untouched. Shortly after 11 P.M. Giancana's housekeeper went to the basement to check on him. He found the mobster on the kitchen floor, lying face up in a pool of blood. Giancana had been shot seven times in the face and neck.

A PUZZLING MURDER

On the surface, the murder looked like a gang execution. Standing inches from his victim, using a silencer on an automatic weapon, Giancana's killer first shot him once in the back of the head. Then he rolled him over to fire six more bullets from beneath his chin up into his jaw and brain. (Since a single bullet in the head is not always deadly, hired assassins fire multiple shots into their victims.) There were no signs of struggle. Giancana was found with a money clip containing $1,400 in his pants pocket—ruling out robbery as a motive for the killing. Apart from some shell casings, the killer left no clues. And after the murder, the Mafia's head boss, **Carlo Gambino** (see entry), reportedly ordered a contract on the killer—a typical precaution to cover up all traces of involvement following Mafia executions.

But a few things about Giancana's killing caused officials to question whether it really was a mob hit. Giancana was shot with a .22-caliber weapon—unlike the heavy guns usually chosen by Mafia hitmen. And Giancana had been shot in the back of the head—not the sort of "respectful" execution that a former Mafia boss should receive, according to the mob's code of honor.

A number of theories circulated about who had killed Giancana. The CIA might have wanted his role in the Castro plot kept quiet—but CIA director William Colby declared his agency had nothing to do with the killing. The Chicago Crime Commission came up with three reasons why other mob heads might have wanted him dead. Giancana might have tried to muscle his way back into power in Chicago rackets; he might have cheated other bosses by keeping all the profits from his Latin American operations; and they might have been afraid of what he would reveal at his upcoming hearing before the Senate committee. But Mafia heads publicly denied any involvement in Giancana's murder. Some people speculated that the onetime Chicago boss had been shot down by a former girlfriend—of whom he had many. No one was ever arrested for Giancana's murder.

Take a look at this!

Hoodlum (1996) tells the story of the 1930s Harlem gang war in which "Bumpy" Johnson, Dutch Schultz (played by Tim Roth in an over-the-top performance), and Lucky Luciano (played by Andy Garcia) battled for control of the area's numbers racket.

Career criminal Giancana was once detained by an FBI agent in an airport. When the agent asked what he did for a living, Giancana responded, "Easy. I own Chicago. I own Miami. I own Las Vegas."

Sources for Further Reading

Brownstein, Ronald. *The Power and the Glitter.* New York: Pantheon Books, 1990, pp. 152–167.

"The Demise of a Don." *Time* (June 30, 1975), p. 26.

"Giancana, Gangster, Slain." *The New York Times* (June 21, 1975), pp. 11–12.

Jackson, Kenneth T. *Dictionary of American Biography.* Supplement 9. New York: Charles Scribner's Sons, 1971–1975, pp. 306–307.

Sifakis, Carl. *The Mafia Encyclopedia.* New York: Facts on File, 1982, pp. 138–140.

John Gotti

Born: October 27, 1940

John Gotti graduated from a youth gang and moved quickly through the ranks of the Mafia. Fond of wearing $1,800 suits and hand-painted ties, he became a powerful don (Mafia leader) at a relatively young age. He seemed immune to the government's attempts to convict him—until a close associate betrayed him.

ROUGH, TOUGH, AND DIRT POOR

Named after his father, John Joseph Gotti was born in the Bronx in New York on October 27, 1940. The son of a construction worker, he had five brothers. The Gotti family moved to Sheepshead Bay, Brooklyn, when John was in the fourth grade. Already street tough, Gotti and his brothers held their own against the neighborhood's reigning hoodlums, the Santoro brothers. A bright student, Gotti attended P.S. (Public School) 209 through the end of the sixth grade.

When Gotti was twelve his family moved to Brownsville-East, New York. The area supported a thriving underworld (Mafia activity). The breeding ground for the mob's hit squad called Murder, Inc., it was the former stomping ground of gangsters such as **Bugsy Siegel** (see entry) and "Kid Twist" Reles. Gotti attended P.S. 178 and, together with his friend Angelo Ruggiero, joined a gang known as the Fulton-Rockaway Boys. Soon recognized as a bright and tough opponent, he fought members of rival gangs such as the Liberty Park Tots and New

Tough childhood

"You had to be two-fisted in order to survive, and the younger ones always followed
the older ones and that's the way it was. It was
rough and they were tough and that's all."

—Anthony Barretta, a parish priest
in Gotti's childhood neighborhood

Lots Boys. Gotti's public school education
ended on June 7, 1954, when he was suspended from the eighth grade. He never
returned to school.

IN AND OUT OF JAIL

Even as a teenager, Gotti was confident
and self-assured—attributes that attracted
the notice of the neighborhood's older gangsters. Gotti's adult criminal record began at
the age of eighteen, when he was picked up
for frequenting a gambling location. A favorite pupil of the local
Mafia heads, Carmine and Danny Fatico, Gotti also made a
favorable impression on the mob's Gambino family before he
was twenty years old.

In 1960, Gotti married Victoria DiGiorgio, the daughter of
an Italian construction contractor and a Russian-Jewish
woman. The couple eventually settled in Queens, in Howard
Beach-Ozone Park, a blue-collar Italian-American neighborhood. Still a young struggling petty criminal, Gotti was arrested
in January 1965 for bookmaking and again, two months later,
for attempted burglary. (A bookmaker, or bookie, is someone
who accepts and pays off bets.) He spent one year in jail. He was
arrested again in December 1967 for stealing a truckload of
electrical equipment and clothing from Kennedy airport in New
York—and again, the following month, for the same offense.
When he was released after serving three years in prison, Gotti
moved in to replace the Fatico brothers, who were stepping
down as the neighborhood mob leaders. Soon he was reporting
to Aniello Dellacroce, Angelo Ruggiero's uncle, a powerful
underboss in the Mob's Gambino family.

A MADE MAN

On May 22, 1973, a man named James McBratney was killed
by three men in Snoopy's Bar in Staten Island, New York. The
reason for McBratney's murder has been the subject of debate.
The killing might have been payback for a number of thefts for
which McBratney was responsible. And it might have been
intended as punishment for his supposed role in the kidnapping

and murder of Manny Gambino, the nephew of Mafia boss **Carlo Gambino** (see entry).

Although most of the seven witnesses claimed not to have seen the McBratney murder, the killers were finally identified as Angelo Ruggiero, Ralphie "the Wig" Galione, and John Gotti. More than two years later, on June 2, 1975, Gotti pleaded guilty to attempted manslaughter in the second degree, for which he was sentenced to four years in prison. Paroled (released from prison early) a little more than two years later, Gotti returned home on July 28, 1977.

The McBratney killing had helped Gotti move up within the Mafia. Soon after his release from prison he was formally initiated into the Mafia to become what is known as a "made man." He continued to report to Dellacroce, the Gambino family underboss. But he began to express dissatisfaction with the chain of command. Carlo Gambino, the mob's overall boss, had been replaced by Gambino's brother-in-law, "Big Paul" Castellano. Gotti disliked Castellano, and felt that Dellacroce was more deserving of the position of overall boss.

Bad memory

Three men approached John Favara as he walked to his car after work in Hyde Park, Long Island. One hit him with a board, while the others pushed him into a van. The owner of a nearby diner saw the incident. A couple of days later, the three men arrived at the diner. They drank coffee and said nothing. And they stared at the diner owner—who suddenly developed a memory problem that prevented him from identifying Favara's kidnappers.

UNNEIGHBORLY BEHAVIOR

On March 18, 1980, Gotti's neighbor, a fifty-one-year-old factory worker named John Favara, headed to his home in Howard Beach. As he drove down 157th Avenue, he was blinded by the sun. He never saw Frank Gotti, John Gotti's youngest son, pull into the street on a motor bike. Favara struck and killed the twelve-year-old boy.

Taking the advice of a priest he consulted, Favara did not attend Frankie's funeral. Nor did he contact Frankie's parents to offer his sympathy. Within days of the accident, Favara began to receive threats against his life. He ignored the warnings and continued about his business, working a regular shift at the Castro Convertible factory on Long Island. And he continued to drive the car that had killed Frankie Gotti. On May 28, Favara was forced into a van by three men after he left work. He was never seen again.

Questioned about Favara's disappearance, Gotti said that he and his wife had been in Fort Lauderdale, Florida, when his neighbor was abducted. The police, meanwhile, received a tip saying that Favara had been hacked to death with a chain saw—and entombed in a car that was compacted into a square-foot block of scrap metal. Many people concluded that Gotti was behind the apparent murder. But others—including police detectives—suspected that the kidnapping had been performed without Gotti's blessing—as an attempt to win approval from Gotti and his crew. Favara's body was never found—and no one was ever charged in his kidnapping.

A KISS IS JUST A KISS

In December 1985, FBI agents who kept Gotti under surveillance noticed that he had begun to receive unusual respect from other mobsters. They approached him politely, embraced, and kissed him—a Mafia custom to show respect to a leader. Gotti's status within the mob had changed.

And with good reason. Gotti's mentor, Dellacroce, had died on December 2, 1985. Two weeks later—on December 16, 1985—seventy-two-year-old Gambino boss Paul Castellano was killed in a hail of gunfire outside a Manhattan steak house. And Gotti—who was undoubtedly behind the killing—stepped in to replace the slain mobster as the head of the nation's largest and most powerful Mafia family. No charges were ever brought in Castellano's murder.

THE "TEFLON DON"

By the late 1980s Gotti was on the federal government's wanted list. Brought to trial on charges of racketeering, he faced the possibility of an extended jail term that would inevitably end his reign as one of the youngest dons (bosses) in the history of the Mafia. But on March 13, 1987, Gotti was acquitted of all charges. The U.S. Attorney told the press, "The jury has spoken.

Obviously they perceived there was something wrong with the evidence." But he knew better. The jury had been tampered with. The jury's foreman had been bribed to make sure that Gotti was not convicted. Gotti, who seemed immune (protected) from the law, became known as "the Teflon don" because government prosecutors were unable to make criminal charges against him stick.

That is, until 1992. The Justice Department, which had spent an estimated $75 million to monitor the Mafia don's private conversations, had tapes that provided evidence of Gotti's involvement in mob-related murder and racketeering. A federal judge ruled that Bruce Cutler, Gotti's attorney in the previous trial, could not defend him. Because Cutler was included in some of the recorded conversations used as evidence against

John Gotti, in the doorway, leaves the Ravenite Club in New York City after a party on February 9, 1990, celebrating his being found not guilty of conspiracy and assault. Underboss Salvatore Gravano is seen in front of Gotti.

"Sammy the Bull"

Gotti's top aide, "Sammy the Bull" Gravano, was indicted—along with his boss—for racketeering and murder. Before standing trial, Gravano became an informant against Gotti—in exchange for a guarantee that he would receive no more than a twenty-year sentence. (Without making a deal with the government, Gravano faced a probable sentence of life imprisonment with no possibility of parole.) While he waited to testify, Gravano was held in a safe house (secret location used to keep witnesses safe) in Virginia to ensure that he was not assassinated by Mafia hitmen before the case went to trial.

Gotti, his participation in the trial was considered to be a conflict of interest. The jury was sequestered (put in seclusion) to prevent any tampering. And Salvatore "Sammy the Bull" Gravano—Gotti's right-hand man—was prepared to testify against his former boss.

By the end of the trial, every one of the fourteen counts against Gotti had stuck. James Fox, the assistant director of the FBI in New York, told the press, "The Teflon is gone. The don is covered with Velcro [a material to which almost everything sticks] and every charge stuck." Convicted of racketeering and murder charges, Gotti was sentenced to life imprisonment without the possibility of parole.

Sources for Further Reading

Angelo, Bonnie. "Wanted: A New Godfather." *Time* (April 13, 1992), p. 30.

Blum, Howard. "How the Feds Got Gotti." *New York* (October 25, 1993), pp. 50–59.

Blum, Howard. "How the Feds Got Gotti." *New York* (November 1, 1993), pp. 42–49.

Daly, Michael. "The New Godfather, The Rise of John Gotti." *New York* (June 23, 1986), pp. 28–39.

"John Gotti, Cultivating a Commanding Presence Both Inside and Outside the Courtroom." *The New York Times Biographical Service* (March 1987), p. 216.

Rogers, Patrick. "Don's Delight." *People Weekly* (March 3, 1997), p. 110+.

Sifakis, Carl. *The Mafia Encyclopedia.* New York: Facts on File, 1982, pp. 143–145.

Stone, Michael. "After Gotti." *New York* (February 3, 1992), pp. 22–30.

Virginia Hill

Born: 1918
Died: March 25, 1966

Referred to by newspapers as "the Queen of the Mob," Virginia Hill never actually wielded any authority in the underworld. Rather, she was infamous for her series of gangland husbands and lovers—and for acting as a Mafia go-between and courier.

POOR AND SHOELESS

Virginia Hill was the sixth of ten children. Her family lived in Liscomb, Alabama—an impoverished steel town where her father worked as a livery stableman. Hill's family was reportedly so poor that, as a child, Virginia never owned or wore a pair of shoes. As an adult, Hill told many stories about her life. She claimed to have been born in the Netherlands and sometimes said that her father was half Native American. She often said she had been married as a teenager. She also claimed that she had become rich by investing an annulment settlement (a payment that results from a marriage that is nullified, or canceled). But no one was ever able to find any record of her supposed first husband, George Rogers.

At age sixteen, Hill ran away from her Alabama home. Settling in Chicago, she worked at the Worlds' Fair—either as a dancer or short-order cook. There she met Joe Epstein, an accountant who was closely involved with the Mafia. A bookie and a gambler, Epstein worked as a tax expert for **Al Capone**'s

The Kefauver Committee

Formed as the Senate Special Committee to Investigate Organized Crime in Interstate Commerce, the Kefauver Committee, as it was known, was named after Senator Estes Kefauver. Looking to make a name for himself in his first term in the Senate, Kefauver sponsored the resolution that created the committee. He also served as the committee's chairman. A Texas Democrat, Kefauver had to overcome stiff opposition from older senators who distrusted their junior colleague's ambitions. The Kefauver Committee has been called "probably the most important probe of organized crime" in the history of the United States. The committee's hearings revealed criminal operations that earned millions of dollars yearly. The hearings also exposed the activities of corrupt public officials who helped the operations to thrive.

During the hearings, many of the crime figures questioned called on their constitutional right against self-incrimination (offering testimony that would prove them guilty of a crime) guaranteed in the Fifth Amendment. In fact, so many criminals cited their constitutional right that "taking the Fifth" became part of the national vocabulary. Others tried to avoid appearing before the committee altogether. "Kefauveritis" was the name given to the variety of mysterious ailments that suddenly afflicted gangsters on the day they were scheduled to testify.

Probably the most dramatic hearings in the Kefauver investigation were those held in New York City. Frank Costello, considered the head of the New York-Miami syndicate (association), testified only on the condition that his face not be shown on television. The cameras focused on his hands for the duration of his appearance. But the ploy failed to protect the gangster's identity. By the time the committee was through with him, Costello was a ruined man. His testimony

(see entry) gang. After he introduced Hill to many prominent members of the Chicago underworld, she quickly became well-known in Mafia circles in Chicago as well as New York and Hollywood.

In the late 1930s, the "new" Mafia was in the process of transforming its activities from small, local operations to large-scale organized crime that linked together criminals throughout the country. A natural actress and diplomat (a skilled negotiator), Hill worked as a go-between and courier for the Mob. On trips between Chicago and New York, she brought news from one Mafia boss to another—so that they were able to communicate

had made him an unwelcome presence among both his legitimate and underworld associates. The other star of the New York hearings was Virginia Hill—whom newspapers called the "Queen of the Mob."

The mobsters who testified at the hearings did not freely provide details about the Mafia's activities. In fact, most of the gangsters who testified denied ever having even *heard* the word Mafia before. But committee members nonetheless managed to piece together a picture of organized crime in America in the 1950s. It was dominated by two syndicates, one operating in New York and the other based in Chicago. Both also had operations in Florida. The committee claimed—but was never completely able to prove—that both of these syndicates were governed by Lucky Luciano.

After the end of the hearings, Kefauver claimed that the committee had done the nation a service. Many of the methods and faces of organized crime had been exposed to the public for the first time. Privately funded crime committees were formed around the country to address criminal activity at the local level. The Justice Department and Internal Revenue Service stepped up efforts to prosecute mobsters on racketeering charges—as well as for failing to pay income taxes. And voters rejected candidates with links to the underworld. Still, for all the public interest generated by the hearings, concrete results were harder to measure. As William Howard Moore wrote in *The Kefauver Committee and the Politics of Crime* (1974), "So inadequate are crime statistics and definitions . . . no one can document whether organized crime and corruption declined or increased during the 1950s."

with one another without fear of being observed by government officials. Hill also worked as a "bag woman." Traveling to Europe with enormous sums of Mafia money, she deposited the funds into Swiss bank accounts and other secret shelters. By having a bag woman hide the money in secret accounts, the Mafia was able to avoid having the sources of its income traced—sources that would reveal the mob's illegal activities.

A MAFIA MAGNET

Hill was linked with a number of powerful Mafiosi (members of the Mafia), including Tony Accardo, Joe Adonis, **Frank**

Here's a book you might like:

Prizzi's Honor, 1982, by Richard Condon

A man who is an enforcer for the Prizzi mob falls in love with a woman who has just stolen a million dollars from the gangsters who employ him. Made into a movie in 1985 starring Jack Nicholson and Kathleen Turner.

Costello, (see entry) the Fischetti brothers, Murray Humphreys, Frank Nitti, and **Bugsy Siegel** (see entry). Siegel was said to be her true love. She once commented, "I just seem to be drawn to underworld characters like a magnet."

Handsomely paid for her mob activities, her life was far removed from her impoverished childhood. She lived in lavish houses and threw parties that cost thousands of dollars. She bought extravagant evening gowns and hundreds of pairs of shoes. She traveled to high-priced resorts and tipped so well that bellboys reportedly fought to carry her bags.

A PUBLIC FIGURE

Hill first attracted the public's notice in 1947 when her boyfriend, mobster Bugsy Siegel, was shot to death in a gangland killing in the living room of her house in Beverly Hills, California. Hill was out of the country at the time—which led many people to speculate that the hit was about to take place. The mob suspected that Siegel had been pocketing mob money while he was building the Flamingo Hotel and Casino in Las Vegas, Nevada. Further, they suspected that Siegel used Hill to move the money to Switzerland.

Hill later became a household name when she appeared as a key witness before the Senate Special Committee to Investigate Organized Crime in Interstate Commerce—commonly known as the Kefauver Committee (see box). In a May 1951 appearance that was seen by millions of people who watched the televised coverage, Hill claimed to have a very poor memory, and was therefore unable to explain how she was able to afford her extravagant lifestyle. Much of her testimony was made up. And when she was questioned on her association with Mafia members, Hill shocked the committeemen with an off-color response. Hill also attracted attention for her behavior outside of the hearings. Angered by the press who hounded her, she punched New York reporter Marjorie Farnsworth in the jaw. And she told the others, "I hope an atom bomb falls on all of you!"

THE END OF THE LINE

Hill left the United States later in 1951 to avoid being questioned by the government about back taxes (unpaid tax bills). On June 23, 1954, a federal grand jury formally charged her with income tax evasion for failing to pay more than $160,000 in back taxes. The following year, the Internal Revenue Service (IRS) issued a notice for her arrest. It described her as: "White; female; height 5 feet 4 inches; complexion fair; hair auburn; eyes gray." The notice listed no occupation for Hill, but referred to her as "paramour [lover] and associate of racketeers and gangsters," and gave *twenty-two* aliases, or false names, that she used.

Living in Austria, Hill continued to enjoy a comfortable existence. She experimented with gourmet cooking and looked

Virginia Hill's home in Beverly Hills, where Bugsy Siegel was slain on June 20, 1947.

Bugsy (1991) stars Warren Beatty as the 1940s gangster who built the Flamingo Hotel in Las Vegas, Nevada, when the area was still desert land. Annette Bening plays Bugsy's moll (mistress of a gangster), Virginia Hill, who inspired him to carry out his dream of building the Flamingo (which was her nickname).

Married to the Mob (1988) is the comic story of an attractive Mafia widow (Michelle Pfeiffer) who tries to escape mob life. She ends up fighting off amorous advances from the current mob boss while she is wooed by an undercover cop.

after her teenage son, who was studying to be a waiter. Often recognized by American tourists, she once complained, "All these jerks watch me like I was on exhibition." Hill attempted to commit suicide several times and finally succeeded in March 1966. After she had been missing for two days, her body was found in the snow in the village of Koppl, near Salzburg, Austria. Having taken an overdose of sleeping pills, she died at the age of forty-nine.

Sources for Further Reading

"The Auction Party for Virginia Hill." *American Mercury* (November 1951), pp. 124–128.

Mortimer, Lee. "Virginia Hill's Success Secrets." *American Mercury* (June 1951), pp. 662–669.

Sifakis, Carl. *The Mafia Encyclopedia.* New York: Facts on File, 1982, pp. 152–153.

"Virginia Hill." *The New York Times Obituaries* (March 25, 1966), p. 57.

Meyer Lansky

Born: 1902
Died: January 15, 1983

The newspapers called Meyer Lansky "the Godfather's Godfather" because he was considered to be the genius behind many of the mob's profitable operations. Described as nearly invisible, his role in the Mafia was sometimes downplayed, although some historians believe he was equal—and perhaps superior—to Mafia godfather Lucky Luciano.

BORN ON THE FOURTH OF JULY

Lansky was born in Grodno, Poland, in 1902. When he was nine years old he immigrated to the United States with his parents, Yetta and Max Suchowljansky, and his younger brother and sister. Because his parents could not remember their son's birth date, an immigration officer at Ellis Island, New York, made one up. Lansky was given a July 4 birthday. Born Mair Suchowljansky, he later Americanized his name, calling himself Meyer Lansky.

The Suchowljanskys settled into the Lower East Side of New York City, on the Brooklyn side of the East River. The poor and crime-ridden immigrant neighborhood was dominated by groups of petty criminals, including Kid Dropper's and Little Augie's gangs. Lansky attended Public School 34, where he was a good student whose teachers and fellow classmates saw him as a sharp, self-assured young man. Lansky graduated from the eighth grade in 1917 and soon went to work in a tool and die shop on the Lower East Side. Already involved in shady (criminal) activities, he added to his income by organizing a floating dice game. (A floating dice game is held at different locations in order to prevent law enforcers from breaking it up).

THE BUGS-MEYER GANG

Lansky was first arrested at the age of sixteen. On October 24, 1918, he rushed into an abandoned tenement (housing unit), where someone was screaming. He found a young man attacking a woman and boy. The police arrived just in time to see him strike the young man. Charged with assault, Lansky was let go after he paid a $2 fine. But the incident did not end there. The young man he had struck—Lucky Luciano—and the boy he had saved—**Bugsy Siegel** (see entry)—would both become important criminal associates in Lansky's adult life.

During the 1920s, as Prohibition (when the Eighteenth Amendment outlawed the manufacture and sale of alcohol) went into effect, Lansky and Siegel worked side-by-side in the bootlegging business. Working as shotgun riders, they protected illegal shipments of alcohol as they were transported by various gangs operating in New York and New Jersey. Lansky and Siegel also hijacked the liquor shipments of other gangsters—a practice that required violent methods. By 1928 the two had formed a gang of their own—called the Bugs-Meyer Mob. In addition to transporting illegal liquor—an activity known as rumrunning—the gang sold its services to bootleggers and other criminals. Some described the Bugs-Meyer Mob as the most violent Prohibition-era gang in the East. Lansky and Siegel eventually joined a group of East Coast gangs that banded together to coordinate rumrunning in the area. Lansky was made the controller (financial supervisor) of the group, which was called the Eastern syndicate.

THE LAUNDRY BUSINESS

When Prohibition ended in December 1933, Lansky and Siegel were wealthy men. Lansky invested his profits in both legal and illegal enterprises, and soon became involved in crooked gambling casinos in Florida, New Orleans, and upstate New York. By 1934 he had become an important figure in the mob's efforts to re-invent itself as a nation-wide crime syndicate. A loose assembly of various gangs, the syndicate was governed by a board of top mobsters who coordinated the activities of gangs across the country. The syndicate's first top man—called the "first among equals"—was Lucky Luciano. A longtime associate of Lansky's, Luciano respected his sharp intellect and shrewd (cunning) ability to look ahead. Under Luciano's supervision, Lansky devised numerous schemes to transform the syndicate into a bigger, more diversified—and more profitable—enterprise.

Chairman of the board

According to an FBI agent who was familiar with the mobster's brilliant plans and financial scams, "[Lansky] would have been chairman of the board of General Motors if he'd gone into legitimate [legal] business." But Lansky devoted his efforts to underworld activities. Some people referred to him as the "Chairman of the Board of the National Crime Syndicate."

Lansky moved immediately into organized gambling. A mathematics genius, he provided the basic groundwork of modern resort gambling—a wildly profitable source of income. Mobsters reaped huge profits by "skimming" funds from the counting rooms of the casinos. But the syndicate needed to cover its tracks. The skimmed money was worthless until its illegal origins could be hidden.

Lansky came up with ingenious methods for "laundering" money (taking money illegally obtained and using it for legitimate purposes)—which was then hidden or invested. He developed a network of bankers, couriers, go-betweens, and frontmen that extended throughout the world. He arranged to route the profits of gambling and other illegal activities to foreign banks, through layers of dummy (fake) corporations.

By the time the money returned to the United States, its origins were untraceable. Sometimes it was invested in legitimate (legal) businesses. Often it was "lent" to gangsters, who were, in essence, lending money to themselves. Middlemen sometimes lent syndicate money to legitimate businessmen—who repaid the loans plus a steep interest rate (an additional fee that increased over time). Lansky's schemes were the work of a financial whiz. The syndicate was free to enjoy hundreds of thousands of dollars that could not be traced to the organization's illegal activities.

November 17, 1952. Meyer Lansky (second from right) confers with (from left to right) attorneys Edward Sullivan, Thomas Clancy, and Moses Polakoff. Lansky was about to go on trial on charges of conspiracy, gambling, and forgery.

A CUBAN GOLD MINE

Lansky also masterminded what was for a while the syndicate's most profitable endeavor—gambling in Havana, Cuba. He convinced Cuban dictator Fulgencio Batista to guarantee him a monopoly (exclusive control) of gambling in the country. He also managed to have a law passed that permitted gambling only in hotels that were worth at least $1 million. He then oversaw the construction of the only million-dollar establishments in Havana—and placed syndicate friends in control of the gambling operations. Lansky reportedly deposited $3 million in a Swiss bank for Batista—in addition to paying the military leader 50 percent of the casino profits. Havana was for a while a gambling paradise. But when Batista was over-thrown by Fidel Castro (who became the Cuban premier in 1959), Lansky's dream went up in smoke. Castro's revolutionaries wanted no part of the syndicate's money-making schemes.

THE TAX MAN

In 1970 the federal government set out to convict Lansky. Many gangsters, like Lansky, enjoyed money that had been skimmed from casinos in Las Vegas that were secretly owned by the syndicate. And many were convicted for income tax evasion. But Lansky was not an easy target. He did not flaunt (show off) his wealth: he led a quiet, modest life.

Clean money

Lansky arranged for middlemen to deposit hundreds of thousands of dollars in mob profits in secret accounts in Switzerland. Because Swiss banks do not reveal the name of depositors, there is no way to find out to whom the money belongs. Money laundered through Swiss bank accounts was said to have been washed clean in the snow of the Alps.

Rather than face two federal indictments, Lansky left the country. (The U.S. government was also attempting to have Lansky deported as an undesirable alien). Traveling to Israel, he hoped to remain in the country under the Law of the Return—which gives anyone who was born to a Jewish mother the right to claim Israeli citizenship. Lansky reportedly invested millions of dollars in the country while his application for citizenship was being considered. But Israeli officials were concerned that the mobster might move his criminal activities to his adoptive country. U.S. officials were strongly opposed to his bid for Israeli citizenship. Some historians claim that the administration of President Richard M. Nixon threatened to hold back Phantom jets that had been promised to Israel if Lansky were allowed to stay. After much public debate, Lansky was forced out of the country in 1972.

The following year Lansky went to trial in Miami, Florida. Charged with income tax evasion, he was acquitted (found not guilty). Following the trial, the government abandoned its crusade to convict the man who was sometimes called the "Godfather's Godfather." Lansky lived peacefully with his wife in a high-security condominium for almost another decade. He died of cancer in a New York hospital on January 15, 1983. He was eighty-one years old.

Sources for Further Reading

Fried, Alfred. *The Rise and Fall of the Jewish Gangster in America.* Austin, TX: Holt, Rinehart and Winston, 1988, pp. 229–286.

Take a look at this!

The Godfather, Part II (1974) continues the story of the Corleone family. Hyman Roth, a character played by Lee Strasberg in the film, was modeled after Meyer Lansky. Soon after the movie was released in 1974, the actor received a phone call from a man who did not identify himself. "You did good," the man said. "Now why couldn't you have made me more sympathetic?"

Gage, Nicholas. "The Little Big Man Who Laughs at the Law." *Atlantic Monthly* (July 1970), pp. 62–69.

"Meyer Lansky." *The New York Times Obituaries* (January 16, 1983), p. 29.

"Meyer Lansky: Mogul of the Mob." *The New Republic* (January 19, 1980), pp. 36–38.

Sheppard, R. Z. "Low Profile, Little Man: Meyer Lansky and the Gangster Life." *Time* (November 4, 1991), p. 93.

Sifakis, Carl. *The Mafia Encyclopedia.* New York: Facts on File, 1982.

The Purple Gang

Active: c. 1918-c. 1932

Made up of the children of poor Jewish immigrants, the Purple Gang started out as a small band of street thugs. But with the prohibition of the sale of liquor in Michigan, the gang rose to the top of the Detroit underworld.

LITTLE JERUSALEM

The Purple Gang was considered to be one of the most ruthless and violent gangs of the Prohibition era (when the Eighteenth Amendment outlawed the manufacture and sale of liquor from 1919 to 1933). Most of the original members came from the lower east side of Detroit, Michigan. The area—a ghetto referred to as "Little Jerusalem" because of the number of Jewish immigrants who lived there—was impoverished, crime-ridden, and plagued by violence. Prior to 1918, the gang consisted entirely of Jewish youths. Most were the children of hardworking Russian Jews who had recently immigrated to the United States. The gang was led by four brothers, Abe, Isadore (Izzy), Joe, and Raymond Bernstein, along with Harry and Louis Fleischer.

A BOOTLEG EMPIRE

Prohibition was enacted in Michigan in May 1918. The city—separated from Canada by the Detroit River—was an

Harry Fleisher.

important center for bootleggers who smuggled booze across the border from Canada, where the production of alcohol was not outlawed. The Purple Gang quickly established itself as a powerful criminal force in Detroit. Formerly a loosely organized group of street hoodlums, the Purples had the seeds of an organized criminal network when Prohibition hit Detroit. The gang soon moved into extortion (obtaining money through force or intimidation), armed robbery, hijacking, gambling, jewel robbery, prostitution, loan-sharking, and bootlegging.

The Purple Gang first entered the liquor racket by offering "protection" to bootleggers. Bootleggers were often preyed on by other gangsters who hijacked their cargoes. The Purples collected a fee—or a share in the profits—for protecting more established gangsters as they unloaded shipments of alcohol on the Detroit waterfront. Gangsters who refused to pay for protection were often robbed of their shipments by the very gang that had promised them protection. The Purples earned a reputation as ruthless killers who readily murdered other gangsters in order to hijack their illegal loads. The gang eventually became involved in transporting liquor to Chicago and other large Midwestern cities. **Al Capone** (see entry), who ruled the Chicago underworld, relied on the Purple Gang to deliver Canadian whiskey to his organization. Aware of the Purple Gang's savage reputation, Capone allowed them to operate as his agents—rather than risk a bloody battle in an attempt to take over their operations.

By the late 1920s, the Purple Gang had expanded to include recruits from Chicago, New York, and St. Louis. No longer an exclusively Jewish organization, the gang had many Italian members, such as Frank and Vincent Camerata, James and Peter Licavoli, Joseph Massei, and Joseph Zerilli—all of whom later became prominent criminal figures.

THE MILAFLORES MASSACRE AND THE CLEANERS' WAR

In March 1926, Purple Gang members were responsible for a machine-gun ambush in the Milaflores Apartments at 106 Alexandrine Avenue East in an apartment belonging to Abe Axler and Edward Fletcher. The three men who died in the ambush—Frank Wright, Reuben Cohen, and Joseph Bloom—were suspected of killing a Purple Gang liquor distributor. Although the Purple Gang was blamed for the slayings, the police were never able to locate the killers, who included Fred "Killer" Burke (later a participant in the St. Valentine's Day Massacre in Chicago) and two other gunmen.

The Purples profited from a period of unrest in the cleaning industry in Detroit. Working as hired muscle for dishonest labor leaders, they bullied union members. They also threatened non-union (independent) workers in what became known as the Cleaners and Dyers War. Paid well to enforce the union's policy, they relied on violent methods—such as beatings, bombings, kidnappings, theft, and murder—to keep the workers in line. In 1928, the Purple Gang trial ended the union dispute. But all of the Purple defendants were eventually found not guilty of extortion and released, and the gang continued to thrive as Detroit's foremost criminal organization.

Eddie Fletcher.

THE COLLINGWOOD MANOR MASSACRE

By the 1930s, members of the Purple Gang had begun to fight among themselves. Three Purples—Joe Lebowitz, Hymie Paul, and Isadore "Joe" Sutker—formed what was called the "Little Jewish Navy." Using several boats, they transported liquor from Canada—a practice known as "rumrunning." They also practiced hijacking, and had begun to expand their operations beyond the area that was assigned to them by the leaders of the Purple Gang. Lebowitz, Paul, and Sutker planned eventu-

Bloody valentine

The Purples had a reputation as a bloody, violent gang. Al Capone reportedly called on three of the Purple Gang's hitmen--George Lewis and Phil and Harry Keywell--to help pull off the St. Valentine's Day Massacre in 1929.

Detroit, Michigan, as seen across the Detroit River from Windsor, Ontario, Canada, in the early 1900s.

ally to form their own organization—something that seriously displeased the leadership of the Purples.

On September 16, 1931, the three men attended what they believed to be a peaceful meeting at an apartment on Collingwood Avenue. They were escorted by a bookie named Sol Levine. When they arrived at the apartment, a brief discussion followed—after which the three unarmed men were shot to death by Purple gangsters. Arrested by the police shortly thereafter, Levine became a state's witness in the affair. Based on his testimony, three Purple gangsters were arrested and tried for first-degree murder. Raymond Bernstein, Harry Keywell, and Irving Milberg were convicted and sentenced to life in prison for their role in what became known as the Collingwood Manor massacre.

Eventually, the Purples were invited to join the national crime syndicate that had been formed in the 1930s under the leadership of Lucky Luciano and **Meyer Lansky** (see entry). The gang was absorbed into the larger syndicate, and became an important aspect of the mob's gambling activities.

Sources for Further Reading

Carpozi, Balsamo and George Carpozi. *Under the Clock, The Inside Story of the Mafia's First Hundred Years.* Far Hills, NJ: New Horizon Press, 1988, pp. 36–39.

Fried, Albert. *The Rise and Fall of the Jewish Gangster in America.* Holt, Rinehart and Winston, 1988, pp. 103–122.

A History of Detroit Organized Crime. [Online] Available http://detnews.com/1998/metro/9801/25/01250053.html, November 19, 1997.

Nash, Jay Robert. *Bloodletters and Badmen.* New York: M. Evans, 1973, pp. 454–455.

Sifakis, Carl. *The Mafia Encyclopedia.* New York: Facts on File, 1982, pp. 268–269.

A colorful name

There are a number of theories about how the Purple Gang received its name. Some say the Purples were named after an early leader, Samuel "Sammy Purple" Cohen. Others cite the gangsters' workout wardrobe. Gang member Eddie Fletcher regularly wore a purple jersey when he worked out at a local gym, and the gang's other members soon followed his example. Probably the most popular theory is that the name was coined by street merchants in Detroit's Hasting Street quarter. The shopkeepers referred to the gangsters as Purples because they were "tainted," or "off-color"—like the color of spoiled meat.

Bugsy Siegel
(Benjamin Siegel)

Born: February 28, 1906
Died: June 20, 1947

As a gangster who ran gambling rackets, Bugsy Siegel was something of a forward-thinker. As part of an expansion of gambling activities in the West, he is credited with putting the small Nevada town of Las Vegas on the map as the kingdom of world gambling capitals.

A HELLION IN HELL'S KITCHEN

Benjamin "Bugsy" Siegel was born on February 28, 1906, in Brooklyn, New York. His poor Jewish parents lived in a crime-ridden slum known as Hell's Kitchen—the breeding ground for many criminals of that era. Among Siegel's boyhood friends were George Raft, who later established a movie career playing gangster roles, and Bo Weinberg, later a top aide to gangster **Dutch Schultz** (see entry).

In a manner similar to fellow gangster **Louis Lepke** (see entry), Siegel began his criminal career by preying upon push-cart peddlers on the Lower East Side with a sidekick named Morris "Moey" Sedway. Unlike Lepke, Siegel did not usually beat the vendors he was trying to convince to buy protection from him. Rather he would simply have Sedway pour kerosene (a fuel oil) over the vendors' merchandise and then light it on fire. It usually only took a vendor one lesson to decide to pay the "insurance."

By the time he was fourteen years old, Siegel was in charge of his own gang of criminals. He joined forces with **Meyer Lan-**

sky (see entry), another rising young New York gangster, to create the Bugs-Meyer Mob. Members of the mob hired their services as enforcers for the large bootlegging mobs. Less than ten years later, the enforcement arm of the mob known as "Murder, Inc." took over responsibility for gangland killings. The Bugs-Meyer Mob was involved in a number of other activities as well. The young mobsters ambushed rival gangsters and took their liquor shipments. They also dealt in stolen cars, prostitution, drug trafficking, and gambling rackets in New York, New Jersey, and Pennsylvania.

A SEASONED HIT MAN

Throughout the 1920s and 1930s, Siegel continued to climb up the underworld ladder. At the same time, Luciano and a number of other Italian gangsters began to organize criminal mobs into a national organization, or syndicate. Siegel and Lansky—who were both Jewish—were included in the organization. The mob's reorganization required some "housecleaning"—the killing of veteran gangsters who stood in the way of the syndicate's progress. Siegel was an eager participant in the new mob's clean-up jobs. In 1931, he was one of the hit men who assassinated Joe "the Boss" Maseria— an old-guard gangster—at a restaurant in Coney Island, New York. Siegel was often accompanied by killer Frankie Carbo, who later became the head of the mob's prizefighting (boxing) racket.

Not all of Siegel's killings were ordered by the national syndicate. In 1935, the government charged syndicate member Dutch Schultz with income tax evasion. Certain Schultz's career would be cut short by imprisonment, fellow syndicate members Luciano and Vito Genovese took over "the Dutchman's" profitable numbers rackets in Harlem. They did this with the help of Schultz's top lieutenant, Bo Weinberg. Tried in upper New York State, Schultz managed to avoid conviction. When he returned to New York City, he found his empire sacked. Aware that his former aide had turned traitor, he ordered Weinberg's assassination. Siegel— who had grown up with Weinberg—was the hit man.

The top man at Murder, Inc.

Louis Lepke (see entry) had the questionable distinction of being executed as the indirect result of founding and building a very successful, though illegal, business. A famous gangster of the 1930s and 1940s, he is perhaps best known by the name of his business, Murder, Inc.

Criminal Education

Lepke, as he was popularly known, was born Louis Buchalter in Manhattan, New York. His only known occupation was as a criminal. He graduated from simple pushcart robberies at the age of seventeen. Lepke was short—five feet seven and one-half inches tall. To threaten those he sought to "protect," he joined forces with Jacob Gurrah Shapiro, a huge man he had met when both gangsters tried to rob the same pushcart. They joined the Lower East Side gang and worked in establishing control over the city's garment industry.

On October 15, 1926, Lepke machine-gunned Jacob "Little Augie" Orgen to death and assumed the position of undisputed leader of the city's garment and business rackets. Often described as the "brains of the operation," Lepke began recruiting mainly Jewish criminals from other gangs to establish his own hit teams.

He also continued to intimidate unions. At one point, his organization controlled the four-hundred-thousand member Clothing Workers Union as well as trucking and motion-picture operators unions. By 1932, Lepke had helped establish a national crime syndicate with other notable gangsters such as Bugsy Siegel, Meyer Lansky, Lucky Luciano, **Frank Costello** (see entry), and Albert Anastasia. In 1933, he proposed the establishment of a national enforcement division of the syndicate, made up of hired killers who would go anywhere to assassinate

"Bugsy"

Few people called Benjamin Siegel "Bugsy" to his face. The gangster hated the nickname--which he had acquired for his sometimes crazy behavior and cold-blooded willingness to kill.

CALIFORNIA DREAMING

Eventually, Siegel became the target of numerous attempts against his life. With the heat turned up, he reportedly approached syndicate leaders regarding a plan to combine criminal undertakings in California with Jack Dragna, who at the time controlled the underworld in that state. With Dragna's help, Siegel operated various gambling establishments, including a floating casino.

The gangsters' other activities included drug smuggling. Using a series of relay points, they were able to transport narcotics from Mexico into the United States without being detected by legal authorities. They also employed a relay system to establish a bookmaking wire service. The wire service transmit-

those who opposed the syndicate. Murder, Inc. was born.

The Fix is In

By the end of the 1930s, Lepke's crime operation was so large that he was having trouble controlling all of it. Murder, Inc., employed so many hired killers that it was only a matter of time before some of them began to crack and provide information to the authorities when they were caught for murdering someone. One of the killers, Max Rubin, eventually implicated Lepke in the killing of Joseph Rosen.

In 1939, Moey Wolinsky had advised Lepke that the syndicate board had decided that he should turn himself in to be tried on narcotics charges, taking the police pressure off the mob. Wolinsky also told him that, as part of the deal, the "fix was in" and Lepke would not be turned over to the New York authorities to be tried for Rosen's murder.

Execution

While Lepke was serving a fourteen-year sentence on narcotics charges, he was tried and found guilty of the murder of Rosen. He was sentenced to die in the electric chair. As it turned out, there was no deal to prevent Lepke from being turned over to the New York authorities. He had been double-crossed.

Lepke fought the guilty verdict sentence for years. During that time he continued to issue orders through Murder, Inc., to kill those who had betrayed him—including Abe "Kid Twist" Reles, one of the first to implicate him for murder. Reles later fell from a hotel window while under police protection. Lepke also ordered the murder of Wolinsky, who was shot to death in 1943. Lepke was electrocuted in Sing Sing prison in New York on March 4, 1944. He was the only highly placed member of the national crime syndicate ever to be legally executed.

ted the results of West Coast horse races to bookies who collected bets in the East and elsewhere.

In California, Siegel contacted his boyhood friend, actor George Raft, who reportedly liked the gangster and was happy to introduce him to various actors and studio directors. A well-dressed, handsome man, Siegel had a boyish, charming personality. He rubbed elbows with many Hollywood stars, including Clark Gable, Jean Harlow, Cary Grant, and Gary Cooper.

A DESERT OASIS

By the mid-1940s, Lansky had gained a reputation as the "chairman of the board" of the national crime syndicate. In

1945, Lansky and Siegel decided to establish a gambling hotel in a small town called Las Vegas, Nevada. According to reports, Siegel borrowed $3 million from the syndicate and eventually spent $6 million in building the Flamingo Hotel. (Flamingo was the nickname of one of Siegel's girlfriends, **Virginia Hill** [see entry].) As the first legalized gambling casino in the United States, the Flamingo became famous nationwide, and Siegel drew enormous profits from it.

But the syndicate members suspected—with good cause—that Siegel was pocketing money that was not his. They believed that the money—which came from building funds and gambling income—had been stashed in Swiss bank accounts by Siegel's mistress, Hill.

A BAD ROLL OF THE DICE

On behalf of the syndicate, Luciano contacted Siegel and instructed him to meet with syndicate members in Havana, Cuba. Havana was at that time one of the gambling centers of the world and a gangster haven. At the Havana meeting in December 1946, Siegel denied that he had stolen mob money. Apparently syndicate members did not believe him.

On June 20, 1947, as Siegel sat in the living room of Hill's Beverly Hills mansion, he was gunned down by shotgun fire. (Hill was in Europe at the time.) Struck three times, he died instantly. When law enforcement officials arrived at the scene of the slaying, they found the gangster's right eye in the dining room, five yards from the corpse. The forty-one-year-old mobster was buried in a closed casket.

Although Lansky and Luciano denied involvement in the hit, there is little doubt that Siegel was murdered on syndicate orders. Carbo is commonly believed to have been the gunman who fired into the living room of Hill's mansion on Linden Drive. Shortly after Siegel's assassination, Sedway and several syndicate members appeared at the Flamingo Hotel and informed the manager that they were taking over.

Sources for Further Reading

Nash, Jay Robert. *Bloodletters and Badmen.* New York: M. Evans, 1973, pp. 501–504.

Sifakis, Carl. *The Mafia Encyclopedia.* New York: Facts on File, 1982, pp. 302–304.

Racketeers
and Gamblers

Underworld figures have for a long time engaged in racketeering, a form of extortion. Today, mobsters practice racketeering to collect substantial kickbacks—and to control certain industries and unions. A steady source of vast power and income, racketeering is a mainstay of modern-day mobsters.

In the mid-1940s, Las Vegas, Nevada, was nothing more than a remote desert town. Through a scheme masterminded by mobster Meyer Lansky—and in part implemented by Bugsy Siegel—the area soon became a gambler's mecca. Today, gambling operations—which produce immense quantities of easily-skimmed cash—constitute a substantial portion of the Mob's activities and income.

In this section you'll meet some of the nation's early racketeers and gamblers. Among those included are Louis Lepke, who murdered his way to the top of New York's labor racketeering empire, and later played a critical role in the formation of a national crime syndicate; Arnold Rothstein, a brilliant organizer—considered by many to be the father of organized crime in America—who was himself a compulsive gambler; and Diamond Joe Esposito, an early practitioner of labor racketeering and political fixing. You'll also read about the formation of Murder, Inc.—a hit squad assembled to carry out the mob's violent dirty work.

Frank Costello

Born: January 26, 1891
Died: February 18, 1973
AKA: Frank Saverio, Francisco
Seriglia, Frank Stello

Frank Costello rose from a poor immigrant background to play a critical role in the formation of the national crime syndicate (association). A close associate of the mob's top bosses, he mediated disagreements and earned a reputation as a "fixer" who could take care of any legal difficulties.

A YOUTHFUL OFFENDER

Born Francesco Castiglia in Lauropoli, Calabria, in southwest Italy, Costello was the sixth child of a poor farmer. When he was four he moved with his family to New York's East Harlem, an Italian slum plagued by street crime. His father opened a small grocery on East 108th Street. Costello quit school at the age of eleven to sell newspapers and run a crap game for kids. (Craps is a game in which the participants place bets on the throw of dice.) Running the game required the young Costello to pay-off a neighborhood policeman—a practice that he would use throughout his criminal career.

A petty (small-time) thief by his teens, Costello was arrested for assault and robbery on April 25, 1908. The case was dismissed. When he was twenty-one he was arrested again—for robbing a woman of $1,600 on the street—the charges were also dropped. In 1914, Costello followed his brother, Edward—who was ten years older—into a ruthless Manhattan street gang

Natural born criminal

When Costello became a U.S. citizen in 1925, he listed his occupation as real estate operator. He was, in fact, a bootlegger at the time. Decades later, when government officials found it difficult to convict the mobster of other crimes, they tried to have his citizenship taken away on the grounds that he had lied about his occupation. This, in turn, would have led to his deportation (forcible return) to Italy as an undesirable alien. But Italian authorities protested. Costello, they said, was a product of American society: when he left Italy as a four-year-old, he had no criminal record.

called the "Gophers," run by gangster **Owney Madden** (see entry). As a member of this gang, Costello began to carry a gun.

Arrested a third time, in 1915, Costello was charged with illegal possession of a pistol. At trial he encountered Edward Swann, a strict judge who intended to teach the young hoodlum (criminal) a lesson. According to court records, the judge said:

> I have got it right from his [Costello's] neighbors that he has the reputation of being a gunman and in this particular case he . . . had a very beautiful weapon and was . . . prepared to do the work of a gunman. He was charged on two other occasions with doing the work of a gunman and, somehow or other, got out of it. Now I commit him to the penitentiary for one year. . . .

Costello served ten months in prison on Welfare Island. In spite of accusations of criminal acts and numerous arrests, it would be another thirty-seven years before he returned to prison.

Kewpie dolls and rumrunning

Costello's criminal career blossomed after his release from Welfare Island. Using money and favors to gain political protection, he ran Harlem crap games. He used fruit stores as fronts to hide illegal gambling activities that took place in the back rooms. He became rich from his numerous gambling enterprises, and shared his wealth with policemen and politicians to ensure that his activities would not be hindered by the law. In 1917, after he was drafted into the U.S. Army, Costello used his political contacts to avoid service.

In 1919, Costello became a partner in something called the Horowitz Novelty Company, which produced Kewpie dolls as prizes for punchboard players. Players paid as much as twenty-five cents per punchboard to punch holes in a card to find out whether they had winning numbers. Although the Horowitz

Novelty Company went bankrupt (reduced to financial ruin), it reappeared as the Dainties Products Company, which quickly earned Costello a small fortune.

By 1920, Costello had enough money to invest into the area's booming bootlegging business (illegal manufacture and sale of alcohol). At first he purchased liquor through his various contacts in the city. With his brother's help, he used the threat of violence to force bar owners to purchase his booze. Costello eventually carved out a role as a wholesale supplier to larger, more established gangs. He ran his bootlegging operations like a big business. He traveled to Montreal, Quebec, Canada, to purchase a fortune in high quality whiskey from Canadian and European exporters. He was responsible for the scheduling of speed boats and trucks that carried liquor shipments into New York City under the noses of Prohibition officers. He oversaw staffs of salespeople and bookkeepers who tallied the day-to-day operations. And he supervised the bribery (paid-off) of thousands of policemen who were paid to look the other way.

A FORTUNE IN NICKELS AND DIMES

Aware that Prohibition (when the Eighteenth Amendment outlawed the manufacture and sale of alcohol) was doomed to fail, Costello expanded his operations. During the early 1920s, he controlled the city's developing slot machine business. Between 1928 and 1934, his slot machine business operated as many as five thousand machines—whose profits were estimated at about $600 per machine each year. With a profit of $3 million each year, Costello made a fortune on the nickel-operated machines.

NEW ORLEANS

Costello—whose influence was far-reaching—wasn't about to abandon such a profitable business. At the invitation of Demo-

A day in the life . . .

Costello's routine, as the don (Mafia leader) of the New York underworld, was highly predictable. He once remarked, "I go places so regular they call me Mr. Schedule." A typical day went as follows:

10 a.m.
Shave, manicure—and sometimes a haircut at the barbershop in the Waldorf-Astoria Hotel.

Late morning
Business conversations in the Waldorf lobby.

Lunch
Usually at the Norse Grill in the Waldorf. (Costello was a good tipper.)

Late afternoon
A movie at a theater on Broadway (in Manhattan) or in the suburbs

Evening
Cocktails at the Madison Hotel (never more than three). More business conversations.

In the bag

Manhattan district attorney Frank Hogan obtained permission to place a wiretap (listening device) on Costello's phone in 1943. The mobster's conversations revealed much about his role in New York politics—including his part in helping Thomas Aurelio to the Democratic nomination for state supreme court judge. Hogan taped an August 23 conversation between Costello and Aurelio that revealed the political fix:

Aurelio: "How are you, and thanks for everything."

Costello: "Congratulations. It went over perfect. When I tell you something is in the bag, you can rest assured."

Aurelio: "It was perfect. It was fine."

Costello: "Well, we will all have to get together and have dinner some night real soon."

Aurelio: "That would be fine. But right now I want to assure you of my loyalty for all you have done. It is unwavering."

After the conversation was made public, authorities attempted to have Aurelio disbarred (expelled from the bar, a professional organization of lawyers). They failed. Costello was never punished for his role in the fix, either. The evidence against him relied on the wiretap, which was inadmissible as evidence in court.

cratic Louisiana senator Huey E. Long—who promised to legalize the slot machine trade—Costello set up shop in New Orleans within months of being forced out of New York. Having made a relatively small cash investment, Costello remained in New York while he raked in the profits of his Louisiana enterprise.

Costello's vast profits nearly landed him in jail. In 1939, the federal government tried him in New Orleans on charges of evading (avoiding) taxes on thousands of dollars in hidden income. The government's case was based on the discovery that Costello's declared income could not possibly support his expensive lifestyle. But Costello remained free to purchase expensive pajamas and hand-tailored suits. The government lost its case because of lack of evidence.

ON TOP OF THE WORLD

By the end of the 1920s, Costello had become a top adviser to Lucky Luciano, one of the most powerful crime bosses in the country. Together with **Meyer Lansky** (see entry), Costello and Luciano helped to create a national crime syndicate during the 1930s. Lansky and Luciano organized the activities of criminal gangs that had previously acted independently. Costello continued to do what he did best—ensuring friendly relations with policemen and politicians. He made sure that complaints disappeared, cases were dropped, and sentences shortened. As a skilled negotiator who dealt with policemen, politicians, and judges, he became known as the "Prime Minister" (official head) of the underworld.

By the 1950s, Costello had become one of the most powerful crime figures in the United States. He was an important member of the national syndicate's crime board, which made decisions that governed the actions of gangsters across the country. He is believed to have been responsible for shielding the crime syndicate from the Federal Bureau of Investigation, whose leader, J. Edgar Hoover, denied the existence of organized crime in America.

That is, until the mayor of New York, Fiorello La Guardia, a fellow Italian, took office. La Guardia objected to the gambling machines—some of which were equipped with ladders so that little children could reach the coin slot to play. Formerly protected by an injunction against police seizure, the machines were seized at the mayor's bequest. (An injunction is a court order forbidding a certain act.) Swinging a sledge hammer, La Guardia personally demolished dozens of machines. The rest he had destroyed and thrown into the sea. By 1935, La Guardia had driven the slot machine business out of New York. And he dismissed crime boss Costello as a bum and a punk.

CONTEMPT

In 1951, a Senate Crime Investigating Committee headed by Senator Estes Kefauver met to investigate organized crime in America. Questioned for eight days in February and March of

My fair lady

Even behind bars, Costello was an influential man. One day in late 1957, his lawyer, Edward Bennett Williams, visited him in the Federal House of Detention in New York. Williams made an off-hand remark that he had been unable—at any price—to purchase tickets to "My Fair Lady." Williams wanted to attend the popular theater play to celebrate his thirty-fifth wedding anniversary with his wife and her parents.

Williams left the detention center and shortly after he arrived home, his doorbell rang. A husky man handed him an envelope and left. When he looked inside, he found four tickets to that evening's performance of the play.

Frank Costello's home on Sands Point, Long Island.

that year, Costello testified about his role in New York City politics. The committee ultimately labeled Costello "the number-one racketeer in the country." Among other things, it revealed that the gangster had played an important role in the Democratic nomination of Thomas Aurelio for the New York Supreme Court some eight years earlier.

Costello insisted that his face not be shown on the televised hearings. But the camera recorded his nervous hand movements and raspy voice. Having carefully avoided the limelight throughout his criminal career, Costello found himself thrust into the public eye. On March 15, Costello left the courtroom claiming that he had a sore throat. His refusal to testify further earned him a conviction for contempt (disobeying a legal order) of the committee, for which he was sentenced to eighteen months in prison with a $5,000 fine.

UNCLE FRANK

When he was released from prison, Costello discovered that the unwanted publicity and time behind bars had weakened his position as head of the Luciano crime family. (Costello had assumed leadership after Lucky Luciano was deported for operating a prostitution ring.) Vito Genovese, a rival crime boss, was eager to take over Costello's territory. For a while, Costello managed to stall Genovese, who arranged for the assassination of Costello's aide, Willie Moretti, and his ally (a helpful associate), Albert Anastasia.

On May 2, 1957, Genovese sent Vincent "the Chin" Gigante to ambush his rival. As Costello entered his Central Park West apartment building, Gigante shouted, "This is for you Frank!" and fired several shots. Only slightly wounded by a bullet that grazed his head, Costello survived. But he understood Genovese's message—whether the shooting was intended to be fatal, or, as some claimed, merely a warning. Costello soon began to step back from his gambling operations, and by the early 1960s had officially retired from crime.

Costello and his wife, Loretta "Bobbie" Geigerman Costello, lived quietly, spending time in their Manhattan apartment and Long Island summer home. Fond of being called "Uncle Frank," the former gangster tended a small peach orchard on his summer property, and displayed flowers he had grown in local shows. Despite occasional newspaper stories that claimed he had resumed his position as don of the New York underworld, Costello insisted that he was a law-abiding retiree. When he was legally summoned by a subpoena (pronounced suh-PEE-na) to testify before a grand jury that was investigating gambling, in May, 1970, he told reporters, "I'm retired. I don't know any more about this than you do." Costello died of natural causes on February 18, 1973, at the age of eighty-two.

An honest New Yorker

After he retired, Costello had a hard time convincing the public that was nothing more than a law-abiding citizen. He once told reporters, "Right now I'm cleaner than 99 percent of New Yorkers. Now I don't want you to get the wrong impression—I never sold any Bibles."

Sources for Further Reading

"Costello, Frank." *The New York Times Obituaries* (February 19, 1973), pp. 1, 21.

"Manners & Morals." *Time* (November 28, 1949), pp. 15–18.

"The Men Behind the Tiger." *The Nation* (October 31, 1959), pp. 265–269.

Sifakis, Carl. *The Mafia Encyclopedia.* New York: Facts on File, 1982, pp. 185–188.

Who's Who in the Mafia. [Online] Available http://home1.pacific.net.sg/~seowjean/Mafia/mafia.html, November 7, 1997.

Legs Diamond
(John Thomas Diamond)

Born: 1896
Died: December 17, 1931

A former member of a vicious youth gang, Legs Diamond muscled his way to the top of the bootlegging business in Prohibition-era New York. At one time rumored to be impossible to kill, he died in a gangland execution.

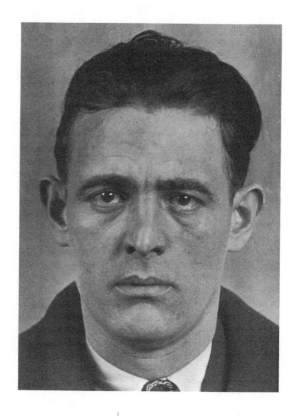

THE SON OF IRISH IMMIGRANTS

John Thomas Diamond was born in 1896, in Kensington, a poor enclave (area) of Irish immigrants in Philadelphia, Pennsylvania. His parents had one other child, Edward, who was born in 1899. With only a limited education, Diamond quickly became street-smart, and by his teens, had become a thief.

Diamond's father moved his sons to New York City after his wife, Sara, died in 1913. John Diamond Sr. settled in Brooklyn, where he worked as a laborer. At the time, New York City was plagued by numerous gangs that attracted poor young boys to their ranks. Both John and Eddie Diamond became involved in a gang known as the "Hudson Dusters," which specialized in robbing packaged goods from delivery trucks. John Diamond quickly earned a reputation as an aggressive young thug. By the time he was seventeen, he had a long list of arrests for assault, burglary, and robbery. A few brief sentences at a reformatory school in New York did not convince him to lead a law-abiding life.

Why John Diamond was called "Legs" is the subject of much debate. Some say he earned the nickname as a teenage thief—because he was consistently able to outrun police. Others say that Diamond, an accomplished dancer, acquired the moniker because of his prowess (ability) on the dance floor. There is also a theory that he was given the name by other gangsters, who regarded Diamond as a man who would run out on just about anyone.

Diamond's criminal career was interrupted in 1918, when he was drafted to serve in the U.S. Army during World War I (1914-1918). After a very short time as a soldier, he went AWOL—absent without leave—an offense that was punishable by imprisonment. Diamond was soon arrested by military police, who delivered him to court. Tried and convicted of desertion, he was sentenced to five years' imprisonment in Leavenworth prison. Diamond was released in 1920, after serving only one year and one day of his sentence.

BACK IN BUSINESS

Shortly after his release, Diamond went to work for Jacob "Little Augie" Orgen, one of New York City's top racketeers (people that gain payments through various illegal methods such as fraud or violence) in the 1920s. Also in Orgen's gang were a number of rising stars in the New York underworld—such as Lucky Luciano, **Louis Lepke** (see entry), and Waxey Gordon. During the early years of Prohibition (when the Eighteenth Amendment outlawed the manufacture and sale of alcohol), Diamond and his brother, Eddie, worked in Orgen's bootlegging business, hijacking shipments of Canadian liquor that were being transported through upstate New York. Daring, calculating, and very good with a gun, Diamond quickly moved up in Orgen's organization. Together with his brother, Diamond took over much of Orgen's narcotics (drugs) and gem smuggling business.

Orgen was not the only gangster to stake a claim in Manhattan's profitable bootlegging business. In the early years of Prohibition, Joseph Weyler (known as Johnny Spanish), Nathan "Kid Dropper" Kaplan (who took the name of Jack the Dropper—or Kid Dropper—a boxer he admired), and Orgen fought for control of the same New York territory. On July 29, 1919, Spanish dropped out of the competition after he was murdered by Kaplan on his way out of a restaurant. With Spanish gone, Orgen and Kaplan battled for control of the enterprise.

A Plan to Eliminate Kaplan

Orgen enlisted Diamond to help him dispose of his arch rival. But Kaplan, who surrounded himself with gunmen, was not an easy target. A clever schemer, Diamond did not plan to commit the assassination himself. Instead, he convinced Louis Kushner, a small-time gangster, to do the actual dirty work. Kushner was being blackmailed by Kaplan and was eager to kill the man who was taking his money on a monthly basis. What's more, Diamond convinced Kushner that the killing would help him to move up in Orgen's organization.

The clay pigeon

Diamond was shot so often during his criminal career that he became known as the "clay pigeon [a shooting target] of the underworld." He survived so many shootings, that it was rumored that he was impossible to kill. The gangster reportedly boasted, "The bullet hasn't been made that can kill me." He was wrong.

Diamond came up with a plan that allowed Kushner to ambush Kaplan when he would have little opportunity to protect himself. First, he convinced a man named Jacob Gurrah Shapiro to file a complaint against Kaplan, who had assaulted him three years earlier. Shapiro had been wounded by Kaplan as he returned fire at Orgen's men in a battle that took place on Essex Street. The incident left two bystanders dead.

A Sitting Duck

Shapiro signed the complaint and on August 28, 1923, Kaplan was tried for the assault. Before he entered the courtroom, he was stripped of his gun, in spite of his objections that it was protection against would-be assassins. Diamond's plan fell in place exactly as he had intended. He knew Kaplan's whereabouts—and he knew he would be unarmed. Kaplan had become a sitting duck (easy target).

Kaplan left the West Side Court surrounded by policemen. He was led to the back seat of a squad car, where police captain Cornelius Willemse sat beside him. Kushner, who watched from across the street, crossed over to the car. Mounting the bumper on the back of the car, he fired several shots into the rear window, shattering the glass. The driver was wounded, but both Willemse and Kaplan were unharmed. Kaplan's wife attempted to stop Kushner as a crowd of police and onlookers watched. But Kushner pushed her aside, broke a side window in the squad car, and fired directly at Kaplan's head. The gang leader

Hard to find

Although Diamond boasted that he was impossible to kill, he made sure that he wasn't an easy target. He surrounded himself with gunmen who were loyal only to him. He also hid his whereabouts when he was visiting out of town by renting several rooms in the city—so that a gunman who wanted to kill him would not be sure where to find him. On the night of his death, Diamond slept in one of the several seedy (run-down) rooms he had rented in Albany, New York.

reportedly uttered "They got me" just before he died. Bragging that he had killed Kaplan, Kushner asked police for a cigarette and posed for newspaper photographers.

THE END OF "LITTLE AUGIE" ORGEN

While Kushner sat in jail, Diamond enjoyed his new standing in Orgen's gang. As a reward, he was given a large portion of the narcotics and bootlegging business that had belonged to Orgen's onetime rival. Diamond was not a modest man. A flashy dresser, he showed off his new wealth by purchasing expensive automobiles and lavish apartments. He became part-owner of a speakeasy (saloon) called the Hotsy Totsy Club, on the second floor of a building on Broadway between 54th and 55th Streets. And he showered money on his numerous girlfriends—one of whom was a chorus dancer named Marion Strasmick, known as Marion "Kiki" Roberts. (Although he was a married man, Diamond still had numerous affairs.)

Within a few years, Diamond had become a kingpin (chief) in the New York crime network as one of Orgen's most feared and trusted lieutenants. But in 1927, Orgen's reign came to an abrupt end. On October 15, he left his headquarters on the Lower East Side. Diamond accompanied his boss as his bodyguard. When the two approached a taxi, the cab door opened, and someone in the back seat opened fire with a machine gun. Orgen fell dead, with a dozen bullet wounds. Diamond was struck twice, but managed to drag himself down the street. After he arrived at Bellevue Hospital by ambulance, doctors announced that he had lost too much blood and would not survive his wounds.

But Diamond recovered—as he did many other times. He knew the men who had shot him and killed his boss. Louis Lepke and Jacob Shapiro—two young members of Orgen's gang who wanted to take over part of the business—had been the shooters. But Diamond refused to name the gunmen. He reportedly told police "Don't ask me nothin'! You hear me? Don't ask!

And don't bring anybody here for me to identify. I won't identify them even if I know they did it!"

At War with Dutch Schultz

After he recovered from his wounds, Diamond made peace with Lepke and Shapiro by promising to stick with his original piece of Orgen's business—bootlegging and narcotics sales. He vowed not to attempt to claim any of his former boss's other rackets. But this agreement did not protect his claim to Orgen's bootlegging territory. **Dutch Schultz** (see entry), a powerful gangster, wanted to muscle in on Diamond's turf. Diamond and Schultz waged war for two years, until Joey Noe, Schultz's right-hand man, arranged for the two to discuss a truce (peace agreement).

In a meeting at the Harding Hotel, Diamond and Schultz discussed the particulars of a peace agreement. Diamond agreed to give Schultz the rights to the midtown beer territory. But he wasn't willing to give up the territory for free. Diamond reportedly collected $500,000 before the meeting ended. The peace treaty lasted only minutes. After Schultz and Noe left the Harding Hotel, two shooters opened fire on them. Noe was killed. When Schultz returned fire, the gunmen ran away. The war was on: Schultz swore that he would make Diamond pay for the ambush.

Difficult Man to Kill

Diamond had already proved that he was a difficult man to kill. But his brother, Eddie, was an easier target. Schultz's gunmen traveled to Colorado, where Eddie was trying to recover from a lung ailment. Although he was ambushed in a hail of bullets, Eddie survived the shooting—only to die later of tuberculosis (a lung disease). Diamond was furious about the attack on his brother—the only person, some people say, to whom the gangster ever showed any loyalty. None of Eddie's attackers lived out the year.

The room where Legs
Diamond was shot: the
window on the extreme
right, one floor below
the top.

ANOTHER BRUSH WITH DEATH

The war between Diamond and Schultz grew hotter. Diamond spent large sums of money to supply himself with deadly gunmen such as Salvatore Aricicio, Tony Fusco, John Herring, A. J. Harry Klein, Gary Scaccio, and Paul Quattrochi—as well as Joe McDonald, a deadly submachine gunner. The list of Schultz's men who had been slain by Diamond's artillery included James Ahern, James Batto, Antonio Oliverio, Moe Schubert, Harry Vesey, and Tom Walsh.

Schultz retaliated (struck back) by attacking Diamond himself. In October 1929, three of Schultz's men ambushed Diamond and his girlfriend, Kiki Roberts, at the Hotel Monticello as they dined in their pajamas. After they burst through the door they let loose a volley of submachine gun fire that ripped through the walls of the hotel suite. Roberts was unharmed. Diamond was shot five times—and lived.

In 1930, Diamond took a break from his feud with Schultz to travel to Europe on the *Baltic*. When he returned to New York he moved with his wife, Alice, to Acra, New York. In April 1931, as Diamond left the Aratago Inn, where they lived, he was shot several times in a drive-by ambush. Again he lived to tell about it.

A Hollow Victory

Several months after the shooting, Diamond traveled with some of his men to Albany, New York, to try to recruit two local bootleggers, James Duncan and Grover Parks. The two men wanted no part of Diamond's business—but the gangster's men convinced them to change their minds. Gary Scaccio and other members of Diamond's gang tortured the men by placing matches under their fingernails. They prodded them with heated fire pokers and cigarettes. Duncan and Parks eventually told Diamond they would work for him. But they went to the police to report the ordeal when they were set free.

Charged with Kidnapping

Diamond and Scaccio stood trial in Troy, New York, for the kidnapping. Notorious (well-known) for making promises he didn't plan to keep, Diamond let Scaccio take the blame—with the promise that he'd get him out of prison after a few months.

The bodyguard

Diamond worked for a while as a bodyguard for **Arnold Rothstein** (see entry), the multimillionaire king of the rackets empire. He earned $1,000 per week for protecting his boss's life from hot-tempered gamblers who lost their money to Rothstein. Diamond was also expected to make sure that customers with a lot of money made it home safely—and he was in charge of "convincing" (forcing) gamblers who owed Rothstein money to pay off their debts.

Hotsy Totsy murders

Diamond owned a speakeasy called the Hotsy Totsy Club with another gangster, Hymie Cohen. A popular spot among the gangster elite, the club was the site of many meetings—and more than a few murders. Many gangsters who were invited to the club for dancing and drinking left the establishment as corpses (dead bodies).

On June 13, 1929, a young crook named William "Red" Cassidy and some of his friends went to the club looking for trouble. Cassidy insulted the service and threatened Diamond and his enforcer, Charles Entratta. Diamond and Entratta shot Cassidy and his friend, Simon Walker, in front of the bar's customers and employees. Both men died.

Diamond and Entratta went into hiding—just long enough to take care of witnesses who could identify them as the killers. The two gangsters eventually surrendered, but they were released by the police because of "lack of evidence." None of the several witnesses were available to testify against the killers.

Diamond never made any effort to help Scaccio out of his ten-year sentence at Sing Sing prison.

On December 17, 1931, Diamond celebrated his victory in court with his friends and wife at a speakeasy in Albany. From there he went to visit his girlfriend, Kiki, in her apartment at 21 Broeck Street. He left after a few hours. Drunk, he ordered his driver, John Storer, to take him to a seedy boarding house at 67 Dove Street.

Sometime after Diamond fell asleep, a couple of men entered his room. As one of the gunmen held his head, the other shot him at point-blank range. Mrs. Wood, the landlady, heard the shots and called the police. When the medical examiner arrived, he pronounced Diamond dead.

WHO KILLED DIAMOND?

Although no one was ever convicted of Diamond's slaying, there are several theories about who killed him. Many assumed that Schultz's men had finally succeeded in killing their boss's rival. Others believed that Salvatore Spitale and Irving Bitz—two gangsters who had given Diamond money to set up narcotics connections on his trip to Europe—had ordered the killing after Diamond spent the money on himself. Still others speculated that the killers might have been hired by mobsters who feared that Diamond would try to take over their business—such as Lucky Luciano or **Meyer Lansky** (see entry).

Diamond's wife claimed to know nothing about the killing. In fact, she claimed that she didn't know that her infamous husband was a gangster. Alice Diamond was murdered two years later, in Brooklyn.

Diamond's girlfriend, Kiki Roberts, contacted the *New York American* after she learned of the gangster's death. She told reporters: "I was in love with Jack Diamond. I was with him in Albany, New York, before he was killed. But I don't know who killed him or anything about the murder." Roberts disappeared shortly thereafter. She later turned up—living under her real name, Marion Strasmick.

Sources for Further Reading

Nash, Jay Robert. *Bloodletters and Badmen.* New York: M. Evans, 1973, pp. 153–158.

Sifakis, Carl. *The Mafia Encyclopedia.* New York: Facts on File, 1982, pp. 107–108.

Who's Who in the Mafia. [Online] Available http://home1.pacific.net.sg/~seowjean/Mafia/mafia.html, November 7, 1997.

Diamond Joe Esposito
(Joseph Esposito)

Born: March 28, 1872
Died: March 21, 1928

Once a dirt-poor immigrant, Diamond Joe Esposito amassed a fortune by participating in bootlegging and racketeering ventures.

A BAKER ON THE MOVE

Esposito was born near Naples, Italy, in the small town of Accera. He grew up in poverty and immigrated to the United States in 1895, when he was twenty-three years old. Scrounging a living by taking whatever work he could find, he collected garbage, dug ditches, and carefully saved his money. After a few years he moved from Boston, Massachusetts, to Brooklyn, New York. At the age of thirty-three, he settled in Chicago, where he opened a bakery in the Nineteenth Ward, an area known as Little Italy.

Esposito continued to hustle, working odd jobs to supplement his income from the bakery. He worked for a while as a hod carrier—hard physical labor that required him to carry heavy loads of bricks to bricklayers and stonemasons. He soon organized his fellow workers into a union known as the International Hod Carriers' Building Construction Laborers' Union. Esposito was the union's treasurer and agent.

Esposito also helped establish the Circolo Accera Club, whose members came from his native village in Italy. As the club's president, he provided start-up money for a number of small businesses in the community—for which he collected a large share of the profits after the business was underway.

As the money rolled in, Esposito took care to improve his standing in the community. He threw expensive parties and helped to feed the poor. He donated money to help other Italians immigrate to America and he played Santa Claus during the Christmas holiday. Well before his fortieth birthday, Esposito had become a wealthy and influential man in Chicago's Italian community.

A BARBERSHOP BRAWL

Always heavily armed, Esposito was involved in a shooting in August of 1908. At the time, he and his barber, Mack Geaquenta, were dating the same woman. Esposito went to the barber shop for a shave and hair cut. As he sat in the barber's chair, with his face covered with lather, he began to argue with Geaquenta. The barber started toward him, but Esposito jumped up—his face still smeared with shaving cream—and pulled a gun. He ended the argument by shooting Geaquenta dead.

Esposito's trial did not take place until May of the following year. During the nine-month wait, the witnesses who had seen the shooting either lost their nerve or vanished. With no one to testify against him, Esposito was released.

DIAMOND JOE

Esposito was not a modest man. Fond of flashy displays of wealth, he was nicknamed "Diamond Joe" (or "Dimey"). A heavyset man who stood six feet tall, he wore a large belt with a buckle that spelled out his name with $50,000 worth of diamonds. He dressed himself in diamond rings, diamond cuff links, and diamond shirt studs (buttons). Like his friend, Big Jim Colosimo—who was also fond of diamonds—Esposito

Big trouble at the Bella Napoli

Many gangsters frequented Esposito's ritzy cafe, the Bella Napoli. Cuono Coletta, a well-known killer, was among the establishment's underworld clientele. One evening Coletta fired his gun in the cafe, blasting the tip off of one of Sam Esposito's fingers. Joe Esposito took grave offense at his brother's injury. One of Esposito's enforcers promptly shot Coletta in the head.

The police raided Bella Napoli in 1923 for serving wine illegally. The establishment was closed down for one year. Esposito was fined $1,000—a mild slap on the hand to a man as wealthy as Diamond Joe.

opened an upscale cafe. The Bella Napoli, on South Halsted, was a popular establishment, especially among gangsters.

In 1913, Esposito threw a three-day party to celebrate his marriage. He invited the entire Nineteenth Ward neighborhood (now the Twenty-fifth Ward) to the festivities, which cost the newlywed a whopping $65,000—$40,000 of which was for wine. Forty-one years old at the time, Esposito married a sixteen-year-old girl named Carmela Marchese.

POLITICS AND BOOZE

Esposito enjoyed a great deal of political clout (power). He was able to influence the voters in his neighborhood to the extent that he could guarantee political friends that the entire Nineteenth Ward would follow his lead. In 1920, when Esposito was forty-eight, his friend, republican Senator Charles S. Deneen, convinced him to run for a political office. In a landslide victory, Esposito won the post of ward committeeman.

Esposito celebrated his election by throwing a lavish party—even more extravagant than his wedding had been. Several people who hadn't been invited to the affair tried to crash the party. Esposito's enforcer, Tony "Mops" Volpe—one of Chicago's most ruthless killers—beat them up and threw them out.

At the time of Esposito's election, Prohibition (when the Eighteenth Amendment outlawed the manufacture and sale of alcohol) had gone into effect. Esposito, like many other gangsters, made a fortune by taking part in the bootlegging industry that produced, supplied, and transported illegal booze. Once in office, he appointed Volpe as the county's deputy sheriff. In so doing, he protected illegal liquor production operations he had installed throughout Chicago and the suburbs of Chicago Heights and Melrose Park.

Esposito employed thousands of illegal Italian immigrants, who worked for very low wages for fear of having their lack of U.S. citizenship exposed. The inexpensive hard liquor, beer, and wine that Esposito produced was delivered throughout the city—in spite of the efforts of Prohibition agents to turn Chicago into a dry (alcohol-free) town. Some of Esposito's enormous stills (machines used to make liquor) produced alcohol that bordered on poison. Esposito also supplied other bootleggers with the sugar to produce alcohol. The **Genna brothers** (see entry), who ran stills in the city, relied heavily on Esposito.

UNHEEDED WARNINGS

As rival bootleggers, the Genna brothers became embroiled (involved) in a battle with infamous gangster **Al Capone** (see entry). Esposito's loyalty to Capone angered the Gennas. To demonstrate their displeasure, they arranged the murder of two of Esposito's brothers-in-law. John Tucillo and Philip Leonatti were ambushed in a hail of machine-gun fire as they bought cigars. The murders were a warning to Esposito to abandon his allegiance (loyalty) to Capone.

Frank Nitti.

Esposito ignored the warnings and the Gennas were eventually destroyed by their rivals. By the spring of 1928, Esposito was on bad terms with Capone. Most of his underworld friends had been forced out of the business—or killed. On the morning of March 21, 1928, Esposito received a phone call from Frank Nitti, one of Capone's top aides. Nitti reportedly warned him, "Get out of town or get killed."

Again, Esposito ignored the warning. He suspected that someone was attempting to scare him off in order to take over his profitable businesses. Ralph and Joe Varchetti, Esposito's bodyguards, tried to convince their boss to retire to his farm on Cedar Lake where he could support himself raising chickens. But Esposito refused to leave his profitable rackets.

FIFTY-EIGHT BULLET HOLES

Later in the evening, Esposito walked toward his home on Oakley Boulevard with his bodyguards. A sedan approached the three men from the rear, and unleashed a round of machine gun fire. The Varchetti brothers survived. But Esposito, who took fifty-eight bullets in all, died on the spot. Ralph Varchetti later described the episode in court:

> Then there were more shots, and Joe says, 'Oh, my God!' and I knew he was hit. I dropped to the sidewalk and lay flat, with my face in the dirt. The shots came in bursts of fire from an automobile. . . . When the firing stopped a second, I looked up and they fired again. I dropped flat, and this time waited until they were gone. I got near Dimey [Esposito] and tried to wake him. He was gone.

The coroner's investigation produced no evidence to charge anyone with Esposito's murder. Esposito left behind a wife, who was then thirty-one, and three young children. His killers were never identified.

Sources for Further Reading

Nash, Jay Robert. *Bloodletters and Badmen.* New York: M. Evans, 1973, pp. 153–158.

Sifakis, Carl. *The Mafia Encyclopedia.* New York: Facts on File, 1982, pp. 107–108.

Who's Who in the Mafia. [Online] Available http://home1. pacific.net.sg/~seowjean/Mafia/mafia.html, November 7, 1997.

Louis Lepke
(Louis Buchalter)

Born: 1897
Died: March 4, 1944

One of several Jewish gangsters in the New York underworld, Louis Lepke rose to the highest level of the newly formed national crime syndicate (association). A multi-millionaire by the end of his career, he was eventually betrayed by fellow mobsters.

LITTLE LOUIS

Like many other gangsters who eventually rose to the top of the New York underworld, Lepke started out as a teenager robbing packaged goods from delivery carts in Manhattan. At the age of sixteen he was arrested for the first time. Lepke was so poor that, according to the police report, he wore stolen shoes. He got his nickname from his mother. "Lepke" is an affectionate Yiddish name meaning "Little Louis." But the gangsters who referred to him by his nickname did not do so with affection.

In the 1920s, during the early years of Prohibition (when the Eighteenth Amendment outlawed the manufacture and sale of alcohol), Lepke worked for crime boss **Arnold Rothstein** (see entry). While most other young gangsters of the era were involved in the profitable bootlegging business (illegal manufacture and sale of alcohol), Lepke decided to work in an area that had longevity—that is, an activity that would outlive Prohibition. Lepke chose labor racketeering (manipulating laborers through intimidation) as his specialty. Together with his boyhood pal Jacob Gurrah Shapiro, he joined the gang of "Little Augie" Orgen, who controlled labor racketeering in New York at that time.

UNGRATEFUL STUDENTS

Orgen trained Lepke and Shapiro in the rackets—and they were quick studies. Orgen's gang sold its services to both employers and unions in the garment industry—services that relied on muscle to put an end to labor strikes. Lepke soon grew restless. He wanted a share of his leader's business, and he wanted to have the freedom to explore many other racketeering opportunities that Orgen had ignored.

Orgen was aware that Lepke wanted a piece of the business for himself. He told his associates that he needed to put the young gangster in his place. But on October 15, 1927, as Orgen left his gang headquarters with his associate **Legs Diamond** (see entry), he was shot dead in a hail of machine gun fire that came from the back seat of a taxi cab. Lepke was the shooter. His friend Shapiro had been the driver.

A TAXING MAN

Lepke and Shapiro took over Orgen's rackets immediately. Although Orgen had offered strikebreaking services to both employers and unions, Lepke began to focus on labor unions. He helped local unions meet their demands by blackmailing (using threats to gain payment) employers. He also raised the fee for belonging to the union—and skimmed money from the dues members paid.

Lepke expanded his rackets empire to a number of other businesses. In exchange for payment, he offered "protection"—which amounted to nothing more than allowing workers to operate as usual. Bakery drivers had to pay a "tax"—one cent for each loaf of bread—to make sure that their bread was delivered before it became stale. Workers in numerous other businesses also paid Lepke's tax—from dry cleaners to poultry raisers, restaurant owners to shoe and handbag manufacturers. Lepke built a racketeering empire that pulled in some $10 million each year. Thomas E. Dewey, who eventually became governor of New York and a candidate for the presidency, referred to Lepke as the worst industrial racketeer in America.

MURDER, INC.

At the height of his career, Lepke was a member of the criminal elite that controlled the newly formed national crime syndicate. He acted as chairman of the board for the syndicate, which included Joe Adonis, **Frank Costello** (see entry), **Meyer Lansky** (see entry), Lucky Luciano, and **Dutch Schultz** (see entry) among its leaders. As such, Lepke—who was also known as Judge Louis—ordered the assassination of Schultz, who was being hounded by officials. A junior member of the board, Schultz had suggested that the gangsters arrange the murder of Dewey—who was at that time an aggressive special prosecutor—because he was putting too much pressure on Schultz's New York rackets. But Lepke realized that Dewey's murder would only make the situation worse by increasing police pressure on the gang's rackets. Schultz was murdered in 1935, in a restaurant in Newark, New Jersey, by a group of syndicate hit men.

Lepke—who had a reputation as a man who enjoyed hurting people—was also placed in charge of the syndicate's enforcement arm, which carried out the gang's violent activities. As the head of "Murder, Inc.," he was responsible for ordering and approving hundreds of killings. Lepke placed trusted associates in top positions in the organization. Shapiro, who had helped him ambush Orgen, was given a key role in Murder, Inc., as was another eager killer named Albert Anastasia.

LEPKE TAKES A POWDER

Dewey soon began to focus on Lepke's racketeering activities—particularly in the bakery business. At the same time, the federal government was investigating Lepke's involvement in restraint of trade (a form of racketeering). And the Federal

Working in Sing Sing

Even from prison, Lepke continued to influence the New York underworld. From behind the walls of Sing Sing prison, he ordered the execution of two of the men who had betrayed him. Abe Reles, the "canary" (person who informs on illegal activity) who tied Lepke to the murder of a candy store owner, was forced out of a window in a hotel on Coney Island. Moe "Dimples" Wolinsky—who had been instrumental in the double-cross that convinced Lepke to surrender—was shot to death in a restaurant in Manhattan.

Setting the record straight

On March 2, 1944, Governor Thomas E. Dewey issued a forty-eight hour stay of execution for Lepke, who claimed to have information that would reveal the criminal activities of a number of politicians. But the mobster wanted to make it clear to his associates that he would not inform on the syndicate's activities. He issued a statement through his wife:

> I am anxious to have it clearly understood that I did not offer to talk and give information in exchange for any promise of commutation of my death sentence. [A commutation changes a legal penalty to a lesser one.] I did not ask for that! The one and only thing I have asked for is to have a commission appointed to examine the facts. If that examination does not show that I am not guilty, I am willing to go to the chair, regardless of what information I have given or can give.

Lepke didn't need to worry about mob retaliation. He went to the chair on March 4, 1944.

Narcotics Bureau began to look into his role in large-scale narcotics (drug) smuggling. Lepke was arrested. Released on bail, he did not wait for authorities to arrest him on other charges. He went into hiding—staying in a number of different hideouts in Brooklyn. The federal authorities, who had no idea where to find the gang kingpin (chief), conducted a nation-wide manhunt.

Lepke's associates were not happy with the state of things. The gangster's disappearance had stepped up police pressure in New York—and throughout the country. The syndicate would not be able to return to business as usual until the authorities stopped searching for Lepke. Lucky Luciano—who ruled the mob from prison—was convinced that Lepke had to surrender. But Lepke faced the possibility of life imprisonment and would probably object to an order to turn himself in. So Luciano arranged for Lepke to be tricked into surrendering.

THE BIG FIX

Some of Lepke's trusted associates convinced him that the syndicate had "fixed" his problem. If he turned himself in, he would receive a light sentence with early parole—or so they said. Further, they claimed, he would not be prosecuted for his most serious crimes, which could easily land him in prison for life. Lepke agreed to surrender.

On August 24, 1939, Lepke surrendered. He met with Walter Winchell, a newspaper columnist who had repeatedly pub-

lished stories asking the gangster to contact him. Winchell delivered him to his friend, J. Edgar Hoover, who was in charge of the Federal Bureau of Investigation (FBI). Winchell reportedly introduced the two by saying, "Mr. Hoover, meet Lepke." Lepke realized immediately that he had been double-crossed by his associates. Hoover, who called Lepke "the most dangerous criminal in the United States," had no intention of showing leniency (tolerance) to the infamous racketeer.

Mrs. Louis Buchalter and her son, Harold, arrive at Sing Sing to visit her husband in his cell on death row, March 1, 1944.

DEATH ROW

Lepke received a fourteen-year sentence for his narcotics dealings, which had involved bribing U.S. customs officials. New York district attorney Dewey was responsible for adding another thirty-nine years to Lepke's imprisonment. But the worst was yet to come.

Dewey had begun to investigate the activities of Murder, Inc. Abe Reles, a former killer in the organization, made his job a great deal easier. In exchange for leniency, Reles informed on other members of the murderous association—including Lepke, who was responsible for the murder of Joe Rosen, a candy store owner who had once been a trucker in the gangster's territory in the garment industry.

In 1940, Lepke was taken from federal custody to New York to be tried for Rosen's murder. He was found guilty, along with two other gangsters, Louis Capone and Mendy Weiss. All three were sentenced to death.

NOT A PRETTY SIGHT

Lepke did not believe that his death sentence would actually be carried out. He had detailed knowledge of the involvement of politicians in syndicate activities—knowledge he hoped to use to his advantage. Lepke told newspaper reporters that he had damaging information about an important labor leader's involvement in criminal activities. "If I would talk," Lepke bragged, "a lot of big people would get hurt. When I say big, I mean big. The names would surprise you." Lepke's ploy worked for a while. He earned several stays (delays) of execution—including a forty-eight hour reprieve (postponement) that was granted on the day he was to be killed. But on March 4, 1944, his luck ran out.

Lepke ate his last meal—roasted chicken and shoestring potatoes—still convinced that he would receive a last-minute pardon. He was in good spirits until late in the evening. Burton B. Turkus, who prosecuted the Murder, Inc. case recalled: "Only late in the evening, with the final minutes of his life ticking away, did he slowly begin to realize that maybe he had relied on the wrong miracle-maker."

Shortly after 11 P.M., Lepke, Capone, and Weiss were escorted to the electric chair at Sing Sing prison. Capone went first. He was pronounced dead three minutes after he received

Wealthy man in a hot seat

Lepke--who was a millionaire many times over--is said to be the wealthiest man ever to have been executed in the electric chair.

the 2,200-volt shock. Weiss followed. Before he was fastened into the chair, he said, "All I want to say is I'm innocent. I'm here on a framed-up case. Give my love to my family and everything." At the warden's signal, the electric shock coursed through electrodes fastened on his head. In less than two minutes, he was dead.

Lepke said nothing before thrusting himself into the chair. According to reporters, his body jerked before becoming limp. His skin turned blue. One newspaper account of the execution concluded: "It is not a pretty sight."

Sources for Further Reading

Nash, Jay Robert. *Bloodletters and Badmen.* New York: M. Evans, 1973, pp. 85–90.

Sifakis, Carl. *The Mafia Encyclopedia.* New York: Facts on File, 1982, pp. 185–188.

Who's Who in the Mafia. [Online] Available http://home1.pacific.net.sg/~seowjean/Mafia/mafia.html, November 7, 1997.

Arnold Rothstein

Born: 1882
Died: November 6, 1928
AKA: Mr. Big, the Big Bankroll, the Brain, the Fixer, the Man Uptown

*Widely considered to be the father of organized crime in America, Arnold Rothstein was a tutor to a number of powerful mob bosses, including **Meyer Lansky** (see entry) and Lucky Luciano. Always operating in the background, he parlayed his mob activities into multiple millions.*

THE SON OF ROTHSTEIN THE JUST

Rothstein was born in New York City in 1882 to well-established immigrant parents. His family lived in a comfortable brownstone building on 47th Street west of Lexington Avenue. Rothstein's father, a respected Jewish merchant, was known as "Rothstein the Just" because of his fairness in business dealings. Having started with nothing, Rothstein's father eventually became so well trusted in the New York garment industry that he was called on to settle a labor dispute in 1919.

But Rothstein did not choose to follow in his father's footsteps. He left school at the age of sixteen, after having spent only two years at Boy's High School in New York. By the time he quit school, he was a gifted pool shark (someone who earns money by beating others at pool). Rothstein played in a pool hall that was run by John McGraw, the manager of the New York Giants. He also gambled compulsively—shooting craps (a dice game) in alleyways and playing poker with other hard-core gamblers. A math whiz, he was able to calculate odds in his head, and kept his skills sharp by adding, subtracting, and multiplying large numbers throughout the day. Rothstein's ability to calculate the odds of winning helped him to amass a small fortune before he reached the age of twenty. Just out of his teens, he became a co-owner of a lavish gambling house in New York, which reportedly earned him in excess of $10,000 per week.

Rothstein used his wealth to finance a loan-sharking business. He lent large sums of money to clients who repaid the loans—plus an outrageous interest payment (a fee that increased with time). Rothstein employed **Legs Diamond** (see entry) to collect the loans—using threats and violence to force reluctant clients to pay. But Rothstein discovered that it was in his interest not to force all of his clients to repay their debts. He lent large sums of money to politicians, police captains, judges, and other influential people whose favors were more valuable than cash.

Father crime

Rothstein was a pioneer in a number of criminal rackets. Although he remained in the background, he masterminded and bankrolled a number of criminal empires—including labor racketeering and narcotics smuggling. Because he thought in terms of a national crime syndicate (association), Rothstein has been called the "spiritual father" of modern organized crime.

THE BLACK SOX SCANDAL

Although his involvement was never proven, Rothstein was called the mastermind of the 1919 gambling fix that became known as the Black Sox scandal. Considered to be the greatest scandal in the history of American sports, the Black Sox incident involved the fixing of the 1919 baseball World Series, for which the Chicago White Sox became known as the "Black Sox." Eight White Sox players were bribed to throw—or lose—the first and second games of the series. Rothstein's associates, who had bet heavily on the White Sox's opponents, stood to make a fortune. Abe Attell, a featherweight boxing champion who worked for Rothstein, handled the bribing of the eight players: Eddie Cicotte, Oscar "Happy" Flesch, Chick Gandil, "Shoeless" Joe Jackson, Freddie McMullin, Charles "Swede" Risberg, George "Buck" Weaver, and Claude Williams. The bribes reportedly amounted to around $70,000.

Although Rothstein was publicly accused of the fix, no one ever proved that he was behind the bribery. In 1920, a grand jury convened (met) in Chicago to investigate the scandal. On

Quite a character

Writer F. Scott Fitzgerald created a fictional character who was based on Rothstein. The character, Meyer Wolfsheim, is described in *The Great Gatsby* as "a gambler . . . the man who fixed the World Series back in 1919."

97

the advice of his lawyer, William Fallon, he voluntarily testified before the grand jury. Rothstein immediately took an offensive approach, accusing the court and the press of treating him as a criminal. Although he never denied having been involved in the affair, he was never indicted (formally charged).

AN ENTERPRISING CROOK

Rothstein, like other members of the underworld, made a fortune during Prohibition (when the Eighteenth Amendment outlawed the manufacture and sale of alcohol). A shrewd (sharp) criminal, he claimed a portion of the bootlegging business (illegal manufacture and sale of liquor) that was both profitable and low risk. Working with associates in Europe, he imported liquor from distilleries abroad, where the manufacture of alcohol was legal. Rothstein purchased a Norwegian freighter to bring in whiskey from Scotland. His business was massive: the freighter imported twenty thousand cases at a time. Since other gangsters relied on Rothstein's shipments of liquor, he played an important role in bootlegging in New York—and therefore had little risk of being killed by his peers.

Rothstein used his vast wealth to help other bootleggers who were in trouble with the law. But he always did so for a price. Between 1921 and 1924, he put up an amazing $14 million in bail for liquor prosecutions. Of approximately 6,900 liquor-related cases during his lifetime, fewer than 500 went to trial without being dismissed. Through his political ties and police contacts—and vast sums of persuasive money—Rothstein became known as a "fixer" who could make any problem disappear.

Rothstein was also credited with changing the way that graft (illegal payments) was collected in New York. Prior to Prohibition, policemen had been responsible for collecting payoffs from politicians to gangsters. But this made the gangsters vulnerable to policemen who occasionally shifted their loyalty. Rothstein and his associates began to collect payoffs directly from the politicians—eliminating the policeman as middle man. When the gangsters wanted "favors" from the police department, they simply asked the politicians to see to their requests.

DEALING IN DRUGS

Rothstein knew that Prohibition would not last forever. And without Prohibition, the bootlegging business would disappear. To ensure continued success, he diversified (varied) his business investments. Rothstein bought nightclubs, gambling casinos, and racehorses. He fixed the odds on bets that he and his associates made, and when possible, he fixed the outcome. He was the mastermind behind a $1 million stolen-bond racket and he used blackmail (threats to gain payment) and violence to profit from labor racketeering (manipulating laborers through intimidation). He financed diamond smuggling. And he is considered to be the man who invented the modern narcotics (drug) industry.

Rothstein moved into the narcotics industry at a time when access to drugs was severely limited. Aware of a growing drug problem in American cities, Congress passed the Harrison Narcotics Act in 1914, which abruptly cut off the ready supply of cocaine, heroin, and morphine in the United States. By the middle of the 1920s, the market for illegal drugs far surpassed availability. Using his vast amounts of capital and political connections, Rothstein created a new system for the supply of narcotics. He bought drugs in Europe through legitimate pharmaceutical firms (companies that develop medical drugs), and then shipped his orders back home—while disguising the true nature of his shipment. Using his ties to various gangs throughout the country, he started a system to distribute drugs to a large network of gangsters.

A GAMBLING MAN

Throughout his life, Rothstein remained a compulsive gambler. He once said, "I always gambled. I can't remember when I didn't. Maybe I gambled just to show my father he couldn't tell me what to do, but I don't think so. I think I gambled because I loved the excitement."

In 1928, Rothstein took part in a two-day poker game that had been arranged by George "Hump" McManus. Also playing

Take a look at this!

Eight Men Out (1988) is a moving account of the infamous 1919 "Black Sox" scandal in which members of the Chicago White Sox team purposely lost the World Series for a bribe of around $70,000. It provides an interesting look at the "conspiracy" that ended "Shoeless" Joe Jackson's major-league career. Based on Eliot Asinof's book, it includes first-rate baseball scenes.

Drug smuggling in disguise

To cover his drug-smuggling operation, Rothstein bought an import-export firm as a front--and, purely by accident, became a successful art dealer.

December 11, 1928. Police examine the files of Arnold Rothstein, in hopes of finding evidence to help solve his murder.

were two gamblers from California, Nate Raymond and "Titanic" Thompson. The game lasted for two days. By the end of the game, Rothstein owed $320,000. According to some stories, he tore up his IOUs (written promises to pay). According to another version, he claimed the game had been fixed and refused to pay. Whatever his reasons, Rothstein did not pay his $320,000 debt.

BETTING ON THE ELECTION

On November 4, 1928, Rothstein placed a large bet that Herbert Hoover, and not Al Smith, would win the presidential election. Also that day, he received a phone call summoning him to a room at the Park Central Hotel in New York. He informed his associates that he was going to see McManus. Thirty minutes later, a hotel employee found Rothstein at the foot of the service stairs. He had been shot in the groin.

Rothstein was taken to Polyclinic Hospital. He died two days later—on election day—before he was able to collect his $500,000 in winnings when Hoover was elected as president of the United States. Rothstein refused to name his killer.

A number of gangsters were suspected in the slaying. McManus was tried and released for lack of evidence. Raymond had an alibi (proof that he was elsewhere) at the time of the killing. Some people believed that rival gangster, **Dutch Schultz** (see entry), had planned the killing in order to take over Rothstein's rackets. And still others speculated that Legs Diamond had arranged the hit following a drug deal in which his employer double-crossed him. Rothstein's killer has never been identified. After his death, Rothstein's estate was appraised (valued) at almost $2 million. But no one knew the value of his hidden assets—which have been estimated at $50 million.

Here's a book you might like:

The Great Gatsby, 1925, by F. Scott Fitzgerald

A vulgar, yet romantic wealthy young man crashes Long Island society in the 1920s and finds his heart captured by an impulsive and emotionally impoverished girl. Made into a movie in 1974 starring Robert Redford and Mia Farrow.

Sources for Further Reading

Jonnes, J. "Founding Father: One Man Invented the Modern Narcotics Industry." *American Heritage* (February-March, 1993), pp. 48–49.

Nash, Jay Robert. *Bloodletters and Badmen.* New York: M. Evans, 1973, pp. 475–478.

Sifakis, Carl. *The Mafia Encyclopedia.* New York: Facts on File, 1982, pp. 285–287.

Smith, Sherwin. "35 Years Ago." *The New York Times Magazine* (October 27, 1963), pp. 96–98.

Robbers

A gentleman stagecoach robber who left a poem at the scene of the crime. A murderous widow who lured bachelors to their deaths. A cigar-smoking lady bandit who enjoyed the celebrity of a star. A bank robber who reportedly broke out of prison using a wooden gun. These are just some of the robbers whose life stories you'll learn about in this section.

Was Ma Barker the vicious "she-wolf" that FBI director J. Edgar Hoover claimed she was? Did Belle Gunness die in the fire that burned down her farmhouse—or did the headless corpse found in the ruins belong to another woman? How was kidnap-victim-turned-robber Patty Hearst finally captured? What did Clyde Barrow have to say in his letter to automaker Henry Ford? And who was the infamous "Lady in Red" who informed FBI agents of the whereabouts of bank robber John Dillinger? The stories of the robbers covered here are filled with intrigue—and more than a few unanswered questions.

Ma Barker
(Kate Barker)

Born: 1871?
Died: January 16, 1935

To the FBI, Kate "Ma" Barker was the mastermind behind her sons' criminal careers. To her sons, she was a dowdy, middle-aged woman who liked the movies. In spite of these vastly differing accounts, one thing seems sure: she was a fiercely protective mother who was deeply attached to her sons.

ARIZONA DONNIE CLARK

Arizona Donnie Clark—who later became Kate Barker—was born to Scottish-Irish parents sometime around 1871 near Springfield, Missouri, in the Ozark Mountains. As a child she had once seen **Jesse James** (see entry), who was also a native of the area. The experience reportedly had a profound impact on her. The young Barker mourned the murder of James—who was, to many people, a folk hero like Robin Hood.

As a young woman, Barker played the fiddle, read the Bible, and regularly sang in church on Sundays. In 1892, she married a farm laborer named George Barker, who seemed to be resigned to a life of poverty. What is known about her married life is that it was hard, unhappy, and taken up with the raising of her four sons, Herman, Lloyd, Arthur (who was called "Doc"), and Fred. A wild bunch, the boys grew up in extreme poverty and soon fell into constant trouble with the law. Barker's loyalty to her children and the fierceness with which she protected them from the consequences of their delinquent

The fabulous Barker boys

Whether or not Ma Barker was a cold-blooded criminal is a question that will never be settled. But there's no doubt that her four boys were a nasty bunch.

Herman Barker. Born 1894. First of the Barker boys to get in serious trouble. Died in 1927 from a self-inflicted gunshot wound during a shootout with police.

Lloyd Barker. Born 1896. Sentenced to twenty-five years at Leavenworth prison for holding up a post office. Released in 1947. Worked at a gas station snack shop until 1949, when he was shot to death by his wife.

Arthur "Doc" Barker. Born 1899. Probably the gang's leader and deadliest killer. Sentenced to life imprisonment for killing a night watchman. Paroled. Captured on January 8, 1935 and sentenced to time at Alcatraz. Killed in January 1939, during an attempted jail break.

Fred Barker. Born 1902. Ma Barker's favorite son. Killed a police officer while attempting to steal a car. Fred died in 1935 with his mother during a shootout with FBI agents.

behavior, became something of a legend itself in the Ozark Mountains where they lived.

CONFLICTING IMAGES

As a historical figure, Barker is something of a puzzle. Never arrested for committing a crime, she was nevertheless suspected of being the leader of a gang that J. Edgar Hoover (1895-1972), director of the FBI, considered to be one of the deadliest of the era. Hoover portrayed Ma Barker as a cold-blooded woman. He once wrote that she was:

> . . . [the] most vicious, dangerous, and resourceful criminal brain of the last decade. . . . The eyes of Arizona Clark Barker always fascinated me. They were queerly direct, penetrating, hot with some strangely smoldering flame, yet as hypnotically cold as the muzzle of a gun. That same dark, mysterious brilliance was in the eyes of her four sons.

—Persons in Hiding, *published in 1938.*

But not everyone saw Ma Barker as the evil mastermind behind her sons' criminal activities. The public, fed on newspaper stories that detailed the escapades of her "boys" and their friends, perceived Barker as a mother whose love for her children was so extreme that it twisted both her conscience and her judgment. To the members of the gang, or so those who survived would later relate, she was no more than a simple-minded, middle-aged woman whose use to them was limited to her

Creepy Karpis

After his friends, Fred and Ma Barker, were killed in a hail of gunfire, Alvin "Creepy" Karpis (1907-1979) notified FBI director J. Edgar Hoover that he planned to kill him in the same way Hoover's agents had slain the Barkers. He never made good on his word, but he did manage to cause Hoover grief.

In 1935, Karpis robbed a train. This distressed Hoover, who saw the resurrection of this outdated crime as an insult to his professional reputation. When the FBI received information about the outlaw's whereabouts in May 1936, Hoover made certain that he was present at the arrest. As agents surrounded Karpis in his New Orleans hideout, the FBI director himself placed Karpis under arrest. Two years earlier, few Americans knew what the FBI was. And fewer still had heard of the agency's director Hoover. But by 1935, after the Karpis capture—and Hoover's supposed role in it—made headlines, Hoover and the FBI had become national institutions.

Hoover was praised as a hero and hard-hitting lawman. But Karpis told another story. He later wrote, "[Hoover] didn't lead an attack on me. He hid until I was safely covered by many guns. He waited until the coast was clear Then he came out to reap the glory. . . . That May day in 1936, I made Hoover's reputation as a fearless lawman. It's a reputation he doesn't deserve."

Karpis was sentenced to life imprisonment at Alcatraz, a brutal penitentiary on an island in San Francisco Bay, in California. In 1962, after twenty-six years at the institution known as "the Rock," Karpis was transferred to another penitentiary. Karpis endured more time at Alcatraz than any other man. Paroled in January 1969, he was deported (expelled from the country) to Canada, his birth country. Karpis, who once shared the leadership of the Barker gang, outlived all of the Barkers. He retired to Spain, where he died in 1979, at the age of seventy-two.

willingness to hide them from the law, raise bail money (money paid as a guarantee that an arrested person will appear for trial), or otherwise to secure their release on parole.

Alvin "Creepy" Karpis, who shared the leadership of the Barker gang, described Barker as a harmless—and even clueless—old woman. In his memoirs, published in 1971, he wrote:

> Ma was always *somebody* in our lives. Love didn't enter into it really. She was somebody we looked after and took with us when we moved from city to city, hideout to hideout.

Jelly Nash

Frank "Jelly" Nash—a bandit, bootlegger, and murderer—was one of the many outlaws who was given shelter by the Barkers. In 1924, Nash and a criminal named Al Spencer attempted to rob a mail train outside of Okesa, Oklahoma. The robbery was a failure. Nash was captured and sentenced to time in Leavenworth prison. He left the Kansas prison six years later—before he'd served his entire sentence. In prison, he worked as a cook at the warden's home. One day he simply strolled out the warden's back door. And he didn't leave empty-handed. He took an edition of William Shakespeare, an English playwright and poet, with him.

The rest of Nash's story was less poetic. The escaped train robber was later arrested at the White Front Pool Hall in Hot Springs, Arkansas. Federal agents took him to Union Station in Kansas City, Missouri, where he was to board a train headed toward Leavenworth. In the parking lot, three men ambushed Nash and the federal agents. Caught in machine-gun fire, Nash and four agents died.

It's no insult to Ma's memory that she just didn't have the brains or know-how to direct us on a robbery. It wouldn't have occurred to her to get involved in our business, and we always made a point of only discussing our scores when Ma wasn't around. We'd leave her at home when we were arranging a job, or we'd send her to a movie. Ma saw a lot of movies.

To the FBI, she was a criminal brain. To Karpis and others, she didn't have the know-how to direct a robbery. What, then, was the truth?

SPREE OF VIOLENCE

In the 1920s, Barker could no longer shield her sons from the law—or the punishments they received for increasingly serious offenses. Doc was arrested in Oklahoma for killing a night watchman during a burglary and sentenced to life imprisonment. In 1927, Herman was stopped by two officers outside of Wichita, Kansas, for questioning in connection with a recent robbery. Pulling his gun, he shot one of the policemen in the head. Herman was then shot by the other officer. Badly wounded and afraid of capture, Herman killed himself. Barker grieved for weeks afterward.

Struggling to find some motive for Barker's criminal activities, the FBI later explained that the death of her eldest child drove her into a vengeance-seeking spree of violence. According to Hoover, the incident caused Barker to change "from an animal mother of the she-wolf type to a veritable [genuine] beast of prey." She was reputed to have carried out a series of bank robberies and kidnappings unequaled in the history of modern crime. The truth was probably quite different, but by then it hardly mattered.

FUGITIVES AND NEW MEMBERS

After the death of Herman, little more was heard concerning the Barkers until 1932, the year Lloyd was arrested for mail robbery and sentenced to a twenty-five year term. Fred had been serving a term in prison for the shooting of a town constable (law officer) who had caught him attempting to steal a car. In 1933, under conditions that suggested his freedom may have been purchased, Fred was released and returned home to Barker in the company of Karpis. Fred was probably the first of the Barker brothers to form an alliance (relationship) with Karpis, who quickly became one of Barker's favorites.

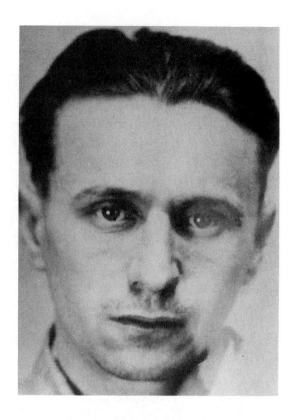

Ma Barker's favorite son, Fred, shown here in a 1934 mugshot.

The gang's membership was constantly shifting. At the time, Barker provided shelter to several wanted men, including Francis Keating (who was later captured by federal agents as he played golf), Frank Nash, an Oklahoma bandit and bootlegger, Al Spencer, a cattle rustler and bank robber who belonged to Henry Starr's gang, and bank robber Ray Terrill (whose gang was later destroyed after trying to rob two banks at once).

KIDNAPPED MILLIONAIRES AND A SILENCED GANGSTER

In a move that gave Hoover fits, the state of Oklahoma pardoned Doc, who promptly rejoined the gang and assumed, with Karpis, a leadership role. Shortly after Doc's return, Barker's

The arsenal of guns used by Ma and Fred Barker during their fatal standoff with federal agents on January 16, 1935.

lover, Arthur Dunlop, was killed. The gang suspected Dunlop of being an informant. A year later, in 1934, the gang reportedly gunned down George Ziegler, one of its own members.

In 1933, Ziegler had joined the gang. He was a veteran of World War I (1914-1918), a college graduate and engineer, and a gunman who had worked for Chicago mobster **Al Capone** (see entry). Ziegler, who had connections throughout the Great Lakes region, participated in two kidnappings engineered by the Barker-Karpis gang. In 1933, the gang abducted William Hamm, the founder of Minneapolis's largest brewery. (The FBI first accused gangster **Roger Touhy** [see entry] of Hamm's abduction.) Just six months later, they kidnapped Minneapolis banker Edward Bremer, for whom they received a $200,000 ransom (money paid for the release of a captive). Following the second kidnapping and ransom payment, Ziegler revealed the gang's participation to friends. He clearly posed a danger to the other members of the gang. Ziegler was murdered in Cicero, Illinois, on March 22, 1934.

While FBI agents searched Ziegler's belongings and tracked the leads they provided, Barker was sent to visit Ziegler's widow. She convinced the woman to turn over the money her late husband had hidden. FBI agents concluded that Barker was the brains of the Barker organization. It was a reputation that would outlive her.

The End of Ma Barker

By 1935, the Barker gang was doggedly pursued by the FBI. On January 8, Doc was captured by the special agent in charge of the FBI's Chicago field office, Melvin Purvis. Doc was captured without a struggle, as he was taking a walk—unarmed. Eight days after Doc's arrest, Fred was tracked to a rented cottage near Lake Weir, Florida, about fifty miles northwest of Orlando. On the morning of January 16, 1935, the house was quickly surrounded, and at the end of a six-hour gun battle both Barker and Fred were found dead.

Fred's body was riddled with fourteen bullets. But according to reports, Barker was struck by no more than three bullet wounds—and possibly only one. Some claimed that Barker had gone down in a blaze of gunfire as she fired a machine gun at the agents who surrounded the house. But if she had been firing at lawmen, she would have been in their line of fire—and would surely have received more than three wounds from the fifteen-hundred rounds of ammunition that were fired into the cottage. Some people speculate that Barker's fatal shot was not fired but lawmen—but by a woman who had just witnessed the death of her favorite son. The mystery of Barker's place in the gang was never solved, but the story of her death took a permanent place in the bandit lore of the day.

Sources for Further Reading

Nash, Jay Robert. *Bloodletters and Badmen*. New York: M. Evans, 1973, pp. 33–39.

Prassel, Frank Richard. *The Great American Outlaw, A Legacy of Fact and Fiction.* Norman: University of Oklahoma Press, 1993, pp. 282–283.

Sifakis, Carl. *The Encyclopedia of American Crime.* New York: Facts on File, 1982, pp. 51–53, 386.

Vandome, Nick, *Crimes and Criminals.* New York: Chambers, 1992, p. 15.

Black Bart
(Charles Boles)

Born: c. 1829
Died: ?
AKA: Charles Bolton, C. E. Benson,
Charley Barlow, T. Z. Spaulding,
and others

An older, distinguished gentleman, Black Bart robbed stagecoaches over an eight-year period in northern California and Oregon. Known as a robber who never harmed his targets, Bart sometimes left poetic notes to tease his pursuers. He was eventually caught and imprisoned. Released from prison early, he disappeared from the public eye.

FROM FARM FIELDS TO GOLD MINES

Charles Boles—who came to be known as Black Bart—was born in England around 1829. His parents, John and Maria Boles, were married on June 27, 1807, and had seven children—including Charles, who was their seventh child—before they left their native country for America. In the summer of 1830, the family left London on a boat that was bound for New York City. The family settled on a one-hundred-acre farm in Jefferson County, in rural upstate New York, near the St. Lawrence River. After they settled in New York, John and Maria Boles had two more children.

Not much is known about Boles's early life in the farming community of Jefferson County. Some historians assume that he was probably a good student. As an adult, Boles was well-spoken and well-read—and he had excellent penmanship (handwriting). At about the age of twenty, Boles left New York with his cousin, David Boles. They spent the winter in Van Buren County, Iowa, with Charles Boles's older brother,

William, who had settled there eight years earlier, in 1841. The following summer, Charles and David arrived in California, eager to seek their fortunes in the gold mines. Disappointed with their small success, they decided to return to New York. A little over one year after their arrival, in the fall of 1851, they returned East by ship. After months at sea, the Boles cousins arrived in New York in January of 1852.

But Boles wasn't cured of gold fever. Within three months, he was on his way back to the California gold rush. For two years, he panned (gold and gravel are separated by washing in a pan) and mined for gold—with little success. In 1854 he returned by land to New York no richer than he had started. But he had become very familiar with the layout of much of northern California, something that he would use to his advantage later in life.

A MAN OF IRON NERVE

After Boles returned to New York, he married Mary Elizabeth Johnson, probably in 1856. In 1857, they moved to the town of New Oregon in the northeastern portion of Iowa, near the Minnesota border. Boles's youngest brother, Hiram, had already settled there. On April 26, Charles and Mary's first child, Ida Martha, was born. Their second child, Eva Ardella, was born May 17, 1859. By 1861, Boles had moved his family to Macon County, near Decatur, Illinois. There, the couple's third daughter, Frances Lillian, was born on the sixth of June. Boles probably made his living as a farmer, as his father had—although it's possible that he was a schoolteacher.

The Boles's family life was interrupted by the Civil War (1861-1865). Within one year after the first shots were fired, Boles enlisted in the Union (Northern) Army on August 13, 1862. During his three-year term, he fought in seventeen battles and was injured three times, including a bullet wound in the abdomen near the hip. Having volunteered to join the army as a private, Boles became his unit's third highest-ranking soldier. By the end of the war, he had been promoted to first sergeant. He distinguished himself as a disciplined and courageous soldier. One of his fellow soldiers, a man named Christian Reibsame, said this about him:

> [He] was one of the bravest men in the regiment. . . . He was always at the front in every fight, and was wounded several times. He was a reticent [quiet] fellow, but was well liked. He was inclined to sport, and played a good game of poker. . . . He was a perfect specimen of a good soldier and a man of iron nerve.

After Boles returned from the war, he rejoined his family in New Oregon. They soon moved to Minnesota, where a relative of Mary's lived. There, the couple's fourth child, a boy named Arian, was born (probably in 1866). But Boles did not remain long with his family. On May 1, 1867, he set out to try again to strike it rich in the gold mines of the West. His family never saw him again. Although Boles wrote to Mary on a regular basis and spoke of a time when they would be reunited, he never returned home. After twelve years of regular correspondence, he suddenly stopped writing letters to his wife. His family assumed he was dead.

Quaker guns

Boles's experience in the Union Army during the Civil War might have helped him to formulate his battle-plan for stagecoach robbery. Both sides in the Civil War used "Quaker guns" (sticks that had been peeled and painted black to look like real guns) to deceive the enemy. Although Boles always worked alone, he sometimes convinced his victims that he was not alone by using a similar trick.

STAGECOACH ROBBER

Boles was far from dead. On July 26, 1875, a few miles east of Copperopolis, California, he committed a stagecoach robbery. It was the first in a series of successful holdups. At sunrise, as the four horses pulling the Sonoma-Milton stage were struggling up a steep section of road known as Funk Hill, Boles stepped onto the road—in front of the lead horse. He wore light-colored pants and linen duster (coat worn to kept dust off clothes). His face was covered by a flour sack that had holes poked through so that he could see. He also carried a double-barreled shotgun. Boles used this method in all of his robberies. The strange outfit disguised his identity and allowed him to startle the horses, so that they would ignore the stagecoach driver's instructions. And by stepping in front of the lead horse, he shielded himself from gunfire. (In fact, most drivers and guards

Who said that?

A boyhood acquaintance of the robber claimed that, in his youth, Boles had been a skillful amateur ventriloquist (someone who can "throw" his voice to make it seem like someone else is speaking). This could explain part of Black Bart's success as a robber. By throwing his voice, he would have been able to convince his targets that he was not working alone.

didn't dare to shoot at him, even when they had a weapon. They didn't want to risk shooting the valuable lead horse.)

Driven by John Shine, the stagecoach held the usual contents: ten passengers, a U.S. mail pouch, and a Wells Fargo strongbox (a small safe). Boles ordered Shine to throw down the Wells Fargo box, but the driver hesitated. Boles then shouted, "If he dares to shoot, give him a solid volley [round of gunfire], boys." Seeing what looked like several shotgun barrels pointed at him from the brush, Shine threw down the strongbox as well as the mail pouch. After he ordered Shine to drive on, Boles broke into the safe and mail pouch, escaping with more than $300 in gold and cash. Shine drove a little way down the road and then returned to the scene of the crime. The masked robber was gone, but a half-dozen shotgun barrels were still positioned in the bush—or so it seemed. As it turned out, the "shotguns" were really sticks that had been propped up to look like guns.

A POET IN DISGUISE

No one had a clue who the masked robber was. Boles had a gentlemanly manner and appearance that didn't attract suspicion. He was well-dressed and very polite, with a mustache and graying hair that was receding at the temples. A fit man who was capable of hiking long distances, he was able to walk away from the scenes of his crimes—dressed as a hobo. In all, Boles committed between twelve and twenty-nine stagecoach robberies between 1875 and 1883. While he might have been given credit for some robberies he wasn't involved in, it's possible he wasn't blamed for others that he did commit.

In addition to his distinctive method of robbing stagecoaches, Boles added another "signature" to his crimes: he left a note of poetry behind. After his fourth robbery, on August 3, 1877, in Sonoma County, California, Boles left a note that was scribbled on a Wells Fargo ticket. It said:

> I've labored long and hard for bread
> For honor and for riches

Wells, Fargo & Company

In the nineteenth century, the U.S. government was not able to handle all mail delivery on its own. Private delivery companies took over some of the delivery responsibilities—for a price. In 1843, two men who had experience delivering freight, a Vermonter named Henry Wells and a New Yorker named William G. Fargo, combined their expertise to deliver freight and mail in Illinois and Ohio. Charging only six cents a letter—compared to the twenty-five cent fee charged by the U.S. Post Office—Wells and Fargo's company was a success. In fact, it was so successful that the government ordered them to stop undercutting its prices (charging a cheaper rate).

In July of 1852, after merging with another delivery company, Wells, Fargo & Company opened for business in San Francisco, California. Wells and Fargo's company became the leading mail deliverer, express agency, and bank in the West. The company ensured its position by taking over rival businesses—or forcing them to fail. In less than ten years, Wells, Fargo & Company had more than one hundred and twenty offices in the West, where people mailed anything from private letters to cash and gold dust. A large part of the company's business involved shipping gold bullion (gold still in raw or unrefined form) from California to mints (a place where the government makes coins) on the East Coast.

The express company used a number of methods to transport goods: it employed men on foot and horseback, mule trains, freight wagons, and steamers. The company also delivered shipments using stagecoach wagons—which soon became popular targets for robbers. During its most successful years, Wells Fargo maintained its own detective and police force in an effort to eliminate stagecoach robberies. It is estimated that Wells Fargo detectives captured nearly two hundred and fifty highway robbers, including Black Bart, who was probably the most successful Wells Fargo bandit ever.

But on my corns too long you've tred
You fine haired Sons of Bitches.

Each line of the poem was written in different handwriting, and it was signed "Black Bart, the PO 8." (Black Bart was a character from one of the robber's favorite books, and the PO 8 is probably a play on the word "poet.") Almost one year later, after his fifth robbery, Boles left behind a second poem. Inside the broken Wells Fargo safe was a poem that read:

here I lay me down to sleep
to wait the coming morrow

Boles committed his twentieth robbery in Yuba County, California, on December 15, 1881. The *Marysville Appeal,* a small-town newspaper, carried this account of the robbery written by George Sharpe, the driver of the Downieville-Marysville coach that was robbed.

"I was driving slowly up a bit of rising ground when suddenly a man jumped out from behind a tree by the side of the road and yelled 'Hold on there you . . . .' I pulled up the horses pretty quick and set the brake. Then I sat still and looked at the man. I had never been stopped on the road before, and was surprised-like. The man was about my size (pretty stoutly built and about 5 feet 10 inches high). His face was covered with white cotton cloth, but one corner of the cloth was torn so that I could see that his eyes were blue. He had on a long linen duster and a pair of blue overalls. On his head was a little whitish felt hat, with some light colored hair sticking through the crown. That's about all I remember of his looks."

perhaps success perhaps defeat
and everlasting sorrow.
Let come what will, I'll try it on,
My condition can't be worse,
But if there's money in the box,
It's munny in my purse.

—*Black Bart the PO 8*

Although a number of fake Bart poems appeared during Boles's lifetime, only these twelve lines are considered to be genuine.

THE HANDKERCHIEF CLUE

Boles's success as a stagecoach robber was unmatched. He continued to rob stages throughout northern California and Oregon—covering ten counties over a three-hundred-and-fifty-mile area. Usually he struck between June and November, taking a break from his profession during the winter months. He often returned to the scene of previous crimes: nine times he committed robberies within a few miles of earlier stick-ups. With more stagecoach hold-ups to his credit than any other robber, Boles—known only as Black Bart—was at the top of the Wells Fargo wanted list. The company offered a large reward for

He spoke in a clear, ringing voice, without any brogue or foreign accent. There was a double-barreled muzzle-loading shotgun in his hands. . . . I saw all these things in a good deal less time than it takes to tell about them. As soon as I stopped the horses the robber got back behind the tree so as to keep out of range of any guns that passengers might have. He kept his shotgun bearing on me from the word "Hold."

"Throw out that box," was his next order. I supposed he meant the Wells-Fargo box, but I didn't stop to make particular inquiries, and I threw it out on the side of the road towards him. . . . "Now drive on, you . . . ." he said. I drove on. . . . There was [a boy] on the box seat with me. He was badly scared. After I had driven on a piece, he said to me, "I'm glad that robber didn't get my parcel," showing me a little package wrapped up in a newspaper. "What have you in that?" I asked him. "I've got my lunch in it," he said. And that was all the poor little cuss did have in it.

his capture. Even so, Boles managed to slip away from the lawmen who pursued him.

On November 3, 1883, Boles's luck changed. He stopped a coach on a steep portion of Funk Hill, where he had committed his first robbery. But a young man with a gun—possibly a passenger who had gotten off the coach to hunt—returned to the coach as Boles was trying to open the strong box. He fired at the robber. Slightly wounded, Boles was forced to flee, leaving behind a number of personal items. When a posse (a group of people with legal authority to capture criminals) searched the area, they found a derby hat, a little food, flour sacks, a leather case for opera glasses—and a handkerchief. That handkerchief proved to be the undoing of Black Bart.

Wells Fargo had hired a number of detectives who were eager to collect the reward for the capture of Black Bart. The detectives attempted, with no success, to trace the opera glasses. They had better luck with the handkerchief, which had an ink laundry mark—FXO 7. Although there were over ninety laundries in San Francisco, the detectives managed to locate the laundry that used that identification mark. The handkerchief was soon traced to a man known as Charles Bolton, who had been living quietly in a boarding house in San Francisco. The man was in fact Charles Boles, who had informed his landlady

Military pension

Something about Charles Boles's background puzzles historians. As a soldier in the Civil War he was wounded three times, including a serious bullet wound to his stomach. His injuries should have qualified him for a military pension that would have provided him with money later in life. But Boles never applied for a pension, choosing instead to rob stagecoaches.

and others that he was a mining executive who was often called out of town to visit his mines.

At first, Boles protested that he was not a stagecoach robber. Finally, he confessed to *one* crime—the final robbery. In November 1883, he pleaded guilty to robbery, and was sentenced to six years in the San Quentin penitentiary (prison). After just over four years, when he was nearly sixty years old, Boles was released—probably because of his age. He promptly disappeared and a new rash of stagecoach robberies began. Following a holdup in November of 1888, James B. Hume, the chief of detectives for Wells Fargo, sent word to his detectives: "We have reason to believe that [a robbery] was committed by the notorious C. E. Boles . . . alias Black Bart." The detectives were never able to prove that he was involved in any robberies after his release. The date of Boles's death is uncertain, although a New York City newspaper mysteriously ran his obituary (death notice) in 1917. It's possible the death notice was real. On the other hand, it might have been written by the poet himself, who wanted the public—and lawmen—to believe that he was dead.

Sources for Further Reading

Adventure of Wells Fargo. [Online] Available http://wellsfargo.com/about/stories/ch3/, January 18, 1997.

The American West, A Cultural Encyclopedia, Volume 1. Danbury, CT: Grolier Educational Corp., 1995, pp. 121–122.

Collins, William and Bruce Levene. *Black Bart: The True Story of the West's Most Famous Stagecoach Robber.* Mendocino, CA: Pacific Transcriptions, 1992.

Nash, Jay Robert. *Bloodletters and Badmen.* New York: M. Evans, 1973, pp. 61–62.

Prassel, Frank Richard. *The Great American Outlaw, A Legacy of Fact and Fiction.* Norman, OK: University of Oklahoma Press, 1993, pp. 123–125.

Bonnie and Clyde
(Bonnie Parker and Clyde Barrow)

Bonnie Parker: 1911-1934
Clyde Barrow: 1909-1934

Romanticized for their devotion to each other and their devil-may-care lives on the run, Bonnie Parker and Clyde Barrow were headline-makers. They robbed banks and stores—but not very successfully. They killed—with no sign of remorse. And they captured the public's imagination— both then and now.

BONNIE MEETS CLYDE

Clyde Barrow was born in Telice, Texas, on March 24, 1909. His parents, Henry and Cumie Barrow, had seven other children. The Barrow family was extremely poor. As a youth, Barrow was sent to the Harris County School for Boys, a reformatory, where he was deemed to be "an incorrigible truant [absent from school without permission], thief, and runaway." After he was released, Barrow joined a gang of petty thieves in Houston, Texas, known as the Square Root Gang. While still in his teens, he joined his older brother Ivan Marvin "Buck" Barrow in stealing cars and robbing grocery stores and gas stations.

In 1928, after the pair robbed a gas station in Denton, Texas, police pursued the Barrow brothers in a high-speed chase. Buck Barrow was shot and severely wounded during the chase. Although he was a skilled driver, Clyde eventually crashed into a ditch. He left his bleeding brother behind, possibly to ensure that he received needed medical attention. Buck Barrow received a

Car talk

Barrow once wrote a letter to automobile manufacturer Henry Ford (1863-1947). "I have drove [driven] Ford's exclusively when I could get away with one. For sustained speed and freedom from trouble, the Ford has got every other car skinned." Barrow concluded by adding, "even if my business hasn't been strictly legal it don't hurt anything to tell you what a fine car you got in the V-8 [a car with an eight-cylinder engine] ." Barrow and Parker took pictures of each other posing with their pride and joy, a 1932 V-8 they had stolen in Texas.

five-year sentence at the Eastham prison farm, while his brother remained at large.

Less than two years later, Barrow met a woman who would change his life. Bonnie Parker was the daughter of a modestly well-off family from the farming community of Rowena, Texas. At the age of sixteen, she married a schoolmate, Roy Thornton. After Thornton was sentenced to a life term in prison for murder, Parker became restless. In 1930, she moved to Dallas, Texas, where she took work as a waitress. She later described her state of mind at the time as "bored crapless." That is, until Barrow walked into her life. Later that month, Parker met Barrow at the cafe where she worked. The pair immediately became inseparable.

BURNING HELL

Parker and Barrow moved in together and tried, for a while, to earn an honest living. Soon, however, Barrow was arrested for a burglary in Waco, Texas. There was no denying the crime: Barrow had left his fingerprints at the scene. He was sentenced to two years in a Waco jail.

Before long, Barrow walked out of jail brandishing the revolver Parker had smuggled to him during a visit. But Barrow's freedom was short lived. In Middleton, Ohio, police arrested him. An escaped convict, Barrow received a harsh sentence. He was sent a prison known as "the Burning Hell"—the Eastham prison farm.

Prison conditions at Eastham were savage. Barrow was whipped and forced to withstand vicious punishments. Brutalized by the experience, he became a more hardened criminal during his imprisonment. Barrow reportedly killed his first victim while in prison—a man named Ed Crowder, who informed prison authorities that Barrow had been gambling.

Barrow's mother, Cumie Barrow, fought to have her son released from Eastham. In January 1932, she visited Texas gov-

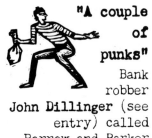

"A couple of punks"

Bank robber **John Dillinger** (see entry) called Barrow and Parker "a couple of punks" who gave bank robbing a bad name.

ernor Ross Sterling to ask him to pardon her son. On February 2, 1932, Barrow walked away from Eastham—vowing that he would die before he ever returned to prison.

ROBBERIES AND KILLINGS

Barrow returned to Parker—and criminal activity—after his release from prison. The two committed a number of robberies until the police caught up with them during a botched theft. According to one story, after their car broke down while they were attempting to escape, Barrow and Parker attempted to "flee" on mules. Although Barrow escaped, Parker was captured in Mabank, Texas. It was an unusual situation, because Barrow was fiercely loyal to Parker. During the couple's many encounters with police, he often fought to help her to escape, risking his own capture.

During Parker's absence, Barrow committed several more robberies, killing two law officers in Atoka, Oklahoma. It was the first time he had killed lawmen, but it would not be the last. Shortly after Parker returned, the couple hooked up with Ray Hamilton, a gun-crazy thief and killer. The three robbed small banks and stores, killing lawmen and others. Hamilton eventually left the criminal company of Barrow and Parker, but he continued to commit crimes. In 1935, after having escaped from jail a number of times, he was put to death in the electric chair.

WANTED KILLERS

Buck Barrow walked out of prison after Miriam "Ma" Ferguson, the governor of Texas, granted him a pardon. Following his release, Buck rejoined Parker and his younger brother, bringing his wife, Blanche, with him.

In Joplin, Missouri, police surrounded the house the outlaw's were living in. A shootout followed, leaving two policemen dead, but the four criminals escaped.

The incident marked a turning point for Barrow and Parker. After police found photographs that the fugitives left behind,

Take a look at this!

Bonnie & Clyde (1967) tells the story of the violent careers of Bonnie Parker and Clyde Barrow, who roamed the Southwest robbing banks during the Depression era. The winner of many awards, it stars Faye Dunaway and Warren Beatty in the title roles.

The ballad of Bonnie and Clyde

On the day that Barrow and Parker were killed, the news of their death received front-page coverage in Dallas, Texas, newspapers. The *Daily Times Herald* printed a long poem about Bonnie and Clyde, claiming that it "came into the hands of the *Daily Times Herald* several months ago with the understanding that it was not to be released until the death of the Parker girl." In many ways, the poem, which was written by Parker, accurately foretold the death of Bonnie and Clyde:

> You have heard the story of Jesse James,
> Of how he lived and died.
> If you still are in need
> of something to read,
> Here is the story of Bonnie and Clyde.
> Now Bonnie and Clyde are the Barrow gang.
> I'm sure you all have read
> How they rob and steal,
> And how those who squeal,
> Are usually found dying or dead.
> There are lots of untruths to their write-ups,

> They are not so merciless as that;
> Their nature is raw;
> They hate all the laws,
> The stool-pigeons, spotters and rats.
> They class them as cold-blooded killers,
> They say they are heartless and mean, But
>   I say with pride,
> That I once knew Clyde
> When he was honest and upright and clean.
> But the law fooled around, kept tracking
>   him down,
> And locking him up in a cell,
> Till he said to me,
> "I will never be free,
> So I will meet a few of them in hell."

> This road was so dimly lighted
> There were no highway signs to guide,
> But they made up their mind
> If the roads were all blind
> They wouldn't give up till they died.

> The road gets dimmer and dimmer,
> Sometimes you can hardly see,

their pictures were printed nationwide. *The New York Times* wrote about them. Newspapers and wanted posters provided physical descriptions, photographs, and information about their relatives. Bonnie and Clyde had gone public.

In November 1932, a gas-station attendant, William Daniel Jones, joined the outlaws—after they kidnapped him during a robbery. At first, he willingly joined them in robberies. But he

Still it's fight, man to man,
And do all you can,
For they know they can never be free.
If they try to act like citizens,
And rent them a nice little flat,
About the third night
They are invited to fight,
By a submachine gun rat-tat-tat.
If a policeman is killed in Dallas
And they have no clues to guide—
If they can't find a fiend,
They just wipe the late clean,
And hang it on Bonnie and Clyde.
Two crimes have been done in
      America
Not accredited to the Barrow mob.
For they had no hand
In the kidnapping demand,
Or the Kansas City depot job.

A newsboy once said to his buddy:
"I wish old Clyde would get jumped;
In these awful hard times,
We'd make a few dimes,
If five or six cops would get bumped."

The police haven't got the report yet,
Clyde sent a wireless today
Saying, "We haven't a peace flag of white
We stretch out at night,
We have joined the NRA."

They don't think they're too tough or
      desperate,
They know the law always wins,
They have been shot at before,
But they do not ignore,
That death is the wages of sin.
From heartbreaks some people have
      suffered,
From weariness some people have died,
But take it all in all,
Our troubles are small,
Till we get like Bonnie and Clyde.
Some day they will go down together,
And they will bury them side by side.
To a few it means grief,
To the law it's relief,
But it's death to Bonnie and Clyde.

later described the time he spent with the Barrow gang as "eighteen months of living hell."

The band of outlaws went on a crime spree that spread from Texas into Iowa. None of their robberies was highly successful: they never collected more than $3,500. But what they lacked in profits they made up for in violence. By the end of their criminal careers, Barrow and Parker were blamed for the deaths of at least twelve people.

A NARROW ESCAPE

In July 1933, their luck began to fail. Hiding at an empty fair grounds, the outlaws were surprised by police. Buck was fatally wounded, and Blanche was captured. The remaining gangsters managed to escape—although Parker and Jones had been wounded. Shortly after the incident, Jones left Barrow and Parker, and was later sent to prison.

The outlaw couple continued their spree of violence. Within a few months, four more law officers were dead. In January 1934, they pulled a daring prison break to free their former partner, Ray Hamilton. During the raid they freed another prisoner, a convict named Henry Methvin. The incident only increased the pressure on the fugitives, who were now pursued by a special squad of lawmen headed by Frank Hamer, a captain in the Texas highway patrol and former Texas Ranger. Hamer's sole responsibility was to locate the notorious couple.

DEATH TO BONNIE AND CLYDE

Barrow and Parker avoided capture until May 23, 1934. The couple drove down a backroad near Arcadia, Louisiana, to meet Methvin, with whom they had arranged a meeting. Parker ate a sandwich. Barrow sat in the driver's seat of the stolen Ford V-8, wearing only socks on his feet. Methvin was nowhere near the appointed meeting spot: he had sold them out.

In exchange for leniency, Methvin had informed police where to find Barrow and Parker. With five other lawmen, Hamer created an ambush post near the supposed meeting spot. Hidden from view, the posse (a group of people with legal authority to capture criminals) waited with rifles and shotguns. When the outlaws' gray Ford approached, the lawmen fired. Both Barrow and Parker died on the spot. Their bodies were riddled with bullets: Barrow had received twenty-five bullet wounds, while Parker had twenty-three.

Inside the outlaws' car, police found an arsenal of weapons. They recovered two Browning shotguns, three Browning rifles,

The bullet-riddled car that Bonnie and Clyde died in.

one revolver, eight automatic pistols, and more than two thousand rounds of ammunition. A large crowd gathered at the scene of the killings. Souvenir hunters reportedly tore bits of clothing from the victims, and cut locks of Parker's hair. They also chopped trees to get at bullets and picked up bits of shattered glass.

It's unlikely that Barrow and Parker would have surrendered to the police. But it's unclear whether they were ever given the chance to do so. In any case, the ambush received official approval. Thomas L. Blanton, a Texas congressman, later said "Hamer's method is the quickest and most effective way of disposing of them. We do not capture alive and try rattlesnakes. We shoot their heads off before they strike."

POST MORTEM

Reporters rushed to interview members of the victims' families. On the day of the shootings, the *Dallas Daily Times Herald* printed their reactions. Parker's mother fainted when she heard the news, while Cumie Barrow questioned, "Mister, is my son really dead?" The following day, the same newspaper ran a story in which Parker's aunt said, "I am glad she is dead," adding that her niece was "surely in hell." Blanche Barrow, Clyde's sister-in-law, was quoted in the same story as saying, "I'm glad they were both killed. It was the easiest way out." Captain Hamer felt similarly. He later said, "I never had the slightest regret. I never killed anyone except human vermin that deserved killing. . . . I hate to have to shoot her, but, as they drove up that day and I pulled down on Barrow, knowing that some of my rifle bullets were going to snuff out her life along with his, I recalled how she had helped Barrow kill nine peace officers . . . you can't afford to feel mercy for such murdering rats, whether they are male or female."

While the bodies of Barrow and Parker rested inside a funeral home in Dallas, twenty thousand people waited outside. Some offered to donate money to purchase wreaths of flowers for their funerals. Hot dog vendors set up stands to feed the crowds of onlookers. Barrow and Parker were buried separately, at the request of Parker's mother. Barrow was buried next to his brother in West Dallas cemetery, while Parker was interred at Fish Trap Cemetery. (She was later taken to Crown Hill Memorial Park.)

Sources for Further Reading

Bruns, Roger. *The Bandit Kings From Jesse James to Pretty Boy Floyd.* New York: Crown, 1995, pp. 168-169.

Nash, Jay Robert. *Bloodletters and Badmen.* New York: M. Evans, 1973, pp. 39-45.

Prassel, Frank Richard. *The Great American Outlaw, A Legacy of Fact and Fiction.* Norman: University of Oklahoma Press, 1993, pp. 297-300, 342-344.

Sifakis, Carl. *The Encyclopedia of American Crime.* New York: Facts on File, 1982, pp. 85-87.

Vandome, Nick. *Crimes and Criminals.* New York: Chambers, 1992, pp. 32-33.

Margie Dean

Born: 1896
Died: 1918

*Although a minor criminal, Margie Dean is remembered as one of the first getaway drivers in the history of bank robbery in the United States. Killed in her car during a shootout with police, she died just as **Bonnie and Clyde** (see entry) did—some sixteen years earlier.*

A GETAWAY DRIVER

Dean was born Margie Cellano in a ghetto in Paris, France, in 1896. As a young girl she emigrated to New York City and quickly turned to shoplifting. Having left New York City for Chicago, Illinois, she was arrested for stealing diamonds from a jewelry store. While serving out her sentence at Joliet Penitentiary in Illinois, she met inmate Eva Lewis, who was a member of a criminal gang headed by Frank "Jumbo" Lewis and Dale Jones. After they were released from prison, Dean and Lewis joined the gang of bank robbers, which also included Roscoe Lancaster and ex-convict Roy Sherrill. Dean quickly took a liking to gang leader Jones, and the two were eventually married. (It is unknown how she ended up with the name "Dean.")

Using Dean as their getaway driver, the Lewis-Jones Gang robbed banks throughout the Midwest. A skillful driver, Dean kept the car running while her fellow gangsters held up the bank. As the robbers fled, she let them into the car and raced out of town before police or investigators had a chance to trail them. The Lewis-Jones Gang is considered to be responsible for mastering the art of the automobile getaway.

THE MYSTERIOUS MRS. FORBES

On September 24, 1918, the gang's luck began to run out. Pursued by the Kansas City, Missouri, police, Dean, Jones, and Lancaster were trapped together in a house on Mount Gall Avenue. Surrounded, they attempted to shoot their way out of the house. Dean and Jones managed to slip out as Lancaster shot at the police who were charging through the front door. After wounding two officers, he was fatally wounded. Just before dying, Lancaster reportedly told police, "Jones is nuts! He wants to get in the movies."

Lancaster's statement helped police track the fugitive couple. Police and Pinkerton (a famous detective agency) detectives focused on Los Angeles, California—near Hollywood, the center of the nation's fledgling movie-making industry. The Pinkerton detectives had been investigating the gang for some time. Due to careful research, they knew that Dean liked one brand of perfume in particular. With the help of the owner of an upscale perfume shop in Los Angeles, detectives located a woman, who used that particular perfume, who called herself "Mrs. Forbes."

Herman K. Lamm, bank robber extraordinaire

Although the members of the Lewis-Jones Gang were innovative bank robbers, they were not very successful. One of the greatest daylight bank robbers of all time was Herman K. Lamm. Although daylight bank robberies were common in the western states in the 1800s, few East Coast robbers ventured into banks during business hours with the intention of withdrawing money illegally. That is, until Lamm came along.

A former Prussian army officer, Lamm carefully plotted his robberies. He made a floor plan of his target and memorized it. He staged fake robberies with his crew in order to practice every movement, and he mapped out an escape route in mind-boggling detail. The dashboard of the getaway vehicle contained detailed descriptions of the roads and notes about other possible routes. "The Baron," as he was called, was an expert driver who had car racing experience. He even tested his escape routes in bad weather conditions to determine how long it would take to reach his destination.

Lamm's career lasted more than a dozen years—much longer than the average bank robber's lifespan as a criminal. He was killed in 1930, but his legend did not end there. Two of Lamm's associates joined forces with a group of men who would later form the ranks of **John Dillinger**'s (see entry) gang. The gangsters met in prison. Dillinger's men allowed the bank robbers to take part in their prison break on one condition: they had to reveal their methods for successful bank heists.

The getaway car

The Lewis-Jones Gang has been given credit for perfecting the use of the getaway car in bank robberies. Before the introduction of the automobile, bank robbers had to flee on foot or on horseback—both of which were risky means of escape. With Dean posted outside the bank in an idling car, the Lewis-Jones robbers had a leg up on pursuing policemen.

LEADED GAS

Police and detectives staked out Mrs. Forbes's address on November 24, 1918. What they saw at the small house on Sierra Madre Avenue confirmed their suspicions: Dean was, in fact, Mrs. Forbes. After Dean and Jones drove away from the house, two police cars followed them. The gangsters stopped at a gas station in Arcadia, a suburb of Los Angeles. Before they were able to refuel their car, the police pulled in behind them.

A fierce gun battle followed. Dean fired at the police with a shotgun that rested on a swivel, while Jones pulled out an automatic weapon. Deputy Sheriff George Van Vliet was struck in the face by Dean's shotgun fire—and was blasted clear out of his car. The police fired back. Surrounded by twelve officers, Dean and Jones died as their car was hammered by gunfire.

Sources for Further Reading

Nash, Jay Robert. *The Encyclopedia of World Crime.* Wilmette, IL: Crime Books, 1990, p. 891.

Nash, Jay Robert. *Look for the Woman: A Narrative Encyclopedia of Female Poisoners, Kidnappers, Thieves, Extortionists, Terrorists, Swindlers, and Spies from Elizabethan Times to Present.* New York: M. Evans, 1981, pp, 117–118.

Sifakis, Carl. *The Encyclopedia of American Crime.* New York: Facts on File, 1982, pp. 47–48.

John Dillinger

Born: June 22, 1903
Died: July 22, 1934

Dillinger liked to say that he robbed banks, not people. Known as "Gentleman Johnnie," he was said to have been pleasant—and often flirtatious—during his many bank robberies. Although there is no evidence that he ever killed anyone, he became the subject of what was at the time the greatest manhunt in American history.

Raised in Indiana

John Herbert Dillinger was born in Indianapolis, Indiana, in 1903. Four years later, his mother, Mollie, died. His father, John Wilson Dillinger, a grocer, was left to raise his son and fifteen-year-old daughter, Audrey. In 1912 Dillinger's father married Elizabeth Fields, who was from Mooresville, a farming community about twenty miles southwest of Indianapolis. When Dillinger was eleven years old, his half-brother, Hubert Dillinger, was born. Two year's later, in 1916, his half-sister, Doris, followed.

Dillinger's early life was quite normal. As a student, his grades were better than average. An outstanding athlete, he enjoyed playing baseball. He sometimes worked in his father's store, and was well liked by his neighbors. But Dillinger eventually became involved with a youth gang known as the Dirty Dozen. As a member of the gang, he was charged with stealing coal from carts belonging to the Pennsylvania Railroad, and selling the stolen coal to neighbors. He was in the sixth grade

The man who stopped Dillinger

In 1934 Melvin Purvis (1903–1960), special agent in charge of the FBI's office in Chicago, received word that the nation's most notorious bank robber, John Dillinger, had driven a stolen car across a state line, a violation of federal law, to make good his escape from an Indiana jail. Purvis and the bureau's efforts to locate and apprehend America's "Public Enemy Number One" were closely followed by both press and public for some four months—a chase filled with all the melodrama of an exciting and violent adventure story. On July 22, acting on a tip, Purvis and a squad of agents shot Dillinger as he reportedly attempted to resist capture outside a movie theater in Chicago. Later that year, Purvis was voted eighth in a poll of the year's outstanding world figures conducted by *Literary Digest*.

Dillinger was not the only criminal whose career was cut short by special agent Purvis. He was in charge of the manhunts that stopped Pretty Boy Floyd, Baby Face Nelson, Thomas H. Robinson Jr., and Verne Sankey. The prestigious *New York Times* once praised the famous G-man as the downfall of public enemies.

A Career Filled with Ups and Downs

Purvis was born in Timmonsville, South Carolina, to a plantation family. He earned a law degree from the University of South Carolina in 1925 and practiced for two years before joining the Department of Justice. Prior to his appointment as special agent in charge of the Chicago office, Purvis served in the FBI's field offices in Dallas, Texas, and Kansas City, Missouri. In 1932, after five years of service in various field offices, he was assigned to Chicago. There he was charged with capturing Dillinger—dead or alive.

Purvis's career was punctuated by a number of devastating failures. In 1933, he arrested **Roger Touhy** (see entry) and three others for the kidnapping of William Hamm, a St. Paul, Minnesota, millionaire. Soon after Touhy was cleared of that kidnapping, Purvis arrested the gangster for the kidnapping of Jake "the Barber" Factor. Although Touhy was sentenced to ninety-nine years in prison, it was later revealed that he

when he was taken to court for his first offense. Soon afterward, Dillinger's father bought a farm in Mooresville.

A STIFF SENTENCE

Shortly after his twentieth birthday, Dillinger enlisted in the U.S. Navy—possibly to avoid being arrested for having stolen a car. He completed basic training and was assigned to work as a

had not been involved in the incident. The kidnapping had been engineered by the Capone mob, which had manipulated the bureau to rid itself of a rival.

The manhunt for Dillinger, too, had encountered disaster. In April 1934, Purvis set a trap to ambush the gangster at the Little Bohemia resort in Wisconsin. The incident, which failed to deter Dillinger, left one innocent man dead and two others wounded. Reacting to the disaster, newspapers urged the FBI to terminate Purvis. But director J. Edgar Hoover refused to accept Purvis's resignation. If Hoover had accepted it, it would have tarnished the bureau's already troubled image.

Trouble with His Boss

Purvis's career was marked by conflict with Hoover, his superior. Throughout the country, the Bureau's field offices sent out press releases that began, "J. Edgar Hoover announces. . . ." But not in Chicago. Special agent Purvis took credit for news from the regional office—a bold practice that did not sit well with the FBI director. Hoover reportedly played a role in Attorney General Homer Cummings's decision not to allow Hollywood to produce a movie about the special agent's career.

The tug-of-war between Purvis and Hoover did not end when Purvis resigned from the FBI in July 1935 "for personal reasons." The situation was such that Hoover issued a statement to deny that he and the special agent had fallen out. But when Purvis took a job as the announcer of the *Post Toasties Junior Detective Corps*—a radio show that was later renamed the *Melvin Purvis Law and Order Patrol*—Hoover insisted that Purvis be identified as a *former* FBI agent. And when Purvis died in 1960, Hoover (on the advice of his assistants) sent no letter of condolence to the former special agent's family.

Purvis died on February 29, 1960, at the age of fifty-six. Using the .38 Police Special he had carried on the night of the Dillinger shooting, he shot himself. Purvis's wife later sent a telegram to Hoover. It read: "We are honored that you ignored Melvin's death. Your jealousy hurt him very much but until the end I think he loved you."

fireman third class on the battleship U.S.S. *Utah*. Military life apparently did not agree with him. He was punished several times for being absent without leave (AWOL). In December 1923—less than five months after he enlisted—Dillinger left the navy for good. After he abandoned ship outside of Boston, he was labeled a deserter. The navy posted a $50 reward for the capture of Dillinger. It would not be the last reward posted for his capture.

By the spring of 1924, Dillinger had married a sixteen-year-old girl from Indiana named Beryl Ethel Hovius. The following autumn, he fell into serious trouble with the law. On September 6, 1924, Dillinger and Edgar Singleton robbed a sixty-five-year-old grocer named Frank Morgan. During the robbery, Morgan was struck on the head and a shot was accidentally fired.

The two robbers were soon caught. Dillinger pleaded guilty to two charges—conspiracy to commit a felony (a serious crime) and assault with intent to rob—having been assured by the prosecuting attorney that he would receive a light sentence. Dillinger's sentence was anything but light. Judge Joseph W. Williams made an example of the twenty-year-old robber by sentencing him to ten to twenty years in prison. Singleton, meanwhile, was tried before another judge. He received a lighter sentence and was paroled in less than two years.

AN EAGER STUDENT

When he entered the Indiana State Reformatory at Pendleton, Dillinger reportedly informed the warden that he would cause no trouble—except to escape. He made good on his word. Dillinger tried repeatedly to escape from Pendleton, and failed every time. While in prison he met a number of bank robbers, including Harry Pierpont and Homer Van Meter, both of whom were eventually sent to the state prison at Michigan City to serve out the remainder of their terms.

When Dillinger's parole hearing was held in 1929 (the year his wife divorced him), he was not released. But the parole board did listen to his plea to be sent to the Michigan City prison—supposedly to play on the prison's superior baseball team. In truth, Dillinger requested the transfer in order to rejoin Pierpont, who had much to teach him about the art of robbing banks.

Dillinger was transferred to the Michigan City prison on July 15, 1929. There he met several of Pierpont's associates, including Russell Lee Clark, John Hamilton, and Charles "Fat

Charley" Makley. When Dillinger was released on May 22, 1933—thanks, in part, to a petition signed by friends and neighbors—he left with a list of banks that were prime targets for robbery. Shortly after his release, Dillinger set about robbing the banks on Pierpont's list. But he did not rob the banks for personal gain. He was attempting to raise enough money to engineer the escape of Pierpont and some of his bank-robbing associates.

"X" MARKS THE SPOT

Over the course of three weeks, Dillinger robbed around ten banks in five mid-eastern states. Sometimes he worked alone, sometimes with others. But he was always well-dressed, and his *modus operandi*—or method of operation—rarely varied. An agile and athletic man, he was known for his ability to jump to the other side of a bank counter in a single bound.

Once Dillinger had gathered enough money to organize the escape of his prison buddies, he traveled to Chicago. With some of the stolen funds, he bribed a foreman at a thread-making company to hide guns in a thread barrel that was to be delivered to the shirt-making shop at the Michigan City prison. The barrel was marked with a red "X" so that Pierpont would know where to look for the guns. On September 26, 1933, using the smuggled guns, ten prisoners escaped from the Michigan City penitentiary. The escapees, led by Pierpont, included Joseph Burns, Jim "Oklahoma Jack" Clark, Russell Clark, Walter Dietrich, Joseph Fox, John Hamilton, James Jenkins, Charles Makley, and Edward Shouse.

THE FIRST DILLINGER MOB

Dillinger was not able to celebrate his friends' new-found freedom. As Pierpont and the nine other inmates broke out of the Indiana institution, Dillinger—who had been captured at a

The Pierpont Gang?

Dillinger worked with an assorted group of bank robbers known as the Dillinger Gang. But Dillinger was probably one of the least experienced bank robbers in the gang. Harry Pierpont, whom he had met in prison, was far more experienced and probably played a role in the leadership of the gang. Dillinger did not start pulling heists until after he had spent several years in jail, where he met a number of veteran bank robbers. The mob was reportedly dubbed the Dillinger Gang by a law official named Matt Leach—who wanted to create tension between Dillinger and Pierpont. The plan failed.

The Dillinger Squad

Intent on capturing the infamous bank robber, Chicago police assembled a "Dillinger Squad." The team consisted of forty officers who were permanently assigned to tracking the man known as "Gentleman Johnnie."

girlfriend's address in Dayton, Ohio—was in jail waiting to be charged for the robbery of the Bluffton Bank. But not for long. On October 12, Pierpont, Clark, and Makley returned Dillinger's favor. They broke into the Lima Jail where the bank robber was being held, fatally shot the sheriff, and escorted Dillinger to freedom.

Pierpont and Dillinger joined forces to create the first Dillinger mob. Using Chicago as their base of operations, they robbed between ten and twenty banks. Their method was nearly flawless. Walter Dietrich, one of the members of the Dillinger mob, had once belonged to a gang led by master bank robber Herman K. Lamm. The veteran bank robber shared Lamm's successful formula with the Dillinger gangsters in exchange for being allowed to participate in the Michigan City jail break. Lamm's method stressed careful planning and timing.

A SURE-FIRE METHOD

The Dillinger Gang based their bank-robbing method on the Lamm formula. They cased banks beforehand in order to find out where the money was kept, where guards were positioned, and where the alarm button was hidden. The gangsters reportedly made up some unusual cover stories in order to gain access to the bank. For instance, one of the mobsters supposedly posed as a movie director who was scouting out locations for a film shoot. After casing the bank, the gangsters drew up floor plans of the institution.

Time was an important factor. The gangsters calculated how much time they needed to relieve the bank of its money—and how much time they could operate without police interference. Like Lamm, Dillinger's gang used a stopwatch during a robbery. Normally, one of the gangsters was charged with keeping his eye on the stopwatch, calling out to the others when their time was up. The heist was abandoned—no matter how much money was left in the bank—after a certain amount of time had passed. Dillinger reportedly boasted that he could clear a bank out of money in less than five minutes.

The gang's getaway was also planned out precisely. Street lights were timed. Backroads and alternate routes were noted in the plans. Often, the Dillinger gangsters did not race out of town on well-paved roads. Rather, they casually motored through a series of little-used back roads at a very modest speed.

The house in Tucson, Arizona, where John Dillinger was captured in January 1934. Three officers who participated in the capture stand in front of the house.

THE WOODEN GUN INCIDENT

In January 1934, the first Dillinger Gang fell apart. Taking a break from robbery, the mobsters traveled to Florida and then to Tucson, Arizona. There, several members were arrested by police. Dillinger was extradited (sent to trial) to Indiana—or, as he claimed, "kidnapped" by a squad of Chicago detectives. The gangster was flown to Chicago and then escorted to the Crown

Point Prison in Indiana, which enjoyed a reputation as an "escape-proof" jail.

Dillinger was held on a charge of shooting a policeman named William O'Malley during a bank robbery in East Chicago. He claimed that he was innocent (the charge was never proven). Choosing not to wait to go to trial, he broke out of jail. According to the newspapers of the day, Dillinger used a "wooden gun" to escape. After carving a gun out of the top of a wooden washboard, he colored it black with shoe polish. A later investigation carried out by the Hargrave Secret Service in Chicago provided another version of Dillinger's escape. According to the investigation, a well-bribed judge agreed to smuggle a real gun into the prison.

Whether the gun was fake or not, prison guards thought it was genuine. Dillinger captured several guards at gunpoint, locked them up, and took hold of two machine guns. He escaped with Herbert Youngblood, a thirty-five-year-old prisoner who was awaiting trial for murder, and two hostages, Deputy Sheriff Ernest Blunk and a mechanic named Ed Saager. Once they were safely away from the prison, Dillinger released the hostages—and gave them $4 for their trouble.

Lots of Trouble at the Little Bohemia

Youngblood and Dillinger separated after their escape from Crown Point. Less than two weeks later—on March 16, 1934—Youngblood was killed by police in Port Huron, Michigan. Dillinger, meanwhile, assembled a second mob of bank robbers. The group, which is considered to be the "real" Dillinger Gang, included veteran bank robber Homer Van Meter and two of his associates, Tommy Carroll and Eddie Green. Also in the new gang were John Hamilton and a young man who had worked in the Chicago gangs of **Al Capone** (see entry) and **Bugs Moran** (see entry). The man was Lester Gillis—better known as Baby Face Nelson. An experienced bank robber and bootlegger, Nelson had a short temper and violent disposition.

Beginning on March 6, 1934—just three days after Dillinger's escape—the new gang set off on a bank robbing spree. Dillinger, who had driven across state lines in a stolen vehicle, was now hunted by federal officials. The Federal Bureau of Investigation (FBI) mounted what would become the largest manhunt in American history. Acting on a tip, FBI agents surrounded the Little Bohemia Lodge in the woods fifty miles outside of Rhinelander, Wisconsin. Inside the deserted vacation lodge was the bank robber's gang. It looked like Dillinger's time had come.

Barking dogs warned the gangsters of the intruders. Dillinger and the other gang members escaped. Unaware that the gangsters had fled, FBI agents continued their stakeout. When three men stepped out of the lodge and into a car, agents called out to the men—and then fired. Two of the men were wounded and the third, Eugene Boiseneau, was killed. All three were innocent bystanders.

The federal bureau of unpopular investigations

Following Dillinger's death, FBI press releases announced that the gangster had been shot after he resisted arrest and attempted to draw a pistol. FBI director J. Edgar Hoover later wrote in his memoirs, *Persons in Hiding*, that "living true to his real character of a sneak and a coward, [Dillinger] had attempted to throw a woman in front of him to act as a barricade as he attempted to draw his gun."

But witnesses did not support the FBI's story. Not for the first time, the public was outraged by the FBI's handling of the Dillinger manhunt. A Virginia newspaper echoed this sentiment: "Any brave man would have walked down the aisle [of the movie theater] and arrested Dillinger. . . . Why were there so many cowards afraid of this one man? The answer is that the federal agents are, for the most part, cowards."

ENEMIES IN THE BUREAU

The public was outraged by the FBI's inability to capture Dillinger, and by the agency's failure to protect law-abiding citizens. In particular, bureau director J. Edgar Hoover and agent Melvin Purvis, who was responsible for the Little Bohemia disaster, received harsh criticism for their role in the Dillinger manhunt. Dillinger was making a mockery of the bureau. Hoover increased the reward offered for the bank robber's capture—and issued an order for his agents to shoot to kill.

In July 1934, Chicago police informed federal agents that Dillinger's whereabouts had been established. And a friend—a Romanian immigrant named Anna Sage—had agreed to betray him. In exchange, Sage wanted the reward money and assurance that immigration authorities would not follow through on her deportation (expulsion from the country). Melvin Purvis received word that on the evening of July 22, 1934, Sage and a waitress named Polly Hamilton would attend a movie at the Biograph Theater on the North Side of Chicago—accompanied by the fugitive bank robber.

A NIGHT AT THE MOVIES

The government agents were not sure that they would be able to identify Dillinger. Although his photograph had been printed in newspapers, wanted posters, and detective magazines throughout the country, he had recently undergone plastic surgery to alter his appearance. Sage (later known as "the Lady in Red") wore a red dress to make sure that she could be easily identified. Agents watched as Dillinger and the women entered the theater. At Hoover's command, they waited until the movie was over to make their move.

Inside, Dillinger watched *Manhattan Melodrama*—the story of the rise and fall of a good-looking and likable gambler, played by Clark Gable. The movie ends as Gable heads for the electric chair. At about 10:40 P.M., Dillinger left the theater with his companions. He was wearing his customary straw hat and dark glasses. Three men followed them closely. Suddenly, the women stepped away from Dillinger, and federal agents fired. The gangster was shot dead in an alley next to the theater. (A woman bystander was wounded as well.)

Immediately after the shooting, bystanders collected souvenirs of Dillinger's death—even dipping their handkerchiefs in the dead gangster's blood. Two days later, on July 24, Dillinger's body was buried in the outskirts of Indianapolis. Five thousand people attended the funeral ceremony. In order to prevent souvenir-hunters from disturbing the grave, Dillinger's father had it covered with reinforced concrete.

THE END OF THE SECOND DILLINGER GANG

For a while, Nelson took over Dillinger's role as "Public Enemy Number One." He died the following November from wounds he received in a gun battle with FBI agents. Van Meter was killed after he, too, was betrayed by friends. Green died at the hands of FBI gunmen. Less than five months after Dillinger's death, the second Dillinger Gang was destroyed.

Pierpont and Makley were sentenced to death for the murder of a sheriff in 1931. Using guns carved from soap, they fought their way out of Ohio State Prison in Columbus. Ambushed by a riot squad, Pierpont was wounded and Makley was killed. Pierpont was executed the following month.

Purvis was unable to intervene in Sage's deportation proceedings. The infamous "Lady in Red" was deported to Europe. She died in 1947.

Take a look at this!

Dillinger (1991) stars Mark Harmon as the Depression-era bank robber, who became Public Enemy Number One. Sherilyn Fenn plays girlfriend Billy Frenchette, with Will Patton as G-man Purvis.

Sources for Further Reading

Bruns, Roger. *The Bandit Kings from Jesse James to Pretty Boy Floyd.* New York: Crown, 1995, pp. 176–210.

Dartford, Mark, ed. *Crimes and Punishment,* Volume 6. Tarrytown, NY: Marshall Canvendish, 1985, pp. 866–877.

Nash, Jay Robert. *Bloodletters and Badmen.* New York: M. Evans, 1973, pp. 159–178.

Nash, Jay Robert. *The Encyclopedia of World Crime.* Wilmette, IL: Crime Books, 1990, pp. 2513–2514.

Prassel, Frank Richard. *The Great American Outlaw, A Legacy of Fact and Fiction.* Norman: University of Oklahoma Press, 1993, pp. 277–283.

Sifakis, Carl. *The Encyclopedia of American Crime.* New York: Facts on File, 1982, pp. 206–210, 596–597.

Vandome, Nick. *Crimes and Criminals.* New York: Chambers, 1992, pp. 80–81.

Belle Gunness

Born: 1859
Died: ?

A middle-aged widow who lured men to her home with promises of marriage, Belle Gunness made a business out of murder—and then disappeared.

THE WIDOW SORENSON

Born in Norway, Gunness moved to the United States at the age of twenty-four. Her family background is sketchy. Her father may have been a stonemason (a builder who works with stones) or a traveling magician. She probably had a sister who also moved to America. In 1884, shortly after she left Norway, Gunness married Mads Albert Sorenson in Chicago. Gunness and Sorenson had three children—Jennie, Myrtle, and Lucy (one or all of whom had been adopted).

In 1900, Mads Sorenson died. Although Gunness claimed her husband died of heart failure, his family suspected foul play. Adding to their suspicion was the fact that Gunness had tried to collect on her husband's $8,500 life insurance policy—just one day after the funeral. Although the family is believed to have ordered an inquest (inquiry), there is no evidence that the coroner pursued the case. Gunness collected a handsome sum from her husband's insurance policy.

"Come prepared to stay forever"

Belle Gunness lured men to her farm in La Porte, Indiana, by placing personal ads in newspapers. When a suitable candidate responded, she began corresponding with him, eventually inviting him to her home. Andrew Hegelein was among the men Gunness wrote to. In a letter dated January 13, 1908, she wrote:

To the Dearest Friend in the World: No woman in the world is happier than I am. I know that you are now to come to me and be my own. I can tell from your letters that you are the man I want. It does not take one long to tell when to like a person, and you I like better than anyone in the world, I know.

Think how we will enjoy each other's company. You, the sweetest man in the whole world. We will be all alone with each other. Can you conceive of anything nicer? I think of you constantly. When I hear your name mentioned, and this is when one of the dear children speaks of you, or I hear myself humming it with the words of an old love song, it is beautiful music to my ears.

My heart beats in wild rapture for you, My Andrew, I love you. Come prepared to stay forever.

Andrew Hegelein never returned from his trip to La Porte. In May of 1908, his remains were found buried on the grounds of the Gunness farm.

In 1902, at the age of forty-two, Gunness appeared in La Porte, Indiana. She purchased a farm near town and soon married a local man, Peter Gunness, who was also a native of Norway. Shortly after their son, Philip, was born in 1903, Peter died. According to Gunness's story, Peter—who was a butcher—had been killed when a heavy instrument fell from a shelf, splitting his skull. Again, Gunness's story was questioned and again there was no evidence to indicate that she was a murderer. Gunness pocketed another $4,000 in insurance money, in spite of the local coroner's insistence that Peter's "accident" had been planned.

OBJECT: MATRIMONY

Gunness's fourteen-year-old daughter, Jennie, reportedly told people that her mother had killed her father with a meat cleaver—although she denied saying so when the coroner questioned her. Two years after Peter's death, in September 1906, Jennie disappeared. Gunness told neighbors that she had sent

A bad poem about a bad woman

Gunness's exploits were described by an anonymous poet whose rhymes were sometimes far-fetched:

Belle Gunness lived in In-di-an;

She always, always had a man;

Ten, at least, went in her door—

And were never, never seen no more.

Now, all these men were Norska [Scandinavian] folk

Who came to Belle from Minn-e-sote;

They liked their coffee and their gin:

They got it—plus a mickey finn [a drugged drink].

And now with cleaver poised so sure

Belle neatly cut their jug-u-lar [a vein in the neck]

She put them in a bath of lime

And left them there for quite some time.

There's red upon the Hoosier [Indiana] moon

For Belle was strong and full of doom;

And think of all them Norska men

Who'll never see St. Paul again.

the girl to a boarding school in Los Angeles, California.

Gunness continued to raise and butcher hogs using the skills she had probably learned from her second husband. She hired a Canadian farmhand named Ray Lamphere (or L'Amphere) to help her run the farm, and by the end of 1906 had begun to place matrimonial (marriage-related) personal ads in newspapers in Chicago and other cities in the Midwest. She also placed some ads in Norwegian-language papers. In her ads, Gunness claimed to be a young, attractive, well-to-do widow who was looking for a financially secure man to marry: "Rich, goodlooking widow, young, owner of a large farm, wishes to get in touch with a gentleman of wealth with cultured tastes. Object, matrimony. No triflers need apply." She also added that her prospective suitor had to be willing to pay off the $1,000 mortgage on her farm.

John Moo (or Moe), a Wisconsinite, was one of the first to reply. A middle-aged Norwegian native, he arrived in La Porte with more than $1,000—and vanished within days of his arrival. Other marriage-minded men followed. Ole Budsburg, a widower from Wisconsin, and Andrew Hegelein, a single farmer from South Dakota, were among the men who traveled to the Gunness farm and were never heard from again.

On April 6, 1907, Budsburg left the La Porte Savings Bank with thousands of dollars in cash. It was the last time he was seen alive. When his sons, Matthew and Oscar, wrote to Gunness to ask about their father, she replied that she had never

The Gunness farm, where many dead bodies were found. The letters A through E indicate individual graves—each hole contained from one to four bodies.

seen the man. Similarly, Hegelein disappeared in January 1908, shortly after he was seen with Gunness depositing a $2,900 check at the Savings Bank.

A TIMELY FIRE

On February 3, 1908, Gunness fired Ray Lamphere, who was reportedly in love with her. She hired Joe Maxon in his place. Asle Hegelein, meanwhile, had become concerned about his brother's failure to return home. He wrote to Gunness, who informed him that Andrew was not on her farm—although she would be willing, for a price, to help look for him.

No doubt Gunness was concerned about mounting questions and loose ends. Pesky relatives, nosey neighbors, and a disgruntled former employee who knew too much about her matrimonial scam. Gunness approached a lawyer named M. E. Leliter to ask him to draw up a will. She claimed that she was afraid for her life because Lamphere, she said, had threatened to set her farmhouse on fire. Gunness paid off the mortgage on her house and drew up a will that left everything to her children. But she didn't inform the police that Lamphere had threatened her life.

On April 28, 1908, Gunness's farmhouse burned to the ground. Joe Maxon, the handyman, escaped by jumping from the second floor. Gunness and her three children died in the fire—or so it seemed. Four bodies were found in the basement, beneath the rubble of the collapsed house. Three of the corpses were those of children, and the fourth was the badly burned body of a woman—a decapitated (beheaded) woman. Without a head, the corpse (body) could not be positively identified as the body of Gunness.

A PIGSTY FULL OF BONES

A number of things led people to question whether Belle Gunness had died in the fire. Two farmers viewed the body and stated that it couldn't possibly have been the remains of their neighbor. A number of Gunness's friends, some of whom had come from Chicago, agreed. What's more, Gunness was a tall woman who weighed about 200 pounds. The corpse was that of a woman who stood five feet, three inches tall—five inches shorter than Gunness—and weighed under one hundred and fifty pounds. Physicians compared measurements taken from the corpse with those taken by tailors who made Gunness's clothing. Their findings were clear: the headless body was not the corpse of Belle Gunness. The body was then examined by Dr. J. Meyers, who determined that the unknown woman had died of strychnine poisoning.

On May 3, 1908, Sheriff Albert H. Smutzer sent a crew of men to Gunness's farm. Digging around the area where the hogs were fed, they uncovered a grisly patchwork of shallow graves. They found the body of Gunness's daughter, Jennie, as well as the corpses of two other unidentified children. The remains of Moo, Budsburg, and Hegelein were also uncovered. By the end of the search, the bodies of at least fourteen men had been discovered. And not all in one piece: an expert butcher, Gunness had cut up many of the bodies.

Ray Lamphere was arrested and charged with murder and arson. Although he admitted to setting the fire, he pleaded innocent to the charges of murder. Tried on May 22, 1908, he was acquitted of murder. He was, however, convicted of arson, and was sentenced to up to twenty years in prison. Lamphere died after less than two years in prison, but not before he confessed to Reverend E. A. Schell.

FIFTY WAYS TO LOSE YOUR LOVER

Lamphere outlined the gruesome details of his service as Gunness's employee. Although he continued to deny killing anyone, he confessed to helping Gunness bury the bodies of a number of men. He also described Gunness's methods. Sometimes she drugged her victim's coffee, waited for him to lose consciousness, and split his head with a cleaver (large butcher knife). Others she simply poisoned with strychnine. Some bodies she buried intact, and others she dissected. She also threw victims' corpses into a vat of hot water (which was used to scald slaughtered hogs) and then covered them with quicklime (substance that burns, like acid). Lamphere claimed that Gunness had taken thousands of dollars from her victims, some of whom had come the farm with their life savings.

Lamphere also claimed to know about the bodies in the basement. The woman, he said, had been hired as a housekeeper—only to serve as Gunness's stand-in during the blaze. Gunness dressed the woman in her clothes, dragged her to the basement, and left her own false teeth behind. The three other corpses belonged to Gunness's children. Prior to the fire, she had knocked them unconscious using chloroform (liquid anesthetic). She then suffocated them and placed them in the basement next to the headless woman.

Lamphere claimed that he was supposed to meet Gunness after the fire. He never saw her again and died in jail on December 30, 1909.

No teeth, no name
A headless woman was found in the ashes of the Gunness farmhouse. This made identification impossible: the head would have contained teeth and dental work that could have been traced.

149

Sources for Further Reading

Nash, Jay Robert. *Bloodletters and Badmen.* New York: M. Evans, 1973, pp. 252, 382–387.

Nash, Jay Robert. *The Encyclopedia of World Crime.* Wilmette, IL: Crime Books, 1990, pp. 1400–1405.

Nash, Jay Robert. *Look for the Woman, A Narrative Encyclopedia of Female Poisoners, Kidnappers, Thieves, Extortionists, Terrorists, Swindlers, and Spies, from Elizabethan Times to the Present.* New York: M. Evans, 1981, pp. 176–178.

Vandome, Nick. *Crimes and Criminals.* New York: Chambers, 1992, p. 102.

Pearl Hart

Born: 1871
Died: 1925?
AKA: Mrs. L. P. Keele

Had Pearl Hart pulled a stagecoach robbery thirty years earlier, she probably would not have earned a spot in the history books. But because she and her accomplice botched a robbery in 1899—at the end of the stagecoach era—she staked her claim to fame as the perpetrator of the last American stagecoach robbery.

MARRIED LIFE AND OLD WEST SHOWS

Pearl Taylor was born into to a well respected middle-class family in Lindsay, Ontario, Canada. One of several children, she was educated at an all-girl boarding school in Toronto. At the age of seventeen she eloped (ran away to marry) with Frederick Hart—a man who liked to gamble and had no steady job.

In 1893 the Harts attended the Columbian Exposition in Chicago, Illinois—a large fair with many sideshows. For some time Frederick worked at the Columbian Exposition while Pearl worked various jobs. Pearl was captivated by the Wild West shows—exciting dramatizations of life on the frontier—and she reportedly learned to ride a horse and shoot a gun from some of the show's performers. When the Exposition ended Pearl left her husband and headed West, to Trinidad, Colorado. There she worked briefly as a hotel maid and gave birth to a son. Returning to Lindsay, she left the boy with her mother and set off to Phoenix, Arizona. Pearl worked as a cook and took in laundry to support herself.

In 1895, Frederick traveled to Phoenix hoping to get back together with his wife. The couple reconciled and Frederick took work as a hotel manager and bartender. But their second attempt to live together didn't last long. Within three years, after the birth of a daughter, Frederick left Pearl. According to one version, he left to join the army fighting the Spanish in Cuba. Another report claims that he left after Pearl shot at him. Whatever his reasons, Frederick left in 1898, and never returned.

THE LAST ARIZONA STAGE

After leaving her second child with her mother, Hart returned to the West, working as a cook in mining camps. During this time, she met her future partner in crime, Joe Boot—a man who has been described in conflicting accounts as a miner, a town drunk, and a dashing British bandit. Historians are also unclear about who was responsible for setting the robbery in motion. Whether it was Boot's quick-fix scheme or Hart's plan to come up with money for her ailing mother, the two devised a plot to rob a local stage in 1899.

The stagecoach that traveled the sixty-five miles between Florence and Globe was the last of its kind in the Arizona Terri-

away, sit still and take your chances; if you jump nine times out of ten you will be hurt. . . . Don't smoke a strong pipe inside especially early in the morning, spit on the leeward side of the coach [the side of the coach the wind blows *away* from]. If you have anything to take in a bottle, pass it around; a man who drinks by himself in such a case is lost to all human feeling. . . . Be sure and take two heavy blankets with you; you will need them. Don't swear, nor lop [lean] over on your neighbor when sleeping. Don't ask how far it is to the next station until you get there. Take small change to pay expenses. Never attempt to fire a gun or pistol while on the road; it may frighten the team and the careless handling and cocking of the weapon makes nervous people nervous. Don't discuss politics or religion, nor point out places on the road where horrible murders have been committed, if delicate women are among the passengers. . . . Don't imagine for a moment you are going on a pic-nic; expect annoyance, discomfort and some hardships. If you are disappointed, thank heaven.

tory. The Globe stage hadn't been robbed for years—and with good reason. At the turn of the century, stagecoaches were an outdated form of transportation—and they no longer carried Wells Fargo strongboxes that had been the targets of earlier highway robbers. In fact, there was so little of value on board the stagecoaches of that era that most didn't even bother to carry a "shotgun rider" to protect the passengers and cargo.

Hart and Boot went ahead with the robbery anyway. Holding guns on the driver, Boot and Hart (who was dressed in pants and wore her hair short) took the driver's gun and relieved the passengers of the contents of their wallets. With a little over $400 for their efforts, the two bandits sent the stage on its way— and promptly got lost. They had neglected to plan their escape. Within three days of the robbery, local lawmen found Hart and Boot asleep. According to one account, they were found within *one mile* of the spot where they had stopped the stagecoach.

THE LADY BANDIT

The robbery had been a miserable failure, but that didn't matter to Hart's contemporaries, who treated her like a star. Crowds of onlookers and autograph-seekers gathered at the Globe jail, where the "Lady Bandit" was held before her trial.

Tried separately from Boot, she was acquitted by a jury that was probably swayed by her hard-luck story. The judge was not pleased. After ordering her to be tried on a separate weapons charge, Judge Doan sentenced Hart to five years in the Yuma Territorial prison. Boot, meanwhile, was sentenced to a thirty-year stay at the same prison.

Hart served only a portion of her sentence. Some say she suddenly "got religion" and started preaching that crime doesn't pay. Others claim that Governor A. W. Brodie gave in to public pressure to release her. Still others suggest that she was quietly pardoned to cover-up an embarrassing—and difficult to explain—pregnancy. In any case, on December 19, 1902—after only eighteen months in prison—Hart left Yuma prison a free woman.

For the most part, Hart stayed out of the public eye after she was released except, possibly, for a brief stint in Buffalo Bill's Wild West Show. In Kansas City, Missouri—under the name of Mrs. L. P. Keele—she was arrested and jailed for a short time. The details of her death are uncertain: there is no way to verify whether she died in Kansas City when she was in her fifties, as some historians claim—or whether she lived into her nineties on a ranch in Globe, as other sources suggest.

Visiting the past

Hart reportedly returned to the Globe jailhouse in 1924 to survey her former lodging. When the guard asked who she was, she replied--so the story goes--"Pearl Hart, the lady bandit."

Sources for Further Reading

The American West, A Cultural Encyclopedia, Volumes 5 and 9, Danbury, CT: Grolier Educational Corp., 1995, pp. 756, 825, 1507-1511.

Collins, William and Bruce Levene. *Black Bart: The True Story of the West's Most Famous Stagecoach Robber.* Mendocino, CA: Pacific Transcriptions, 1992, pp. 24-39.

Davis, William C. *The American Frontier.* New York: Smithmark, 1992, pp. 32-33, 180.

Lewis, Jon. *The Mammoth Book of the West.* New York: Carroll & Graf, 1996, p. 335.

Metz, Leon Claire. *A Gallery of Notorious Gunmen from the American West: The Shooters.* New York: Berkeley Books, 1996, pp. 247–250.

Nash, Jay Robert. *Bloodletters and Badmen.* New York: M. Evans, 1973, pp. 61–62.

Ross, Stewart. *Fact or Fiction: Cowboys.* Surrey, British Columbia: Copper Beech, 1995, p. 31.

The Wild West. [Online] Available http://www.calweb.com/~rbbusman/women/hart.htm, February 7, 1997.

The bandit actress

After Hart was released from prison, she starred—very briefly—in a play called *The Arizona Bandit.* She was a natural in the role: the play, written by her sister, was about her life as an outlaw.

Patty Hearst

Born: February 20, 1954
AKA: Tania

Kidnapped as a young woman, Patty Hearst was transformed into "Tania" during her nineteen-month odyssey as a captive—and then a member—of the Symbionese Liberation Army. A participant in a number of robberies, she later claimed to have been brainwashed. Although convicted and imprisoned, she eventually received a pardon.

THE HEARST LEGACY

The middle child of five daughters, Hearst was born in San Francisco, California, on February 20, 1954. Her father, Randolph Apperson Hearst, was chairman of the board of the Hearst Corporation—the largest privately owned media conglomerate (a business coporation made up of a number of companies) in the United States. Hearst's mother, Catherine Wood (Campbell) Hearst, was a member of the governing board of the University of California. Her position earned her a reputation as an outspoken conservative. Hearst's legendary grandfather, William Randolph Hearst Jr., amassed a fortune as the founder of the Hearst newspaper empire.

Hearst grew up on family estates in Beverly Hills and Hillsborough, California. She spent vacations at family ranches, such as Wyntoon and San Simeon. A one-hundred-and-forty acre estate, San Simeon is the largest single piece of privately owned land on the Pacific Coast. The grounds include an enormous castle that was commissioned by Hearst's eccentric grandfather.

In an autobiography published in 1982, Hearst recalled that her family's wealth helped her develop self-assurance: "I grew up in this affluent [wealthy] and sheltered environment sublimely self-confident," she wrote. "But we were never spoiled. . . . What I remember most keenly about those years was my parents' strictness."

CATHOLIC SCHOOL AND BERKELEY

Hearst attended Catholic boarding schools as a girl. She graduated from the Convent of the Sacred Heart in Menlo Park, California, and then began high school at Santa Catalina School in Montery, California. While she excelled in English and History, she received average grades in subjects she did not enjoy, such as French and Math. As a junior, she transferred to an exclusive day school in Hillsborough, the Crystal Springs School for Girls. Hearst's grades improved at Crystal Springs, and she graduated in June 1971, one year ahead of the rest of her classmates.

While at Crystal Springs, Hearst was tutored by Steven Weed, a young teacher at the school. The two eventually moved in together and eventually became engaged. During Hearst's first year at Menlo College, she lived with Weed in an apartment two miles from campus. She earned all As and was named the school's best student of the year. After spending the summer in Europe, Hearst moved to Berkeley, California, where Weed had been awarded a teaching grant to pursue his graduate studies. Hearst enrolled in the University of California for the winter and spring terms of 1972 to 1973. Majoring in veterinary science (the treatment of animals), she took courses in chemistry, math, and zoology. Again, her grades were average. The following school year she changed her major to art history, and immediately began to earn high marks.

KIDNAPPED BY THE SLA

At 9:20 P.M. on February 4, 1974—two months after Hearst and Weed had announced their engagement—two men and one

The high cost of living

The kidnapping of Patricia Hearst—and its aftermath—cost the Hearst family a fortune. Randolph Hearst spent at least $2 million trying to get his daughter ransomed—in the form of a food program to feed poor people in California. After Patty's capture, Randolph posted $1.5 million in bail—of which he paid $100,000 in cash. Fearing for his daughter's life during the trial, he hired bodyguards to watch her around the clock—for a fee that is estimated at $200,000 (plus a very expensive guard dog). Legal fees and expenses added more than $1 million more to the tab.

woman broke into their apartment on Benvenue Street. Weed was beaten and knocked unconscious with a wine bottle. Hearst, who was screaming and partially clothed, was abducted at gunpoint.

Hearst's kidnappers were members of the Symbionese Liberation Army (SLA), a left-wing terrorist group. (Left-wing terrorist groups pursue political goals by extreme, revolutionary, and sometimes violent means.) Founded in Berkeley, the group was headed by Donald Defreeze, an African American petty criminal who had escaped from Soledad prison in 1972. Appointing himself "general field marshal" in the army, Defreeze called himself Cinque Mtume, a Swahili name meaning "Fifth Prophet." Defreeze originally recruited nine members to his radical organization, including Russell Little (known as Bo) and Joseph Romero (known as Osceola). The SLA first captured public attention on November 6, 1973, after members murdered Marcus Foster, the first African American superintendent of schools in Oakland, California. Little and Romero, the only gang members captured in the slaying, were sentenced to serve terms at San Quentin penitentiary outside San Francisco, California.

Originally, SLA members planned to organize a hostage exchange in which they would trade their "prisoner of war," Hearst, for Little and Romero. But the kidnapping generated so much publicity that they decided to change their plan. They decided to hold on to their hostage indefinitely.

BRAINWASHING, BANK ROBBERY, AND DISNEYLAND

First, Hearst was subjected to fifty-seven days of confinement. Bound and blindfolded in a closet, she was also raped and psychologically tortured. Hearst later claimed that her kidnappers used control and abuse to brainwash her. (Brainwashing involves replacing an individual's beliefs with opposing beliefs.)

Opposite page: Patty Hearst in front of the Symbionese Liberation Army symbol, brandishing an automatic weapon.

An artist turned terrorist

Wendy Misako Yoshimura was born in a California detention camp, where Japanese Americans were forcefully detained during World War II (1939-1945). The daughter of gardeners, she was a prize-winning artist who turned to terrorism in the early 1970s.

In March 1972, a police raid uncovered a stash of bombs, explosives, rifles, and shotguns in a garage that Yoshimura had rented under the name of Annie Wong. Formally charged with illegal possession of weapons in connection with a plot to blow up a Navy Reserve Officers Training Corps building on the University of California campus, she pleaded guilty—and disappeared. Her former boyfriend, William Brandt, was imprisoned at Soledad prison on the same charges. Yoshimura managed to avoid capture for more than three years. During that period she joined with SLA members—sometime after the Los Angeles shootout. Yoshimura's odyssey ended on September 18, 1975, when FBI agents and police arrested the Japanese American terrorist along with Hearst. During her trial and sentencing, Hearst informed on many of her former underground associates—including Yoshimura, a woman she reportedly once adored.

On April 5, 1974, she recorded a message to announce publicly that she had joined the SLA. Claiming to have joined the organization of her own free will, she took the name of "Tania."

Ten days later members of the SLA robbed the Hibernia Bank's Sunset District branch in San Francisco, California. Hearst was among the robbers. Later that day, the evening news carried surveillance footage that showed Hearst wearing a beret and carrying a rifle. William Saxbe, the U.S. attorney general, publicly labeled her a "common criminal." Once considered a victim, Hearst had become a villain in public opinion.

Pursued by the police, the SLA moved from San Francisco to the Compton ghetto in Los Angeles, California. Hearst next surfaced on May 16, 1974, when she and two other SLA members—William and Emily Harris—stopped at Mel's Sporting Goods on Crenshaw Boulevard. After security guards began to wrestle with William Harris, who had been accused of attempting to shoplift a pair of socks, Hearst fired an automatic rifle at the store from a van parked outside. The trio fled in the van and then quickly abandoned it. Using other vehicles, they drove thirty miles south of Los Angeles, to Anaheim, where they rented a motel room at Disneyland.

MORE VIOLENCE

The abandoned van contained something the bank robbers had overlooked: a parking ticket. The ticket lead police right to the SLA's doorstep. Moving from their safehouse to a home on East 54th Street, SLA members engaged in a violent shootout with police. After the house was demolished by fire, the remains of Defreeze and five other SLA members were found among the ashes.

Hearst and the Harrises watched the shootout on the television in their room in Anaheim. Within a few days, the three surviving SLA members issued a taped statement. Reading a script written by Emily Harris, Hearst denounced (rejected) her parents, whom she called "the pig Hearsts." She also professed love for William Wolfe, an SLA member who had died in the shootout.

The three criminals avoided capture by hiding in various safe spots across the country. Aided by outsiders who were sympathetic to their cause, they hid in a farmhouse in South Canaan, Pennsylvania, in the early summer of 1974. In July, they moved to a farm in Jeffersonville, New York, returning to California at the end of the summer.

In Sacramento, the group gathered a small number of new recruits, including a brother and sister, Kathleen and Steven Soliah. In February 1975, the new group robbed the Guild Savings and Loan Association near Sacramento, and in April they hit the Crocker National Bank in the Sacramento area. A bank customer died in the Crocker robbery, after having been shot by Emily Harris. Hearst drove the getaway vehicle. Returning to San Francisco, the group bombed a number of police cars—both in the San Francisco area and in Los Angeles.

A MASSIVE MANHUNT

Meanwhile, SLA members were tracked by a manhunt that involved more than three thousand Federal Bureau of Investigation (FBI) agents who interviewed, followed, or background-checked almost thirty thousand individuals from coast to coast.

Lights, camera, action!

With her kidnapping and trial behind her, Hearst tried her hand at acting. The one-time terrorist appeared in *Serial Mom* (1994)—in which she plays "juror number eight," who is beaten to death by the serial mom herself, Kathleen Turner. Hearst also appeared in *Cry Baby* (1990)—as Traci Lords's crossing-guard mom—and supplied a radio call-in voice for a 1997 episode of the television show, *Frasier.*

The investigation also involved local police from Alaska to New York—and even Hong Kong. After receiving a tip, the FBI located the two-story farm house in Pennsylvania where Hearst and the Harrises had hidden. Police dogs picked up Hearst's scent in one of the beds. After dusting rooms for evidence, agents found fingerprints belonging to William and Emily Harris as well as those of another person—Wendy Yoshimura, a Japanese American woman who was wanted in a Berkeley, California, bombing conspiracy.

With a new lead to pursue, the FBI began to look into Yoshimura's background. After learning that Yoshimura's former boyfriend, William Brandt, was imprisoned at Soledad penitentiary, the FBI monitored the visitors he received. Kathleen Soliah was among Brandt's visitors.

Next agents began to check out Soliah—as well as her younger brother, Steven. Investigating the activities of the twenty-seven-year-old house painter, agents discovered that Steven Soliah had rented an apartment at 625 Morse Street. The investigation also led to another San Francisco address—288 Precita Street, a few miles away—into which a young couple had recently moved.

TIME RUNS OUT

FBI agents suspected that the Harrises were living at the Precita Street apartment. From surveillance vehicles parked on the street, they thought they saw William Harris leaving the apartment. In order to make a positive identification, one agent, dressed as a hippie, followed the man to a laundromat. Convinced that they had located the SLA fugitives, FBI agents had local police seal off the block surrounding the Precita Street apartment. Shortly after 1 P.M. on September 18, 1975, William and Emily jogged around the corner toward their apartment. They were arrested.

Less certain about who they would find at the other address, the FBI sent only two agents to investigate the apartment at 625 Morse. Arriving with two policemen, they ordered the occupants to open the door. At gunpoint, Wendy Yoshimura opened the apartment door. Agents caught another woman as she tried to escape. The woman—who weighed less than ninety pounds—was Hearst. A later search of the apartment turned up four pistols (in addition to two that were hidden in the women's purses), two sawed-off shotguns, and a marijuana plant.

URBAN GUERILLA

Hearst's arrest received tremendous publicity. Taken to the federal building in San Francisco in handcuffs, she smiled and lifted her clenched fist. Hearst's militant (combative) pose appeared nation-wide—and around the world—in newspapers and on television. On the jailhouse booking form she listed "Urban Guerrilla" (terrorist) as her occupation. But Hearst's jailhouse swagger did not last long. She later told a reporter, "The more I talked to psychiatrists, I just started breaking down. I started realizing that I was terribly confused."

On May 9, 1977, Hearst was sentenced to five years' probation on state charges involving the incident at the sporting goods store. (A convict who is sentenced to probation is given a trial period in which he or she is expected to abide by the law.) But the federal charges—armed robbery and the use of a firearm—were much more serious. In spite of all the money and resources at the Hearst family's disposal, she was found guilty on both counts. On April 12, 1976, she was temporarily sentenced to twenty-five years for robbery and ten years for the use of a firearm—the maximum sentence for each offense. On September 24, she received her final sentence: two seven-year terms, to be served one after the other.

RELEASED FROM PRISON

The Hearst family did not give up easily. After the U.S. Supreme Court refused to hear the case, a national Committee for the Release of Patricia Hearst circulated a petition that was signed by forty-eight congressmen. In January of 1979, President Jimmy

Costly manhunt

The nineteen-month nation-wide manhunt for Patty Hearst cost taxpayers an estimated $5 million.

163

Randolph and Catherine Hearst, Patty's parents, plead with their daughter's abductors for her safe return.

Carter commuted (lessened) Hearst's sentence. On February 1, after serving only twenty-two months and seventeen days in prison, Hearst was released. Interviewed after her sentence was commuted, she wore a T-shirt bearing the words "Pardon Me."

On April 1, 1979, Hearst married Bernard Shaw, a policeman who worked as her bodyguard during the trial. (Her maid of honor was Trish Tobin, a childhood friend whose father owned the Hibernia Bank that Hearst and the SLA robbed.) The couple moved to New England with their two daughters.

Sources for Further Reading

Contemporary Authors Volume 136. Detroit: Gale Research, 1992, pp. 184-185.

Earl Blackwell's Celebrity Register 1990. Detroit: Gale Research, 1990, p. 195.

Fosburgh, Lacey. "Patty Today." *The New York Times Biographical Service* (April 1977), pp. 545–549.

Lovece, Frank. "Heiress Human." *Entertainment Weekly* (April 22, 1994), p. 37.

Matthews, Tom, et al. "The Story of Patty." *Newsweek* (September 29, 1975), pp. 20–40.

Nash, Jay Robert. *Look for the Woman: A Narrative Encyclopedia of Female Poisoners, Kidnappers, Thieves, Extortionists, Terrorists, Swindlers, and Spies, from Elizabethan Times to the Present.* New York: M. Evans, 1981, pp. 188–189.

Sinclair, Tom. "Patty Hearst Turns Symbionese: The Kidnapped Heiress' Ordeal Of Torture and Terror Held America Captive 22 Years Ago." *Entertainment Weekly* (September 12, 1997), p. 152.

Here's a book you might like:

Every Secret Thing, 1982, by Patty Hearst and Alvin Moscow

Hearst gives a first-person account of her ordeal in this autobiography. "It's a personal story," she says, "and I hope it will give people the feeling of what happened and how they might react in the same situation. I want people to understand what I experienced."

Hearst has also published a novel (which was co-written with Cornelia Frances Biddle). *Murder at San Simeon,* published in 1996, is a mystery based on some 1924 events at the mansion of multi-millionaire William Randolph Hearst Jr., the newspaper heiress's grandfather.

Marion Hedgepeth

Born: ?
Died: January 1, 1910

Operating at the end of the era of American train robbers, Marion Hedgepeth enjoyed a certain degree of popularity until he was shot and killed in a botched robbery attempt.

THE HEDGEPETH FOUR

Born and raised in Cooper County, Missouri, Hedgepeth headed West as a teenager in hopes of becoming a cowboy. He traveled to Colorado, Montana, and Wyoming, and by the 1880s had earned a reputation as a robber, rustler, and killer. An expert shooter, he reportedly had lightning-fast reflexes. It was said that he could draw and shoot a man who had *already* drawn a pistol on him.

By 1890, Hedgepeth had formed a group of outlaws known to lawmen as the "Hedgepeth Four." The gang included Hedgepeth, Charles "Dink" Burke, James "Illinois Jimmy" Francis, and Albert "Bertie" Sly. After committing a number of holdups and muggings, the gang pulled their first train robbery on November 4, 1890. Stopping the Missouri Pacific train near Omaha, Nebraska, they got away with about $1,000. The following week they headed to Wisconsin, where they robbed the Chicago, Milwaukee & St. Paul train line just outside of Milwaukee on November 12, 1890. Without pausing to allow the guard to surrender, they dynamited the express car in order to get at its contents. The gang ran away from the wrecked railway car with $5,000. The express guard somehow survived the ordeal.

Within weeks, the gang organized another robbery. After boarding a St. Louis train, they stopped it near Glendale, Missouri. Without firing a shot, they emptied the express car safe of $50,000—their most successful haul ever. Leaving the site, the gang members deliberately created trails that would mislead the detectives who followed them. They returned to St. Louis and rented rooms to wait for the posse (a group of people with legal authority to capture criminals) activity to die down.

But the Hedgepeth Four had made a fatal mistake. Before retreating to St. Louis, they had buried their weapons—and envelopes that had contained the money from their last theft—inside a shed. Shortly after the robbery, a young girl who was playing in the shed dug up the evidence. The newly discovered clues enabled lawmen to trace Hedgepeth to his room in St. Louis.

JAILED IN ST. LOUIS

Awaiting trial in St. Louis, Hedgepeth was a bit of a celebrity. A slim, six-foot-tall man, he was a sharp dresser who wore well-tailored suits, a derby hat over slicked-back hair, and a large wing collar with a cravat, or tie, that was kept in place by a diamond stick-pin. Women admirers reportedly sent him flowers as he waited for the trial to begin.

Held in a St. Louis jail until his trial, Hedgepeth shared a cell for a while with a man who called himself Harry Howard Holmes. Imprisoned on a swindling charge (obtaining money through cheating a person), Holmes asked Hedgepeth to recommend a good attorney—for a fee. In exchange for a promise to pay $500, Hedgepeth introduced Holmes to a well-respected criminal attorney named J. D. Howe. Soon released from jail on bail, Holmes did not pay Hedgepeth the money he had promised. But he did confide details of his criminal activity to Hedgepeth—a big mistake that would later haunt him.

NO SURRENDER

After a long delay and much publicity, Hedgepeth's trial was held in 1892. He was convicted and sentenced to twelve to

The legend of Herman Webster Mudgett

Harry Howard Holmes was one of the many aliases (fake names) used by Herman W. Mudgett. Born and raised in Gilmantown, New Hampshire, he attended medical school at the University of Michigan. There he discovered an easy way to make money. After taking out large insurance policies under various names, he stole corpses (dead bodies) from the medical school's dissecting rooms. Having taken care to burn the bodies—and then using acid to dispose of the parts that would not burn— to keep them from being correctly identified, he then left the cadavers where they would eventually be discovered. Once his victim was officially pronounced dead, he collected the insurance money. Mudgett collected a small fortune before he was caught pilfering (stealing) the body of a young woman, for which he was expelled (kicked-out) from school.

Mudgett drifted to Chicago, where he took a job in a drugstore. Having saved enough money, he hired builders to construct a three-story structure that had trap doors, concealed rooms, hidden stairways, and doorways that led to brick walls. The basement was equipped with a large dissecting table, an immense stove, and a couple of pits.

twenty-five years in the state penitentiary (prison). After he had served only a few years of the sentence, some important Missourians began to work to have him released. Double-crossed by his former cell-mate, Hedgepeth had informed on Holmes. Because he had been an important witness in Holmes's conviction, Hedgepeth was praised as a "friend of society." In spite of the these efforts, the campaign to release Hedgepeth was unsuccessful. The train robber remained in prison until July 1906, by which time he had become very ill with tuberculosis (a deadly disease that affects the lungs).

One year and two months after his release, Hedgepeth was arrested for robbing a safe in Omaha, Nebraska. Caught in the act, he was sentenced to two more years in prison. After he was released, he organized another gang of robbers. They pulled a number of small robberies in the West, and Hedgepeth eventually drifted to Chicago, Illinois. On January 1, 1910, he pulled a gun on a saloon owner and robbed the cash register. A policeman saw the robbery and drew his gun, demanding that Hedgepeth surrender. The robber reportedly coughed once and shouted, "Never!" Hedgepeth and the policeman shot at the same time, but only the robber was hit. Struck in the chest by a

Claiming to be a businessman in need of secretarial help, Mudgett contacted several employment agencies. Once a young woman was sent to work for him, he reportedly convinced her that he wanted to marry her—and that she should sign over her belongings to him. Once the young woman complied (agreed), he killed her—and dissected the body in the basement. The stove was sometimes used to burn the bodies, while the pits, filled with quicklime, burned them beyond recognition. Many murders later, Mudgett became discouraged because his earnings were not what he had hoped. He set the building on fire, expecting to collect an insurance settlement.

When police officials insisted on examining the building's remains, Mudgett left town. He eventually arrived in St. Louis, where a simple swindle landed him in jail. Calling himself Harry Howard Holmes, he shared a jail cell with Marion Hedgepeth, who was awaiting the start of his trial.

Mudgett eventually confessed in detail to the murders he had committed at his Chicago residence, which became known as Murder Castle. He described the killings in his "memoirs" (a book about a person's life), which went unfinished. On May 7, 1896, he was hanged.

bullet, he fell to his knees, fired his gun's remaining bullets into the ground, and died.

Sources for Further Reading

McLoughlin, Denis. *Wild and Woolly, An Encyclopedia of the Old West.* New York: Doubleday, 1975, pp. 218–219.

Nash, Jay Robert. *Bloodletters and Badmen.* New York: M. Evans, 1973, pp. 252, 382–387.

Nash, Jay Robert. *The Encyclopedia of World Crime.* Wilmette, IL: Crime Books, 1990, p. 1506.

Bill Miner

Born: 1846
Died: September 2, 1913
AKA: George Budd, California Bill,
George Edwards, John Luck, William Morgan

In a career that spanned from the Civil War years (1861–1865) to the twentieth century, Bill Miner robbed trains and stagecoaches in five states and Canada. Regarded as a gentleman robber, he spent much of his life behind bars.

A FICTIONAL LIFE

Imprisoned toward the end of his life, Miner recorded his life story while serving a sentence in a Georgia jail. His autobiography (the story his life) provided contemporary newspapers with engaging stories of his bandit exploits and later writers with ample material for detailed biographies. The trouble was, Miner was a bit of a storyteller.

Miner claimed to have been born in Kentucky in 1847. Deserted by his father at the age of ten, he ran away from home when he was thirteen to become a cowboy. After a daring trip across land that was populated by hostile Apache Indians, he started up a daring one-man pony express business. Unable to support himself with his earnings, he became a criminal—finding time in between jobs to travel the world.

But Miner's story doesn't match historical records. One of several children, he was born near Onondaga, in Ingham County, Michigan in 1846. After his father died, Miner—who was still a boy—moved with his mother, Harriet J. Miner, to Yankee

Jims, a gold-mining town in Placer County, California. There he earned miserable pay working as a laborer. In his teens, Miner enlisted in the Union Army as a private with the California Cavalry Volunteers. His military career was short-lived: on July 22, 1864, less than three months after he had enlisted, he deserted his post.

"ON THE ROB"

By December of 1865, Miner was, as he told one of his victims, "on the rob." After renting a horse several miles outside of Yankee Jims, he rode to the town of Auburn, where he stole an expensive suit and a store clerk's watch. He rode back to the mining camp and never returned the rented horse. Heading for San Francisco, he met a fifteen- year-old named John Sinclair. Together they "rented" two more horses and, on January 22, 1866, held up a ranch-hand named Porter as he drove a wagon near Stockton. Although Porter told the robbers he had no money, he eventually handed over $80— $10 of which Miner returned so that Porter could buy new boots.

By evening, Porter had informed the police of the holdup. Captured the following morning—as they slept in a hotel— Miner and Sinclair were taken into custody at the Stockton County jail. They attempted to escape by digging their way out of jail, but a wall reinforced by a metal plate defeated their effort. Tried after one month in jail, they were convicted of armed robbery. Miner and Sinclair were each sentenced to three years' imprisonment. On April 5, 1866, Miner entered San Quentin penitentiary. In the meantime, however, he had been tried for horse theft. Convicted of grand larceny, he landed another five-year sentence at the San Quentin prison.

Guilty verdict overturned

Captured shortly after they robbed a stagecoach near San Andreas, California, Miner and Harrington were taken to a jail in Calveras County to await trial. There, they were chained to the floor of the cell with forty-pound irons. Harrington managed to saw through his irons—and had started to work on Miner's fetters (another name for iron chains)—before the guards found out.

To prevent their escape, Miner and Harrington were forced to wear heavy iron chains in court when they were tried. Later, their ten-year sentences were appealed and overturned. The California Supreme Court ruled that they hadn't received a fair trial: because they wore chains, the jury was more inclined to find them guilty. On March 21, Miner and Harrington were tried again—and convicted. Each was committed to thirteen years in prison—adding four years to their original sentences.

Read all about it!

After having been convicted of armed robbery and horse theft, Miner and his accomplice were sentenced to three years in the San Quentin penitentiary. Boarding a steamship that was to take them to prison, they acted as if they were about to embark on a pleasure cruise. Here's how a local newspaper described their departure:

> John Sinclair and William Miner were taken off, in charge of Deputy Sheriff J. M. Long, on the steamer *Julia* yesterday, en route for San Quentin to serve a term of three years for highway robbery. The prisoners were chained together, and stood on the upper dock until the steamer left the wharf. They were jovial and appeared unconcerned. When the steamer moved off they threw apples into the crowd on the wharf, and waved their pocket handkerchiefs, as if bidding adieu [goodbye] to friends.
>
> **—The Stockton Daily Independent**

THE STONES REVISITED

While serving his term at the penitentiary, Miner became friends with another prisoner—"Alkali Jim" Harrington, a burglar and stagecoach robber who was serving his third term at San Quentin. After serving a little over four years of his sentence, Miner was released from San Quentin on July 12, 1870. Together with Harrington, who had been released before him, he participated in a number of burglaries and robberies in northern and southern California.

In January of 1871, Miner returned to stagecoach robbery. First Miner, Harrington, and a young Easterner named Charlie Cooper broke into a hardware store to steal shotguns and pistols. Then they traveled to San Andreas, where Miner studied the comings and goings of local stagecoaches. On January 23 they struck. After Miner stopped the coach, pretending to need a ride, Cooper and Harrington stepped in front of the horse team—with shotguns aimed at the driver. Miner then directed the driver to throw down the Wells Fargo strongbox. Taking a hatchet (small axe) to the box, the robbers collected more than $2,500 in gold dust and coins.

But Miner hadn't worn a mask. By June—after less than one year of freedom—he was back behind the walls of San Quentin. Tried on June 22, Miner and Harrington were each sentenced to ten years in the state prison. Cooper—who had informed on his companions by turning state's evidence—was not convicted.

OLD HABITS DIE HARD

After serving nine years, Miner was released on July 14,

1880. Shortly after he headed to Colorado Springs—to see his older sister, Mary Jane Wellman—he met an Iowa farm worker named Arthur Pond. The pair staged a number of coach robberies. In less than one month, they pulled three holdups which yielded thousands of dollars in loot.

Traveling to Michigan with his share of the booty—and suitcases full of new clothes—Miner posed as a successful California businessman named William A. Morgan. He stayed in Onondaga at the Sherman House, the town's finest hotel, and became engaged to marry a young woman from a prosperous family. In February 1881, he left abruptly, claiming that his ill mother needed him.

Miner returned to Colorado, where he rejoined Pond—who now went by the alias (fake name) of Billy LeRoy—and Pond's brother, Silas. After the threesome pulled two more stagecoach robberies, they were hunted by a posse (a group of people with legal authority to capture criminals). The Pond brothers were captured. In jail awaiting trial, they were lynched (killed illegally) by angry locals who broke into their cell. Miner—who had gone into town to retrieve supplies—remained at large.

Joining forces with Stanton T. Jones, Miner continued to rob stages in Colorado and New Mexico. In California the two hooked up with Jim Crum—Miner's friend from San Quentin—and Bill Miller, who was part of Crum's successful gang of horse thieves. Early in the morning of November 7, the newly formed gang stopped a stagecoach near Angels Camp. Armed and masked, the robbers referred to each other by numbers to avoid being identified. Breaking open two Wells Fargo strongboxes and a safe, they found more than $3,000 in gold—to which they added another $500 worth of gold dust that a passenger had hidden.

No Exit

Pursued by lawmen from five counties, Miner and two others were soon captured. On December 21, 1881, Miner returned to San Quentin—after having spent less than a year and a half

---

Take a look at this!

Loosely based on the story of Bill Miner, *The Grey Fox* (1983) follows a gentlemanly old stagecoach robber as he tries to pick up his life after thirty years in prison—as he is suddenly thrown into the twentieth century. Unable to resist another heist, he tries train robbery, and winds up hiding out in British Columbia.

"Hands up!"

According to the Pinkerton detectives who pursued him, Miner was the first bandit to use the phrase "Hands up!" in a robbery.

173

Hard time

San Quentin, referred to as "the Stones," was a brutal prison in Miner's day. Prisoners faced a number of inhumane punishments—including whippings and "showers" that consisted of being blasted in the face by a high-pressure water hose. Convicts were often thrown into the dungeon—a dank, dark, filthy hole with no windows or fresh air. Fed meager rations of bread and water, they slept on the dungeon's cold stone floor.

Prison reforms that brought about slightly more humane conditions gradually crept into the Stones. In 1864—two years before Miner's first trip to prison—the Goodwin Act allowed prisoners time off their sentences for good behavior. Prisoners accumulated "coppers," or credits, that were subtracted from the prison sentence. After 1880, prisoners were no longer whipped, and the practice of "showering" ended two years later. The dungeon, however, was not abandoned until after Miner had served three separate terms at San Quentin.

in freedom. Before he had served the first year of his sentence, Miner attempted to escape—*twice*. In his second attempt, on November 29, 1892, Miner and his cellmate, Joe Marshall, managed to escape onto a balcony that surrounded their cell block. Ambushed by guards who knew of their plans, they were fired on with no warning. Marshall was shot dead and Miner was wounded.

Miner later described the shooting in an interview:

[Marshall] opened the door and looked out and nobody was to be seen. Then we slid out and started toward the steps. There was no guard in sight and we calculated to slip by one man in a guardhouse near where we had to go down the steps. Joe was ahead and I was close behind. Just as we got to the corner of the stone building and Joe had gone down a step or two the shot came and you bet it was a surprise when I hear that gun. Joe tumbled down and I started to run, but the guard sent in another shot and I did not know much for some time after. . . . The guard did not call out or make any noise to let us know he was there. If he had we should have gotten back to 47 [the number of their cell], because it is no use to go up against buckshot.

In spite of his efforts to flee, Miner received time off his sentence for good behavior. (On one occasion, he helped put out a fire in the shop building.) On June 17, 1901—eight years, five months, and nineteen days after his last failed attempt to escape—Miner left San Quentin a free man. He never returned.

Oh, Canada!

A grey-haired man of fifty-five, Miner could no longer support himself as a stagecoach robber—not because of his age, but because stagecoaches had become outdated. During his long stay at San Quentin, he took advantage of the resources at hand to learn a new trade: jailed with a number of experienced train robbers, Miner learned what he could about their methods.

A little more than two years after his release from prison, Miner and two others held up the Oregon Railway and Navigation Company express train. He then moved north to Canada, with Jake Terry, a counterfeiter who had shared a cell with him at San Quentin. A former railway engineer, Terry was familiar with Canadian train routes. Miner and Terry plotted to rob a train near Mission Junction in British Columbia. First, they tapped the telegraph lines to find out which trains carried large shipments of gold. On September 13, 1904, Miner, Terry, and a man named Shorty Dunn struck the Canadian Pacific railway's transcontinental express forty miles outside of Vancouver. The gang collected thousands of dollars in gold dust and currency. They also pocketed $50,000 in U.S. bonds that were being shipped to Seattle—in addition to thousands of dollars in Australian securities.

His next Canadian train robbery was far less successful than the first. On May 8, 1906, Miner held up the Canadian Pacific's Imperial Limited near Kamloops, British Columbia. He left with about $15—and a handful of cough tablets. Six days later, Miner and two of his accomplices were captured by the Royal North-West Mounted Police.

Tried and convicted, Miner was sentenced to life imprisonment at the New Westminster penitentiary in British Columbia.

A staged escape?

Sometime after Miner escaped from the New Westminster prison in British Columbia, local newspapers claimed that the train robber had been *allowed* to escape. A number of things made Miner's disappearance look suspicious. First, Miner had met with detectives during the weeks prior to his escape. After the escape, police officials claimed that no man could have crawled through the tunnel the convict had supposedly used. What's more, Miner had a foot injury that would have limited his mobility.

Journalists suggested that Miner had worked out a deal with Canadian officials: freedom in exchange for the bonds he had stolen from the Canadian Pacific railway in September 1904. Although the matter was debated in the Canadian Parliament, Miner's escape was never fully investigated by the Canadian government. And Miner never confessed.

First and last

Miner's career began in the Civil War era—and ended in the twentieth century with an automobile ride to jail. Even in his day, he was considered to be one of the last frontier outlaws. But he was also known for a number of firsts: he is credited with having committed the first train robbery in the state of Georgia. And he was the *first* robber ever to hold up a train in all of Canada.

Popular with many local people who despised the railroads, he became a bit of a celebrity: large crowds surrounded him after the trial. Some admirers even tossed him cigars. Miner served less than one year of his sentence at the New Westminster prison. On August 8, 1907, he escaped.

TIME TO RETIRE

At the age of sixty-four, Miner committed his last train robbery—the first ever in the state of Georgia. Working with two accomplices, he struck a Southern Express train at White Sulfur Springs on February 22, 1911. A couple of thousand dollars richer, the three men were hunted by local and federal lawmen. Within a few days, Miner faced a twenty-year sentence at a state prison.

On March 15, Miner was sent to work on a chain gang at Newton County Convict Camp. Claiming that he was old and in ill health, he petitioned the prison commission to transfer him to a low-security prison farm in Milledgeville. With the help of public support, he was transferred. Within months, he escaped.

Just over two weeks later, Miner was captured and returned to Milledgeville, where he was met by crowds of locals. Eight months later, on June 29, 1912, he escaped again. After three days in the Georgia swamps, Miner was captured. Again he was greeted by cheering crowds. Back in prison, Miner reportedly told guards, "I guess I'm getting too old for this sort of thing." On September 2, 1913, he died in the prison hospital.

Sources for Further Reading

Boessenecker, John. *Badge and Buckshot, Lawlessness in Old California.* Norman, OK: University of Oklahoma Press, 1988, pp. 158–177.

Bruns, Roger. *The Bandit Kings from Jesse James to Pretty Boy Floyd.* New York: Crown, 1995, pp. 132–133.

Dugan, Mark and John Boessenecker. *Grey Fox: The True Story of Bill Miner, Last of the Old-Time Bandits.* Norman, OK: University of Oklahoma Press, 1992.

Irene Schroeder

Born: 1909
Died: February 23, 1931

*Irene Schroeder's career shared many things with that of two more famous outlaws. But she enjoyed none of the notoriety that surrounded **Bonnie and Clyde** (see entry). A minor robber, Schroeder became most famous after death—as one of very few women to have been put to death in the electric chair.*

ONE DEAD COP

Toward the end of 1929, when she was a twenty–year–old housewife, Schroeder met a salesman and Sunday school teacher named Walter Glenn Dague. She left her husband to accompany Dague, who deserted his wife and children in West Virginia. Traveling in a stolen car with Schroeder's four–year–old son, Donnie, the couple robbed a number of stores and small banks.

Schroeder and Dague's final robbery took place in Butler, Pennsylvania. After robbing a grocery store, they left by car—and were soon chased by two highway patrolmen, Ernest Moore and W. Brady Paul. With Donnie in the back seat of the car, Dague and Schroeder fired at the patrolmen as they sped through the Pennsylvania countryside. Patrolman Paul was killed by a bullet Schroeder had fired and Moore was wounded by Dague. The patrolmen's car veered off the road and into a ditch.

The outlaw couple managed to avoid capture—in spite of road blocks that had been erected by police. Hundreds of miles south, in Arizona, they were finally surrounded by a posse (a

The death penalty

Not all countries that embrace capital punishment (the death penalty) permit the execution of women. Russia, for example, excludes women from the death penalty.

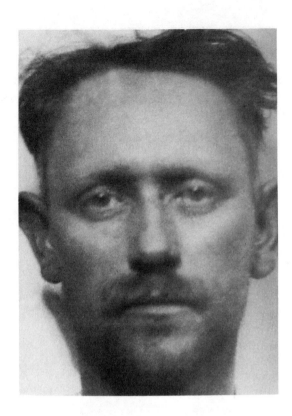

Walter Dague,
Schroeder's
partner-in-crime.

group of people with legal authority to capture criminals) as they traveled down a back road. A shootout followed. Eventually—after they had run out of bullets—Schroeder and Dague surrendered.

TRIED, CONVICTED, AND EXECUTED

Tried for the murder of patrolman Paul, Schroeder admitted that she was guilty—and she tried to claim that she had been responsible for the robberies and other crimes that Dague had committed with her. Her attempt to save Dague failed. Both were convicted and sentenced to be executed.

Schroeder was taken to the Rockview Penitentiary in Center County, Pennsylvania, to await execution. On February 23, 1931, a prison chaplain visited her before she was led to the electric chair. She reportedly told him, that she would be all right—but that he should check on Dague, who needed the clergyman more than she did. Just before she died she is said to have had a final request: that prison cooks prepare Dague's eggs the way he liked them—fried on both sides. Schroeder died in the electric chair less than three minutes after the current was administered. She was the first of only two women to have been electrocuted in the state of Pennsylvania. Dague was executed a few days later.

Sources for Further Reading

Kadish, Sanford, ed. *Encyclopedia of Crime and Justice,* Volume 1. New York: Free Press, 1983, pp.133–142.

Nash, Jay Robert. *Look for the Woman: A Narrative Encyclopedia of Female Poisoners, Kidnappers, Thieves, Extortionists, Terrorists, Swindlers, and Spies from Elizabethan Times to Present.* New York: Evans, 1981, pp. 339–341.

Sifakis, Carl. *The Encyclopedia of American Crime.* New York: Facts on File, 1982, pp.238–240.

A public spectacle

In 1824, a hatchet murderer named John Johnson was hanged in New York City. The event was a public spectacle. Later, newspapers reported that fifty thousand people had attended Johnson's hanging. At the time, executions—and hangings, in particular—had a long history as public entertainment. Pirate hangings, which were intended to serve as a warning to others, often attracted enormous crowds. In the Old West, hangings were sometimes scheduled on weekends to guarantee a well-attended execution. Far from a solemn event, hangings were the cause for celebration.

Today, executions are always performed behind prison walls. But public executions were not outlawed until the 1930s. The final public executions in the United States took place in 1936, when a man was hanged in Kentucky for rape, and 1937, when a murderer was hanged in Missouri.

Since television was introduced in the 1950s, some people have argued in favor of televised executions. They believe that televised executions—like public hangings—would serve as a deterrent (a preventive measure) to other would-be criminals. Others—who oppose capital punishment—support televised executions as a means to turn the public against what they believe to be an inhumane practice. In 1977, the federal courts considered whether prison authorities in Texas should be forced to allow public television to cover an execution. The courts decided against television coverage.

Still, there is a public aspect to many executions. When Karla Faye Tucker was executed in February 1998, hundreds gathered outside the Huntsville, Texas, institution where she died. Some were protesting the taking of a life. Others, in the spirit of the bygone revelers who attended pirate hangings and outlaw executions, were there to see the show—and to express their approval of the ax murderer's fate. One person carried a sign that said, "Axe and ye shall receive." When officials announced that Tucker was dead, the crowd let out a cheer. Some cried, while others sang the song whose refrain is "Na na na na, hey, hey, hey, goodbye."

Veitz, Dee Tabone. *Irene.* Punxsatawney, PA: Spirit, 1985.

Verhovek, Sam Howe. "Dead Women Waiting: Who's on Death Row." *The New York Times* (February 8, 1998), pp. A1, 3, 17.

Computer Criminals

In 1823, English visionary Charles Babbage (1792–1871) persuaded the British government to finance an "analytical engine." This would have been a machine that could undertake any kind of calculation. It would have been driven by steam, and the program of operations would have been stored on a punched tape. The system was not completed. Although he never built a working computer, Babbage thought out many of the basic principles that guide many computers today.

But chances are he never envisioned the criminal possibilities that the computer age provides. Stolen secrets and data theft. Unauthorized wire transfers. Illegal access to phone company products and services. The computer age provides unprecedented opportunities for far reaching criminal applications. Some of the computer criminals you'll read about in this chapter were interested primarily in proving what they were capable of. Others used their skills for personal gain—and even to spy for a foreign government. And in most cases, the investigations that led to their capture offer a fascinating look at a high tech game of cat and mouse.

Marcus Hess

Active: 1986-1989

*Between 1986 and 1989—at a time when computer security was an unexplored field—
a West German named Marcus Hess and a number of other computer hackers took
advantage of loopholes in computer systems to gain unauthorized access to sensitive
information. Pioneers in computer espionage, they reportedly sold that information to
Soviet officials.*

A RECIPE FOR CHAOS

In the late 1980s Marcus Hess worked as a computer programmer for a small computer company in West Germany. He also belonged to a computer group known as the Chaos Computer Club, based in Hamburg, West Germany. As a member of Chaos, Hess and a number of other West German hackers became involved in a computer-based espionage ring. Hess—who was known as "the Hanover Hacker" (because he lived in Hanover, West Germany)—started with a telephone call from his home phone. By making a local computer modem call in Hanover, he tapped into a European data network called Datex. From there he entered a library computer at the University of Bremen in West Germany. Tampering with the system's software, he fooled the computer into thinking that he was an authorized user with special privileges. Through the Bremen account, he connected to the Tymnet network in the United States. From there, he entered a computer at Lawrence Berkeley Laboratories in California that gave him access to other systems across the country.

The cyber hound who hunted the "Hanover Hacker"

A scientist by training, Clifford Stoll viewed the pursuit of a hacker as an interesting "problem." At a time when computer security was an unexplored field, he discovered a trail that indicated that the hacker was reading—and copying—extremely sensitive information concerning national security.

"I wasn't interested in the hackers," Stoll later reported in *Compute* magazine. "To come across people who believe that it's their right or responsibility to break into computers doesn't interest me at all. I'm a physicist. I do science. It struck me as more interesting technically—[I began wondering] what's happening? What's the connectivity here? What's permitting this? Here is a field of study no one has worked on before: how do insecure networks, through holes in security, allow exploitation of databases in a way that nobody's ever talked about before?"

Small change

In 1986, Stoll, who held a Ph.D. in astronomy, had a job designing software for the Keck Observatory in Berkeley, California. But when the project's grant money ran out in August of that year, he was transferred to another job—managing computers in the same building. On the second day of his new job at Lawrence Berkeley Laboratories, Stoll received a simple assignment. He was to find out why the computer's accounting system showed a seventy-five cent deficit (shortage).

First, Stoll examined the computer's accounting programs to find out whether the software was responsible for the billing error. He found nothing wrong with the program—but he did find something suspicious. An unfamiliar user named Hunter had logged onto the system briefly—just long enough to use seventy-five cents worth of time. Since the computer center had no record of Hunter, Stoll erased the account from the system.

A hacker in their midst

But the mystery did not end there. Next Stoll received a report from the National Computer Security Center, a unit of the National Security Agency (NSA). Someone from Lawrence Berkeley Laboratory had attempted to break into an NSA computer system in Fort Meade, Maryland. After looking into the incident, Stoll discovered that the break-in attempt had originated from the account of someone named Joe Sventek. But

An appetite for military data

Hess operated like a burglar who goes from one house to another attempting to find an unlocked door. In all, he tried to

Sventek was not in Berkeley at the time of the break-in: he was in England.

At first, Stoll suspected that a student at the nearby University of California was attempting to hack his way into NSA computers—using an account at Lawrence Berkeley Laboratory—to pull an elaborate prank. To find the culprit, he created a monitoring station that allowed him to trace the intruder's online movements.

Looking at a spy

Stoll set up programs that were able to determine every time the hacker entered the Berkeley computer. When he was not in the computer laboratory, he wore a pocket pager that alerted him when the hacker was online. Stoll programmed the computers in his surveillance station to monitor and record every keystroke the intruder made—without the intruder's knowledge.

What he found led him to believe that the hacker was not local—nor was he a novice (inexperienced beginner). The hacker communicated over a worldwide network and had created a program that acted as a master key to unlock protected files—which allowed him to gain entry into hundreds of other computer systems on the networks the Lawrence Berkeley Lab employed, including academic, industrial, and military computers.

Little help from the feds

Because the hacker was secretly gaining access to sensitive documents, Stoll felt it was his duty to inform the government organizations of the intruder's activities. At first he encountered resistance. "When we first took it to the FBI, they laughed at us," he told *Science* magazine. FBI agents claimed that they could not become involved unless classified information had been stolen or more than $500,000 in computer resources had been lost. All Stoll could produce was the seventy-five cent shortfall. A scientist at the National Computer Security Center informed him that it was the agency's job to design computers that are theoretically secure—not to help out those who had already experienced hacker attacks.

Acting on a suggestion from his girlfriend (and later wife), Martha Matthews, Stoll managed to bait the hacker into revealing his home base. Stoll's investigative work ultimately led to the arrest of Marcus Hess and other members of the Computer Chaos Club. Later offered jobs as a computer-security specialist at the CIA and elsewhere, Stoll turned them down to return to his first love, astronomy. He accepted a job as an astronomer at Harvard's Smithsonian Observatory in Cambridge, Massachusetts.

enter about four hundred and fifty computers—of which he was able to enter approximately thirty. Much of Hess's activity involved the Milnet—a computer network that involves defense contractors and military installations. Administered by the Pentagon, the Milnet contains vast quantities of sensitive information. Hess's many targets included computers at an Air Force space division in El Segundo, California; army bases in Alabama and Georgia; the Buckner Army Base in Okinawa, Japan; the Mitre Corporation, a Virginia defense contractor; the Navy Coastal Systems command in Panama City, Florida, and others.

Once he hacked his way into a computer system, Hess was very deliberate and methodical in his attack. To look for sensitive information about military, nuclear, and space research projects in the United States and elsewhere, he used keywords such as "nuclear" and "SDI" to search documents. (SDI stands for "Strategic Defense Initiative"—a defense program also known as "Star Wars.") Hess located information on intelligence satellites, semiconductor design research, space shuttle missions, navy missiles, and plans for chemical warfare. He also examined systems he entered for passwords to other computers.

Clifford Stoll, astronomer and spy tracker.

A TRAP IS SET

Hess's interest in military information is ultimately what led investigators to his doorstep. Clifford Stoll, an astronomer who tracked Hess's movements for eighteen months, decided to lay a trap to entice the hacker to stay online long enough for the origin of the modem call to be traced. Stoll planted phony national security files that supposedly contained information on the Strategic Defense Initiative in the Lawrence Berkeley computer. The file was called "SDI Network Project."

Hess took the bait. Intrigued by the information he saw, he downloaded the file to his home computer. The process took more than one hour—more than enough time for authorities to trace the call. West German police, working with the FBI, were able to trace the hacker's call to an apartment in Hanover—at #3A Glocksee Strasse. On March 2, 1989, Marcus Hess was arrested at the apartment. The West German police also seized Hess's computer, records of computer passwords, and computer logs that contained the protocols (first draft) of a much-publicized, July 27, 1987 invasion of a National Aeronautics and Space Administration (NASA) computer.

Hess and two other West Germans, Peter Carl and Kirk-Otto Brezinski, who were also reportedly members of the Chaos Computer Club, were formally charged with selling software, military computer passwords, and other sensitive data to the KGB—the Soviet intelligence agency. In all, eight young men were suspected of selling secrets to the Soviets.

United States officials turned the matter over to German authorities. As far as U.S. government officials could determine, the hackers had not provided the Soviets with information that seriously compromised the nation's security. German authorities eventually released Hess because they did not have enough evidence to hold him. Jim Christy, the assistant chief of computer crime at the U.S. Air Force Office of Special Investigations in Washington, D.C., later charged that Hess's attorney had used a little-known loophole in the legal system. The loophole prevented the government from looking at important files that were contained on Hess's computer—files which might have provided ammunition for his prosecution.

Who are you gonna call?

Why did Clifford Stoll, an astronomer, become involved in an eighteen-month investigation tracking a computer spy? He later explained, "I was walking along one of the basement corridors and I happened to glance up. The open ceiling was brimming with wires, pipes, and cables. Most of them were clearly marked: hot water, cold water, waste water, gas, steam, electric conduit. And then I saw a bright orange Ethernet cable [a cable over which computers communicate in a local area network]. It was unlabeled but I knew what it was. And then it struck me. If the Ethernet cable broke, there'd be a puddle of bits and bytes on the floor and who would I call? If someone was stealing electricity, we had an electrician. If someone was purloining [stealing] water, there was a plumber on staff. But who is responsible for protecting the Lab's information, which is far more valuable commodity than electricity or water? It came into my head that I was responsible."

Sources for Further Reading

Elmer-DeWitt, Phillip. "A Bold Raid on Computer Security." *Time* (May 2, 1988), p. 58.

Hoffman, Russell D. *High Tech Today*. [Online] Available http://www.animatedsoftware.com/hightech/cliffsto.htm, December 11, 1997.

Kunen, James S. "Astronomer Cliff Stoll Stars In the Espionage Game, But For Him Spying Doesn't Really Compute." *People Weekly* (December 11, 1989), pp. 118–120.

Lehmann-Haupt, Christopher. "On the Electronic Trail of a Computer Spy." *The New York Times* (October 19, 1989), p. C23.

Marshall, Eliot. "German Spy Ring Broken." *Science* (March 24, 1989), p. 1545.

McCartney, Robert J. "West German Charged with Espionage In Computer Intrusion Investigation." *The Washington Post* (March 4, 1989), p. A16.

Mckeeman, Darren P. "Cliff Stoll Tells All." *Compute* (January 1992), p. 144.

Richards, Evelyn. "Computer Detective Followed Trail to Hacker Spy Suspect; Work Called Key to West German's Arrest." *The Washington Post* (March 4, 1989), p. A1.

"West Germany Arrests Computer Hackers." *Facts on File World News Digest* (March 10, 1989), p. 157F3.

Katya Komisaruk
(Susan Alexis Komisaruk)

Born: 1958

As an anti-nuclear protest, Komisaruk destroyed a government computer—a crime for which she later said she expected to go to court. In committing a crime for which she intended to be caught and punished, she hoped to bring the anti-nuclear cause into the public eye and help steer the United States away from nuclear war.

RADICAL BEGINNINGS

Born in the late 1950s, Susan Alexis Komisaruk was raised in Michigan and California. Her parents, a psychiatrist and homemaker who later divorced, were well-educated liberals who taught their daughter to question authority. Born to a Jewish family with roots in the Ukraine, Komisaruk had relatives who died in the Holocaust (the period of persecution and extermination of European Jews by Nazi Germany). Her parents, who were Zionists, instilled in their daughter a sharp awareness of the Holocaust and of the events that led up to it. (Zionism is a movement interested in recovering for Jewish people the historic Palestinian homeland.)

An intelligent young woman, Komisaruk—who received the nickname "Katya" as a child—became bored with high school after just one year. She quit high school at the age of sixteen and attended Mills College in California. One year later, she transferred to Reed College in Oregon, where she majored in the classics—the study of Greek and Latin literature. In 1978, when she was just nineteen years old, she graduated from college.

Next, Komisaruk enrolled in the business school at the University of California at Berkeley. The experience transformed her. Raised by parents who were not politically active, Komisaruk found herself becoming increasingly politicized. Early in her first term as a business student, she became convinced that American business is part of a corrupt system that exploits (makes unethical use of) workers and destroys the environment.

She also concluded that politics were unduly affected by money, and that military spending was destroying the nation's economy.

CIVIL DISOBEDIENCE

Komisaruk later told the *Los Angeles Times,* "All of this left me extremely politicized. It came to me I had to do something. I felt I should go to a rally and protest." And protest she did. In 1982, she joined a demonstration at Lawrence Livermore Laboratories. Although she was arrested and detained for two days, the experience left her convinced of the power of activism.

After graduating from the University of California with a master's degree in business administration, Komisaruk worked as an administrator at the Graduate Theological Union in Berkeley, California. She lived with other activists and contributed half of the money she earned to the cause. She became increasingly involved in a number of issues—especially those involving anti-nuclear activities. She also helped establish the Community Defense, Inc., an organization that was established to provide legal assistance to people involved in civil disobedience—or nonviolent protests.

After one year, Komisaruk quit her job at the Graduate Theological Union. She worked at part-time jobs and continued to organize and participate in anti-nuclear activities. In 1983, she was arrested for taking part in a protest movement at Vandenberg Air Force Base in California. Komisaruk spent a short period in jail for her role in attempting to prevent the launching of an MX missile at Vandenberg.

THE VANDENBERG INCIDENT

As Komisaruk became more involved in anti-nuclear activities, so did her conviction that her activism would eventually result in long-term imprisonment. On June 2, 1986, she

The margin of error

Komisaruk believed that she was destroying a computer whose global positioning system provided the U.S. with first-strike superiority over the Soviet Union. But the U.S. government claimed that the computer was no longer in use and was being stored as surplus. What is more, government officials claimed that the satellite navigation system had been moved to Colorado more than one year earlier. Further, Pentagon officials announced that any claims that the NAVSTAR system was intended to provide first-strike capability are "flatly wrong." Assistant U.S. Attorney Nora Manella, who prosecuted the case, claimed that Komisaruk was misinformed. She told reporters, "We have here a woman whose zeal exceeded her level of knowledge by a wide margin."

Flowers, cookies, and a poem

Komisaruk visited the Vandenberg Air Force Base armed with tools with which she planned to destroy a government computer. She also carried a bag of cookies, a bouquet of flowers, and a poem—as gifts for soldiers she might encounter. She was afraid that well-armed soldiers who discovered her on the base without permission in the middle of the night might shoot first and ask questions later. Komisaruk's poem read,

> I have no gun
> You must have lots.
> Let's not be hasty
> No cheap shots.
> Please have a cookie and a nice day.

Komisaruk later explained why she had left behind such an odd assortment of items. "I was afraid," she said, "that the guards would respond to an alarm—that there might be these soldiers dashing in with their automatic weapons, and it would be like Kent State [on May 4 1970, four Kent State University students were shot and killed by national guardsmen during an anti-war protest], where young panicky men who had been through boot camp and had a lot of brainwashing were suddenly faced with an emergency and did what they were trained to do, which was pull the trigger. I didn't want to be the target. I thought one way to get around that was to have them come across the flowers, poem, and cookies first, anything to distract them and make them stop and think for a few minutes before they went swarming in there." Komisaruk never faced any soldiers during her two-hour visit to Vandenberg.

returned to Vandenberg Air Force Base by a back-road route—armed with a hammer, crowbar, cordless drill, and bolt cutters—aware that the action she was about to take would probably earn her an extended prison sentence.

Komisaruk's target was a sophisticated Air Force navigation computer housed in a building on the base. She believed that the computer's NAVSTAR global positioning system, which had the ability to locate Soviet missile silos (underground shelters for missiles), was intended to give the U.S. "first-strike" nuclear capability. By destroying the computer, she intended to prevent the U.S. government from mounting a first-strike attack against the Soviet Union. In short, she believed she was acting to prevent the possibility of nuclear war.

Komisaruk walked onto the Air Force base in the middle of the night. Although the compound was surrounded by a barbed wire fence, the gate stood wide open. She entered through the open gate, closed it from the inside—and then locked it with a bicycle lock she had brought with her. She also squeezed epoxy (a type of glue) into the lock to make it more difficult for security personnel to enter. She placed a bouquet of flowers, cookies, and poem at the gate to evoke compassion from guards who might try to stop her.

After breaking into a building that contained the navigation computer, she went to work. Using the tools she brought with her, she hammered and pried at the valuable computer. She later reported that she was terrified throughout the experience: "I was afraid; I'd never done anything like this before. At any minute, I expected to be caught; my stomach was churning, and I had to run into the bushes more than once."

Two hours later, the twenty-eight- year-old activist walked off the base, leaving behind a wrecked computer and satellite dish. The computer chips were piled on the floor, where Komisaruk had done a dance over them. Next, she hitchhiked back to the San Francisco area, where she consulted with lawyers. The following day a press release appeared. It said: "Peace activist destroys satellite control center, gives self up, press conference noon Wednesday, San Francisco Federal building." At the news conference, Komisaruk told reporters, "You're a party to mass murder if you don't get out there and try to stop it." Further, she defended her actions under international law—such as the Nuremberg Treaty, signed by the United States. Under the treaty, nations agree never to prepare for or initiate a war of aggression. Komisaruk admitted to destroying the government computer, and surrendered to authorities.

Komisaruk's lead defense attorney, Leonard Weinglass.

TRIAL STRATEGIES

Komisaruk was arrested and charged with two crimes: destruction of government property and sabotage (a deliberate effort to harm an endeavor). She was tried in November 1987. Her defense team was made up of Leonard Weinglass, a respect-

The White Rose

Komisaruk called the Vandenberg Air Force Base incident the "White Rose Action." The name was inspired by a group of young German activists known as "The White Rose" about whom Komisaruk had learned when she was fourteen years old. Active during World War II (1939–1945), the Christian members of the White Rose group urged their countrymen not to participate in the Nazi persecution of Jews. In 1943, the protesters were arrested and executed.

During Komisaruk's trial, her supporters in the court room held white roses to demonstrate their solidarity (unity). They also distributed the following statement at a pre-trial press conference: "During the Third Reich [Germany's Nazi era] a small group of gentile [Christian] students, calling themselves 'The White Rose,' chose to resist [Adolf] Hitler. They tried to tell their fellow citizens what horrors were being committed in their name."

ed New York civil rights attorney, Dan Williams, William Simpich, and others. Komisaruk's defense relied on international law that prevents the U.S. from planning a war of aggression—such as a first-strike nuclear attack against the Soviet Union. The government filed a motion to limit Komisaruk's defense. Government attorneys argued that Komisaruk's motives should not enter into the trial—and the computer's purpose should not be taken into consideration.

Federal district judge William J. Rea approved the government's motion. Defense attorneys were not allowed to argue that Komisaruk was justified under international law that prevents nations from planning or launching wars of aggression. That is, Komisaruk's attorneys could not claim that their client was acting to prevent a crime of nuclear aggression—a crime against humanity. One day before the trial started, prosecuting attorneys dropped the count of sabotage, which involves the "willful destruction with intent." In order to prove intent, the government needed to examine Komisaruk's motive for destroying the computer—something prosecuting attorneys did not want discussed at the trial. All that remained to be settled at trial was the question of whether Komisaruk had destroyed the government computer.

A HARSH SENTENCE

Komisaruk's trial lasted just four days. After less than two hours' deliberation, the federal court jury found Komisaruk guilty of one count of destroying government property. Soon after the verdict was announced, security guards forcibly removed several of Komisaruk's supporters from the courtroom because they created a disturbance by attempting to make speeches. The guilty verdict carried a maximum sentence of ten years in prison. (If Komisaruk had been found guilty of the additional charge of sabotage, she could have faced another ten years' imprisonment.) Major General Donald O. Aldridge, the commanding officer of Vandenberg Air Force Base, sent a letter to the court urging the judge to issue a harsh sentence to discourage other activists from taking similar steps.

Aware that she was about the be sentenced to a long imprisonment, Komisaruk decided to inform Judge Rea of her opinion of the trial. She said:

> I'm in a delicate position. I believe I am expected to plead for understanding, for mercy . . . and the stakes are very high. What does one say to ward off the nightmare of ten years in prison? . . . I don't think we can have an honest dialogue, because I stand here below your platform and I'm afraid of you . . . and my stomach hurts and my mouth is dry and my heart is pounding and I wish I were anywhere but your courtroom. Yet there's one thing that bothers me more than my fear of what punishment you're going to pronounce. And that's the fact that I made a coward's choice during my trial. Like the sycophants [someone who flatters important people] who assured their naked emperor that he was beautifully dressed, I pretended that the trial was a fair and just proceeding. I was so intimidated [frightened] by this huge courtroom, by all the marshals and officials, by the formal language and ceremony, and by you, Your Honor, that I failed to speak the truth. I never really stated just how ludicrous [laughable] the proceeding was. . . . Your robes and bench are transparent, Your Honor. They cannot cover up injustice. They only hide it for a while.

On January 11, 1988, Judge Rea sentenced Komisaruk to five years in federal prison. He also ordered her to pay

An unfair trial?

Tried for destroying government property, Komisaruk was not allowed to appeal to international law to defend her actions. Her attorneys believed that the court's decision was unfair—and presented jurors with a one-sided version of the incident. Komisaruk's lead attorney, Leonard Weinglass, later complained, "We didn't get a right to have a jury trial in this case. We got a right to be present when the government presented its case to twelve people."

The making of a martyr

Komisaruk's attorney argued that his client's stiff sentence would not discourage other activists from similar acts of disobedience. He told reporters, "They have succeeded in making a martyr, not in deterring anyone.'

Nuclear holocaust

"When my mother was young, her worst nightmare was that the Nazis would come," Komisaruk once explained. "Mine was the flash of light signaling the explosion of a nuclear bomb. I am Jewish, and for a long time, I worried that anti-Semitism [hostility toward Jews] could again become a destructive force. Later, I feared that we Americans could be the ones to unleash a holocaust [total destruction—such as Nazi Germany's attempt to destroy European Jews], this time nuclear."

$500,000 in restitution (to make good for a loss)—the estimated replacement cost of the computer. Rea explained the harsh sentence as something intended "to pass the word along that you can't do these things and get a slap on the wrist." Dozens of Komisaruk's supporters were present at the sentencing—many of whom cried when the sentence was announced.

THE JUDGE RESPONDS

After Komisaruk's sentencing, Judge Rea announced, "[Komisaruk] says she has obeyed a higher law. Well, if every person in this country could take [the law] into his or her hands . . . we would have a society of anarchy [choas]. We cannot permit you and others motivated as you are to destroy taxpayers' property merely because you feel that what is going on in this country is not to your liking."

Sources for Further Reading

Davis, Cheryl A. "Five Years for the 'White Rose.'" *Progressive* (March 1988), pp. 14–15.

Hendrix, Kathleen. "Katya Komisaruk's Revolution: Why a Berkeley MBA Trashed a Multimillion-Dollar Air Force Computer in the Name of Peace." *Los Angeles Times* (November 11, 1987), View section, p. 1.

Murphy, Kim. "Anti-War Activist Gets Five Years for Junking Computer." *Los Angeles Times* (January 12, 1988), p. 1.

Murphy, Kim. "'Higher Law' Behind Attack on Computer, Activist Says." *Los Angeles Times* (November 14, 1987), p. 32.

Murphy, Kim. "Peace Activist Guilty of Wrecking Computer." *Los Angeles Times* (November 17, 1987), Metro section, p. 1.

Murphy, Kim. "Woman Who Destroyed Computer Denied Anti-Nuclear Defense." *Los Angeles Times* (October 27, 1987), p. 25.

Kevin Mitnick

Born: 1965?

Kevin D. Mitnick made a name for himself by hacking his way into telephone networks and vandalizing corporate, government, and university computers. For a while, according to assistant United States attorney Kent Walker, "He was arguably the most wanted computer hacker in the world."

A YOUTHFUL PHONE PHREAK

Mitnick grew up in the San Fernando Valley near Los Angeles, California. After his parents divorced when he was three years old, he lived with his mother, who worked long hours as a waitress at a delicatessen. As a youth he had few friends. He rarely saw his father and grew up lonely and isolated.

While in his teens, Mitnick got into phone phreaking—using electronic techniques to gain illegal access to telephone services. He became friends with other phone phreaks and often hung out with a group that met at a Shakey's Pizza Parlor in Los Angeles to plot ways to break into local computer and communications systems. Together with other phone phreak friends—such as a young woman who called herself Susan Thunder and a young man who went by the name of Roscoe—he searched the dumpsters behind phone company offices for manuals that would provide vital information about company computers.

Mitnick first got into trouble with the law during his teens. As a student at Monroe High School in North Hills, California,

Susan Thunder

Mitnick met Susan Thunder as a teenager, when both were involved with a phone phreaking group in Los Angeles. (Susan Thunder was the young woman's online name.) Thunder dropped out of school in the eighth grade, worked as a prostitute in Hollywood, and later got into phone phreaking and computer hacking. In 1982, she testified in a case that landed the seventeen-year-old Mitnick on probation for stealing computer manuals from the Pacific Bell Telephone Company. She also described to a U.S. Senate Subcommittee how she and other phone phreaks had used their personal computers to change their victims' credit ratings—and replace them with obscenities. What's more, she claimed the group had attempted to shut down the telephone system in all of California. After a brief period in Las Vegas, Nevada, as a professional poker player, Thunder returned to California. In 1994, she was elected city clerk in a small town in the desert.

 **Public servants**

Hackers rely on flaws in computer systems to gain access to off-limits information. Many hackers believe that by bringing these flaws to light, they are performing a sort of public service.

he broke into the computer system of the Los Angeles Unified School District. He could have changed students' grades, but he did not. He also reportedly hacked his way into the military's North American Air Defense Command computers in Colorado just for fun. When Mitnick, just seventeen years old, was caught stealing valuable technical manuals from the Pacific Bell Telephone Company, a judge sentenced him to probation (a trial period to test his good behavior). In spite of his brush with the law, Mitnick returned to hacking. After he was caught breaking into computers at a local university, he was sentenced to six months in jail.

A COMPUTER ADDICT

When Mitnick was twenty-three, he met Bonnie Vitello, who worked for the phone company. A short while later, Mitnick and Vitello were married. Mitnick's computer hacking created a strain on the relationship, and the couple eventually divorced.

Mitnick attracted the attention of security experts in December 1988, when he was charged with breaking into MCI telephone computers and stealing long-distance codes. By secretly reading the electronic mail of security officials at MCI and Digital Equipment Corporation, Mitnick discovered how the companies' computers and phone equipment were protected against hackers. In July 1989, he was convicted and sentenced to one year in federal prison at Lompoc, California—followed by a period at a rehabilitation center. One of Mitnick's defense attorneys had managed to convince the judge that his

198

client was "addicted" to computers—and that, like an alcoholic, he was not able to control his behavior.

Following his release from federal prison, Mitnick was sent to Gateways Beit T'Shuvah, a residential program designed to help addicts overcome their addictions. (The program's name is Hebrew for "house of repentance.") There he followed a Twelve-Step program modeled after Alcoholics Anonymous. He spent six months at the rehabilitation center—during which time he was forbidden to use a computer or a modem.

Mitnick was released early from Beit T'Shuvah, in the spring of 1990. One of the conditions of his parole specified that he was forbidden to use computers until he could demonstrate that he was able to control his behavior. Mitnick returned to Los Angeles in early 1992, following the drug-related death of his half-brother. He was employed for a while with his father, Alan, who was a general contractor. When that did not work out, he took a job with a private investigation agency called Tel Tec Investigations.

In September 1992, federal officials, armed with a search warrant, raided Mitnick's apartment. Mitnick, who was suspected of breaking into a Pacific Bell computer, was nowhere to be found. But coded disks and documents provided proof of his activities. In November, a federal judge issued a warrant for the hacker's arrest. Mitnick had violated the conditions of his parole. Aware that the heat was on, Mitnick went went into hiding.

MERRY CHRISTMAS, MR. SHIMOMURA

For more than two years, Mitnick managed to elude federal officials. But on Christmas Day 1994, he committed a fatal mistake. Mitnick broke into the home computer of Tsutomu Shimomura, a computational physicist who worked as a computer security expert at the Supercomputer Center in San Diego. Using a modem, Mitnick "spoofed" his way into Shimomura's networked databases. "Spoofing" involves fooling a computer into thinking that it is communicating with a friendly computer.

Cat meets mouse

When Mitnick finally met Tsutomu Shimomura, the man who led the FBI to his doorstep, he said, "Hello, Tsutomu. I respect your skills." Shimomura said nothing in reply. Later, when asked what he thought about Mitnick's remark, he told a *Newsweek* reporter, "You know, I feel sorry for him. But he's caused a lot of people a lot of grief, and his behavior is clearly unacceptable. I don't know what's wrong with him, but he keeps getting in trouble. Throwing him in prison isn't a very elegant solution, but I don't have a better idea."

Tsutomu Shimomura

Shimomura was born in Nagoya, Japan, on October 23, 1964. Both his father, Osamu, and mother, Akemi, were biochemists. In the 1960s, Shimomura and his younger sister, Sachi, moved to the United States with their parents. Osamu Shimomura took a position as a research faculty member at Princeton University in New Jersey.

Shimomura's parents taught him the value of experimentation. Describing his upbringing in the book *Takedown* (a record of his pursuit of Mitnick), he wrote: "From my first steps my family encouraged me to be curious. I was provoked to ask questions, to which I never received "because" replies. My parents' response was often to suggest an experiment through which I could determine for myself the answer."

An exceptionally bright student, Shimomura skipped several grades. He entered his first year of high school when he was just twelve years old. Bored with school, he dropped out before he graduated in order to work at the astrophysics department at Princeton University. Next, he enrolled at Caltech in Pasadena, California, as a physics major.

While still an undergraduate student, he received a call from a team of researchers at Los

Mitnick took over a computer that was "friendly" to the computer he wanted to enter. Once inside the target computer, he stole hundreds of documents and software programs that contained sensitive information about computer security. The attack lasted from 2 P.M. on Christmas Day until 6 P.M. the following evening.

Shimomura was on his way to Lake Tahoe, California, for a ski vacation, when he was informed that someone had broken into his databases. He returned home and immediately set out to discover the identity of the intruder. On December 27, he received a mocking message on his office voice mail. A man's computer-altered voice said: "My technique is the best. Damn you. I know sendmail technique. Don't you know who I am? Me and my friends, we'll kill you." Next, another voice said, "Hey, boss, my kung fu is really good." Before the end of the month, Shimomura had received another message: "Your technique will be defeated," the voice said. "Your technique is no good."

After Shimomura made the voice messages available on the Internet (in computer audio files), he received yet another mes-

Alamos National Laboratory in New Mexico. The team was building a specialized computer for physics research and they wanted to know if Shimomura was interested in working on the project. In 1984, Shimomura accepted a postdoctoral position at Los Alamos. He was just nineteen years old—and had not even graduated from high school.

By the time he was twenty-five, Shimomura was recruited to work at the San Diego Supercomputer Center, a federally funded operation. He gained a reputation as a brilliant, driven (and somewhat difficult) trouble-shooter. Having become an expert in computer security, Shimomura also worked as a consultant for the U.S. Air Force, the Federal Bureau of Investigation (FBI), the National Security Agency, and others.

After Kevin Mitnick broke into his computer on Christmas Day 1994, Shimomura relentlessly tracked the intruder's every move. For more than two years, Mitnick had managed to elude federal authorities. Seven weeks after Mitnick tangled with Shimomura's computer, the man who has been called the "Eliot Ness of the Internet" led FBI agents to the fugitive hacker's hideout. He later claimed that Mitnick's hacking involved nothing new or imaginative. Mitnick, he told reporters, "wasn't very hard to catch."

sage. This time, the computer-altered voice said, "Ah Tsutomu, my learned disciple. I see that you put my voice on the Net. I'm very disappointed my son." The messages provided little information about the intruder's identity. But they indicated that he viewed the situation as a game of wits.

THE HUNT FOR THE HACKER

For most of the following month, no new clues appeared. On January 27, 1995, Bruce Koball, a computer programmer, received notice from an online service called WELL. The notice informed him that his account was taking up too much disk space: Koball's account suddenly claimed hundreds of millions of bytes of storage space. But Koball had not been using his account. When he looked at the files in his account, he found Shimomura's name. The next day, when he read a newspaper story about the theft of files from a computer expert named Shimomura, he realized what had happened. The computer thief had stashed Shimomura's files in his account. And that was not all. The WELL account included secret codes for various companies, password files, and more than twenty-one thousand credit card numbers.

Shimomura and a few other computer experts formed a surveillance team at the WELL headquarters in Sausalito, California, in order to track the hacker's online movements. Using sophisticated programs, they were able to monitor every key-stroke the intruder made. By February 8, the team had determined that their subject was gaining access to WELL through Netcom, another Internet provider. The team of cyber-sleuths moved to Netcom's headquarters in San Jose, California. There, they monitored the intruder's modem calls. Using Shimomura's complicated security programs, they unraveled the tangled computer connections that allowed the hacker to connect to the Internet without being identified.

But the intruder's identity was slowly coming to light. Mitnick was already a well-known hacker—whose habits and interests were familiar to computer security experts such as Shimomura. Like Mitnick, the intruder was a night-owl who often remained online into the early morning. What's more, the information stashed in the WELL accounts included software that controls the operations of cellular phones made by various manufacturers—exactly the sort of information that interested Mitnick.

SHIMOMURA GETS HIS MAN

Working with government investigators, Shimomura's team compared telephone company records with records of the intruder's activity on the Internet. Soon, they determined that the hacker was using a telephone switching office in Raleigh, North Carolina, to re-route phone calls—making it difficult to trace calls from his cellular phone modem. On Sunday, February 12, Shimomura flew to Raleigh, where he met a Sprint cellular technician. The pair drove through the streets of suburban Raleigh with high-tech scanning and homing equipment designed to locate the origin of the cellular modem activity. By early Monday morning, Shimomura and the technician concluded that the calls originated from an apartment complex near the Raleigh airport.

Earlier that month, a man who identified himself as Glenn Thomas Case had rented a one-bedroom apartment at the Players Club complex. When federal agents knocked on the door of apartment 202 at 2 A.M. on February 15, they found Kevin Mitnick. Although it took him five minutes to open the door to his apartment, Mitnick surrendered without a struggle. As he waited to be charged in a North Carolina jail, he was allowed a few phone calls—to his attorney, his mother, and his grandmother. All of his calls were monitored. Charged with computer fraud and illegal use of telephone-access devices, Mitnick faced up to thirty-five years in prison.

Burning the midnight oil

Mitnick was a night-owl who liked to sleep late. He typically logged on in the mid-afternoon and remained active (except for a dinner break) through the night and into the following morning. Because of his unusual schedule, the surveillance team that monitored his activities often had to work twenty-hour days.

Sources for Further Reading

Hafner, Katie. "Kevin Mitnick, Unplugged." *Esquire* (August 1995), p. 80+.

Hafner, Katie. "A Superhacker Meets His Match." *Newsweek* (February 27, 1995), p. 61+.

Hafner, Katie and John Markoff. *Cyberpunk: Outlaws and Hackers on the Computer Frontier.* New York: Simon & Schuster, 1991.

"Interview with the Cybersleuth." *Newsweek* (March 6, 1995), p. 76.

Kennedy, Dana. "Takedown: The Pursuit and Capture of Kevin Mitnick." *Entertainment Weekly* (February 2, 1996), p. 50+.

Littman, Jonathon. "Hacked, Cracked and Phreaked." *PC Week* (January 27, 1997), p. 1+.

Markoff, John. "How a Computer Sleuth Traced a Digital Trail." *The New York Times* (February 16, 1995), p. D17.

Markoff, John. "A Most-wanted Cyberthief is Caught In His Own Web." *The New York Times* (February 16, 1995), pp. A1, D17.

A hacker's revenge

Mitnick sometimes used his hacking skills to pay back people who offended him. For example, the judge who sentenced him to serve time in a juvenile hall detention center for stealing technical information from Pacific Bell Telephone Company later discovered that his credit information had been altered. A probation officer who was involved in the case reported that his telephone was disconnected with no explanation. And police computers mysteriously lost all record of Mitnick's crimes.

Meyer, Michael. "Is This Hacker Evil or Merely Misunderstood? Two Writers Clash Over the Crimes of Kevin Mitnick." *Newsweek* (December 4, 1995), p. 60.

"Mitnick Confesses: 'No One is Secure.'" *Datamation* (January 15, 1996), p. 6+.

O'Brien, Miles. "Book Presents Two Sides of Super-Hacker Mitnick." [Online] Available http://www.cnn.com/tech/9602/hacker/index.html, January 7, 1997.

Quittner, Joshua. "Kevin Mitnick's Digital Obsession." *Time* (February 27, 1995), p. 45.

Shapiro, Andrew L. "Cyberscoop!" *The Nation* (March 20, 1995), p. 369+.

Shimomura, Tsutomu. *Takedown: The Pursuit and Capture of Kevin Mitnick, America's Most Wanted Computer Outlaw, By the Man Who Did It.* New York: Hyperion, 1996.

Sussman, Vic. "Gotcha! A Hard-core Hacker is Nabbed." *U.S. News & World Report* (February 27, 1995), p. 66+.

Stanley Rifkin

Born: 1946

Stanley Mark Rifkin, a mild-mannered computer wizard, used his skills to pull off the largest bank robbery in the history of the United States. Adding insult to injury, the bank was unaware that it had been victimized until federal officials informed them of Rifkin's scam.

AN ARTFUL SCHMOOZER

In 1978, Rifkin operated a computer consulting firm out of his apartment in the San Fernando Valley in southern California. The balding thirty-two-year-old had numerous clients, including a company that serviced the computers of the Security Pacific National Bank, headquartered in Los Angeles, California. Located in a room on the bank's D-level was Operations Unit One—a wire transfer room. A nationwide electronic wire network allows banks—including Security Pacific—to transfer money from one bank to another. Operated by the Federal Reserve Board, a government agency, the network allows banks to transfer funds throughout the United States and abroad. Like other banks, Security Pacific guarded against wire theft by using a numerical code to authorize transactions. The code changed on a daily basis.

Rifkin used his position as a consultant at the bank—and his knowledge of computers and bank practices—to rob the institution. In October 1978, he visited Security Pacific, where bank employees easily recognized him as a computer worker. He took an elevator to the D-level, where the bank's wire transfer room was located. A pleasant and friendly young man, he managed to talk his way into the room where the bank's secret code-of-the-day was posted on the wall. Rifkin memorized the code and left without arousing suspicion.

Soon, bank employees in the transfer room received a phone call from a man who identified himself as Mike Hansen, an employee of the bank's international division. The man ordered a routine transfer of funds into an account at the Irving Trust Company in New York—and he provided the secret code numbers to authorize the transaction. Nothing about the transfer appeared to be out of the ordinary, and Security Pacific transferred the money to the New York bank. What bank officials did not know was that the man who called himself Mike Hansen was in fact Stanley Rifkin, and he had used the bank's security code to rob the bank of $10.2 million.

DIAMONDS: AN UNTRACEABLE COMMODITY

Officials at Security Pacific were not aware of the theft until Federal Bureau of Investigation (FBI) agents informed them of the robbery. The heist went through without a problem—until the second part of Rifkin's plan came into play. Rifkin had actually begun preparations for the robbery in the summer of 1978, when he asked attorney Gary Goodgame for advice in finding an untraceable commodity. Goodgame suggested that Rifkin should speak to Lon Stein, a well-respected diamond dealer in Los Angeles.

In early October, Rifkin laid the groundwork to convert stolen funds into diamonds. Claiming to be a representative of a reputable firm—Coast Diamond Distributors—he contacted Stein. He claimed to be interested in placing a multi-million dollar order for diamonds. Suspecting nothing, Stein ordered diamonds through a Soviet government trading firm called Russalmaz.

On October 14, the Russalmaz office in Geneva, Switzerland, received a phone call from a man who claimed to be an

employee of the Security Pacific National Bank. The man, who called himself Mr. Nelson, informed the Russalmaz firm that Stein was acting as a representative of Coast Diamond Distributors. Further, he confirmed that Security Pacific had the funds to finance the multi-million dollar transaction. The man who called himself Mr. Nelson called again, to say that Stein would stop by Russalmaz's Geneva office on October 26 in order to look over the diamonds.

FBI agent Roger Young displays $12,000 and some of the diamonds seized in Rifkin's arrest.

ON THE ROCKS

On October 26, Stein arrived at the Geneva office of Russalmaz. He spent that day inspecting diamonds and returned the following day with another man. (The identity of the second

An incredible problem

People who knew Rifkin found it hard to believe that the pleasant computer whiz was the mastermind of a multi-million dollar bank robbery. Gerald Smith, a professor of management science at California State University at Northridge told reporters, "The guy is not a bank robber, he's a problem solver. I have a feeling Stan viewed the thing as an incredible problem. He's always five years ahead of anything else going on."

Rifkin sues magazine

In 1982, Rifkin sued *Esquire* magazine for libel (a written statement that damages a person's reputation) and invasion of privacy because they had printed a story that dramatized his theft. The suit was eventually dismissed.

man is unknown. According to physical descriptions of the man, he did not resemble Rifkin.) Stein agreed to pay the Soviet firm $8.145 million in exchange for 43,200 carats of diamonds. (Diamonds are weighed by a basic unit called a carat, which is two hundred milligrams. A well-cut round diamond of one carat measures almost exactly one-quarter inch in diameter.)

Somehow Rifkin managed to smuggle the diamonds into the United States. Five days after he robbed Security Pacific, he began to sell the Soviet diamonds. First, he sold twelve diamonds to a jeweler in Beverly Hills—an exclusive suburb of Los Angeles, California—for $12,000. Next, he traveled to Rochester, New York, where he attempted to sell more of the diamonds. There Rifkin's plot hit a snag.

On November 1, he visited Paul O'Brien, a former business associate. He informed O'Brien that he had received diamonds as payment for a West German real estate deal—and that he wanted to exchange the diamonds for cash. Before he had a chance to act on Rifkin's request, O'Brien saw a news item on television describing a multimillion-dollar bank heist in Los Angeles. The story named Rifkin as the thief. O'Brien wasted no time in contacting the FBI.

CONVICTED OF WIRE FRAUD

Rifkin flew to San Diego, California, to spend a weekend with Daniel Wolfson, an old friend. He informed Wolfson that he planned to surrender. But he never had the opportunity to give himself up. O'Brien had given the FBI permission to record calls from Rifkin. On November 5, Rifkin called O'Brien. The conversation contained information that allowed FBI agents to track Rifkin to Wolfson's Carslbad, California, address.

Around midnight on Sunday, November 5, FBI agents Robin Brown and Norman Wight appeared at Wolfson's apartment. At first, Wolfson barred their entry with outstretched arms. When the agents informed him that they would force their way inside if necessary, he allowed them to enter. Rifkin surrendered without a struggle. He also turned over evidence to the federal agents: a suitcase containing the $12,000 from the Beverly Hills diamond sale and several dozen packets of diamonds that had been hidden in a plastic shirt cover.

Rifkin was taken to the Metropolitan Correctional Center in San Diego. Soon after he was released on bail, he got into more trouble with the FBI. He had begun to target the Union Bank of Los Angeles—using the same scheme that had worked at the Security Pacific National Bank. What he did not know was that someone involved in the scheme was a government informant who had set him up. Rifkin was arrested again on February 13, 1979. Federal agents also arrested Patricia Ferguson, who was helping Rifkin set-up the bank. Tried on two counts of wire fraud, Rifkin faced the possibility of ten years imprisonment. He pleaded guilty, and on March 26, 1979, was sentenced to eight years in federal prison. In June 1979, Ferguson was convicted of three counts of conspiracy.

A picture worth a thousand words

Rifkin was picked up by FBI agents at the home of Daniel Wolfson. Wolfson, a photographer, shot pictures of his old school pal as federal agents escorted him into custody. He sold the photographs the following day for $250. One of the photographs was purchased by UPI (United Press International). The picture included the caption: "Stanley Mark Rifkin, 32, smiles in this picture, taken minutes after his arrest, by Dan Wolfson, who rented the apartment where Rifkin was arrested. Rifkin, a computer wizard, is charged with defrauding a Los Angeles bank of $10.2 million. Wolfson was also arrested . . . during the telephone interview with UPI." Wolfson was later charged with harboring a criminal.

Sources for Further Reading

Nash, Jay Robert. *The Encyclopedia of World Crime.* Wilmette, IL: Crime Books, 1990, pp. 2582–2583.

"The Ultimate Heist." *Time* (November 20, 1978), p. 48.

Jerry Schneider

Active: Early 1970s

Working a loophole in the system to his advantage, Jerry Neal Schneider employed the telephone to steal thousands of dollars worth of products from the Pacific Bell Telephone & Telegraph Company. He ordered at will, never paying for the products—until two of his employees blew the whistle on his illegal operation.

A PHONE FANATIC

By the time he was four years old, Schneider was shy and overweight. Growing up he had no real friends. Other children called him "fatso." He loved telephones and by the time he was ten, he had built a telecommunications system in his family's home. A few years later, he received a telephone repair worker's belt and hat—so that he could pretend to be a repair man. Talented in science, Schneider won prizes at science fairs. First a ham radio operator, Schneider eventually became a "phone phreak"—someone who illegally uses telephone company services.

As a student at Hamilton High in Los Angeles, California, Schneider was president of the radio club. He once asked officials at Pacific Telephone & Telegraph (PT&T) Company to give him phone company equipment for his electronics class. The phone company refused. He later applied for a job with PT&T— and again, he was refused.

Fifteen minutes of fame-- and then some

Catapulted to fame by his brazen use of electronics to steal hundreds of thousands of dollars worth of computer equipment from the Pacific Telephone & Telegraph Company, Schneider instantly became a media hit. On October 10, 1976—more than four years after he was released from prison—Schneider appeared on a *60 Minutes* television segment called "Dial E for Embezzlement." (Embezzlement involves swindling money by violating a trust.)

Dan Rather, the host of *60 Minutes,* introduced the segment with these words: "The way a banker makes money is to move money around as fast as he can. Bankers are hell-bent to speed up their systems with instant communications and electronic wizardry. Trouble is, the bank thieves are as up-to-date as the bankers, and sometimes a step ahead. . . . Faster banking can lead to faster stealing, as some sadder and wiser banks are beginning to learn."

Next, Rather introduced Schneider, a convicted computer thief. "Sometimes," Rather said, "it takes a thief to catch a thief." By the end of the segment, Schneider had used his phone phreaking skills to prove Rather's point. Armed with nothing more than a phone number and a credit card number, Schneider had gotten the bank to raise Rather's credit limit from $500 to $10,000!

IN BUSINESS FOR HIMSELF

In spite of the obstacles he encountered, Schneider was determined to get into the telephone business. While in high school, he regularly passed by the PT&T warehouse. He examined the contents of the warehouse dumpster and found operating manuals and specific instructions for ordering computer equipment by phone. After graduating, he studied engineering and used the PT&T materials to start up a small business.

Pretending to be a company supplier, Schneider ordered computer equipment over the telephone—using the ordering guidelines from the instructions he had taken from the dumpster. First, he consulted a PT&T catalog for the seven-digit code number for a product he wanted to order. Next, he punched in his order using a PT&T telephone that allowed him to order directly through the company's computerized inventory system. Schneider and his employees then picked up the merchandise that had been ordered. To almost everyone concerned, the business appeared to be legitimate. Assisted by ten employees,

Phone phreaking

Schneider once told a reporter at the *Los Angeles Times,* "Phone phreaking didn't prove to be any great challenge to me. . . . I was more into setting up large-scale computer systems."

211

Schneider conducted his business out of a six-thousand- square-foot warehouse.

DISGRUNTLED EMPLOYEES

Not everyone was convinced that Schneider's business was legal. Special agents at the phone company had received word from one of Schneider's customers that he was selling phone company merchandise. For nearly three months they tracked his activities, but were unable to gather solid evidence against him.

Just before Christmas 1971, one of Schneider's employees, John Nicholas, contacted PT&T officials. Nicholas claimed that Schneider had hired him in September as a warehouse manager. Soon after he started his new job, he began to suspect foul play. Nicholas said that Schneider claimed to have received a shipment of phone company equipment from a salvage center—but many of the products looked brand-new. Schneider loaded shipments into a truck that was the same make and style as phone company vehicles—but it was not an official PT&T vehicle. He told officials that he was given an official PT&T purchase order form—but he never signed any receipts for the shipments he picked up.

Eventually, Nicholas and another employee, Earl Eugene Watson, confronted Schneider. The two men gave Schneider a choice: either abandon all illegal practices or suffer the consequences. Schneider reportedly told the two employees that it would be impossible to turn a profit by running a legitimate business. He promised to close down his operation. When he didn't, Nicholas and Watson informed the authorities about their former boss's illegal activities.

A COMPUTER-AGE SHERLOCK HOLMES

Based on these reports, Los Angeles district attorney investigators Frank Kovacevich, Ron Maus, and others arrived at Schneider's office with a search warrant. They found a stash of inventory. Schneider immediately became front-page news. The February 9, 1972, edition of the *Los Angeles Times* carried a story whose headline—"Massive Phone Thefts Uncovered"—stretched across the entire front page. One article called Schneider a computer-age Sherlock Holmes; another was titled "How to Steal a Million from a Computer."

Officials at PT&T filed a lawsuit against Schneider's operation—based only on the inventory that had been found at Schneider's office. (Early estimates placed the phone company's losses at hundreds of thousands of dollars.) Schneider pleaded guilty to receiving stolen property. He was sentenced to less than two months at a low-security prison farm in southern California and was ordered to pay the PT&T company $8,500.

Following his release from prison, Schneider claimed to have gone into computer security consulting (although no one ever actually paid him for his services). Next, he became involved in offshore banking—an enterprise that sometimes treads a fine line between legitimate and illegal business.

Phone phreaks

A phone phreak is a hacker who specializes in breaking into telephone systems. Among other things, phone phreaks figure out how to use the telephone company's long distance service without paying for it. In the early days of phone phreaking, hackers used a "blue box"—a device that imitated a high-pitched tone in the switching system—to trick the telephone service into providing toll-free long-distance calls. (The founders of the Apple Computer Company—Stephen Jobs and Steve Wozniak—were among the many college students who sold home-made blue boxes for spending money.) By the middle of the 1970s, phone phreaking was so widely practiced that the American Telephone & Telegraph company (AT&T) reported losing about $30 million each year to phone fraud.

Sources for Further Reading

Nash, Jay Robert. *The Encyclopedia of World Crime*. Wilmette, IL: Crime Books, 1990, p. 2696.

Parker, Donn B. *Crime by Computer*. New York: Charles Scribner's Sons, 1976, pp. 59–70.

Reen, Brian. *True Hackers are not Dangerous*. [Online] Available http://www.cedarville.edu/student/s1143400/hack.htm, December 2, 1997.

Spies

Spying entails watching in secret—usually for hostile purposes. The spy's motives may involve political and ideological concerns—or simple financial gain. And his or her methods often involve exploiting a position of trust. Elizabeth Van Lew used her position in the community to spy on the Confederate war effort. Christopher Boyce took advantage of his job at an aerospace firm to pass classified information to Soviet agents. Julius and Ethel Rosenberg used a family connection to gain access to the nation's top-secret atomic bomb project. Some spied for profit and others believed they were acting for the greater good. They were regarded as heroes, or traitors—or both. In this section you'll encounter a CIA mole, an FBI double-agent, a Soviet agent who disappeared without a trace from her New York apartment, and others. You'll find out what they did, why they did it, and the price they paid for engaging in espionage.

Aldrich Ames

Born: May 26, 1941

During his thirty-two year career at the CIA, Aldrich Hazen Ames was known as a mediocre agent who tended to drink too much. What Ames's superiors did not know was worse than that: he was, from 1985 to 1994, a mole (spy) who passed top-level national secrets to the Soviet Union.

First Contact

Ames's role as a Soviet mole began in April 1985. In order to create a legitimate reason to visit the Soviet embassy in Washington, D.C., he arranged to meet with Sergei Chuvakin, an embassy diplomat who was an expert on nuclear weapons. Ames told the Soviet diplomat that he wanted to meet in order to discuss foreign policy issues. He told his superiors at the CIA that he had arranged the meeting in order to attempt to recruit Chuvakin (to spy for the U.S.). But in truth, he arranged the meeting to provide a cover for the real reason he visited the Soviet embassy: to contact the Soviet secret police (known as the KGB) and offer his services.

Before Ames met with Chuvakin at the Soviet embassy, he stopped briefly at the desk of the embassy receptionist. Without speaking, he passed her an envelope. Addressed to a senior KGB officer, the envelope contained three items: the names of three Soviets who had offered to work for the CIA; a page from the CIA directory, with Ames's name highlighted; and a demand for

Double jeopardy

From late 1985 to early 1986, the Central Intelligence Agency (CIA) lost most of its agents in the Soviet Union. Three dozen operatives were sent to prison—or executed—as a result of information that Ames provided to the Soviet espionage service (also known as the KGB). The execution of two operatives—Valeri Martynov and Sergei Motorin—alerted the CIA to the possibility that a mole (spy) was leaking government secrets to the Soviets.

In the summer of 1980, U.S. officials had persuaded Sergei Motorin, a young major in the KGB, to spy for them. FBI officials knew that Motorin had been involved in a car accident—and that a prostitute had been a passenger in his car. They also knew that the Soviet agent had attempted to trade his government allotment (allowance) of vodka and cigars for stereo equipment in a store in downtown Washington. Motorin's superiors would frown on such behav-ior. Armed with this information, FBI officials convinced the Soviet to spy for them. Although slow to agree, Motorin eventually provided agents with the name of every KGB operative in the Soviet embassy in Washington, D.C. Motorin returned to Moscow at the end of 1984, six months before Ames provided information to the Soviets that identified him as a double-agent. He was executed.

Valeri Martynov arrived in Washington, in November 1980, to assume the post of third secretary of the Soviet embassy there. Martynov's title was a cover for his real position as a lieutenant colonel in the KGB. The Soviet agent began to supply United States intelligence officials with secret information after he was recruited in the spring of 1982. Ames provided the KGB with information about Martynov's activities. Ordered to return to Moscow in November 1985, Martynov remained in jail until he was executed by a firing squad on May 28, 1987, at the age of forty-one.

$50,000. The names offered proof that he had access to valuable information. The directory page provided evidence that he was in a position to gather more information. And the demand for payment made clear his intentions.

Two days after his first meeting with Chuvakin on April 16, 1985, Ames deposited $9,000 in cash into one of his two accounts at the Dominion Bank of Virginia. Two months later, he marched by security guards at the CIA headquarters with plastic bags filled with several pounds of classified documents. He delivered the bags to the KGB. The documents contained a wealth of valuable information, including the names of ten Soviets who were acting as double agents (agents working for a government that they were actually spying on), providing Western intelligence agencies with Soviet secrets.

On August 10, 1985, Ames married a Colombian woman named Maria del Rosario Casas. (He had recently divorced his first wife, Nan, who was also a CIA employee.) By the time he and his new wife traveled to Rome, Italy, where Ames would spend a three-year term in a program to recruit more spies from the Soviet embassy, his bank deposits amounted to $123,500—a rather sudden increase in income for a $69,000-a-year government agent.

Garbage pickers

FBI agents regularly inspected Ames's trash. But they had to be discreet. One night in September 1993, agents pulled up in front of Ames's residence in a van. They placed a trash can just like Ames's on the street—and they lifted the full container into the vehicle. Sifting through the trash they found a torn note that indicated Ames was planning to meet with his Soviet contact.

AN INFORMATION LEAK

The Soviets did not ignore the information that Ames passed to them. They jailed and executed the men who were identified as double agents. Eventually the CIA received news that two Soviet agents—Valeri Martynov and Sergei Motorin—had been returned to Moscow and executed. Officials began to suspect a leak within the CIA. At first they investigated the possibility that the Soviets were intercepting CIA communications. In order to test this theory, officials sent a number of phony messages that were designed to stir up a reaction in the KGB organization. But the KGB did nothing.

Slowly, CIA officials admitted that someone within their own organization was responsible for the leak. In January 1986, the agency attempted to reduce the possibility of further leaks by limiting access to top-secret information to a small group of officers. The new procedure might have worked—had Ames not been one of the officers who received top-level clearance.

AT THE TOP OF THE SPY LIST

U.S. investigators were not sure whether they were looking for one spy or more. The Federal Bureau of Investigation (FBI) worked with the CIA to investigate the problem. FBI agents compiled two "bigot lists" of possible suspects. One list contained "single suspects" who might have worked alone, while

Murderous intent

"[Ames] has the blood of a dozen officers on his hands. He would have had my blood, too, had I not managed to escape."

--Oleg Gordievsky, KGB officer working for the British, who claimed he was betrayed by Ames

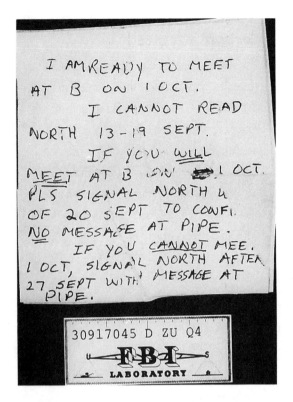

I AM READY TO MEET AT B ON 1 OCT.

I CANNOT READ NORTH 13-19 SEPT.

IF YOU WILL MEET AT B ON 1 OCT. PLS SIGNAL NORTH 4 OF 20 SEPT TO CONFI. NO MESSAGE AT PIPE.

IF YOU CANNOT MEE. 1 OCT, SIGNAL NORTH AFTER 27 SEPT WITH MESSAGE AT PIPE.

30917045 D ZU Q4

FBI

LABORATORY

This torn note, found in Ames's garbage, was the first evidence that he was meeting with the Russians.

the other list provided the names of agents who might have worked together to spy for the Soviets. Ames was on both lists.

To be named on a list, an agent must have had access to information on a case that failed. Investigators also took into account other factors—such as a drinking or drug problem, unexplained time away from work or home, or a lifestyle that exceeded the suspect's income. Ames had a well-documented drinking problem. He drove an expensive red Jaguar and had paid cash for a luxurious $540,000 home. He had expensive tastes—which ranged from original art work to Swiss-made watches. And his bank accounts showed numerous large cash deposits. Ames began to move to the top of investigators' lists of suspects.

A MOLE HUNT

The FBI began to focus on Ames. On May 12, 1993, they opened a criminal investigation of the Soviet mole suspect. In an operation whose codename was "Nightmover," agents monitored Ames's telephone conversations at home and in his car. They raided his garbage on a regular basis. Posing as lawn workers and tree trimmers, they installed a small video camera in a neighbor's tree to monitor Ames's comings and goings. And finally they entered his home.

On October 9, 1993—while Ames and his wife and child spent a long weekend in Florida—agents entered his house with a search warrant that had been authorized by Attorney General Janet Reno. One agent examined Ames's bank books to look for suspicious deposits. A computer whiz named Tom Murray broke into Ames's personal computer. He found messages about message relays, meetings, and document transfers. And he found file after file of top-secret CIA information that should never have found its way to Ames's home computer. What they found left no doubt: Ames was the Soviet mole.

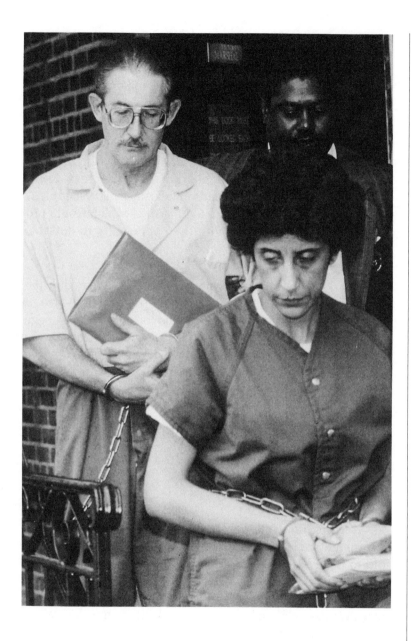

Aldrich Ames and his wife, Rosario, are escorted from the courthouse by federal marshals on March 10, 1994.

A CONVICTED TRAITOR

Agents were reluctant to arrest Ames. Although they had plenty of evidence against him, they had not caught him in the act of selling national secrets to the Soviets. But they couldn't afford to wait until Ames tipped his hand. Involving more than one hundred special agents, the spy-catching operation could

Officials in the CIA and FBI are not sure whether to believe Ames about when he was recruited by the Soviets—and why he became a double-agent. Ames claimed that he became a Soviet spy in 1985—and that he was motivated primarily by greed. But when Ames underwent a polygraph (lie-detector exam), he failed questions about his recruitment and his motivations.

not be hidden from Ames indefinitely. And even if Ames didn't become suspicious, his neighbors were bound to notice odd activities around the government man's house.

And there was the question of whether Ames planned to defect (to desert one's country). The FBI noticed that Russian intelligence officers had been passing through Ames's neighborhood with increasing frequency. What's more, Ames had scheduled a business trip to Moscow—which would provide him with the opportunity to defect to the Soviet Union.

Ames was arrested on a quiet suburban street on February 21, 1994, as he drove from his home to CIA headquarters. Ames pleaded guilty, was convicted of espionage, and was sentenced to life imprisonment. His wife, Rosario, who knew of Ames's activities, was sentenced to five years and three months. Unapologetic about the deaths he caused, Ames claimed that money was his main motivation, coupled with a strong disregard for the foreign policy of President Ronald Reagan's administration and a conviction that spying for the CIA had no meaning. He was quoted as saying, "This is the great myth of espionage: that it makes a difference. Of course, it doesn't."

DEADLY INFORMATION

Over the nine-year period during which Ames acted as a government mole, he collected $2.5 million for information he sold to the Russians. The information he sold exposed more than one hundred intelligence operations and led to the execution of at least ten top spies. "They died," former CIA Director James Woolsey claimed, "because this warped, murdering traitor wanted a bigger house and a Jaguar."

Sources for Further Reading

"The Aldrich Ames Holiday Shopping Guide." *Time* (December 5, 1994), p. 25.

Corn, David. "A Talk with Aldrich Ames." *The Nation* (September 11, 1995), p. 238+.

Duffy, Brian. "The Cold War's Last Spy." *U.S. News & World Report* (March 6, 1995), p. 48+.

Earley, Pete. *Confessions of a Spy: The Real Story of Aldrich Ames.* New York: G. P. Putnam's Sons, 1997.

Pound, Edward T. "The Spy Who Picked the CIA's Pockets." *U.S. News & World Report* (May 9, 1994), p. 49.

Thomas, Evan. "Spooking the Director." *Newsweek* (November 6, 1995), p. 42+.

"Victims of Aldrich Ames." *Time* (May 22, 1995), p. 56.

Waller, Douglas. "For Your Disinformation." *Time* (November 13, 1995), p. 82.

Hundreds of suspects

When the FBI began to investigate the intelligence leaks that had led to the execution of two operatives, Ames was only one of hundreds of suspects. Edward Lee Howard, an agent who had defected to Moscow in September 1985, was an early prime suspect.

Christopher Boyce and Andrew Daulton Lee

Christopher Boyce: 1953–
Andrew Daulton Lee: 1952–

Boyhood friends Christopher Boyce and Andrew Daulton Lee shared several things—including a privileged upbringing, involvement with drugs, and discontent with the U.S. government. Together, they spied for Soviet intelligence, for which U.S. officials estimated they received $17,500. Discovered by chance, each turned against the other—and both earned extended prison terms.

PALS IN PALOS VERDES

Boyce and Lee both grew up in Palos Verdes—one of the wealthiest suburbs in southern California. Lee's adoptive father was a successful physician; Boyce was the son of an Federal Bureau of Investigation (FBI) agent who later took a higher paying job as the security director of McDonnell Douglas Corporation, an airplane manufacturer. The two boys met at a local Catholic church while serving as altar boys and soon became good friends. They spent much of their free time with one another, and both shared an intense interest in falconry—the art of training falcons, or hawks.

Lee, a gifted woodworker, had little interest in school. He became increasingly involved with drugs as a teenager, and eventually went into business selling them with a young man named Cameron Adams. Buying and selling cocaine and marijuana, the pair earned $2,000 a week. By 1977, Lee had been arrested five times for possessing and selling drugs—and three times for driving under the influence of alcohol or drugs. He also had one arrest for suspicion of robbery and resisting arrest.

One of Lee's arrests—for selling cocaine to undercover agents working for the Los Angeles County sheriff's department—earned him a one-year jail sentence. From jail, he wrote to a judge begging to be set free so that he could continue his education. He wrote, "My incarceration [imprisonment] has helped me to evaluate my life and made it possible for me to formulate plans for the future." Released after seven months in prison, Lee enrolled in a nearby junior college—and then dropped out. He returned to selling drugs and, since he violated the terms of his probation, a warrant was issued for his arrest.

Boyce had no police record. He was an intelligent young man whose IQ (intelligence quotient) of 142 was well above average. When he put his mind to it, he earned straight-As in school. The oldest of nine children, he was a devout Catholic and was well-liked by neighbors who saw him as an idealistic young man. Although he was a bright student, Boyce was not eager to attend college. After enrolling and dropping out three times over the course of three years, he took a job in nearby Redondo Beach, California.

INSIDE THE BLACK VAULT

On July 29, 1974, Boyce began work at TRW Systems, Inc., an aerospace firm that worked on many classified military programs. TRW was one of two companies that manufactured most of the "spy" satellites for the Central Intelligence Agency (CIA). Boyce earned $140 per week as a communications clerk at TRW. Within months, he was responsible for running the company's "black vault"—a high-security operation that involved top-secret information. Awarded top-secret clearance, he supervised secret communications between TRW and the CIA headquarters in Langley, Virginia. Boyce operated two types of coding systems that transmitted information involving TRW satellites. He also handled coded material concerning top-secret Air Force, Army, and Navy communications.

Take a look at this!

The Falcon and the Snowman (1985), based on the book by the same name, tells of boyhood friends Christopher Boyce and Andrew Daulton Lee. The movie features Sean Penn as Lee and Timothy Hutton as Boyce.

U.S. Espionage Act

Boyce and Lee were both tried under the United States Espionage Act--the same law that sent convicted spies, **Ethel and Julius Rosenberg** (see entry) to their deaths.

Andrew Daulton Lee.

Few people received the security clearance required to enter the black vault. And fewer still received clearance to handle coded material contained in the vault. CIA officials routinely conducted extensive background checks of employees before granting them security clearance. Why Boyce—a twenty-one-year-old high school graduate—received clearance has puzzled authorities. Many have suggested that it was no coincidence that Boyce's father was a friend of Regis Carr—a former FBI agent who was in charge of "special projects" security at TRW.

Code name "Luis"

At some point in 1975, Boyce and Lee devised a plan to provide Soviet agents with top-secret information. How the plan started—and whose idea it was—has become the subject of debate. During 1975, Lee traveled to the Soviet embassy in Mexico City, Mexico, a center of Soviet espionage activities. He informed the Russians that he was working with someone who had access to top-secret information on U.S. spy satellites. Further, he said that he wanted to sell them classified information, and offered two documents as proof that he could deliver valuable information.

After five hours of questioning, the Soviets informed Lee that they were interested in his proposition. Lee's contact was Boris A. Grishin, the embassy's science attaché. Grishin was, in fact, an agent in the KGB—the Soviet espionage service. Grishin informed Lee that they were to refer to each other by code names: the Soviet agent would go by the name "John," while Lee would take the code-name "Luis."

Over the course of eighteen months, Lee provided Soviet agents with information Boyce smuggled out of TRW. He made several trips to Mexico, and traveled to Vienna, Austria, where Soviet agents had arranged to meet him to avoid surveillance. Using a camera Lee had purchased with money from the Soviets, Boyce photographed sensitive documents in the security vault. Some documents he smuggled off company grounds by placing them inside potted plants.

Trouble in Mexico

In December 1976, Boyce left TRW. But Lee had one final delivery to make to the Soviet embassy. On January 6, 1977, he followed the usual procedure to arrange a meeting with "John." First he taped a large "X" on a lamp post, as he had many times before. Later that evening, he waited for Grishin at the Viva Pizza Restaurant. After his contact failed to appear, he followed a backup plan: he returned to the pre-arranged meeting spot the following morning. Again, Grishin did not appear.

Next, Lee went to the Soviet embassy—although he had been specifically warned not to. The Soviet embassy was normally monitored by Mexican police. When he threw an envelope over the embassy's fence, police suspected that he might have thrown a bomb onto the embassy grounds. Lee was taken to police headquarters and forced to empty his pockets. What the Mexican police found aroused their interest: inside an envelope Lee was carrying were twenty strips of film that contained photographs of documents—all of which were marked "TOP SECRET." The film reportedly contained a feasibility study (a study to determine whether something can be accomplished) of a spy communications satellite network that operated through miniature receiver/transmitters in the Soviet Union and China.

At first Lee protested that the films were part of an ad campaign for the General Electric Company. But Mexican police notified officials at the U.S. Embassy in Mexico City, who in turn notified the CIA. Boyce and Lee's spy operation immediately began to unravel. Lee informed on Boyce, who was picked up ten days later by FBI agents in Los Angeles. Boyce, in turn, confessed that he had copied the documents that Lee provided to the Soviets.

Christopher Boyce.

Letter from prison

On the night before his trial began, Boyce wrote a letter to his father from prison. It explained, in part, why he had gotten involved in espionage.

Dear Dad:

I thought of you all long and hard today and have decided I owe you an explanation of my feelings. In reality I owe you so much more than that, but at this point it is all I can give.

I wish I could bring myself to convey my love to my family from this place but I cannot and so I leave it up to you. I realized many dozens of months ago that there could be no coming back from the decisions made and I do not propose to pick up the pieces now. I regret none of my actions except for the deceptions that I played upon you [and] any subsequent loss of face. For that I am truly sorry, more now than ever. If we never understood each other, the fault is mine. . . .

To my perceptions, the foundations of this country are a sham. It was designed by the few for the few and so it will remain. Western culture is in decline now and the trend cannot be reversed. We are grasping alone in a headless insanity that will continue to consume until nothing is left.

CONVICTED SPIES

Boyce and Lee were accused of spying for the Soviets. Although they were tried separately, both were prosecuted under the United States Espionage Act in April 1977. Boyce claimed that he had been bullied by Lee into spying for the Soviets—and that he was afraid of being blackmailed by his former partner. He even volunteered to take a lie detector test to prove that he was telling the truth. Boyce was convicted—on eight counts of espionage, conspiracy to commit espionage, and theft of official documents—and sentenced to forty years in prison.

Less than three years later—in January 1980—he escaped from a high-security federal prison in Lompoc, California, by cutting through barbed wire fences. Nineteen months later—after a series of robberies—he was captured by FBI agents in a fishing port sixty miles north of Seattle, Washington. When Boyce returned to prison, ninety years had been added to his sentence for additional charges of conspiracy, firearms violations, and robbery.

Time and time again I watched the destruction of those things and places I love and I was disgusted. I believe we are on the edge of a poisoned horrible darkness. Industrialism and technology are dragging humanity toward universal collapse and will take most life forms with it. . . .

I would give anything to be out of this place and be able to feel sunshine and to just even run again. I think there is small chance of that now so I have detached myself from what goes on here.

Being alone all the time leaves one much time to turn thoughts inward. As I think back upon my beliefs that put me here in the first place, they are strengthened more than ever. I could never make of my life that which you would have wanted.

That is no reflection on you. I chose freely my response to this absurd world, and if given the opportunity again, I would be even more vigorous. Please give all my love to mom and Kathy and everyone and tell them for me to see them would just make a bad situation worse.

Respectfully,

Chris

Lee's defense was widely viewed as ridiculous. He claimed that he thought that he was part of an undercover CIA operation to provide Soviet agents with inaccurate information. He was convicted of espionage and sentenced to life in prison.

Sources for Further Reading

Lindsey, Robert. *The Falcon and the Snowman.* New York: Simon & Schuster, 1979, pp. 356–357.

Lindsey, Robert. "To be young, rich—and a spy." *The New York Times Magazine* (May 22, 1977), p. 18.

Nash, Jay Robert. *Spies: A Narrative Encyclopedia of Dirty Deeds and Double Dealing from Biblical Times to Today.* New York: M. Evans, 1997, pp. 113–115.

"Stealing the Company Store." *Time* (May 9, 1977), p. 19.

Steele, Richard. "The 'Pyramider' Spy Case." *Newsweek* (April 18, 1977), p. 29.

Juliet Stuart Poyntz

Born: November 25, 1886
Died: 1937?

A former member of the Communist Party, Juliet Stuart Poyntz was trained in Soviet espionage. After brief service as a spy for the Soviets, she became disillusioned and announced her plan to retire—and was never heard from again.

A WELL-EDUCATED WOMAN

Poyntz was born on November 25, 1886, in Omaha, Nebraska, to an Irish Catholic family. Her parents were Alice E. Poyntz and John J. Poyntz, a lawyer. An intellectually gifted young woman, Poyntz graduated from Barnard College with high honors in 1907. In 1910, at a time when few women pursued graduate degrees, she earned a master's degree from Columbia University in New York. She also attended the prestigious London School of Economics at London University in England (1910–1911) and Oxford University, in Oxford, England (1911–1912).

Poyntz's education enabled her to land research positions in a number of organizations. She was a special investigator for the U.S. Immigration Commission from 1908 to 1909, and a researcher for the American Association for Labor Legislation from 1910 to 1913. In 1914 she became the director of the Bureau of Labor Research at the Rand School, a position she held until 1915. She was the educational director of the International Ladies Garment Workers Union for four years, from 1915

Red September

Americans in the 1940s did not look kindly at communist teachers. Although communist teachers, especially in New York, had proven themselves no better or worse than teachers of any other political persuasion, many Americans feared that teachers would use their influence with students to expose them to communist ideas—and to recruit them to the cause. As early as 1941, the American Federation of Teachers banned two teachers' unions in New York for communist activities.

The anti-communist hysteria did not reach American universities until 1947 or 1948, but its impact was just as pronounced as it was in the nation's secondary schools. Harvard University was a favorite target for anti-communists. In 1948, several faculty members at the University of Washington were expelled from the university for refusing to cooperate with anti-communist investigators. Western Illinois State University fired two "liberalists" as a result of anti-communist pressures. Oklahoma began a loyalty oath for university instructors in 1949, leading to the dismissals of thirty-one professors the following year. Such cases did far more than ruin the careers of academics. They paved the way for the gray conformism of American education in the 1950s.

to 1919. She also taught for a while at Columbia University, one of the nation's leading educational institutions.

Interested in social questions and social reform, Poyntz was a spokesperson for women's suffrage (right to vote). While still in her twenties, she lectured at various suffrage organizations in New York City. She also contributed articles to a number of magazines and professional publications. Awarded the first scholarship to be given by the General Federation of Women's Clubs of the United States of America, she was a member of numerous professional organizations, including the American Historical Association and the Oxford Anthropological Association.

COMMUNIST ACTIVITY

Poyntz became a member of the American Communist Party (ACP) in New York in 1921. An educated and persuasive speaker, she became a distinguished member of the ACP. Although she never rose to the highest level of leadership, she was one of the most influential women leaders in the ACP. She was a candidate for public office on the Communist Party ticket

Who killed Carlo Tresca?

The answer to that question is, most likely, the Mafia. Carlo Tresca was born the son of a wealthy landowning family in Sulmona, Italy, in 1879. By the middle of the 1890s, however, the family had lost its land and privileged status due to a series of bad investments and a poor economy. Tresca was deeply disappointed by these events. He eventually turned to anarchism as a political philosophy.

Tresca found employment as editor of the Socialist Party newspaper in Italy, but was forced to flee to America when his critical writings earned him too many enemies. In America he eventually became well known as an anticommunist and anti-fascist. (Fascism is a dictatorship of the extreme right.) In that role, he used much of his energy to rage against Italian dictator Benito Mussolini (1883–1945) in the Italian-language newspaper that he published, *Il Martello*. Mussolini had Tresca's name placed on a death list in 1931, but it was not until 1943 that the sentence was actually carried out.

Vito Genovese, a leader of the New York Mafia, had been forced to leave the United States for Italy in the 1930s in order to escape a murder charge. There he managed to develop a friendly relationship with Mussolini and the Fascist cause. After Mussolini complained to him about Tresca's anti-fascist activities in America, Genovese informed the Italian leader that he would take care of the problem.

On January 11, 1943, as Tresca crossed Fifteenth Street in New York with his friend Giuseppe Calabi, they paused under a streetlamp. Another man stepped from the darkness and shot Tresca once in the back and once in the head, killing him instantly. For several years the crime was listed as an unsolved political assassination. It is now commonly believed that Genovese ordered the killing to improve his relationship with Mussolini. The murder was reportedly carried out by Carmine Galante—who later became a Mafia leader and was himself killed in 1979.

and directed the New York Workers School. She also led the organization's Women's Department and served for a time as national secretary of the International Labor Defense.

Poyntz was an active member of the Communist Party throughout the 1920s and into the 1930s. She helped organize the Friends of the Soviet Union and the Trade Union Unity League. Her work with the Workers Committee Against Unemployment would be her last public contribution to the Communist Party.

232

A SOVIET SPY

At a time when the Soviet Union was attempting to increase its espionage (spy) base in the United States, Poyntz was recruited to work as a Soviet spy. As was routine for spies recruited from the United States, she first dropped out of the ACP—although she continued to maintain ties with her communist associates.

Sometime around 1934 or 1935, Poyntz reportedly traveled to Moscow in the Soviet Union to be trained in espionage. Poyntz was seen in Moscow in 1936. She was in the company of George Mink, an American who had been convicted of espionage in 1935 for his role as a Soviet agent. When she returned to New York, Poyntz was established in an apartment and provided with funds that allowed her to lead a comfortable existence as a spy for the Soviet Union.

Poyntz did not remain with Soviet intelligence for long. At first a devoted agent, she began to find herself at odds with Soviet policy. In 1936 and 1937, Soviet leader Joseph Stalin (1879–1953), carried out a series of "purges" to rid himself of opponents. In 1937, the Trial of the Seventeen allowed Stalin to do away with the leader of his potential opponents—that is, those who were still living. Around that time, Poyntz informed her friend Carlo Tresca that she planned to discontinue her espionage activities.

THE LADY VANISHES

Fifty years old when she announced her resignation, Poyntz left her New York apartment. She moved into an inexpensive room at the Women's Association Clubhouse at 353 West 57th Street in New York. Sometime in late May or early June, she left her room. No one saw her leave, but she obviously planned to return. The light was on. She left all her belongings in the room. The memoirs she had been working on were spread out on a table. No note indicated where she was going or when she would return.

Poyntz never returned. And no evidence of what happened to her has ever been found. But many had theories about the

> **Here's a book you might like:**
>
> *Who Was That Masked Man, Anyway,* 1992, by Avi Wortis
>
> A boy pretends that he is a master spy as he and his friend reenact their favorite radio serials. They spend much of their time trying to do away with the family lodger, nicknamed "the evil scientist," and to marry off the boy's older brother, a World War II veteran.

fate of the former spy. Many of Poyntz's friends blamed the Soviets for her disappearance. It was not an unusual situation: various people who were associated with communist parties in the United States and other parts of the world had been assassinated—or had vanished. Soviet agents were frequently blamed for these killings and disappearances.

Tresca, an American anarchist who often gave speeches, blamed Mink for his friend's disappearance. (Anarchists believe that all forms of government are oppressive and should be abolished.) Mink, who was believed to be an agent in the Soviet Union's secret police, had been seen in New York at the time of Poyntz's disappearance. It was not an outrageous suggestion. Mink had previously been openly accused of arranging the assassinations of two Italian anarchists. Tresca was not alone in accusing Mink of playing a role in Poyntz's disappearance. Benjamin Gitlow, a former prominent member of the ACP, also accused Mink. Tresca was assassinated in 1943.

Sources for Further Reading

Johnpoll, Bernard K. and Harvey Klehr, eds. *Biographical Dictionary of the American Left*. Westport, CT: Greenwood Press, 1986, pp. 317–318.

Leonard, John William, ed. *Woman's Who's Who of America*. Detroit: Gale, 1976, p. 659.

Nash, Jay Robert. *The Encyclopedia of World Crime*. Wilmette, IL: Crime Books, 1990, p. 2495.

Seth, Ronald. *Encyclopedia of Espionage*. London, England: New English Library, 1975, pp. 488–491.

Ethel and Julius Rosenberg

Ethel Rosenberg: 1915-1953
Julius Rosenberg: 1918-1953

Ethel and Julius Rosenberg were convicted of conspiracy to commit espionage for their supposed roles in passing atomic secrets to the Soviets. The fact that they were convicted on circumstantial evidence, and the resulting severity of their sentences, emphasizes the seriousness of the two greatest fears of the 1950s: communism and the atomic bomb.

A COMMUNIST COUPLE

Julius Rosenberg grew up in a poor and strictly religious Jewish family in New York. Although he had been trained to become a rabbi, he became involved in radical politics by the time he was a teenager. In 1936, he met his future wife, Ethel Greenglass, at a New Year's Eve benefit for the International Seamen's Union. Greenglass was a politically active New York native who helped organize labor groups. Born on New York's Lower East Side, she was the only daughter of Austrian-born Tessie Felt Greenglass and Barnet Greenglass, a Russian immigrant who repaired sewing machines from the basement of the family's tenement. Ethel had three brothers: an older half-brother, Samuel, and two younger brothers, Bernard and David.

Rosenberg, a student in electrical engineering at City College of New York, joined the Young Communist League in 1934. After he graduated from college in 1939, the couple married and moved into a small Brooklyn apartment. Rosenberg found a civilian (non-military) job as an engineer inspector for the U.S.

Army Signal Corps. For a while, both Rosenbergs were active participants in the Communist Party. They brought Ethel's brother David into the party and, later, David's wife, Ruth.

Rosenberg lost his position at Signal Corps in early 1945, for alleged (supposed) communist activities. Later that year, he took a job with Emerson Radio—and was soon laid off. Next, he attempted to start a non-union machine-shop business in Manhattan with his brother-in-law, David Greenglass. The business failed and both partners lost money.

In the mean time, Rosenberg had severed contacts with the Communist Party and stopped subscribing to the *Daily Worker*, a party publication. But he did not abandon his communist activities. In 1943, Rosenberg had been recruited by Aleksander Feklisov, a KGB (Soviet intelligence) officer, to spy for the Soviet Union. He began by stealing manuals for radar tubes and proximity fuses (a device that substantially increases the ability of air force fighters to shoot down enemy planes), and by the late 1940s, had two apartments set up as microfilm laboratories. He had become the coordinator of a large spy network involved in atomic, industrial, and military espionage.

A JELL-O BOX TOP

Greenglass was stationed as an assistant foreman at a machine shop in Los Alamos, New Mexico, where the lens mechanism for the atomic bomb (A-bomb) was developed. While Greenglass was on leave from his duties in Los Alamos, the Rosenbergs reportedly convinced him to provide them with secret drawings. The materials were to be passed to a spy in Los Alamos.

Later, Rosenberg gave Ruth Greenglass the torn half of a Jell-O box top, with instructions to deliver it to her husband in Los Alamos. In June 1945, a man visited Ruth and David Greenglass at their home in Los Alamos. He presented the second half of the Jell-O box top and said that he came from Julius. That man was Harry Gold, a Swiss immigrant who worked in Philadelphia, Pennsylvania, as a chemist.

In August 1949, American officials were stunned to learn that the Soviets had tested an atomic bomb. The A-bomb, which had been developed by scientists in the United States, was considered to be a national secret. The news that the Soviets had developed their own atomic weapon caused American officials to suspect an intelligence leak. It appeared that the Soviets had been able to create an atomic weapon ahead of schedule because they had obtained secret information about the U.S. atomic project.

THE DOMINO EFFECT

The U.S. government immediately set out to find the source of leaked information. A network of espionage soon came to light. First, Russian defector Igor Gouzenko informed British intelligence of the activities of a German-born scientist named Klaus Fuchs. A high-level atomic scientist on the Manhattan Project (the code name for the project to develop an atomic bomb), Fuchs had passed atomic secrets to the Soviets. In February 1950, Fuchs was arrested in England. He confessed after Soviet messages that implicated (involved) him were decoded. Partly due to Fuchs's confession, Harry Gold was arrested the following May. He admitted to receiving atomic data, which he passed to a Russian contact. He also identified the source of that information as David Greenglass

On June 15, 1950, Greenglass confessed to the Federal Bureau of Investigation (FBI) that he had passed information about the atomic bomb project to Harry Gold. He also claimed that he had handed over documents to his twenty-six-year-old sister, Ethel, and her husband, Julius. The next day FBI agents showed up at the Rosenbergs' apartment.

The Rosenbergs were listening to a radio broadcast of the *Lone Ranger* with their two young sons, Michael and Robert, when someone knocked on the door to their Manhattan apartment. Twelve FBI agents entered the apartment and arrested Julius Rosenberg as a spy. Unlike Fuchs, Gold, and Greenglass,

The world protests

The Rosenbergs' death sentence caused world-wide controversy. Scientist Albert Einstein and French president Vincent Auriol were among those who publicly urged the United States government to offer the couple clemency (mercy). After the Rosenbergs were put to death, French novelist Jean-Paul Sartre, a Nobel prize winner, called the case "A legal lynching which smears with blood a whole nation." In a form of protest, Spanish artist Pablo Picasso drew a sketch of the couple sitting in a pair of electric chairs holding hands.

Agent Gold

Harry Gold was born in Berne, Switzerland, to Russian parents. As a child, he moved to the United States with his family. The family, whose name was Golodnotzky, took the more American-sounding name of Gold. In the U.S., Harry Gold received a college education and technical training. A communist sympathizer, he was recruited by agents from the Soviet Union in 1935. Gold agreed to work as a Soviet spy and eventually specialized in stealing industrial chemical secrets. Gold was chosen by his Soviet superior, Anatoli Yakovlev, to act as a courier (a person who transports goods) for Klaus Fuchs. Fuchs provided vital information about atomic bomb preparations in the U.S. After Fuchs named Gold as a go-between, Gold was arrested. Tried for conspiracy, he was sentenced to thirty years' imprisonment.

Rosenberg protested that he was innocent. He told reporters that the FBI's story was "fantastic—something like kids hear on the *Lone Ranger* program."

THE NOOSE TIGHTENS

Rosenberg told the agents that his brother-in-law was a liar. His refusal to cooperate convinced the FBI that he was hiding something and that they were about to uncover an important spy ring. Intensifying and broadening its investigation, the FBI found Max Elitcher, who told agents that Rosenberg had approached him various times during the mid-1940s, attempting to obtain classified information that Elitcher had access to through his work with air force and navy contracts. The FBI felt it now had its case.

Ethel Rosenberg was called to appear before a grand jury (a group of people that decide if enough evidence exists to warrant a trial) on August 2, 1950. Nine days later she was called to appear again. She was arrested and sent to the Women's House of Detention in New York City. On August 17, 1950, a federal grand jury formally charged the Rosenbergs with conspiracy to commit espionage. Lack of direct evidence kept them from being charged with the more serious crime, treason. Their trial began on March 6, 1951. Morton Sobell, a former college classmate of Rosenberg's who had been implicated by Elitcher as an accomplice (someone who assists in a criminal act), was the third defendant.

A QUESTIONABLE TRIAL

From the start, the trial attracted national attention. Prosecutor Irving Saypol and his assistant, Roy Cohn, decided to keep the scope of the trial as narrow as possible. They set out to simply establish the Rosenbergs' guilt. Exposing their spy ring was a lesser concern. Even so, the trial was punctuated by numerous arrests of spies associated with the Rosenbergs, some of whom appeared in court to testify against them.

Unfair publicity and questionable procedures by Saypol jeopardized the fairness of the trial. Saypol told the jury that "the evidence of the treasonable acts of these three defendants you will find overwhelming"—even though the defendants were not accused of treason. During the trial, Saypol announced in a national news conference that he had secured sworn affidavits (statements) from an old friend of the Rosenbergs, William Perl, which proved the conspiracy beyond any doubt. Saypol decided against putting Perl on the stand, however, when Perl admitted to lying in his affidavits.

GUILTY!

One by one, Greenglass, his wife, Gold, and Elitcher took the stand and testified that the Rosenbergs were involved in a spy ring. Although Elitcher admitted that he never actually passed any documents to Julius Rosenberg, Greenglass damaged the Rosenbergs by testifying that Julius had arranged for him to give Gold the design of an atomic bomb. When Gold testified, he named Anatoli Yakovlev as his contact. This directly tied the Rosenbergs to a known Soviet agent.

The Rosenbergs denied any wrongdoing on their part. When Saypol questioned them about their past association with the Communist Party, they pleaded the Fifth Amendment and refused to answer. (The Fifth Amendment prevents an individual from being forced to offer testimony that may prove his or her guilt in a crime.)

Sobell never took the stand. A large part of Saypol's case rested on Sobell's flight to Mexico and Julius Rosenberg's attempt to obtain a passport after Fuch's confession. The defendants' attempted flight made them appear guilty in the eyes of the jury. After about eighteen hours of deliberating (deciding innocence or guilt), the jury found all three defendants guilty of conspiracy.

"WORSE THAN MURDER"

Judge Irving Kaufman had the responsibility of sentencing the Rosenbergs. Although the defendants had not been convicted of treason, the judge appeared to pass sentence on unproven acts and an uncharged crime. Announcing that the crime was "worse than murder," he explained that "putting into the hands of the Russians the A-bomb has already caused, in my opinion, the communist aggression in Korea, with its resultant casualties exceeding fifty thousand and who knows but what that millions more innocent people may pay the price of your treason." (The Korean War, 1950–1953, was a conflict between communist and non-communist powers.) The Espionage Act of 1917 gave the judge the power to impose the death sentence. On April 5, 1951, Kaufman sentenced the Rosenbergs to die in the electric chair—a sentence more fitting a treason conviction than the lesser charge of espionage. Sobell received a sentence of thirty years in prison.

INTERNATIONAL PROTESTS

The Rosenbergs unsuccessfully appealed their convictions for two years, eventually taking their case to the U.S. Supreme Court. Meanwhile, the public interest in their case reached international proportions. Many people protested the hysteria (excessive panic) of the trial and the extreme harshness of the punishment. Demonstrators urged the government to commute (to reduce it to a lesser sentence) the Rosenbergs' death sentence. Supreme Court justice William O. Douglas, issued a temporary stay (postponement) of execution.

Some supporters were against the idea of executing a woman. Others maintained that Ethel, who knew of her husband's work, but was not directly responsible for espionage, had been condemned to death as a means to pressure Julius to reveal the identities of other spies. Some protesters believed

that the Rosenbergs had been falsely accused by Greenglass and then framed by the government. Many felt the Rosenbergs were being persecuted (unfairly harassed) because they were Jewish (although both the prosecuting attorney and the judge were Jewish).

The Rosenbergs were held in Sing Sing prison in New York for two years. The institution's only woman prisoner, Ethel was kept in what amounted to solitary confinement throughout her imprisonment. The couple were allowed one weekly visit with each another—with a wire screen between them. On June 16, 1953, Ethel wrote to President Dwight D. Eisenhower asking him to grant them their lives. She addressed him as an "affectionate grandfather," "sensitive artist," and "devoutly religious man."

February 23, 1953. Police watch to see that there is no clash between protesters seeking clemency for the Rosenbergs (left) and those picketers, like the man in front, who favor their executions.

Executed for espionage

Ethel and Julius Rosenberg were the first Americans to be executed for espionage. Ethel was the second woman in the history of the United States to be put to death. A woman named Mary Surratt, who had been involved in the assassination of President Abraham Lincoln, was the first American woman to be executed.

Ethel's pleas fell on deaf ears. Eisenhower maintained that reducing their sentences would only encourage future spies. On June 18, 1953, there were demonstrations in support of the couple in Paris, France, and New York City. The following evening, shortly before 8:00 P.M., the Rosenbergs were electrocuted in Sing Sing prison. Both died refusing to confess. In one of the many letters Ethel Rosenberg wrote in prison, she told her sons, "Always remember that we were innocent and could not wrong our conscience." Recent studies of the Rosenbergs' activities, however, show that the evidence against them was overwhelming.

Sources for Further Reading

Arms, Thomas S. *Encyclopedia of the Cold War.* New York: Facts on File, 1994, p. 491.

Cohen, Jacob. "The Rosenberg File: What Do We Really Know about the Rosenbergs and the Case Against Them?" *National Review* (July 19, 1993), p. 48+.

"Espionage." *Time* (July 31, 1950), pp. 12–13.

Gertz, Bill. "Early Cold War Spies Exposed." *Insight on the News* (August 7, 1995), p. 35.

Nash, Jay Robert. *Spies: A Narrative Encyclopedia of Dirty Deeds and Double Dealing from Biblical Times to Today.* New York: M. Evans, 1997, pp. 428–430.

Radosh, Ronald. "Final Verdict: The KGB Convicts the Rosenbergs." *The New Republic* (April 7, 1997), pp. 12–13.

Radosh, Ronald. "The Venona Files." *The New Republic* (August 7, 1995), p. 25+.

Seth, Ronald. *Encyclopedia of Espionage.* London England: New English Library, 1975, pp. 597–599.

Sicherman, Barbara, Carol Hurd Green, et al., eds. *Notable American Women: The Modern Period* Cambridge, MA: Belknap Press. 1980, pp. 601–604.

Elizabeth Van Lew

Born: October 17, 1818
Died: September 25, 1900

During the Civil War, Elizabeth Van Lew lived in the heart of the Confederacy (southern states that supported slavery). A Northerner by birth, however, she was sympathetic with the Union (northern states that opposed slavery) cause. Spying for the Northern army, she became one of the Union's most valuable sources of military intelligence.

OPPOSED TO SLAVERY

The Van Lews were a prominent Virginia family. Elizabeth's father, a native of Jamaica, New York, had moved to Richmond to start a hardware business. During a trip to Philadelphia, Pennsylvania, he met a woman named Elizabeth Baker—the daughter of Hillary Baker, the city's former mayor. The couple returned to Richmond, where they were married in St. John's Church. Some time after Elizabeth was born, the Van Lews had a son, John.

As a young girl, Van Lew led a privileged existence that included tutors, dance instructors, music teachers, and riding lessons. She was sent to private school in Philadelphia, Pennsylvania, where she lived with her mother's family. At a time when Northern and Southern states were increasingly divided over the question of slavery, the Southern-born Van Lew was exposed to an environment where slavery was openly condemned. After she returned home from Philadelphia, she convinced her father to free the family's fifteen slaves. And she did not stop there. She convinced her family to purchase other slaves in order to free them. Van Lew sent one of the former slaves—Mary Elizabeth Bowser—to school in Philadelphia.

LIFE IN CHURCH HILL

The Van Lews lived in a large white mansion, in an area of Richmond known as Church Hill. The family entertained Richmond society at their home—hosting garden parties in the terraced gardens, horseback rides in the country, and elaborate formal balls. They received many prominent guests, including poet and short story writer Edgar Allen Poe, who read his eerie poem, "The Raven," aloud in the family's library.

Sometime around 1855, Van Lew's brother, John married. When their father died in 1860, he left behind a substantial fortune. John took over the family's hardware business, and Van Lew, who never married, continued to live at the family's mansion with her mother and a number of servants.

CIVIL WAR

On April 12, 1861, the conflict between Northern and Southern states erupted into civil war. While their neighbors wholeheartedly embraced the Confederate cause, the Van Lews openly stated that they supported the Northern abolitionists who fought to do away with slavery. (The eleven states of the Confederacy wanted to secede, or withdraw, from the Union.) It was a daring move. Because of their beliefs, Van Lew and her mother were outcasts in their community. They were shunned on the street and publicly ridiculed. Accused of being traitors, they received threats against their lives. Threatening messages were posted on the front door of their house, and they were warned that their home would be set on fire during the night.

In spite of resistance from Confederate officials, Van Lew received permission to visit jails where Northern soldiers were imprisoned. A pass allowed her to visit prisoners and to bring them books to cheer them up, clothing, and food to supplement their meager diets. She also tended to sick prisoners—one of whom later remembered that she had given him grapes to eat when he was burning with a fever. During the four years of the Civil War, Van Lew visited Northern soldiers at the Confederate prisons of Belle Isle, Castle Goodwin, Castle Thunder, and Libby Prison. At some point during that time, she became a spy for the North.

A UNION SPY

Because she was able to travel freely through Confederate prisons, Van Lew had access to inside information about the Southern war effort. The information she received came from a number of sources. Northern soldiers gathered valuable information about the enemy's troops as they were transported to prison. They saw where the troops were positioned—and they counted men, horses, and weapons. They also took into account the soldiers' state of mind—something that could affect their performance on the battlefield. In prison, the soldiers counted horses, men, cannons and weapons that left for battle. And they listened to prison guards who let slip details about Confederate battle plans—sometimes even baiting their captors into providing information about enemy troops. All this information was passed to Van Lew, who, as far as the prison guards were concerned, was nothing more than a harmless woman who sympathized with the Northerners.

But Van Lew was far from harmless to the Confederate cause. After collecting vital military intelligence from Northern prisoners, she relayed the information—in coded reports—to Union officers in the North. She accomplished this by forwarding messages through a network of five posts—the first of which was the Van Lew family's mansion on Church Hill in Richmond. To relay messages she used a number of spies, including servants who carried messages in their shoes. Some reports were hidden in baskets of fruit or eggs that were carried by servants from one location to another. Others were sewn into clothing by a dressmaker who worked for Van Lew. Conveyed through common daily activities, Van Lew's messages reportedly reached

Don't judge a book by its cover

The Van Lew home contained an enormous library filled with books. When she visited imprisoned Union soldiers, she often brought bags full of books for them to read. But the books did not simply help the prisoners pass time. After Van Lew returned home with books she had lent to prisoners, she carefully examined them. Often she found marks over letters and lightly underlined words. After she pieced together the messages, she compiled reports which she forwarded to Union officers.

Secret code and invisible ink

Van Lew knew better than to attempt to pass information to Northern leaders herself. She used a network of spies—many of whom were loyal servants who relayed information during their daily routines. But not all her spies were in her employ. An unknown associate described how she relayed some of her messages through enemy lines:

> She had many ways of sending this information through the Rebel lines; sometimes she would send it by persons who were comparative strangers to her. In that case, she wrote out her cipher [code] in invisible ink, a liquid which looked like water and could be brought out by milk and heat.

(The unsigned note was found among Van Lew's papers, which have been preserved. It was written in pencil on a piece of ledger paper—in handwriting that is not Van Lew's.)

Northern leaders within twenty-four hours.

ESCAPED PRISONERS

Van Lew did not limit her activities to spying for the North. Appalled by the conditions that the Union prisoners lived, she helped soldiers who escaped by hiding them in the secret room in the family's mansion.

In January 1864, Van Lew learned that all Union prisoners in Richmond were scheduled to be relocated to Andersonville—a hellish prison further south, in Georgia. On January 30—using her code name, "Mr. Babcock"—Van Lew relayed the following message to Brigadier General Ben Butler:

> It is intended to remove to Georgia very soon, all the Federal [Union] prisoners; butchers and bakers to go at once. They are already notified and selected. Quaker [one of Van Lew's spies] knows this to be true. . . . Beware of rash [hasty] councils. This I send to you by direction of all your friends. No attempt should be made with less than 30,000 cavalry [soldiers on horseback], with 10,000 to 15,000 infantry [foot soldiers] to support them, amounting to all 40,000 or 45,000 troops. Do not underrate their strength or desperation.

The following month, Union soldiers organized a raid to free Union soldiers imprisoned in Richmond. One unit was organized to liberate the prisoners at Belle Isle. The unit was led by twenty-one-year-old Colonel Ulric Dahlgren—the youngest colonel in the Union army. But as Dahlgren's men approached Richmond, they were encircled by Confederate troops. The young colonel was killed and the raiding party destroyed.

Van Lew did not abandon her efforts to help imprisoned Union soldiers. In the winter of 1864, one hundred and nine Union inmates escaped from Libby Prison by burrowing through a fifty-eight-foot tunnel. Union officers credited Van Lew with planning and assisting the escape. The Richmond newspapers also blamed Van Lew for the daring escape. One newspaper, the Richmond *Times Dispatch,* published the following account of Van Lew's role:

> Following Miss Van Lew's instructions, the fugitives, led by Colonel Streight [Colonel Abel Streight, a Union officer], scurried to a number of unfrequented spots about the closely guarded city, where her agents met them and placed them in temporary shelters, providing them with clothes—farmers, laborers, civilians and women. When their escape was discovered alarm guns were sounded and churchbells rung. Many were quickly recaptured but those who followed her [Van Lew's] instructions, safely passed through the lines. . . .

Union general Ulysses S. Grant.

STARS AND STRIPES FOREVER

By April 1865, it was clear that the South was losing the war. Confederate troops retreated to Richmond from territories that had been taken over by Union soldiers. Amid rumors that the city would be evacuated (cleared of people), the residents of Richmond watched helplessly as the city fell into riot. Mobs overwhelmed the city's police, looting stores and setting fires. Van Lew wrote in her diary:

> The city was burning. Our beautiful flour mills, the largest in the world and the prize of our city, were destroyed. Square after square of stores, dwelling homes, factories, warehouses, banks, hotels, bridges, all wrapped in fire—all filled the city with clouds of smoke as incense from the land for its

Letitia Van Lew Smith

Van Lew was not the only spy in the family. Her father's great-aunt, Letitia Van Lew Smith, was a hero of the American Revolution (1775–1783). She carried messages to General George Washington (1732–1799) in New York. Captured by the British, she was imprisoned in an old church that was used as a jail.

deliverance. What a moment. Avenging wrath appeased in flames!

As Richmond burned, Van Lew raised a twenty-by-nine-foot flag from her home on Church Hill. It was the Union flag—whose thirty-four stars represented the states of the Union *including* the eleven states of the Confederacy. It was the first such flag to be raised in Richmond since 1861. Hours later, the city surrendered to Union commander Ulysses S. Grant (1822–1885). The war was over on April 9, 1865, when the Confederate States of America formally surrendered. The last of the Confederate troops surrendered at Shreveport, Louisiana.

AN OUTCAST

Grant became president in 1869. Fifteen days after his inauguration, his first official act was to appoint Van Lew as postmaster of Richmond. Van Lew, who had spent her family's fortune in her wartime efforts, was awarded a yearly salary of $4,000. But the appointment did not change the way the people of Richmond felt toward Van Lew. She continued to be treated as a traitor. When Grant's term in office ended, she lost the postmastership—and the small salary she depended on. Eventually she was forced to accept a small pension from the family of one of the Union soldiers she had helped during the war.

Having outlived her mother, brother, and even her two nieces, Van Lew died on September 25, 1900, at the age of seventy-two. She was buried two days later at the family plot in Shockhoe Cemetery. Two years later, a 2,000-pound grave marker arrived at the cemetery. In the center was an inscription that read:

Elizabeth Van Lew

1818–1900

She risked everything that is dear to man—friends, fortune, comfort, health, life itself, all for the one absorbing desire of her heart, that slavery be abolished and the Union be preserved.

This Boulder From the Capitol Hill in Boston, is a tribute from her Massachusetts friends.

Sources for Further Reading

Horan, James. *Desperate Women.* New York: Putnam, 1952, pp. 125–168.

Kulkan, Mary-Ellen. *Her Way: Biographies of Women for Young People.* Chicago: American Library Association, 1976, p. 289.

Seth, Ronald. *Encyclopedia of Espionage.* London, England: New English Library, 1975, pp. 358–360.

Umlauf, Hana. *The Goodhousekeeping Woman's Almanac.* New York: Newspaper Enterprise Association, 1977, p. 455.

Swindlers

W*ebster's Unabridged Dictionary* (10th ed.) defines the verb *swindle*: "to obtain money or property by fraud or deceit." In short, swindlers practice the fine art of fooling people—for personal gain. Why did Clifford Irving write a phony biography of reclusive billionaire Howard Hughes? What made Cassie Chadwick pretend that she was the illegitimate daughter of steel magnate Andrew Carnegie? What made Joseph "Yellow Kid" Weil hire actors to pose as bank employees? The answer to each of these questions is simple: they did it for the money—and maybe, just a little, for the thrill of it. Meet the swindlers who perpetrated hoaxes, set scams in motion, and otherwise bilked their victims out of money, property—and in some cases, pride.

Cattle Kate
(Ella Watson)

Born: c. 1861
Died: 1888
AKA: Kate Maxwell

Caught in the battles between cattle barons and small ranchers, Ella Watson was a cattle rustler who paid for her thefts with her life.

HEADING WEST

The oldest of ten children, Watson was born in Lebanon, Kansas. Her father was a wealthy farmer. When she was about sixteen years old, Watson ran away to join the carnival in St. Louis, Missouri. When the family found her, she was forced to return to Lebanon. At the age of eighteen she married a middle-aged widower, who was also a farmer. Less than two years later, she left her husband, who had been unfaithful.

Watson headed for Kansas City, Missouri, where she worked as a maid for a prominent banker. After a brief stay there, she left Missouri for Red Cloud, Nebraska, where she worked as a dancer and saloon hostess. After about one year in Red Cloud, she headed for Denver, Colorado, where she spent several months. Next she headed to Wyoming, where she worked for a while in a Cheyenne dance hall. She finally landed in Rawlins, Wyoming—in the middle of cattle country.

A dark devil in the saddle

When Ella Watson arrived in Sweetwater Valley in the Wyoming Territory, cowboys and ranchers outnumbered the area's women residents. A few months after she arrived in the valley, the *Cheyenne Mail Leader* published a disapproving description of the unconventional woman known as "Cattle Kate:"

She was one of the most unforgettable women on the range. She was of robust [strong] physique, a dark devil in the saddle, handy with a six shooter and a Winchester [rifle], and an expert with the branding iron and lariat [rope]. Where she came from no one knows, but all agree, she was a holy terror. She rode straddle [not side-saddle, as women of that era were expected to], always had a vicious bronc[o] [wild horse] for a mount, and seemed never to tire of dashing across the range . . . .

THE BIG PLAINS OF WYOMING

The territory of Wyoming was created in 1868 out of sections of the Dakota, Idaho, Oregon, and Utah territories. The name "Wyoming" came from a Delaware Indian expression meaning "at the big plains." The plains (grasslands) of Wyoming provided ideal conditions for raising cattle, which were left to roam on open ranges.

The Homestead Act, enacted in 1860, was meant to bring settlers into the area. Under the Act, individuals were permitted to claim up to 160 acres of public land. After working the land for five years, they could register the land and claim the title (proof of ownership). If a man wanted to claim ownership in less than five years, he was required to work the land for six months. At the end of that time, he was offered the option to purchase the claim at the cost of $1.25 per acre.

MOUNTING TENSION

Because Wyoming was ideally suited to raising cattle, the Homestead Act was abused by greedy cattle barons (cattle ranchers that controlled large areas of land). Staking illegal claims, they established enormous ranches in the area. They claimed vast areas of government land, making it very difficult for individual homesteaders to stake their claims—and even more difficult for them to raise cattle. Many of the cattle barons were absentee land owners who rarely—if ever—showed up to survey their claims. Some were the heirs (recipients) of English fortunes, such as the Powder River Land and Cattle Company, which controlled 100,000 acres and 50,000 head of cattle. The Scottish-owned Swan Company consisted of 500,000 acres of land and more than 100,000 cattle. Independent ranchers, on the other hand, owned only a couple of hundred head of cattle.

The large cattle empires and small homesteaders soon became rivals. They clashed over land and water use, and each accused the other of stealing livestock. Many of the large ranches freely plundered the settlers' herds. With the assistance of the Wyoming Stock Growers' Association—a collection of wealthy cattle men and powerful politicians—the ranchers passed the "Maverick Law." The law enabled members of the association to claim any unbranded calf that was found on his property. But the association offered an unusual definition of "unbranded" stock. Any calf that did not have the brand of one of the cattle outfits in the Stock Growers' Association was considered to be unbranded— even if it was marked with the brand of an independent owner. The Maverick Law gave association members the right to claim a small rancher's herd as property of the association.

Many of the small herd owners responded by stealing cattle from the large cattle outfits who, in their view, had stolen government lands. They then rebranded the cattle, and claimed them as their own. Angered by their losses, the cattle barons hired detectives to spy on the small ranchers—and to catch rustlers.

Handy with a gun and iron

Stolen cattle were kept in the corral next to Cattle Kate's cabin. She was said to be handy with a gun and a branding iron, and took an active role in the rustling.

CATTLE KATE'S CORRAL

Somewhere around the time of Watson's arrival in Johnson County, a general store and saloon owner named James Averill had begun to speak out against the cattle barons. In letters to the editor of the *Casper Weekly Mail,* he called them "land-grabbers" and "land mad men." He complained that there were "four men alone claiming the Sweetwater [a river in Sweetwater Valley] seventy-five miles from its mouth [where a river begins]." He urged lawmakers to alter the area's irrigation (watering system) so that farms would thrive. In short, Averill became the hero of the independent ranchers—and the enemy of the cattle empires.

Shortly after Averill became the unofficial leader of the smaller ranchers, he met Watson at a saloon in Rawlins, and

The Johnson County War

The lynching of James Averill and Ella Watson—and the local government's failure to punish their killers—divided the residents of Johnson County. Those who sympathized with the large cattle barons felt that the vigilantes deserved to have been set free. Independent ranch owners, on the other hand, felt that Averill and Watson were innocent victims whose killers had gone unpunished.

After the six vigilantes were acquitted of the double hanging, the area's small independent ranchers increased their efforts to rustle cattle from the stockgrowers' empire. And the large cattle barons, in turn, continued to seize cattle from the independent ranchers. Tensions mounted until April 1892, when forty-one vigilantes—who called themselves "Regulators"—spread through Johnson County on a mission to kill many of the area's rustlers. Made up of Wyoming cattlemen and their detectives, the Regulators also included twenty-one Texas gunmen who had been hired to break-up the independent ranchers.

The Regulators killed two known rustlers, Nick Ray and Nate Champion. A third man escaped and informed William "Red" Angus, the Johnson County Sheriff. An enemy of the Stock Growers' Association, Angus had been elected by the area's numerous independent ranchers. On April 10, Sheriff Angus and some three hundred men headed to the TA Ranch, where the Regulators were hiding. A shoot-out followed, but to little effect. On April 13, the battle ended suddenly when U.S. Cavalry troops arrived from Fort McKinney. After a ceasefire (when both sides agree to stop fighting) was arranged, the Regulators surrendered. Of the forty-six Regulators only one was killed and none were punished for the deaths of Champion and Ray.

asked her to travel with him to Sweetwater Valley. He set her up on a homestead (working farm) within one mile of his saloon and hired workers to build a single-story log cabin on the property. He also sent a fourteen-year-old boy named Gene Crowder to help her take care of a couple of cows. Once Watson was established, he sent men who frequented his saloon to visit her. Watson's home soon became the site of an illegal business. Working as a prostitute, she sometimes received livestock as payment, for which she became known as "Cattle Kate."

Many of the animals Watson received had been stolen from the herds of the cattle barons. What's more, by the spring of 1889, Averill had organized a group of men to roundup the mavericks in the large ranchers' herds. The stolen cattle were then branded with Watson's mark and kept in her corral. Next, they were driven to a ranch used by rustlers and then to the railroad, where they were boarded onto trains to be shipped to slaughterhouses in the Midwest. The plan seemed to be foolproof. If the ranchers found Watson with stolen cattle in her corral, she could claim that she had received them as payment—and that she had nothing to do with their theft.

SOMETHING AWFUL

Angered by the repeated thefts, members of the Stock Growers' Association took the law into their own hands. On July 20, 1889, a powerful rancher named Albert J. Bothwell organized a group of association members to put a stop to Watson and Averill's rustling. Having lost a battle with Averill over his right to fence off government land, Bothwell had become the rustlers' most recent target. Adding to his desire to put Averill and Watson out of business was the fact that their homesteads were on land that Bothwell had claimed illegally.

A group of vigilantes (self-appointed doers of justice) kidnapped Averill and Watson and headed for a canyon about four miles from Watson's cabin. Averill's foreman, Jim Buchanan, had seen the kidnapping, and followed them to the south bank of the Sweetwater River. The two captives, who had been ordered to stand on boulders in the rock-strewn gully, seemed to take the kidnapping lightly. They reportedly insulted the ranchers and laughed at their threats.

Buchanan fired on the vigilantes. Outnumbered, he managed only to anger the men further. Tying a noose around the necks of their two victims, the vigilantes hanged Averill and Watson from the branch of a cottonwood tree. Buchanan had witnessed the lynchings from his hiding place and later described the scene:

> The murderers divided into two groups. Each group took the other end of the lasso and slowly pulled Jim and Kate into the air. Their necks weren't broken by a fall. They were strangled. Kate was the worst and took the longest. She kicked so hard her beaded moc-

casins flew through the air. . . . She struggled for about fifteen minutes before she became dead. After she died, I looked at Jim and he was already dead.

The *Casper Weekly Mail*—which had once printed Averill's complaints against the ranchers—reported the hangings: "A point overlooked by the amateur executioners was tying the limbs of their victims. The kicking and the writhing of these two people was something awful. . . ."

THE CORONER'S VERDICT

Buchanan eventually found his way to a ranch, where he reported the lynchings. (He later claimed to have gotten lost on his way back from the site of the murders, but some historians think it is more likely that he had taken time to decide whether he should risk his own life by reporting the incident.) The rancher then rode fifty miles to the town of Casper to summon the sheriff. On his way there, he informed several ranchers of the double-murder.

With Buchanan to direct him, the sheriff rode with a posse (a group of people with legal authority to capture criminals) of independent ranchers to the spot where Averill and Watson had been killed. According to the *Casper Weekly Mail,* they found "the bodies swaying to and fro by the gentle breeze which wafted the sweet odor of the prairie flowers across the plains." An inquest (inquiry) into the killings was held. Based on the testimony of Buchanan, Crowder, and another employee of Averill's, the coroner's jury ruled that Averill and Watson had died by hanging—and that several ranchers, including Bothwell, were responsible. Six ranchers were charged with murder and held in the Casper jail.

The lynching party was tried in Rawlins before the town's only judge—who happened to be employed by a Cheyenne law firm responsible for handling legal matters for the Stock Growers' Association. The judge set bail for each of the defendants at $5,000. And he allowed each one to sign another's bond. In short, he allowed them to go free.

CASE DISMISSED

Bothwell and the other posse members were summoned to court on July 26. As they awaited trial before the Carbon County Grand Jury, the county coroner wrote a letter to the governor of Wyoming. He claimed that the case would not be treated fairly because the legal officials—as well as Governor Warren—were "interested parties." That is, because of their involvement with the association, they would not be capable of rendering (giving) a fair verdict. Governor Warren and the prosecutor's office insisted that the ranchers would be given a fair trial. But the coroner was suspicious of their notion of fair play. He told a reporter, "By fair trial they mean that none of the accused ever will spend a day in jail. All state officials, legislature [lawmakers], even the governor, have been corrupted by the association."

And he was probably right. Of the six defendants, only Bothwell was indicted (formally charged). The grand jury released the other vigilantes because of a lack of evidence against them. Because his bond had been paid, Bothwell remained free until his trial. By mid-December, all the prosecution witnesses disappeared. Gene Crowder was found dead, and then Jim Buchanan vanished. (Buchanan's remains—which were found near Casper four years later—were identified by a tie fastener that he always wore.) And a third witness, who had seen the kidnapping, was mysteriously shot and killed.

With no witnesses to testify against Bothwell, the case was dismissed for lack of evidence. But the double-hanging did not go unnoticed. A newspaper that supported the independent ranchers announced "If it's lynching they want, two can play the game." The small ranchers grew increasingly resentful of the cattle barons, and by April 1892, the conflict erupted into the Johnson County War. The lynching of Watson and Averill is considered to have been a major contributing factor to the tensions that sparked that war.

CHEAP LAND

Sometime after he was cleared of the murder charges, Bothwell contested (challenged) the homestead claims of Averill and

Watson. Because their taxes had not been paid, Bothwell was allowed to purchase their land for a total of $14.93. Bothwell had Watson's cabin taken apart and reassembled on his ranch, where he used it as an icehouse.

Sources for Further Reading

The American West, A Cultural Encyclopedia, Volume 5. Danbury, CT: Grolier Educational Corp., 1995, pp. 833–837.

Horan, James. *Desperate Women.* New York: G. P. Putnam's Sons, 1952, pp. 227–241.

Lamar, Howard Roberts. *The Reader's Encyclopedia of the American West.* New York: Harper & Row, 1977, p. 182.

McLoughlin, Denis. *Wild and Woolly, An Encyclopedia of the Old West.* New York: Doubleday, 1975, pp. 542–543.

Nash, Jay Robert. *Bloodletters and Badmen.* New York: M. Evans, 1973, pp. 595–596.

Ward, Geoffrey. *The West, An Illustrated History.* Boston: Little, Brown, 1996, pp. 368–370.

Cassie Chadwick

(Elizabeth Bigley)

Born: 1859
Died: October 10, 1907
AKA: Constance Cassandra Chadwick,
Cassie L. Hoover, Lydia D. Scott,
Lydia Springsteen, Lydia de Vere

As a young woman and well into middle age, Cassie Chadwick used her elegant manner and acting ability to pull off confidence schemes that earned her thousands of dollars—and a prison term.

FORGERY AND FRAUD

Chadwick was born Elizabeth Bigley, near London, Ontario, Canada. The daughter of a railway worker, she was from a poor family. Chadwick began her career as a con woman and swindler (person who cheats people out of money) when she was still in her teens. At the age of sixteen, she attempted to forge a check for $5,000. (Forgers pass off fake checks as real. Sometimes they forge, or fake, the signature of somebody else. Other times they write checks drawn on accounts that don't exist.) Caught forging the check, Chadwick was not jailed because the court found her temporarily insane.

When she was twenty-five years old, she married W. S. Springsteen, a physician. Using his name as a reference and his property as collateral (property that is pledged to protect the lender), she borrowed money. Springsteen eventually had to sell his home in order to repay Chadwick's debts. One year after they were married, the couple divorced. Chadwick then moved

Cassie Chadwick's extravagant diningroom at her home in Cleveland. Some of her silverware was studded with rubies.

to Toledo, Ohio, where she started a business as a fortune teller named Lydia de Vere. She claimed that she could make sick men healthy—and poor men wealthy. Chadwick would hire private detectives to find out what they could about her clients. Armed with embarrassing information that her clients wanted to keep secret, she collected thousands of dollars by blackmailing her victims. (Blackmail is a form of extortion in which threats are used to gain payment.) After one of her clients threatened to take her to court, Chadwick abandoned her fortune-telling scam. But she soon landed in court anyway. Caught with $20,000 in forged bills, she was convicted of fraud (deliberate deception) and forgery. Although she was sentenced to nine years in prison, she was released in 1897, after serving only three years behind bars.

The Carnegie scam

After she was released Chadwick settled in Cleveland, Ohio, where she adopted the identity of Cassie L. Hoover, a widow. She met and married Dr. Leroy Chadwick, a wealthy and well-respected older man. After they were married, Chadwick threw lavish parties in their stylish home on Euclid Avenue. She also traveled out of town on extravagant trips.

During a trip to New York City, Chadwick set in motion an elaborate scam that involved the famous millionaire Andrew Carnegie. First, Chadwick rented expensive rooms at the exclusive Holland House. There she managed to bump into James Dillon, a Cleveland lawyer who knew her slightly. As far as Dillon knew, their meeting was accidental. But Chadwick had arranged the coincidence. She knew that Dillon was scheduled to be in New York on business and arranged her trip accordingly.

Following their "accidental" meeting, Chadwick asked Dillon to join her on an errand. At Chadwick's instruction, they rode in a coach up Fifth Avenue in a wealthy section of Manhattan. Chadwick ordered the coach to stop in front of a residence, telling the lawyer that she would only be a few minutes. Almost everyone—especially bankers and lawyers—knew that the spacious quarters belonged to the multi-millionaire Andrew Carnegie.

The scam develops

Chadwick knocked at Carnegie's door and was admitted. Posing as a wealthy New Yorker, she pretended that she wanted to check the reference of a maid who claimed to have worked for Carnegie. In order to make her story more believable, she carried a fake letter of application from the make-believe job applicant. The housekeeper informed Chadwick that no such maid had ever worked for Carnegie. When Chadwick acted puzzled, the housekeeper checked her files to find out whether the woman had ever worked at any of the millionaire's other homes. Chadwick thanked the housekeeper for her time and left.

Steel magnate

Andrew Carnegie (1835–1919) earned millions of dollars as a steel magnate (successful business person). Chadwick borrowed hundreds of thousands of dollars by pretending to be the millionaire bachelor's daughter. But Carnegie had no children. What's more, he never even met Chadwick, his supposed daughter.

Spending spree

Cassie Chadwick had no trouble spending thousands of dollars of "borrowed" money. She once reportedly purchased *twenty-seven* grand pianos on credit.

263

Chadwick had no interest in hiring a maid. She simply needed a legitimate reason to gain entry into Carnegie's home—with James Dillon as a witness. When she returned to the carriage, after about a half hour in the Carnegie residence, she "accidentally" dropped a piece of paper in front of the lawyer. Dillon picked up the slip of paper, which was a note promising to pay two million dollars. The note was signed by Andrew Carnegie.

Pretending to be embarrassed that Dillon had seen the promissory note (a note that promises to pay a sum of money), Chadwick "confessed" that she was Carnegie's daughter. This surprised him since Carnegie had never married and had never acknowledged having any children. Chadwick explained that the note was one of many that Carnegie had written to help support his "illegitimate daughter."

Dillon was appalled to hear that Chadwick had several promissory notes signed by Carnegie at home. He convinced her that the notes belonged in the bank, and offered to make arrangements to secure a safe deposit box at one of the banks he represented. Chadwick agreed. After she turned over the forged Carnegie notes, Dillon gave her a receipt for $7 million—without ever checking the authenticity of the notes.

A PAUPER'S END

Chadwick wasted no time using the $7 million receipt to her advantage. With the forged notes as collateral, she borrowed hundreds of thousands of dollars from a number of bankers who were eager to lend her money—for an outrageous fee. Chadwick enjoyed the high life, purchasing expensive gowns, jewelry, paintings, and tapestries (decorative wall hangings). She bought a mansion and carriages and hired servants to work for her.

Chadwick's scheme worked smoothly until she encountered Henry Newton, a Cleveland millionaire. Borrowing $500,000 from Newton, she promised to pay a high interest (a fee that increases over time) on the loan. But Newton was not as trusting as the banks had been. He demanded that Chadwick pay the interest she owed. When Chadwick informed him that she had

Criminal activities caused grief

Following Chadwick's arrest, one newspaper claimed, "The suicide of more than one man, and the impoverishment [poverty] of probably hundreds of families, may be laid at her door."

tens of thousands of dollars worth of promissory notes in the bank, he demanded to see them. The notes—which had never been examined by any of the bankers—were soon discovered to be forgeries. And Andrew Carnegie offered no support. He denied ever having fathered a child and stated "I have never heard of Mrs. Chadwick!"

On December 7, 1904, Chadwick was arrested in the Holland House in New York—where she had first set the scam in motion. She was wearing a money belt stuffed with more than $100,000. Guards escorted her on a train back to Cleveland where she stood trial in March of the following year. She protested that she was an innocent victim who was being persecuted because she was a member of the upper class. But the prosecutor informed the court that Chadwick had a long history of forgeries, frauds, and arrests.

Take a look at this!

Set in New York in the 1980s, *Six Degrees of Separation* (1993) is based on the true story of a young man who claims to be the son of Sidney Poitier, a famous actor. Posing as the young Poitier, David Hampton (played by Will Smith) hustles his way into the lives of a number of wealthy Manhattan couples.

THE END OF A LIFE OF CRIME

The trial was brief. Convicted of six charges of fraud, Chadwick was sentenced to ten years in the Ohio State Penitentiary in Columbus. Dr. Chadwick had his marriage annulled (declared invalid) and moved to Florida. After two and a half years in prison, Cassie died in the penitentiary hospital at the age of forty-eight. Although she was scheduled to be buried in a pauper's (poor person's) grave, an unidentified man reportedly paid to have her body shipped to Canada to be buried.

Sources for Further Reading

De Grave, Kathleen. *Swindler, Spy, Rebel.* Columbia: University of Missouri Press, 1995, pp. 57–73, 144–157.

Dressler, David. "Cleveland's Queen of Society Swindlers." *Coronet* (May 1950), pp. 71–74.

Nash, Jay Robert. *The Encyclopedia of World Crime.* Wilmette, IL: Crime Books, 1990, p. 1506.

Stein, Gordon. *Encyclopedia of Hoaxes.* Detroit: Gale Research, 1993, pp. 33–34.

D. B. Cooper

Active: November 24, 1971

The identity of a man referred to as "D. B. Cooper" has never been discovered. No one knows who he was or what became of him. But on November 24, 1971, he stepped out of a plane and into history as the only hijacker in the United States to escape capture.

THE PASSENGER IN SEAT 15D

On the day before Thanksgiving in 1971, a man who identified himself as Dan Cooper (a journalist erred in reporting his name as "D. B.," and it was never cleared up) was one of thirty-six passengers who boarded Northwest Airlines flight 305. The plane, a Boeing 727, was headed from Portland, Oregon, to Seattle, Washington—a flight that would normally take less than one hour. Shortly after takeoff, when the plane had climbed to thirty thousand feet, the passenger in seat 15D gave one of the two stewardesses a note. The stewardess, Florence Schaffner, did not read the note at first. But the passenger, a middle-aged man who wore a business suit and dark glasses, insisted that she read it.

The hand-written message on the note indicated that the man had a bomb in his briefcase. Further, it said that if he did not receive $200,000 in $20 bills, along with four parachutes, he would blow up the aircraft. When pilot William Scott spoke to the man, he was convinced that the hijacker was serious.

THE HIJACKER'S DEMANDS

The crew contacted Seattle Airport Traffic Control, who in turn contacted the Seattle police. Next the Federal Bureau of Investigation (FBI) was alerted. Soon, the airplane was pursued by two F-106 fighter planes that departed from nearby McChord Air Force Base, and a National Guard helicopter that was flown by Ralph Himmelsbach, a Portland FBI agent and former World War II fighter pilot.

Cooper's conditions made sure that law enforcement authorities did not have time to devise traps. He insisted that the money and parachutes be delivered to Seattle Airport before the plane landed. With only a limited amount of fuel, the plane could not circle the airport indefinitely. This lack of time prevented FBI agents from marking the money so that it could be identified when the hijacker spent it. And by asking for four parachutes, Cooper led authorities to believe that he might not jump alone. They dared not boobytrap (purposely dismantle) any of the parachutes.

Hijacking instructions manual

In 1971, commercial airline hijackings were unheard of in North America. None of the airlines' procedure manuals—which instructed the crew how to handle certain situations—provided any information on how to deal with a hijacking.

With no other hijacking cases to look to, the president of Northwest Airlines had to decide for himself how to handle the Cooper hijacking. His decision became the industry standard for dealing with hijackers: he gave Cooper exactly what he asked for.

FLIGHT INSTRUCTIONS

At 5:40 P.M., after the plane had circled Seattle Airport for almost an hour, the crew was notified that the money and parachutes had arrived and that the aircraft was cleared to land. Cooper allowed all of the passengers and one stewardess to exit the plane. Still on board were one stewardess, the pilot, and two other crew members.

Cooper had the plane refueled for the next leg of its journey. It was to head south, toward Reno, Nevada. And it was to head there slowly, and at a low altitude. Cooper specified that the aircraft was to climb no higher than ten thousand feet. (Any higher would require a parachutist to jump with oxygen.) To make sure that the plane remained below the ten thousand-foot ceiling, Cooper wore an altimeter, a device that measures altitude, on his wrist. He also ordered the crew to leave the cabin unpressurized—probably as a precaution against climbing higher than the safe-jump zone.

Cooper insisted that the plane be flown no faster than 150 knots per hour. By limiting the speed at which the plane traveled, Cooper made sure that the aircraft would be difficult to follow. While the Boeing 727 was capable of maintaining altitude at that speed, many other planes would stall if the pilot tried to maintain such a sluggish (slow) pace. At best, pursuing planes would have to double back and forth to maintain contact with the skyjacked aircraft. Cooper also instructed the crew to leave the flaps and landing gear down. Once the aircraft reached ten thousand feet, Cooper ordered the four crew members to close themselves into the cockpit. It was the last they saw of him.

INTO THIN AIR

Sometime before Northwest flight 305 arrived in Reno, Nevada, Cooper parachuted into a storm in the cold, mountainous southwest Washington wilderness. He jumped at a high altitude into freezing rain, with winds that blew up to seventy miles per hour. No one knows what happened next. Some investigators believe Cooper did not survive the skydive. Of the two parachutes he took, one was a non-working training parachute that had been supplied by mistake. If he relied on that chute, he undoubtedly fell to his death.

And even if his parachute did work, Cooper's chances of surviving the jump would have been slim. Agent Himmelsbach—who worked the case from 1971 until he retired from the FBI in 1980—noted, "[Cooper] didn't ask for a helmet, gloves, flight jacket, jumpsuit, or boots. It was seven below zero outside, it was dark, and the plane was going 196 miles per hour." When he hit the air at that speed, Cooper probably tumbled head-over-heels. The wind resistance would have given him black eyes and his shoes were probably blown off.

What's more, the landing conditions where Cooper jumped would have scared away even the most experienced jumpers. Cooper's choice of parachutes (he left behind the two best chutes) suggests that he was a novice (beginner) skydiver. "Whatever Cooper would have hit down there, he would have hit hard," Himmelsbach said. "Even if he'd just sprained his leg it'd be a death sentence in that kind of environment."

Dead or not, Cooper was the subject of intensive manhunts. FBI agents, U.S. Air Force pilots, National Guardsmen, army

What happened? If Cooper died in the forests of Washington, there wouldn't be much evidence. Small animals would have eaten his flesh and scattered his bones so that investigators would have had a hard time identifying his remains.

troops, and civilian (non-military) volunteers searched the area where Cooper might have landed. They found no trace of the hijacker.

Found money

For almost a decade, investigators found nothing to shed any light on the 1971 hijacking. But in February 1980, a young boy discovered a package containing several dozen $20 bills. The wet and shredded money—whose serial numbers were traceable to the ransom payment—was the only real clue that had appeared since Cooper jumped out of the jetliner. But it was a clue that led nowhere. Authorities searched the area for further clues. Again they found nothing.

None of the remaining $194,000 was ever found—nor have the serial numbers appeared in circulation. (If large sums of the money had been spent, banks, which keep track of the serial numbers on bills, would have records indicating that the cash was in use.) In spite of repeated intensive searches, no parachute was ever found. Although he apparently never enjoyed the money he ransomed, the man who called himself Dan Cooper remains the only U.S. hijacker who was never caught.

Part of the money that was paid to Cooper in 1971 was found near Portland, Oregon, on February 10, 1980, by eight-year-old Brian Ingram, who was on a family picnic.

Sources for Further Reading

Angeloff, Sam. "The FBI Agent Who Has Tracked D. B. Cooper for Nine Years Retires, But the Frustrating Search Goes On." *People Weekly* (March 3, 1980), pp. 45–46.

Gates, David. "D. B. Cooper, Where Are You?" *Newsweek* (December 26, 1983), p. 12.

Schroeder, Andreas. *Scams, Scandals, and Skulduggery.* Toronto, Ontario, Canada: McClelland & Stewart, 1996, pp. 178–191.

Williams, Geoff. "Have You Seen This Man?" *Entertainment Weekly* (November 24, 1995), p. 120.

Clifford Irving

Born: 1930

Formerly a minor author—who had trouble sticking to the truth—Clifford Irving convinced his publisher to hire him to write The Autobiography of Howard Hughes. *The trouble was, Howard Hughes had no involvement in his supposed memoirs. Irving faked the life story of the reclusive billionaire—and almost got away with it.*

EARLY LIFE

Born in New York City in 1930, Irving grew up on the Upper West Side of Manhattan. His father, Jay Irving, was a cartoonist who drew a comic strip called "Pottsy," a friendly, overweight policeman. Irving did not get along well with his father, who pressured his son to be successful. As a boy, Irving lived in his parents' New York apartment and attended public schools in Manhattan. His boyhood friends included William Safire, who later became a speechwriter for President Richard Nixon (1969–1974) and a prominent contributor to the *New York Times.*

Irving enrolled in New York's prestigious Cornell University in 1947, with the intention of becoming an artist. After he read some of the works of novelist Ernest Hemingway (1899–1961), however, he decided to become a writer. Having taken college courses in creative writing, Irving was awarded a one-year creative writing fellowship. He remained at Cornell for one year after receiving his bachelor's degree in 1951.

In the spring of his senior year, he married Nina Wilcox, a student. Irving soon became restless and the marriage fell apart. Traveling around the country, he took odd jobs to support himself. In Detroit, Michigan, he took a job in a machine shop. In Syracuse, New York, he worked as a door-to-door salesman for the Fuller Brush company. He traveled overseas, and even lived on a houseboat in Kashmir (a former princely state in northwest India and northeast India).

NOVELS AND WIVES

Irving's first novel, *On a Darkling Plain,* was published in 1956. Irving's first novel is considered to be largely autobiographical (based on the author's life). Completed during a visit to Ibiza (a Spanish island in the west Mediterranean Sea), *On a Darkling Plain* portrays the difficulties three school friends have adjusting to life in the United States after war. The following year, Irving published *The Losers,* a fictional story—told in the words of a cartoonist—about a businessman who becomes an artist. In 1961, he produced a western tale titled *The Valley.* During 1961 and 1962, Irving taught creative writing at an extension school of the University of California in Los Angeles. He later worked on various television projects and sold a script to the western series, *Bonanza.* In 1966, *The Thirty-Eighth Floor* appeared in bookstores. Irving's fourth novel concerned an African American's rise to the position of acting secretary-general of the United Nations.

Irving, in the meantime, met and married three other women. His second wife, Claire, died in a car crash in Monterey, California, in the late 1950s. She was eight months pregnant at the time. Next, Irving married a former fashion model named Fay Brooke. Wed in 1961, the couple had one son, Josh. Irving was anything but a model husband. He was a hard-core drinker, he had affairs with other women, and he beat his wife. Brooke and Irving divorced in 1965. Two years later he married a divorced painter named Edith. Born in Germany, she was the daughter of the owner of a clock factory. The couple had two children, Ned and Barnaby.

Until his role in the Howard Hughes scandal, Irving was best known as the author of *Fake!*—the supposed biography of a Hungarian art forger named Elmyr de Hory. Published in 1969, the novel received some favorable reviews. Others were less forgiving of the author's inability to stick to a factual account of the art forger's life. Although Irving was a friend of de Hory, he had invented much of his story.

THE HOAX TAKES SHAPE

With several books to his credit, Irving approached McGraw-Hill, his regular publisher, with the idea for another biography. The book was to be the authorized biography of billionaire Howard Hughes (1905–1976). A fiercely private and eccentric (unconventional) man, Hughes had not been photographed or interviewed since 1958. Irving's editors were intrigued.

But Irving had no intention of producing an authorized or factual work. (An authorized biography is an officially approved story of the subject's life.) First, Irving convinced the publishers that he was in contact with the billionaire. Using a piece of a Hughes letter that had been published in *Newsweek* magazine, Irving created fake letters from the billionaire to himself.

While he was in New York to attend his mother's funeral, Irving stopped at McGraw-Hill and showed them the phony material. The publisher was convinced that Hughes had agreed to supply the little-known author with the first and only authorized version of his life story—and convinced that such a book had the potential to earn a fortune. On March 23, 1971, Irving signed a contract with McGraw-Hill to write the authorized biography of Hughes. The contract provided an immediate advance of $100,000.

A WELL-RESEARCHED STORY

Next, Irving had to put together a manuscript of Hughes's "tell-all" account of his life. He needed some accurate material in order to lend credence (believability) to the story. He had to be able to duplicate Hughes's manner of speaking so that the words he attributed to the billionaire would sound authentic. And he needed to provide inside information and little-known details that would set his book apart from countless other works about the mysterious Mr. Hughes.

Working with a research assistant, Richard Suskind, Irving pieced together a plausible (believable) account of the life of Hughes. He consulted countless books and articles written by other authors and journalists. He researched his subject at the New York Public Library. He went to Washington, D.C., where he uncovered a useful file on the Hughes Aircraft Company at the Pentagon. At the Library of Congress, he found congressional testimony by Hughes, and a thesis that discussed the role of Trans World Airlines (TWA)—which was at that time a Hughes company—in the development of Ethiopian Airways. Suskind and Irving also examined the files of Time-Life publishers and the *Los Angeles Times*—as well as newspaper files in Houston, Texas, and Las Vegas, Nevada, for material concerning Hughes or his family. And they traveled to Los Angeles, California, to gather information about Hughes's Hollywood years.

STOLEN RESEARCH, PHONY INTERVIEWS, AND MAKE-BELIEVE MEETINGS

Much of Irving's inside information was derived from the research of another author, James Phelan, whose work on Hughes had not yet been published. Irving was approached by his friend, Stanley Myers, to rewrite a book on Hughes. Based on material provided by Noah Dietrich—who had been the billionaire's chief of staff for thirty-two years—the manuscript was filled with insider information not available in other sources. The original manuscript was compiled by Phelan, an experienced investigative reporter who had already written five magazine articles on Hughes. Irving informed Myers that he was not interested in the project. What he failed to tell Myers was that he planned to steal much of Phelan's material for his own book on Hughes.

Since their work was supposed to be from tapes dictated by Hughes, Suskind and Irving took turns dictating what they had learned into a tape recorder. The exercise helped Irving create the feeling of a book that had been dictated. It also allowed Irving to produce transcripts of the tapes to prove to McGraw-Hill that the conversations had taken place. The transcripts of the "interviews" produced nine hundred and fifty pages of typed material—which Irving copied and provided to his publishers. The original tapes were destroyed.

In order to make absolutely sure that his publishers were convinced that his story was authentic, Irving traveled to far-away destinations to "meet" with Hughes. He claimed that his first meeting with Hughes had taken place from high atop a mountain in Oaxaca, Mexico. He made trips to Florida, California, the Bahamas, Mexico, and Puerto Rico, and often called his editors. He even sent postcards from distant places to relatives—scribbling made-up stories about his fictitious (made-up) meetings with Hughes.

SWISS BANKS AND THE MYSTERIOUS HELGA HUGHES

Irving's original contract with McGraw-Hill provided for $500,000 in advances. Some of the money was to be paid to Irving. The rest was to be paid directly to Hughes. Within six months, Irving informed his publishers that Hughes—one of the richest men in the world—wanted more money for the book. Afraid that the duo would take the autobiography elsewhere, McGraw-Hill increased their offer to $750,000.

Irving's wife, meanwhile, had been busy taking care of finances. In Barcelona, Spain, she acquired a fake Swiss passport under the name of Helga Rosencrantz Hughes. Next she opened a bank account—under the name "H. R. Hughes"—at Credit Suisse in Zurich, Switzerland. Wearing a wig and dark glasses, she deposited 1,000 Swiss francs—equivalent to $260—on May 12, 1971. The following day—using the same Credit Suisse bank teller—she deposited a check from McGraw-Hill for $50,000. The check was made out to H. R. Hughes.

Two weeks later—after the check cleared—Edith withdrew the $50,000 from Credit Suisse. She then deposited the money in a numbered account in another Swiss bank. The Irvings had established a way to convert any money paid to Hughes by

McGraw-Hill (or other publishers involved in the deal) into their own account.

Edith repeated the procedure with two more checks from McGraw-Hill. She deposited $275,000 at Credit Suisse on September 30. On October 19, she appeared with an airline bag—and withdrew the entire amount in 1,000-franc notes. By withdrawing the money in francs rather than dollars, she avoided additional paperwork. The phony Mrs. Hughes made her final deposit—$325,000—toward the beginning of December. By the end of the month, she appeared at the bank—in wig and sunglasses—to claim the money.

A STATEMENT TO THE PRESS

On December 7, 1971, publisher McGraw-Hill announced that it would publish *The Autobiography of Howard Hughes*. The press release explained that Hughes had spent much of 1970 working on his memoirs with the help of Clifford Irving, an American writer. The two men reportedly spent one hundred work sessions together—often in parked cars.

The memoir, which was 230,000 words long, was to be published on March 27, 1972. *Life* magazine would publish three 10,000-word installments of the book, in addition to a separate article by Irving on the interviews. At a publishing party, it was announced that the Book-of-the-Month Club had agreed to feature the Irving book, and to pay a $350,000 advance for the right to do so. Dell Publishing Company bought the rights to publish the book in paperback for $400,000.

HUGHES CRIES *HOAX!*

Immediately after McGraw-Hill's press statement was released, a spokesman for Hughes rejected the book in no uncertain terms. A short time later, Frank McCulloch—the New York bureau chief of *Time* magazine and the last journalist to interview Hughes—was informed that the billionaire wanted to talk to him on the phone. McCulloch agreed.

To make sure that he was speaking to the *real* Hughes, McCulloch asked him two trick questions. Hughes answered the questions correctly. He also said that he had never met or heard of Irving—and that he was definitely not working on his memoirs with the man.

But McCulloch still was not convinced that Irving's book was a scam. He was convinced that the biography was genuine because Irving was able to quote what Hughes had said to him on the phone during their last conversation in the late 1950s. McCulloch thought that only he and Hughes knew what was said at that time. He had apparently forgotten that a transcript of the conversation had been made for the president of Time-Life, Inc. As Hughes's employee, Dietrich had seen the transcript. Irving had read about the conversation in the Dietrich-Phelan manuscript. With McCulloch's endorsement, McGraw-Hill decided to stand by the authenticity of the Irving book. And no one checked with the Swiss bank to find out if there was anything unusual about the person who made deposits—and withdrawals—from the H. R. Hughes account.

INCREASING SUSPICION

Irving passed a number of other "tests." All of the material supposedly written by Hughes was reexamined. The writings were inspected by a firm that had a reputation for being the finest handwriting experts in the United States. They compared the McGraw-Hill samples with the material written by Hughes when he was in Las Vegas, Nevada. They, too, confirmed that Hughes had written all of the McGraw-Hill material. Irving was given a last-minute lie-detector test. The results proved nothing—and the test was not repeated.

In January 1972, Irving was informed that Hughes was planning to hold a telephone news conference with seven journalists from Los Angeles. During the conference, the man who claimed to be Hughes told the journalists that he did not know Irving—and that he had never worked with him on a book. Irving responded that the voice was not that of Hughes—although it was a fairly accurate imitation of how the billionaire once sounded.

THE JIG IS UP

Irving's hoax began to collapse after Swiss authorities began to take a closer look at H. R. Hughes. They discovered

Dead men don't write

Some people believed that Howard Hughes was dead. They speculated that the "autobiography" was a hoax engineered by a group of Hughes employees to gain control of the billionaire's assets.

that "H. R. Hughes"—who opened the bank accounts and deposited the checks intended as payment to the billionaire—was not Howard Hughes. They knew that the deposits had been made by a woman—a woman who looked very much like Irving's five-foot-six, hazel-eyed, thirty-something wife. By the first week of February, Swiss authorities issued warrants for the arrest of Clifford and Edith Irving.

At first, Irving denied that he knew the woman who went under the name of Helga R. Hughes. He even threatened to bring a lawsuit against reporters who suggested that his wife was involved in a hoax. Eventually, he was forced to admit that Helga was, in fact, his wife. But he denied being involved in a hoax. He claimed that Hughes had provided Edith with the fake passport—and that he had instructed them to open the Swiss bank accounts. He also claimed that Edith had not endorsed any of the checks. She simply deposited the checks in the Swiss accounts after the billionaire had signed them.

But Irving's credibility (believability) had been destroyed. McGraw-Hill and *Life* magazine delayed publishing Irving's manuscript. Reporters continued to search for the truth. Soon after the Swiss authorities charged the Irvings, the author received a phone call from a reporter from *Time* magazine. The reporter had a copy of the Dietrich-Phelan manuscript. This time there was no way out. Irving could not deny that he had borrowed—or stolen—material from the unpublished biography.

THE TRUTH AT LAST

Irving was investigated from every angle. The New York County district attorney, United States Postal Service, and the Justice Department all had him under investigation. Rumors began to circulate that Irving was about to be arrested. Finally, he confided in a friend, attorney Philip Lorber. (Irving's lawyer, Martin Ackerman, had quit shortly after the bank scam was discovered. He told his client to hire a criminal lawyer.) Irving admitted to Lorber that the biography was a hoax.

After Irving was formally charged, prosecuting attorneys offered to cut him a deal if he would plead guilty. They would not prosecute Edith, who was little more than a courier. And Suskind would be given a light sentence.

On May 21, 1989, Ray
Simpson (pictured here)
of Simpson's Auction
Galleries in Houston,
Texas, held an auction
for Howard Hughes
memorabilia, including
the original manuscript
of Irving's fake
autobiography.

JAIL TIME

On March 9, 1972, Irving was formally charged with federal
conspiracy to defraud, forgery, and the use of forged instru-
ments (documents), using the mail to defraud, and perjury
(lying under oath in court). Suskind was charged only as a co-
conspirator on the federal charges. In New York State court,
both Irvings and Suskind were charged with grand larceny

(theft), conspiracy, and a few minor charges. They pleaded guilty to all charges.

Clifford Irving was sentenced to two-and-a-half years in jail. After serving about seven months in Allenwood Federal Prison in Pennsylvania, he was paroled (released from jail before his sentence was fully served). Edith Irving was sentenced to two years—of which all but two months were suspended. Richard Suskind was sentenced to six months in prison.

The Swiss authorities at first refused to drop charges against Edith, who had used false documents to enter the country, open bank accounts, and conduct transactions. The authorities later agreed to drop the charges—and then changed their minds again. In Zurich, Edith was tried and convicted of forgery, embezzlement (taking money by illegal means), and theft. Sentenced to two years in jail, she served the entire term.

What Really Happened?

Irving's hoax biography of Hughes has never been published. But his account of his involvement in the scandal—called *What Really Happened*—was available for public consumption in 1972. (McGraw-Hill would not publish it.) A reviewer in *Time* magazine noted that it would be difficult to view Irving's work (co-authored with Suskind) as a true story. "To believe the confessions of Clifford Irving," the author writes, "is a little like believing the confessions of Baron Munchausen." (Baron Karl Friedrich Hieronymus von Munchausen was a German soldier and hunter who lived from 1720 to 1797. He was famous not for his military exploits—but for the wild lies he told about his adventures.)

Sources for Further Reading

"Clifford & Edith & Howard & Helga." *Time* (February 7, 1972), pp. 20–22.

"The Fabulous Hoax of Clifford Irving." *Time* (February 21, 1972), pp. 12–17.

Friedrich, Otto. "Caper Sauce." *Time* (September 18, 1972), pp. 92–93.

"The Great Hughes Fiasco." *Newsweek* (February 7, 1972), pp. 18, 20, 23.

"Irving's Latest Cliff-Hanger." *Newsweek* (February 14, 1972), pp. 20–22.

Nash, Jay Robert. *The Encyclopedia of World Crime.* Wilmette, IL: Crime Books, 1990, pp. 1665–1666.

Sophie Lyons

Born: December 24, 1848
Died: May 8, 1924
AKA: Fannie Owens,
Kate Wilson, Mary Wilson

A petty (small-time) thief from the time she could walk, Sophie Lyons eventually earned a reputation as "one of the cleverest criminals the country has ever produced."

A CRIMINAL EDUCATION

Born Sophie Levy in New York City on December 24, 1848, she was the daughter of criminals. Her mother—who used the names Julia Keller and Sophie Elkins—was an old-time shoplifter. She saw little of her father, Sam Levy, who spent much of his life in prison for robbery. Sophie's mother taught her to shoplift at an early age. She also instructed her in the practice of picking pockets—which was considered to be an art among criminals of that time. Taught various ways to steal to help support her family, Sophie never attended school.

As a teenager Sophie married a pickpocket named Maury Harris, who was caught and jailed soon after they married. Having left her husband, she met and married Ned Lyons, a burglar and bank robber who was highly respected in the criminal community. Born in England in 1837, Ned participated in a number of successful robberies—including the theft of nearly $800,000 from the Ocean Bank in New York on June 27, 1869. He also led a group of burglars who collected $150,000 from vaults in the Philadelphia Navy Yard in 1870.

A TALENTED ACTRESS

A successful thief, Ned reportedly wanted his wife to give up crime. He bought an extravagant home on Long Island, New York. He hired servants and purchased expensive furniture, china, and other household items. Lyons no longer needed to steal to survive—but she continued to steal anyway. During one of her outings, Lyons was arrested by a detective who caught her picking pockets at a fair. The arrest report describes how Lyons's behavior at the jailhouse helped her to regain her freedom:

> She was then only nineteen years old, but her phenomenal [exceptional] talent as an actress was already developed. She could mold her face to every shade of emotion. She could make her eyes at will a fountain of tears. She treated us to a moving display of her art. She was by turns horror-stricken, proudly indignant [angered by something unjust], heartbroken, and convulsed with hysterics. Who could press a charge against such a blushing, trembling, sobbing young beauty piteously claiming that it was a dreadful mistake, painting the agony of her dear husband and parents at the bare suspicion of her spotless innocence, and subtly hinting at the grave censure [severe criticism] that would surely fall on her maligners [those who spoke ill of her]? It was her shrewd [cunning] calculation that the authorities in charge of her case would prefer to let it drop quietly, and so they did.

Lyons was set free.

ESCAPE FROM SING SING

Lyons was arrested again in early 1871 when she was caught stealing from a jewelry store in New York—for which she was sent to prison on Blackwell's Island, New York. Soon after she was released she was tried for grand larceny (theft). Con-

victed on October 9, 1871, she was sentenced to five years in Sing Sing state prison.

Sing Sing prison, in Ossining, New York.

But prison might have been part of Lyons's master plan. At the time of her trial, Ned was serving a long sentence in Sing Sing. Many people believe that Lyons was arrested on purpose—so that she could help her husband to escape. Soon after she arrived at the prison, Lyons became a personal assistant to the matron (female supervisor) of the women's division at Sing Sing. She wore a maid's outfit instead of prison clothes, and walked freely outside of prison walls with the matron's children. Taking advantage of her freedom, she managed to have clothing, a wig, and a forged (faked) prison pass smuggled to her. Dressed in street clothes and armed with a prison pass, Ned simply walked out of jail. On December 19, 1872, Sophie also

Sophie Lyons operated at a time when criminal society was as class-conscious as law-abiding citizens—perhaps even more so. *The New York Times* explained the underworld hierarchy (ranking of importance) in Lyons's 1924 obituary:

There is nothing like that world today, but at the time there was a conscious pride about the big crooks, and they married as in a caste [a social class] and often passed their craft from father to son or from mother to daughter. Sophie, then, was something of a catch. So was Ned Lyons.

walked to freedom, using a key her husband had made from a wax impression.

But their freedom was short-lived. After a brief stay in Canada, where the couple robbed a pawnbroker (person who loans money on items left as a security deposit) of more than $40,000, both the Lyons were arrested for pickpocketing at the Suffolk County fair on Long Island. On October 26, 1876, they returned to Sing Sing state prison.

BLACKMAIL AND BANK ROBBERY

After her release from prison, Lyons expanded her criminal activities to include more profitable endeavors, such as blackmail (a form of extortion in which threats are used to gain payment) and bank robbery. Following circuses from one town to another, she and a partner in crime robbed small banks while the employees watched the circus parade pass by. She also robbed banks by posing as a wealthy woman who was considering opening an account. First she and her accomplice waited until one clerk was alone in the bank. Her partner then convinced the clerk to speak to Lyons, who waited outside in an elegant carriage. Once the clerk was outside, Lyons held a long conversation with him—while her accomplice robbed the empty bank.

Lyons also employed blackmail to bolster her bank accounts. In one instance, she accompanied a married man to a room in a Boston hotel. She hid his clothing and threatened to expose him if he didn't agree to her demands. The man wrote her a check for several thousand dollars.

As her wealth mounted, Lyons took it upon herself to make up for the education she had not received as a child. Once illiterate, she hired tutors to teach her to read and write. She read literature and studied art and music—and reportedly learned to speak four languages. Traveling often to Europe, she moved among the upper class and pulled off a number of successful heists—from robbing banks to smuggling stolen gems.

THE BANK OF SOPHIE

In the early 1890s, Lyons opened the New York Women's Banking and Investment Company with another con artist, Carrie Morse. Lyons later described Morse in her memoirs (book about a person's life), in a chapter titled "Women Criminals of Extraordinary Ability with Whom I Was in Partnership." Morse had, according to Lyons, "well-bred cordiality which was such an important part of her stock in trade [an important part of her success as a con woman]." She further described her extraordinary partner: "In every detail, her well kept hands, her gentle voice, her superb complexion, and the dainty way she had of wearing her mass of chestnut hair—she was the personification [embodiment] of luxury and refinement." Lyons, meanwhile, posed as the bank's elegant president, Mrs. Celia Rigsby. Together they preyed on wealthy women—as well as poor elderly widows. Before the "bank" closed, it had collected at least $50,000 from unsuspecting victims. But Lyons did not profit from the scam. A veteran swindler, Morse double-crossed her partner and ran off with the money.

The queen of crime

By the 1880s, Lyons had such a famous criminal reputation that the chief of the New York Police Department, William S. Devery, held a special press conference to denounce the "Queen of Crime." He told newspaper reporters:

Sophie Lyons is one of the cleverest criminals that the country has ever produced. She has carried her operations into nearly every quarter of the civilized globe and is known to the police of every European capital. She has been arrested hundreds of times since she was first picked up by the police in 1859 at age twelve. And don't you believe that nonsense about her reforming. For her that's impossible.

RETIREMENT FROM A LIFE OF CRIME

Lyons soon retired from crime. Her long career as a criminal earned her the reputation as "the Queen of Crime"—and it had taken away her ability to operate anonymously (without being noticed). One police official commented, "Of late years, she has had little opportunity for plundering, for her face is so well known in all the large cities of America and Europe that she is constantly watched for, if she is not arrested on site." Adding to her difficulties was the fact that she was addicted to opium (a narcotic drug made from the poppy plant).

Claiming to be a reformed criminal, Lyons became a society columnist for the *New York World* newspaper. She also wrote an autobiography, titled *Why Crime Does Not Pay*. Published in

1913, it provided numerous accounts of crimes that paid—and paid well. Nonetheless, Lyons urged other criminals to give up their crooked occupations. She hoped that fellow swindler **Ellen Peck** (see entry) would read her book, and that the experience would help Peck to mend her criminal ways.

But not all of her subjects wanted to be reformed. On May 8, 1924, she let three men into her home—supposedly in the hope of reforming them. They asked her for the money and valuables that were reportedly hidden around her house. She refused. Her neighbors found her on the floor, in a coma. Her skull had been crushed. Taken to Grace Hospital in Detroit, Michigan, Lyons died later that evening of a massive brain hemorrhage. She was seventy-six years old.

Sources for Further Reading

Byrnes, Thomas. *1886 Professional Criminals of America.* Broomall, PA: Chelsea House, 1969, pp. 205–206.

De Grave, Kathleen. *Swindler, Spy, Rebel.* Columbia: University of Missouri Press, 1995, pp. 57–73, 144–157.

Nash, Jay Robert. *Look for the Woman: A Narrative Encyclopedia of Female Poisoners, Kidnappers, Thieves, Extortionists, Terrorists, Swindlers, and Spies from Elizabethan Times to Present.* New York: M. Evans, 1981, pp. 321–322.

Ellen Peck
(Nellie Crosby)

Born: 1829
Died: 1915

*Referred to as the "Queen of Confidence Women," Ellen Peck came up with ingenious
(creative) plans to swindle wealthy victims—even as an old woman.*

WORTHLESS INFORMATION

Born Nellie Crosby in Woodville, New Hampshire, in 1829,
Peck eventually settled in New York City. She was an ordinary
swindler until 1878, when she gained notoriety (attention) for
cheating B. T. Babbitt, a wealthy soap manufacturer, out of
$19,000. Babbitt had recently been robbed of more than
$500,000 and was eager to recover his lost money. Posing as a
female detective, Peck promised to produce valuable information in the robbery. But she needed a cash advance. The elderly
millionaire advanced her the money—and soon discovered that
the information she provided was worthless. Although Babbitt
attempted to bring Peck to trial, she continued to swindle
(cheat people out of money) unsuspecting victims—including
other swindlers.

Samuel Pingee, a man who dealt with patented (certified)
drugs, paid her for inside information on stock investments.
Claiming that she received stock tips from a friend in the office
of Jay Gould, a wealthy investor, Peck collected $2,700 from

Pingee. Again, the information Peck provided was worthless. John D. Grady, a shady diamond dealer, was also among Peck's victims. A veteran swindler, Grady lent the confidence woman (female con artist or swindler) a large sum of cash in exchange for the receipt to a safe deposit vault that supposedly contained valuable diamonds. The vault was empty.

STOLEN JEWELRY

Four years after the Babbitt affair, detectives caught up with Peck. Although she was formally charged with the crime, her trial received several postponements. When the date of her trial approached, she claimed—repeatedly—to be ill. When that ploy no longer worked, she pretended to be insane and was sent to an asylum (a type of hospital that treats the mentally ill) in Pennsylvania. On July 18, 1879, she was tried in the Kings County Court of Sessions on another charge—obtaining several thousand dollars' worth of jewelry under false pretenses. But she managed again to avoid a conviction.

NEW SCAM

Peck soon engaged in other scams in which she passed herself off as Mrs. Eliza Knight, a woman who held a large bank account at a New York bank. First she introduced herself as Mrs. Knight to John H. Johnson, a Manhattan jeweler. She selected $150 in jewelry, for which she gave Johnson $25. Using the bank where Knight had an account as a reference, she promised to pay the remaining $125 at a later date. Convinced that her credit was worthy, Johnson allowed Peck to leave with the jewelry. But he soon found out that the woman who visited him was not the Mrs. Knight who enjoyed good credit at the bank.

Peck borrowed Mrs. Knight's identity again on March 4, 1884, when she introduced herself to a diamond dealer named John Bough. Claiming to be a businesswoman who dealt in precious stones, she selected a diamond ring valued at $75. She said the ring was for a woman friend. Peck returned the next day to pay Bough the money she owed. Hoping that she might bring him additional business, he offered to pay her a commission (fee). Peck refused, saying that the purchase was insignificant. But she promised, however, to return soon to place a more important order.

The following month Peck informed Bough that she was going to meet with a wealthy woman from Brooklyn. Claiming that she could sell the woman some jewelry, she chose $400 worth of diamond earrings and rings. Bough waited several days for Peck to return with either a payment or the jewelry, but she never appeared.

The jeweler reported the incident to the police, who discovered that the missing diamonds had been left at a pawnshop called Simpson's. Sometime after the jewelry had been exchanged for $130, Peck entered the shop with a claim ticket. She told the shopkeeper the jewels had been stolen from her, and that she had received the claim ticket in the mail. When the shop owner refused to turn over the jewelry, Peck brought the matter to court. The suit was tried on September 12, 1884. But the result was not what she had hoped: the judge postponed making a decision in the case and Bough, meanwhile, had identified the jewelry as his missing property.

BORROWED MONEY

Soon Peck swindled another victim, a woman named Ann McConnell. Posing as a woman named Mrs. Crosby, Peck claimed that she needed money to help her son start a business. She also claimed that she had a substantial income, but would not have access to her next payment until May and that she had a house on Putnam Avenue in Brooklyn that was filled with furniture that could be used as collateral (property that is pledged to protect the lender). Impressed by Peck's elegant manner, McConnell lent her $250. "Mrs. Crosby" agreed to pay back the loan—plus a $75 interest fee—in thirty days.

A little over two weeks later, McConnell read about a woman who had been arrested for swindling a jeweler. The woman lived on Putnam Avenue. She wondered if it could be the "Mrs. Crosby" who had borrowed money from her. When McConnell left the Tombs Police Court, where Peck was being held, there was no doubt. Peck was the woman who had introduced herself as Mrs. Crosby.

McConnell was not surprised when, at the end of thirty days, Peck had not repaid the loan. On December 6, 1884, the con woman was again led into police custody. The charge was larceny (theft). Her lawyer, Henry A. Meyenborg, argued that his client's failure to pay the debt and interest was not equal to the charge of larceny. She was set free.

A JAILBIRD AND A CON

Finally, on October 6, 1885, Peck received her first conviction. Charged with forging (faking) a document in order to obtain $3,000 from the Mutual Life Insurance Company of New York City, she was sentenced to four and a half years in prison. When she heard the sentence, Peck reportedly started to faint and then wept uncontrollably. At the age of fifty-six, she headed for the penitentiary on Blackwell's Island in New York.

Prison did not convince Peck to abandon the life of a con woman. In 1894 she played the role of an admiral's wife. Posing as the spouse of a Danish Navy officer, Admiral Johann Carl Hansen, she collected more than $50,000 in loans from various banks. Shortly thereafter she managed to swindle $10,000 from an elderly Brooklyn physician named Dr. Christopher Lott. She was arrested one last time in 1913 for cheating a Latin-American businessman who had given her the title to several coffee plantations. Peck died two years later, at the age of eighty-six.

Large savings account

Peck reportedly had more than $1 million stashed in numerous bank accounts when she died at the ripe old age of eighty-six.

Sources for Further Reading

Byrnes, Thomas. *1886 Professional Criminals of America*. Broomall, PA: Chelsea House, 1969, pp. 316–321.

De Grave, Kathleen. *Swindler, Spy, Rebel*. Columbia: University of Missouri Press, 1995, pp. 57–73, 144–157.

Nash, Jay Robert. *Look for the Woman: A Narrative Encyclopedia of Female Poisoners, Kidnappers, Thieves, Extortionists, Terrorists, Swindlers, and Spies from Elizabethan Times to Present.* New York: M. Evans, 1981, pp. 321–322.

Charles Ponzi

Born: 1883
Died: 1949

Sometimes referred to as the "Boston Swindler," Charles Ponzi set in motion one of the largest financial hoaxes of the twentieth century. Although he was widely regarded as a financial genius, he was nothing more than an inept (foolish) risk taker who enjoyed a brief bout of good luck.

POOR BEGINNINGS

Born in Italy in 1883, Ponzi emigrated (moved) to the United States when he was about twenty years old. Having entered his adoptive country with only $2.50, he became a waiter, but was soon fired. Still very poor, he took a train to Canada, where he was arrested for forging (faking) a check. Ponzi was sentenced to a brief term in a Montreal prison, after which he returned to the United States. In Atlanta, Georgia, he came up with a scheme to help Italians enter the country illegally—without following proper immigration procedures. Ponzi soon found himself in prison again—this time for smuggling aliens (transporting people illegally) into the United States.

Ponzi headed north to Boston, Massachusetts, in 1914. After marrying a woman named Rose, he assumed control of his father-in-law's grocery business. When that failed, he took a job as a translator for an import-export firm, which paid only $16 per week. While working at the firm, Ponzi came across something that gave him an idea for a scheme to earn money quickly.

Ponzi discovered that International Postal Union reply coupons could be purchased in Europe at a low rate, because the economies of European countries were depressed. The coupons could then be redeemed in the United States—which was not suffering from an economic depression at that time—for a much higher rate. Ponzi used these reply coupons as a foreign exchange system: buying inflated foreign currencies, swapping the money for international exchange coupons, and reconverting these coupons into dollars.

THE SECURITIES EXCHANGE COMPANY

Ponzi was convinced that he had found his calling. He quit his job to focus on the postal coupon business and borrowed money to purchase his first batch. His plan was slow to develop because various rules and regulations made it difficult to redeem the coupons. But eventually the scheme began to pay off—handsomely. For example, Ponzi was able to purchase coupons from his native country, Italy, at a cost of one cent each. He then had the coupons mailed to him in the United States, where he redeemed them for five cents each—for a profit of four cents per coupon.

Ponzi was not content to limit himself to a one-man operation. He convinced other investors to take part, promising them an astonishing 50 percent profit within three months. Ponzi's offer was too good to refuse. Investors flocked to his seedy (run-down) office at 27 School Street in Boston's financial district. So much money passed through the Securities Exchange Company that his employees stashed it in trash cans, drawers, and closets. And Ponzi made good on his promise. He paid old investors with cash supplied by new investors, doubling their money within six months. Hailed as the "Wizard of Finance," Ponzi collected *$15 million* from forty thousand investors over an eight-month period that began in December 1919. His best single-day take amounted to more than $2 million.

The greatest Italian of them all

When Charles "Get Rich Quick" Ponzi was called to a hearing to investigate his financial operations, he was tremendously popular among the people of Boston—many of whom he had helped to collect a small fortune. As he entered the city's State House—wearing a straw hat, walking stick, and boutonniere (a lapel flower)—he was cheered by enthusiastic crowds. Some onlookers reportedly praised him as "the greatest Italian of them all." Ponzi is said to have responded, "No, [Christopher] Columbus and [Guglielmo] Marconi were greater. Columbus discovered America, Marconi discovered the wireless." To this, a voice in the crowd added, "But you discovered money!"

Crowds gather outside
Charles Ponzi's Boston
office, 1920.

Ponzi was so successful that he opened branch offices throughout New England, New Jersey, and New York. He bought an extravagant mansion, a chauffeur-driven limousine, hundreds of expensive suits and ties, gold-handled walking canes, and diamond stickpins. Having made thousands of other investors wealthy, he enjoyed the respect and affection of the community—for a while.

BORROWING FROM PETER TO PAY PAUL

Ponzi's plan worked without a hitch—as long as there was a ready flow of incoming cash. But after about six months of money-trading, the local newspapers began to look into his operations. At first, Ponzi stalled the investigations by striking

294

back with large lawsuits. Before long, the *Boston Post* newspaper uncovered Ponzi's criminal record, which included convictions for forgery and smuggling aliens.

The news startled Ponzi's investors. The company's steady flow of new clients came to an abrupt end—and former investors demanded their money back. Without incoming cash to pay out interest on old investments, Ponzi's scheme fell to pieces. He ordered his clerks to pay off his clients, but there was not enough money to cover his debts. The Securities Exchange Company paid out $15 million—leaving about $5 million in unpaid debts.

State investigators were appalled at the state of Ponzi's bookkeeping. Instead of careful records of cash receipts and payments, they found pages of random entries—some of which were missing dates, names, or amounts. Soon federal agents arrested Ponzi. Because he had written letters to clients asking them to reinvest, he was charged with using the U.S. mails to commit fraud, or deliberate deception. He served four years in a Plymouth, Massachusetts, prison for mail fraud. Released in 1925, Ponzi was arrested again for his swindle, but this time he was charged with theft. Sentenced to a nine-year term, he posted bail and fled to Florida.

A FLORIDA LAND SCAM

Ponzi arrived in Florida at a time when the southern state was in the midst of booming real estate speculation and land sales. He set up a land swindle, promising a 200-percent profit to his clients—and was soon arrested and convicted. After serving one year in a Florida prison he was released. He was then forced to return to Massachusetts to serve out his original nine-year sentence for theft. Ponzi was paroled (granted early release) in 1934—and deported to Naples, Italy, as an undesirable alien.

What Ponzi did next is not entirely clear. He seems to have secured a position in the government of Italian dictator Benito Mussolini (1883–1945). Within a few years he left Italy for South America. Sources vary on the reasons for his departure.

According to one version, he traveled to Rio de Janeiro, Brazil, to manage Italy's LATI Airlines. According to another story, Ponzi was forced to flee from his native country because he had been discovered skimming money from the government's treasury. In any case, Ponzi settled in Rio de Janeiro. Partially blind and paralyzed, he eventually landed in the charity ward of a Brazilian hospital, where he died in January 1949, at the age of sixty-six. Ponzi's funeral reportedly took his last $75.

Sources for Further Reading

"Charles Ponzi." *Newsweek Obituaries* (January 31, 1949), p. 55.

Nash, Jay Robert. *Bloodletters and Badmen.* New York: M. Evans, 1973, pp. 252, 382–387.

"One of the Slickest of Them All." *Newsweek* (April 1, 1957), pp. 93–94.

Sifakis, Carl. *The Encyclopedia of American Crime.* New York: Facts on File, 1982, pp. 582–583.

"Take My Money!" *Time* (January 31, 1949), p. 21.

Joseph Weil

Born: 1875 or 1877

Died: February 26, 1976
AKA: Dr. Tourneur St. Harriot,
Walter H. Weed, James R. Wilson,
The Yellow Kid

Considered to be one of the greatest con men of the twentieth century, Joseph Weil posed as a number of characters to pull off elaborate scams. Looking back on his career Weil once commented: "Men like myself could not have existed without the victims' covetous [desirous], criminal greed."

THE YELLOW KID

Although Weil claimed to have been born in Chicago in 1875, some records indicate that the year of his birth was actually 1877. He was raised in Chicago and began to associate with crooks at an early age. As a teenager, Weil was fond of reading a popular comic strip, "Hogan's Alley and the Yellow Kid," which appeared in the *New York Journal*. He soon picked up a nickname—the Yellow Kid—that would follow him throughout his life.

Weil was married at an early age. Although his wife wanted him to lead an honest life, he was involved in numerous scams over a period of about forty years. A well-dressed, impressive looking man, he wore a carefully groomed beard and either a monocle (an eyeglass for one eye) or pince-nez (eyeglasses that are clipped to the bridge of the nose). Sometimes he dressed in a beaver hat and cape and yellow gloves. Weil's dignified and affluent (wealthy) appearance helped him to convince his victims that he was a banker, millionaire, or whatever role his scam required him to play.

Weil often worked with other con men who helped him pull off elaborate scams. In 1908, he first hooked up with Fred "the Deacon" Buckminster—a man who would become a longtime criminal associate. The two reportedly met when Buckminster, who was a Chicago policeman, arrested Weil, who had duped (tricked) clients into paying him to paint buildings with a phony "waterproofing" substance. But before Weil arrived at the precinct house, he convinced the policeman that he had earned thousands of dollars through confidence scams (scams that rely on the victim's trust). Tempted by the prospect of easy money, Buckminster teamed with Weil in a number of schemes over the next twenty-five years.

MAN'S BEST FRIEND

Weil once appeared in a Chicago bar with a dog. He informed the bartender that he had an errand to run, and asked the man to watch his dog. He claimed the animal was a valuable, prize-winning pedigreed (pure-bred) hunting dog—and he had the papers to prove it.

Weil left the dog with the bar owner. Soon another man appeared. The man—who was actually working with Weil—admired the dog and offered to pay the bartender as much as $300. The bartender informed him that he could not sell the dog because it was not his. The man then offered him $50 as a deposit. He also left a phone number where the bartender was to call him in case the dog's owner was willing to sell his pet.

When Weil returned to the saloon, the bartender offered to buy the dog. At first Weil objected—to make sure that the man did not become suspicious. Eventually, he accepted $250 from the bartender, who planned to call the man who had offered him $300 for the dog. But the man's phone number was fake—as were the dog's awards and papers.

A FREE LAND FLIMFLAM

When he was still in his twenties, Weil teamed with a former riverboat gambler named Colonel (pronounced KER-nel)

Jim Porter. First, the pair purchased land in Michigan for $1 per acre. Then Weil introduced Porter as an eccentric (unconventional) millionaire who was giving away valuable land *for nothing.* Bartenders, waiters, prostitutes, and even policemen accepted free parcels of land from Weil's supposed millionaire friend. Once the victim accepted the land, Weil made a point of asking him or her to keep quiet about it—since there were not enough free lots to go around.

Weil and Porter also opened a phony sales office that displayed a lavish plan to turn the land into a large, expensive vacation area. Convinced that the free land would soon become even more valuable, Weil's victims followed his advice to record the land transaction at the Michigan county seat. Recording the land transfer would allow them to prove that they owned the lots when they were ready to sell the parcels to the supposed vacation area developers.

It was no coincidence that the county recorder was Porter's cousin. The usual recording fee was just $2. But the recorder raised the price to $30—of which $15 went to Weil and Porter. The pair reportedly earned well over $15,000 in recorder's fees in what became known as the "Great Michigan Free Land Swindle."

A COLOSSAL BANK SCAM

Many of Weil's scams involved numbers of other participants and elaborate props. In one of his most complicated schemes, Weil learned that the Merchants National Bank in Muncie, Indiana, was vacating its original building to move to another location. After arranging to rent the original building—which still contained the tellers' cages—he stocked it with deposit and withdrawal slips that had been stolen from other banks as well as salt sacks for money bags. His associates posed as bank tellers, security guards, and regular customers.

Weil, in the meantime, had been trying to convince a millionaire to invest $50,000 in a phony land deal. To close the deal, he told the millionaire that the president of the Muncie bank was in favor of the transaction. The man was not from Muncie and was therefore unaware that the bank had moved—and that the

Honor among thieves

In 1956, Weil was called to testify before a Senate subcommittee, led by Senator Estes Kefauver, that was investigating juvenile delinquency (crimes committed by young people). Eighty-one years old and retired from swindling, Weil was appalled at the lack of honor among swindlers. He claimed that in his day, a swindler never left his victim penniless. "Our victims were mostly big industrialists and bankers," he testified. "The old-time confidence men had a saying: 'Never send them to the river [leave them with nothing].' We never picked on poor people or cleaned them out completely. Taking the life savings from poor old women is just the same as putting a revolver to her head and pressing the trigger!"

Weil also told the committee that he regretted his crimes. "I see how despicable [hateful] were the things I did," he said. "I found out a man is responsible not only for himself but for the other lives he wrecked."

supposed bank president was a con artist and friend of Weil's. When the millionaire visited the bank, he was impressed by its apparent success. The bank's "president" had no trouble convincing him that the land deal was a worthwhile investment. Weil collected some $50,000 from his victim and then closed the "bank."

A MINING MILLIONAIRE

Weil often made his scams appear more believable by using forged (faked) documents. In order to convince victims that he was a mining millionaire, he devised an elaborate ruse (deception) with an associate who was a printer. Weil gave the printer a copy of *McClure's,* a financial magazine. The issue included a story about Pope Yateman, a man who had earned millions from an abandoned gold mine he had purchased in Chile, a country in South America. The printer substituted Weil's photograph for that of Yateman—and then reprinted the page and rebound the magazine.

Weil traveled to various cities in the Midwest with the doctored (altered) magazine issue. First he visited the town library, where he replaced the library's copy with his phony reprint. Next he posed as a mining millionaire who was passing through town. He targeted wealthy victims and informed them that he had made a fortune by investing in an abandoned gold mine. And he suggested that they read about it in the local library. Impressed by the article in *McClure's,* a number of people gave Weil money to invest for them. Once he had collected sufficient funds, Weil left town—but not until after he replaced the reprinted magazine with the authentic library copy so that no one could identify him after the scam was discovered.

An Honest Citizen

Weil's victims rarely reported him to the authorities. Over the course of forty years of operations, he served only three prison terms, which amounted to less than six years' imprisonment. He was last convicted in 1940, when he was sentenced to three years for a mail-fraud (using the mail service as a means to deliberately deceive) charge involving phony oil leases. Released after only twenty-seven months, he settled in Chicago, where he abandoned swindling to live a law-abiding life.

In 1948, Weil wrote his memoirs—*The Autobiography of Yellow Kid Weil*—with the help of a Chicago journalist named W. T. Brannon. In his autobiography he claimed that he had earned about $8 million in four decades of international operations. (Some authorities believe he exaggerated his earnings, estimating that he collected only $3 to $5 million—still, a large amount of money.) At the time of his death, Weil had no money left. The cost of operating his scams had been enormous, and his attempts to invest in legitimate businesses had failed. Weil entered the Chicago Lake Front Convalescent Center on welfare (public relief) when he was in his nineties. He often said that he wanted to live to be one hundred years old. Weil died on February 26, 1976. Newspapers listed his age as one hundred— although records suggest that he was only ninety-nine.

Sources for Further Reading

"Joseph Weil." *The New York Times Obituaries* (February 27, 1976), p. 34.

"Joseph Weil." *Newsweek Obituaries* (March 8, 1976), p. 37.

"Joseph Weil." *Time Obituaries* (March 8, 1976), p. 81.

Nash, Jay Robert. *Bloodletters and Badmen.* New York: M. Evans, 1973, pp. 598–601.

"One of the Slickest of Them All." *Newsweek* (April 1, 1957), pp. 93–94.

Sifakis, Carl, *The Encyclopedia of American Crime.* New York: Facts on File, 1982, pp. 751–752.

"The Yellow Kid Returns." *Newsweek* (December 24, 1956), pp. 20–21.

Take a look at this!
Dirty Rotten Scoundrels (1988) features Steve Martin and Michael Caine as con men who attempt to rip off a suddenly rich woman--and each other.

Terrorists

Terrorists employ violence to intimidate, to protest, to incite revolution. Their motives are many but their methods invariably rely on the use of deadly force. They commit appalling acts of violence against innocent victims for which they are regarded by some as enemies of mankind.

Included in this section are profiles of four terrorists: JoAnne Chesimard, an African American revolutionary accused of murdering a New Jersey state trooper; Gordon Kahl, a tax protester who died in an explosive battle with FBI agents; Timothy McVeigh, who was convicted of what is considered to be the worst act of terrorism on American soil; and Diana Oughton, who perished when the bomb factory belonging to a terrorist group known as the Weathermen exploded.

You'll read about Timothy McVeigh's childhood, his wartime experiences, and his disturbing obsession with weapons. You'll learn about the right-wing belief system that led Gordon Kahl to shoot at agents who served him papers for tax evasion. And you'll find out much about the social climate of the 1970s—an era marked by peaceful civil rights demonstrations, student protests, and antiwar activities, as well as violent terrorist acts committed by radical organizations.

JoAnne Chesimard
(Assata Shakur)

Born: July 16, 1947
AKA: Joan Davis, Justine Henderson

To the FBI, JoAnne Chesimard is an armed robber, a cop-killer, and a dangerous escaped criminal. To her supporters, she is a woman of action who has never received fair treatment from the law. Whatever she may be to others, Chesimard is—by her own description—a black revolutionary.

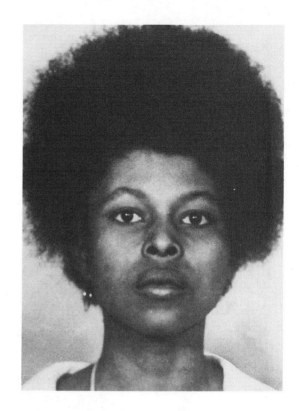

FROM NEW YORK TO NORTH CAROLINA

Chesimard was born JoAnne Deborah Byron in New York City on July 16, 1947. Until she was three, she lived with her parents, her aunt, and her grandparents in a house in Flushing, New York. Her father was an accountant for the federal government and her mother taught elementary school. When her parents divorced, Chesimard accompanied her grandparents, Frank and Lulu Hill, to Wilmington, North Carolina.

In a place where African Americans were barred from public beaches, her grandparents owned property and became small business owners. They ran a beach-front restaurant with lockers and changing rooms that provided a vacationing spot for many people who had never seen the ocean. Chesimard helped out at the restaurant and spent much of her time playing on the beach and reading the stacks of books her grandfather had brought her from the "colored" library.

DIFFERENT FORMS OF RACISM

Because Chesimard's grandparents were afraid that the segregated (racially separated) North Carolina school system was providing their grandchild with an inferior education, they sent her back to New York to live with her mother and stepfather. The eight-year-old was shifted from one extreme to another. She left a segregated, all-African American community in the South for a middle-class, heavily Jewish, and nearly all-white area of Queens, New York.

There she encountered a new kind of racism. In third and fourth grades, Chesimard was the only African American child in her class. In the fifth grade she was one of only two. As one of a very small minority in her school, she ran into teachers and students who assumed she was inferior because of her color. She attended schools where African American children were sometimes automatically placed in slow classes because teachers and administrators assumed they were not as bright and capable as white students.

Like most African American children of the 1950s, she was never allowed to forget that she was different because she was black. "When I was growing up," she revealed in her autobiography, "being called 'Black,' period, was ground for fighting."

ASSATA SHAKUR

Chesimard dropped out of high school and began running away from home. She searched for odd jobs and tried to make it on her own, but life on the streets brought its own kind of education. She stayed briefly with a family of professional shoplifters, and found herself in more than one dangerous situation. When her aunt, a lawyer named Evelyn Williams, found her and took her home, the thirteen-year-old was working in a bar hustling drinks. Chesimard credited her aunt for expanding her education by introducing her to culture, museums, and theater, and for seeing to it that she got her Graduate Equivalent

Degree (GED) after she quit high school at the age of sixteen.

In the late 1960s, Chesimard entered Manhattan Community College. She planned to major in business administration, but was immediately drawn to the school's expanding black studies program and the activities of the student body. At a time when the African American struggle and consciousness were on the upswing, she began to read about black history, culture, politics, and ideology (belief systems). She attended civil rights meetings and took part in passionate discussions. She joined a black students' group called the "Society of the Golden Drums," where she met her husband, Louis Chesimard. She even changed her hair and dress to reflect her African roots. She also took on a Muslim name, Assata Shakur. "It was like being born again," she wrote. "It was then that I decided that the most important thing in my life was for me to struggle for the liberation of black people."

THE BLACK LIBERATION ARMY

In 1970, Chesimard joined the Black Panther Party (BPP) and was assigned to provide assistance to the African American community through medical care and the breakfast program. But like many other members, she soon became disappointed with the BPP. She left the party after coming to the conclusion that its lack of a unifying philosophy made the party weak and ineffective.

Chesimard turned to a more radical (revolutionary) organization—the Black Liberation Army (BLA). Members of the informally organized BLA believed that change would come about through revolution. From 1971 to 1973, the BLA was held responsible for a series of sniper shootings and bank robberies in New York, New Jersey, Missouri, and Michigan. JoAnne Chesimard, as the news media continued to call her, was considered to be the guiding force behind the BLA.

LEGAL TROUBLES

Chesimard was personally charged with six different crimes, including bank robbery and the attempted murder of police officers. In 1974, she and Fred Hilton, another reputed member of the BLA, were tried for robbing a bank in the Bronx, New York, in September of 1972. (They had already been tried once for the robbery. The trial resulted in a hung jury—a jury that cannot agree on a verdict—with eleven of the twelve jurors in favor of a guilty verdict.) During the second trial, both Chesimard and Hilton were forced to leave the courtroom because they shouted insults at the judge. They also claimed to reject the U.S. legal system. Chesimard acted as her own lawyer through part of the trial, and helped to show that some of the testimony against her was inconsistent. Both Chesimard and Hilton were acquitted (found not guilty).

But Chesimard remained in jail on charges of murder. On May 2, 1973, the car that she and her two companions were traveling in was stopped by the police on the New Jersey turnpike. Gunfire was exchanged. A New Jersey state trooper and a former Black Panther information minister lay dead. Chesimard was wounded in both arms and a shoulder. The second man fled. The following day the *New York Times* reported that, at the time of her arrest, Chesimard was wanted by the Federal Bureau of Investigation (FBI) for armed bank robbery and by the New York police in connection with the 1972 slaying of two policemen, as well as for a hand-grenade attack on a police car.

During the beginning of the state trooper murder trial, Chesimard had discovered that she was pregnant. The father was Fred Hilton, her co-defendant in the bank robbery trial. The news of her pregnancy made headlines, but it did not improve her living conditions. She was taken from the prison on Rikers Island to the Middlesex County jail, where she spent more than twenty months in solitary confinement. (A prisoner in solitary confinement is not allowed contact with other inmates.) On September 11, 1974, she gave birth to her daughter, Kakuya Amala Olugbala Shakur, at a local hospital. A few days later, Chesimard was returned to Rikers Island.

A mistrial was declared because of Chesimard's pregnancy. But three years later a new murder trial was held. On March 25, 1977, Chesimard was convicted of the murder of the New Jersey state trooper. Because she was found guilty of murdering a law enforcement official, the sentence was severe. Chesimard was sentenced to life in prison—plus twenty-six to thirty-three years, to be served one after the other. (Sometimes life sentences are shortened, and the convict is paroled, or released before serving out the full sentence. In some cases, time is added to a life sentence to make sure that the convict spends a life term in prison.)

JAIL BREAK

In 1978, Chesimard was transferred to a maximum security prison for women in West Virginia. But because the facility was being closed down and other prisons considered her too great a security risk, she was shipped back to the New Jersey Corrections Institute for Women. Then, on November 2, 1979, three visitors seized two prison guards at gunpoint and took control of a prison van. Chesimard escaped. The following day she was named to the FBI's most wanted list.

With the help of her supporters, Chesimard managed to avoid capture for five years. Authorities suspected that the Weathermen (a violent and extreme group of radicals) might have helped her hide from police. In 1984, Chesimard was granted political asylum (political protection) in Cuba. She slipped out of the United States—and beyond the jurisdiction (authority) of U.S. law. Because the FBI kept her friends and family under close surveillance, Chesimard could not risk contacting them until she was out of the country. But once in Cuba, she was visited several times by her mother and her Aunt Evelyn. And in 1987, her daughter, Kakuya, by then a pre-teen, went to live with her.

At the time, Chesimard was reportedly pursuing a master's degree and living in a government-paid apartment in Havana, Cuba. Also in 1987, Chesimard published her autobiography. On

The building in Pittsburgh, Pennsylvania, where FBI agents found evidence that JoAnne Chesimard had been using a second-floor apartment as a hideout.

March 29, 1998, New Jersey governor Christie Whitman announced that she would be appealing to Cuba for Chesimard's return.

Sources for Further Reading

Bacon, John. "Governor to appeal for convict's return." *USA Today* (March 31, 1998), p. 3A.

"Extremists Acquitted." *Time* (January 7, 1974), p. 24.

Shakur, Assata. *Assata: An Autobiography.* Chicago: Lawrence Hill Books, 1987.

"Then and Now, Revisiting the Radicals." *Newsweek* (September 27, 1993), p. 60.

"Three Still At Large." *Newsweek* (November 2, 1981), p. 33.

Gordon Kahl

Born: 1920
Died: June 4, 1983

A member of a right-wing fringe group, militant tax protestor Gordon W. Kahl vowed he would never be taken alive—and he was right.

A MAN WHO WOULD NOT PAY TAXES

Kahl, a retired North Dakota farmer, joined an extremely conservative survivalist group—an organization of militant individuals who do not recognize the government's authority. The group was known as the Posse Comitatus (Latin for "power of the county"). As a member of the organization, he was opposed to income taxes and most forms of government authority above the county level. To protest government taxation, Kahl refused to report his income to the federal government. In 1977, he was convicted of failing to file federal income tax returns, for which he was placed on probation. Like the other members of the Posse Comitatus, Kahl insisted on his right to carry firearms.

On February 13, 1983, federal marshals approached Kahl in Medina, North Dakota, to serve him with a warrant for violating his parole. (A prisoner who is placed on parole is expected to meet certain conditions.) A shootout followed—in which two marshals were killed. On May 11, Kahl, his twenty-three- year-old son Yorivon, and a man named Scott Faul were formally charged with the murders. Within three weeks, on May 28, Yorivon and Faul were convicted of two counts of second- degree murder. But Kahl, who had avoided capture, remained at large.

MANHUNT

The nationwide hunt for Gordon Kahl began in February 1983 and ended almost four months later, when Federal Bureau of Investigation (FBI) agents received a tip that someone answering to the fugitive's description was sighted near Smithville, Arkansas—a hilly area one hundred and twenty-five miles northeast of Little Rock. The informant recognized the man from a wanted poster. (It was not difficult to recognize a stranger in the area: Smithville at that time had only one hundred and thirteen residents.) The man who looked like Kahl was riding in a car that belonged to Leonard and Norma Ginter—a couple who were reportedly sided with tax protesters.

Officials knew that Kahl had spent the previous year living in Arkansas under a false name. In late May they set out to gather evidence that Kahl was residing with the Ginters in their bunker-like house four miles outside of Smithville—a hilly area populated by more than twenty tax protesters. Once they had adequate evidence to suggest that the Ginters were harboring the fugitive, officials obtained a search warrant. On June 2, federal officials staked out the Ginter home, which stood at the end of a mile-long dirt road. Constructed of concrete, the house was built partly underground. Ginter was known to collect large quantities of explosives, weapons, and ammunition.

After a two-day stakeout, federal marshals organized a raid on the Ginter house. At about 3 P.M. on June 4, heavily armed agents formed a large circle around the bunker—out of sight of its occupants. Backing them up were sheriff's deputies and state troopers. As an extra precaution, a fire truck and ambulance stood by as well.

Almost three hours later agents stopped Leonard Ginter as he drove away from his house—with a loaded and cocked gun in his lap. In the back seat was a loaded rifle with a telescopic sight—a weapon that allows the shooter to fire accurately from

a great distance. Before he was taken into custody, Ginter told officials that his wife was alone in the house.

SHOOTOUT NEAR SMITHVILLE

The Ginter house had only one door. After Ginter was stopped, Sheriff Gene Matthews led a state police investigator and two Federal agents through the door. As soon as they entered the house, Norma Ginter ran outside. And Kahl, who had been hiding behind a refrigerator, fired a high-powered rifle—striking the thirty-eight-year-old sheriff on his left side, between the flaps of his bullet-proof vest. Severely wounded, Matthews fired at Kahl as he crawled outside. The three other officers fired on Kahl as they left the house.

313

Once Matthews had been dragged away from the house, officers let loose a hail of automatic gunfire. They also fired smoke bombs through the windows of the home, hoping to force the fugitive outdoors. But the tactic backfired. One of the tear-gas canisters fell down an air vent and caught on fire, setting off an explosion of thousands of rounds of ammunition that had been stockpiled in the Ginter home. Inside the bunker, Kahl was trapped in a fireworks of exploding dynamite and ammunitions that went on for nearly two hours. The final ammunition explosion took place at 8:10 P.M.

The Ginter home continued to burn after the explosions ceased. Attempting to put out the blaze, fire fighters emptied the fire truck of its water supply. When officers entered the house at about 10 P.M., flames still smoldered in the ruins. Wearing face masks to avoid being overcome by the smoke, they found Kahl's body lying face down. An automatic weapon lay near his corpse. Around the same time that Kahl's body was being taken out of the fire-gutted house, Sheriff Matthews died of his wounds.

Sources for Further Reading

Corcoran, James. *Bitter Harvest: Gordon Kahl and the Posse Comitatus.* New York: Viking, 1990.

"Shootout In a Sleepy Hamlet." *Time* (June 13, 1983), p. 16.

Rawls, Wendell Jr. "Man Dead in Gunfight Identified as Dakota Fugitive." *The New York Times* (June 5, 1983), p. 18.

Timothy McVeigh

Born: April 23, 1968

When a bomb exploded in Oklahoma City, Oklahoma, in 1995, it killed and injured hundreds of innocent victims. The nation was stunned to discover that the attack had not been committed by international terrorists, but by an American whose background was hardly cause for concern.

A SCRAWNY KID FOND OF GUNS

Students in McVeigh's high school referred to their classmate as the school's "most talkative" student. They were kidding. Raised in a suburb of Buffalo, New York, McVeigh was a quiet boy who kept to himself. His classmates picked on him, calling him "Chicken McVeigh" and "The Wimp."

By the time he graduated from high school in Pendleton, New York, McVeigh had become obsessed with guns. He lifted weights in order to add muscle to his scrawny physique. And he became increasingly fascinated with extremist organizations (radical, right-wing groups that favor revolutionary changes in the government). An accomplished computer student, McVeigh earned a scholarship to a state college after taking an advanced placement course in programming. But he dropped out of college within a few months because it took time away from his real interests: guns and the extremist underworld. McVeigh read right-wing materials and conversed with others who shared his increasingly paranoid world-view—a world-view that saw the federal government as evil and the citizens as victims who would soon be enslaved.

IN THE ARMY

McVeigh enlisted in the army in 1988, hoping to find his way into the Special Forces (an elite branch of the military). At Fort Riley in Kansas, he was a disciplined, model soldier. There he became increasingly interested in extremist publications—including a book called *The Turner Diaries,* which tells a bloody story of race war and right-wing revolution. When the Gulf War erupted, McVeigh served as a gunner on a assault vehicle in Kuwait. He earned a Bronze Star for his wartime service—which has been the subject of conflicting accounts. For example, McVeigh informed his mother that Iraqi soldiers surrendered to him with their arms in the air. But friends heard gorier tales of his Desert Storm experiences, which included blowing up an Iraqi soldier. Also, an army pal reported that McVeigh had shot an enemy soldier—even though the captured soldier held his arms in the air as a gesture of surrender.

After McVeigh returned from the Gulf War, he went to Fort Bragg, North Carolina, to participate in a course to qualify for Special Forces training. In April 1991, he dropped out of the difficult three-week course, and resigned from the army. He served briefly in the National Guard, but soon found other ways to feed his fascination with guns and other weapons.

THE NICHOLS BROTHERS

By 1993, McVeigh had drifted to the farming community of Decker, Michigan, where James and Terry Nichols lived. He had met Terry Nichols, a quiet, aloof man, in the army. The two men shared a hatred for the federal government. Terry Nichols claimed that he wanted to secede (to withdraw formally from an organization) from the United States and gave up his citizenship. He turned in his voter-registration card claiming that he was a "nonresident alien" (an outsider).

Terry's older brother, James—an organic farmer—also despised the government. To show his contempt, he defaced

(spoiled the appearance of) U.S. money and gave up his passport. When his ex-wife sued for child support, he told the court that he was no longer a citizen of "your Defacto . . . government." Regarded as strange by other members of his community, he used peroxide (a bleaching agent that contains oxygen) to bathe and amused himself by building homemade bombs. James and Terry Nichols belonged to an extremist group called the Patriots—an organization of gun-carrying anarchists who do not recognize any of the government's laws or authority.

During his stay in Decker, McVeigh became immersed in the Nichols brothers' anti-government philosophy. He attended Patriots meetings where members warned that bankers and politicians would soon take over the country and plant comput-

The front of the Alfred P. Murrah building was turned to rubble when the bomb went off, killing 168 people.

A timeline to death row

November 1994
$60,000 in guns and valuables are stolen from an Arkansas gun dealer.

December 1994
McVeigh and Michael Fortier visit each floor of the nine-story Murrah federal building in Oklahoma City.

January 1995
McVeigh and Fortier travel to Kansas, where they pile guns into a rented car. Fortier drives the car to Kingman, Arizona.

February 1995
McVeigh joins Fortier in Kingman. The two men reportedly sell the stash of guns.

April 14, 1995
McVeigh arrives in Junction City, Kansas. He sells his car and makes a phone call to reserve a Ryder rental truck for April 17.

April 18, 1995
McVeigh reportedly assembles an ammonium nitrate bomb with the help of Terry Nichols.

April 19, 1995
The Murrah building is destroyed by a bomb. McVeigh is stopped by a highway patrolman and arrested for a routine traffic violation.

April 21, 1995
Just as he is about to be released from the Perry jail on $500 bail, McVeigh is identified as "John Doe Number One."

April 1997
McVeigh's trial begins.

May 29, 1997
The prosecution and defense teams present closing arguments to sum up their cases.

May 30–June 2, 1997
The jury decides on a verdict.

June 2, 1997
A federal jury finds McVeigh guilty of eleven counts of murder and conspiracy. Later that month he is sentenced to death.

er chips in enslaved citizens. As his hatred for the government grew, he became increasingly paranoid.

A LETHAL EXPLOSION

On April 19, 1995, a bomb exploded in the Alfred P. Murrah Federal Building in Oklahoma City, Oklahoma. Within eight seconds, the building was utterly destroyed. Each of the nine floors collapsed on top of one another. Inside were government employees and small children who were playing in the building's day-care center.

Rescue workers attempted to save victims who had narrowly escaped death and were trapped in the rubble of the destroyed building. The broken remains of concrete, glass, and metal stood twenty-seven feet deep. After the dust had settled, one hundred and sixty-eight corpses were identified—nineteen of which were children.

At first, investigators suspected that the bombers were international terrorists—possibly Islamic fanatics who were known to use car bombs such as the one that had blown up the Murrah building. Immediately after the crash, federal agents began to sift through the debris for clues about the bombing.

A COUPLE OF JOHN DOES

Shortly after the explosion, the first significant clue appeared. Richard Nichols, a maintenance worker, was parked two blocks away from the Murrah building when the explosion occurred. Just as Nichols and his wife were about to get into their car, a large piece of metal landed on top of the vehicle. When investigators examined the metal scrap, they discovered that it was a piece of the axle of a truck. (An axle is a supporting shaft on which a wheel revolves.) But the axle had not come from just any truck. It had come from the vehicle that contained what investigators were calling the "OK Bomb." (OK is the abbreviation for Oklahoma.)

The truck axle contained a vehicle identification number (VIN). (Every car and truck has a VIN, which must be recorded with every new owner.) Using the truck's VIN, investigators traced the truck to a 1993 Ford that was registered to a Ryder rental agency in Miami, Florida. Further investigation placed the truck closer to the bombing. The Ryder agency had assigned the vehicle to a body shop in Junction City, Kansas—just two-hundred seventy miles from Oklahoma City.

Looking for a target

McVeigh and his friend Michael Fortier cased the Murrah building in December 1994. They stopped on each of the nine floors. There is little doubt that they saw the America's Kids day-care center on the second floor, where dozens of children were playing when the bomb exploded on April 19, 1995. Nineteen children died in the explosion.

It's possible that McVeigh did not intend to stop with the bombing of the Murrah building in Oklahoma City. Witnesses saw him and another man wandering around federal buildings in Phoenix, Arizona, and Omaha, Nebraska. It's possible the two men were casing the buildings to determine whether they were suitable targets for future bombings.

Pancho Villa rides again

Even as a high school student, McVeigh was obsessed with guns. After graduating he took a job as an armored car guard. Armed like a soldier, he rode in an armored car that took money from department stores to a nearby bank. His everyday work weaponry included three guns: one holstered in a black military belt, one tucked into a strap on his leg, and a third concealed in a handbag. A former co-worker recalled that the scrawny McVeigh once showed up "looking like **Pancho Villa**" (see entry). He had belts of ammunition strapped across his chest and he carried an arsenal of firearms that included two pistols, a sawed-off shotgun, and a rifle equipped with a scope. McVeigh's boss eventually told his gun-crazy employee that he would have to shed some of his weapons if he wanted to continue work as an armed guard.

The truck helped agents move closer to the bombing suspects. On April 17—two days before the bombing—two men had rented the truck that was used in the bombing at Elliott's Body Shop in Junction City. Investigators quickly traced the driver's license numbers the men had used to rent the truck. The licenses and other pieces of identification were fakes. But based on the descriptions of employees, FBI artists sketched a likeness of both men. In no time, the drawings of the bombing suspects were televised across the world. Investigators did not know the real names of the suspects, who became known as "John Doe Number One" and "John Doe Number Two." (John Doe is a name that is often assigned to someone whose true identity is unknown.)

A ROUTINE TRAFFIC STOP

Less than two hours after the explosion, state trooper Charlie Hanger pulled over a young man for a routine traffic violation on Interstate 35 in Perry, Oklahoma—about sixty minutes north of Oklahoma City. The driver of the 1977 yellow Mercury had no license tags. But he did have a gun—a nine-millimeter semiautomatic pistol was tucked under his jacket. It was loaded with Black Talon bullets, commonly known as "cop killers," because they can penetrate bulletproof vests worn by law enforcement officers. Hanger arrested the man on traffic and weapons charges.

Without realizing it, Hanger had arrested the prime suspect in the Oklahoma bombing case. At the time of his arrest, McVeigh was wearing a T-shirt that said, "The tree of liberty must be refreshed from time to time with the blood of patriots and tyrants." His car contained further clues about his state of

320

mind, such as sections of *The Turner Diaries* that describe the bombing of FBI headquarters and a piece of paper containing a quote from the eighteenth-century American Revolutionary leader Samuel Adams (1722–1803). It said, "When the Government fears the people, there is liberty. When the people fear the Government, there is tyranny [power that is exercised unjustly]." McVeigh had written something beneath the quote: "Maybe now, there will be liberty."

McVeigh was held at the small jail in Perry while the minor traffic and weapons charges were processed. After two days, he came within moments of being released. But before he was allowed to leave the jail, the results of a computer search arrived. McVeigh had been identified as one of the men who had rented the Ryder truck. Investigators believed that he was John Doe Number One.

The McVeigh Bill

Soon after McVeigh, a decorated Gulf War veteran, was convicted of the Oklahoma City bombing, the Senate passed a bill that denies veterans' benefits to persons convicted of federal capital offenses (offenses that are punishable by death). The bill is known as the "McVeigh Bill."

A TON OF FERTILIZER

McVeigh was formally charged with the destruction of federal property. As investigators looked into his background and activities, they discovered a trail of evidence that linked him to the bombing. When they searched the home of Terry Nichols (who had moved to Kansas), they found a slip of pink paper in a drawer. It was a receipt for two thousand pounds of ammonium nitrate—a fertilizer that can be used as a key ingredient for bomb making. Although the receipt was made out to "Mike Havens," it provided a critical link to McVeigh: it contained his fingerprints.

The evidence against McVeigh was damning: neither he nor Nichols were farming at the time the fertilizer was purchased. With no crops, he had no real reason to purchase two thousand pounds of fertilizer. What's more, the bomb that destroyed the Murrah building contained a large quantity of ammonium nitrate. And the clothing McVeigh was wearing when he was arrested contained traces of a substance similar to the explosive.

The evidence against McVeigh mounted. Investigators also found his fingerprints on a rental contract for a storage unit where the ammonium nitrate was reportedly kept before the bomb was assembled. And the damp ground in front of the stor-

Recipe for disaster

Investigators determined that an ammonium nitrate bomb—sometimes called an "anfo"—destroyed the Murrah building in Oklahoma City. The Oklahoma bomber mixed 4,800 pounds of the fertilizer, ammonium nitrate, with fuel oil in twenty blue plastic drums. The bomb's destructive power was made even more deadly by the addition of metal containers of hydrogen or acetylene (a highly explosive gas).

age unit contained tire tracks that could have been made by a Ryder truck—such as the one McVeigh had rented in Kansas City.

POSING AS JOB HUNTERS

The fact that the Murrah building was so totally destroyed was no accident. The bomber—who was thoroughly familiar with the layout of the building—knew exactly how much explosive material to use and where to place it. Soon after McVeigh's arrest, federal investigators learned that witnesses had seen him casing the building (examining a building carefully in order to plan a crime) with another man.

Michael Fortier, an army buddy of McVeigh's, quit his job at the True Value Hardware store in Kingman, Arizona, on December 22, 1994. Later that month, he and McVeigh traveled to Oklahoma City, where they visited each of the nine floors of the Murrah building. They avoided attracting attention by posing as men looking for jobs at the offices of various federal agencies—such as the Small Business Administration and the Internal Revenue Service.

THE CASE AGAINST MCVEIGH

After two years of pretrial proceedings—which produced seven thousand pounds of physical evidence and twenty-five thousand interviews—McVeigh's trial began in Denver, Colorado, in April 1997. (Terry Nichols was tried in a separate trial.) U.S. assistant attorney Joseph Hartzler, who led the prosecution team, promised to try the case in just six weeks. Many people thought Hartzler would not be able to keep his promise.

The trial lasted a little less than six weeks. First, the prosecution team presented its case. Over the course of eighteen days, one hundred and thirty-seven witnesses contributed to the prosecution's account of the events that led to the Oklahoma City bombing. According to government attorneys, McVeigh was motivated by a burning hatred of the federal government. He spent months gathering the ingredients to make an ammonium nitrate bomb and planning the attack. He rented the truck used in the bombing, and drove the truck to Oklahoma City. The government's case was strong and detailed, but it was not without flaws. No one testified to having seen McVeigh constructing the bomb, and no one had actually seen him at the scene of the disaster. Most of the prosecution's evidence was circumstantial (evidence that is based on circumstances rather than facts).

Guilty!

Faced with a detailed timeline of McVeigh's activities prior to the bombing, defense lawyers needed to present an alternative account of their client's activities during the period leading up to the incident. But McVeigh's lawyers could offer no such proof. No friend, relative, or stranger was able to provide evidence that McVeigh was not in Oklahoma City on the day of the bombing. And McVeigh did not testify in his own defense. After just three and a half days of testimony, the defense rested its case. After closing arguments (summary statements by the defense and prosecuting attorneys), the seven men and five women of the jury were sequestered (secluded) while they decided the eleven charges of murder and conspiracy against McVeigh.

On June 2, 1997—after just twenty-three hours of discussions—the jury arrived at a verdict. The jurors returned to a courtroom packed with fifty bombing survivors and relatives of the victims who had died. McVeigh entered the courtroom smiling. None of his family was present. When the verdict was announced, he showed no emotion. McVeigh was found guilty of all eleven charges against him, including eight counts of first-degree murder of federal agents. Later that month, the jury decided on McVeigh's sentence. Each of the twelve jurors voted for the death penalty.

Sources for Further Reading

Annin, Peter, Tom Morgenthau, and Randy Collier. "Blowing Smoke." *Newsweek* (February 19, 1996), pp. 28–31.

Here's a book you might like:

Trader Wooly and the Terrorist, 1988, by Tom Townsend

When a seventh-grader takes a liking to a new girl in school, he brings her into his circle of friends, which includes a number of "army brats" (children of American soldiers) at the American School in Munich, Germany. But they don't know that the girl is the youngest member of a terrorist group whose mission is to poison the school's students.

Dead man waiting

In 1996, Congress implemented legal changes to speed up the execution of criminals on death row. But experts estimate that it will take four to six years to put McVeigh to death.

Gun money

The bombing of the Murrah building was an expensive undertaking. It involved purchasing thousands of pounds of fertilizer and other explosive agents. The bomber also had to pay storage, vehicle rental, and travel expenses. Federal investigators believe that the bombing was financed by the sale of guns—including stolen weapons.

On November 5, 1994, Roger E. Moore, an Arkansas gun dealer, was robbed by a man wearing camouflage battle dress and a black ski mask. Armed with a shotgun, the man taped Moore's legs and feet and swept through the house, stealing pistols and rifles, gold, silver, and cash. The robber escaped with $60,000 in cash and valuables.

When FBI agents raided the home of Terry Nichols, they found a number of things that had been taken from Moore during the robbery—including guns, gold coins, a bag of money, and the key to Moore's safety deposit box. Federal investigators believed that McVeigh and Nichols masterminded the robbery and used the money to finance the bombing.

Bragg, Rick. "McVeigh Guilty on All Counts in the Oklahoma City Bombing; Jury to Weigh Death Penalty." *The New York Times* (June 3, 1997), p. A1

Collins, James. "The Merits of the Case." *Time* (June 9, 1997), pp. 28–29.

Kifner, John. "U.S. Case Against 2d Defendant May Not Go as Smoothly." *The New York Times* (June 3, 1997), p. A19.

Stickney, Brandon M. *All-American Monster: The Unauthorized Biography of Timothy McVeigh.* Buffalo, NY: Prometheus Books, 1996.

Terry, Don. "Steel with Soft Surface." *The New York Times* (June 3, 1997), p. A19.

Thomas, Evan et al. "Inside the Plot." *Newsweek* (June 5, 1995), pp. 24–27.

Thomas, Evan et al. "The Plot." *Newsweek* (May 8, 1995), pp. 28–34.

Thomas, Jo. "Six Weeks, One Theory." *The New York Times* (June 3, 1997), p. A1.

Thomas, Jo. "Verdict Is Cheered." *The New York Times* (June 3, 1997), p. A1.

Watson, Russell and Evan Thomas. "Cleverness—and Luck." *Newsweek* (May 1, 1995), pp. 30–35.

Diana Oughton

Born: January 26, 1942
Died: March 6, 1970

Once a promising young student and social activist, Diana Oughton became increasingly radical during the political turmoil of the Vietnam era. Never identified as a prominent terrorist, she died in a bomb factory of the Weathermen—a terrorist organization to which she belonged.

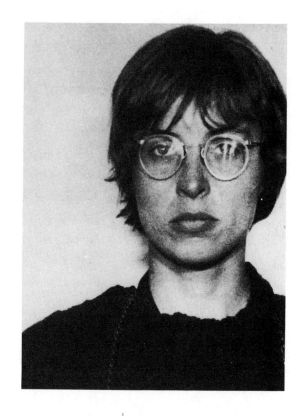

A SOLID FAMILY

Born on January 26, 1942, Oughton was the first of her parents' four daughters. She was raised in Dwight, Illinois, a small farming community in the northern part of the state. Oughton's family was respected for its history of social consciousness. Her father's great-great-grandfather founded the Keeley Institute for alcoholics. And her mother's great-grandfather, W. D. Boyce, was responsible for establishing the American Boy Scouts. Oughton's father, James Oughton, turned to the restaurant business after completing an Ivy League education. Conservative and Episcopalian, the Oughton family stood out in the community of just over three thousand people.

Oughton enjoyed an upper-middle class childhood. She swam, played tennis, and was an accomplished horseback rider. She learned to play the flute and piano. The Oughton family ate dinner together in the evening, and the children were included in discussions on an equal basis with adults. Even as a child, Oughton expressed strong opinions. Her father later remem-

Students for a Democratic Society

Although the members of the Students for a Democratic Society (SDS) played a minor role in demonstrations against American involvement in the Vietnam War as early as September 1963, its major focus during the first half of the 1960s was on domestic issues (problems within the United States). In 1963, the organization began its Economic Research and Action Project (ERAP) to enlist the involvement of the urban poor in the democratic system. The project was established in ten cities, among them Baltimore, Maryland; Boston, Massachusetts; Chicago, Illinois; Cleveland, Ohio; Newark, New Jersey; and Philadelphia, Pennsylvania. Most ERAP projects were short-lived, although new ones sprang up as soon as old ones died.

In late 1964, while leaders of the first generation of SDS were still involved in grassroots domestic issues, the second generation was already starting to focus on the Vietnam War. They planned an antiwar campaign that included an April 1965 protest march in Washington, D.C.

The bombing of North Vietnam, which began in February 1965, triggered an increase in opposition to the war. In December 1964, SDS had hoped to draw 2,000 demonstrators to its April march. As many as 25,000 protesters

bered that she was an independent thinker who always had her own ideas—about anything from movies to how animals should be treated.

A SOCIAL CONSCIENCE

As a young woman, Oughton attended the Madeira School in Greenway, Virginia. Later, she was enrolled at Bryn Mawr College, an exclusive women's school, where she began to take an interest in community affairs and social injustices. She became active in voter registration, helping underprivileged individuals register to vote. Many activists then and now see voter registration as the first step in addressing the social problems of the poor and of minority groups who are not well-represented in political issues.

Oughton also began to tutor underprivileged students. Over the course of two years, she took a train at night to a ghetto area in Philadelphia, Pennsylvania, where she tutored two junior high school boys. The experience was eye-opening. Oughton's younger sister, Carol, later told *Time* magazine, "I remember how

showed up. SDS had been growing steadily, from 250 members in December 1960, to 2,500 in December 1964. As the war rose to new heights, so did SDS membership. By October 1965, 25,000 people claimed SDS membership.

The original members of the SDS believed that the political system could be forced to reform itself. But many of the newcomers to the organization in 1965 and 1966 lacked that faith. As the war heated up, many members of the old guard began to agree. By late 1967, the SDS had entered a new phase, focusing on resistance to the war and military draft. The new SDS leadership dismissed plans for the antiwar demonstrations at the 1968 Democratic National Convention as insufficiently revolutionary. The small number of SDS members who went to Chicago played a role in heading up the demonstrations. They came away believing that the young people of America were ready for revolution on the streets.

Although the SDS no longer kept careful records, its membership was estimated between 80,000 and 100,000. But just as the SDS should have been at the height of its influence, two rival groups began to battle for its control. In June 1969, at an SDS convention, the Weathermen and Progressive Labor Party—who followed the Chinese Communism of Mao Tsetung (1893–1976)—split the organization in two.

incredulous [disbelieving] she was that a seventh- or eighth-grade child couldn't read, didn't even know the alphabet."

Oughton spent her junior year in Germany, as a student at the University of Munich. There she chose to turn away from the trappings of a privileged existence. She pedaled around town on a bicycle instead of hiring a taxicab. And when she traveled, she chose inexpensive rooms over expensive hotels.

LIVING IN GUATEMALA

When a football player from Princeton University proposed marriage to her, Oughton turned him down. She said that she was not ready to marry because she had too many things to do. After graduating from Bryn Mawr, she joined the American Friends Service Committee, an organization devoted to social relief. After taking an intensive course in the Spanish language, Oughton traveled to the Latin American country of Guatemala, where she taught Guatemalan Indians the language she had recently learned. (Many of them spoke only a native dialect. Their inability to speak and understand Spanish, the official

Bill Ayers.

language of Guatemala, made it even more difficult to rise out of the poverty and oppression in which much of the country lived.)

Stationed in the town of Chichicastenango, Oughton was shocked by the area's terrible poverty—and by the bitter hatred between the large class of poor people and the very small group of wealthy individuals. What's more, she was disturbed by the fact that the United States supported the Guatemalan regime—a government she considered to be unjust and oppressive.

RADICAL IDEAS

After she returned to the United States, Oughton enrolled at the University of Michigan in order to earn a teaching certificate. As a student, she participated in the Children's Community School, an experimental school for children ages four to eight. The school offered an open and informal approach to education, but the institution collapsed in 1968, when its funding disappeared.

While involved in the Children's Community School, Oughton met Bill Ayers, who later became one of the prominent leaders of a political group known as the Students for a Democratic Society (SDS). Oughton joined the SDS and became more political and radical (revolutionary). When she discussed politics with her father, she argued in favor of revolutionary approaches to social problems—approaches that often involved violence. Oughton's relationship with her family became increasingly strained. Convinced that his daughter had become completely carried away with radical ideas, her father and the rest of the Oughton family lost touch with Diana.

JOINS RADICAL GROUP

For two years, beginning in 1968, Oughton's family knew next to nothing about her whereabouts. The legal establishment, on the other hand, became increasingly familiar with Oughton's activities. In 1969, the SDS had splintered into sepa-

328

The Weathermen

By 1970, small groups of extremists turned from protests to street riots and terrorist violence. In 1969, the Weathermen formed a radical splinter group from the Students for a Democratic Society (SDS). The words "You don't need a weatherman to know which way the wind blows," taken from a Bob Dylan song, "Subterranean Homesick Blues," were the source of the Weathermen's name. The Weathermen organized street riots in Chicago and attacked federal buildings around the country, calling for revolution in the United States. In October of that year, the Weathermen group stormed through Chicago streets, destroying property and beating up people who got in their way—supposedly to protest the trial of the organizers of the Chicago demonstrations at the Democratic National Convention in August 1968, and to "bring the war back home."

But the Weathermen's "days of rage" rampage failed to mobilize the large numbers of young Chicagoans who had turned out for the defendants' protest marches. The Weathermen suffered more injuries and financial damage than their targets. Two hundred Weathermen were arrested.

In June 1970, the Weathermen bombed the New York City police headquarters, inflicting substantial damage. They took credit for seven other bombings from 1970 to 1972. Weathermen bombings destroyed the army's mathematics lab center in Madison, Wisconsin, killing one person. Another bomb blew up part of the U.S. Capitol.

Many Americans were frightened by the violence—and violent words—of the Weathermen. By 1970 they had almost no public support. On March 6, 1970, the explosion of a Weathermen bomb factory in the basement of a New York townhouse killed three members, and the discovery of antipersonnel explosives in their arsenal further destroyed their limited base of support. Charged with several offenses, the Weathermen went underground. Some took on new identities. Others joined forces with Black Panther Party members who were in exile in Algeria.

rate camps. Oughton and Ayers joined the most violent and extreme group of radicals, known as the Weathermen. As a member of the Weathermen, Oughton established a criminal record. Caught passing out pamphlets to high school students, she was arrested in Flint, Michigan. In Chicago, Illinois, she was arrested for raids against the police that were known as the Weathermen's "days of rage."

In December 1969, a small group of Weathermen held a secret meeting in Flint. The meeting reportedly ended in a plan

The Democratic National Convention

In Chicago, Illinois, during the Democratic National Convention of 1968, city police beat thousands of demonstrators protesting the war in Vietnam. At the time, an official government report labeled the incident a "police riot." The televised pictures of the Chicago police clubbing demonstrators angered many young Americans—some of whom turned to violence in response to the brutal police action. A poll taken after the convention, revealed that 368,000 young people called themselves revolutionaries.

to begin a wave of terrorist bombings. The Detroit police claimed that Oughton was present at that meeting.

Although bomb threats worried the country throughout the following year, Oughton was never accused in any bombing or conspiracy to plot a bombing. On March 6, 1970, a house on 11th Street in Manhattan, New York, was destroyed by a bomb. The address was determined to be a bomb factory where the Weathermen put together the explosives they intended to use in bombings. As police scoured the ruins of the shattered house, they concluded that three people had died in the explosion. Having found a severed finger, they identified one of the victims as twenty-eight-year-old Diana Oughton.

Sources for Further Reading

Franks, L. and T. Powers. "Destruction of Diana." *Reader's Digest* (November 1970), pp. 49–58.

"Memories of Diana." *Time* (March 30, 1970), p. 21.

Powers, Thomas. *Diana: The Making of a Terrorist.* Boston: Houghton Mifflin, 1971.

"Seeds of Terror." *The New York Times Magazine* (November 22, 1981), pp. 34–38.

Bandits
and Gunslingers

"**O**utlaws are made, not born," lawman Wyatt Earp once said. Was Jesse James a born bandit who was destined to rob trains? Did Billy the Kid's upbringing turn him into a killer? Would Butch Cassidy have been a crook if he'd been born in Boston? These aren't questions that can be answered. But they're questions that provide an interesting glimpse into the life and times of the bandits and gunslingers who contributed to the legend of the Wild West.

In this section you'll read all about outlaws—from legendary gunslinger Clay Allison to Pancho Villa, the Mexican revolutionary who became a hero to some and a villain to others. You'll find out about their early lives, the people they met, the circumstances they encountered—and the details involving their final days.

Clay Allison
(Robert Clay Allison)

Born: 1840 or 1841
Died: July 3, 1887

Gunslinger Clay Allison was once asked what he did for a living. "I am a shootist" was his response. Although in reality he killed fewer men than many other outlaws, he has gone down in history as one of the most infamous gunslingers in the West.

A SOUTHERN BOY

Born in the Tennessee countryside, Allison received little schooling. Almost twenty years old when the Civil War erupted in 1861, Allison served in the Confederate Army—both as a spy and as a scout for Confederate General Nathan Bedford Forrest (1821–1877). After the war ended, he headed south to Texas to find work as a cowboy. He drove cattle from Texas to Kansas and worked on ranches in Colorado and New Mexico—and trouble followed wherever he went.

During the 1870s, Allison worked for many wealthy cattle owners in the border state of New Mexico. In 1874 he committed his first killing—his first *recorded* killing, that is—when he shot a man near the Canadian River in New Mexico. Allison was probably also involved in a number of other killings that took place in Colorado, Kansas, New Mexico, and Texas around that time. He justified his killings by claiming that he was protecting property holders from thieves and murderers. And he made no

Bat Masterson 1853-1921

Bartholomew "Bat" Masterson wasn't a man to back down from a fight. A member of the infamous "Dodge City Peace Commission"—which included **Wyatt Earp** (see entry), Doc Holliday, and Charlie Bassett, among others—he was one of the most prominent lawmen in the Old West.

Masterson had deadly aim with a gun. Describing what was required to become an accurate shooter, Masterson wrote this:

To accustom his hands to the pistols of those days, the man who coveted [desired] a reputation started in early and practiced with them just as a card shark practices with his cards, as a shell game man drills his fingers to manipulate the elusive pea, or a juggler must practice to acquire proficiency [to become skilled]. When he could draw, cock and fire all in one smooth lightning-quick movement, he could then detach [remove] his mind from that movement and concentrate on accuracy.

There is no question that Masterson was a well-practiced pistol shooter. "It was not magic which enabled Bat Masterson to produce some wizard-like effects with the draw. It was hard and unrelenting practice," a journalist named Arthur Chapman wrote in the January 3, 1930, edition of the New York *Herald-Tribune.* Chapman interviewed a man named John L. Amos, who, as a young man, had been Masterson's roommate in Dodge City, Kansas. Apparently, sharing a room with the gunslinger was a nerve-racking experience. Amos told the journalist:

The only complaint I had against my roommates [Masterson and Conk Jones, another gunslinger] was that they were always practicing gunplay. For at least an hour every day, they would practice with unloaded guns, draw and click, draw and click. . . . Masterson and Conk practiced their gunplay in the room and generally, I was the target. I would hear a click behind me and would turn around to find that one of them had snapped his

apologies for his chosen occupation. He reportedly once said, "I never killed a man who didn't need it."

TALL TALES

A tall, good-looking man with brown hair and blue eyes, Allison was a drunk. Although there's no doubt that he was deadly with a gun and played a role in killing a number of men, many of the stories about his exploits are either far-fetched exaggerations—or utterly untrue. In one such story, a drunken

revolver at me. If I came in the door, perhaps both of them would go through the motion of drawing and firing at me as I entered. I liked both of them a lot, but finally I had to tell them that my nerves were going to pieces, and I would have to hand in my official resignation as their target.

Before he became a peace officer, Masterson dabbled in a number of occupations. Born in St. George, Quebec in Canada, and raised in the Midwest, he left for Kansas in 1872 with his brother, Ed, to join a railroad gang in Dodge City. After one year of railroad labor, he took work as a buffalo hunter—something many other noted gunfighters had done.

Back in Dodge City, Masterson was employed as a city policeman. In 1877, he was elected sheriff of Ford County, Kansas. Here are some of the highlights of his career:

- Captured Dave Rudabaugh and Edgar West after they attempted to rob a train near Kinsley, Kansas

- Led a posse (a group of people with legal authority to capture criminals)—which included Wyatt Earp among its ranks—that captured James W. Kennedy, who was accused in the slaying of a woman who worked in a dance-hall

- Was appointed a deputy U.S. marshal in 1879; after serving his term, Masterson was defeated for re-election

Masterson was also an avid gambler. In 1881, he moved to Tombstone in the Arizona Territory to work for Wyatt Earp as a card dealer at the Oriental Saloon. He ended his career in New York City—as a journalist. Masterson earned a favorable reputation as a writer and sports editor for the *New York Morning Telegraph,* and was recognized as an authority on prizefighting (boxing). Masterson died of a heart attack on October 25, 1921.

Allison gallops through the streets in a Texas town—wearing nothing but his boots and his hat—as he empties his guns into storefront windows. Another tale recounts an episode with a dentist who mistakenly pulled the wrong tooth. As revenge, the story goes, Allison pulled a gun on the dentist—as well as one of the dentist's teeth.

Allison apparently shot his friend-turned-enemy Chuck Colbert. In one account of the shooting, Allison and Colbert meet at a restaurant in Texas for dinner. Following a stare-down, during which the outlaws stir their coffees with the muzzles of their

Bat Masterson.

guns, Allison draws on Colbert, shooting him in the forehead. As his former friend's body is carried away, the hard-hearted shootist continues his meal—without even looking up. Francisco "Pancho" Griego, a Mexican outlaw, met a similar fate. When Allison realized that Griego was using his sombrero to hide a gun, he shot him without asking any questions.

Other stories have Allison forcing various lawmen—including Wyatt Earp and Bat Masterson—to back down. But there is no evidence to support any such meetings. In fact, Allison probably avoided face-to-face confrontations with lawmen. Ironically, Allison didn't die in a blaze of gunfire. Drunk, he fell out of a heavy freight wagon, and was killed when the wheel rolled over him. Allison's grave is in Peco, Texas.

Sources for Further Reading

The American West, A Cultural Encyclopedia, Volumes 1 and 6. Danbury, CT: Grolier Educational Corp., 1995, pp. 28–29, 968–971.

Nash, Jay Robert. *Bloodletters and Badmen.* New York: M. Evans, 1973, pp. 18–19.

Rosa, Joseph. *The Taming of the West: Age of the Gunfighter.* New York: Smithmark, 1993, pp. 120–121.

Wukovits, John. *The Gunslingers.* Broomall, PA: Chelsea House, 1997, p. 17.

Richard Barter

Born: 1834
Died: July 11, 1859
AKA: Rattlesnake Dick

A small-time outlaw, Richard Barter organized a gang of thieves that robbed a mule train carrying thousands of dollars in gold. The robbery was a success—but the gold was lost—and none of the thieves ever profited from the heist.

A GOLDEN OPPORTUNITY

The son of a British officer, Richard Barter was born in either England or Quebec, Canada. He moved to the United States when he was young. In his teens, he headed for California to pan for gold—only to find himself employed by large companies that made it difficult for an individual gold-digger to strike it rich. Barter soon turned to theft—and was soon caught. Found guilty of stealing horses, he was jailed for two years. Soon after his release, Barter, who was known as "Rattlesnake Dick," formed a gang made up of George Skinner, his brother, Cyrus Skinner, a horse thief called Big Dolph Newton, Bill Carter, who had a reputation as a fast shot, and a man named Romero. Barter first had the gang commit small robberies—as practice for a larger job he had in mind.

During the gold-rush era, thousands of dollars worth of gold bullion (gold still in raw or unrefined form) were transported out of the hills by mule trains that were accompanied by armed guards. After studying the movements of shipments in

All that glitters--the California gold rush

In 1848, Alta, California, was a modest frontier outpost with a population of about 14,000. The following year Alta's population skyrocketed and by 1850, the area's population had grown to about 100,000 residents. The reason for the population explosion: gold fever.

John Augustus Sutter, a German-born Swiss immigrant, created a 50,000-acre agricultural empire in northern California. On his lands were orchards, fields, and a fort (manned with an army). In January 1848, his foreman—James Wilson Marshall, a thirty-eight-year-old carpenter from New Jersey—had instructions to build a sawmill on Sutter's property, at a bend of the South Fork of the American River. As his crew deepened the millrace (a canal in which water flows to and from a mill wheel), Marshall spotted something shiny. He later recalled, "My eye was caught by something shining in the bottom of the ditch . . . I reached my hand down and picked it up; it made my heart thump, for I was certain it was gold."

Indeed it was. Marshall brought the nugget back to Sutter's Fort, where he and his employer tested it—according to methods outlined in an encyclopedia. Although Sutter tried to keep the discovery secret, word soon spread through California and beyond. On March 18, 1848, a San Francisco newspaper announced "Gold Mine Found." Sometime later a young Mormon named Sam Brannan stirred up public interest when he marched through the streets of San Francisco with a bottle filled with gold dust shouting, "Gold! Gold! Gold from the American River!" Within one month, thousands of men abandoned San Francisco in hopes of striking it rich in the gold fields. News of the bonanza hit New York before summer—when it was announced in the *New York Herald*.

In 1849, the peak year of the California Gold Rush, about 80,000 "Forty-niners" (the name refers to the year the California Gold Rush

Wet gold claims

Miners in California worked gold claims that stretched over 400 miles of rivers and streams including the American, Feather, Mercedes, Stanislaus, and Yuba.

the area, Barter came up with a plan to steal a fortune in gold by stopping the Wells Fargo mule team that carried bullion out of the Trinity Mountains. He sent his men to ambush the mule train—but he didn't join them.

BURIED TREASURE

Barter's plan was a success. The gang members headed down the mountain pass with $80,000 worth of gold—an enormous amount of money in that day. But what Barter hadn't real-

began) arrived in California. Nine-tenths of the miners were men—and more than half of them were under twenty years old. Most of them had been tradesmen or farmers before taking up the shovel and pan. Some were military men. Infected by gold fever, soldiers deserted their posts and sailors jumped ship. The majority of miners were from the United States—two-thirds of whom came from the eastern states of New England. Many of the Forty-niners were foreign-born. Mining camps became a melting pot of Chinese, Mexicans, Irish, Russians, West Indians, Italians, French, and Australians.

Life in the dismal mining towns was expensive. Forced to pay outrageous prices for food and supplies (the price of a common shovel was reported to have increased by 800 percent), the miners lived in squalid (poverty-ridden) conditions. In a letter home, one miner reported, "You can scarcely form any conception of what a dirty business this gold digging is and of the mode of life which a miner is compelled to lead. We all live more like brutes than humans." Not surpris-

ingly, violence was a problem in mining regions: miners were stoned to death in arguments over gambling, well-armed claim stakers readily shot intruders, and dead bodies were sometimes seen floating down rivers. Historians estimate that the homicide rate in the mining frontier was several times higher than it is in today's major American cities.

The work was back-breaking. Eroded (worn away) into dust, nuggets and flakes, the gold combined with sand and gravel in the bottom of stream beds. In order to sift the gold from worthless sludge, miners had to "wash" the contents of streambeds. They used a variety of methods. Gold panning entailed shoveling sand and gravel into a rocker or cradle. Some used a sluice (a long trough) called a "Long Tom" that allowed them to wash greater quantities. During the peak years of the gold rush, gold sold for $15 to $16 an ounce. Although some miners struck it rich, the odds were poor: it is estimated that only one out of every one hundred miners earned more than $16 a day.

ized was that the mules—which were clearly marked with the Wells Fargo brand—would not be able to complete the difficult trip out of the mountains. Somewhere near Ureka, the three robbers were forced to abandon what they couldn't carry. They buried most of their haul.

Barter and Cyrus Skinner were supposed to meet the rest of the gang at Folsom to divide the gold. But before they were able to rejoin their accomplices, they were thrown in jail for stealing mules. Since lawmen didn't suspect them of being involved in the gold robbery, their sentence was short. Meanwhile, posses

That's a lot of money!

It is estimated that between 1848 and 1857, $500 million in gold was mined in California.

(groups of people summoned by a sheriff to aid in law enforcement) of lawmen and Wells Fargo detectives had been hunting the countryside for the thieves who robbed the mule train. When the lawmen found the thieves, a shoot-out erupted. George Skinner was killed and Romero was severely wounded. Newton and Carter surrendered. While Carter gave up the remaining gold in exchange for his freedom, Romero and Newton were sent to prison.

After they were released from jail, Barter and Cyrus Skinner searched the foothills for the buried gold. They found nothing. Having earned nothing from the gold heist, they turned to stagecoach robbery and were soon pursued by local lawmen. On July 11, 1859, Barter encountered Sheriff J. Boggs, who shot and killed him with a single bullet. He was twenty-five years old. Skinner was wounded and later sentenced to a lengthy imprisonment.

Sources for Further Reading

The American West, A Cultural Encyclopedia, Volume 4. Danbury, CT: Grolier Educational Corp., 1995, pp. 634–636.

Courtrigt, David T. "Violence in America." *American Heritage* (September 1996), p. 36+.

Louis, Ted. "Hidden California Gold Treasure." *Stamps* (January 7, 1995), p. 12.

Nash, Jay Robert. *Bloodletters and Badmen.* New York: M. Evans, 1973, p. 46.

Nash, Jay Robert. *The Encyclopedia of Western Lawmen and Outlaws.* New York: DaCapo, 1994, p. 25.

Nash, Jay Robert. *The Encyclopedia of World Crime.* Wilmette, IL: Crime Books, 1990, p. 265.

Ward, Geoffrey. *The West, An Illustrated History.* Boston: Little, Brown, 1996, pp. 120–165.

Sam Bass

Born: July 21, 1851
Died: July 21, 1878

"Sam Bass was not much of an outlaw as outlaws go. He was no gunman, nor was he a killer," wrote Charles L. Martin in A Sketch of Sam Bass, the Bandit. But somehow, he was transformed into a folk hero even before he was betrayed by a gang member.

A ROUGH CHILDHOOD

One of ten children, Sam Bass was born in Indiana on July 21, 1851. Two of his siblings died as infants, and one of his brothers was killed fighting as a member of the Sixteenth Indiana Regiment during the Civil War (1861–1865). His mother, Elizabeth Sheeks Bass, died at the age of thirty-nine, shortly after her tenth child was born. Sam was just ten years old at the time.

Sam's father, Daniel Bass, married a woman who had two children from an earlier marriage. Together the couple had a son. Shortly thereafter, on February 20, 1864, Daniel died of pneumonia. He was forty-two. Having sold the family farm, Sam's stepmother was forced to send the children to live with relatives. Twelve-year-old Sam went with two of his brothers and three of his sisters to live with an uncle, David Sheeks.

Sam's uncle put the children to work on his farm. Sam plowed, hoed corn and potatoes, harvested, butchered, and sheered sheep. He rarely went to school and he never learned to read and write. And he soon grew tired of working for no pay on his uncle's farm.

FAST PONIES AND CATTLE SCAMS

At the age of eighteen, Bass ran away. He left with no money and only the clothes on his back. Taking odd jobs to support himself, he made his way west, where he hoped to become a cowboy. In Denton, in northeastern Texas, he worked as a hired hand for the sheriff, W. F. "Dad" Egan.

Horse racing was a popular pastime in Denton. Bass enjoyed betting at the race track and eventually purchased a horse—Jenny, a mare (female horse)—with the sheriff's younger brother. Egan didn't approve of the people who were associated with horse racing, and offered to lend Bass the money to buy out his brother's share in the mare.

Bass eventually quit his job and devoted his time to horse racing. He traveled through southwest Texas, the Indian territories, and Mexico with his friend, Henry Underwood, to enter his horse in races. Jenny—who became known as "the Denton Mare"—won most of the races she ran in.

Bass started out as a hard-working, honest young man who handled his money well. But he soon began to gamble at cards and drink heavily. On a trip to San Antonio, Texas, he made friends with Joel Collins, a former cowboy who owned a bar in town. Collins had been tried and acquitted in 1870 for murdering a man named Bedal Rosalees. Soon after meeting Bass, Collins sold his bar, and the two came up with a scheme to use the Denton Mare to win even more money.

Collins posed as the owner of the Denton Mare, while Bass pretended to be a horse trainer. After he hired on to work for another man who owned a race horse, Bass would test the horse to see if it was capable of beating the Denton Mare. If he thought the mare could beat the other horse, Bass encouraged the owner to enter the horse in a race against the Denton Mare. He also urged the owner to bet heavily on his horse. The Denton Mare always won—earning Bass and Collins easy money.

Bass and Collins eventually sold the Denton Mare. In the summer of 1876 they bought several hundred cattle in order to make money trail-herding them to Kansas. Since they didn't have enough cash to pay for the entire herd, they left for Kansas heavily in debt. North of Dodge City, Kansas, Bass and Collins sold the cattle. They made a handsome profit and could easily have repaid their debt. Instead, they kept all the money, and headed for Deadwood, in the Black Hills of the Dakota Territory. There, they gambled and made poor investments. In no time they lost all their earnings.

EASY MONEY

Bass and Collins decided to try their luck at stagecoach robbery. They formed a gang with three other men, and tried to stop the Deadwood Stage, which was carrying $15,000. When they yelled, "Halt!" the driver tried to stop—but the horses were scared and continued to run. One of the robbers shot the driver, killing him.

Hunted as wanted outlaws, Bass and Collins attempted a few more stagecoach robberies, with little success. One robbery yielded as little as $3. Next they turned to train robbery, which turned out to be much more rewarding. Joining with four other outlaws, they planned to rob an express train that had departed from San Francisco with a Wells Cargo freight car. After consulting the railroad's timetable, they met the train at Big Springs, Nebraska, and stopped it as it labored uphill. The robbers never managed to break into the safe, which contained about $200,000. But they did ride off with $60,000 in $20 gold pieces that had been stored in wooden boxes—and about $1,300 in loot taken from passengers.

Wells Fargo offered a reward for their capture. Dozens of railroad detectives and posses (groups of people with legal authority to capture criminals) soon hounded the robbers as they tried to make their way back to Texas. To throw their pursuers off their trail, the outlaws split into pairs. Bass went with Jack Davis, while Collins rode with a man who called himself Bill Heffridge. Collins and Heffridge were both killed in a shoot-out with soldiers. Davis disappeared, never to be heard from again. Another gang member, Tom Nixon, also vanished—even though the Pinkerton Detective Agency was conducting a nation-wide manhunt for the outlaws. Bass managed to make it back to Denton, Texas, where he organized another band of outlaws.

GROWING SUSPICION

After committing a few moderately successful stagecoach robberies, Bass decided that it was time to return to train robbery. He organized a gang that included his friend, Henry Underwood, and some new recruits: Frank Jackson, Seaborn Barnes—who had been acquitted of a shooting when he was seventeen years old—and Tom Spotswood. In the spring of 1878, Bass and his gang staged four train holdups around Dallas.

Alarmed by the robbers' repeated offenses, the governor of Texas called out the Texas Rangers. Pinkerton Detectives from Chicago joined the manhunt, as did a number of other law officers. But none of them was able to capture Bass, who hid for some time in Cove Hollow—a steep, hilly area near Denton. Many of the local people defended Bass, while others began to suspect that he was one of the outlaws who had robbed the Big Springs train. Each of the stolen $20 gold pieces—which were called double eagles—had the same date, 1877. Sam Bass had been going around town for some time spending $20 double eagles stamped with that date.

A TRAITOR IN THE GANG

Bass never managed to match the success of the first train robbery at Big Springs. Hungry for some quick cash, he decided to try his hand at bank robbery. Together with his bandit recruits, he planned to rob a bank in Round Rock, Texas. One of the new members of Bass's gang was Jim Murphy, whose family had hidden Bass after one of his train robberies.

Goodnight little doggies

Shortly after Sam Bass was killed, a ballad that described his life and betrayal appeared. The song was a favorite among cowboys on the range, who sang it as they rode slowly around their cattle at night. The final four verses below describe Sam's betrayal at the hands of Jim Murphy, the gang-member-turned-traitor:

Jim Murphy was arrested and then
  released on bail;
He jumped his bond at Tyler and took the
  train for Terrell.
But Major Jones had posted Jim and that
  was all a stall;
'Twas only a plan to capture Sam before
  the coming fall.

Sam met his fate at Round Rock, July the
  twenty-first;
They pierced poor Sam with rifle balls and
  emptied out his purse.

Poor Sam he is a corpse and six foot under
  clay;
And Jackson's in the bushes, trying to get
  away.

Jim had used Sam's money and didn't
  want to pay;
He thought his only chance was to give
  poor Sam away.

He sold out Sam and Barnes and left their
  friends to mourn—
Oh, what a scorching Jim will get when
  Gabriel blows his horn!
And so he sold out Sam and Barnes and
  left their friends to mourn.
Oh, what a scorching Jim will get when
  Gabriel blows his horn!

Perhaps he's got to heaven, there's none of
  us can say;
But if I'm right in my surmise, he's gone
  the other way.

What Bass didn't know was that Murphy had made a deal with Major John B. Jones, a Texas Ranger. In exchange for dropping charges against his family—and a handsome reward—Murphy agreed to report on Bass's whereabouts.

Some of the other members of the Bass gang were suspicious of Murphy, but he managed to get word to Jones that the outlaws were planning to hit the Round Rock bank. On the afternoon of July 15, 1878, Bass and three others rode into Round Rock. A group of Texas Rangers were there waiting for them. As Jim Murphy watched from his hiding spot, the outlaws shot it out with two of the town's deputy sheriffs and a gang of rangers. Shot in the stomach, Bass fled on horseback. But Murphy had seen that Bass was seriously wounded, and set the rangers on the outlaw's trail.

The rangers soon found Bass, whose right hand had also been hit by a bullet. Two of his fingers had been shot off. But that was the least of Bass's troubles. He had lost a great deal of blood from his stomach wound. A doctor who arrived with the posse said that he wouldn't survive. The doctor was right. Bass died two days later—on his twenty-seventh birthday—having refused to inform on the other gang members. Asked who had planned the raid with him, Bass reportedly said "It's agin [against] my trade to blow [tell] on my pals. If a man knows anything, he ought to die with it in him."

Jim Murphy, the gang member who turned against Sam Bass, died under strange circumstances one year after the outlaw's death. He swallowed atrophine, an eye medication. Some said it was an accident, while others claimed it was suicide.

Sources for Further Reading

The American West, A Cultural Encyclopedia, Volume 1. Danbury, CT: Grolier Educational Corp., 1995, pp. 80–81.

Nash, Jay Robert. *Bloodletters and Badmen.* New York: M. Evans, 1973, pp. 46–49.

Prassel, Frank Richard. *The Great American Outlaw, A Legacy of Fact and Fiction.* Norman, OK: University of Oklahoma Press, 1993, pp. 139–142, 338–340.

Ross, Stewart. *Fact or Fiction: Bandits & Outlaws.* Surrey, British Columbia: Copper Beech Books, 1995, p. 37.

Billy the Kid
(William Bonney)

Born: September 17, 1859
Died: July 14, 1881
AKA: Henry Antrim,
Kid Antrim, Henry McCarty

One of the most famous outlaws of the Old West, Billy the Kid never robbed a bank or a stagecoach and probably killed no more than a half-dozen men. However, when the man responsible for killing the Kid wrote a sensationalized book about him, fact and fiction became forever blurred.

A SKETCHY PAST

Everyone has heard of Billy the Kid—but no one knows who he really was. It's generally accepted that he was born in the slums of New York City, although other sources place his birth in Indiana. (One version of Billy's life claims that he was born in Ireland to a peasant father and Native American mother.) William Bonney was probably an alias (assumed name), that he took later in life. Some authorities believe that his real name was Henry McCarty—the son of Patrick Henry McCarty and Catherine Devine McCarty. The couple also had an older son, Joseph.

Billy's father died sometime in the 1860s—possibly while fighting in the Civil War (1861–1865). Billy's widowed mother moved West, and eventually married a man named William Antrim. Antrim moved the family to the boom town of Silver Springs, New Mexico, where he worked as a miner. With no school to attend, Billy, who was still just a boy, received little education.

Billy's mother died when he was fifteen years old, and his reputation as a killer seems to have developed shortly thereafter. Some sources claim young Billy left Arizona to flee from a petty theft charge. Others claim he murdered a man with a pen knife. Whatever really happened, Billy left Silver Springs. In Arizona, in 1877—when Billy was just seventeen years old—he shot and killed a blacksmith named "Windy" Cahill in a saloon fight. It was the Kid's first documented killing. The *Arizona Citizen* published the coroner's verdict concerning the killing. The coroner concluded that the killing was "criminal and unjustifiable, and that Henry Antrim, alias Kid, was guilty thereof." The legend of the Kid was off and running.

CATTLE WARS AND KILLINGS

The Kid soon resurfaced in Lincoln County, in southeastern New Mexico. At the time, Lincoln County covered a great deal of territory (several times more than it does today). It was the land of cattle barons, where rival factions were waging war with one another. The violence came to a head in 1878 in what has come to be known as the Lincoln County War.

Billy worked on the ranch of John Tunstall, an educated Englishman. A number of other wealthy cattle owners were native to the area, and resented Tunstall as a newcomer who threatened their livelihood. Lawrence Murphy and James Dolan were among the men who opposed Tunstall. The Englishman withstood threats and harassment. But on February 18, 1878, he was killed.

The Kid seems to have been very fond of Tunstall. Some sources claim that Billy adopted the Englishman as a father-figure. But in truth, the two didn't know each other for long before Tunstall was killed. Whatever his motivation, Billy joined forces with Tunstall's men to seek revenge for his murder. The group, known as the "Regulators," tracked and killed many of Murphy and Dolan's associates. On April 1, 1878, Billy took part in the ambush killing of Sheriff William Brady, who had set in motion the plot against Tunstall.

The killing of Brady—who was also a deputy U.S. marshal—did not go unnoticed. A huge posse (a group of people with legal authority to capture criminals) and a troop of cavalrymen tracked Billy and his companions. When the lawmen found the Regulators hiding in the home of one of Tunstall's associates, a tremendous gun battle followed. After days of shooting, some members of the posse set the house on fire. When Billy and the others fled the burning building, some were killed—but Billy managed to escape.

NO PARDON FOR THE KID

Billy somehow arranged to make a deal to be pardoned by Governor Lew Wallace, who had been appointed by President Rutherford B. Hayes with specific instructions to bring law and order to Lincoln County. According to some sources, Billy was to receive a full pardon in exchange for testifying against three men who had killed a lawyer. Billy still had to stand trial for the sheriff's murder, but the governor promised he would go free—no matter what the verdict was.

The governor was surprised at Billy's popularity with the people of Lincoln County. In a letter to a friend, he wrote, "A precious specimen nicknamed 'The Kid' whom the Sheriff is holding here in the Plaza, as it is called, is an object of tender regard. I heard singing and music the other night; going to the door, I found the minstrels [musicians] of the village actually serenading the fellow in his prison." Billy testified against the lawyer's killers, but he didn't wait to find out if the governor was a man of his word. Billy left town before his own trial began.

By now, Billy needed money. He asked John Chisum—a cattle baron he had worked for—to pay him back wages. When Chisum refused, Billy organized a gang of outlaws to steal his livestock. For a year and a half, from the summer of 1879 to the end of 1880, Billy headed a band of horse and cattle thieves. Governor Wallace, who was angry that Billy had run away from

Captured: A Boy with Winning Ways

Billy's capture was big news. Newspapers around the country reported the details of his last stand (although many false accounts of his capture had already been published). The incident was front-page news in Las Vegas papers—one of which printed:

> He looked and acted a mere boy. He is about five feet eight or nine inches tall, slightly built and lithe [graceful], weighing about 140; a frank open countenance [expression], looking like a school boy, with the traditional silky fuzz on his upper lip; clear blue eyes, with a roguish snap about them; light hair and complexion. He is, in all, quite a handsome looking fellow, the only imperfection being two prominent front teeth slightly protruding like squirrel's teeth, and he has agreeable and winning ways.

his trial, posted a $500 reward for the capture of the Kid.

SURRENDER AT STINKING SPRINGS

In November of 1880, a new player entered the picture. Patrick Floyd Garrett, a former acquaintance of Billy's, was elected as sheriff of Lincoln County. An expert gunman, Garrett knew the area well and was supported by the cattle ranchers. And he was determined to rid the county of the notorious Billy the Kid. Because he had known Billy, some people in the county regarded Garrett as a traitor, who had turned against a friend.

For a while, Billy's informants managed to help him avoid capture. But in December, Garrett learned that the outlaws would be riding near Fort Sumner. A former army post, Fort Sumner was used as a ranch by a friend of Billy's. On December 18, Garrett organized a number of detectives and ambushed Billy and members of his gang at Fort Sumner. One of the outlaws—the Kid's friend, Tom O'Folliard—was killed in the gunfire, while Billy and the others escaped.

The Garrett posse had little trouble tracking the outlaws in the snow. Their trail led to a deserted cabin east of Sumner, at Stinking Springs. There, the sheriff's men surrounded the cabin, demanding that the outlaws surrender. Refusing, the outlaws fired their guns at the posse. Rather than risk the lives of his men, Garrett decided to try a different approach. The posse waited until the outlaws had run out of food. Within a few days, Billy and his associates surrendered.

JAIL BREAK!

After he was taken to Mesilla, New Mexico, Billy was tried for murder. Since he had broken the terms of his agreement with Governor Wallace, he no longer had any hope of a pardon.

Convicted of murder by a jury, Billy was sentenced to hang in Lincoln on May 13, 1881. As the story goes, the judge sentenced Billy to hang "until you are dead, dead, dead," to which the outlaw responded, "And you can go to hell, hell, hell."

A couple of Garrett's men took Billy back to Lincoln, where he was kept under guard on the top floor of the court house. He sent many letters to Governor Wallace demanding a pardon—but his pleas fell on deaf ears. On April 28, 1881—just a couple of weeks before his execution was to take place—Billy escaped from jail. No one is sure exactly how the jail break occurred. But *somehow,* Billy managed to get hold of a pistol. (Some say a girl who was in love with the outlaw hid the gun in an outhouse, while other sources claim he managed to wrestle the pistol away from one of the guards after his handcuffs had been loosened at mealtime.) In any case, Billy shot and killed James Bell, one of the guards, and then killed Deputy Bob Ollinger when he ran into the room to see what had happened. Sheriff Pat Garrett was out of town at the time.

Pat Garrett, the man who took out Billy the Kid.

Billy escaped with a couple of guns and a Winchester rifle. After he forced a blacksmith to remove the shackles on his hands and feet, he stole a horse and roared out of town. Hiding in familiar territory, Billy remained in the area of Fort Sumner—something that has puzzled historians since the day he died. Why didn't he flee to an area—such as Old Mexico—where he wasn't well known? Some say a girlfriend kept him from leaving, but he was known as a man who always looked out for himself above anyone else. Others think that hopes of revenge might have kept him from vanishing from the territory.

THE END OF THE LINE

Whatever his reasons, Billy didn't leave the area. On July 14, 1881, Garrett went to the home of Pete Maxwell, a sheep rancher who lived near Fort Sumner—perhaps in response to a tip that the outlaw was hiding there. What happened next varies

Pat Garrett: The Man Who Shot Billy the Kid

Patrick Floyd Jarvis Garrett was born in Alabama in 1850. Raised in Louisiana, he moved to Texas when he was in his twenties in order to work as a cattle herder and buffalo hunter. By 1878, hunting was no longer a productive occupation since much of the buffalo population in Texas had been killed off. Garrett—an expert shot and skilled horseman—moved West to New Mexico, where cattle owners were battling rustlers who were stealing their stock.

Garrett tried a number of activities, includ-ing ranching and tending bar. Eventually, the citizens of Lincoln County, New Mexico, asked the six-foot-five-inch former buffalo hunter to be the sheriff. Immediately after he was appointed to the office, Sheriff Garrett made clear his intention to bring in the notorious Billy the Kid. With the help of detectives from the cattle lands in Texas, Garrett relentlessly tracked the Kid and killed him.

Some people praised Garrett as a hero for killing the Kid, while others criticized him for failing to give the outlaw a fair chance in a fight. The sheriff later described how he felt the evening he from one story to another, but the ending is always the same: Garrett shot and killed Billy the Kid. According to some sources, Garrett killed the Kid in cold blood—possibly in his sleep. According to the sheriff himself, he bravely faced the fugitive outlaw in a darkened room at the Maxwell home. In Garrett's own words, this is how it happened:

> Maxwell whispered to me. "That's him!" Simultaneously [at the same time] the Kid must have seen, or felt, the presence of a third person at the head of the bed. He raised quickly his pistol, a self-cocker, within a foot of my breast. Retreating rapidly across the room he cried: *"Quien es? Quien es?"* ["Who's that? Who's that?"] All this occurred in a moment. Quickly as possible I drew my revolver and fired, threw my body aside, and fired again. The second shot was useless; the Kid fell dead.

—**The Authentic Life of Billy the Kid** *(1882), by Pat Garrett*

Billy was dead at the age of twenty-one. Although legend claimed that he had killed a man for every year of his life, the actual figure was probably between six and nine. A local judge immediately ruled that Garrett had shot Billy in the line of duty.

Billy's grave

Today, the exact location of Billy's grave is unknown-- the original wood marker has disappeared. According to legend, no flowers will grow there.

killed the Kid: "Scared? . . . Wouldn't you have been scared? . . . Well, I should say so. I started out on that expedition with the expectation of getting scared. I went out contemplating the probability of being . . . killed; but not if any precaution [a measure to prevent harm] on my part would prevent such a catastrophe [disaster]."

With the help of writer Ash Upson, Garrett wrote *The Authentic Life of Billy the Kid,* published one year after the outlaw's death. The purpose of the book was not to document history—but to make money. Filled with fictional and exaggerated accounts of Billy's exploits, it is the source of many of the inaccuracies in the legend of Billy the Kid. (Many of Billy's later biographers relied on *The Authentic Life* for the "facts" of the outlaw's life.) In spite of everything, the book was a financial failure.

Garrett's career after the killing of Billy the Kid was anything but noteworthy. He tried his hand at farming and ranching, and also served a two-year term as a customs collector in El Paso, Texas. On February 29, 1908, he was shot to death. Historians still argue about who his killer was. No one was ever convicted of the crime.

The outlaw was buried in a military cemetery at Fort Sumner. At his grave was a marker that bore the words, *"Duerme bien, Querido,"* meaning "Sleep well, beloved."

Sources for Further Reading

The American West, A Cultural Encyclopedia, Volumes 1 and 4. Danbury, CT: Grolier Educational Corp., 1995, pp. 102–105, 612–613.

Nash, Jay Robert. *Bloodletters and Badmen.* New York: M. Evans, 1973, pp. 66–71.

Prassel, Frank Richard. *The Great American Outlaw, A Legacy of Fact and Fiction.* Norman, OK: University of Oklahoma Press, 1993, pp. 144–161, 327–330, 340.

Rosa, Joseph. *The Taming of the West: Age of the Gunfighter.* New York: Smithmark, 1993, pp. 76–83.

Shenkman, Richard and Kurt Reiger. *One Night Stands with American History.* New York: Quill, 1982, p. 197.

Vandome, Nick. *Crimes and Criminals.* New York: Chambers, 1992, pp. 30–31.

Wukovits, John. *The Gunslingers.* Broomall, PA: Chelsea House, 1997, pp. 25–32.

The Buck Gang

Active: July 28-August 10, 1895

In July of 1895, a small gang led by Rufus Buck embarked on a thirteen-day crime spree. For reasons that have never been explained, the group of five young, uneducated men committed a series of robberies, rapes, and murders in the Indian Territory to the west of Arkansas.

THIRTEEN DAYS OF DEVASTATION

The gang's rampage began on July 28 when they met in Okmulgee, Oklahoma, to arm themselves with guns and rifles. John Garrett, an African American U.S. deputy marshal, approached the young men to ask why they were heavily armed. Rufus and the others opened fire on the deputy, killing him.

Traveling between Muskogee and Fort Smith, Arkansas, the young men robbed a number of shopkeepers and ranch owners. Later they raped at least two women—a widow named Wilson and Rosetta Hassan, a farmer's wife. Next they robbed a drummer named Callahan, killing a boy who worked for him by shooting him in the back. The young men showed no sympathy for their victims: they threatened to harm infants and reportedly made some of their victims "dance" by shooting at their feet.

THEY HANGED THEM HIGH

News of the Buck gang's activities soon reached the territory's lawmen and a large posse (a group of people with legal

authority to capture criminals) of federal marshals was sent to capture the outlaws. With them went a company of Creek Indian police—or Creek Lighthorsemen. Trapped near Muskogee, the gang attempted to shoot their way past the posse, but they were outnumbered. On August 10, 1895, all five gang members were captured and taken into custody.

The five men were taken to the town of McDermott, Oklahoma—near the site of two of the gang's robberies—where angry citizens threatened to lynch them. (Lynchings, usually performed by mobs, are illegal killings. Most often, the victims are hanged.) Chained to one another to prevent escape, they were secretly taken out of town to Fort Smith, Arkansas, a town they had previously terrorized. Although the Creeks wanted to try the gang members under tribal law, the young men went to

The Buck Gang, with Rufus Buck in the center, await their trial in 1895.

Judge Isaac Parker's court of the damned

Rufus Buck and the four other members of his gang weren't the only criminals to be sentenced to death by Judge Isaac Charles Parker. During his twenty-one years on the bench, Parker sentenced over one hundred seventy-two men to death—of whom eighty-eight were killed. (The numbers would have been higher if it weren't for presidential pardons and other acts.) Known as the "hanging judge," Parker sentenced more men to death than any other judge of his time. When pronouncing a death sentence, Parker reportedly said, "I do not desire to hang you men. It is the law." (He was also said to cry when he delivered the sentence.)

Although hanging was not the only sentence prescribed for murder, Parker always condemned convicted murderers—for which his court became known as the Court of the Damned. Concerning the sentencing of murderers, Parker stated, "This court is but the humble instrument to aid in the execution of that divine justice which has ever decided that he who takes what he cannot return—the life of another human being—shall lose his own."

Parker studied law on his own and was admitted to the Missouri bar in 1859. Following brief service in the Civil War (1861–1865), he became an attorney in St. Joseph, Missouri, in 1862. After serving four years as Missouri's republican congressman, Parker was appointed as a federal judge by President Ulysses S. Grant in 1875. (Parker had already turned down an offer to assume the position of chief justice of the Utah Territory.) Parker's jurisdiction, or territory—the Western District of Arkansas—included the Indian Territory (now Oklahoma), an area ravaged by crime. In his first eight-week session, Parker tried eighteen defendants for murder; of the fifteen who were convicted, six were sentenced to death. A man who stood six feet tall, weighing two hundred pounds, Parker reportedly held court six days a week, from 8:30 in the morning until after dark.

Parker appointed two hundred deputy marshals—many of them African Americans and

trial before Judge Isaac Parker, who was known as the "hanging judge." A number of their victims testified, including Rosetta Hassan and her husband. At the end of the brief trial, one of the defense lawyers reportedly concluded his argument saying, "May it please the court and the gentlemen of the jury, you have heard the evidence. I have nothing to say."

Each of the gang members was convicted of rape. The jury reportedly handed down its verdict without even sitting in the

Native Americans. Bass Reeves, an African American who served as federal marshal for thirty-five years, was one of Parker's most effective deputies. Charged with policing a rough territory, "the men who rode for Parker" were paid by a fee system. For bringing in prisoners, marshals earned ten cents a mile, one way. The "guardsmen" earned two dollars a day. Many of these men paid a high price for their work. Over the twenty-one years Parker was in office, at least sixty-five of his marshals were killed in the line of duty.

Parker's court also had a record-setting conviction rate. The judge issued 8,600 convictions and 1,700 acquittals—which means *5 out of 6* prisoners tried in Parker's court were found guilty. Although judges are expected to be impartial, Parker was in the habit of "leading" the jury, or letting the jurors know what he thought about a case. He once said: "I have been accused of leading juries. I tell you a jury should be led! If they are guided they will render justice." Parker also had his own ideas about evidence—which forced members of the Supreme Court to remind him that the government's rules of evidence applied to

his court as much as any other. Objections such as these prompted Parker to complain about the Supreme Court's "laxity" (lack of authority) and concern for the "flimsiest technicalities."

Up until 1889, the Supreme Court did not allow prisoners who were convicted in Parker's court to appeal the judge's decision. That year, forty-six cases were reconsidered by the Supreme Court. The High Court decided that *thirty* of the men Parker had condemned to die had received an unfair trial. In 1895, Congress removed the Indian Territory from Parker's jurisdiction. He died the following year—the year the Buck gang was executed—before the formal transfer of the territory took place.

During his lifetime many people across the country had disapproved of Parker's justice—which often attracted large crowds to multiple public hangings. But after his death, many praised Parker—who had championed Women's Suffrage (the women's rights movement) and had supported the rights of Native Americans—as one of the greatest judges in the American West.

jury room. After the verdict was announced, Judge Parker informed the gang members that he considered the crime they were convicted of to be equal to murder. He said:

> I want to say in this case that the jury, under the law and the evidence, could come to no other conclusion than that which they arrived at. Their verdict is an entirely just one, and one that must be approved by all lovers of virtue. The offense of which you have

been convicted is one that shocks all men who are not brutal. It is known to the law as a crime offensive to decency, and as a brutal attack upon the honor and chastity of the weaker sex . . . it has been by the law-makers of the United States deemed equal in enormity and wickedness to murder, because the punishment fixed by the same is that which follows the commission of the crime of murder.

Parker sentenced the five young men to hang on October 31, 1895. But sometime after the trial, Rufus Buck claimed that he was not involved in the crimes and could provide an alibi—proof that he was elsewhere when the rapes were committed. Parker delayed the execution while the gang's lawyers appealed the verdict. (In an appeal, a case is taken to a higher court to be reheard.) After the U.S. Supreme Court declined to hear the case, Parker set a new date for the mass hanging: July 1, 1896. The execution was not postponed. Almost one year after they were captured, the five gang members were hanged—together, on one large scaffold—at Fort Smith. While three of the gang members were said to have died instantly, of broken necks, Rufus Buck and Lucky Davis struggled on the gallows as they slowly strangled to death.

Following the execution, a prison guard found a poem that Rufus Buck had written on the backside of a photograph of his mother. The poem, titled "My Dream," was full of odd spellings, punctuation, and misplaced capitals. Here is Rufus Buck's poem:

> MY, dream. —1896
> i, dremp'T, i, was, in heAven,
> Among, The, AngeLs, Fair;
> i'd, neAr, seen, none, so HAndsome,
> THAT, Twine, in golden, HAir,
> They, looked, so, neAT, and; sAng, so, sweeT,
> And, PLAY'd, The, The, goLden, HArp,
> i, wAs, About, To, Pick An, ANgeL, ouT,
> And, Take, Her, To, mY, HeArT,
> BuT, The, momenT, i, BegAn, To, PLeA,
> i, THougHT, oF, You, mY, Love,
> There, wAs, none i'd, seen, so BeAuTiFuLL,
> On, eArTH, or HeAven, ABove,
> gooD, By, My. Dear. Wife, AnD. MoTHer
> all. so, My, sisTer

RUFUS BUCK
youse. Truley
1 Day. of. JUly
Tu, The, Yeore
off 1896

TRANSLATION:

I dreamt I was in Heaven
Among the Angels fair;
I'd never seen any so handsome,
That are entwined in golden hair.
They looked so neat and sang so sweet
And played the golden harp.
I was about to pick an angel out
And take her to my heart.
But the moment I began to plea,
I thought of you, my love.
There was none I'd ever seen so beautiful
On earth or Heaven above,
Goodbye my dear wife and Mother.
Also my sister.
Rufus Buck,
Yours truly.
July 1, Tuesday, 1896

Sources for Further Reading

The American West, A Cultural Encyclopedia, Volume 7. Danbury, CT: Grolier Educational Corp., 1995, pp. 1193–1194.

Cusic, Don. *Cowboys and the Wild West, An A to Z Guide from the Chisholm Trail to the Silver Screen.* New York: Facts on File, 1994, p. 220.

Nash, Jay Robert. *Bloodletters and Badmen.* New York: M. Evans, 1973, p. 90

Nash, Jay Robert. *Encyclopedia of World Crime.* Wilmette, IL: Crime Books, 1990, pp. 531–532.

Rosa, Joseph G. *The Taming of the West: Age of the Gunfighter.* New York: Smithmark, 1993, pp. 136–137.

Sifakis, Carl. *The Encyclopedia of American Crime.* New York: Facts on File, 1982, p. 105.

Calamity Jane
(Martha Jane Cannary)

Born: May 1, 1852?
Died: August 1, 1903
AKA: M. E. Burke

Calamity Jane—although not exactly an outlaw—was unconventional. At a time when women did not wear men's clothing, go to bars, or appear in public drunk, she did so— and then some. A hard-bitten alcoholic, she died in her early fifties, aged far beyond her years.

AN UNCONVENTIONAL CHILDHOOD

Like many other frontier figures, Calamity Jane was a legend in her own time. Tall tales about her exploits traveled from town to town throughout the West. Dime novels published in the East printed episodes from her life—most of which had little to do with the truth. And Calamity Jane's autobiography (a biography written by the subject) was no more reliable. Printed and distributed when Calamity Jane was a theatrical attraction, the "autobiography" presented a sensational—and often fictional—account of her life.

Even the simplest details about Calamity Jane's life are uncertain. She might have been born in Illinois, Missouri, or Wyoming. Her father could have been a minister, an army man, or a gambler. According to one version, she was born near Fort Laramie, Wyoming, and orphaned at an early age when Indians killed and scalped her parents.

In spite of the many stories, it is generally accepted that Calamity Jane was born on May 1, 1852, near Princeton, Missouri, to a farmer named Robert Cannary (or Canary) and his wife, Charlotte. The original Cannary farm was purchased by Cannary's grandfather in 1855. Four years later, Robert Cannary added 108 acres to the family's plot—at a cost of $500. He worked the farm with his father until the older man died in 1859. Thornton Cannary, Robert's brother, lived on the opposite side of Mercer County and established himself as one of the state's largest landowners. The oldest of five children, Martha Jane—who was later known as "Calamity Jane"—soon earned a reputation as a wild and high-spirited child.

What's in a name?

Calamity Jane probably received her nickname sometime in the early 1870s. Historians disagree as to how she came to be known as "Calamity." Cannary reportedly claimed that she had gotten the name from Army captain Pat Egan, whom she had saved from an Indian attack. "Jane," he supposedly said, "you're a wonderful little woman to have around in time of calamity. From now on your name's Calamity Jane." The story is now part of the Calamity Jane myth—but Cannary made it up.

Some historians speculate that the name "Calamity" came about as a reference to what would happen to those who did not take sharpshooter's guns seriously. Others still consider it to be a reference to Jane's calamitous, hard-luck life.

According to Calamity Jane's autobiography—if portions of it can be believed—Martha Jane Cannary traveled with her family on the Overland Route to the gold-rush town of Virginia City, Montana, in 1865. During the five-month journey that covered approximately two thousand miles, Cannary learned to drive teams of oxen. She became an expert at using a bullwhacker—a thirty-foot whip that teamsters used to drive animals. According to her autobiography, she spent much of her time with men. She wrote that she was "at all times with the men when there was excitement and adventures to be had."

By the age of fifteen, Cannary was orphaned—after both parents died within a year of one another. Little is known of her activities until the early 1870s, when she surfaced in Rawlins, Wyoming. Tall and solidly built, she dressed in men's clothing and worked at jobs that were not usually available to women—such as railroad work, which entailed swinging a heavy pick and laying railroad ties; bullwhacking, or driving teams of bulls carrying supplies to mining camps; and mule skinning, or driving mules from one point to another.

Calamity's daughter

In June 1941, a woman who called herself Mrs. Jane Hickok McCormick, a native of Billings, Montana, claimed that she was the daughter of Calamity Jane and Wild Bill Hickok. To prove her identity, she produced a diary and confession that were supposedly written by her mother. The diary consists of a series of letters that are sometimes years apart. The first letter, addressed to her daughter, is dated September 25, 1877. It reads in part:

My Dear:

This isn't intended for a diary and it may even happen that this may never be sent to you. But I would like to think of you reading it someday, page by page, in the years to come after my death. I would like to hear you laugh when you look at these pictures of meself. I am alone in the shack and tired. I rode sixty miles yesterday to the post office and returned today. This is your birthday. You are four years old today. Jim [James O'Neil, the man who reportedly adopted Cannary's daughter] promised me he would always get a letter to me on your birthday each year. Was I glad to hear from him. He sent a tiny picture of you. You are the dead spit of meself at the same age. . . .

The diary and confession have never been authenticated. And Mrs. McCormick's relationship to Calamity Jane and Hickok has never been proven.

A GIRL SCOUT

Cannary wrote in her autobiography that she spent the years between 1868 and 1876 serving as an Army scout on various expeditions. She claimed to have worked with General George Armstrong Custer and other renowned Army officials—but Army records fail to mention her service. The many errors in Cannary's accounts of her scouting expeditions have caused historians to doubt their truth. There is no real evidence that she ever worked as an Army scout.

But Cannary did accompany Army expeditions—possibly as a bullwhacker or simply as a hanger-on. According to some sources, she traveled with General George Crook's expedition against the Sioux Indians in 1875—and was forced to return home when her gender was found out as she swam in the nude. Cannary herself claimed to have delivered messages from General Crook to General Custer by swimming across the Platte

River. Another story has her following a young soldier she met while working in a brothel. Dressed as a man, she followed the soldier's detachment into the Black Hills of Dakota. It seems likely that she did venture into the Black Hills with Crook's soldiers in 1876: one of Crook's men reported that "Calamity Jane is hear [here] going up with the troops." Cannary spent the next four years in the Black Hills—at a time when gold fever was at its peak.

WILD BILL

Historians generally agree that Cannary was associated with Wild Bill Hickok in Deadwood, Dakota Territory, in 1876. But they don't all agree on the nature of their relationship. Cannary claimed in her autobiography to have been married to Hickok. Despite evidence to the contrary, the legend that the couple was secretly married continues to thrive. Some biographers claim that she was little more than a bar-room acquaintance of the famous shootist known as "the Prince of the Pistoleers." Still others argue that there is no evidence that the two ever met.

Hickok, who claimed to be devoted to his wife, Agnes, was shot and killed by a man named Jack McCall on August 2, 1876. Cannary later boasted that she had helped to hang McCall. In truth, however, McCall was legally hanged after a court at Yankton, South Dakota, found him guilty of murder.

CALAMITY JANE, MEDICINE WOMAN

Cannary had a reputation as a hard-drinking, rowdy, foul-mouthed ruffian. But she was also known as a generous, kind-hearted woman who was never mean-spirited, even when drunk. When a smallpox epidemic struck Deadwood in 1878, she stepped forward to help take care of the sick miners by providing them with food, drink, and clean clothing.

The testimony of her contemporaries prevents this incident from being written off as part of the legend of Calamity Jane: a man named Babcock, the town's only doctor, later confirmed that Cannary volunteered to help the smallpox-stricken people

A young girl stands over the grave of Calamity Jane in Deadwood, South Dakota.

who were housed in a shack on the outskirts of town. A number of Deadwood natives were later quoted as saying that they owed their lives to Cannary.

Mrs. Burke

Cannary left Deadwood in 1880. For the next fifteen years, she traveled around the Dakotas, Kansas, Montana, and Wyoming. In August 1885, according to her autobiography, she married a hack driver (horse-drawn carriage driver) from Texas named Clinton Burke—although there is no legal evidence of any such marriage. (She apparently had a habit of referring to any man she lived with as her husband.) Later in life, Cannary called herself Mrs. M. E. Burke—a name that is inscribed, beneath "Calamity Jane" on her tombstone.

Cannary also claimed to have had a child—a daughter, who was born on October 28, 1887—although many people believed that the girl was in fact Burke's child by another woman. According to popular theory, the child was raised by Burke's relatives. Before long, Burke disappeared from Cannary's life.

Take a look at this!

The Paleface (1948), starring Bob Hope and Jane Russell, is the story of a cowardly dentist who becomes a gunslinging hero when Calamity Jane starts aiming for him. A nutty comedy, it turns conventions of the Old West upside down. And if you like that, check out the sequel—*The Son of Paleface* (1952).

ALL THE WORLD'S A STAGE

Cannary continued to drift from one town to another. She worked at various jobs to support herself—and sometimes turned to prostitution. Her drinking binges sometimes lasted for days, and her physical condition began to deteriorate. In 1896 she worked for an amusement company in Minneapolis, Minnesota, appearing on stage dressed as an Army scout—in a buckskin outfit and moccasins, carrying six-shooters and a Winchester rifle. In order to stir up public interest, she sold copies of her seven-page autobiography, in which she spun sensational tales about her exploits as a scout.

Suffering from alcoholism, Cannary missed many performances and was eventually fired from her job. In May 1900, a newspaper editor and novelist reportedly found her living in a brothel. They convinced her to travel east to Buffalo, New York, where she took a job performing in a western show at the Pan-American Exposition. She did not stay long. According to legend, "Buffalo Bill" Cody, a western showman, sent her back to the West after Cannary complained that she was homesick for her native land. Whether Cody was responsible or not, Cannary returned to the West, where she continued to drift and drink.

In July 1903, she arrived at the Calloway Hotel in Terry, near Deadwood, in Dakota Territory. Ravaged by alcoholism and impoverished, she died in early August of "inflammation of the bowels." Local women dressed her body in a clean dress and an undertaker donated a pine coffin. On August 4, Cannary was buried at Mt. Moriah Cemetery—in one of the largest funerals the residents of Deadwood had ever seen. She was buried next to Wild Bill Hickok.

Sources for Further Reading

Horan, James. *Desperate Women.* New York: Putnam, 1952, pp. 171–200.

James, Edward T., ed. *Notable American Women,* Volume 1. Cambridge, MA: Belknap Press, 1971, pp. 267–268.

Johnson, Thomas H., ed. *The Oxford Companion to American History.* New York: Oxford University Press, 1966, p. 129.

Lamar, Howard Roberts. *The Reader's Encyclopedia of the American West.* New York: Harper & Row, 1977, pp. 146–147.

The McGraw-Hill Encyclopedia of World Biography. New York: McGraw-Hill Book Company, 1973, pp. 320–321.

Butch Cassidy
(Robert Leroy Parker)

Born: April 6, 1866
Died: ?
AKA: George Cassidy, Jim Ryan

A likable and intelligent young man, Butch Cassidy participated in a number of successful bank and train robberies in the American West at the end of the nineteenth century. He was a member of a group of outlaws known as the Wild Bunch—most of whom were either killed or imprisoned.

A MORMON CATTLE THIEF

Robert Leroy Parker was born in 1866 in the Sevier River country near Circleville, Utah. Ten years before he was born, his father and grandparents had crossed the Great Plains as "hand-cart pioneers." They carried their possessions across the plains by walking and pulling carts behind them. One of ten children, Robert was raised on a small ranch. Like many of the people who settled in Utah, his parents were Mormons—a group of Christians that follows strict moral guidelines. (Although Parker's father, Maximillian Parker, was said to have had a rebellious streak.)

Growing up, Parker received no formal education. Instead, he was "educated" in the art of cattle rustling by Mike Cassidy, a cowboy-rustler who worked for his father. Under Cassidy's supervision, Parker learned how to rope and brand animals, and he became an expert rider and marksman. In short, he learned all the skills required to become a horse and cattle thief. While still a teenager, Parker accompanied Cassidy on long cattle drives in the neighboring mountain ranges.

The Wild Bunch:
(standing, left to
right) William Carver,
Harvey Logan; (sitting,
left to right) the
Sundance Kid (Harry
Longbaugh), Ben
Kilpatrick, and Butch
Cassidy.

Frequently in trouble with the law, Cassidy headed south after the shooting of a Wyoming rancher. Parker—who had been Cassidy's right-hand man—took over his cattle-rustling business. And he took his last name, too. (In Parker's day, it was common for an outlaw to adopt the name of another criminal whose crimes and misdeeds he admired.) Robert Leroy Parker went by the name of George Cassidy. Later—after brief work as a butcher—he became known as Butch Cassidy.

En Route to the Robbers' Roost

Butch Cassidy soon left Utah and took an honest job in Telluride, in southwest Colorado. For a while, he packed ore by muleback from the mines to the mill. But it wasn't long before

The Sundance Kid

After his release from the Wyoming penitentiary, Butch Cassidy helped to rob a bank in Montpelier, Idaho, and fled to the Robber's Roost. The Robber's Roost was an isolated hideout in southeastern Utah. There, he met Harry Longabaugh—better known as the Sundance Kid. The two soon struck up a lifelong friendship.

Not much is known about Longabaugh's background. He was probably born in Pennsylvania in 1863, and eventually headed West. As a young man, he served an extended sentence for horse theft. Imprisoned in Sundance, Wyoming, Longabaugh later became known as the Sundance Kid.

Longabaugh became a member of the Wild Bunch—also known as the Hole-in-the-Wall Gang, named after one of the gang's favorite hideaways. An expert gunslinger, he had lightning reflexes, and was known as one of the fastest and most accurate shooters in the West. Unlike many of his counterparts, he is said to have worn only one gun. In spite of his deadly aim, Longabaugh was said to be a quiet man who was slow to draw his weapon.

After the Wild Bunch broke up, Longabaugh escaped with Butch Cassidy to South America, where they continued to rob banks and trains. What became of the two outlaws has become the subject of much debate. Some historians believe that Longabaugh and Cassidy died in a shoot-out with Bolivian soldiers. Others believe Longabaugh escaped. According to one story—made popular by a man who claimed to be the son of the Sundance Kid—Longabaugh fled to the United States, where he married his girlfriend, Etta Place, and lived happily ever after until 1957, when he died peacefully at the age of ninety-four.

he fell in with a group of bandits known as the McCarty gang—run by the McCarty brothers, Tom and Bill. They asked Cassidy, who was twenty at the time, to help them rob a train. Cassidy joined the gang as they stopped the Denver and Rio Grande Express on November 3, 1887. The robbery was a complete failure. When the guard refused to open the safe, the outlaws were forced to ride away empty-handed.

The gang's next jobs were more successful. On March 30, 1889, they struck the First National Bank of Denver. Before a single shot was fired, the outlaws made off with $20,000 in bank notes. During this heist, Cassidy was said to have threatened to blow up the bank with a small bottle of nitroglycerin (liquid explosive). The bottle apparently contained nothing

Oddly, authors and screenwriters ignored the story of Butch Cassidy for decades after the outlaw disappeared from the public eye. But in 1969 that changed. *Butch Cassidy and the Sundance Kid* (1969)—starring Robert Redford as Sundance and Paul Newman as Cassidy—was wildly successful at the box office and soon became one of the most popular Westerns ever produced by a Hollywood film studio. About one billion people have seen the movie. Loosely based on the facts of Cassidy's life, the screenplay—written by William Goldman—takes many liberties with the truth. The opening sequence informs viewers: "Not that it matters, but most of what follows is true."

The story's ending prevented the studio from producing a sequel. In 1978, however, a *prequel* appeared, in which the story relates the early exploits of Butch and Sundance. *Butch and Sundance: The Early Days* (1979), featuring Tom Berenger and William Katt, was less successful than the first film.

The Wild Bunch, directed by Sam Peckinpah, is considered to be one of the best American films of all time. Released in 1969, it portrays the last days of the group of outlaws who associated with Butch Cassidy and the Sundance Kid. An influential film, it won many awards and nominations, including an Academy Award for Cinematography.

more than water. Cassidy and the other gang members headed for the Star Valley, a remote area on the Wyoming-Idaho border where bandits often hid.

Three months later—on June 24—the gang robbed a bank in Telluride. They struck at noontime and they struck fast. Without firing a shot, the outlaws left the bank with a sack filled with more than $10,000 in currency. Pursued by large posses (groups of people with legal authority to capture criminals), they escaped across rocky terrain by wrapping their horses' hooves in gunny sacks—a coarse fabric that allowed the horses to keep their footing on the slippery rock. The outlaws hid in canyons in an area called Robbers' Roost, along the lower Green River in southeastern Utah.

But more posses followed. Cassidy and the other gang members decided to lay low. For two years—from 1890 to 1892—Cassidy made an honest living, working as a cowboy in Colorado and Utah and as a butcher in Rock Springs, Wyoming.

TROUBLE WITH THE LAW

Eventually Cassidy tangled with the law. First, he was briefly jailed for disturbing the peace in a fight with a drunken man who had provoked him. After he was released, he went into business with Al Rainer, a cattle rustler. Together, they came up with a plan to make easy money. They rode from ranch to ranch in Colorado, promising the ranchers that they would protect their herds from cattle rustlers—for a fee. If the ranchers refused to pay the "protection" fee, Cassidy and Rainer resorted to "plan B." They stole the ranchers' cattle. Sometime in 1892 they were caught. That year, Cassidy's name appeared for the first time in court records.

Because of court delays, Cassidy's trial did not begin until July 4, 1894. Found guilty of cattle rustling, he was sentenced to two years in the Wyoming State Penitentiary. He was released early, thanks to a pardon issued by Governor William A. Richards. Cassidy is said to have made a deal with the governor in exchange for his pardon. According to some stories, he promised never to rustle cattle or rob another bank in Wyoming—although he said nothing about robbing trains or planning robberies for other outlaws in the state. Cassidy was released on January 19, 1896.

What's in a name?

Butch Cassidy and the Sundance Kid weren't the only outlaws in the Wild Bunch who went by assumed names. Many of the other gang members went by colorful nicknames—such as Deaf Charley (Camillo Hanks), the Tall Texan (Ben Kilpatrick), and Blackjack Ketchum (Thomas Ketchum). Often, they took a name that honored another outlaw. For example, Kid Curry (Harvey Logan) took his alias from an older bandit—Flat Nose George Curry (George Parrott).

A WILD BUNCH

Freed from jail, Cassidy headed straight for the Hole-in- the-Wall—an isolated hideout in the Colorado mountains where bandits and gunmen gathered. By the spring of 1896, Cassidy had joined up with a group of about twenty outlaws. "The Wild Bunch," as they were called, included ex-convicts Elza Lay and Bob Meeks, and Harvey Logan, a deadly man who was also known as Kid Curry. Sometime later, Harry Longabaugh—better known as the Sundance Kid—joined the Wild Bunch. Active in Wyoming, Colorado, and Utah, the Wild Bunch robbed about a dozen trains and banks over the next five years.

Many train robbers had failed because of stubborn guards or time-locked safes that prevented them from getting at their loot. But Cassidy and the Wild Bunch favored dynamite, which allowed them to get at the contents of locked safes by blowing them up. In one robbery, the gang used too much dynamite, and had to run up and down the railroad tracks to collect the bills that had been thrown from the train in the explosion.

Most of the Wild Bunch raids were very successful. (Although the Union Pacific train holdup at Tipton, Wyoming, brought the outlaws only fifty dollars.) The gang owed much of its success to intelligent planning—thanks largely to Butch Cassidy—and smooth execution, in which each robbery was carefully carried out according to plan. They studied the floor plans of banks and consulted timetables for trains they planned to rob. They bribed railroad workers to find out about shipments. They positioned fresh horses along the escape route so that they would be able to outrun the lawmen who pursued them. And they had carefully chosen hideouts along the "outlaw trail," where the gang members could come and go without being seen—and cross state borders to avoid capture.

THE END OF AN ERA

The Wild Bunch raided the Great Northern Flyer train near Wagner, Montana, on July 3, 1901. It would be the last heist they worked together. At Malta, Montana, Kid Curry boarded the train. When the Great Northern reached Wagner, he stepped into the engine room with a six-shooter (type of pistol) in each hand, and ordered the engineer to stop the locomotive. The Sundance Kid, who had been sitting in a coach car, kept passengers at bay by running up and down the aisles firing his guns. When the train came to a stop, Cassidy and other gang members boarded the train. Using dynamite to blow open the safe, the outlaws collected $40,000 in bank notes. But there was one problem: the notes weren't signed. In order to cash the notes, gang members had to forge the signature of the president of the bank.

By now the gang was being closely followed by lawmen and detectives from the Pinkerton Agency, who had been hired by the railroad companies. The detectives even had a photograph

of some of the outlaws. During a trip to Fort Worth, Texas, five members of the Wild Bunch had dressed in brand-new clothes to have their picture taken. As the story goes, Cassidy mailed a copy of the picture to the bank they had just robbed to thank them for their "contribution." The picture fell into the hands of Pinkerton detectives who were then able to identify the individual outlaws.

The Wild Bunch gang's days were numbered. New inventions like the telephone and the telegraph made it more and more difficult for the outlaws to escape from lawmen. Armed with modern technology, detective agencies and law officers were able to relay messages from one town to another, improving their ability to track the movements of the bandit gang. Within a year of the Great Northern raid, most of the Wild

Robert Redford (left) and Paul Newman star in *Butch Cassidy and the Sundance Kid* (1969).

According to legend, Butch Cassidy was a kind and generous outlaw. As the story goes, some of the other gang members wanted to shoot the stubborn guard who refused to open the safe on the Denver and Rio Grande Express train. Cassidy suggested that they vote on the matter, and the guard was allowed to live.

Leader of the bunch

Although Butch Cassidy planned many of the raids performed by the Wild Bunch, he probably wasn't the gang's leader. Harvey Logan--who was known as Kid Curry--was a hardened killer who had more authority among the band of outlaws.

Bunch had been tracked down by lawmen—and either killed or imprisoned.

TIME TO MOVE ON

Cassidy and Longabaugh managed to escape—with Longabaugh's girlfriend, Etta Place. In New York City, they shopped at Tiffany's jewelry store and again had their pictures taken. Then they boarded a boat bound for South America. The three settled in Argentina—a South American country popular with outlaws because it did not have a treaty with the United States that required them to return American criminals to their homeland.

The details of their activities in Argentina are sketchy. At first, they quietly raised cattle, sheep, and horses on a ranch in Chubot Province—far from the long arm of the American law. But in 1906, they abandoned the ranch, possibly because Pinkerton detectives had rediscovered their trail. Next they turned to banditry, robbing banks in Argentina and Chile and a payroll in Bolivia. The heists were successful, bringing the robbers tens of thousands of dollars in loot. Cassidy and Longabaugh also worked for a while in tin mines near La Paz, Bolivia. For two years they worked as day laborers in the mine—and again they left abruptly.

Sometime around 1907, Place—who had been acting as a scout in the bank robberies—returned to the United States. Longabaugh went with her to New York, where she had an operation for appendicitis (an inflamed appendix). Shortly thereafter, the two parted—some say forever. No one is certain where Etta Place went or what she did thereafter. Longabaugh returned to South America where he rejoined Cassidy.

THE END?

There are plenty of stories about the final days of Butch Cassidy and the Sundance Kid—and none of them can be proven: sometime between 1909 and 1911, Cassidy and Longabaugh died in a shoot-out with soldiers in Bolivia—or Argentina, Chile, or Uruguay; Cassidy shot himself in the head when he saw Sundance felled by Bolivian soldiers; Cassidy escaped to work as a soldier-for-hire in the Mexican Revolution; he changed his name to William K. Phillips and moved to Spokane, Washington, where he died in 1937.

The Bolivian shoot-out is the most widely accepted version of how the outlaws died. But nothing in army and police files at San Vicente supports the story—not even the corpses that were dug up from the local cemetery and examined.

Hole-in-the-wall hideout

The Hole-in-the-Wall was one of the Wild Bunch gang's favorite hideouts. A valley in the Wyoming wilderness, it was shielded by a mountain passage. The trail was so narrow that riders were forced to enter it single file— which discouraged many posses and lawmen from pursuing the outlaws into the area.

Sources for Further Reading

The American West, A Cultural Encyclopedia, Volumes 7 and 10. Danbury, CT: Grolier Educational Corp., 1995, pp. 1199–1201, 1691–1692.

Nash, Jay Robert. *Bloodletters and Badmen.* New York: M. Evans, 1973, pp. 114–118.

North, Mark. "To Hell You Ride, On the Trail of Butch Cassidy." *Bicycling* (October 1997), pp. 77–83.

Prassel, Frank Richard. *The Great American Outlaw, A Legacy of Fact and Fiction.* Norman, OK: University of Oklahoma Press, 1993, pp. 308–314.

Rosa, Joseph. *The Taming of the West: Age of the Gunfighter.* New York: Smithmark, 1993, pp. 69, 72.

Ross, Stewart. *Fact or Fiction: Bandits & Outlaws.* Surrey, British Columbia: Copper Beech Books, 1995, p. 39.

Steckmesser, Kent. *Western Outlaws: The "Good Badman" in Fact, Film, and Folklore.* Claremont, CA: Regina Books, 1983, pp. 115–124.

Curly Bill
(William Brocius)

Born: 1857
Died: 1882?

A number of outlaws and lawmen had reputations for being fancy shooters. Some were able to spin a pistol around their index finger, cock it, and fire. Billy the Kid and Pat Garrett were both rumored to be skilled at the spin-and-cock method—but Curly Bill was rumored to be the best.

A TOMBSTONE GUNSLINGER

Born William B. Graham in 1857, Brocius—who stood six feet tall and had curly black hair—was a cattle thief in Arizona as a young man. As a member of the Clanton-McLaury clan in Tombstone, he rustled livestock and earned a reputation as a drinking man who was easily provoked. He quickly became the enemy of **Wyatt Earp** (see entry) and his brothers. When the Earp brothers and Doc Holliday met the Clantons and McLaurys at O.K. Corral in October 1881, Brocius did not take part in the shoot-out. But that same month, he was involved in another incident.

Brocius was one of a number of cowboys who were disturbing the peace in Tombstone by racing their horses up and down the main street while firing their guns into the air. The town's sheriff, Fred White, appointed a deputy in an attempt to quiet things down. The deputy was Virgil Earp, Wyatt's brother. The troublemakers left town, but White and Earp trailed Brocius and cornered him in an alley. White asked for the outlaw's gun, and Brocius held out his six-shooter (a type of pistol) with the butt, or handle, facing the sheriff. Before White could take the gun from him, Brocius reportedly spun the gun around his index finger so that it was pointing directly at the sheriff. What happened next is the subject of debate. Some sources say the pistol went off when White tried to grab it from the outlaw. Others say Virgil Earp, who approached from behind, had startled Brocius, causing the hair-trigger of his gun to fire. Others say it was a cold-blooded act of violence. However it happened, Brocius shot Sheriff White.

Earp pistol-whipped (beat with a pistol) Brocius until he was unconscious, and then dragged him to jail. Within a few days, he was moved to Tucson, Arizona, where he was tried for the murder of White, who had died from his gunshot wound. Before dying, however, the lawman stated that the shooting had been accidental. Brocius was acquitted [found not guilty] of White's death.

MORE TROUBLE

The outlaw tangled with the law again on May 25, 1881, when an argument with lawman William Breakenridge ended in gunfire. Brocius was shot in the mouth in an incident that was described on the front page of the next day's newspaper the *Arizona Star:*

> The notorious Curly Bill, the man who murdered Marshal White at Tombstone last fall, and who has been concerned in several other desperate and lawless affrays [fights] in South Eastern Arizona, has at last been brought to grief, and there is likely to be a vacancy in the ranks of our border desperadoes. The affair occurred at Galeyville Thursday. A party of eight or nine cowboys, Curly Bill, and his partner Jim Wallace among the number, were in town enjoying themselves in their usual manner, when Sheriff Breakenridge of Tombstone, who was at Galeyville on business, happened [came] along.

Wallace made some insulting remarks to the deputy at the same time waving his revolver in an aggressive manner. Break-

Take a look at this!

Filmed on location in Santa Fe, New Mexico, *Wyatt Earp* (1994) tells the story of the tarnished lawman (played by Kevin Costner), his brothers, and his sickly friend Doc Holliday (played by Dennis Quaid, who lost forty pounds to play the role). Originally planned as a television miniseries, it also portrays Earp's early life.

Wyatt Earp, sworn enemy of Curly Bill.

enridge did not pay much attention to this gesture of aggression from Wallace but quietly turned around and left the party. Shortly after this, Brocius, who it would seem had a friendly feeling for Breakenridge, insisted that Wallace should go and find him and apologize for the insult given. Wallace never did and instead accompanied Brocius back to the saloon where the rest of the cowboys were drinking.

By this time Brocius, who had had just enough to drink to make him quarrelsome, was in one of his most dangerous moods and evidently looking to increase his record as a man killer. He started to verbally abuse Wallace, who, by the way, had some pretensions himself as a desperado and bad man generally. Wallace immediately went outside the door of the saloon, Brocius following close behind him. Just as Brocius stepped outside, Wallace, who had meanwhile drawn his revolver, fired, the bullet entering the left side of Brocius's neck and passing through, came out the right cheek, not breaking the jawbone. The town erupted in wild excitement.

SHOT TO PIECES

The outlaw's wound wasn't fatal. But his feud with Wyatt Earp probably was. Earp believed that Brocius was one of the outlaws responsible for the murder of his brother, Morgan, some years earlier. In the "Vendetta Ride" of 1882, Earp hunted down the suspected murderers. On March 27, the *Tombstone Epitaph* published an account of "one of the most desperate fights that ever took place on Arizona soil"—between Wyatt Earp and his brothers and a gang led by Curly Bill Brocius. Brocius, the article claimed, had been shot off his horse.

Wyatt Earp later described the incident in an August 1896 edition of the *San Francisco Examiner*:

> We had ridden twenty-five miles over the mountains with the intention of camping at a certain spring. As

we got near the place I had a presentiment [felt beforehand] that something was wrong and unlimbered [untied] my shotgun. Sure enough nine cowboys sprang up from the bank where the spring was and began firing at us. I jumped off my horse to return the fire, thinking my men would do the same, but they retreated. One of the cowboys who was trying to pump lead into me with a Winchester was a fellow named Curly Bill, a stage-robber whom I had been after for eight months, and for whom I had a warrant in my pocket. I fired both barrels of my gun into him, blowing him all to pieces.

Here's a book you might like:

The Righteous Revenge of Artemis Bonner, 1992, by Walter Dean Myers

When a young man receives a request from his aunt to punish his uncle's murderer, he quickly leaves New York City and heads West. Among the Old West towns he visits are Tombstone, Arizona; Lincoln, New Mexico; and Juarez, Mexico.

But not everyone believed that the outlaw was dead. Shortly after the killing was supposed to have taken place, the *Nugget,* an Arizona newspaper, offered a $1,000 reward to anyone who could prove that Brocius was dead. To this day, historians question whether the one-time lawman really killed Brocius. Some sources speculate that Brocius moved to Texas, where he lived as William Graham.

Sources for Further Reading

Horan, James. *The Lawmen of the Authentic Wild West.* New York: Crown, 1980, pp. 237–238, 241, 262, 267.

Nash, Jay Robert. *Bloodletters and Badmen.* New York: M. Evans, 1973, p. 84.

Nash, Jay Robert. *The Encyclopedia of World Crime.* Wilmette, IL: Crime Books, 1990, pp. 494–495.

Wyatt Earp

Born: March 19, 1848
Died: January 13, 1929

Although he's one of the most famous lawmen of the American West—best remembered for his role in the shoot-out at the O.K. Corral—Wyatt Earp spent only six of his eighty years working as a peacemaker. To this day, Earp has been branded as both a hero and a killer.

EARLY YEARS

Born in Monmouth, Illinois, Wyatt Berry Stapp Earp was one of five brothers. Wyatt had two older brothers—James C. (1841–1926) and Virgil W. (1843–1906)—and two younger siblings—Morgan (1851–1882) and Warren B. (1855–1900). The Earp boys spent most of their youth in Illinois and Iowa. As the end of the Civil War approached, the boys moved West with their parents to San Bernardino, California.

When Wyatt was twenty, he and his brother Virgil worked on a Union Pacific Railroad crew. They rejoined the rest of the Earp family, who had returned to Illinois. Wyatt soon relocated to Lamar, Missouri, where he married his first wife, Urilla Sutherland. In February of 1870, just one month after his marriage, Earp was appointed as the town's constable—his first job as an officer of the law. But Wyatt didn't stay long in Lamar. When Urilla died of typhoid fever (a deadly and contagious disease), Earp left town.

After leaving Missouri in 1871, Earp drifted from job to job in Indian Territory (present-day Oklahoma) and a number of towns in Kansas (where he reportedly forced a number of Texas gunmen who were causing trouble to back down). He worked as a police officer in Wichita, Kansas (1875–1876), and later took a post as the chief deputy of Dodge City, Kansas (1876–1877), where two other well-known lawmen, Bat and Jim Masterson, worked as his aides. From Dodge City, Earp headed for the gold rush in the Black Hills in the Dakota Territory—only to find that the area had already been nearly stripped of gold. Returning to Dodge City, he assumed the post of assistant marshal (1878–1879). During his days in Dodge City, Earp met two people who would become important figures in his life: Cecelia "Mattie" Blaylock, who would later become his second wife, and John "Doc" Holliday, a gunman who would become his lifelong friend.

TOMBSTONE

Tombstone, Arizona, had become a boomtown (a town that experiences sudden growth and prosperity) almost overnight. In 1877, Edward Schieffelin, a prospector, found silver in the area. (The town's name supposedly came from a friend of Schieffelin's who warned the prospector that instead of a mine, he'd find a tombstone.) Schieffelin found a motherlode (principal source or supply) of silver that eventually yielded millions of dollars in silver. Soon, the town was filled with fortune-seeking miners—as well as con artists, claim jumpers, gamblers, and gunmen. A haven for outlaws, the area often erupted with gunfights and riots. To the rest of the country, Tombstone represented chaos and lawlessness—and every other negative stereotype of the Wild West.

In December of 1879, Wyatt and Mattie arrived in Tombstone, and were soon joined by Wyatt's brothers James, Morgan, Virgil, and Warren. The following year, Virgil was appointed town marshal, and he sometimes called on Wyatt to serve as his deputy. A hard-core gambler, Wyatt also worked as a guard in the very successful Oriental Saloon.

Tombstone troublemakers

At the time of the gunfight at O.K. Corral, Tombstone, Arizona, had a population of 10,000—and a reputation for chaos. The town remained a lawless place even after the feud between the Earps and the Clanton-McLaury gang was over. Less than one year after the shoot-out, on May 3, 1882, President Chester Arthur (1829–1886) issued a proclamation stating that "it has become impracticable to enforce by the ordinary course of judicial proceedings the laws of the United States" in Tombstone. He urged the trouble-makers to "retire peacefully to their respective abodes." President Arthur was threatening Tombstone with martial law—a state of emergency in which the military takes over law enforcement.

Never a Sheriff

Wyatt Earp was never a full sheriff in Tombstone, Dodge City—or anywhere else, for that matter.

Doc Holliday
(1851 or 1852-1887)

On his way to fight the Clanton-McLaury gang with his brothers at the O.K. Corral, Wyatt Earp tried to tell his friend, Doc Holliday, that he shouldn't join the fight. Holliday didn't listen, and received a gunshot in the hip while fighting with the Earp brothers. Although sometimes an embarrassment to the lawmaker, Holliday stood by Earp through difficult times.

John Henry Holliday was born to a genteel southern family in Griffin, Georgia, in 1851 or 1852. His father was a major in the Confederate Army during the Civil War (1861–1865). When Holliday was eleven years old, his family moved to Valdosta, Georgia, and he left home about five years later. He enrolled at a college of dental surgery on the East Coast, and at the age of twenty, set up a practice in Atlanta, Georgia. Holliday's profession as a dentist earned him the nickname "Doc." Easily angered, he earned a reputation as a dangerous man. It was said that he was well-drilled (skilled) in the art of dentistry, but for those who doubted his ability, he would drill (shoot) them for free.

Holliday suffered pulmonary tuberculosis (a deadly disease that affects the lungs), the disease that took his mother's life. A sickly man throughout his life, he was thin and weak, and often fell into terrible coughing fits. Bat Masterson, a lawman who was an acquaintance of Holliday's, said this about him: "Physically, Doc Holliday was a weakling who could not have whipped a healthy fifteen-year-old boy in a fight."

As his health grew worse, Holliday was forced to leave Georgia for a drier climate. A

Wyatt brothers

Wyatt's older brother Virgil was considered to be the leader of the Earp brothers during their stay in Tombstone, Arizona. His younger brother Morgan had a reputation as the hothead in the family.

By 1881, the Earps were involved in a feud with a gang of outlaws led by Joseph Isiah "Ike" Clanton. Operating from their ranches west of town, on the San Pedro River, the Clantons—Ike and his younger brother Billy—and the McLaury brothers—Tom and Frank—rustled cattle and robbed stagecoaches in the area. The Clantons and McLaurys were a powerful gang that wanted to rid Tombstone of the Earp brothers, who threatened their livelihood.

THE GUNFIGHT AT O.K. CORRAL

It was simply a matter of time before the feud between the Clanton-McLaury gang and the Earp brothers ended in violence. Frank McLaury challenged Morgan Earp to a shoot-out,

gambler and a heavy drinker, he drifted from one town to another. In Texas, he reportedly killed for the first time. He also stopped in a number of western boomtowns, including Tucson, Tombstone, and Dodge City—where he probably met and befriended Wyatt Earp. Historians have never been able to explain Earp's loyalty to Holliday—although some speculate that Holliday saved the lawman's life sometime during their stay in Dodge City.

Earp was impressed by Holliday's ability to handle a gun. He claimed that the dentist was "the nerviest, speediest, deadliest man with a six-gun that I ever knew." But he wasn't a man to argue with. Bat Masterson said that Holliday had "a mean disposition and an ungovernable temper, and under the influence of liquor was a most dangerous man." The list of his dangerous activities was long. In Las Vegas, New Mexico, he killed a man in a saloon fight. In another fight, he killed a bartender. Holliday was also suspected of stagecoach and train robbery. Free on bail at the time of the O.K. Corral gunfight, Holliday later helped the Earps to track down and kill two men suspected of the murder of Morgan Earp.

Liquor contributed to Holliday's poor health. Weakened by alcoholism, he fell into uncontrollable coughing fits that left him helpless. In May of 1887—less than six years after the gunfight at O.K. Corral—he entered a hospital in Glenwood Springs, Colorado. Six months later, as the story goes, he propped himself up in bed and yelled to a nurse, "Dammit, put them back on." Holliday wanted to die *with his boots on*. But the nurse was too late. At 10 A.M. on November 8, 1887, Doc Holliday died. Although he was in his mid-thirties, his illness had made him look like a man in his eighties.

but Earp refused. But when Ike Clanton got into an argument with Doc Holliday in a saloon on the afternoon of October 25, 1881, he set in motion a series of events that would lead to a showdown—the gunfight at O.K. Corral.

The morning after the argument, Ike Clanton was still angry. He made threats against the Earps and he waved a gun in town. Virgil Earp, the town marshal, deputized his brothers Wyatt and Morgan, as well as Doc Holliday. Then he arrested Clanton for carrying guns within the city limits. Clanton was taken to court and fined. Outside the courthouse, Wyatt and Tom McLaury broke into an argument—which ended when Earp "buffaloed" McLaury by hitting him on the side of his head with a pistol.

Inside the O.K. Corral
at Tombstone, Arizona.

Later that day, the Earps learned that the Clantons and McLaurys were gathered near the O.K. Corral. Convinced that a shoot-out was in the making, the Earp brothers headed to a vacant lot on Fremont Street where the outlaws awaited them. Doc Holliday joined the Earps, although Wyatt had tried to discourage him from joining the fight.

The shoot-out was short but brutal. In very little time—somewhere between thirty seconds and three minutes—three of the eight men involved were dead. Among the dead were Frank and Tom McLaury, and nineteen-year-old Billy Clanton, who had wounds in his chest, head, and wrist. Of the four lawmen involved, only Wyatt Earp was uninjured. Ike Clanton was the only other man to escape without being shot. Clanton had run into Fly's photographic studio when the shooting began.

Beyond O.K.

Although the town had been rid of three troublesome outlaws, the people of Tombstone were not happy about the violent events of October 26. Many believed that the gunfight was murder disguised as crime fighting. Immediately after the shoot-out, town sheriff John E. Behan issued warrants for the arrest of Wyatt Earp and Doc Holliday. Justice of the Peace Wells Spicer reviewed the case for thirty days, and finally decided that there was not enough evidence to charge Earp and Holliday with murder. They were released. Although Virgil Earp was not arrested, he was dismissed from his duties as town marshal and criticized for having deputized his brothers.

The violence was far from over. On November 28—just over one month after the gunfight—Virgil was ambushed on his way into the Oriental Saloon. Shot by an unidentified gunman, he was disabled for life. In March of 1882, Morgan was shot and killed. Wyatt and his brother Warren tracked and killed a number of men they believed to be responsible for the shootings.

Now labeled a murderer, Wyatt fled first to Colorado and then to assorted boomtowns in the West—from Idaho to Arizona and Alaska. In 1888, after Mattie Earp died, he married his third wife (and longtime girlfriend) Josephine Sarah Marcus. Wyatt eventually settled in California, where he became a familiar figure at the horse racing tracks. He mingled with movie stars and lived to a ripe old age. He died on January 13, 1929, at the age of eighty—having outlived every one of his four brothers.

> ### Waxed pockets
>
> A tall, well-groomed man who never left home without his coat and tie, Wyatt Earp didn't wear the traditional gun belt and holster. Instead, he had tailor-made waxed pockets in his suit coat that allowed him to remove the gun easily.

Sources for Further Reading

The American West, A Cultural Encyclopedia, Volumes 3 and 8. Danbury, CT: Grolier Educational Corp., 1995, pp. 468–471, 1345.

"Brave, Courageous and Bold." *New York Times Book Review* (November 9, 1997), p. 72.

Nash, Jay Robert. *Bloodletters and Badmen.* New York: M. Evans, 1973, pp. 423–428.

Rosa, Joseph. *The Taming of the West: Age of the Gunfighter.* New York: Smithmark, 1993, pp. 120–121, 128, 134, 179–180, 184–185.

Ross, Stewart. *Fact or Fiction: Bandits & Outlaws.* Surrey, British Columbia: Copper Beech Books, 1995, pp. 24–25.

Wukovits, John. *The Gunslingers.* Broomall, PA: Chelsea House, 1997, pp. 37–39.

Jesse James

Born: September 5, 1847
Died: April 3, 1882
AKA: "Dingus," J. D. Howard

Together with his brother Frank, Jesse James made a career out of robbing banks and trains. Although he was a ruthless killer, he was also a religious family man. Even before he was murdered by a gang-member turned-traitor, the legend of Jesse James was larger than life.

A PREACHER'S SON

Zerelda Cole was just sixteen when she left a Catholic convent to marry Robert James, a well-educated Baptist minister. The couple left Kentucky in the early 1840s to try their luck at running a small farm in Clay County, Missouri, about twenty miles northwest of Kansas City. The couple's first son, Alexander Franklin James, was born in 1843. Nearly five years later, on September 5, 1847, Jesse Woodson James was born.

Robert James left his family to join the California gold rush. Jesse, who was three years old at the time, never saw his father again. A few weeks after he arrived in California to seek his fortune, Robert James died of pneumonia, at the age of twenty-six. Zerelda soon remarried, but quickly divorced her fifty- year-old second husband. She gave her boys a religious upbringing, and in 1857 married her third husband, Reuben Samuel, who was a farmer and doctor.

AN UNCIVIL WAR

Frank and Jesse were teenagers when the Civil War erupted in 1861—the same year that Kansas became a state. It was also a time of brutal border wars between Kansas "Red Legs" or "Jayhawkers"—who opposed slavery—and Missouri "Bushwackers"—who were in favor of continuing the practice of slavery. Both sides formed guerrilla forces, which employed "irregular" methods of warfare such as violent surprise attacks.

The James brothers had no trouble choosing sides. Their family owned several black slaves, and they were committed to supporting the Confederacy. (The Confederacy was a group of eleven pro-slavery Southern states that broke away from the Union in 1860–1861 to form their own government.) Frank, who had enlisted in the Confederate army, was jailed by Federal militia for taking part in the Confederate cause. He was released from prison after he signed an oath pledging his loyalty to the Union—a promise he did not intend to keep.

As the Civil War raged, Frank, and later Jesse, took part in the vicious guerrilla (outlaw soldier) battles between Confederate and Union supporters. Frank joined the army of William Clarke Quantrill, a Southern guerrilla leader, and participated in a bloody raid on Lawrence, Kansas, on August 20, 1863. About one year later, Jesse joined the guerrilla band under one of Quantrill's lieutenants, "Bloody Bill" Anderson. Jesse soon became an expert marksman and horseback rider. By his eighteenth birthday, he had participated in many violent raids on anti-slavery towns. These raids left countless Union soldiers dead. At Centralia, Missouri, in 1864, for example, Jesse and other Confederate guerrillas murdered dozens of unarmed Union soldiers.

FALSE PARDON

At the end of the Civil War, Southern troops were pardoned. But guerrilla fighters were tracked and killed. The James brothers continued to live as hunted outlaws until 1865, when the government offered all guerrilla soldiers amnesty (pardon). According to legend, on April 1, 1865, Frank and Jesse James rode into the small town of Lexington, Missouri, waving the white flag of surrender. They were met by a group of cavalry soldiers who ignored their attempt to surrender and opened fire on the former guerrillas. Both James brothers managed to escape—although Jesse was shot in the chest and nearly died.

Popular reading material

The public loved to read about the real and fictional exploits of Jesse James and his gang. Their adventures were written up in books, dime novels and weeklies (newspapers). In just two years (between 1901 and 1903), the Street and Smith publishing house sold *six million* copies of 121 Jesse James novels.

Weak and wounded, Jesse was helped back to his family by Southern sympathizers. Because of their strong support of the Confederate cause, Zerelda and Reuben Samuel had been forced to leave Missouri for Nebraska. But Jesse, who was afraid that he might die, insisted that the family return to its native state. He is said to have vowed, "I don't want to die in a Northern state." In the fall of 1865 he was brought by covered wagon back to Clay County, where his uncle, John Mimms, ran a boardinghouse. Jesse's cousin, also named Zerelda, helped to nurse him back to health. After a nine-year engagement, Jesse married Zerelda—or "Zee," as she was called.

A NEW CAREER

At eight o'clock on the morning of February 13, 1866, four men strolled into the Clay County Savings and Loan Bank in Liberty, Missouri. Six others stayed outside on their horses. Minutes later the men—including Frank James and his cousin Cole Younger—rode out of town with a wheat sack filled with $60,000 in bonds and currency. One man was dead. The Clay County heist was the first bank robbery committed by the James-Younger gang. But it was far from the last. For more than ten years, the James boys and their cousins, the Younger brothers—Cole, James, John, and Robert—were the central figures in a criminal gang that made off with hundreds of thousands of dollars in stolen goods.

The gang covered a lot of territory, robbing banks in seven states: Arkansas, Iowa, Kentucky, Minnesota, Missouri, Texas, and West Virginia. Using some of the skills they had learned as

Will the real Jesse James please stand up!

A number of people believe that Jesse James faked his own death. After the outlaw's supposed corpse was exhumed (dug up) and examined, scientists determined that DNA extracted from the corpse's hair was nearly identical to that of the outlaw's sister's descendants. But that didn't stop would-be relatives from claiming that James did not die in Missouri at the hands of Bob Ford.

Some claimed that James had lived out his days in Granbury, Texas—where he died at the age of 103. In the 1920s and 1930s, circuses often staged sideshows featuring the "real" Jesse James. And for years, the descendants of J. Frank Dalton have claimed that their bearded ancestor was, in fact, Jesse James. Supporting their claim was a 1951 autopsy report that identifies Dalton as the infamous gunslinger. The report states that the corpse of Dalton is missing the tip of the left forefinger. (During the Civil War, James accidentally shot off the tip of his finger.) Dalton's body also contained more than thirty bullet wounds. Most of the evidence, however, relied on statements from friends and family who claimed to have overheard the old Texan boast that he was the former outlaw.

More recently, a Texas woman named Betty Dorsett Duke entered her claim as the great-

Imposters

After the Northfield disaster, Frank and Jesse James disappeared into the Dakota Territory. They sometimes posed as law officers--and told several citizens that *they* were going to capture the James boys.

guerrilla fighters, the outlaws arrived at a successful formula for robbery. They planned their hits carefully and attacked suddenly and violently. And they always plotted their escape before they struck their targets. Most years, the gang staged only one or two robberies, which left the James brothers plenty of time to live peacefully as farmers.

In 1873, the gang added train robbery—a relatively new and very profitable form of robbery—to its growing list of illegal activities. They pulled off their first theft by loosening a rail at a blind curve in order to stop the train. The robbers made off with only $2,000. But future train robberies would be more profitable. One of the gang's most successful robberies took place in 1875, when the James brothers and seven others robbed the Missouri-Pacific Express train of $75,000.

SHOWDOWN IN NORTHFIELD

The gang's next target was the First National Bank in Northfield, Minnesota. On August 7, 1876, eight members of the gang

granddaughter of Jesse James. Her great-grandfather, a farmer named James Lafayette Courtney, lived in Texas to the ripe old age of ninety-six. After he died on April 14, 1943, he was buried in a cemetery in Falls County. The evidence Duke presents was surprising:

- A portrait of James Lafayette Courtney was surprisingly similar to a famous photograph of Jesse James that was taken in Nebraska in 1866.

- Many photos of Courtney showed him with his left hand curled in. Jesse James reportedly used the same pose to hide his injured finger.

- A photograph of Courtney's mother, Dianah Andruss Courtney, appeared to be identical to a photo of Jesse's mother, Zerelda James Samuel. Like Zerelda Samuels, Dianah Courtney's left arm ended at the elbow.

- Many other Courtney family photographs resembled photographs of Jesse's relatives.

- Courtney's diary mentioned Bill Wilkerson, a member of the James gang. And Wilkerson's brother sometimes lived with the Courtneys.

- Courtney had a lot of money for a farmer. He bought a farm for every one of his eight children. And he paid cash.

rode into the peaceful Minnesota farming town. The group included both James brothers and three of their cousins—Bob, Cole, and Jim Younger—as well as Charlie Pitts, Clell Miller, and Bill Chadwell. They all wore new boots and well-pressed suits, and rode handsome, well-kept horses.

The robbery didn't go well from the start. The bank teller claimed the safe was time-locked and couldn't be opened. (As it turned out, the safe was *open*—but the robbers hadn't looked.) Two men in the street had noticed the activity by the bank, and started shouting to alert the townspeople. Gunfire broke out inside the bank, and the outlaws were fired on by citizens when they abandoned the heist. Miller and Chadwell were shot dead in the street, and most of the others were wounded.

Followed by an angry posse (a group of people with legal authority to capture criminals), the surviving members of the gang split up. Frank and Jesse struck out together, while Pitts joined the three Younger brothers. Two weeks later, a posse caught up with the Youngers, and a shoot-out followed. Pitts was killed and the three brothers were captured. The Younger

Bob Ford, killer of
Jesse James.

boys were all wounded (Cole had been hit by eleven bullets), but they recovered and were each sentenced to life in prison.

THE SECOND JAMES GANG

Frank and Jesse James were the only gang members who weren't dead or in prison. For three years they laid low. They lived in Nashville, Tennessee, and hid their identities by taking new names. Frank James and his wife lived as the Woodsons, while Jesse and Zee called themselves the Howards. But by October 1879, the James brothers returned to Missouri and organized a new gang that specialized in train robbery. The gang included Tucker Basham, Wood Hite, Dick Liddel, Ed Miller (who was Clell's brother), and Bill Ryan.

The gang's first hit was successful. On October 7, 1879, it robbed a train near Glendale, Missouri, of $35,000. For two years gang members continued to rob and kill, but the second James gang soon began to fall apart. They were ruthlessly pursued by lawmen and hired detectives. The gang's new members were outsiders who weren't loyal family members, as the Youngers had been. They fought among themselves over the loot they had stolen. And they betrayed one another.

THE MAN WHO SHOT JESSE JAMES

Charles Ford and his brother Robert were two new recruits who sometimes accompanied the James gang on their raids. They disliked Jesse and argued with him. And they had no problem planning to stake their claim to the $10,000 reward that Thomas T. Crittenden, the governor of Missouri, had offered for the capture and conviction of Jesse James.

In the spring of 1882, the James brothers and the Fords were the only living gang members who had escaped capture. On April 3, the Fords met Jesse at his home in St. Joseph, Missouri, to plan another robbery. Jesse's wife Zee fixed breakfast

An American Robin Hood

Many people saw Jesse James as a hero. In a popular song composed shortly after his death, Jesse's life was glorified:

Jesse James was a lad who killed many a man.

He robbed the Glendale train.

He stole from the rich and he gave to the poor,

He'd a hand and a heart and a brain.

Although many people viewed Jesse James as a modern-day Robin Hood, there is no real evidence that he gave to the poor. But there were plenty of unconfirmed stories that portray him as a brave and kind gentleman thief. In one such story, James gives a widow $3,000 to prevent a banker from taking over her run-down cabin. The widow pays the banker and regains ownership of her home. A few miles from the widow's cabin, James robs the banker of the $3,000 and his watch, and rides away laughing to himself. It's possible that James was the Robin Hood of this story. Then again, versions of the story have been told about a number of other outlaws—including Butch Cassidy, who told it about himself.

Jesse's choice of targets probably contributed to his popularity. The James gangs robbed from banks and railroad companies, both of which were unpopular among poor country dwellers. Many viewed banking houses as crooked institutions. Railroad companies were the enemy of poor farmers, who believed they were run by robber barons who cheated honest people out of their property.

for them. Jesse and Zee's son, Jesse Jr. and Mary, their daughter, played outside. After breakfast, Jesse stood on a chair to straighten a picture on the wall. Before he stepped on the chair, he removed his jacket—and both gun belts.

Standing about six feet from the outlaw, Bob Ford shot him in the back of the head. Jesse James was dead at the age of thirty-four. When Zee ran into the room, Ford claimed that the gun—a revolver that Jesse had given him a few days earlier—had gone off accidentally.

Two weeks after the shooting, Ford brothers were convicted of murder and sentenced to death. Hours later, Governor Crittenden issued a pardon that spared their lives. The governor denied that he had plotted with Robert Ford—who received a little over $600 of the $10,000 reward. Having lost the respect of an entire nation for shooting an unarmed man in the back, he

The house in St. Louis, Missouri, where Jesse James was killed on April 3, 1882, is a popular tourist attraction.

was remembered in a ballad (a popular song) that was composed shortly after Jesse's death. One verse of the song went:

It was Robert Ford, that dirty little coward,
I wonder how he does feel,
For he ate of Jesse's bread and he slept in Jesse's bed,
Then he laid Jesse James in his grave.

THE END OF THE OUTLAWS

Within a few months of his brother's death, on October 5, 1882, Frank James surrendered to the authorities. He was a beaten man who was sick of running. Asked why he had surrendered, he said, "I was tired of an outlaw's life. I have been hunted for twenty-one years. I have literally lived in the saddle. I have never known a day of perfect peace." In three separate trials for murder, robbery, and armed robbery, Frank James was tried and set free. He never served a prison sentence for his crimes, and led a peaceful life on the family farm. He died on February 18, 1915, in the room in which he had been born. He was seventy-two years old.

Nearly twenty years after Jesse's death, Jim and Cole Younger were paroled from prison. They had served almost twenty-five years when they were released on July 11, 1901. Their brother, Bob, had died of tuberculosis (a disease that affects the lungs) while still in prison. One year after their release, Jim Younger committed suicide. Cole made a career giving lectures about the evils of crime. He died at the age of seventy-two, bearing the scars of twenty bullet wounds.

Charles Ford committed suicide in 1884. Jesse's killer, Robert Ford, performed for a while in traveling shows such as *The Outlaws of Missouri* and *How I Killed Jesse James.* He eventually became a saloonkeeper in Creede, Colorado. There, his past caught up with him. Ed Kelly, a relative of the Youngers, shot Ford to death during a quarrel in 1892.

Here's a book you might like:

Mamaw, 1988, by Susan Dodd

Zerelda Samuel—the mother of the infamous James boys, known as Mamaw—is raised in a convent, marries at sixteen, rescues one husband from hanging, loses her hand to a Pinkerton bomb meant for her sons, and then watches as her sons are hunted down.

Sources for Further Reading

The American West, A Cultural Encyclopedia, Volume 5. Danbury, CT: Grolier Educational Corp., 1995, pp. 822–826.

Dingus, Anne. "Body of Evidence." *Texas Monthly* (August 1997), p. 22+.

Nash, Jay Robert. *Bloodletters and Badmen.* New York: M. Evans, 1973, pp. 265–285.

Prassel, Frank Richard. *The Great American Outlaw, A Legacy of Fact and Fiction.* Norman, OK: University of Oklahoma Press, 1993, pp. 125–138.

Rosa, Joseph. *The Taming of the West: Age of the Gunfighter.* New York: Smithmark, 1993, pp. 40–45.

Son or daughter?

After the Northfield disaster, Frank James and his wife Annie called themselves Mr. and Mrs. B. J. Woodson. The couple had a son, Robert Franklin James. To throw his enemies off his trail, the "Woodsons" dressed their son as a girl and called him Mary.

Ross, Stewart. *Fact or Fiction: Bandits & Outlaws.* Surrey, British Columbia: Copper Beech Books, 1995, pp. 38–39.

Steckmesser, Kent. *Western Outlaws: The "Good Badman" in Fact, Film, and Folklore.* Claremont, CA: Regina Books, 1983, pp. 43–68.

Vandome, Nick. *Crimes and Criminals.* New York: Chambers, 1992, pp. 119–120.

Belle Starr
(Myra Belle Shirley)

Born: February 5, 1848
Died: February 3, 1889

Sometimes called the female Jesse James, Belle Starr was an expert rider and a good shot. A foul-tempered cattle and horse thief, she lived with a number of outlaws and earned a reputation as a Bandit Queen in Texas and the Indian Territory.

BORDER WARS AND BANDITRY

Myra Belle Shirley was born in a log cabin near Carthage, Missouri, in 1848. Her father, a farmer and tavern owner, came from a wealthy and aristocratic (socially exclusive) Virginia family. At the age of eight, Belle enrolled in the Carthage Female Academy, where she attended classes through the eighth grade. Because the Kansas-Missouri border had become a battleground for people who were fighting over slavery, Belle's father decided to move his family away from the violence—to Scyene, Texas, not far from Dallas.

Several years after her family moved to Texas—after the Civil War had ended—Belle met an outlaw named Cole Younger, a former Confederate guerrilla (outlaw soldier), who was the cousin of Jesse James and a member of the Younger-James gang. Younger was hiding from the law following a Missouri bank robbery. Belle ran away with Younger in 1866, and the two lived together in a cabin on the Oklahoma Strip. Younger eventually rejoined his brothers and the rest of the

Western outlaw Belle
Starr on horseback.

James gang. Shortly after he left, Belle had a daughter, Pearl. Most historians assume that Younger was Pearl's father.

Belle soon had a son, Edward, whose father was another outlaw, Jim Reed. Belle and Reed left Texas in 1869 because lawmen were on their trail. In California, near the North Canadian River, they pulled a robbery. According to some sources, they forced a prospector to tell them where he had hidden a large stash of gold. In other reports, they tortured a Creek Indian chief into telling them where his tribe's government subsidy (a grant of money) was hidden. In any case, Belle and Reed left California $30,000 richer.

Returning to Texas, Belle enjoyed her new-found wealth. She sometimes wore velvet dresses, shiny boots, and feathered hats—and often strapped a gun belt over her skirt. And she rode an expensive black race-horse named Venus (side-saddle, as women of that era were expected to). Reed was killed in a gun fight in August of 1874, and Belle reportedly refused to identify his body so that his killer would not be able to collect the reward that had been offered for his capture.

An infamous first

In 1883, Belle Starr became the first woman ever tried for a major crime in Judge Isaac Parker's infamous "court of the damned." Belle was sentenced to less than one year in a federal prison in Detroit—a light sentence, given Parker's reputation as the "hanging judge."

MRS. SAM STARR

After Reed's death, Belle left her two children with her mother and helped to run a horse- and cattle-stealing ring in the Indian Territory. She lived briefly with a Native American rustler named Blue Duck, and then in 1880 met and married Sam Starr, a Cherokee outlaw who was four years her junior. Married according to Cherokee custom, Belle took an oath of allegiance to the Cherokee Nation. She kept the Starr name throughout the rest of her life.

The Starrs settled near the Canadian River, in an area she named Younger's Bend—in memory of her former love, Cole Younger. Housing outlaws in guest rooms, the couple ran a hideout for fugitives. Jesse James reportedly stayed with the Starrs following a train robbery in 1881.

Three years after they were married, Starr and Belle were both tried for horse theft by Isaac Parker—the so-called "hanging judge." Starr was sentenced to less than one year in prison. Belle—whom Parker called the "leader of a notorious band of horse thieves"—enjoyed a reputation in the newspapers as "the petticoat of the planes" and "the lady desperado." Belle played up her role as the Lady Bandit, posing for numerous pictures before serving time in a prison in Detroit, Michigan.

Released from prison, the Starrs returned to Younger's Bend and resumed their careers as horse and cattle rustlers. After they were arrested by U.S. marshals in 1886 they were tried. Judge Parker released the couple because there was not enough evidence to convict them of theft. But their freedom was short-lived. Sam Starr was killed later that year by a Native American police officer. (According to some sources, the shooting took place at a dance. Others claim that Sam and one of the officers who arrested him got into a barroom fight that left both men dead.)

A LEGEND IN THE MAKING

After Starr's death, Belle remained at Younger's Bend and became involved with Jim July, a Creek Indian who was wanted for robbery. A few months after the two were married, in 1889, Belle was killed in an ambush. No one is sure who killed her—although there are several theories concerning her killer's motives and identity. Some believed that an angry former lover was responsible for the killing. Others believed the culprit to be a neighbor named Edgar Watson, who had quarreled with her about land. Some suspected Belle's eighteen-year-old son, Edward, who had a difficult relationship with his mother. At the time, R. P. Vann—a neighbor and former member of the Indian police—suggested that Edward had a motive in the killing: "Among the people in the Belle Starr country," Vann reported, "it is commonly accepted belief that there were incestuous relations [sexual relations between people who are related] between Belle and her son and that she complicated this with extreme sadism [delight in cruelty]." Some historians have concluded that—given the surroundings—Belle must have seen her shooter. Although a neighbor found her before she died, she never named her killer.

Belle was buried at Younger's Bend, in a Cherokee ceremony: jewelry was laid in her coffin and a revolver (possibly one given to her by Cole Younger) was placed at her hand. Her daughter, Pearl, had a monument placed at the grave. It was inscribed with the words:

> Shed not for her the bitter tear,
> Nor give the heart to vain [useless] regret,
> 'Tis but the casket that lies here,
> The gem that fills it sparkles yet.

Shortly after Belle was buried, her grave was robbed. Within three years, Jim July died in an Arkansas jail.

Thanks to a New York author, Belle Starr became a legend soon after she died. *Belle Starr, the Bandit Queen, or the Female Jesse James: A Full and Authentic History of the Dashing Female Highwayman,* by Richard Fox (a dime-novel author), was billed as the authentic biography of the woman rustler. In reality, it was a sensationalized adventure tale that had little to do with the truth. Fox painted a heroic picture of Belle: "Of all women . . . the universe produced none more remarkable than Belle Starr, the Bandit Queen. Her character was a combination of the very worst as well as some of the very best traits of her sex. She was more amorous [loving] than Anthony's mistress, more relentless [harsh] than Pharaoh's daughter, and braver than Joan of Arc." And Fox didn't stop there. He made up diary entries that were supposed to have been written by the notorious Bandit Queen.

Confederate supporters

Belle's twin brother, Ed, was reportedly a captain in the Confederate Army, serving under the notorious outlaw leader William Clarke "Bloody Bill" Quantrill. Hunted by Union troops, Ed was killed. Belle also worked for the Confederate "irregulars": she was arrested as a Confederate courier.

Sources for Further Reading

The American West, A Cultural Encyclopedia, Volume 9. Danbury, CT: Grolier Educational Corp., 1995, pp. 1514–1516.

Bruns, Roger. *The Bandit Kings from Jesse James to Pretty Boy Floyd.* New York: Crown, 1995, pp. 166, 217.

Horan, James. *The Lawmen of the Authentic Wild West.* New York: Crown, 1980, p. 171.

Lewis, Jon E. *The Mammoth Book of the West.* New York: Carroll & Graf, 1996, pp. 334–335.

Nash, Jay Robert. *Bloodletters and Badmen.* New York: M. Evans, 1973, pp. 527–529.

O'Neal, Bill. *Encyclopedia of Western Gunfighters.* Norman, OK: University of Oklahoma Press, 1979, pp. 260–261, 297–298, 346–347.

Pirotta, Saviour. *The Wild, Wild West.* Austin, TX: Raintree Steck-Vaughn, 1997, pp. 28–29.

Prassel, Frank Richard. *The Great American Outlaw, A Legacy of Fact and Fiction.* Norman, OK: University of Oklahoma Press, 1993, pp. 188–190, 227–229.

The children of Belle Starr

Edward Reed, the son of Belle Starr and outlaw Jim Reed, was convicted of bootlegging and later served a term as a deputy federal marshal. He was killed in a barroom fight in 1896. Belle's daughter, Pearl, became a well-known prostitute at Fort Smith, Arkansas. She died in 1925.

Ross, Stewart. *Fact or Fiction: Cowboys.* Surrey, British Columbia: Copper Beech, 1995, p. 23.

Sifakis, Carl. *The Encyclopedia of American Crime.* New York: Facts on File, 1982, pp. 683–685.

Ward, Geoffrey. *The West, An Illustrated History.* Boston: Little, Brown, 1996, p. 356.

Dallas Stoudenmire

Born: December 11, 1845
Died: September 18, 1882

A former Texas Ranger, Dallas Stoudenmire began his career as a well-respected U.S. marshal, but he soon acquired a reputation for drinking too much and shooting too freely. He has been remembered as one of the most sensational lawmen of the West— and as a man who sometimes stood on the wrong side of the law.

A CONFEDERATE RANGER

A Southerner by birth, Dallas Stoudenmire was born in 1845 in Aberfoil, Alabama. He grew up in a large family, and when the Civil War broke out in 1861, he didn't wait long to join the fighting. Stoudenmire is reported to have joined the Confederate army in 1862, when he was just sixteen years old. (The Confederate army fought for the eleven Southern states that broke away from the Union in order to form their own government.) Although he received many severe wounds, he survived the war and later settled in Texas. He tried his luck—very briefly—as a farmer near Columbus, Texas.

Stoudenmire joined the Frontier Battalion of the Texas Rangers, where he soon became known as a man who was fearless to a fault—and who was easily provoked to violence and showed no remorse for killing. An imposing man who stood over six feet tall, he was feared by the outlaws he pursued—as well as the citizens he protected.

"The cure"

In the summer of 1882, Stoudenmire took "the cure"—a treatment for alcoholism—at the hotsprings near Las Vegas, New Mexico. The lawman's hands reportedly shook so much that a friend had to sign the guest register for him.

By the time he left the Texas Rangers, Stoudenmire had a reputation as a gunslinger who shot first and asked questions later. He became the marshal of Socorro, New Mexico, where he participated in a number of gunfights—some of which led people to question which side of the law he represented. In 1881 he returned to Texas, presumably at the request of his brother-in-law, Samuel "Doc" Cummings, owner of the city's finest restaurant, the Globe. He served imported food and advertised "No dust, no noise, no flies." Having married Stoudenmire's sister in Columbus, Texas, Cummings farmed in the panhandle, ran a hotel in San Marcial, New Mexico, and then traveled by stagecoach to El Paso—a town he'd never even visited. He arrived there on Christmas Eve of 1880.

The El Paso that Cummings and Stoudenmire encountered was a lawless and violent boomtown (a town that experiences sudden growth and prosperity). The town's mayor, Solomon Schutz, showed more concern for his personal interests than for El Paso's welfare, and city marshals—who seldom stayed in office long—had a difficult time attempting to maintain law and order within the city limits. Adding to the border town's troubles were frequent and ongoing disputes between Mexicans and Americans.

After his predecessor (the former marshal) was forced to resign, Stoudenmire became marshal of El Paso on April 11, 1881. Involved in two shoot-outs within days of his appointment, he quickly made a number of enemies. But he also had his supporters. El Paso's city leaders were pleased with his ability to intimidate the town's many criminals.

During his brief term in office, Stoudenmire developed a personal feud with the wealthy Manning brothers—George, Frank, and Jim. The Mannings owned one of the state's largest cattle ranches and controlled most of the town's thriving saloon business. George Manning, was a well-respected doctor in El Paso. Adding fuel to the feud was a shoot-out between Stoudenmire and John Hale, an associate of the Manning brothers. Stoudenmire gunned down Hale. He also shot an innocent bystander and George Campbell—a former city marshal and friend of the Mannings. Campbell protested during the gunfight that he was not involved in the dispute and claimed, on his deathbed, that the marshal had murdered him.

A FAILED AMBUSH

Stoudenmire and Cummings were frequently attacked, and they believed the Mannings had hired assassins to kill them. On April 17, 1882, Bill Johnson—who had resigned as city marshal before Stoudenmire arrived—attempted to ambush the two lawmen. Hiding behind a pile of bricks that were to be used in the construction of the State National Bank, he waited for his targets to pass on their nightly rounds. When Stoudenmire and Cummings approached, he fired, missed, and was shot dead by his intended victims. Stoudenmire was then wounded in the heel by one of a group of shooters who were hiding across the street. Following the shooting, he retreated to a Texas Ranger camp. Stoudenmire returned to El Paso one week later to find the town divided for and against him. Although he blamed the Manning brothers for the incident, he had no evidence that tied them to the attack.

DEAD DEPUTY

In February 1882, Stoudenmire deputized Cummings in order to help a Kansas sheriff who was trailing a rapist to Chihuahua, Mexico. When Cummings returned, both Stoudenmire and his deputy, James Gillett, were ill with the flu—leaving Cummings in charge. Later that month, Stoudenmire left town on a honeymoon with his new wife, Isabella Sherrington. With Gillett still ill, Cummings continued on as the town's deputy.

Before Stoudenmire returned, Cummings was shot dead at the Coliseum saloon. Jim Manning was the shooter. Although a judge later ruled that Manning had acted in self-defense, the killing raised a number of questions. The deputy's corpse had two bullet wounds and a fractured skull. Although Manning claimed to have shot twice, only one of the cartridges in his pis-

Ready, set, jump!

When El Paso city council members gathered to fire Stoudenmire from his post as marshal, they were afraid of how the lawman might react. Some of the councilmen sat on window sills in front of open windows—to make sure they could escape in case the marshal flew into a rage.

Fighting like the very devil

The Texas Rangers were established long before Dallas Stoudenmire was even born. Texas was colonized in 1823 by Stephen Austin (1793–1836), who ordered a group of "rangers" to handle hostile Mexican and Native American raiders. John S. "Rip" Ford, a well known Texas Ranger, once boasted that a ranger was required to "ride like a Mexican, trail like an Indian, shoot like a Tennessean, and fight like the very devil."

Within twelve years, the Texas Rangers became official law enforcers. They also fought in the Texas War of Independence (1835) and in the Mexican War (1846–1848). When the group broke up during the Civil War (1861–1865), many former rangers fought in the Confederate army. By 1874, the rangers were reorganized to combat outlaw gangs, livestock rustlers, stagecoach and bank robbers, and other criminals.

Never governed by military or local laws, Texas Rangers were able to travel freely across the entire state. While most rangers in the Old West were employed in areas that had no local government, Texas Rangers were called on when local officers were unable to maintain peace. Texas Rangers still exist—and they continue to work with Texas law officers.

---

tol had been fired (which suggests there was a second shooter). What's more, the coroner testified that Cummings's skull fracture could not have occurred simply by falling to the ground (which raises the possibility that he was hit on the head before he was shot).

Unfriendly feelings

Stoudenmire was furious about Cummings's murder and wanted to punish the Mannings. Noting the growing hostility, the El Paso *Lone Star* newspaper printed that the city streets could be "deluged with blood at any moment." Concerned about the growing feud between the marshal and the wealthy Mannings, the El Paso city council convinced Stoudenmire—after three weeks of negotiating—to sign a truce (peace agreement) with the brothers. The agreement was signed on April 16, and was published, word-for-word, in the El Paso *Herald:*

> We the undersigned parties having this day settled all differences and unfriendly feelings existing between us, hereby agree that we will hereafter meet

and pass each other on friendly terms, and that bygones shall be bygones, and that we shall never allude [refer] in the future to any past animosities [ill will] that have existed between us.

The truce was short-lived. A heavy drinker, Stoudenmire often taunted and threatened the Mannings. City officials passed an ordinance making it illegal for city officers to indulge in drunkenness—a law that was clearly aimed at the town's unruly marshal. Public sentiment was against Stoudenmire as well. The *Lone Star* published the following editorial, which called on city officials to "stop dilly-dallying" and:

> to make a proper investigation, to do it with open doors, and then remove or reinstate the marshal. If he has not done his duty, or if his continuance in office is a threat to the city, he ought to be removed. Public policy dictates that, even if a man be a good peace officer, if he be obnoxious in the community, or if his continuance in office is liable to provoke serious trouble, perhaps even a riot, he ought to be replaced. Let the city act only from a high sense of duty and quit dilly-dallying.

On May 27, 1882, the city council met to dismiss Stoudenmire. When Stoudenmire appeared, he cursed and threatened them—and the meeting was called off. The following week he submitted a letter of resignation. Although he apologized for his behavior, he complained that he had been wronged by the city's politicians. In a unanimous vote (a vote in which everyone agrees), James Gillett was approved as the city marshal.

SHOWDOWN AT THE MANNING SALOON

On September 18, 1882, Stoudenmire (who was said to be drunk) got into an argument at the Manning saloon. According to some accounts, he was looking for a fight. Others report that he entered the Manning saloon with a warrant hoping to locate a wanted criminal. The Mannings, hearing that Stoudenmire

City marshal: job description

In the Old West, the city marshal was usually appointed by the mayor and the town council. Acting as a chief-of-police, the marshal usually appointed a deputy and a number of assistant lawmen. In emergencies, the marshal was authorized to enlist the help of citizens. The marshal's authority extended only to the city limits (in theory, at least), and the town council had the power to dismiss him if they were displeased with his performance. Depending on his reputation, a city marshal in the middle of the nineteenth century earned between $50 and $250 a month.

had been to their saloon, assumed that he was stirring up trouble. The following day, the Mannings picked a fight with Stoudenmire.

However the fight started, it ended in gunfire. George Manning got off the first shot. The bullet ricocheted into Stoudenmire's chest, and then another shot struck him in his shirt pocket. Although the second bullet didn't wound him—since it had been stopped by the papers in his pocket—it did send him crashing through the saloon doors.

Stoudenmire, meanwhile, had managed to fire a shot that forced Manning to drop his gun. Before Stoudenmire could shoot again, Manning wrestled him into a bear hug. At that point, Manning's brother, Jim, arrived. He fired once and missed: his sawed-off revolver was missing the trigger. Jim fired a second shot using his thumb to trigger the hammer. It struck Stoudenmire in the head, killing him. Still enraged, George Manning pistol-whipped Stoudenmire's corpse until lawmen pulled him away. Tried individually for the murder of Dallas Stoudenmire, George and Jim Manning were each acquitted (found not guilty). The judge ruled that Jim had acted in defense of his "unarmed" brother. Having died a poor man, Stoudenmire was buried in a suit and coffin that were paid for by El Paso freemasons. His grave, in Columbus, has since been lost.

THE MANNING BROTHERS

Frank Manning became El Paso's marshal in April 1883. After he was dismissed for threatening a citizen, most of the Manning brothers left town. Frank turned to prospecting, and was eventually committed to a state-run institution.

Jim Manning moved from Arizona to Washington state. He married Lenor Isabelle Arzate, a woman from Juarez, Mexico. In April 1915 he died from cancer and the effects of a bullet wound he'd received earlier in life.

George Manning moved to Flagstaff, Arizona, where he continued to practice medicine. He never recovered use of the arm that had been wounded in the gunfight with Stoudenmire.

Sources for Further Reading

Collins, James L. *Lawmen of the Old West.* New York: Franklin Watts, 1990, pp. 27–35.

Metz, Leon Claire. *A Gallery of Notorious Gunmen from the American West.* New York: Berkeley Books, 1996, pp. 87–110.

Nash, Jay Robert. *The Encyclopedia of World Crime.* Wilmette, IL: Crime Books, 1990, pp. 2864–2865.

O'Neal, Bill. *Encyclopedia of Western Gunfighters.* Norman, OK: University of Oklahoma Press, 1979, pp. 78–79, 214, 302–305.

Rosa, Joseph. *The Taming of the West: Age of the Gunfighter.* New York: Smithmark, 1993, pp. 169–173.

Sifakis, Carl. *The Encyclopedia of American Crime.* New York: Facts on File, 1982, p. 691.

Old West nightlife

The Coliseum Saloon and Variety Theatre—one of the many drinking establishments owned by the Mannings—was a class establishment. It advertised a "seating capacity of 1,500, a stage 30 by 40 feet, and carpeted private boxes with elegant lace curtains."

Pancho Villa
(Doroteo Arango)

Born: June 5, 1878
Died: July 19, 1923

A gifted soldier and strategist, Pancho Villa (pronounced VEE-yah) spent a decade fighting for Mexico's freedom. But Villa was also a killer who was capable of tremendous cruelty. He was both loved and feared by his countrymen, and, by the end of his career, had few admirers north of the border.

HEAD FOR THE HILLS!

Born on June 5, 1878, Doroteo Arango was the son of a field laborer in San Juan de Río, Mexico. His parents—Augustín Arango and Micaela Arambula—died when he was very young, and the orphaned Arango took charge of protecting his siblings. As a field worker, he was forced to work long, back-breaking hours that allowed him no time for school.

When one of the owners of the estate where he worked assaulted his sister, Arango killed the man and fled to the mountains. Still just a teenager, he lived as a fugitive from the law, calling himself "Francisco Villa"—the name of an earlier outlaw. Soon, he became known as "Pancho Villa." Villa spent years in the mountains, living off the land—and robbing, looting, and raiding banks, trains, mines and more. Because he shared his spoils with the poor, he soon became popular with the people of northern Mexico—something that would serve him well later in life.

A CALL TO ARMS

In 1909, Villa joined Francisco Madero's uprising against Porfirio Díaz, who had proclaimed himself the temporary dictator of Mexico. Quickly recognized as a brave soldier, Villa helped lead Madero and his supporters to victory over Díaz in 1911. Once his enemy had been toppled, Villa continued to fight to protect Madero's government, which had come under attack.

A suspicious man by nature, Villa sometimes aroused the suspicion of others—including his commanding officer, General Victoriano Huerta. In 1912, during the rebellion of Pascual Orozco, the general condemned the thirty-four-year old revolutionary to death. When Madero discovered that his loyal soldier was to be killed, he ordered a stay of execution. With the execution stopped, Villa was sentenced to prison in Mexico City.

But not for long. Four months later, Villa escaped to El Paso, Texas, where he began to reorganize his followers. In February of 1913, Huerta had Madero killed, and took over as dictator. Villa saw this as a call to arms. Within a month, he and eight followers crossed the muddy waters of the Rio Grande at midnight—on horses they had stolen in El Paso—in order to recruit an army from Villa's native territory.

AN UNEASY ALLIANCE

Villa's army—called the *División del Norte,* or the Division of the North—was mostly made up of *peons* (poor, landless workers) who came from cattle ranches and small towns in northern Mexico. Criminals, soldiers of fortune, miners, gamblers and even some women—who were called *soladera*—joined the ranks. A rebel army, Villa's band survived as young Doroteo Arango had—by stealing, rustling, and extorting.

Revolutionary leader Pancho Villa and his troops in Mexico City, 1914.

Victoriano Huerta was a harsh dictator and he was responsible for the death of Madero, who had inspired Villa to fight for a Mexico free from oppression. Villa was determined to overthrow the man who had once condemned him to die. Joining forces with Venustiano Carranza, another rebel military leader, he scored a number of victories over Huerta and gained control of northern Mexico. By the end of 1913, Villa had become the most powerful general in northern Mexico. As governor of the state of Chihuahua, he attempted to address some of the needs of the poor: his troops cleaned the streets in Chihuahua City, he built schools, gave land to peons and printed money—even though he had nothing to back it up. In the United States, President Woodrow Wilson was so impressed with Villa's potential as a candidate for the Mexican presidency that he sent his personal representative, George C. Carothers, to visit the former bandit chieftain.

In June of 1914, Villa and Carranza succeeded in deposing (removing from power) Huerta, who had become Mexico's president—even though the United States did not recognize him as such. With Huerta removed from power, Villa and Carranza entered Mexico City as allies. By December 1914, however, Villa—by then Carranza's bitter enemy—was forced to flee the city with Emiliano Zapata, a revolutionary leader who opposed Carranza. The two exiles waged a series of guerrilla attacks against the Carranza government.

A survivor's story

Jessie L. Thompson was four years old at the time of the Columbus massacre. Her grandfather, William Taylor Ritchie, owned the Commercial Hotel, one of the targets of the ambush. By the end of the raid, William Ritchie and three of his guests had been shot dead. Here's what his granddaughter recalls:

On March 9, 1916, at about 4:00 A.M. the Ritchie family was awakened by shouting and shooting in the street. Peering cautiously out of the window, as stray bullets ricocheted off the stovepipes and walls of the rooms, they could dimly see horses and hear the pounding of hooves. . . . Bandits on foot were running and shooting in every direction and smashing storefronts with the butts of their rifles. Entering the stores, they bayoneted bags of flour and unrolled bolts of cloth in the streets. They swept what had been orderly rows of merchandise on the shelves into ruined piles of trash.

—*excerpted from* American Heritage *magazine,*
December 1996

But Villa had met his match. After losing a number of battles, Villa and Zapata were forced to retreat to the mountains of the north. Then came the death-blow to Villa's military power: in April 1915, Alvaro Obregón—a general in Carranza's army—defeated Villa's troops at the Battle of Celaya. A savvy strategist, Obregón applied what he had learned from reports of the war in Europe—World War I, which changed the face of modern warfare. Instead of old-fashioned cavalry-style warfare such as Villa used—attacking his enemy on horseback—Obregón fought a modern battle—choosing a battleground and defending his ground. He directed his troops to wait for Villa—that is, after they had dug trenches, positioned barbed-wire entanglements, and posted machine guns. Three times Villa attacked, and three times his cavalry was cut down.

Pancho Villa was a much-married man. By some accounts, he had as many as twenty-nine wives—many of whom he had "married" by his own proclamation. In 1946, the Mexican legislature recognized Soledad Seanez la Viuda de Villa (later known as Soledad Seanez Holguin) as Villa's lawful wife after proving that they'd had a civil and a church wedding on May 1, 1919. Soledad outlived her husband by some seventy-three years. Villa's widow died on July 12, 1996—at the ripe old age of one hundred.

BAD BLOOD

Once again a bandit leader, the former General of the North withdrew to Chihuahua, where many people still viewed him as a Mexican Robin Hood. No longer a contender as a national leader, Villa watched as his countrymen shifted their loyalty to Carranza—whose government was officially recognized by the United States. This, along with the U.S. embargo on his munitions (supplies), infuriated Villa.

Villa—who had once made it a point to protect American lives and property—turned his anger against the people whose government he felt had betrayed him. In January of 1916, a gang of *Villistas* (followers of Villa) stopped a train from Chihuahua City. On board was a group of American mining engineers who planned to reopen a mine at Cusihuiriachic, in the state of Chihuahua. Most were executed. Although Villa protested that he was not to blame, many assumed that the massacre was intended to prove that Carranza didn't control the North.

Two months later, another slaughter ensued. On March 9, 1916, the small New Mexico border town and military camp of Columbus was visited by a band of guerrillas who rode through the streets, shooting out windows as they shouted "*Viva Villa! Viva México! Muerte a los americanos!*" ("Long live Villa! Long live Mexico! Death to the Americans!") Ambushed in their sleep, the Americans fought back with butcher knives, baseball bats and boiling water. By the end of the raid, the city had become a smoking ruin, and seventeen Americans—including nine civilians—were dead.

Black Jack Pershing's Wild Goose Chase

Within days, U.S. president Woodrow Wilson had sent Brigadier-General John "Black Jack" Pershing to Mexico with strict orders: capture Villa—*dead or alive*. Pershing's Punitive Expedition—the last true cavalry action to be mounted by the U.S. army—led some ten thousand American soldiers into the mountains and deserts of Villa's native Chihuahua. Pershing's troops pushed 400 miles into Mexico, as far south as the city of Parral, where they were forced, after a battle, to retreat to bases in northern Mexico.

Eleven months after American troops crossed the Mexican border, the expedition was abandoned. Pershing's epic chase had cost U.S. taxpayers a whopping $130 million—and Villa was still at large. In fact, no U.S. soldier had even seen the fugitive *bandido!* Worse yet, the failed expedition had strained relations between the United States and Mexico, whose people resented the very presence of the U.S. military on Mexican soil. In an ironic twist of fate, Pershing's expedition had managed not to capture Villa—but to help *him* capture the imagination of the Mexican people, who viewed the infamous Pancho Villa as a hero for resisting the Americans.

Meanwhile, Back at the Ranch . . .

As long as Carranza was in office, Villa continued his attacks against the Mexican government. In 1920, however, he retired from the guerrilla life (fighting as an outlaw soldier). After Carranza died in the rebellion of Agua Prieta, his government was overthrown. In his place, the Mexican legislature had appointed Adolfo de la Huerta, a Sonoma governor. During his brief tenure, Huerta granted a pardon to all Mexicans—including Villa—who were in exile due to their political actions. What's more, Villa was given full pay as a retired military general and a 25,000-acre *hacienda* (ranch) in Chihuahua, along with fifty state-funded bodyguards. But there was one catch: Villa had to agree to lay down his arms and to refrain from participating in Mexican politics.

Villa made good on his promise. For three years, the onetime guerrilla fighter led a peaceful rancher's life. But on July 19, 1923, he was involved in a final ambush. As he returned from the christening of the child of one of his men, Villa was shot to death in a hail of fire. More than three dozen bullets riddled his car, killing four of the five bodyguards with him. His assassins had been signaled—in an ironic echo of the Villistas' battle cry—by a pumpkin seed vendor who cried out *"Viva Villa!"*

Sources for Further Reading

The American West, A Cultural Encyclopedia, Volume 10. Danbury, CT: Grolier Educational Corp., 1995, pp. 1651–1652.

Carroll, Bob. *The Importance of Pancho Villa.* San Diego, CA: Lucent Books, 1996.

The Grolier Library of International Biographies. Vol. 1. Danbury, CT: Grolier Educational Corp., 1996, pp. 369–370.

"Pancho Villa Rides Again—in Tucson." *Newsweek* (August 2, 1982), p. 42.

Thompson, Jessie L. "A Visit from Pancho." *American Heritage* (December 1996), p. 28+.

Bootleggers

On January 16, 1920, the Eighteenth Amendment to the U.S. Constitution went into effect, outlawing the manufacture, transport, and sale of alcoholic beverages. Almost overnight, America went "dry." But vast numbers of Americans from all walks of life never lost their thirst for beer and spirits. No sooner had Prohibition gone into effect, when bootlegging gangs set up operations throughout the country to meet the public's demand for illegal alcohol.

Bootlegging—which involved the illegal production of beer and alcohol, smuggling spirits from outside of the country, and distributing illegal spirits—was an extremely profitable business. Rival gangs fought bitterly to retain control of—or to expand—their vast empires. On December 5, 1933, when the Eighteenth Amendment was officially withdrawn, Prohibition came to an abrupt end—and with it ended a criminal era.

In this section you'll read about some of the major bootlegging gangs and gangsters—such as "the terrible Gennas" and Hymie Weiss in Chicago, Owney Madden and Dutch Schultz in New York, and many others. Some became casualties of the gang wars, others earned prison terms—and a number of former bootleggers went on to illustrious careers in the reorganized gangs of post-Prohibition America.

Two Gun Alterie
(Louis Alterie)

Born: 1886
Died: July 18, 1935

The owner of a ranch in Colorado, Alterie was rare among bootleggers in his wild-west approach to gangster life in Chicago. Hot-tempered and often brutal, he was murdered by an unidentified killer years after retiring from his criminal rackets.

A Chicago racketeer

All that is known about Louis Alterie's background is that he was born Leland Varain in 1886. Other details about his life may—or may not—be true. He was probably born in either Denver, Colorado, or Los Angeles, California. According to some accounts, he boxed in the early 1900s, using the name of Kid Haynes. Other reports have him working on the right side of the law in Colorado, where he earned the position of lieutenant in the Denver police department.

By 1922, Alterie had settled in Chicago, Illinois, where he was arrested with the leader of the Lake Valley Gang, Terry Druggan, for robbery. They were charged with stealing $50,000 worth of jewelry from two Chicagoans. Although the victims had gotten a good look at Alterie and Druggan, neither was willing to identify the thieves.

Alterie eventually joined the mostly Irish gang of Charles Dion O'Banion (see box, page 467), which controlled the North Side of Chicago during the early years of Prohibition (when the

Eighteenth Amendment outlawed the manufacture and sale of alcohol). Part of his duties involved fixing union elections by using violence to sway the outcome. Alterie roughed up union leaders in order to convince them to elect him and his associates to the presidency of several unions. Some of the terms were for life. In one incident, Alterie and other gangsters beat the leaders of the Theatrical and Building Janitors' Union. Following a brief election, Alterie was voted into a life term as the union's president. Alterie's union activities reportedly earned him $50,000 each month—not including the money he passed on to gang leader O'Banion.

Alterie quickly became a wealthy man. He bought real estate with his earnings, including nightclubs, restaurants, apartment buildings, and even theaters. And he purchased a ranch near Gypsum, Colorado—a three-thousand-acre piece of property that would serve him well during the Chicago gangland wars.

AN O'BANION GANGSTER

For a long time O'Banion's gang enjoyed the protection of politicians and police, who received large bribes (money gained by dishonest means) for their assistance. Judges, police officials, and politicians all lined their pockets with O'Banion's money. Even Chicago mayor William "Big Bill" Thompson was on the gangster's payroll. O'Banion expressed his thanks with more than money. He used his position to influence voters. In some cases, he guaranteed that entire wards (sections of a city) would vote for his man.

As one of O'Banion's top mobsters, Alterie took part in gang wars to control bootlegging activities during Prohibition. The O'Banion gang battled with rival gangsters from **Al Capone**'s (see entry) gang, the Druggan-Lake Valley Gang, the O'Donnell Brothers, and the **Genna brothers** (see entry). As an O'Banion gunman, Alterie reportedly killed more than twenty gangsters in numerous shootouts.

A HANDSHAKE MURDER

In 1924, O'Banion was slain in what became known as the "handshake murder." O'Banion owned a flower shop on North State Street, which served as a front (cover) for his criminal activities. When three men arrived at the shop, supposedly to pick up wreaths of flowers for a funeral, one shook hands with him, while the others shot him. The three men—who worked for Capone—left the North Sider dead in his flower shop.

Alterie was enraged, and he made no effort to hide it. When police captain John Stege had Alterie brought in for questioning, he reportedly boasted, "If those cowardly rats have any guts they'll meet me at noon at State and Madison and we'll shoot it out." In front of police officials and reporters, Alterie proposed an Old-West-style shootout at high noon at Chicago's busiest intersection. Captain Stege was not amused.

Stege was not the only one who disapproved of Alterie's grand threats. The surviving leaders of the O'Banion gang—such as **Hymie Weiss** (see entry) and **Bugs Moran** (see entry)—disapproved of the attention Alterie's threats drew to the gang. But Alterie did not let up. At O'Banion's funeral, he staged a tearful performance for reporters beside the coffin of his former boss. "I have no idea who killed Deanie [O'Banion]," he said. "But I would die smiling if only I had the chance to meet the guys who did, any time and any place they mention and I would get at least two or three of them before they got me. If I knew who killed Deanie, I'd shoot it out with the gang of killers before the sun rose in the morning and some of us, maybe all of us, would be lying on slabs in the undertaker's place."

Chicago mayor William Dever did not appreciate Alterie's flair for dramatic remarks, which had been printed in the daily newspapers. He reportedly demanded, "Are we still abiding by [following] the code of the Dark Ages?" Following Dever's instructions, Chicago police began to hound Alterie and other O'Banion gangsters. They stormed saloons and gambling houses that were run by Weiss and Moran, ending the gang's former protection from such police raids.

Lousy neighbors

Alterie has been given credit for inventing a particular type of ambush assassination. First, he rented a second-floor room that faced the street. Across the street was an address his target visited regularly—such as an apartment or business. Next, he installed heavy artillery in front of the apartment windows. From his second-story perch, Alterie simply picked off his victim when he came into sight.

Prohibition--the Eighteenth Amendment and the Volstead Act

By 1909, there were more saloons in the United States than there were schools, libraries, hospitals, theaters, parks, or churches. There was one saloon for every three hundred Americans, and the saloons were mainly concentrated in cities. (These establishments were not distributed evenly across the United States. There were more bars in Chicago than there were in the entire South, for instance.)

Medical evidence suggested that alcohol was seriously harmful. Adding to the social problem was a political one: most taverns were controlled by brewers or the liquor trust. Many in the era came to consider those two as an interest group, like the railroads, insurance companies, or other manufacturers who were more concerned with profit than with the public welfare.

In the years before World War I (1914–1918), the temperance movement (a movement that advocated refraining from consuming alcoholic beverages) had succeeded in convincing the legislatures (groups of individuals empowered to make laws) of twenty-six states to enact laws banning the manufacture and sale of alcoholic beverages. The long campaign was at first directed against saloons, and later against the production of alcoholic beverages. The movement's success was dramatically affected by the nation's preparations for war.

The need to conserve grain and the importance of maintaining some appearance of discipline and devotion to a patriotic cause added to the success of the movement. Toward the end of 1917, both houses of Congress had approved a resolution to amend (alter) the U.S. Constitution to outlaw the manufacture, transportation, or sale of alcoholic beverages. By January 1919, forty-six of the forty-eight states had ratified (formally approved) this proposal. Only Rhode Island and Connecticut had not. The amendment became effective on January 16, 1920. Meanwhile, the Volstead Act was passed to provide for the enforcement of the amendment.

The Eighteenth Amendment was officially withdrawn on December 5, 1933, when the Twenty-first Amendment was ratified, allowing the legal manufacture and sale of alcohol.

HOME ON THE RANGE

Alterie had become a hindrance to the O'Banion gang. His boasting had brought the gang's activities under public scrutiny (examination). What's more, his threats against O'Banion's killers angered the gang's leaders, who wanted to wait until the time was right to strike back at Capone's men. Weiss and Moran reportedly ordered Alterie to retire to his ranch in Colorado.

Alterie left Chicago's gangland wars in the mid-1920s, when he moved with his wife to his Colorado ranch. While he reportedly continued to control the unions he had ruled in Chicago, his former associates were killed in the gangland wars. Weiss was murdered in 1926. Seven others were slaughtered in the notorious St. Valentine's Day Massacre in 1929. Moran's power in the underworld faded. His former rival, Capone, was still living—although he was jailed for failing to pay taxes on his income.

LOOSE LIPS SINK SHIPS

In 1935, Alterie was called as a government witness in the trial of Ralph "Bottles" Capone—who, like his brother, Al, had been charged with tax evasion. At first, Alterie said nothing to help the government convict Capone. But when he was threatened with charges of perjury (lying in court, under oath), he testified against Ralph.

It was not long before Alterie was gunned down in a gangland ambush. On July 18, 1935, the former gangster was caught in a blast of machine-gun fire. His wife, who had been behind him, was unharmed. As he lay on the sidewalk mortally wounded, Alterie reportedly said to his wife, "I can't help it, Bambino [Baby], but I'm going." Alterie's murder was never solved.

What goes around comes around

Alterie eventually suffered the consequences of introducing the ambush murder to gangland Chicago. He was gunned down in front of his union offices—from the second-story window of an apartment across the street. Inside, investigators found machine guns poised at the windows facing the street. Alterie had been killed by a gunman who used the same method Alterie himself had used to eliminate enemies.

Sources for Further Reading

Nash, Jay Robert. *Bloodletters and Badmen*. New York: M. Evans: 1973, pp. 104–106.

Sifakis, Carl. *The Encyclopedia of American Crime*. New York: Facts on File, 1982, pp. 7–8.

Sifakis, Carl. *The Mafia Encyclopedia*. New York: Facts on File, 1982, pp. 17–18.

The Genna Brothers

Active: 1912-1925

The six Genna brothers were among the first gangsters in the city of Chicago to build an empire that took advantage of the prohibition of alcohol. Once key players in the bootlegging wars, the brothers faded from importance. Three met violent deaths, while the others lived out unremarkable lives.

Rough Kids

The Genna brothers—Angelo, Antonio, Jim, Mike, Pete, and Sam—were born in Marsala, Sicily. After immigrating to the United States in 1910, the Genna family settled in Chicago, Illinois. When they were still young boys, their mother died, leaving their father, a railroad worker, to care for them. The Genna boys grew up in a violent and crime-ridden environment. They ran around the neighborhood with little supervision. The area, known as Little Italy, was populated by Sicilian immigrants and plagued by criminals who readily committed bombings and murders.

When their father died, the teenaged Genna brothers looked to **Diamond Joe Esposito** (see entry) for guidance. A Sicilian immigrant himself, Esposito tutored the Gennas in the use of violence as a means for self-advancement. By 1912, three of the Genna brothers were involved in the **Black Hand Society** (see entry)—using violence and the threat of violence to force the residents of Little Italy to pay extortion fees. The other three brothers—Antonio, Jim, and Peter—carved out their own business in the Chicago underworld. Jim opened a house of prostitution, using his two brothers as pimps.

THE BOOTLEG EMPIRE

When Prohibition (when the Eighteenth Amendment outlawed the manufacture and sale of alcohol) was enacted in January 1920, scores of gangsters seized the opportunity to make money producing illegal alcohol. The Gennas realized that this moonshine (illegally distilled liquor) business would be much more profitable than their extortion and prostitution rackets. They put many fellow immigrants to work producing illegal alcohol. Soon, Little Italy became a vast moonshine operation under the direction of the Genna brothers.

At first, the Gennas entered into an agreement with the powerful criminal duo of Johnny Torrio and **Al Capone** (see entry), who controlled the South and West sides of Chicago. They sold their cheap alcohol to the Torrio-Capone gang, who then distributed the booze to saloons throughout the area. But the Gennas soon tired of settling for a small percentage of the profits. In less than one year, they claimed a section of the Near West Side of Chicago as their own. Opening their own speakeasies (drinking clubs), they gained exclusive control of the territory. Soon the Genna's booze empire posted staggering returns—which amounted to $350,000 each month.

THE TERRIBLE GENNAS

Torrio and Capone feared the Genna brothers, who became known as "the Terrible Gennas." The Genna brothers employed a gang of ruthless killers, including Sam "Smoots" Amatuna, Guiseppe "the Cavalier" Nerone, and Orazio "the Scourge" Tropea. Also on the Genna hit squad was an infamous pair of assassins: Albert Anselmi and John Scalise. Vicious gunmen, Anselmi and Scalise were known for dipping the tips of their bullets in garlic. They believed—mistakenly—that garlic-tipped bullets would cause a deadly infection in victims who did not die imme-

Cultured killers

The Genna brothers were not uncultured killers. They attended opera performances in front-row seats and ate at fine restaurants. Anthony Genna—who was known as "Tony the Gentleman" and "Tony the Aristocrat"—lived in an exclusive hotel in downtown Chicago, studied architecture, and even constructed model tenements for poor immigrants from his native Italy. The brothers were also deeply religious. Each reportedly carried a crucifix in his pocket—right next to his gun.

Demon alcohol

The Gennas produced cheap, vile-tasting, and sometimes deadly illegal booze. Their awful alcohol reportedly caused several deaths each year and was responsible for blinding dozens of other drinkers.

Final farewells

When Angelo Genna was killed by O'Banion gunmen, his brothers staged an elaborate funeral. Angelo was laid to rest in a $10,000 bronze casket. The men who carried the coffin wore tuxedos. The grave site was festooned with more than $25,000 worth of flowers. Most of the residents of Little Italy attended the solemn affair. Tony Genna's funeral was far less spectacular. Buried just two months after his brother, Angelo, "Tony the Gentlemen" was laid in an inexpensive wood coffin. No flowers adorned the grave site. And no one other than reporters and policemen attended the burial—not even his longtime girlfriend. Tony's mourners were scared off by the prospect of being gunned down by Capone's bloodthirsty hitmen. Ironically, Tony was buried a few feet from O'Banion—the man whose gang had been responsible for Angelo's death.

diately from their wounds. Anselmi and Scalise were also given credit for introducing the "handshake murder." While one gangster pretended to greet their victim with a friendly handshake, the other produced a gun. Unable to draw his own weapon, the helpless victim was then shot at close range.

When Torrio and Capone attempted to unite Chicago gangs under the same leadership, they found the Genna brothers very difficult to manage. Vicious and quick to kill, they ignored the territorial boundaries of rival gangsters. Eventually Chicago splintered into three rival factions: the Torrio-Capone Gang on the South and West sides, the Genna brothers on the Near West side, and the O'Banion mob on the city's North Side.

A BLOODY END FOR ANGELO

In 1924, Anselmi, Scalise, and another gangster named Frankie Uale (known as Yale) reportedly assassinated Charles Dion O'Banion (see box, page 467), the leader of the North Side gang. As O'Banion shook the hand of one of the gangsters, he was gunned down by the others. O'Banion's murder was committed as a favor to Capone.

Soon the Genna brothers began to expand their activities in Chicago's underworld. But the killing of O'Banion had sparked a wave of violence against the West Siders. One after another, the Genna brothers fell in gangland ambush killings. First to die was Angelo—known as "Bloody Angelo" for his murderous temperament. On May 25, 1925, he left his suite at the Belmont Hotel, on the North Side of Chicago. (While he made arrangements to purchase a new home, Angelo was living at the hotel, in the midst of O'Banion territory, with his wife, Lucille Spingola. The couple had been married only weeks earlier.)

As Angelo drove away from the hotel, he was followed by another car. Angelo drove to Ogden and Hudson streets unaware that he was being followed. Suddenly he realized a long black sedan was pursuing him. He sped up and turned a corner so fast that he lost control. Angelo's $6,000 automobile crashed into a post, trapping the gangster behind the steering wheel. Unable to reach his gun, Angelo remained in the car as the sedan approached. Inside was a squad of O'Banion gunmen: Vincent "the Schemer" Drucci, **Bugs Moran** (see entry), **Hymie Weiss** (see entry), and driver Frank Gusenberg. Leaning out the open windows, the gangsters pummeled Angelo's car with gunfire. His body blasted apart by the hail of bullets, Angelo died in his car.

On the take

The Genna organization did not rely on violence alone. They paid Chicago policemen to ensure that the law would not interfere in their illegal activities. The Gennas reportedly paid $200,000 *each month* to the many policemen who were on their payroll. In 1925, when the Genna's office manager made a formal confession, the former employee stated that four hundred uniformed officers and five police captains accepted Genna payments.

A SECOND GENNA FUNERAL

Mike Genna swore revenge for his brother's death. He enlisted the family's top killers, Anselmi and Scalise, to help carry out the hit. But—without Mike's knowledge—Anselmi and Scalise had joined forces with Capone. On June 13, 1925— a little less than a month after Angelo's death—Mike Genna, Anselmi, and Scalise went on a mission to find and destroy Angelo's killers. Or so Mike thought. The outing was actually a setup to allow the traitorous duo to ambush Mike.

But the hitmen never had a chance to strike. A squad car containing four Chicago police officers spotted the gangsters. Convinced that the car contained weapons, they pursued the vehicle. The gangsters' car spun out of control and crashed. Mike, Anselmi, and Scalise fled with their shotguns in hand.

A shootout followed—one policeman was killed and two others were wounded. Anselmi and Scalise fled, leaving Mike alone to battle with officer William Sweeney. After shooting Mike in the leg, Sweeney took the gangster into custody. The wound turned out to be fatal: Mike, who had been struck in an artery, bled to death before doctors could operate.

The bootleg generation

Support for the Eighteenth Amendment remained strong in the years immediately following its ratification. As late as 1928, those calling for its repeal (withdrawal) were a minority. The Volstead Act (1919) seemed to have the intended effect. But there was no doubt that large numbers of people still wanted to drink.

With overall production severely restricted, prices rose dramatically. The situation ushered in an era of lawlessness greater than any in recent memory. Enforcement became increasingly difficult and, much to the disgust of the supporters of Prohibition, unenthusiastic.

Many were prepared to risk arrest to take advantage of the opportunities that bootlegging (the illegal manufacture and sale of alcohol) presented. Closing the legal channels of supply had given thousands the incentive to become bootleggers and operators of clubs that dispensed liquor that became known as "speakeasies." Liquor dealers in Canada, the Caribbean, and Europe provided a ready and uninterrupted source of alcoholic beverages. Local stills (distilleries) often operated day and night to produce cheap and illegal booze.

Toward the end of the Prohibition era, much of the organized effort to transport, sell, and distribute alcohol had fallen under the control of criminal gangs. Many of the gangs reflected a particular ethnic origin and possessed enough wealth and political influence to link cities and entire regions within the networks they had created. As the gangsters gained in power and prominence, and as the perception of public corruption became more pronounced, Americans became more unhappy with the government's efforts to enforce the law. Meanwhile, rival gangs waged war with one another. It has been estimated that more than one thousand people died in the Chicago bootleg wars alone.

THE DEATH OF TONY GENNA

Afraid for his life, Tony Genna refused to leave his suite at the Congress Hotel. There, Guiseppe Nerone contacted him. He informed Tony that Capone was responsible for his brother's death—and he suggested that they meet to decide on a plan to get rid of the South Side mobster. Tony agreed. He was aware that Anselmi and Scalise had joined forces with Capone. But he was not aware that Nerone, too, had deserted him.

On July 8, 1925, Tony met Nerone at Curtis and Grand Avenue. As the two men shook hands, two other men appeared from a doorway and shot at Tony. Struck several times in the back, he was taken to County Hospital, where he died days later. The two shooters were said to be Anselmi and Scalise.

OLIVE OIL AND CHEESE: THE END OF THE GENNA DYNASTY

One after another, Genna supporters were ambushed by Capone hit squads. Henry Spingola—Angelo's politician father-in-law, who had taken over the Genna family's business affairs—was gunned down by Tropea, who had deserted the Genna gang for Capone's camp. Vito Bascone was murdered as he begged, on his knees, for his life. Ecola Baldelli was cut to pieces by his assassins, who threw his remains in a garbage dump. Tony Finalli and Felipe Gnolfo also died at the hands of Capone's killers.

The remaining Genna brothers fled Chicago. After years in hiding, Jim, Peter, and Sam Genna returned to their former home in Illinois—but not to their former rackets. No longer a part of the Chicago underworld, they operated an importing firm that dealt in olive oil and cheese. The three surviving Genna brothers lived the remainder of their lives in obscurity.

The evil eye

The superstitious residents of Chicago's Little Italy believed that Orazio Tropea, a Genna gunman, possessed the "evil eye." They were convinced that Tropea—who was known as "the Scourge"—could bring someone bad luck simply by *looking* at him.

Sources for Further Reading

Nash, Jay Robert. *The Encyclopedia of World Crime.* Wilmette, IL: Crime Books, 1990, pp. 1291–1294.

Sifakis, Carl. *The Encyclopedia of American Crime.* New York: Facts on File, 1982, pp. 278–279.

Machine Gun Kelly
(George Barnes)

Born: 1897
Died: 1954

A likable—although none-too bright—small-time crook, Kelly became a legend in his own time. With the prodding of his image-conscious wife, Kathryn, the non-violent bootlegger was molded into a gun-toting gangster known as "Machine Gun" Kelly. Guilty of only one major crime, a kidnapping, he was eventually captured and imprisoned for life.

A BOOTLEGGER NAMED BARNES

Born and raised in an impoverished Tennessee community, George Barnes received little schooling. A petty (small-time) crook as a teenager, he sometimes produced illegal alcohol. When Prohibition (when the Eighteenth Amendment outlawed the manufacture and sale of alcohol) went into effect, he began a full-time bootlegging business (the illegal manufacture and sale of alcohol). Operating in Memphis, Tennessee, he provided wealthy individuals and clubs with liquor that had been smuggled from Canada—where U.S. Prohibition laws did not apply. Barnes changed his name to Kelly during his bootlegging days.

Criminal gangs fought viciously to retain control of their territories and to expand their profitable bootlegging operations. When Memphis gangsters learned that Kelly was moving in on their territories by selling to speakeasies (drinking clubs), they threatened his life. A non-violent man, he promptly abandoned his bootlegging activities and moved out of state. Kelly eventually landed in New Mexico, where he attempted to

Nobody said he was smart

When Kelly's in-laws were arrested for kidnapping, the gangster sent a threatening letter to Charles Urschel, the man he had kidnapped. He urged Urschel to drop the case, writing:

Ignorant Charles—

If the Shannons are convicted look out, and God help you for He is the only one that will be able to do you any good. In the event of my arrest I've already formed an outfit to take care of and destroy you and yours the same as if I was there. I am spending your money to have you and your family killed—nice, eh? You are bucking people who have cash—planes, bombs, and unlimited connections both here and abroad. . . . Now, sap [sucker]—it is up to you, if the Shannons are convicted you can get you another rich wife in Hell because that will be the only place you can use one. Adios [goodbye], smart one, Your worst enemy, Geo. R. Kelly I will put my prints below so you can't say some crank wrote this.

Kelly sent the damaging letter—with his fingerprints—to Urschel. While his in-laws eventually received light sentences for their role in the kidnapping, Kelly was sentenced to life in prison.

---

resume his bootlegging business. But in 1927, as he made a liquor delivery, he was arrested. Convicted of violating the Volstead Act (drawn up in 1919 to enforce the prohibition of alcohol), he was sentenced to three months' imprisonment. After he was released from the New Mexico State Prison, Kelly moved to Fort Worth, Texas, where he picked up where he had left off— delivering bootleg liquor.

A SHARE-CROPPER'S DAUGHTER

While Kelly worked as a rum runner (transportation of illegal alcohol) between Fort Worth and Oklahoma City, Oklahoma, he met a beautiful young woman named Kathryn Thorne. Born in Saltilo, Mississippi, in 1904, Thorne was the daughter of a poor farm laborer. She later changed her birth name, Cleo, to Kathryn—because she thought the name was more sophisticated. At the age of fifteen she married a local boy, with whom she had a daughter. She soon divorced her husband and moved with her child to Coleman, Texas, where she joined her mother (who had left her father).

Coleman was the home of her mother's family, many of whom were crooks who ran illegal stills and brothels. Thorne's mother eventually married a man named R. G. "Boss" Shannon, who ran a ranch near Paradise, Texas. Shannon added to his income by turning his ranch into a criminal hideout where he housed and fed wanted criminals—in exchange for a fee.

When her daughter was two years old, Thorne left the girl with her mother and moved to Fort Worth, Texas. Working at a hotel as a manicurist, she met many men who were passing through town on business. She sometimes worked as a prostitute, and was arrested two times for soliciting. At the age of twenty, she met and married a bootlegger named Charlie Thorne. Three years later, he was found shot to death, with a note that said, "I can't live with her, or without her, hence I am departing this life." Many people objected that the language in the suicide note did not sound like something Charlie would have written. In fact, it sounded much like his wife, Kathryn, who liked to used formal expressions (such as "hence") to make herself look more sophisticated. Although Thorne had reportedly told a gas station attendant that she was going to kill her husband days before he was found, the death was ruled a suicide. She inherited what remained of the bootlegger's estate.

A THORN IN HIS SIDE

Kelly met Thorne in 1927. At the time, she is said to have been helping bank robbers by making trips to out-of-town banks and reporting back with information about the bank's layout and procedures. Thorne immediately began to mold Kelly into something that he was not: a hardened, big-time crook. She gave him a submachine gun and bragged to others that he was a daring and fearless bank robber. She reportedly made him practice shooting for hours at her family's Texas ranch. Eventually Kelly became a good shot—and even boasted that he could shoot walnuts off a fence at twenty-five yards and *never even damage the fence*. In reality, the easy-going gangster disliked weapons and avoided violence. It's quite possible that "Machine Gun" Kelly never killed anyone.

Still involved in the bootlegging business, Kelly was arrested in 1930, when he drove onto an Oklahoma Indian reservation with a truckload of liquor. He was given a brief sentence at Leavenworth prison, where he was well-liked by inmates as well as guards. A model prisoner, he landed a job in the prison's records office. Thorne pressed him to befriend some of the more important prisoners, who would be able to help him when he was released from jail. Taking her advice, he became acquainted with bank robbers Thomas Holden and Francis Keating. Using his position in the records office, he secured fake passes. The two gangsters used the passes and borrowed clothes to walk out of prison before their terms were up.

When Kelly was released the following year, he married Thorne. Working with a few other gangsters, the couple staged a number of bank robberies from 1931 to 1933. Using Thorne to case the businesses (study the layout of a business to plan a crime), the Kelly gang raided banks in Mississippi, Washington, and Texas. Although most of the holdups went off without violence, a job in Wilmer, Texas, left one guard dead. Thorne bragged that Kelly was the shooter—but it was probably one of the other gang members.

A BUMBLING KIDNAPPER

Kelly's bank robberies did not bring in enough cash to satisfy Thorne, who enjoyed expensive things. They decided to follow the lead of other criminals, who had collected large sums of money by kidnapping wealthy individuals. On July 22, 1933, Kelly and a middle-aged burglar named Albert Bates entered the mansion of Oklahoma City oil millionaire Charles F. Urschel. To their surprise, they found two couples playing cards. Since the kidnappers had neglected to find out what Urschel looked like, they did not know which of the two men was their intended victim. And none of the four card players volunteered to identify him.

Kelly and Bates took both men outside, where Thorne was waiting in a getaway car. As they drove out of town, Kelly col-

433

lected each man's wallet. Once he identified Urschel, he dropped the second man, Walter R. Jarrett, on an empty country road. Urschel was taken, blindfolded, to Thorne's family ranch in Texas, where he was held in a one-room shack.

In spite of a few miscalculations, the kidnappers eventually collected the $200,000 ransom they demanded. A friend of the millionaire, E. E. Kirkpatrick, gave Kelly a briefcase full of money on Linwood Avenue in Kansas City, Missouri—in exchange for a promise that Urschel would be returned home within twelve hours.

WAITING FOR THE POLICE

Thorne reportedly wanted to kill Urschel to make sure that he did not identify his kidnappers, while Kelly and Bates insist-

The Alcatraz rebellion and escape

During Kelly's imprisonment at Alcatraz federal prison, located on an island in San Francisco Bay, California, a number of other inmates staged a rebellion. On May 2, 1945, prisoners started a riot and, securing weapons, fought a gun battle with prison guards in an effort to shoot their way out. For the first time in the history of "the Rock," as Alcatraz was known, inmates were able to obtain firearms during their attempt to escape.

The escape plan began to take shape when three inmates, Bernie Coy, Joseph "Dutch" Cretzer, and Miran "Buddy" Thompson, joined forces in Alcatraz. Coy had designed and built a bar spreader and had figured out a way to gain access to the prison armory (where weapons were kept). The three ringleaders and three other inmates staged an uprising in a cellblock and took nine guards as hostages. U.S. marines were ordered to the island prison to reinforce the officers.

On the second day of the riot, occasional fighting continued between the guards and convicts. The inmate leaders attempted to negotiate a deal with prison officials, but this was refused with a demand for total surrender. On the third day of the uprising, when it became apparent that the inmates would not succeed, Thompson ordered Cretzer to kill the hostages since they were the only ones who could identify Thompson as being involved in the escape attempt.

Against Coy's orders not to kill any hostages, Cretzer shot all nine. During the last stages of the battle, Coy and Cretzer were killed. Secure in the belief that his own involvement in the uprising would remain unknown, Thompson returned to his cell. Surprisingly, only one of the guards shot by Cretzer had actually been killed. Thompson was later convicted of murder and sentenced to death. On December 3, 1948, he became the first person put to death in the California gas chamber.

ed on letting him live. They drove him, blindfolded, to the edge of Oklahoma City, where they left him with $10 for taxi fare. Once the millionaire arrived home safely, Federal Bureau of Investigation (FBI) agents questioned him about the incident. He had an excellent memory, and provided agents with information that eventually led them to the Shannon ranch in Texas.

When FBI agents arrived at the ranch, they found Thorne's mother and her husband, "Boss" Shannon, as well as her son, Armand (Thorne's stepbrother). The three were charged in the kidnapping. Kelly and Thorne, who had driven to Chicago, remained at large. But after Bates was picked up in Denver, Colorado, the couple moved south, to Memphis, Tennessee, near where Kelly had grown up. There, residents recognized him and informed the police where he was hiding.

On September 26, 1933, three Memphis police detectives—Detective Sergeant W. J. Raney and Detectives A. O. Clark and Floyd Wiebenga—captured Kelly and Thorne in the small bungalow they were using as a hideout. After dropping the automatic gun he held, Kelly reportedly told officers, "I've been waiting all night for you."

FATE OF THE KIDNAPPERS

Tried and convicted of kidnapping, Kelly, Bates, and Thorne were sentenced to life in prison. Thorne's family, who had hidden the kidnappers, received lighter sentences. Kelly was jailed at Alcatraz Prison, California, until 1954, when he was transferred to Leavenworth Prison in Kansas. He died from a heart attack later that year. Thorne remained in the Cincinnati Workhouse for Women until she was paroled in 1958.

Sources for Further Reading

Bruns, Roger. *The Bandit Kings From Jesse James to Pretty Boy Floyd.* New York: Crown, 1995, p. 168.

Nash, Jay Robert. *The Encyclopedia of World Crime.* Wilmette, IL: Crime Books, 1990, pp. 1782–1787.

Sifakis, Carl. *The Encyclopedia of American Crime.* New York: Facts on File, 1982, p. 390.

Owney Madden

Born: 1892
Died: 1965

Transplanted as a child to a tough New York neighborhood, Madden soon earned the nickname, "the Killer," because of his reputation as a cold-blooded killer. While violence came back to haunt many of his hot-headed associates, Madden lived quietly—and very comfortably—until the age of seventy-three.

A YOUTHFUL GOPHER

Madden was born in Liverpool, England, in 1892. After his father died, the eleven-year-old moved to New York City to live with his aunt in a poor and violent neighborhood known as Hell's Kitchen. Shortly after his arrival he became a member of a violent street gang called the Gophers. As a young gangster, Madden earned a reputation as a violent and dangerous criminal. He committed muggings—using various weapons, including brass knuckles, a sling shot, and a lead pipe wrapped in newspaper—and fought with members of a rival gang, the Hudson Dusters.

Madden soon rose to the gang's top ranks. As the leader of the Gophers, he planned robberies, killings, beatings and other crimes for which he reportedly collected $200 per day. Barely out of his teens, Madden became involved in an "insurance business." For a fee, he provided bomb insurance to local shopkeepers. Dozens of merchants paid the sum, well aware that if they refused, the gangsters would strike back by bombing their businesses. By the time Madden was twenty-three years old, he was believed to have been responsible for five murders. During his time as a Gopher, he was arrested forty-four times—but he was never jailed. Witnesses to the violent gangster's criminal activities rarely stepped forward to accuse him.

LEFT FOR DEAD

In 1910, a clerk named William Henshaw attempted to date one of Madden's many girlfriends. Madden followed Henshaw onto a Manhattan trolley car, where he shot the man in front of passengers. Before jumping from the trolley, he rang the conductor's bell. Henshaw lived long enough to identify Madden as the shooter. Two weeks later, police arrested the gangster in a daring rooftop chase. Charged with murder, Madden was set free after witnesses refused to testify against him.

Madden announced that he planned to become the boss of the New York underworld. He strengthened his position by hiring a number of deadly gunmen, including Eddie Egan, Chick Hyland, Tanner Smith, and Bill Tammany. But as his power grew, so did the resentment of rival gangs.

On the evening of November 6, 1912, eleven members of the Hudson Dusters followed Madden to the Arbor Dance Hall on Fifty-Second Street. A shootout followed. By the end of the gunfight, Madden had been hit several times. The Dusters left him for dead.

In spite of his several wounds, Madden survived. In the hospital, he refused to identify his attackers. Following the gangster's code of silence, he reportedly told police that the matter was nobody's business but his own. By the time he was released from the hospital, six of Madden's assailants had been gunned down by members of the Gopher gang.

THE MURDER OF PATSY DOYLE

Madden's troubles were not over: a gangster named Patsy Doyle was moving in on his territory. By some accounts, he wanted to take over the leadership of the Gophers. By other accounts, he was angry because Madden had begun seeing his girlfriend, Freda Horner.

Whatever his reasons, Doyle set out to ruin Madden—and Madden knew it. On November 28, 1914, Madden arranged for Doyle to appear at a bar at Eighth Avenue and 41st Street in Manhattan. He shot Doyle three times. Sentenced to twenty years in prison for the murder, Madden was paroled after nine years.

BOOTLEGGING AND BOXING

Released from Sing Sing prison in 1923, Madden discovered that the Manhattan underworld had been reorganized around the bootlegging business (the illegal manufacture and sale of alcohol, which took place when the Eighteenth Amendment was ratified in 1920). In Prohibition-era New York, the remains of the Gopher gang had been absorbed into other rumrunning mobs (gangs that transported illegal alcohol). After a brief period working as a strikebreaker, Madden formed a new gang and staked his claim in the illegal liquor industry. Together with **Dutch Schultz** (see entry), an established bootlegger who headed the numbers racket (gambling) in Harlem, he fought for control of bootlegging activity in New York. Throughout the 1920s, Madden and Schultz battled with other powerful bootleggers, such as Vincent "Mad Dog" Coll, **Legs Diamond** (see entry), and Waxey Gordon.

As Prohibition came to an end, Madden sought out other opportunities. In the 1930s, he became involved in fixing boxing matches. Working with "Broadway" Bill Duffy and "Big

A social butterfly

When a reporter asked Madden how he spent his days, the gangster began to keep a journal to record his activities. The journal revealed a busy social calendar:

Thursday—Went to a dance in the afternoon. Went to a dance at night and then to a cabaret. Took some girls home. Went to a restaurant and stayed there until seven o'clock Friday morning.

Friday—Spent the day with Freda Horner. Looked at some fancy pigeons. Met some friends in a saloon early in the evening and stayed with them until five o'clock in the morning.

Saturday—Slept all day. Went to a dance in the Bronx [an area in New York City] ate in the afternoon, and out to dance on Park Avenue at night.

Sunday—Slept until three o'clock. Went to a dance in the afternoon and to another in the same place at night. After that I went to a cabaret and stayed there almost all night.

Frenchy" DeMange, he promoted Italian boxer Primo Carnera.
A large but untalented fighter, Carnera became heavyweight
champion by winning a series of fixed matches. Carnera held
the heavyweight title until June 14, 1934—when he was severely beaten by one of Madden's associates. The boxer earned nothing from his brief career: Madden reportedly claimed all of
Carnera's earnings, which amounted to $1 million.

The difficult task of enforcing Prohibition

The discovery off the New Jersey coast of a flexible pipeline used to connect the bootleggers' boats to the bootleggers' fleets of trucks said a lot about their boldness and inventiveness. It also revealed the extent to which local and national Prohibition agents had become powerless to do anything meaningful about it.

In 1921, Mabel Walker Willebrandt was appointed an assistant to the U.S. attorney general. Assigned the task of overseeing the Justice Department's efforts to enforce the newly passed Volstead Act (drawn up in 1919 to enforce the prohibition of alcohol), she discovered that few colleagues took this responsibility seriously. Worse still was the fact that her authority did not extend to local police officers who were largely responsible for enforcing the law.

In New York, where a state Prohibition law had been in effect since 1921, sixty-nine hundred arrests had been made during one three-year period—but only twenty convictions had been obtained. Willebrandt's attention soon focused upon the U.S. attorneys in federal districts around the country, many of whom she criticized for their lack of commitment. But corruption ran wild among the Prohibition agents. Willebrandt gave up in 1928.

In 1930, attorney general William N. Mitchell appeared before the Senate Judiciary Committee to criticize Congress for not providing President Herbert Hoover (1874–1964) with the funds he needed to improve the government's ability to enforce Prohibition. Admitting that efforts to enforce the law were losing their power, he called for more prisons and longer prison terms for offenders. Many marveled at the attorney general's persistence. He would have done better, they felt, if he had heeded the advice of his former assistant, Willebrandt, when she concluded that what federal enforcement required was not more men, money, and ammunition but greater respect for its own purpose and responsibility.

THE HIGH LIFE IN HOT SPRINGS

Madden found himself in jail again in 1932, when he was arrested for parole violation. Released after a short time in prison, he was followed by policemen who arrested him frequently on minor charges. Tired of his constant troubles with the law, Madden retired from the New York underworld. A millionaire several times over, he moved to Hot Springs, Arkansas, a favorite vacation spot among mobsters.

Working for mobster **Meyer Lansky** (see entry), Madden opened several casinos in Hot Springs. As one of the leaders of the area's thriving gambling activity, he enjoyed the protection of local police. After marrying the daughter of the postmaster, he became a citizen in 1943. When Madden died in 1965, his estate was estimated to be worth $3 million.

Sources for Further Reading

Nash, Jay Robert. *The Encyclopedia of World Crime.* Wilmette, IL: Crime Books, 1990, pp. 2072–2073.

Sifakis, Carl. *The Encyclopedia of American Crime.* New York: Facts on File, 1982, pp. 459–460.

Sifakis, Carl. *The Mafia Encyclopedia.* New York: Facts on File, 1982, pp. 204–206.

Bugs Moran
(George Moran)

Born: 1893
Died: 1957

Moran was the target of one of the most brutal episodes in gangland Chicago: the St. Valentine's Day Massacre. But, by a stroke of luck, he was not among those slain. Formerly the commander of the North Side's bootlegging empire, Moran died poor, and in prison—for a minor robbery.

A POLISH CROOK IN AN IRISH GANG

A native of rural Minnesota, George Moran moved to Chicago, Illinois, as a teenager. There he found himself in a mostly Irish area on the city's North Side, where Irish street gangs controlled the neighborhood. Pretending to be of Irish rather than Polish descent, Moran joined one of the area's all-Irish gangs.

During his teens, Moran—now known to some as "Bugs"—befriended Charles Dion O'Banion (see box, page 467). The young Irish crook taught Moran what he needed to know about burglary and safe cracking. By the time he reached his seventeenth birthday, Moran was an experienced criminal. Before he was twenty-one, Moran had reportedly committed at least twenty-six known robberies. He was arrested for the first time in 1910, although he was not convicted. During the next several years, he managed to stay out of prison in spite of frequent arrests. But on May 24, 1918, Moran was convicted of armed robbery and sentenced to serve time at Joliet State Prison in Illinois.

ENEMIES OF CAPONE

On February 1, 1923, Moran was released on parole (the release of a prisoner before his time has expired). Fresh out of state prison, he headed back to his former gang. Under O'Banion's direction, the gang had begun to thrive during Prohibition (when the Eighteenth Amendment outlawed the manufacture and sale of alcohol). By bribing policemen and politicians, the gang operated breweries and distilleries without fear of being shut down. The gang also controlled the illegal distribution of alcohol. Soon O'Banion's gang became the most powerful bootlegging gang on the city's North Side.

At the time, bootlegging activities on the South Side of Chicago were controlled by Johnny Torrio and **Al Capone** (see entry). O'Banion's gang often raided the South Siders' territory. Moran and others from O'Banion's gang hijacked the trucks carrying Torrio and Capone's beer and liquor shipments. They beat up bar owners and bartenders who bought their liquor from the rival mobsters to force them to purchase O'Banion's product.

On November 10, 1924, O'Banion was murdered by gunmen from the Torrio-Capone organization. While **Hymie Weiss** (see entry) took over the leadership of the North Side gang, Moran was next in the line of command. First on their agenda—revenge for O'Banion's murder.

TORRIO RETIRES

Torrio, who was responsible for ordering O'Banion's murder, was at the top of the North Side gangsters' hit list. On January 24, 1925, Moran, Weiss, Peter Gusenberg, and Vincent "the Schemer" Drucci ambushed the South Sider as he returned home with his wife. As the couple stepped out of their limousine at their address on South Clyde Avenue, Weiss and Drucci fired at them with shotguns. Wounded, Torrio fell to the ground.

Moran rushed across the street to finish him off. He placed a revolver at Torrio's head and pulled the trigger. But the gun did not fire. By then police were approaching. Moran and the other North Siders fled, leaving Torrio and his wife behind. Although he'd been struck four times, Torrio survived.

Shaken by his brush with death, Torrio retired, leaving Capone in charge of the South Side's thriving bootleg business. The twenty-five-year-old gangster was more than happy to take Torrio's place. In fact, some people suspect that it was Capone who had an informer provide the North Siders with information about Torrio's whereabouts.

AT WAR WITH THE GENNAS

Throughout the rest of the year, the North Side gang continued to kill off rival gangsters who had been involved in O'Banion's murder. Among their targets were the **Genna brothers** (see entry), a rival bootlegging gang that had ties with Capone. The Gennas had reportedly provided two of the three hitmen who had ambushed O'Banion: Albert Anselmi and John Scalise.

The North Siders struck on May 25, 1925. Angelo Genna—who was known as "Bloody Angelo" because of his murderous disposition—was their target. Moran, Weiss, and other members of the O'Banion gang hunted Genna in a car chase through the city's North Side. They opened fire on Genna's car with shotguns and submachine guns. Genna crashed into a post and was trapped behind the steering wheel. The North Siders pulled up beside him in a black sedan and fired three blasts of shotgun fire—Angelo was dead.

For more than a year, the Gennas waged war against the North Side gangsters. On June 13, 1925, they struck on Michigan Avenue, a busy street in the center of town. A car filled with Genna gunmen ambushed Moran and Drucci just as they were about to walk into a building. Caught in a hail of machine-gun and revolver fire, both North Siders were wounded—but not killed. As police rushed to site of the shootout, the hit men fled. Questioned by police, Moran and Drucci refused to name the shooters—even though they knew exactly who they were. Most gangsters followed a code of silence that prevented them from naming their attackers.

FIREWORKS AT THE HAWTHORNE INN

The North and South Side gangs continued to wage war. They engaged in shootouts in full daylight, on streets crowded with innocent bystanders. The violence peaked on September 20, 1926. Ten cars filled with North Side gangsters drove to Capone's headquarters in Cicero, on the southwest side of Chicago. They struck at noon. As the gunmen drove by, they fired thousands of shots into the Hawthorne Inn. They focused on the coffee shop on the first floor—where Capone and his bodyguard were trapped. Caught in the shootout, both gangsters and innocent bystanders shielded themselves against the flurry of shotgun, submachine gun, and revolver fire. Amazingly, no one was killed, and only a few were wounded.

Capone had seen his attackers. Louis Barko, one of the Capone gang's most respected hitmen, soon received clear instructions from his boss: destroy the North Side gangsters. Barko attacked twice—and twice he failed. But on October 11, 1926, Weiss became a casualty of the gang wars when he was shot to death as he crossed the street near Holy Name Cathedral. As luck would have it, Moran was not with him.

MORAN TAKES CHARGE

Moran, who had been second in command, took charge of the North Side gang. He met several times with Capone to arrange a peace treaty—which both gangsters were quick to ignore. While Moran agreed not to interfere with Capone's operations on the South Side, Capone promised not to operate north of the "Dividing Line" (Madison Street, in the heart of downtown Chicago).

Moran made a point of demonstrating that he was not afraid of Capone. After he was married, he drove around town with his wife in an open car. Popular with newspaper reporters, he informed them where he would be—and when. And he took every opportunity to badmouth Capone. He told reporters that the North Side gang were gentlemen bootleggers who simply addressed a public need. Capone, on the other hand, was a "lowlife" whose underworld activities were not confined to bootlegging. Unlike the North Side gang, Capone's mob dealt in prostitution.

A BLOODY VALENTINE

In 1929, Capone began to disregard the "Dividing Line" completely. After the South Sider's gunmen began to invade the North Side, Moran joined forces with mobster Joseph Aiello. An enemy of Capone, Aiello posted a $50,000 reward for the murder of the man known as "Scarface."

A pauper's funeral

Most of Moran's associates were buried in expensive funerals—with lavish floral arrangements, extravagant coffins, solemn processions, costly headstones, and large crowds of mourners. But Moran—who was once a millionaire—was given a pauper's burial when he died in Leavenworth prison in 1957. He was laid in a plain wooden casket and buried in a potter's field—a public burial place for paupers, unknown persons, and criminals.

With two of Moran's top gunmen—Frank and Peter Gusenberg—Aiello murdered Capone's good friend, Pasquilino Lolordo. As the three men sat drinking wine in Lolordo's living room, they shot their unsuspecting victim to death. Capone knew who the killers were—and that the murder had taken place with Moran's blessing. He swore revenge.

First he killed Aiello as he attempted to skip town. Capone reportedly committed the murder himself. Next, he targeted Moran. Using a mobster from Detroit, Michigan, he arranged an ambush at Moran's headquarters at 2122 North Clark Street. The Detroit mobster approached Moran, claiming to have a shipment of hijacked booze for sale. Moran took the bait—and arranged to take delivery at the gang's headquarters on the morning of February 14, 1929—Valentine's Day. But there was no liquor shipment. Instead, a hit squad appeared at Moran's headquarters, killing several of the North Side mobsters.

Moran was not among them. Arriving late to the meeting, he noticed three men dressed as policemen and two others in street clothes entering the gang's garage headquarters. He assumed that a police raid was taking place. Accompanied by his bodyguards, Willie Marks and Ted Newberry, he waited at a nearby

coffee shop. Soon the garage was ablaze with machine-gun fire, which killed six gangsters and one innocent bystander.

DOWN AND OUT

Moran no longer made light of his rival, Capone. He reportedly checked into a hospital, where his bodyguards maintained a constant watch. Once friendly with reporters, he refused to answer their questions. Asked about the massacre, he replied, "I don't know. I don't know anything about it." But newsmen continued to question him until he finally blurted, "Only Capone kills like that!"

The shootout—which became known as the St. Valentine's Day Massacre—marked the end of Moran's career as a gangland boss. Although he continued to maintain political control of the North Side area for the next few years, he never recovered from Capone's vicious attack. By 1940, Moran exercised no power in the Chicago underworld.

His fortune spent, Moran survived by pulling small burglaries. With most of his associates dead—and deserted by his wife—he no longer had ties to Chicago. He moved to Ohio after World War II (1939–1945), where he joined forces with a couple of petty crooks, Albert Fouts and Virgil Summers. In 1946, the three men robbed an Ohio bank messenger of $10,000. Moran was soon arrested by Federal Bureau of Investigation (FBI) agents and sentenced to prison. Released after ten years he was again arrested—for a bank robbery he had committed before he was sent to prison. Moran died of cancer in Leavenworth penitentiary. He was sixty-four.

Sources for Further Reading

Nash, Jay Robert. *The Encyclopedia of World Crime*. Wilmette, IL: Crime Books, 1990, pp. 2213–2215.

Sifakis, Carl. *The Encyclopedia of American Crime*. New York: Facts on File, 1982, pp.498–499.

Dutch Schultz
(Arthur Flegenheimer)

Born: August 6, 1902
Died: October 23, 1935

Unreliable and governed by self-interest, Dutch Schultz was nevertheless included on the board of the national crime syndicate organized by Lucky Luciano and other crime bosses of the era. When his hot temper threatened to attract too much heat to the organization, his associates ordered him killed—with little regret.

YOUNG FLEGENHEIMER

Arthur Flegenheimer—who later took the name Dutch Schultz—was born in New York City, on August 6, 1902. His parents were Emma and Herman Flegenheimer. Raised in the Bronx, Schultz dropped out of school after the fourth grade. He soon joined the Bergen Gang—a gang of juvenile thieves and pickpockets.

When Schultz was just fourteen, his father deserted the family. Emma Flegenheimer supported herself and her teenaged son by taking in laundry for pay. A warm and kind woman, she tried to convince Schultz to return to school. But he looked for his education on the streets of New York.

Armed with burglars' tools, Schultz committed numerous burglaries and holdups as a teenager. He worked for a while as a printer—simply to provide a front for the more profitable business of theft. In 1919, at the age of seventeen, he was arrested for burglary and sentenced to a fifteen-month prison term.

The expensive apartment building in New York's exclusive 5th Avenue neighborhood where Dutch Schultz lived.

BACK ON THE STREET

Time behind bars did little to reform Schultz. After serving out the entire sentence, he returned to his earlier occupation. With the earnings from several robberies, he purchased a bar in the Bronx and began to assemble a fierce gang of thugs. Among the men in his gang were Abe Landau, Julie Martin, Joey Rao,

Headline material

Arthur Flegenheimer was afraid that his given name was too long to appear in newspaper headlines. Following his release from prison, he changed his name to Dutch Schultz—the name of an earlier gang leader. Shortly before the turn of the century, the original Dutch Schultz headed a band of Bronx gangsters known as the Frog Hollow Gang.

Schultz continued to open illegal bars during Prohibition (when the Eighteenth Amendment outlawed the manufacture and sale of alcohol), which he stocked with liquor that had been smuggled from Canada and Europe and whiskey that had been stolen from rival bootleggers. He also served homemade beer, which was considered to be among the area's worst. Schultz's gang soon expanded its operations to include areas of Manhattan. But the new territories did not come easily. A number of rival gangsters were killed in the process.

NUMBERS GAMES AND ONE-ARMED BANDITS

Always on the lookout for new opportunities to make money, Schultz did not limit his activities to the illegal liquor business. In Harlem and other areas of New York, African American gangsters controlled an illegal gambling operation known as the numbers racket—also called the policy racket. Most of Schultz's associates ignored the numbers racket, believing that it was a nickel-and-dime operation that provided little earning potential. But Schultz knew otherwise.

Schultz and his gunmen threatened Stephanie St. Clair, who presided over the numbers racket in Harlem. The cold-blooded mobster gave her a choice: allow him to take over her business, or face Schultz's death squad. St. Clair turned over her operations—and other Harlem numbers leaders followed. The numbers racket was a nickel-and-dime business. But most of Harlem's population wagered nickels and dimes on a daily basis. The business yielded millions of dollars, and Schultz amassed a private fortune.

By the 1930s, Schultz became involved in another money-making enterprise: the slot machine business. Working with **Frank Costello** (see entry) and Joey Rao, he and his gang flooded New York City with gambling machines known as one-armed bandits—some of which were equipped with step-ladders so that children could play. Again, it was a nickel-and-dime business. And again, it reaped millions for Schultz and his colleagues.

DIAMOND LOSES HIS SPARKLE

Schultz hired a number of notorious mobsters to protect his many illegal operations. Gunman Vincent Coll and a number of young gangsters delivered Shultz's beer and liquor to various New York speakeasies (bars that sold illegal alcohol). **Legs Diamond** (see entry), whose gang controlled a portion of Manhattan's bootlegging empire, lent Schultz added muscle.

But Schultz's alliance with Diamond did not last long. By 1930, their partnership had dissolved. Schultz's beer shipments often disappeared: his delivery trucks were hijacked by rival gangsters. When he learned that Diamond was responsible for the thefts, he declared war on Diamond's gang. The gang war claimed several casualties from both sides.

Because he lived through numerous attempts on his life, Diamond became known as the "clay pigeon of the underworld." For a while it looked like he was impossible to kill. But on December 19, 1931, Diamond was killed when two Schultz gunmen tracked him to upstate New York, burst into his hotel room, and repeatedly shot him. Schultz later told reporters that the dead gangster "was just another punk with his hands in my pockets."

THE COLL WAR

Schultz also found himself in a gang war with Vincent Coll and his brother Peter. The Colls' followers beat up bartenders and bar owners who purchased liquor from Schultz. Using violence, they forced their victims to stop buying Schultz's booze—and to purchase their own product instead. Coll also began to take over Schultz's profitable numbers racket.

Although Coll's gang was small, his mobsters killed a number of Schultz's top men. In June 1931, Schultz and his bodyguard, Danny Iamascia, saw two men loitering on a street in Manhattan. They thought they were about to be ambushed by

"You're dead"

Schultz's lawyer, Dixie Davis, was quoted as saying, "You can insult Arthur's [Schultz's] girl, spit in his face, push him around—and he'll laugh. But don't steal a dollar from his accounts. If you do, you're dead."

the Coll brothers. A shootout followed, in which Iamascia was fatally wounded. Schultz fled, and one of the men followed him. The man wrestled him to the ground in an alley and identified himself.

The man was not, as Schultz feared, one of the Coll brothers. He was New York Police Detective Steve DiRosa. The other man was Detective Julius Salke. The two detectives had been following the bootleg czar to find out more about his operations. Booked on charges of attempted murder, carrying a concealed weapon, and resisting arrest, Schultz was not detained long. Thanks to one of the many judges who received bribes from the gangster, he was released on bail and the charges were eventually dropped.

A FATAL PHONE BOOTH

The incident fueled Schultz's grudge against Coll. The following year, one of his men followed Coll to find out more about his daily habits so that he would be more vulnerable to attack. Schultz learned that Coll often used a phone booth inside a drugstore on West 23rd Street. From the drugstore phone booth, Coll made many "business" calls—including ransom calls to **Owney Madden** (see entry), whose partner had been kidnapped.

On February 8, 1932, Coll was making a phone call to Madden when one of Schultz's men saw him. The man contacted Abe and George Weinberg, two gunmen for the Schultz gang. The Weinberg brothers arrived at the drugstore with two other men as backup. First, one man escorted the store clerk and two customers to a room in the back. Then another opened fire on Coll, who was still in the phone booth. Several rounds of bullets shattered the glass booth, killing Schultz's rival.

TRIED FOR TAX FRAUD

Schultz's next battle was with the government. Having earned millions of dollars from his various illegal rackets, the mobster had neglected to pay taxes on his income. After the state of New York estimated that Shultz owed millions of dollars in back taxes, he was charged with income tax evasion.

Many of Schultz's peers had received long jail terms on similar charges. But, with the help of his lawyer, Dixie Davis, Schultz managed to beat the charges. Davis managed to have the trial moved out of New York City—where his client was a high-profile gangster—to a town in rural upstate New York. Schultz also employed a public relations firm that helped to improve his public image in the local community. The agency made sure that everyone in town knew about Schultz's many donations to local charities and other favorable activities. By the time Schultz was tried for tax evasion, Schultz had many supporters. The jury found him not guilty.

WEINBERG'S REWARD

When Schultz returned to New York City, he found that many of his rackets had been taken over by Vito Genovese and Lucky Luciano. What's more, his former aide, Bo Weinberg, had helped Schultz's rivals gain control of his operations. Schultz reacted by moving his headquarters from the Bronx, in New York, to Newark, New Jersey. Schultz also gave the order to kill Weinberg. Some said that Schultz personally shot Weinberg in the head. Others claimed Schultz's former aid was encased in cement and dropped into the Hudson River—while he was still breathing. Evidence suggests that **Bugsy Siegel** (see entry) carried out the hit—by stabbing Weinberg repeatedly.

A SYNDICATE MAN

Schultz returned to New York at a time when crime leaders were busy organizing the underworld into a national crime syndicate. He was offered a position on the syndicate's board of directors—not because he was a loyal associate, but because he would pose a powerful threat as an enemy. Concerned only with his own rackets, Schultz had no regard for the interests of the other board members. The other board members considered "the Dutchman" to be unreliable. And they wanted to gain control of his bootlegging and numbers rackets. In short, they wanted him dead.

Charles Workman, the man who killed Dutch Schultz.

No more slots

By 1935, Schultz saw his vast slot machine empire destroyed. Backed by New York mayor Fiorello La Guardia (1882–1947), New York district attorney Thomas E. Dewey launched an attack on the state's slot machine business. Hundreds of Schultz's one-armed bandits were demolished by sledgehammers and dumped in the East River. Mayor LaGuardia took advantage of every opportunity to have himself photographed as he swung a sledgehammer down on one of the gambling machines—as a symbol of his stance against crime and corruption.

Schultz's partners, Frank Costello and Phillip "Dandy Phil" Kastel, relocated their slot machine business to New Orleans, Louisiana. But Schultz, who remained on the East Coast, arrived at another solution. He planned to have Dewey murdered.

Schultz informed the crime syndicate board of his plan to kill Dewey. Concerned about the attention such a murder would attract, the board members refused to approve the killing. But Schultz planned to make the hit with or without the board's approval. He reportedly left the board meeting shouting that he would do the killing himself—within forty-eight hours.

The board members had little time to react. They voted to have Schultz killed and appointed Albert Anastasia to take care of the matter. Anastasia had recently been put in charge of Murder, Inc. A hit squad for the newly formed national syndicate, Murder, Inc. was charged with taking care of gangsters who challenged syndicate decisions. Anastasia promised that Schultz would not live to see the next day.

The Dutchman's demise

On the evening of October 23, 1935, Schultz and three associates—his accountant Otto "Abbadabba" Berman and two bodyguards, Abe Landau and Lulu Rosencranz—met in the back room of Schultz's favorite hangout, the Palace Chophouse in Newark, New Jersey. Shortly after Schultz left the table for the men's room, three men arrived at the restaurant: Emmanuel "Mendy" Weiss, Charles "the Bug" Workman, and another man, known only as "Piggy." First, one of the gunmen charged into the men's room, where he shot a man to ensure that the gunmen would not be attacked from behind. Schultz was next to be shot. Then, the gunman fired at the men who were seated at the table.

When the gunmen fled, all of the victims were still breathing. Berman, Landau, Rosencranz, and Schultz were all taken to Newark City Hospital, where each one died. Shot in the back

Last words

Police Sergeant L. Conlon questioned Schultz in the hospital to try to find out who shot him. Many gangsters refused to identify their attackers because they followed a code of silence. Schultz was anything but silent—although he never identified his assailant. The dying gangster uttered nonsense that was impossible to understand. Conlon recorded Schultz's ramblings.

Shortly before Schultz died, the policeman asked him again to identify his shooter. The gangster responded:

I don't know. I didn't even get a look. I don't know who could have done it. Anybody. Kindly take my shoes off . . .

No, there's a handcuff on them. The baron says these things. I know what I am doing here with my collection of papers. It isn't worth a nickel to two guys like you or me, but to a collector it is worth a fortune. It is priceless. I am going to turn it over to. . . . Turn your back to me please. Henry, I am so sick now. The police are getting many complaints. Look out! I want that G-note. Look out for Jimmy Valentine for he is an old pal of mine. Come on, come one, Jim. Okay, okay, I am all through. Can't do another thing.

Look out mama. Look out for her. You can't beat him. Police, mama, Helen, mother, please, take me out. I will settle the indictment. Shut up! You got a big mouth! Please help me up, Henry. Max, come over here! French-Canadian bean soup. I want to pay. Let them leave me alone!

After a two-hour silence, Schultz died.

and in the side, Schultz lived the longest. When he was asked who his killer was, his garbled responses made no sense. He died two days later, without ever naming his assassins. Although Schultz never identified him, Charles Workman was convicted of the murder and sentenced to life in prison. He was paroled from the New Jersey State Prison after twenty years.

Sources for Further Reading

Nash, Jay Robert. *The Encyclopedia of World Crime.* Wilmette, IL: Crime Books, 1990, pp. 2699–2705.

Sifakis, Carl. *The Encyclopedia of American Crime.* New York: Facts on File, 1982, pp. 642–643.

Roger Touhy

Born: 1898
Died: December 17, 1959

*Roger "Terrible" Touhy was reportedly one of the few men who could force **Al Capone** (see entry) to blink in a confrontation. Framed for a crime he did not commit, he spent years in jail before he was finally paroled—only to be gunned down by someone who apparently held an old grudge.*

FROM ALTAR BOY TO OIL MAN

The son of a policeman, Touhy was born in Chicago, Illinois, in 1898. When he was ten years old, a kitchen stove exploded, killing his mother. Touhy moved with his father, two sisters, and five brothers from Chicago to the suburb of Downer's Grove, Illinois. There, he and his seven siblings had a respectable upbringing. The young Touhy served as an altar boy at the neighborhood Catholic church and was a student at St. Joseph's grade school, where he graduated from in 1911. Many of his friends went on to become police officers.

As a teenager, Touhy worked as a Western Union messenger. He eventually became a telegraph operator and managed a small Western Union office. After being fired in 1915 for participating in union activities, he moved to Colorado, where he worked as a telegraph operator for the Denver & Rio Grande Railroad.

Touhy enlisted in the United States Navy during World War I (1914–1918). In 1918, he spent the year teaching Morse code to Navy officers at Harvard University. (Morse code is a system of dots and dashes used to communicate by telegraph.) After he was discharged from the military, he again headed West. In Oklahoma, where oil was being drilled from the land, he worked in a number of towns as an oil rigger and engineer. He became involved in the profitable business of buying and selling oil leases. By the time he returned to Chicago in 1922, he had saved $25,000.

A BETTER BREW

Back in Chicago, Touhy married and started a trucking firm with his brother, Tommy, in the early 1920s. The business started off slowly. But when the Touhy brothers began to load their trucks with illegal alcohol (when the Eighteenth Amendment was enacted in 1920, it outlawed the manufacture and sale of alcohol), their business began to boom. The Touhys earned a fortune by distributing illegal beer and liquor. Soon they controlled most of the bootlegging activities in the northwestern section of Cook County in Chicago, including the suburb of Des Plaines. Using cash payoffs and fringe benefits—such as free beer—he made sure that local politicians and police officials did not interfere with his operations.

Much of the alcohol sold during Prohibition was of very poor quality. But Touhy, who had hired a leading chemist to establish a beer brewery, sold top-notch beer and liquor. Together with his partner, Matt Kolb, he manufactured what was widely regarded as the best beer in the Midwest during the Prohibition era. Profiting from his reputation as a quality producer, Touhy charged top dollar for his product. But not everyone was happy to pay a large fee for Touhy's special brew.

TERRIBLE TOUHY

Chicago mobster Al Capone was among Touhy's clients. In one notorious incident, he purchased eight hundred barrels of beer—and then attempted to pressure Touhy into lowering his price. He claimed he would not pay the full price—$37.50 for each barrel—because some of the barrels leaked. But Touhy stood his ground and Capone paid the full amount he owed. Touhy is reportedly the only gangster to have forced Capone to back away from a conflict.

But in reality, Touhy was not the fearsome man he was reputed to be. The newspapers referred to him as Roger "The Terrible" Touhy—but reports of his terror were mostly made up. The leader of what was actually a very small gang, he deliberately created a public image as a gunslinging gangster. When rival gangsters visited his headquarters in the Arch, a road house in Schiller Park, he reportedly relied on police and other associates to help him create the appearance of a large and powerful gang. He borrowed machine guns and other weapons, with which he lined the walls of his headquarters. Policemen, friends, and other locals posed as trigger-happy gangsters who were eager to follow his orders. The ploy is said to have scared away a number of would-be challengers to his bootlegging territory.

A FALL GUY

Because of Touhy's fierce reputation, few gangsters were willing to confront him. But Capone's mobsters were determined to take over Touhy's share of the Chicago bootlegging market. The mobsters reportedly used another method to force Touhy out of power: they set him up—and stood by as he was arrested for crimes he did not commit.

A taxing murder

The former bootlegger's murder was reportedly ordered by Murray "the Camel" Humphreys, a Capone mobster who had been threatened by Touhy years earlier. Six months after Touhy was killed, Humphreys purchased four hundred shares of First National Life Insurance Company stock from Jake Factor—the man Touhy had been wrongly convicted of kidnapping. He bought the stock at a price of $20 a share. Eight months later, he sold the stock back to Factor—for $125 a share. The Internal Revenue Service (IRS) decided to take a look at Humphreys's $42,000 profit. The IRS declared that the money was clearly a payment for services that had been performed. (It was not the business of the IRS to determine what those services were.) Humphreys therefore owed full income taxes on $42,000 he received from Factor. It's quite possible that the government collected taxes on money that had been paid for an execution.

Blood runs down the steps of the home of Touhy's sister where Touhy was shot down.

In 1933, Federal Bureau of Investigation (FBI) agent Melvin Purvis arrested Touhy and charged him with kidnapping William A. Hamm Jr., a millionaire brewer from St. Paul, Minnesota. Although the FBI claimed to have a strong case against him, Touhy—and gang members who had been arrested with him—were found not guilty. Members of the Barker-Karpis gang (see entry on **Ma Barker**) were later accused of the kidnapping. (Alvin "Creepy" Karpis had ties to the Capone gang.) Although it is not clear whether Capone's gang was involved in this incident, there was little doubt that they were the masterminds of a second frame-up.

Later in 1933, Touhy was again charged with kidnapping. This time the "victim" was Jake "The Barber" Factor, a con man who was known to be linked with the Capone mob. Although it was commonly rumored that the kidnapping had been staged by Factor and Capone gangsters, Touhy was taken to court. Although his first trial resulted in a hung jury, he was convicted in a second trial. (A hung jury cannot agree on a verdict.) Sentenced to ninety-nine years in Joliet penitentiary in Illinois, Touhy left the courtroom shouting that he had been framed.

Melvin Purvis, FBI

When Touhy was arrested for the kidnapping of Jake "the Barber" Factor, Melvin Purvis, a special agent in the FBI, boasted that the case had been solved because of outstanding detective work. He said, "This case holds a particular interest for me because it represents a triumph of deductive work. We assumed from the start, with no material evidence, that the Touhy gang was responsible for the crime."

But that was exactly the problem. There *was* no material evidence, because Touhy had been framed for the crime by rival mobsters who wanted to take over his bootlegging territory. The case against Touhy and the three others who were charged in the kidnapping relied on testimony that was later discovered to have been false.

FBI agent Purvis later captured the notorious **John Dillinger** (see entry) and other wanted fugitives. But the Touhy incident remained an embarrassment for him throughout his career. In 1960, just months after Touhy was gunned down, Purvis, who had retired from the FBI, committed suicide.

FREE AT LAST

At first, Touhy was a model prisoner. For years he tried to prove that he had been wrongly accused. He saw his fortune dwindle as high-priced lawyers tried to win an appeal for the former bootlegger. On October 9, 1942, after almost ten years in prison, Touhy joined six other convicts in a prison break. With him were Basil "the Owl" Banghart, Edward Darlak, St. Clair McInerney, Martlick Nelson, Eugene O'Connor, and Edward Stewart. Using a homemade rope ladder, they climbed up a prison wall to a guard's tower. From there they escaped to the outside.

The escaped convicts were soon placed on the FBI's "Most Wanted List." In December 1942, FBI agents tracked them to a boarding house in Chicago. A shootout followed. Two of the escapees died in the gunfire. The others were taken into custody. Touhy found himself back in prison—with one hundred and ninety-nine years added to his sentence.

But Touhy continued to fight his conviction. Supported by a number of reporters who believed that he had not been responsible for the kidnapping, he won another hearing in the 1950s. Touhy's lawyers argued his case in federal court, before Judge John P. Barnes. At the end of the thirty-six-day inquiry, Barnes declared that the kidnapping had been a hoax. Factor, he said, had cooperated in his "disappearance." On November 25, 1959—after close to twenty-five years behind bars—Touhy was released from prison.

The former bootlegger's fortune was gone and he was in poor health. He moved in with his sister in Chicago. On the night of December 16, 1959, as he returned to his sister's home, Touhy was gunned down by shotgun fire. Although the bullets nearly cut his body in two, he did not die right away. Before dying he reportedly said, "I've been expecting it. The bastards never forget!"

Sources for Further Reading

Nash, Jay Robert. *The Encyclopedia of World Crime.* Wilmette, IL: Crime Books, 1990, pp. 2976–2978.

Sifakis, Carl. *The Encyclopedia of American Crime.* New York: Facts on File, 1982, pp. 717–719.

Sifakis, Carl. *The Mafia Encyclopedia.* New York: Facts on File, 1982, pp. 323–325.

Hymie Weiss
(Earl Weiss)

Born: 1898
Died: October 11, 1926

As a member of Charles Dion O'Banion's North Side gang, Earl "Hymie" Weiss was involved in the longstanding territorial disputes between Chicago's North and South Siders. Weiss was killed by the familiar mob method of ambush from a second-story apartment.

THE PERFUME BURGLAR

When Polish-born Earl Wajciechowski moved to the United States with his family as a boy, he took the name of Earl "Hymie" Weiss. He was still just a boy when he was arrested, in 1908, for robbing a pharmacy. Weiss spilled perfume on his clothing during the robbery. When reporters wrote about the incident, they referred to the ten-year-old criminal as the "Perfume Burglar."

By the time Weiss was a teenager, he had become a skilled car thief and burglar. Labor unions hired him to provide muscle in union disputes—and to carry out executions when necessary. An accomplished safecracker, he found his way into the gang of O'Banion—a former alter boy who, like Weiss, was a devout (religious) Catholic who regularly attended Holy Name Cathedral. Operating out of the North Side of Chicago, O'Banion's gang concentrated on jewel thefts and various other safecracking jobs.

With valuable political connections in the North Side wards, O'Banion enjoyed some degree of protection from police and prosecution. In one case, both Weiss and O'Banion were arrested for burglarizing the Parkway Tea Room. Although their fingerprints had been found on the Tea Room's safe, both gangsters were acquitted (found not guilty). The jury had been bribed.

AN O'BANION LIEUTENANT

When Prohibition (when the Eighteenth Amendment outlawed the manufacture and sale of alcohol) went into effect, O'Banion's gang moved into the profitable bootlegging business (the illegal manufacture and sale of alcohol). Joining forces with a number of other mobsters, such as Vincent "Schemer" Drucci, Frank and Peter Gusenberg, and **Bugs Moran** (see entry), they took control of the North Side's thriving bootlegging business. Acting as O'Banion's second-in-command, Weiss convinced saloon owners to purchase the gang's liquor. Thoughtful about planning for the future, Weiss employed bribery freely. Police gave him credit for building his boss's business into a successful large-scale operation. At the height of its success, the O'Banion gang supplied bootleg booze to hundreds of establishments near the lakefront in Chicago's 42nd and 43rd Wards (political districts of a city).

As major players in the city's bootlegging business, O'Banion's gang became involved with territorial disputes with Al Capone's rival organization. Gang warfare was unavoidable. On November 10, 1924, Capone's hitmen gunned down O'Banion at the gangster's flower shop. (O'Banion operated the flower shop, a legal business, as a "front," or cover, for other illegal activities.)

Although Weiss was enraged by the killing, he prevented the gang from striking back at Capone's gang—for a while. The newly appointed gang chief was rumored to have promised O'Banion's widow that he would refrain from violence until after the funeral. Among the mourners who attended O'Banion's burial was Capone, who defiantly watched the ceremony with six of his bodyguards.

In less than two months, violence erupted. On January 12, 1925, Weiss—together with O'Banion gangsters, Drucci and Moran—attempted to ambush Capone. After following Capone's

Charles Dion O'Banion (1891-1924)

In the early 1920s, the illegal rackets on the North Side of Chicago were dominated by an Irish immigrant named O'Banion. On the surface he was a pleasant man who loved to sing the old songs of his homeland, and he spent most days working in his florist's shop on North State Street. He was also a major bootlegger and drug trafficker who was considered "Chicago's arch-criminal" by the Chicago police.

Informed insiders claimed that O'Banion—who always carried three guns concealed in special pockets made by his tailor—arranged for the deaths of at least twenty-five of his enemies. It was O'Banion who began the custom of sending large floral arrangements for the public funerals of slain mobsters. He made most of these funeral wreaths himself.

O'Banion started out as a member of a North Side juvenile street gang. His earliest adult crimes were burglary and safecracking. Because of a leg wound from an early gunfight, O'Banion walked with a pronounced limp. By the time Prohibition (when the Eighteenth Amendment outlawed the manufacture and sale of alcohol) went into effect in 1920, O'Banion's gang—an ethnic mix of Irish, German, and Jewish hoodlums—was well placed to benefit from the newly profitable racket of bootlegging whiskey.

At first, O'Banion and his major rival **Al Capone** (see entry) maintained an uneasy coexistence. But in the summer of 1924, O'Banion's henchmen began hijacking Capone's liquor trucks. They also shot up several speakeasies (bars that sold illegal alcohol during Prohibition) in Capone's South Side territory, wounding some of Capone's men. Capone would have his revenge: at noon on November 10, 1924, three gunmen entered O'Banion's shop and shot him to death. The fact that his usually reliable bodyguards were in the back room at the time raised suspicions that they had been paid to stay out of the way. No one was ever charged with O'Banion's murder.

limousine to State and 55th streets, they drove by while shooting at the parked vehicle. Although twenty-six shots had ripped into the car, only the chauffeur, Sylvester Barton, was wounded. Two bodyguards escaped without injury, as did their boss, who had stepped into a nearby restaurant moments before the shooting began. To protect himself from further attacks, Capone later ordered the construction of an expensive armored car.

Weiss continued to launch attacks against Capone. Just over one week after the restaurant shooting, Drucci and Moran wounded Capone's longtime associate, Johnny Torrio, near his

The first Chicago gangland funeral

In 1920, James Colosimo was the reputed "kingpin" of the Chicago underworld. After arriving in Chicago, Illinois, from Italy in 1895, "Big Jim" started a lucrative loan-shark operation on the South Side. By the late 1910s, Colosimo also dominated prostitution and gambling in Chicago from his headquarters at Colosimo's Cafe on South Wabash Avenue, one of the most popular nightspots in the city. There, gangsters freely mingled with figures from high society.

In 1915, Colosimo brought in his relative, Johnny Torrio, from New York City to help manage his growing operations. Five years later, Torrio arranged for another New Yorker, Al "Scarface" Capone, to join the organization.

With the beginning of Prohibition in January 1920, Colosimo began a sizable bootlegging enterprise. But his role in Chicago's bootlegging skirmishes was short-lived. Colosimo was fatally shot in the lobby of Colosimo's Cafe on the afternoon of May 11, 1920. Some claim that Frank Uale (known as Yale), a former associate, performed the killing in an attempt to "muscle in" on Colosimo's rackets. Others are certain that Capone and Torrio commissioned (ordered) the killing—although both had proof that they were elsewhere at the time. Colosimo's slaying is generally considered to be the first gangland "hit" during the 1920s.

Colosimo was the first mobster to be given a lavish public funeral. His "send-off" at the Holy Name Catholic Cathedral cost $20,000. It was also the first burial for which gangster and florist Charles O'Banion provided the extravagant floral arrangements that became standard displays at mob funerals.

South Side home. On June 13, Angelo Genna—a member of the Capone-friendly **Genna brothers** (see entry) organization—was murdered by Weiss's men.

ALL-OUT WAR

On September 20, 1926, a large contingent of Weiss's men ambushed Capone at the Hawthorne Inn—the Capone gang's headquarters on the West Side of Chicago. Eleven cars full of gunmen drove slowly by as they fired pistols, machine guns, and shotguns into the lobby of the hotel. According to reports, more than one thousand bullets ripped into the building. Capone—who had been thrown to the floor by a bodyguard—again escaped without injury.

Soon the tables turned. The day after the Hawthorne Inn shooting, Capone associates rented a room in a building across the street from Holy Name Cathedral and the O'Banion gang's headquarters at the State Street flower shop. Capone's hitmen settled into the second-floor room and waited for their victim to appear. On October 11, 1926, Weiss appeared with attorney William W. O'Brien and his bodyguards, Benny Jacobs, Paddy Murray, and Sam Peller. Capone's killers fired at them as they crossed State Street, wounding O'Brien, Jacobs, and Peller. Weiss and Murphy were shot dead. When questioned after the slaying, Capone expressed false regret: "That was butchery. Hymie was a good kid. He could have got out long ago and taken his and been alive today."

Take a look at this!

Bugsy Malone (1976) is an offbeat musical spoof of 1930s mobster movies with an all-child cast. The plot loosely concerns a gangland war between sarsaparilla (root beer) bootlegger Fat Sam and an upstart named Dandy Dan, who raids Sam's speakeasies with "splurge guns" that shoot whipped cream. A young Jodie Foster plays a gangster moll (girlfriend).

Sources for Further Reading

Nash, Jay Robert. *The Encyclopedia of World Crime.* Wilmette, IL: Crime Books, 1990, pp. 3119–3120.

Sifakis, Carl. *The Encyclopedia of American Crime.* New York: Facts on File, 1982, pp. 752–753.

Pirates

In 1837, an American named Charles Ellms wrote, "In the mind of the mariner, there is a superstitious horror connected with the name of Pirate; and there are few subjects that interest and excite the curiosity of mankind more than the desperate exploits, foul doings, and diabolical careers in human form. . . ."

Mutinies, stolen cargoes, and battles fought in the high seas. Buried treasure and sunken ships. Cruel and unusual punishments and the pirate code of conduct. There's plenty here to "interest and excite the curiosity"—and then some. In this section you'll read about the desperate exploits and foul doings of a handful of pirates who terrorized ports in the American colonies and elsewhere. Included are Blackbeard—who burned tapers in his beard to create a fiendish appearance; Charles Gibbs and Joseph Baker—mutineers who paid for their crimes on the gallows; and Anne Bonny—one of very few women pirates about whom anything is known.

Joseph Baker

Born: ?
Died: May 9, 1800

A ruthless mutineer, Joseph Baker was duped by the captain of the ship he intended to claim. Returned to the port he departed from, he was hanged in a public execution.

MUTINY ON THE *ELIZA*

Born in Canada, Baker was a pirate and murderer who sometimes worked as a merchant seaman out of the American colonies. On his last voyage he signed onto a merchant ship named *Eliza*. With Captain William Wheland at the helm, the vessel left the harbor in Philadelphia, Pennsylvania, for the warm waters of the Caribbean.

Baker did not intend to help *Eliza* reach its final destination in the Caribbean. Before departing on the voyage, he had recruited two other sailors—Joseph Berrouse and Peter LaCroix—to join him in a mutiny (open rebellion against authority). The three men waited until the ship was far from land and out of range of the assistance of other vessels. The mutineers struck at night—as one seaman watched over the ship while most of the crew slept. Surprised by the attack, the first mate (the crew member next in command to the captain) struggled with Baker and his accomplices. They threw him overboard.

The pirate code of conduct

Although pirates rejected the rules of governments, most followed a democratic organization on board ship and in port. Many pirates were required to swear to observe the rules before setting sail on a voyage. The code was printed in *Captain Johnson's General History of the Robberies and Murders of the Most Notorious Pirates*. Published in 1724, the code lists some of the rules that provided order in the sea rovers' existence. The rules included:

• Everyone may vote on all important decisions.

• Anyone keeping a secret or attempting to desert will be marooned. He may take only a flask of gunpowder, a bottle of water, a gun and some shot [ammunition].

• Anyone found stealing from another member of crew will have his ears and nose slit open, and be set ashore.

• Anyone being lazy or failing to clean his weapons will lose his share of booty.

• No one may leave the crew until each man has made one thousand pounds [British currency] worth of booty.

Having heard signs of a struggle, Captain Wheland went above deck to investigate and was wounded by the mutineers. Baker could not afford to kill Wheland: he had failed to plan a safe route to a port where the mutineers could sell the ship's cargo. Baker needed to Wheland to help him find his way in the high seas.

THE TABLES TURN

Baker informed the captain that, if he helped the mutineers sail to safety, his life would be spared. But Wheland knew that Baker had no intention of keeping his word. He bought time by promising to help the pirates reach the Spanish Main—a haven for sea robbers comprised of parts of Central and South America owned by Spain. When two of the mutineers were below deck, he shut the only entrance that led to the hold—and locked them in. Baker stood at the captain's wheel. When he saw Wheland approaching with an ax in his hand, he fled.

Wheland ordered Baker to climb to the top of the ship's main mast—and to tie himself in place with rope. For two weeks, Baker remained tied to his perch, while Wheland steered the ship toward a safe port. The captain occasionally sent the pirate something to eat and drink by using a rope as a pulley, and he lashed himself to the steering wheel to make sure that he did not accidentally fall asleep and allow the ship to veer off course.

After fourteen days of little sleep and rough seas, Wheland arrived at St. Kitts (an island in the West Indies). There he deliv-

Piracy on the Spanish Main

Shortly after Christopher Columbus sailed to the Americas in 1492, Spain laid claim to a territory known as the Spanish Main—parts of the Central and South American mainlands from Mexico to Peru. The New World territory contained vast riches—including silver mines in Ecuador and Peru and native treasures of the Aztecs and Incas. Having seized the area, the Spaniards plundered the Spanish Main. They loaded ships with jewels, gold, silver, and artifacts, and transported their booty to their native country. The solid gold jewelry of the Aztec natives was crushed and melted down in order to save room on the treasure ships.

The area became a pirate haven. As they made their way from the Caribbean Sea to the Atlantic Ocean, the Spanish galleons (a type of sailing vessel) were looted by privateers—sea robbers who had government approval to plunder enemy ships. Many of the privateers on the Spanish Main were French and English. Most attacks took place early in the return voyage. Waiting in ambush off the North American coast, privateers surprised their victims as they headed north from the Caribbean.

In 1603, King James I (1566–1625) of England attempted to put a stop to privateering in the Caribbean, when he withdrew all letters of marque—a government license that gave privateers authority to pillage (rob) the vessels of rival governments. Then, in 1630, Spain signed a treaty with France and England allowing them to colonize some of the territories in what had been the Spanish Main. By the end of the century, the Spaniards had lost much of their lands and influence in the Caribbean. As Spain's presence in the area declined, so did privateering.

But the Spanish Main soon became the center of renewed pirate campaigns. In 1713, the Treaty of Utrecht put an end to the War of the Spanish Succession among Spain, Britain, and France. Suddenly unemployed, many former sailors turned to piracy. Pirate ports flourished in the Caribbean and on mainland America. The area known as the Spanish Main—which now included the West Indies, the Gulf of Mexico, and the Caribbean (including the various Caribbean islands)—entered a golden age of piracy.

ered Baker, Berrouse, and LaCroix to U.S. Navy officers, who shipped the mutineers back to the port from which they had departed. The prisoners were held on board a war ship, the *Ganges.*

On April 21, 1800, the mutineers' trial began. All three were tried for piracy and murder before the circuit court in Philadelphia, Pennsylvania. The charges of piracy and murder

Piracy and profit-sharing

Pirates lived by articles of agreement that determined how the loot was divided. Historians have found evidence that the standard agreement allotted two shares of the loot to the pirate captain, one and a half shares to the quartermaster, and one share to regular seamen. Pirates who were seriously injured in battle received additional shares.

were punishable by death. Five days later, all three mutineers were found guilty. Each was sentenced to be executed. On May 9, 1800, the pirates were hanged, in plain sight of a large crowd of onlookers who attended the execution.

Sources for Further Reading

Broad, William. "Archaeologists Revise Portrait of Buccaneers As Monsters." *The New York Times* (March 4, 1997), pp. C1, C9.

Nash, Jay Robert. *The Encyclopedia of World Crime.* Wilmette, IL: Crime Books, 1990, pp. 216–217.

Platt, Richard. *Pirate.* New York: Alfred A. Knopf, 1994, pp. 20–21.

Ross, Stewart. *Fact or Fiction: Pirates.* Surrey, British Columbia: Copper Beech Books, 1995, pp. 10–11.

Smith, Simon. "Piracy in Early British America." *History Today* (May 1996), pp. 29–37.

Blackbeard
(Edward Teach)

Born: c. 1680
Died: November 22, 1718
AKA: Edward Tach, Tash, Tatch,
Thatch, Drummond

Blackbeard was a legend in his own time. Born in England, he plundered (robbed) ships traveling to and from the American colonies—as well as vessels in the Caribbean. Although his reign of terror lasted only two years, he became one of the best-known sea robbers in all of history.

FROM PRIVATEER TO PIRATE

Edward Teach was probably born somewhere near Bristol, England. Little is known of his early life—except that he went to sea as a young man. As a privateer (legalized pirate) during the War of the Spanish Succession (1701–1713), he plundered ships in the West Indies. When the war ended in 1713, he turned to piracy, like many other former privateers.

By 1716, Teach was serving under the command of Benjamin Thornigold, a pirate captain. On Thornigold's ship, he sailed from the pirate colony of New Providence in the West Indies to the American mainland. The pirates captured a number of ships, whose cargo ranged from flour and wine to silk and gold bullion (gold still in raw or unrefined form). In 1717, after the pirate crew attacked a large merchant ship headed for the French island of Martinique, Teach took over as the captured vessel's captain. Equipping the boat as a warship, he added some forty guns and renamed it the *Queen Anne's Revenge*.

The year after Teach was killed, the *Boston News Letter* published a detailed account of the pirate's last battle. Here it is:

Maynard and Teach themselves began the fight with their swords, Maynard making a thrust, the point of his sword went against Teach's cartridge box, and bended it to the hilt. Teach broke the guard of it, and wounded Maynard's fingers but did not disable him, whereupon he jumped back and threw away his sword and fired his pistol which wounded Teach. Demelt [another sailor] stuck in between them with his sword and cut Teach's face pretty much; in the interim [in the meantime] both companies engaged in Maynard's sloop, one of Maynard's men . . . engaged Teach with his broad sword, who gave Teach a cut on the neck, Teach saying well done lad; [the man] replied If it be not well done, I'll do it better. With that he gave him a second stroke, which cut off his head, laying it flat on his shoulder.

Shortly after Teach became the captain of his own ship, Thornigold gave up piracy. Captain Woodes Rogers, the British-appointed governor of the Bahamas, had been given the power to pardon pirates who agreed to mend their ways. Thornigold—and other members of Blackbeard's circle—sailed to New Providence to accept the King's pardon. Edward Teach, however, had just begun his short but active career as a pirate.

SMOKING BLACK BEARD

A tall man with a booming voice, Teach deliberately developed a terrifying appearance. He had an enormous black beard, which he tied up with black ribbons and twisted into braids. According to some accounts, it covered his entire face and grew down to his waist. Before going into battle, he tucked pieces of hempen rope (rope made from fibers of the hemp plant)—which were soaked in saltpeter and lit—into his hair. The slow-burning chords of rope gave off clouds of thick black smoke that gave him the appearance of a living demon. Captain Charles Johnson, the author of a pirate history that was published six years after Teach's death, wrote what is probably the best-known description of the infamous pirate:

Captain Teach assumed the cognomen [nickname] of Black-beard, from that large quantity of hair, which, like a frightful meteor, covered his whole face, and frightened America more than any comet that has appeared there in a long time.

This beard was black, which he suffered to grow of an extravagant length; as to breadth, it came up to his eyes; he was accustomed to twist it with ribbons, in small tails . . . and turn them about his ears: in time of action, he wore a sling over his shoulders,

Sunken history

In June of 1718, shortly before Teach was captured, his flagship—the *Queen Anne's Revenge,* a 103-foot forty-cannon vessel—became grounded on a sandbar off the coast of North Carolina. It eventually sank, taking with it secrets about the day-to-day existence of one of the world's most infamous sea robbers. But on November 21, 1996, one day before the anniversary of Teach's death in 1718, archaeologists found what they believe to be Teach's long lost flagship.

The wreck of the *Queen Anne's Revenge* probably doesn't contain any of the pirate's treasure. Historians believe that Teach had already hidden most of his loot, and anything else of value could easily have been stashed by the members of his crew as they jumped ship. What is most valuable about the find is the history that it may reveal—such as insights into the daily workings of life aboard a pirate ship. It may also fill in missing pieces about what is known of the eighteenth-century. For example, the chest full of medicines that the pirates received as a ransom payment could provide valuable clues about medicine and health care in Teach's day.

The wreck was discovered in just twenty feet of water two miles off the North Carolina coast near Beaufort, in an area called the "Graveyard of the Atlantic" because of the number of ships that are wrecked there. Towing an underwater metal detector over an eight-square-mile area, a team of archaeologists discovered numerous metal objects—including a bell dated 1709, large anchors, and a number of cannons. It may take four to five years to determine whether the wreck is what remains of the *Queen Anne's Revenge,* but evidence suggests that the submerged vessel is, in fact, the flagship of the infamous Edward Teach.

with three brace of pistols, hanging in holsters like bandoliers [a belt worn over the shoulder]; and stuck lighted matches under his hat, which appearing on each side of his face, his eyes naturally looking fierce and wild, made him altogether such a figure, that imagination cannot form an idea of a fury, from Hell, to look more frightful.

His actions also contributed to his reputation as a monster. He disemboweled (gutted) captives and fed their entrails to the sharks. He cut off the fingers of victims who were too slow to hand over their rings. He sliced up a prisoner's ears—and then forced him to eat them. What's more, he turned on his crew with no forewarning: he shot randomly at the pirates on his ship

A watery legend

After Teach was beheaded in his final battle on the *Jane,* his corpse was thrown into the sea. According to local legend, his headless body swam around the ship before disappearing into its murky grave.

Hidden treasure

According to legend, "Blackbeard's treasure" is buried at various spots along the eastern seaboard. But chances are, there is no such treasure: a typical pirate's plunder consisted of silk, cotton, tools, and assorted sailing supplies. Archaeologists are still hoping to recover the wreck of the *Adventure*—the vessel that carried the pirate to his last battle—and one other ship in his fleet. In those wrecks they hope to find not chests full of gold and jewels but a treasure of information on the age of piracy.

and marooned them when he didn't feel like sharing the bounty. Although there's no telling where the facts end and legend begins, it is probably safe to say that Blackbeard deserved his reputation as "the devil's brother."

THE CHARLESTON BLOCKADE

Like most pirates, there was a seasonal pattern to Teach's voyages. In the warmer months, his crew robbed ships off the coast of Virginia and the Carolinas. Operating out of Oracoke Inlet—off the island of Oracoke in the Outer Banks chain of islands that extends along the coast of North Carolina—his ships anchored in shallow waters that prevented other ships from attacking. As winter approached, Teach headed south, to the warmer climate of the Caribbean. Sailing on board his flagship, the *Queen Anne's Revenge,* he traveled with a fleet of other boats—many of which, like his, had been stolen and converted to pirate boats.

Having spent the winter of 1717 in the Caribbean, Teach's crew landed in Charleston, South Carolina, in the spring of 1718. With three other pirate sloops (small, one-masted ships), the pirates blockaded the city's harbor and attacked any ship that attempted to leave or enter. They also took prisoners and put ashore a landing party that had instructions to bring back medical supplies to treat diseases that plagued the crew. Teach promised to release the prisoners in exchange for the supplies. After he received a chest full of expensive medicine, he made good on his word (but not until after the captives had been robbed of their possessions). The governor of South Carolina described the incident in a report to officials in London, England:

> [The pirates] appeared in sight of the town, took our pilotboat and afterwards 8 or 9 sail with several of the best inhabitants of this place on board and then sent me word if I did not immediately send them a chest of medicines they would put every prisoner to death,

which for their sakes being complied with after plundering them of all they had were sent ashore almost naked. This company is commanded by one Teach alias Blackbeard has a ship of 40 odd guns under him and 3 sloops tenders besides and are in all above 400 men.

A ROYAL PAIN

Shortly after the Charleston blockade, the *Queen Anne's Revenge* sank. Sailing on another ship, a ten-gun vessel called the *Adventure,* Teach headed up the Pamlico River to the town of Bath in North Carolina—in search not of treasure but of a royal pardon. (England's King George I, who reigned from 1714 to 1727, offered to pardon pirates who gave up their profession. As a British colony, North Carolina was able to extend the king's pardon to pirates.) Charles Eden, the governor of North Carolina, granted Teach a pardon, and then ordered the court to declare him a privateer. As a privateer, Teach was able to continue to plunder ships in Carolina waters with no fear of being punished—provided he shared his loot with Governor Eden and his secretary and collector of customs, Tobias Knight. Sailing up and down the Pamlico River, Teach stole from ships he encountered as well as from local plantations.

Unable to appeal to Governor Eden for assistance, local traders asked Thomas Spotswood, the governor of Virginia, for protection from the pirates. In November 1718, Spotswood issued a proclamation offering rewards for the capture—dead or alive—of Teach and his shipmates. He also enlisted the help of British navy officers to organize an expedition to capture the infamous pirate, even though the Carolina shoreline was well beyond his jurisdiction.

BLACKBEARD'S LAST STAND

Under the charge of Lieutenant Robert Maynard, an experienced officer, two ships sailed to the Carolina coast with specific orders to rout the pirates (to search them out and force them

Privateers

During the War of the Spanish Succession between Spain, Britain, and France, many English seamen became privateers. Awarded a "letter of marque," they were given permission to attack Spanish merchant ships on England's behalf. It was, in effect, legalized piracy. But when the Treaty of Utrecht was signed in 1713—ending the War of Succession—many privateers and seamen lost their livelihood. And many, like Edward Teach, turned to piracy.

Walking the plank

Modern historians believe that pirates never really forced their victims to walk the plank--the punishment that has been associated with sea robbers for centuries.

to leave). Because the pirate ships were anchored in shallow waters that were difficult to navigate, Maynard took small vessels that had no guns, which meant his crew would be forced into hand-to-hand combat with knives and swords. Having learned from other seamen that Teach was anchored in a sheltered area off Oracoke Island, Maynard reached the area on the evening of November 21, 1718. Anchoring his ships nearby, he waited until morning to attack.

Maynard's ships—the *Jane* and the *Ranger*—headed for Oracoke Island at dawn. Spotting the approaching ships, the pirates sounded the alarm and pulled in the anchor. Maynard's vessels chased the pirate ships, using oars since there was very little wind to sail by. Navigating shallow waters that were filled with sand bars and submerged obstacles, Maynard's ships ran aground.

Next came a shouting match between the navy lieutenant and the pirate captain. In his pirate history, Captain Johnson describes the exchange:

> Black-Beard hail'd him in this rude Manner: Damn you for Villains, who are you? and from whence come you? The Lieutenant make him Answer, You may see by our Colours [the flags that identified a ship] we are no Pyrates. Black-beard bid him send his Boat on Board, that he might see who he was but Mr Maynard reply'd thus; I cannot spare my Boat, but

Opposite page: The fierce swordfight between Blackbeard, left, and Lieutenant Maynard.

Pirate skills

In order to succeed at sea roving, pirates needed to be familiar with the layout of coastlines—so that they could safely careen their ships (to run a ship ashore in order to clean the bottom of the vessel) or hide from pursuers. Most sailed close to shore, which required a detailed knowledge of the hazards that were hidden in shallow waters. Pirates also needed an understanding of predominating winds to ensure adequate sail-power.

I will come aboard of you as soon as I can, with my Sloop. Upon this Black-beard took a Glass of Liquor, & [and] drank to him with these Words: Damnation seize my Soul if I give you Quarters [a place to stay], or take any from you. In Answer to which, Mr Maynard told him, That he expected no Quarters from him, nor should he give him any.

Eventually, Maynard's crew managed to free its two vessels. Rowing toward Teach's ship, the crew was hit by a broadside volley that killed several men and wounded others. (Broadsides could be devastating: firing at the enemy, a ship discharged all the guns on one side of the boat at once—and at close range.) Maynard ordered the remainder of his crew to conceal itself below deck.

Teach assumed that most of Maynard's men had been killed by the broadside attack. But when he climbed aboard the *Jane,* he was surprised by Maynard's sailors. The fight that followed was Blackbeard's last battle. According to Captain Johnson's account, he "stood his ground and fought with great fury till he received five and twenty wounds." Of Teach's twenty-five wounds, the last was fatal: the pirate had been decapitated (beheaded). Maynard's crew threw Teach's headless corpse overboard—but the bearded head of the infamous pirate was hung from the bowsprit of Maynard's boat as a warning to other sea robbers. (A bowsprit is a large pole projecting from the front of a ship.) It also offered concrete proof of Teach's death—something that made it easier for Maynard to collect the reward on the pirate's head.

Sources for Further Reading

Broad, William. "Archaeologists Revise Portrait of Buccaneers as Monsters." *New York Times* (March 11, 1997), pp. C1, C9.

Cordingly, David. *Under the Black Flag.* New York: Random House, 1995, pp. 13–14, 20–21, 165–166, 191, 194–201.

"Cutthroat Dogs." *Current Events* (May 5, 1997), p. A2+.

"Devil of a Find." *People Magazine* (March 17, 1997), p. 114.

Nash, Jay Robert. *The Encyclopedia of World Crime.* Wilmette, IL: Crime Books, 1990, pp. 387–388.

Pirotta, Saviour. *Pirates and Treasures.* New York: Thomson Learning, 1995, pp. 27–31.

Platt, Richard. *Pirate.* New York: Alfred A. Knopf, 1994, pp. 30–31, 61.

"Sea May Have Yielded a Piece of Pirate Lore." *New York Times* (March 4, 1997), p. A14.

"Yo ho! Treasure!" *Time for Kids* (March 14, 1997), p. 65.

Anne Bonny

Born: c. 1700
Died: ?

Few women have been recorded in the histories of piracy. Because they were forbidden—by a pirate code—to sail on pirate vessels, they hid their identities. After Anne Bonny was captured in a battle with British naval officers, she became widely known—making her one of the few women whose life as a pirate has been documented.

A SAILOR'S WIFE

Born near Cork, Ireland, Bonny was the illegitimate (born out of wedlock) daughter of William Cormac, a successful lawyer. Her mother was the family's housemaid, Peg Brennan. When the scandal of having a baby out of wedlock affected the married attorney's legal practice, he sailed with Brennan and his daughter to America. Settling in Charleston in the British colony of South Carolina, he earned a fortune as a merchant and purchased a large plantation.

Peg Brennan died when Bonny was still a girl. As a teenager she married James Bonny, a poor sailor, against her father's will. Disowned, she was turned out of her father's house. In 1716 she sailed with her husband to the Caribbean island of New Providence, a safe shelter for pirates who preyed on the area's many merchant ships. The Bahama governor, Woodes Rogers, had been charged with ridding the area of pirates to ensure the safety of British ships. In an effort to reduce piracy, Rogers offered rewards to informants who provided information that led to the capture and conviction of pirates. James Bonny worked as a paid informant—an occupation of which his wife strongly disapproved.

WOMAN PIRATE

Governor Rogers soon changed his approach to the pirate problem: he offered a royal pardon to men who agreed to abandon piracy. Pirates flocked to New Providence to take advantage of the governor's amnesty (pardon). Among them was pirate captain John Rackam—known as "Calico Jack" for the colorful clothes he wore. Having arrived in New Providence in 1719, Rackam met Anne Bonny shortly after he accepted a royal pardon.

Bonny left her husband to live with Rackam—who offered to "buy" a divorce from James Bonny (a fairly common but very illegal practice at that time). James Bonny refused and informed the governor of his wife's infidelity. Rogers threatened to have Bonny flogged if she did not return to her husband, which prompted her to run away with Rackam. Together with some of Rackam's old crew, they overpowered the crew of a ship that was harbored at New Providence.

Bonny became a pirate—despite the pirate code that strictly forbade women to sail on pirate ships. Whether she hid the fact that she was a woman is disputed: the ship's quarters offered little privacy, and witnesses claimed that she sometimes wore dresses on board the pirate ship. According to reports, she was a strong and courageous woman who handled a cutlass (short curved sword) and pistol well. Rackam's crew included another woman pirate, Mary Read, who also wore men's clothing and was a brave fighter. The two women became good friends.

ENEMIES OF ENGLAND

Toward the end of summer in 1720, Rackam's crew attacked and boarded a British merchant ship called the *William*.

Pirate hunting

The governor of the Bahamas, Captain Woodes Rogers, was an experienced sea captain who had sailed around the world. Rogers was commissioned by the British government to break up the network of pirates who operated out of the Caribbean island of New Providence. He arrived in the West Indies in 1718 armed with three warships—and a proclamation from England's King George (1660–1727) that gave him the authority to pardon pirates.

Don't break the bargain

Many pirates took advantage of the pardon that Governor Rogers offered to men who swore to abandon their pirate ways. But the price of failure was high: those who continued to pirate ships were rounded up and hung.

Mary Read

Mary Read was born in England. Her father, a sailor, went to sea and never returned. No one knows what happened to him. Read's early life was in some ways similar to Anne Bonny's childhood. Like Bonny, she was probably an illegitimate child. Born after her father had disappeared, she was probably the daughter of a man who had an affair with her mother. Read's mother had another child—a boy—who died just before Read was born. After her son died, Read's mother dressed her daughter as a boy. By having Read pose as her legitimate son, she was able to collect an allowance from her mother-in-law.

Read's grandmother died when she was thirteen years old. With no allowance to help support her, she went to work. Still disguised as a boy, she was employed as a footman to a French woman. (A girl in a similar position would have been employed as a chambermaid.) Read didn't care for the life of a servant. According to Captain Johnson: "Here she did not live long, for growing bold and strong, and having also a roving mind, she entered herself on board a man-of-war [war ship], where she served some

Angered by Rackam's failure to fulfill his part of their pardon, Governor Rogers issued a proclamation that named Rackam—and the two women pirates—as enemies of England. The proclamation stated: "John Rackam and his said Company are hereby proclaimed Pirates and Enemies to the Crown of Great Britain, and are to be so treated and Deem'd by all his Majesty's subjects." The proclamation specifically named Bonny and Read as members of Rackam's "company."

For two months, Rackam's crew sailed on the stolen *William*. They attacked several fishing boats and merchant ships, and headed to the western side of Jamaica. Anchored in Negril Bay, the *William* encountered Captain Jonathon Barnet, who had been commissioned to round up pirates. Suspicious of Rackam's ship, Barnet approached the *William* at about ten o'clock in the evening. Unprepared for a fight, Rackam tried to flee. Barnet's well-armed boat overtook the pirates, and, firing at the ship, wrecked part of the *William*'s rigging (sailing gear), without which it was unable to escape. When Barnet's crew boarded the *William,* Bonny and Read were reportedly the only pirates who fought Barnet and his crew. Rackam and the entire pirate crew were captured and taken to jail.

time: then she quitted it, went over to Flanders and carried arms in a regiment of foot as a cadet." Involved in a number of skirmishes, Read earned praise from her superiors for her bravery.

Read fell in love with a Flemish soldier in her regiment. After their military campaign ended, she revealed her identity to the regiment and married the Flemish soldier. The couple moved to Breda, in the Netherlands, where they opened a pub (bar) called "The Three Horseshoes," whose main customers were officers from their old regiment. Business flourished for a while. But Read's husband died suddenly and the soldiers left Breda shortly thereafter, taking with them most of the pub's business.

Posing again as a man, Read first joined a foot regiment of soldiers and then signed on board a Dutch ship headed for the Caribbean. The ship was taken over by pirates, and she eventually joined the crew led by John "Calico Jack" Rackam. But Read wasn't the only woman sea rover on Rackam's ship: Anne Bonny was a member of the pirate vessel's crew.

UNFINISHED SENTENCES

The pirates were tried in two separate trials. Rackam and ten of his crew men were tried in Spanish Town, Jamaica (known as St. Jago de la Vega), on November 16, 1720. Although they pleaded not guilty to the charges against them, they were all convicted and sentenced to be executed. Within the next two days, all eleven men were hanged. Before he was marched to the gallows, Rackam was reportedly allowed to see Bonny, who told him, "Had you fought like a man, you need not have been hanged like a dog!" After his execution, the body of Rackam was hung from a gibbet (a wooden frame) on Deadman's Cay—in plain view of passing ships.

Less than two weeks later, on November 28, Bonny and Read were tried for piracy. Dorothy Thomas, a witness at the trial, had been on a ship that was attacked by Rackam's crew. The two women pirates, she said, "wore men's jackets, and long trousers, and handkerchiefs tied about their heads," and "each of them had a machete [large heavy knife] and pistol in their hands." Thomas testified that the two women "cursed and swore at the men"—and urged them to kill her. There was no doubt that

Mary Read.

Bonny and Read had been willing participants in piracy. Convicted on two counts of piracy, they were sentenced to be hanged. Sir Nicholas Lawes sentenced them with these words:

You, Mary Read, and Anne Bonny, alias Bonn, are to go from hence to the place from whence you came, and from thence to the place of execution; where you shall be severally [each] hanged by the neck till you are severally dead. And God of his infinite mercy be merciful to both your souls.

Mercy is exactly what Bonny and Read requested from the court. Both claimed to be "quick with child" or pregnant. The judge postponed their execution until after they could be examined to determine whether they were telling the truth. Both women were found to be pregnant, and both escaped execution: under British law, a pregnant woman could not be executed. Read died in prison shortly after the trial, before her child was born. Bonny somehow disappeared from prison, leaving no record of what happened to her or her child.

Sources for Further Reading

Cordingly, David. *Under the Black Flag.* New York: Random House, 1995, pp. 57–65, 71, 177.

Langley, Andrew. *Twenty Names in Crime.* Tarrytown, NY: Marshall Cavendish, 1988, pp. 10–11.

Nash, Jay Robert. *The Encyclopedia of World Crime.* Wilmette, IL: Crime Books, 1990, pp. 432–434.

Nash, Jay Robert. *Look for the Woman, A Narrative Encyclopedia of Female Poisoners, Kidnappers, Thieves, Extortionists, Terrorists, Swindlers, and Spies, from Elizabethan Times to the Present.* New York: M. Evans, 1981, pp. 35–39.

Pirotta, Saviour. *Pirates and Treasures.* New York: Thomson Learning, 1995, pp. 30–31.

Other women pirates

Anne Bonny and Mary Read weren't the only women to become well-known pirates. The following women were notorious sea rovers in other areas of the world:

- Alvilda, the daughter of a Scandinavian king, organized an all-woman crew to avoid a forced marriage to the Danish prince Alf in the fifth century A.D. According to legend, Alvilda's ship ran into pirates who were so impressed by her that they made her their captain. Later, she was so taken by Prince Alf's ability in battle that she married him after all—and became the Queen of Denmark.

- The daughter of an Irish chieftain, Grace O'Malley was born around 1530. She led crews in a number of raids against other chieftains and she sometimes plundered merchant ships.

- Charlotte de Berry (born in England in 1636) dressed in men's clothes and served in the navy with her husband. After being forced on board a ship that was headed for Africa, she led a mutiny and took over the ship. She reportedly cut off the head of the ship's captain, who had assaulted her. De Berry led a number of attacks on gold-laden ships off the coast of Africa.

- Lady Kiligrew—the wife of Sir John Kiligrew, who was the vice-admiral of Cornwall, England—had pirates on both sides of the family. After engaging in a number of other attacks, she took over a German ship anchored in Falmouth harbor in the spring of 1582. Tried and convicted of piracy, she was sentenced to hang. Queen Elizabeth intervened, and Lady Kiligrew's sentence was reduced to a long imprisonment.

- In the early nineteenth century, a woman named Ching Shih led a large pirate fleet that plundered boats in the China Sea. She was in charge of about 1,800 ships—and 80,000 pirates.

Platt, Richard. *Pirate*. New York: Alfred A. Knopf, 1994, pp. 32–33.

Ross, Stewart. *Fact or Fiction, Pirates*. Surrey, British Columbia: Copper Beech, 1995, pp. 18–19.

Charles Gibbs

Born: c. 1800
Died: April 22, 1831

Although he lived almost one hundred years after the "golden age" of piracy, Charles Gibbs was a highly successful pirate who plundered tens of thousands of dollars in goods—and murdered with little hesitation.

A WANTED MAN

Born in Rhode Island at the end of the eighteenth century, Gibbs went to sea as a teenager. As a seaman during the War of 1812 (a conflict between the United States and Great Britain), he sailed with a number of privateers (legalized pirates), earning a reputation as an able fighter. Later, as a privateer aboard an Argentinean ship, Gibbs looted ships in the Caribbean.

By 1821 Gibbs had crossed the fine line that distinguished privateers from pirates. After signing on as a member of a ship's crew, he determined how he could best profit from his position. Taking advantage of a ship's brief stays in various ports, he stole goods and returned on board. If his ship carried valuable stock, he organized a mutiny (open rebellion against authority). With a help of a few other sailors, he typically murdered the captain and first mate—and any others who presented a threat to him.

Having become a notorious pirate, Gibbs was hunted by the U.S. Navy. The *Enterprise,* a military ship headed by Lieutenant Commander Lawrence Kearney, took over four of the pirate's ships—but Gibbs remained at large. With a hideout in Cuba, Gibbs captured ships throughout the Caribbean and reportedly led a comfortable life in New York City between sea rovings.

Gibbs eluded capture for more than ten years and earned a reputation as a fierce opponent as well as a dangerous ally (a person who joins forces with another). Rumors of his gruesome acts abounded: he was said to have set fire to an entire ship with the crew on board. And he was credited with having cut off the arms and legs of a captain who opposed him. After his capture, Gibbs bragged that by scaring off his co-pirates he was often able to keep all the stolen goods for himself. He also supposed that he had murdered some 400 victims, although historians believe his claim to be exaggerated.

PUBLIC HANGING

On November 1, 1830, Gibbs signed on board the *Vineyard* for a voyage from New Orleans, Louisiana, to Philadelphia, Pennsylvania. Just off Cape Hatteras, North Carolina, Gibbs organized a mutiny. Together with Thomas G. Wansley, the ship's cook, and three others, he took over the leadership of the *Vineyard* by murdering the captain, William Thornby, and first mate William Roberts. The pirates seized the ship's cargo. Valued at $50,000, it was Gibbs's biggest haul.

As the *Vineyard* sailed toward Philadelphia, the bodies of Thornby and Roberts were thrown overboard. Near Long Island, New York, the pirates scuttled (sank) the ship and headed inland. (Pirates scuttled ships by making holes in the bottom of the vessel. They often scuttled stolen ships they wanted to abandon.) The three sailors who had joined in the mutiny went to the authorities, claiming that they had joined Gibbs because they feared for their lives. Shortly thereafter, Gibbs and Wansley were captured and tried. In a sentence pronounced on March 11, 1831, the two were found guilty of murder and piracy.

Here's a book you might like:

Treasure Island, 1883, by Robert Louis Stevenson

Young Jim Hawkins is invited to serve as the cabin boy on a schooner headed for Treasure Island. Hawkins overhears some of the sailors—including the smooth-talking ship's cook, Long John Silver—as they plot a mutiny. But before he can warn the others, Treasure Island comes into view, and the ship's crew, armed with a map, scramble off to find the hidden treasure.

The hempen jig

Hanging was the traditional punishment for pirates. Wooden gallows were usually built for each hanging. Gallows were simple structures made of two upright beams that were joined at the top by a crossbeam. Hung from the crossbeam was the hangman's noose. Helped by the executioner, the prisoner stepped up a ladder that was leaned against the gallows. After the executioner placed the noose around the prisoner's neck, he awaited a signal—and then pushed the prisoner off the ladder.

The hanged man then fell until the rope became tight, which either broke his neck or slowly strangled him to death. Hanging was sometimes called "dancing the hempen jig" because hanged men sometimes "danced"—or convulsed—at the end of the hempen rope (rope made from fibers of the hemp plant) as they died. Sometimes a victim's friends or relatives pulled on his legs in order to hasten death. In some cases, such as the execution of the infamous Captain Kidd, the rope broke, and the half-dead pirate was forced to be hanged a second time.

In England and the colonies, pirates were hanged at the low-tide mark to indicate that their crimes had been committed under the jurisdiction of the Admiralty. Public hangings attracted large crowds, who gathered on the shore and in boats. A pirate's final words and confessions made interesting reading: they were usually printed and sold in the days following the execution.

Urged to confess before he died, Gibbs recounted a long series of horrible murders and other misdeeds, some of which he made up. Many of the terrible deeds he described, however, were true, and the pirate's final confession was printed in New York newspapers. On April 22, 1831, in front of thousands of people who watched from boats, Gibbs and Wansley were hanged on Ellis Island, New York. After the hanging, their corpses were given to the College of Physicians and Surgeons to be dissected (cut up for scientific examination).

Sources for Further Reading

Cordingly, David. *Under the Black Flag.* New York: Random House, 1995, pp. 145–146, 223–240.

Nash, Jay Robert. *The Encyclopedia of World Crime.* Wilmette, IL: Crime Books, 1990, p. 1307.

Pirotta, Saviour. *Pirates and Treasures.* New York: Thomson Learning, 1995, pp. 36–37.

Platt, Richard. *Pirate.* New York: Alfred A. Knopf, 1994, pp. 56–57.

Sifakis, Carl. *The Encyclopedia of American Crime.* New York: Facts on File, 1982, pp. 281–282.

MURDER

Boston Massacre Trials: 1770

Defendants: Captain Thomas Preston; Corporal William Wemms; Privates Hugh White, John Carroll, William Warren, Matthew Killroy, William McCauley, James Hartegan, and Hugh Montgomery

Crimes Charged: Murder and accessories to murder

Chief Defense Lawyers: Both trials: John Adams and Josiah Quincy Jr.; first trial: Robert Auchmuty; second trial: Sampson Salter Blowers

Chief Prosecutors (Attorneys for the Crown): Samuel Quincy and Robert Treat Paine

Judges: John Cushing, Peter Oliver, Benjamin Lynd, and Edmund Trowbridge

Place: Boston, Massachusetts Bay Colony

Dates of Trials: *Rex v. Preston:* October 24–30, 1770; *Rex v. Wemms et al.:* November 27–December 5, 1770

Verdicts: First trial: Captain Preston, not guilty; second trial: Corporal Wemms, Privates White, Carroll, Warren, McCauley, and Hartegan, not guilty; Privates Killroy and Montgomery, not guilty of murder but guilty of manslaughter

Sentences: Branding on the thumbs for Killroy and Montgomery

SIGNIFICANCE: This case was a landmark on the road to the American Revolution. Despite a politically hostile atmosphere, two reasonably fair trials were conducted and the right of self-defense was upheld.

MURDER

On the night of March 5, 1770, three men lay dead and two more were dying, following shots fired by British troops into an angry crowd outside of the Custom House in Boston, Massachusetts. This scene, known as the Boston Massacre, came after months of conflict between Bostonians and the British soldiers sent to the city to protect newly appointed British Customs commissioners. The English king and his advisors viewed Boston as a birthplace of disagreement in the colonies, where hostility increased in the years following the French and Indian War. Quarrels arose over Indian and frontier affairs, import rules, and taxes—especially the

An engraving of the Boston Massacre by Paul Revere, 1770.

British Parliament's tax on the American colonies. Boston, with its unusually stormy Stamp Act riots, seemed to be the center of American political unrest.

B o s t o n
M a s s a c r e
T r i a l s : 1 7 7 0

Although some British troops had remained in the colonies after the Revolutionary War (1775–1783), the placement of a large number of troops in a colonial city was a new and unwelcome development. In the eighteenth century, British citizens and colonists viewed the existence of a war-ready army during peace time as trouble. The British troops in Boston seemed proof that colonists' civil rights and the powers of their political organizations were being ignored.

In such an atmosphere, trouble was certain. Rude behavior, shoving matches, loud arguments, and occasional fistfights occurred between Boston residents and the British soldiers almost from the first day troops arrived in the fall of 1768.

Snowballs, then Musket Balls, Fly

The series of events that led to the clash on March 5, 1770, apparently began with a nasty exchange between Private Patrick Walker of the Twenty-Ninth Regiment and William Green, a local rope-maker.

Soldiers of low rank, who were paid very little, often made additional money with odd jobs. As Walker passed Green on March 2, the rope-maker asked the soldier if he wanted work. When Walker said yes, Green told him to clean his outhouse (outdoor bathroom). Insulted, Walker swore revenge. He walked away and, in a few minutes, returned with several other soldiers.

A fight broke out between soldiers and rope-makers, who had rallied in support of Green. Clubs and sticks were used, as well as fists. The rope-makers won out over the soldiers.

However, the calm after that incident was brief. Fights popped up over the next two days. Rumors flew and tensions mounted. The commander of the Twenty-Ninth Regiment, Lieutenant Colonel Maurice Carr, wrote to Acting Governor Thomas Hutchinson to complain of the abuse his men were forced to take from the citizens of Boston. On March 5, Hutchinson put the letter before his council. Council members all agreed that the people of the town would not be satisfied until the troops were removed.

The evening of March 5 was cold, and a foot of snow lay on the ground. A wig-maker's helper named Edward Garrick insulted Private Hugh White, who was on guard at a watchman's box near the Main Guard, the army's headquarters. White struck Garrick on the head with a musket. Nevertheless, other helpers continued to taunt White and throw snowballs at him.

Cries of "fire" could be heard in the streets, although no buildings were burning that night. Soldiers on Brattle Street carried clubs, bayonets, and other weapons. In Boylston's Alley, a volley of snowballs and insults was halted by a passing officer, who led the British troops to nearby Murray's barracks, where he told their junior officers to keep them inside. Outside the barracks, more angry words were exchanged before Richard Palmes, a Boston merchant, persuaded many members of the crowd to go home. Still, some of the crowd shouted that they should go "away to the Main Guard."

The Crowd Gathers

At about the same time, 200 people gathered in an area called Dock Square. More people joined them as groups flowed in from Boston's North End. Some came carrying clubs. Others picked up whatever weapons they could find in the square. The crowd eventually gathered around a tall man who urged the crowd to storm the Main Guard.

Meanwhile, White retreated from his guard's box near the Main Guard to the steps of the Custom House. From there, he threatened to fire on the approaching crowd and called for the assistance of other soldiers.

When news of the watchman's situation reached Captain Thomas Preston, he led a small group from the Twenty-Eighth Regiment to White's rescue. With bayonets ready, two groups of soldiers managed to reach Private White. When the troops prepared to leave, however, the chances of retreating through the angry crowd appeared more difficult. The soldiers positioned themselves in a semicircle, facing the crowd, with their captain in front of them. Their muskets were loaded. Some in the crowd dared them to fire. Finally, someone hurled a club, knocking down soldier Hugh Montgomery. As he got to his feet, someone ordered the men to fire. Montgomery fired one shot. No one seemed to be hit, and the crowd pulled away from the troops. There was a pause during which Captain Preston might have given an order to cease firing. The pause between the first shot and those that followed could have been as little as six seconds or as long as two minutes, according to witnesses' accounts.

The Massacre Begins

However long the pause, the troops began firing. In the confusion that followed, most people in the crowd believed the soldiers were firing only powder, not bullets. However, two men were hit almost immediately. Samuel Gray fell, shot in the head. A sailor known as Michael Johnson (real name Crispus Attucks) took two bullets in the chest. As some members of the crowd surged forward to prevent further firing, another sailor, James Caldwell, was hit.

A bullet struck seventeen-year-old Samuel Maverick as he ran toward the Town House. He died several hours later at his mother's boarding house. The fifth death was Patrick Carr. Struck in the hip he died nine days later. His dying testimony later helped strengthen the defense attorneys' claim that the soldiers fired in self-defense.

Captain Preston yelled at his men, demanding to know why they had fired. The reply was they thought he had ordered them to shoot when they heard the word "fire." As the crowd, which had fallen back, began to help those who had fallen, the troops again raised their muskets. Preston commanded them to cease fire and went down the line pushing up their musket barrels. The crowd dispersed, carrying the wounded, the dying, and the dead. Captain Preston and his men marched back to the Main Guard. The Boston Massacre was over.

Following a brief interview with Captain Preston, Royal Governor Hutchinson promised a full investigation. He said "The law shall have its course; I will live and die by the law." Thus, the Crown began an investigation into the Boston Massacre.

The Redcoats Are Indicted

That very night, two justices of the peace went to the council chamber, where they spent the next several hours calling up witnesses. By morning, Captain Preston and his eight men had been locked up. A week later, a grand jury was sworn in, and, at the request of Attorney General Jonathan Sewall, Preston and his men were officially charged.

Sewall, a loyalist committed to Britain, busied himself with legal affairs out of town, leaving the prosecution of the soldiers to whomever the royal court appointed. The disappointing choice was another loyalist, Samuel Quincy, the colony's solicitor general. To strengthen the prosecution, radicals led by Samuel Adams persuaded Bostonians at a town meeting to pay the prosecution's expenses, thus making it possible to bring in the successful lawyer Robert Treat Paine.

The choice of loyalist Robert Auchmuty to serve as the senior counsel for Captain Preston was no surprise, but the other two attorneys who agreed to act for the defense were Josiah Quincy Jr. (brother of the prosecutor Samuel Quincy), a fiery radical, and John Adams, who was just as offended as his cousin Samuel Adams by the presence of the king's troops in Boston. For the trial of the soldiers, Auchmuty dropped out, and Adams became senior counsel, with Sampson Salter Blowers as junior counsel.

The decision on whether to hold one trial or two was not announced until the last minute. The troops wanted to be tried with Captain Preston. They believed separate trials would lessen their chances of being found not guilty. If Preston were tried first and found not guilty, the result would indicate that his men were responsible for firing without orders. Additionally, if the Captain and his men were tried together, the prosecution would have a difficult time proving that a bullet from one specific gun, fired by one specific soldier, had hit one specific victim. In the end, though, it was decided there would be two separate trials: the first for Captain Preston, the second for the troops.

Captain Preston's Trial

The captain's trial began October 24, 1770, and was over by October 30, 1770. Even so, it was the first criminal trial in Massachusetts to last longer than a day. Samuel Quincy opened for the prosecution and called as his first witness Edward Garrick, the wig-maker whose taunts had ended with his being struck by Private Hugh White. After describing this incident, Garrick testified that he had seen soldiers in the streets carrying swords before Preston had led his men to the Custom House. The next witness, Thomas Marshall, supported that statement, adding that Preston most certainly did have time to order his men to cease fire after the first shot was fired.

Witnesses who followed also gave damaging testimony. Peter Cunningham said that Preston had ordered his men to load their muskets. Later, he changed his statement slightly, saying that the man who had ordered the troops to fire was definitely an officer because of the way he was dressed. Witnesses William Wyatt and John Cox both insisted that Preston had given the order to fire.

On the following day, the prosecution had a setback. Witness Theodore Bliss said Preston had been standing in front of the guns. Bliss heard someone shouting "Fire," but he did not think it was the captain. Henry Knox testified that the crowd was shouting, "Fire, damn your blood, fire." Meanwhile, Benjamin Burdick said he heard the word "fire" come from behind the men.

The prosecution regained some ground with witness Daniel Calef, who stated that he had "looked the officer in the face when he gave the word" to fire. The next witness, Robert Goddard, also stated firmly that Preston, standing behind his men, had given the order to fire.

The first three witnesses for the defense testified to the threats uttered against the soldiers by those in the street. According to one witness, Edward Hill, after the firing, he saw Preston push up a musket and say, "Fire no more. You have done mischief enough."

On the following day, a string of witnesses clearly described the confusion and anger that dominated the scene on March 5. The first witness for the defense, John Edwards, stated firmly that it was the corporal, William Wemms, who had given the men the order to load their muskets. Another, Joseph Hilyer, said, "The soldiers seemed to act from pure nature . . . I mean they acted and fired by themselves."

Chief defense lawyer John Adams.

Reasonable Doubt

Richard Palmes testified that he had placed his hand on Preston's shoulder just as the order to fire was given. At the time, the two men were in front of the troops. Even though he was standing right next to Preston, Palmes could not be sure whether Preston or someone else had given the order. Palmes' testimony threw a strong reasonable doubt on the Crown's case.

Another major witness for the defense was a slave named Andrew. In great detail, Andrew described the explosive scene on March 5 and testified that the voice that gave the order to fire was different from the other voices calling out at the time. He was sure the voice had come from beyond Preston.

When John Gillespie took the stand, he testified about an event that occurred at least two hours before the massacre. He spoke of seeing a group of townspeople carrying swords, sticks, and clubs, coming from the South End area. The tone of Gillespie's testimony implied a "plot" to expel the troops from Boston.

In presenting closing arguments, defense attorney Adams spoke first. He said, "Self-defence is the primary canon [rule] of the law of nature," and he explained how a homicide was justifiable when an assaulted man had nowhere to retreat. Carefully reviewing the evidence, Adams demolished the Crown's weakly presented case.

In his closing argument for the prosecution, Paine, in an effort to dismiss the idea of self-defense, pointed out that defense witness Palmes had been standing in front of the soldiers' muskets. "Would he place himself before a party of soldiers and risque his life at the muzzles of their guns," Paine reasoned, "when he thought them under a necessity of firing to defend their life?"

The court adjourned at 5:00 P.M. on Monday. By 8:00 A.M. on Tuesday, the jury had reached a verdict. Preston was found not guilty.

The Soldiers' Trial

One month later at the soldiers' trial, the Crown's first witnesses testified about the behavior of troops—who may or may not have been among those on trial—in the hours before the massacre. Prosecution witnesses spoke of off-duty officers, armed with swords, running through the streets and assaulting citizens without reason.

The prosecution seemed to be widening the focus of the trial by describing criminal acts by soldiers unconnected with the massacre itself. This was a questionable move since testimony about other soldiers was not important for the case being tried. Of the Crown's first witnesses, only one made a major point. The town watchman, Edward Langford, described the death of a citizen, John Gray. According to Langford, Gray had definitely been shot by Private Matthew Killroy.

The following day the Crown's witnesses faltered. James Brewer, who denied that the crowd had uttered any threats against the soldiers, admitted that people all around were calling "fire." Asked if he had thought the cry referred to a fire or if it was an order for soldiers to fire, Brewer answered that he could not "tell now what I thought then."

Another witness, James Bailey, stated clearly that boys in the street had pelted the soldiers with pieces of ice large enough to hurt them. Bailey also stated that Private Montgomery had been knocked down and that he had seen Crispus Attucks carrying "a large cord-wood stick."

Like the prosecution's witnesses, the first defense witnesses spoke of extreme behavior throughout the town. A picture emerged of a possible riot in the making. The testimony of William Hunter, an auctioneer who had seen the tall man speaking to the crowd in Dock Square, suggested that some of the crowd's activities may have been organized rather than unprepared. For two days, the defense presented solid evidence that the soldiers at the Custom House had been threatened by a dangerous crowd.

In his closing remarks, Quincy pointed out that even a "moderate" person might seek revenge on the soldiers at the Custom House for the actions of soldiers elsewhere in the town that night. Still, the law did not permit this. The evidence demonstrated that the troops had acted in self-defense.

In his closing summary, which was a brilliant blend of law and politics, John Adams placed much of the blame on "Mother England." He pointed out, "At certain critical seasons, even in the mildest government, the people are liable to run into riots and tumults [disorder]." The possibility of such events "is in direct proportion to the [absolute rule] of the government." Adams turned his attention to a description of the crowd. "And why we should [hesitate] to call such a set of people a mob? . . . Soldiers quartered in a populous town, will always [cause] two mobs, where they prevent one. They are wretched conservators of the peace."

After over two hours of deliberation, the jury found Corporal William Wemms and Privates White, Warren, Carroll, McCauley, and Hartegan not guilty of all charges. Privates Killroy and Montgomery were found not guilty of murder but guilty of manslaughter. The evidence had shown that these two men had definitely shot their weapons. There was not enough evidence to prove which of the other soldiers had fired.

On December 14, 1770, Killroy and Montgomery returned to court for sentencing. They cited "benefit of clergy," a plea for pity originally created for members of religious orders, but later extended to those who could read and write. The court granted the request, and Killroy and Montgomery were branded on the thumbs and released from custody.

CRISPUS ATTUCKS

Crispus Attucks, the first American to die in the Boston Massacre, was born in Framingham, Massachusetts, around 1723. He was enslaved to Deacon William Brown. Although not much is known about Attucks' early life, he apparently escaped from slavery at age twenty-seven, going to work on the whale ships docked along Massachusetts' east coast. He seemed to be a leader who could quickly inspire large numbers of people to action. When the crowd of Americans—both black and white—gathered around the British barracks on March 5, Attucks was in the lead, urging the others forward. When the soldiers ordered the crowd to leave, Attucks convinced them to remain. Then the crowd heard from a man who claimed that a British guard had hit him with a musket. Furious, the crowd surged forward, Attucks in the lead. According to one witness, he actually hit one of the armed British soldiers.

In the fighting that followed, Attucks was shot and killed instantly. Attucks' fame lasted long after his death. Before the Civil War, African American military companies took the name of the "Attucks Guards." From 1858 to 1870, African Americans living in Boston held a Crispus Attucks Day. A Crispus Attucks statue was erected on the Boston Common by the black Boston community in 1888.

The mystery of who actually gave the order to fire was solved after the trials. Shortly before he left Boston, Private Montgomery admitted to his lawyers that it was he who cried "fire" after he had been knocked down by a stick.

The massacre and the following trials persuaded the British that the presence of their troops in Boston was more likely to cause a rebellion than prevent it. Although British troops were soon withdrawn from the city, American patriots continued to refer to the massacre as evidence that the British could not be trusted and to urge their fellow colonists toward rebellion.

Suggestions for Further Reading

Hansen, Harry. *The Boston Massacre: An Episode of Dissent and Violence.* New York: Hastings House, 1970.

Middlekauff, Robert. *The Glorious Cause, The American Revolution, 1763–1789.* New York: Oxford University Press, 1982.

Millender, Dharathula H. *Crispus Attucks, Black Leader of Colonial Patriots.* New York: Aladdin Books, 1986.

Zobel, Hiller B. *The Boston Massacre.* New York: W. W. Norton & Company, 1970.

Charlotte Corday Trial:
1793

Defendant: Charlotte Corday d'Armont
Crime Charged: Murder
Chief Defense Lawyer: Chauveau de la Garde
Chief Prosecutor: Antoine Fouquier-Tinville
Judge: Jacques Montané
Place: Paris, France
Dates of Trial: July 13–17, 1793
Verdict: Guilty
Sentence: Death by guillotine

SIGNIFICANCE: Charlotte Corday's killing of the political leader Jean-Paul Marat began a new and more destructive phase of the Reign of Terror in revolutionary France. To supporters of the king and moderate opponents of the radical Jacobin Party, she became a heroine and a martyr (one who chooses suffering or death instead of giving up their religion or principles).

People fleeing for safety poured into the town of Caen in the Normandy region of France in the late spring of 1793. Members of the violently revolutionary Jacobin party had driven their political opponents out of Paris. These Girondins, members of a moderate republican party, were filling the prisons and providing a steady stream of victims for the new government many called the Reign of Terror because of the enormous number of executions of those believed to be "enemies of the state." In Caen and other local towns, Girondin leaders hoped to regroup, rally, and recruit an army for a march on Paris.

Charlotte Corday was guillotined on July 17, 1793, for the stabbing death of Jacobin leader Jean-Paul Marat.

The Jacobins rose to power after the overthrow of King Louis XVI and his queen, Marie Antoinette. However, their Girondin rivals had reason to believe this rise would not last long. In the cities of Lyons, Marseille, and Toulon, moderate political groups were in revolt against the radicals who held power in Paris. Social and economic conditions were becoming desperate: unemployment had risen, prices were shooting upward, food and other necessities of life were in short supply. Also, the Jacobins' extreme behavior—arrests, blackmail, and an unending series of beheadings by guillotine—had turned many ordinary people away from the revolution.

The Making of an Assassin

In Caen during the summer of 1793, Charlotte Corday d'Armont read newspapers, listened to what others had to say, and decided to act. Born into a family of minor Norman nobility, she was a distant descendant of the playwright Pierre Corneille. Corday was convent-educated, and brought up on the classic works of Plutarch, Voltaire, and Rousseau. She became a champion of the Republic, which she saw as the means of changing France into a country with a better sense of right and wrong. The Jacobins, she believed, were destroying the revolution.

Horrible stories of the Reign of Terror were told in Caen, a center of Girondin strength in mid-1793. Norman leaders wrote a proclamation (public announcement) condemning the revolutionary ruling authority, the Convention, as a "conspiratorial commune engorged with blood and gold." The Girondin press in Caen identified the worst culprit as Marat, the most well-known and bloodthirsty of all the Jacobins:

> Let Marat's head fall and the Republic is saved. Purge France of this man of blood. Marat sees the Public Safety only in a river of blood; well then his own must flow, for his head must fall to save two hundred thousand others.

So Charlotte Corday, twenty-four years old, decided to become a patriotic avenger (one who acts in revenge), a martyr in the Republican cause. "One can die but once," she wrote a friend, "and what consoles me for the horror of our situation is that no one will lose in losing me."

She had a personal motive as well. As her mother lay dying in childbirth in 1782, the priest of the church of Saint-Gilles in Caen, the Abbé Gombault, had given her the last rites. Eleven years later, the Jacobins had forced him from his church, threatened to send him out of the country, and finally arrested him. On April 5, 1793, the Abbé Gombault became the first resident of Caen to go to the guillotine, and Corday sought to avenge his death.

The Killing

Jean-Paul Marat had risen to great power by the summer of 1793. He had been a scientist and doctor before the revolution, interested in the science of vision, flying, and electrical therapy. Europe's popular scientists had not taken his medical talents seriously. With the upheaval of 1789, Marat found his true vocation at last—as well as a means of avenging himself on an ungrateful group of people who had held power for too long. He became a revolutionary writer, the editor of *L'Ami du Peuple,* through which he expressed his anger. Marat's birdlike facial appearance led his friends to compare him to an eagle. To his enemies, he was a vulture.

In July 1793, Marat was suffering intensely from an illness that caused his skin to break out all over his body. He could find relief only in a cool bath, and so he had the tub in the bathroom of his apartment made into an office.

On July 9, Corday boarded a coach in Caen, and arrived in Paris two days later. On the morning of the 13th, a bright, hot Saturday, she set out

Jean-Paul Marat, who was stabbed to death by Charlotte Corday on July 13, 1793.

for the Palais-Royal, stopping at a shop to buy a hat, a dark hat with green ribbons. At another shop she bought a wooden-handled kitchen knife with a five-inch blade.

She had hoped to kill Marat in front of his accomplices. Instead, she had to settle for a visit to his apartment. She took a carriage there, arriving around 11:30 A.M. A woman turned her away at the door, saying Marat was too ill to receive callers. Corday wrote him a brief and interesting note, saying she brought evidence of plans to overthrow the escaped Girondins.

Corday returned at 7:00 P.M. with another note requesting to see Marat. This time, in the confusion of deliveries of newspapers and bread, she managed to reach the head of the stairs before anyone stopped her. She began to speak in a loud voice about treason in Caen, hoping Marat would overhear.

"Let her in," he called out from the bath.

She pulled a chair up next to the tub. For a quarter of an hour they discussed plots to remove the Jacobins from authority, and Corday supplied Marat with a list of the Caen residents who plotted against them. "Good," he told her. "In a few days I will have them all guillotined."

At these words, Corday drew the knife from the top of her dress and plunged the blade into Marat's chest. He sank into the water, now red from the blood pouring from his wound. When he called out, an aide rushed in and threw a chair at the assassin. A neighbor who had heard the cry rushed in from across the street and tried to stop the bleeding. However, within a few minutes Marat was dead.

MURDER

Trial and Execution

Revolutionary justice was swift. Six policemen questioned Corday in Marat's apartment immediately after the killing. She made no attempt to deny her responsibility. She had come from Caen for the sole purpose of killing Jean-Paul Marat, she said, and she had acted alone.

An angry crowd gathered to shout for Corday's death as the police led her from Marat's house to a cell in the Abbaye prison. There, and later in the Conciergerie prison, she continued to claim that she had not been part of a plot, that she had neither needed nor sought help to carry out her assassin's mission.

All the same, the judges of the court, the Revolutionary Tribunal, were certain there were other people involved. "It has been mathematically demonstrated that this monster to whom nature has given the form of a woman is an envoy of. . . all the other conspirators of Caen," the Jacobin Georges Couthon insisted. However, Corday would admit only to having read Girondin newspapers.

"Was it from those newspapers that you learned that Marat was an anarchist?" asked Jacques Montané, the tribunal president.

"Yes, I knew that he was perverting France. I have killed one man to save a hundred thousand. I was a republican well before the Revolution and I have never lacked energy," said Corday.

Montané wondered whether she had practiced before attacking Marat. At first angered by the question, she then admitted it had been a lucky blow.

"Who were the persons who counseled you to commit this murder?" he went on.

"I would never have committed such an attack on the advice of others," she repeated. "I alone conceived the plan and executed it."

Finally, Montané asked Corday what she thought she had achieved: "Do you think you have killed all the Marats?"

"With this one dead, the others, perhaps, will be afraid."

The court moved swiftly to convict and condemn her. Dressed in the red shirt of an assassin, she wrote her last letters from her cell in the Conciergerie prison. "I beg you to forget me or rather rejoice at my fate," she wrote her father. "The cause is good." The executioner came for her in the early evening of July 17. She stood upright in the wagon that was to carry her to her death, knees braced against the tailgate, all the way to the scaffold. A man named Pierre Notelet stood among the street crowds to see her pass. Her image haunted him for a long time.

"THE FRIEND OF THE PEOPLE"

Jean-Paul Marat was known for the newspaper he founded, *L'Ami du peuple,* which is French for "the friend of the people." His publication was devoted to attacking those in power in the name of the poor and powerless. In the political fighting of the French Revolution, Marat found himself outlawed. In 1790 and 1791 he had to flee to England. He also hid in the Paris sewers, which made his skin disease worse. Even while he was in hiding, however, Marat continued to publish his revolutionary writings. Marat was later portrayed in a 1964 play by Peter Weiss, *The Persecution and Assassination of Jean-Paul Marat as Performed by the Inmates of the Asylum of Charenton Under the Direction of the Marquis de Sade,* most often known simply as *Marat/Sade.*

"Her beautiful face was so calm that one would have said she was a statue," Notelet recalled. "For eight days I was in love with Charlotte Corday."

Suggestions for Further Reading

Dobson, Austin. *Four Frenchwomen.* Freeport, NY: Books for Libraries Press, 1972.

Doyle, William. *The Oxford History of the French Revolution.* Oxford: Clarendon Press, 1989.

Schama, Simon. *Citizens: A Chronicle of the French Revolution.* New York: Alfred A. Knopf, 1989.

Wilson, Robert McNair. *Women of the French Revolution.* Port Washington, NY: Kennikat Press, 1970.

Hester Vaughan Trial: 1868

Defendant: Hester Vaughan
Crime Charged: First-degree murder
Chief Defense Lawyer: John Guforth
Chief Prosecutor: No record
Judge: James Riley Ludlow
Place: Philadelphia, Pennsylvania
Dates of Trial: June 10–July 2, 1868
Verdict: Guilty
Sentence: Death

SIGNIFICANCE: More than a century before the United States Supreme Court ruled that women's systematic exclusion from state juries was unconstitutional, women's rights leaders protested a teenage girl's murder conviction without "a trial by a jury of her peers," that is, without a woman's presence on the jury.

In the middle of the nineteenth century, Hester Vaughan left her native England for the United States to marry her American fiancé. A year and a half later, Vaughan discovered that her husband, Harris, had another wife and family. Then he left her. Too ashamed to return to England, Vaughan took back her family name and moved to Philadelphia, Pennsylvania, where she took a job as a housekeeper. A member of her employer's household raped her and she became pregnant. Shamed once more, she left the household, rented a small room, and took in sewing while she waited for her baby to be born.

Elizabeth Cady Stanton, first president of the National Woman Suffrage Association, helped raise funds for Hester Vaughan when the teen was convicted of murder in 1868.

What happened next is not entirely clear. However, on February 8 or 9, 1868, Hester Vaughan gave birth. At the time she was poorly nourished and living alone in an unheated room. Two days later, she asked another resident of the building for a box in which to place her dead baby. Vaughan asked the other woman not to tell anyone about her secret. However, Vaughan's neighbor informed the police. Lawmen immediately arrested Vaughan, charging her with murder.

Tried for Murder

Hester Vaughan's murder trial began on June 30, 1868. The prosecution called several witnesses to the stand to present the case against her. The *Philadelphia Inquirer* summarized their testimony:

> [Vaughan] explained [to the resident from whom she requested a box] that she had been frightened by a lady going into the room with a cup of coffee, and fallen back upon her child, thus killing it. . . . Dr. Shapleigh [of the Coroner's office, charged with investigating the baby's death], who examined the body, found several fractures of the skull, made apparently with some blunt instrument, and also clots

MURDER

of blood between the brain and skull. The lady who took the coffee to the prisoner heard the child give one or two faint cries.

The state of Pennsylvania then rested its case against Vaughan. Judge James Riley Ludlow ordered Vaughan's lawyer, John Guforth, to present the defense witnesses the next morning. However, although Vaughan had given Guforth her last few dollars for his fee, he did not even bother to interview her before the trial. All Guforth presented the next day were a few witnesses who testified as to Vaughan's good character. Guforth added little in summing up Vaughan's case for the jury. He said only that, "the prisoner should not be convicted of murder in the first degree, because in the agony and pain she must have suffered, she may have been bereft of all reason." Thus providing an explanation for his failure to call Vaughan herself as a witness, he added only that the baby's death might have been accidental. Not surprisingly, Vaughan was convicted of first-degree murder and sentenced to death.

Women to the Rescue

Two of America's first female doctors took an immediate interest in Vaughan's case. Dr. Susan A. Smith visited Vaughan in Moyamensing prison in Philadelphia. After interviewing the prisoner several times and performing a medical examination, Smith wrote to Pennsylvania Governor John W. Geary. Of Vaughan's pregnancy, labor, and delivery, Smith said:

> [Hester Vaughan] rented a third story room . . . from a family who understood very little English. . . . She was taken sick in this room at midnight on the 6th of February and lingered until Sunday morning, the eighth, when her child was born, she told me she was nearly frozen and fainted or went to sleep for a long time. You will please remember, sir, throughout this period of agony she was alone, without nourishment or fire. . . . My professional opinion in Hester Vaughan's case is that cold and want of attention produced painful and protracted

labor—that the mother, in endeavoring to assist herself, injured the head of her child at birth—that she either fainted or had a convulsion, and was insensible for a long time.

Both Smith and another female physician, Clemence Lozier, doubted that anyone had heard the child cry. They believed the baby was born dead.

Governor Geary did not respond to Smith's request that Vaughan be pardoned. Then women's rights leaders Susan B. Anthony and Elizabeth Cady Stanton stepped in, along with members of the Working Women's National Association. They held a meeting at New York City's Cooper Institute to protest Vaughan's conviction. Stanton and Anthony strongly objected to Vaughan's "condemn[ation] on insufficient evidence and with inadequate defense." They also voiced their objections to the nineteenth-century ban on women serving on juries and voting. The crowd in attendance voted unanimously to appeal to Governor Geary for either a pardon or a new trial for Vaughan.

Women's rights advocate Susan B. Anthony.

WOMEN'S LEGAL RIGHTS

Eight years before Hester Vaughan's trial, one of her supporters, Elizabeth Cady Stanton, had addressed the New York State legislature, urging equal legal rights for women:

> Just imagine an inhabitant of another planet entertaining himself some pleasant evening in searching over our great national compact, our Declaration of Independence, our Constitutions, or some of our statute-books; what would he think of those 'women and Negroes' that must be so fenced in, so guarded against? Why, he would certainly suppose we were monsters, like those fabulous giants or Brobdingnagians of olden times, so dangerous to civilized man, from our size, ferocity, and power. Then let him take up our poets, from Pope down to Dana; let him listen to our Fourth of July toasts, and some of the sentimental adulations of social life, and no logic could convince him that this creature of the law, and this angel of the family altar, could be one and the same being. Man is in such a labyrinth of contradictions with his marital and property rights; he is so befogged on the whole question of maidens, wives, and mothers, that from pure benevolence we should relieve him from this troublesome branch of legislation. We should vote and make laws for ourselves.

Stanton and Anthony continued to broadcast their case to the public, in their travels across the country and in their own newspaper, the *Revolution*. They condemned the male-dominated American society that resulted in a death sentence for a "young, artless, and inexperienced girl." Women responded. They continued to petition the governor to release Vaughan. They even wrote poems about her case.

Finally Governor Geary did pardon Vaughan in the summer of 1869. The one condition of her release was that she return to England, and that her passage be paid with private, rather than state, funds. Stanton and Anthony raised the money. Vaughan's thank-you letter was published in the *Revolution* on August 19, 1869.

Suggestions for Further Reading

Barry, Kathleen. *Susan B. Anthony.* New York: New York University Press, 1988.

Doten, Lizzie. "Hester Vaughan." *Revolution* (March 25, 1969).

Harper, Ida Husted. *Life and Work of Susan B. Anthony,* Vol. 1, 1898. Reprint. Salem, NH: Ayer Co., Publishers, 1983.

**Hester
Vaughan
Trial: 1868**

Haymarket Trial: 1886

Defendants: George Engel, Samuel Fielden, Adolph Fischer, Louis Lingg, Oscar Neebe, Albert Parsons, Michael Schwab, and August Spies

Crime Charged: Murder

Chief Defense Lawyers: William P. Black, William A. Foster, Moses Salomon, and Sigismund Zeisler

Chief Prosecutor: Julius S. Grinnell

Judge: Joseph E. Gary

Place: Chicago, Illinois

Dates of Trial: June 21–August 20, 1886

Verdicts: Guilty

Sentences: Death by hanging for all but Neebe, who was sentenced to prison for fifteen years

SIGNIFICANCE: The Haymarket Riot was one of the most famous battles between the growing labor movement and industry and government. It was a serious setback for the unions and their efforts to improve industrial working conditions.

After the Civil War, the number of factories in the United States grew. People became famous for building new industries and businesses. Among them was John D. Rockefeller's Standard Oil, the largest company in the new petroleum industry. Another was Andrew Carnegie's Carnegie Steel (later renamed U.S. Steel). Finally there was Marshall Field, named for its founder, which changed the face of the clothing business. However, most wealthy owners did not want to share the wealth with the workers who made this success possible.

The Relationship between Workers and Employers

In the 1880s, every worker was free to bargain individually with his or her employer over wages, working hours, and conditions. In reality, however, the worker's "right to bargain" was meaningless. New workers from Europe and those just off American farms swelled the labor force. Any worker who complained about wages, hours, or sick leave was easily replaced.

The only way for workers to improve their lives was to band together, to "unionize," so that one group representing the whole workforce could push management to change its positions. Naturally, companies resisted. The relations between the union movement and management became strained and often violent. Because union members saw the government as a friend of big business, many were attracted to a political idea called "anarchism," which wanted to do away with government altogether.

Chicago: Hotbed of Radicalism

By the 1880s, Chicago was one of American's factory centers. Workers, many newly arrived from Europe, were unhappy with their jobs. They joined the labor movement and became anarchists. One of the most outspoken members of the movement was August Spies, the editor of a German-language newspaper.

In 1886, most businesses insisted on a ten-hour workday. Even longer shifts were common. Labor demanded that management reduce the workday to eight hours, while keeping the daily wage the same. On May 1, the great labor holiday, unions staged nationwide protests in favor of the eight-hour workday. Two days later, on May 3, Spies spoke before the striking workers at the McCormick farm machinery works. Fights broke out between the strikers and "scab" workers hired to replace them. The police broke up the fights by firing into the crowd and killing two and wounding many others.

Spies told of this incident in his newspaper, calling for a rally the next day in Chicago's Haymarket Square to protest police brutality. At first the meeting was peaceful. Chicago's Mayor, Carter Harrison, showed

MURDER

Police, U.S. military soldiers, and firefighters try to control the turmoil brought on by the Haymarket riots.

up briefly to stand before the working-class voters. The situation became violent after Spies spoke to the crowd and Harrison left. Two of Spies's fellow anarchists, Samuel Fielden and Albert Parsons, gave speeches, blasting business, government, and the Chicago police.

Chicago police captain John Bonfield ordered the 200 officers to advance towards the crowd. Suddenly, someone in the crowd threw a bomb made of dynamite at the police. The explosion killed eight officers and wounded sixty-seven others. Furious, the police struck back, firing into the crowd and killing or wounding dozens of people.

Police Arrest Eight Anarchists

The fighting between the police and labor caused the loss of life following the May Day rallies. After the Haymarket bomb explosion, however, the public blamed labor. A major Chicago newspaper ran the headline "NOW IT IS BLOOD!" Other papers copied it, fanning public fears.

Despite widespread searches and raids on working-class neighborhoods, the police never found the bomber. Prosecutor Julius S. Grinnell, charged with finding those responsible for the Haymarket disaster, needed

people to charge. The police began arresting anarchists and labor leaders. Among them were Samuel Fielden, Michael Schwab, and August Spies. Grinnell supported the arrests. Encouraged, the police arrested five more labor anarchists: George Engel, Adolph Fischer, Louis Lingg, Oscar Neebe, and Albert Parsons. On May 27, 1886, all eight faced murder charges.

The Trial

Because of the public outcry, at first the defendants had trouble finding lawyers who were willing to represent them. Eventually, however, experienced lawyers joined the defense team, and the trial began on June 21, 1886.

Jury selection took three weeks. A total of 981 potential jurors were questioned until twelve were finally selected. There have been accusations that Judge Joseph E. Gary attempted to make sure that the jury favored the prosecution. In any event, none of the twelve finally chosen worked in a factory; they were not expected to sympathize with the union movement, which was the real subject of the trial.

Poster asking for workers to attend a meeting following the previous day's violence at the Haymarket riots.

Attention Workingmen!

------- GREAT -------

MASS-MEETING

TO-NIGHT, at 7.30 o'clock,

------- AT THE -------

HAYMARKET, Randolph St., Bet. Desplaines and Halsted.

Good Speakers will be present to denounce the latest atrocious act of the police, the shooting of our fellow-workmen yesterday afternoon.

THE EXECUTIVE COMMITTEE.

"I WENT TO WORK TO ORGANIZE THEM . . ."

The defendant Oscar Neebe was the first to address the court after the verdict was handed down. He spoke passionately of the "crime" he had committed: "I saw that the bakers in this city were treated like dogs. . . . I helped organize them. That is a great crime. The men are now working ten hours a day instead of fourteen and sixteen hours. . . . That is another crime. And I committed a greater crime than that. I saw in the morning when I drove away with my team that the beer brewers of the city of Chicago went to work at four o'clock in the morning. They came at home at seven or eight o'clock at night. They never saw their families or their children by daylight. . . . I went to work to organize them. . . . And, your Honor, I committed another crime. I saw the grocery clerks and other clerks of this city worked until ten and eleven o'clock in the evening. I issued a call . . . and today they are only working until seven o'clock in the evening and no Sunday work. That is a great crime . . . ."

Prosecutor Grinnell tried to prove that the defendants had conspired to attack the police during the Haymarket rally and to overthrow all government authority. He called several witnesses, but all of them gave poor testimony. They were only able to testify that the defendants had at different times made pro-anarchist and pro-union statements. Such statements did not prove conspiracy or murder. Judge Gary ruled, however, that if the jury believed the defendants were guilty beyond a reasonable doubt of conspiring to attack the police or overthrow the government, they could also find the defendants guilty of murder. Also, the jury merely had to find beyond a reasonable doubt that the defendants had arranged for someone to throw the bomb. According to his instructions to the jury, it did not matter that no one had found the bomb-thrower.

Judge Gary's explanation of the law resulted, on August 20, 1886, in a guilty verdict for all eight defendants. All but Neebe, who received fifteen years in jail, were sentenced to death. The public and press applauded, and most newspapers carried glowing accounts of Grinnell. Despite the efforts of various groups—who were assisted by a young but soon-to-be-famous lawyer named Clarence Darrow—the Illinois Supreme Court upheld the death sentence. A final appeal to the U.S. Supreme Court was also unsuccessful.

Suicide, Hanging, and Pardons

Lingg committed suicide before his scheduled execution. On November 11, 1887, Engel, Fischer, Parsons, and Spies were hanged. Fielden, Neebe, and Schwab sat in jail, Neebe serving out his sentence and the others awaiting execution. Their stay in prison lasted for years. On June 26, 1893, John Peter Altgeld became governor of Illinois. He pardoned the remaining Haymarket defendants. The three left prison as free men.

The Haymarket Riot began with one political conflict and ended with another. Altgeld's pardon harmed his reputation, and he lost the next election for governor. Nevertheless, his pardon strengthened labor's claim that the trial had been unfair from start to finish and that Judge Gary had been biased.

Suggestions for Further Reading

Avrich, Paul. *The Haymarket Tragedy.* Princeton, NJ: Princeton University Press, 1984.

Foner, Philip S. *The Autobiography of the Haymarket Martyrs.* New York: Anchor Foundation, 1978.

Haymarket Remembered Project Staff. *Mob Action Against the State: The Haymarket Remembered. . . . An Anarchist Convention.* Seattle: Left Bank Books, 1987.

Roediger, David and Franklin Rosemont, eds. *Haymarket Scrapbook: A Centennial Anthology.* Chicago: C. H. Kerr, 1986.

Harry Thaw Trials: 1907–1908

Defendant: Harry Kendall Thaw

Crime Charged: Murder

Chief Defense Lawyers: First trial: Delphin M. Delmas, John B. Gleason, Clifford Hartridge, Hugh McPike, and George Peabody; second trial: Martin W. Littleton, Daniel O'Reilly, and Russell Peabody

Chief Prosecutor: William Travers Jerome

Judge: First trial: James Fitzgerald; second trial: Victor J. Dowling

Place: New York, New York

Dates of Trials: First trial: January 23–April 12, 1907; second trial: January 6–February 1, 1908

Verdict: First trial: none, jury deadlocked; second trial: not guilty by reason of insanity

SIGNIFICANCE: Harry Thaw married the glamorous performer Evelyn Nesbit, who had previously been the mistress of the famous architect Stanford White. Thaw shot White during a public performance in Madison Square Garden and later stood trial for murder. Thaw's attorneys took the insanity defense to murder to new extremes. They successfully argued that Thaw suffered from a condition supposedly unique to American men that caused Thaw to develop an uncontrollable desire to kill White after he learned of White's earlier relationship with Nesbit.

Harry Thaw was born in 1872 into a family of wealthy Pennsylvania industrialists. His father made a fortune estimated at $40 million in the Pittsburgh steel business and had also invested heavily in the Pennsylvania Railroad. Thaw's mother spoiled him when he was young and pampered him throughout his life—with tragic consequences.

As a young man, Thaw went to Harvard University, but the school expelled him for playing poker. Thaw's mother provided him with a large allowance and paid off the large gambling debts that he acquired after moving to New York City. Thaw also had a taste for activities even more damaging than gambling. In New York, he developed the habit of physically abusing prostitutes. Although Thaw had several run-ins with the police, his family's money always bought his release.

Evelyn Nesbit

Evelyn Nesbit's background in Pittsburgh was far more modest than Thaw's. Nesbit's parents were poor and could never provide for their daughter's education. Nesbit was beautiful, however, and from an early age she also showed some skill as a singer and dancer. Her family came to rely on the money she earned in New York City as a model and in the theater. Within a short time, Nesbit's career soared, and she became a "Floradora girl," joining the famous all-woman Floradora chorus.

During a performance of the chorus, Nesbit attracted the attention of architect Stanford White. White had made a fortune designing homes for wealthy New Yorkers and had also designed several famous buildings, including Madison Square Garden. White kept private rooms for himself in the Garden's tower. Evelyn Nesbit began to visit White at his apartment and became his mistress; their affair lasted for three years. Nesbit later testified at trial that at one point in their relationship, White got her drunk and assaulted her after she passed out.

Nesbit Marries Thaw

Nesbit left White early in 1905 for Thaw, who, like White, began pursuing Nesbit after he saw her on stage. Whether out of love or a desire for another wealthy supporter, Nesbit married Thaw on April 4, 1905. Thaw took Nesbit to Europe for their honeymoon and reportedly began to abuse her. He became obsessed with Nesbit's earlier relationship with White. Thaw became convinced that he had to avenge Nesbit's humiliation and rid the world of a human monster, Stanford White.

Courtroom Drama

On June 25, 1906, Thaw acted on his obsessions. At Madison Square Garden, where the Thaws were attending the performance of a new musical, Thaw spotted White. Thaw charged up to White's table and pulled out a pistol, then shot White several times while hundreds of people watched in horror. Thaw made no attempt to resist arrest by police officers who rushed to the Garden.

Thaw Is Tried for Murder

Upon learning of his arrest, Thaw's mother rushed to his defense. Declaring that she would spend the family's $40-million fortune to set Thaw free, she paid to have her son represented by one of the most famous lawyers of the age, Delphin Delmas. He brought four other attorneys with him to assist in Thaw's defense. When the trial opened January 23, 1907, however, Delmas played the main role in defending Thaw.

The prosecutor was William Travers Jerome, New York's district attorney, who had once served as a judge and was said to want to become governor. Jerome knew that the press would closely follow Thaw's trial. As *The New York Times* reported, "The Thaw trial is being reported to the ends of the civilized globe."

Thaw wanted to save himself from the electric chair, which was the penalty for murder. He also wanted to avoid spending the rest of his life in an insane asylum—the other penalty he might receive if found guilty. Therefore, Delmas conducted the defense with the aim of proving that Thaw was and always had been sane except for one day: June 25, 1906. On that day, Delmas claimed Thaw temporarily went insane and shot White. Delmas used Nesbit's beauty to appeal to the jury's emotions. He also called Nesbit to the stand and asked her to describe the events of the night on which White assaulted her.

Prosecutor Jerome, who had produced many eyewitnesses testifying that Thaw shot White at point-blank range, watched in frustration while Delmas put White's treatment of Nesbit on trial. Delmas then introduced the defense's argument of temporary insanity by asking Nesbit about Thaw's reaction upon learning about the assault incident. Delmas and Nesbit both carefully avoided the subject of Thaw's own tendency towards physical violence. Nesbit's acting experience combined with Delmas's legal ability to present a picture of a young, pretty, and innocent girl telling the story of her disgrace to her husband, who then flew into a murderous fury: "He would get up and walk up and down the room a minute and then come and sit down and say, 'Oh, God! Oh, God!' and bite his nails like that and keep sobbing."

OPPOSITE PAGE

*Brought to trial for
the murder of
architect Stanford
White, Harry Thaw
was found not guilty
by reason of
insanity at his
second trial.*

MURDER

In his closing argument, Delmas hammered the argument home to the jury:

> And if Thaw is insane, it is with a species of insanity known from the Canadian border to the Gulf. If you expert gentlemen ask me to give it a name, I suggest that you label it Dementia Americana. It is that species of insanity that inspires of every American to believe his home is sacred. It is that species of insanity that persuades an American that whoever violates the sanctity of his home or the purity of his wife or daughter has forfeited the protection of the laws of this state or any other state.

Judge James Fitzgerald reminded the jury that they could only find Thaw not guilty by reason of insanity if Thaw could not understand at the time of the murder that his actions were wrong. On April 12, 1907, the jury reported that it could not reach a verdict. Judge Fitzgerald adjourned the court until Thaw could be retried.

Thaw Is Found Insane

Thaw's second trial began January 6, 1908. Although Jerome was still the prosecutor, Thaw had a new team of defense lawyers: Martin W. Littleton, Daniel O'Reilly, and Russell Peabody. Further, Judge Victor J. Dowling had replaced Judge Fitzgerald. The same witnesses, including Nesbit, testified as in the first trial. Neither Jerome nor the defense team, however, fought as hard over the issue of temporary insanity as they had during the first trial. Perhaps both sides had decided that they would be content with a verdict of not guilty by reason of insanity, which would put Thaw in a mental institution but prevent his execution. On February 1, 1908, after a trial that lasted less than four weeks, the jury found Thaw not guilty by reason of insanity.

After the jury handed down its verdict, Judge Dowling sent Thaw to the Asylum for the Criminally Insane at Matteawan, New York. Thaw's trials had taken the insanity defense to a murder charge to new heights. The publicity surrounding Nesbit and her testimony eventually led to the making of a movie.

Thaw divorced Nesbit in 1915 and spent the rest of his life in and out of insane asylums and the courts. He escaped from Matteawan and

RENAISSANCE ORNAMENT AND INTERIOR DESIGN

Stanford White, whom Harry Thaw killed, was one of the most influential American architects of his time. In 1879, he began a partnership with Charles Follen McKim and William R. Mead. Together they created a firm whose works changed the shape of New York City, designing many new buildings in the classical style. White's specialties were interior design, furnishing, and the decorative aspects of a building, particularly Renaissance ornament. Perhaps his best-known work is the Arch in Washington Square Park. White also designed the Century Club, while his firm was responsible for the Boston Public Library, and, in New York, the Harvard Club and the Pierpont Morgan Library.

fled to Canada, but the Canadian authorities sent him back to New York. Briefly freed from the asylums by the lawyers paid for by his mother, Thaw was arrested in 1917 for kidnapping and whipping nineteen-year-old Frederick Gump nearly to death. Mother Thaw arranged for her son to go to a Pennsylvania insane asylum, where he stayed until 1924. After 1924, he appeared from time to time in the news, in connection with his involvement in wild parties or lawsuits by performers claiming that Thaw had beaten and whipped them. Thaw died February 22, 1947, at the age of seventy-six.

Suggestions for Further Reading

Abramson, Phyllis L. *Sob Sister Journalism.* New York: Greenwood Press, 1990.

Hodge, Clifford M. "The Benefactor at Dorr's Pond." *Yankee* (December 1986): 154.

Lessard, Suzannah. *The Architect of Desire: Beauty and Danger in the Stanford White Family.* New York: Dial Press, 1996.

Nesbit, Evelyn. "Beauty as Evidence." *Life* (June 1981): 10–13.

Leo Frank Trial: 1913

Defendant: Leo Max Frank

Crime Charged: Murder

Chief Defense Lawyers: Reuben Arnold, Herbert Haas, Stiles Hopkins, and Luther Z. Rosser

Chief Prosecutors: Hugh Dorsey, Frank Arthur Hooper, and Edward A. Stephens

Judge: Leonard Strickland Roan

Place: Atlanta, Georgia

Dates of Trial: July 28–September 26, 1913

Verdict: Guilty

Sentence: Death by hanging, changed by Georgia Governor John Slaton to life imprisonment (afterward, Frank died at the hands of an angry lynch mob)

SIGNIFICANCE: The Leo Frank trial was a national scandal that exposed the double standard of Southern justice: one set of laws for whites and one for minorities such as Frank, who was Jewish. Not only was Frank hung by a lynch mob, but his lynching seemed to have helped the racist organization the Ku Klux Klan, which experienced an increase in membership for years afterward.

Leo Max Frank was born in Paris, Texas, in 1884. His family moved to Brooklyn, New York, while he was still a baby. Frank's family was Jewish, and he grew up in New York City's large Jewish community. He was a quiet, shy man, but he had great mechanical ability, and he graduated from Cornell University with an engineering degree. After working for

After Leo Frank's sentence was commuted to life imprisonment, some people who disagreed hung a dummy representing Governor John Slaton as "King of the Jews."

brief periods with several companies, Frank went to work for his uncle, Moses Frank, who was the primary owner of the National Pencil Company. In 1907, when Frank became superintendent, he moved to the company's Atlanta location.

It probably never occurred to Frank that bigotry (prejudice) might be a problem in the South. Atlanta's Jewish community was small by New York standards, but it was still significant and had deep roots in the city's history. In 1911, Frank married Lucile Selig, whose family was also Jewish. Frank spent most of his time supervising the pencil factory, avoided politics and racial issues, and was honored by the Jewish community as one of Atlanta's most promising young businessmen. By 1913 Frank was one of Atlanta's leading citizens and was enjoying a successful career.

Little Mary Phagan Murdered

As was common at the time, Frank's factory employed women and children—both of whom were paid lower wages than men—to perform the light work involved in manufacturing pencils. One such worker was Mary Phagan, a thirteen-year-old girl who lived in the nearby city of Marietta. When she was laid off on April 26, 1913, she went to collect her final paycheck from Frank, who paid her and thought no more of the matter after she left. Shortly before he left for the day, he met another former employee, John Gantt, who asked if he could get some shoes he had left in his locker. Frank allowed Gantt to get his shoes.

Frank's nervous personality made him fear Gantt, who had a reputation as a drunkard and whom Frank had fired for stealing. That night, Frank called the night guard, an African American named Newt Lee, several times to ask if there was any trouble. Frank probably feared some sort of trouble from Gantt, but there was none. In the early hours of the morning, however, Lee discovered Phagan dead in the basement. Someone had raped and killed her after she collected her pay the day before. Afraid that he would be blamed for the crime, Lee went straight to the police and reported the crime. His honesty did him no good: after the police arrived at the factory and investigated the scene of the crime, they threw Lee in jail, holding him without charges for months.

The police then went to Frank's house, took him to the scene of the crime for questioning, and then to the police station for several days of further interrogation. Meanwhile, the murder became public, and the Atlanta newspapers were filled with shocking headlines describing the details of the crime and calling for justice. Hugh Mason Dorsey, the chief prosecutor for that section of Atlanta, had political ambitions that a victory in such a highly publicized case might boost. Dorsey focused on the shy Frank, who was an easy target. On April 29, 1913, police arrested Frank for the murder of Mary Phagan.

Prosecutors Emphasize Frank's Nervousness

When the trial began on July 28, 1913, Newt Lee, still in prison "under suspicion," was one of the first witnesses. Frank's telephone calls to Lee on the night of the murder came back to haunt him. The prosecutors made it look as if Frank had been checking to see if the body had been found that Saturday night. The government lawyers then turned Frank's nervous personality to their advantage. They used the testimony of the police officers who had taken Frank to the scene of the crime on Sunday, April 27, to create suspicion in the mind of the jury. They sought to reason that Frank's nervousness was the result of a guilty conscience.

Next, the lawyers tried to prove that Frank had deliberately planned to get Phagan to come to the factory that weekend. A factory employee named Helen Ferguson testified that she had been Phagan's friend and had in the past picked up her pay for her. However, on the day before the murder, Ferguson said, Frank refused to let Ferguson pick up Phagan's final check:

> [I went to] Mr. Frank on Friday, April 25, about
> seven o'clock in the evening and asked for Mary

Phagan's money. Mr. Frank said, 'I can't let you have it,' and before he said anything else I turned around and walked out. I had gotten Mary's money before. . . .

Prosecution Clinches Case

The government lawyers saved their best witness for last: Jim Conley, an African American who was the factory janitor. Despite some suspicion that Conley might be the actual murderer, the government put him on the stand. It has even been written that Dorsey chose to prosecute a Yankee Jew rather than an African American for purposes of sensationalism, regardless of Frank's innocence. The point of Conley's testimony was that he had been at the factory on the day of the murder and that Frank had confessed to it. The defense lawyers cross-examined Conley for several days but were unable to shake his testimony. Either Conley was a superb liar or the lawyers had coached him about what to say. The defense lawyers also had to deal with spectators in the courtroom who constantly yelled out racist comments—such as "Hang the Jew!"—while the defense attempted to make its case. Although Judge Leonard Roan had once been defense lawyer Luther Rosser's legal partner, he made no serious effort to stop these distractions.

At the conclusion of the defense's case, Frank himself took the stand. For nearly half a day he spoke, and he consistently denied murdering Phagan. He explained his nervousness as the natural result of being dragged out of his home so early on a Sunday morning to learn of the shocking crime. Further, Frank bluntly called Conley a liar. His testimony was of no avail.

Frank Convicted, Commuted, and Lynched

On September 26, 1913, after one of the longest trials in Georgia history, the jury found Leo Frank guilty of the murder of Mary Phagan. Judge Roan sentenced Frank to hang on October 10, but the defense appealed. On February 17, 1914, the Georgia Supreme Court upheld (agreed with) Frank's conviction. The defense lawyers, however, did not give up. They pursued evidence that Conley had committed the murder. Witnesses had seen Conley washing his bloody clothing at the factory after the murder. Conley's girlfriend gave evidence concerning Conley's abnormal sexual tendencies, and Conley's own lawyer told Judge Roan that Conley had confessed to the murder to him.

MURDER

THE KU KLUX KLAN

The Leo Frank case gave a new prominence to the Ku Klux Klan, which experienced a huge growth in membership in the 1910s and 1920s. The Klan had its first meeting in Nashville, Tennessee, in April 1867, in response to the growing political power of African Americans after the Civil War had ended slavery and Reconstruction (period of rebuilding following the end of the Civil War) guaranteed their voting rights. The group was organized by former military and political leaders of the Confederacy (group of Southern states during the Civil War) as well as by religious leaders. Originally, the Klansman spoke of themselves as the ghosts of dead Confederate soldiers, which led to their wearing white sheets. At a time when many former participants in the Confederacy had been stripped of their political power, the Klan attempted to regain that power through sheer terror: beatings, burnings, and lynchings. The Klan declined after 1873, when Northern troops left the South and African Americans could be suppressed through new laws, known as Jim Crow laws. However, it revived during World War I, when the poverty and anti-foreign feeling of the era made the Klan's tactics attractive to a new generation. At this point, the Klan expanded its targets to include Jews, Catholics, and the foreign-born as well as African Americans, and membership spread through the Midwest as well as the South. By 1924, the "new" Klan had from four to five million members.

Despite the evidence of Conley's guilt, Judge Roan refused to overturn the verdict against Frank, which the Georgia Supreme Court reaffirmed (let stand) on October 14, 1914. Frank's scheduled execution moved to January 22, 1915. However, his defense lawyers delayed it again by asking the U.S. Supreme Court for a writ of *habeas corpus* (release from unlawful imprisonment). On April 19, 1915, the court denied the petition.

Frank's last chance was an appeal to the governor of Georgia, John Slaton, for a reduction of his sentence. This appeal began with a hearing on May 31, 1915, before the Georgia Prison Commission. On June 9,

1915, the Commission voted 2–1 against recommending a change in sentence to the governor. Slaton, however, was an independent man and had on several occasions used his power to grant clemency, freeing prisoners when in his opinion justice demanded it, regardless of the unpopularity of his decision. On June 21, 1915, Slaton reduced Frank's sentence to life imprisonment, citing the widespread national criticism of Georgia justice and the many doubts raised about the evidence in the case.

Many in Georgia instantly condemned Slaton's decision. There were demonstrations in Atlanta and in Marietta, Phagan's home town; some people attacked Jewish homes and stores. On August 16, 1915, a vigilante group (people seeking justice on their own without legal authority) drove from Marietta to the Milledgeville Prison Farm outside Macon, Georgia. They overpowered the small crew of prison guards, and took Frank from his cell. The vigilantes then drove back to Marietta, a seven-hour trip, with Frank. In Marietta, a lynch mob of local citizens gathered and watched as Frank was hung from a tree limb on the morning of August 17, 1915.

The racist hatred stirred up by the Frank trial did not end with Frank's lynching. For decades, the Phagan case served as a rallying cry for the white supremacist Ku Klux Klan, which targeted Jews as well as blacks.

In 1982, an old man named Alonzo Mann, who had worked at Frank's pencil factory as a child, publicly declared that he had seen Conley drag Phagan's corpse to the basement. He had kept silent because Conley had threatened to kill him. On March 11, 1986, the Georgia State Board of Pardons and Paroles officially pardoned Frank. The Leo Frank trial had been a national scandal and demonstrated how Southern justice could be a double standard when applied to an unpopular minority.

Suggestions for Further Reading

Dinnerstein, Leonard. *The Leo Frank Case.* Athens: University of Georgia Press, 1987.

Liebman, James S. "Lesson Unlearned." *The Nation* (August 1991): 217.

Lindemann, Albert S. *The Jew Accused: Three Anti-Semitic Affairs (Dreyfus, Beilis, Frank), 1894–1915.* New York: Cambridge University Press, 1991.

Oney, Steve. "The Lynching of Leo Frank; Two Years Ago, and Seventy Years Too Late, a Witness Came Forward to Prove That Frank's Only Crime was Being a Stranger in the Old South." *Esquire* (September 1985): 90–98.

Phagan, Mary. *The Murder of Little Mary Phagan.* Far Hills, NJ: New Horizon Press, 1987.

Sacco-Vanzetti Trial:
1921

Defendants: Nicola Sacco and Bartolomeo Vanzetti

Crime Charged: Murder

Chief Defense Lawyers: William J. Callahan, Herbert B. Ehrmann, James M. Graham, Arthur Dehon Hill, Jeremiah J. McAnarney, Thomas F. McAnarney, Fred H. Moore, Michael Angelo Musmanno, William G. Thompson, and John P. Vahey

Chief Prosecutors: Frederick Gunn Katzmann, Donald P. Ramsey, and Harold P. Williams

Judge: Webster Thayer

Place: Dedham, Massachusetts

Dates of Trial: May 31–July 14, 1921

Verdicts: Guilty

Sentences: Death

SIGNIFICANCE: The Sacco-Vanzetti case began as a simple trial for murder. It ended as an international cause because the world believed that Massachusetts had executed two innocent men for their radical political views. A study of the trial and its consequences provides a superb lesson in how myths are made.

On the afternoon of April 15, 1920, a shoe manufacturer's paymaster (a person assigned to pay employees), Frederick Parmenter, and his guard, Alessandro Berardelli, were carrying a $15,777 cash payroll in South Braintree, Massachusetts. Two armed men shot and killed them. Seizing the money, the men jumped into a car filled with other men and sped away. Eyewitnesses thought the murderers looked Italian.

At the time, police were investigating a holdup attempted in nearby Bridgewater on the previous Christmas Eve. A group of Italians with a car seemed to be the robbers. Police Chief Michael E. Stewart suspected Mike Boda, whose car was now awaiting repairs in Simon Johnson's garage. Stewart told Johnson to call the police when anyone came to get Boda's car.

The Transportation of Red Literature

Stewart also was busy rounding up foreigners who were Communists. After raids made by the U.S. Departments of Labor and Justice, the United States deported many such individuals. In May, a prisoner holding radical political beliefs fell from the fourteenth floor of the New York City Department of Justice. He died on the pavement below. His friends, including Boda, decided they had better hide a large quantity of "Red" (Communist) literature. To move it, they needed Boda's car.

Boda and three others appeared at Johnson's garage. Mrs. Johnson called the police. Johnson refused to hand over the car because it had out-of-date license plates. Boda and another man then left on a motorcycle. The other two boarded a street car. The last two, Nicola Sacco and Bartolomeo Vanzetti, were arrested moments later. Sacco carried a .32-caliber pistol loaded with nine bullets and had twenty-three additional bullets in his pocket. Vanzetti had a fully loaded .38-caliber revolver and four twelve-gauge shotgun shells. Also found on Sacco was a notice, in Italian, of a forthcoming meeting at which Vanzetti was to speak on "the struggle for existence." The two men were active anarchists (those who believe that society can only be truly free if it does not have an organized government).

Anarchists Convicted

Questioned by district attorney Frederick Gunn Katzmann, Sacco said he had bought the gun two years earlier for $16 or $17 and had bought a new box of cartridges. Vanzetti said his gun had cost $18 or $19 four or five years earlier. Neither gun was licensed.

Vanzetti's shotgun shells made him a suspect in the failed holdup on Christmas Eve, when a twelve-gauge shotgun was fired. His alibi (excuse) was that, as a fish peddler, he had spent a busy Christmas Eve selling eels for traditional Italian dinners that night. At his trial, several witnesses identified him as the man with the shotgun at the Bridgewater holdup. He did not take the stand to answer this claim and was convicted

MURDER

Bartolomeo Vanzetti (left) and Nicola Sacco on the day of their sentencing.

and sentenced to twelve to fifteen years in prison. Sacco had a solid alibi: he had been on the job in a shoe factory when the attempted robbery occurred. However, police held him for trial in the South Braintree murders, for on April 15 he had taken the day off.

Defense Committee Organized

Anarchist friends organized the Sacco-Vanzetti Defense Committee. For three months it collected money. Then the committee hired Fred H.

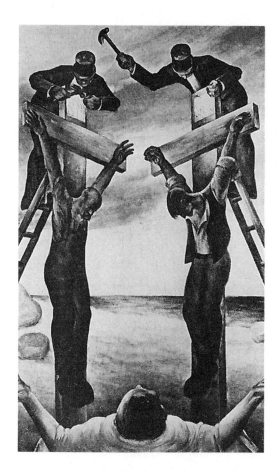

Many people felt that Sacco and Vanzetti were arrested and convicted because they were radicals. This newspaper cartoon depicts them being crucified, like Jesus. The man below represents the people, asking "Why?"

Moore, a left-wing labor lawyer from California. Moore, experienced in handling cases for unpopular political radicals, saw the Sacco-Vanzetti case as a cause. "In saving them," he said, "we strengthen our muscles, develop our forces preparatory to the day when we save ourselves."

Moore spent a busy year writing, traveling, and organizing volunteers. Labor unions such as the United Mine Workers, the Amalgamated Clothing Workers, and the American Federation of Teamsters, as well as the American Civil Liberties Union, were among the many organizations that helped him. Pamphlets protesting the innocence of Sacco and Vanzetti were printed in batches of 50,000. Publicity notices were sent every week to 500 newspapers. In all this literature, the murder charge was depicted as "a mere device to get them [Sacco and Vanzetti] out of the way."

Outdated Bullets and a Cap

Opening May 31, 1921, the trial had revealed that Sacco lied about his gun. It was several years old, and his box of "new" cartridges contained a mixture of old bullets that were all outdated. The bullet that killed Berardelli was so old that the prosecution could locate none like it with which to test Sacco's gun—except the equally outdated bullets taken from Sacco's pocket.

Vanzetti, too, had lied. Although he said he paid $18 or $19 for his gun, the jury learned that it cost $5. Vanzetti had said he bought a new box of cartridges and threw it away when only six bullets were left, which he put in the revolver. However, Vanzetti's gun held only five bullets, and the ones found in it were not all the same make. Further, Vanzetti's nickel-plated pistol was identical to the one that had belonged to the murdered guard, whose gun could not be found after the crime.

Then there was the cap found beside the dead guard. It was not his. Sacco's employer testified that it looked like a cap that Sacco regularly wore. When the government lawyer asked Sacco to put the cap on, the defendant pulled it down over his ears in an attempt to prove it was too big. He threw the courtroom into giggling hysterics. However, the state also introduced as evidence a cap of exactly the same size that had been taken from Sacco's home.

Trial for Murder, Nothing Else

Before the trial opened, Judge Webster Thayer had told the lawyers on both sides that he saw no reason to bring up the issue of anarchism. No one mentioned it during the prosecution's entire presentation to the jury. On the twenty-ninth day, however, Vanzetti himself brought up the question of the defendants' politics. Under direct examination by his attorney, Jeremiah J. McAnarney, Vanzetti explained why the four men sought Boda's car: "We were going to take the automobile for to carry books and newspapers," he said. Why hadn't he told the police that when he was arrested? "Because there was the deportation and the reaction was more vivid than now and more mad than now." In other words, his defense was that he lied out of fear of being expelled from the country because of his radicalism.

Under Massachusetts law, since the defense had brought up the issue, the door was now open for prosecutor Katzmann to cross-examine Vanzetti about all his radical activities. But the jury heard no such questions. "Neither is Radicalism being tried here," the prosecutor told them. "This is a charge of murder and it is nothing else."

Next, Sacco explained that he, too, lied when he was arrested because he feared deportation on a radical charge. And he explained another lie. Upon his arrest, he had said that he was at work all day April 15. Now his boss testified that Sacco had taken that day off to see the Italian consul in Boston about a passport for a trip to Italy. The clerk in the counsel's office testified that Sacco was there at about 2:00 P.M. on April 15, but the alibi was weak: Sacco had been turned down immediately because the passport photo he offered was too large. The jury was told that Sacco had spent an entire day in Boston. (Several witnesses for the defense testified to having seen him there in the morning, at lunch, and in the afternoon.) However, his business at the consulate had taken only ten minutes. Then Sacco noticed a spectator in the courtroom whom he had seen on the late afternoon train home. Sworn as a witness, the man could not remember seeing Sacco but was certain he had been on the train Sacco described.

As with Vanzetti, prosecutor Katzmann refrained from asking any questions that might have led the jury to consider Sacco a dangerous radical.

Bullets Convince Jury

At 3:00 P.M. on July 14, the jury retired. It immediately voted 10–2 to convict both defendants. "Then," said one juror afterward, "[w]e started discussing things, reviewed the very important evidence about the bullets, and everybody had a chance to speak his piece. There was never any argument, though. We just were convinced Sacco and Vanzetti had done what the prosecution had charged them with."

Asked later what evidence impressed him most, another juror said, "The bullets, of course. That testimony and evidence on it sticks in your mind. You can't depend on the witnesses. But the bullets, there was no getting around that evidence."

The guilty verdict brought fierce reactions around the world. American consulates and embassies in Europe and South America were flooded with letters of protest. The *Communist International* newspaper urged all Communists, Socialists, anarchists, and trade union supporters to join together to rescue Sacco and Vanzetti. Demonstrations took place in France, Italy, Switzerland, Belgium, Spain, Portugal, and Scandinavia. It took 10,000 police and 18,000 troops to hold back the crowd surrounding the American embassy in Paris. Bombs exploded in that embassy and in other areas around the world. One destroyed the home of one of the jurors. Judge Thayer's house was put under guard.

Vehement Appeals Follow

Over the next six years, people debated over the convicted men's guilt or innocence. Repeated requests for a new trial were rejected. So-called experts examined the pistols, took them apart, and put them back together incorrectly. Radical leader Elizabeth Gurley Flynn raised $25,000 in two days to pay the legal fee of Harvard Law School lecturer and political insider William G. Thompson, who replaced Moore, the radical outsider, as defense lawyer. Imprisoned criminals volunteered confessions.

In 1926, with "Sacco-Vanzetti" a worldwide battle cry, the Massachusetts Supreme Judicial Court, the state's highest tribunal, rejected an appeal. The International Labor Defense (ILD), set up by the Communists, received only some $6,000 of the millions raised in the names of Sacco and Vanzetti. Harvard law professor Felix Frankfurter (later to serve as a justice on the U.S. Supreme Court), in a magazine article, attacked the jury, witnesses, verdict, and judiciary. The state's supreme court, having already rejected Thompson's appeal, now upheld the judge. He had committed no errors of law or abuses of power.

Lowell Committee Reviews Case

In June 1927, on Thompson's urging, Massachusetts Governor Alvan T. Fuller, who was considering an appeal for mercy, appointed an advisory committee headed by Harvard president Abbott Lawrence Lowell to review the entire case. After two months, and after himself interviewing 102 witnesses in addition to those who testified at the trial, he agreed with the Lowell Committee's conclusion: Sacco and Vanzetti had received a fair trial and were guilty.

Worldwide protests grew more violent. A London demonstration injured forty people. Paris, Berlin, Warsaw, Buenos Aires, and countless other cities experienced riots. Picketers before the State House in Boston, including novelists John Dos Passos and Katherine Anne Porter, humorist Dorothy Parker, and poet Edna St. Vincent Millay, were arrested. All Boston buildings that were open to the public were heavily policed, and for the first time in memory no meetings were permitted to take place on Boston Common. Newspaper columnist Heywood Broun found his column removed from the New York *World* because of his violent comments about Lowell.

By now, Judge Thayer had denied a half-dozen requests for a new trial, the state superior trial court had denied another, and the state supreme judicial court had turned down four appeals. Several petitions requesting the prisoners' release, extensions of time, and delays of execution were denied by the Circuit Court of Appeals for the First Circuit of the United States and by U.S. Supreme Court justices Oliver Wendell Holmes and Harlan F. Stone.

DISSENT OVER THE SACCO-VANZETTI CASE

After the Sacco-Vanzetti trial was over, new information came to light about the government's role in it. Felix Frankfurter cited two affidavits (sworn legal statements), by Lawrence Letherman, head of the Justice Department's Boston office, and Fred J. Weyand, special department agent, both claiming that the Justice Department did not believe in Sacco and Vanzetti's guilt, but rather was trying to deport them for radical activities. Letherman said under oath that "The Department . . . was anxious to get sufficient evidence against Sacco and Vanzetti to deport them but never succeeded. . . . It was the opinion of the Department agents here that a conviction . . . for murder would be one way of disposing of these men. It was also the general opinion of such agents in Boston as had any knowledge of the . . . case, that Sacco and Vanzetti had nothing to do with the South Braintree crime. My opinion, and the opinion of most of the older men in Government service, has always been that the South Braintree crime was the work of professionals." This opinion was corroborated (confirmed by another person) in 1925, when Celestino F. Madeiros, under death sentence for killing a cashier in a bank robbery, sent Sacco a note confessing to the South Braintree crime. Madeiros's confession ended his own chances for appeal, but, he explained, "I seen Sacco's wife come here with the kids, and I felt sorry for the kids."

Sacco and Vanzetti were executed August 23, 1927. In 1977, their names were officially "cleared" when Massachusetts governor Michael Dukakis signed a special decree.

Suggestions for Further Reading

Montgomery, Robert H. *Sacco-Vanzetti: The Murder and the Myth.* New York: Devin-Adair, 1960.

Porter, Katherine Anne. *The Never-Ending Wrong.* Boston: Little, Brown, & Co., 1977.

MURDER

Rappaport, Doreen. *The Sacco-Vanzetti Trial.* New York: Harper-Collins Publishers, 1992.

Russell, Francis. *Sacco & Vanzetti: The Case Resolved.* New York: Harper & Row, 1986.

Russell, Francis. "Why I Changed My Mind about the Sacco-Vanzetti Case." *American Heritage* (June–July 1986): 106–108.

Sifakis, Carl. *The Encyclopedia of American Crime.* New York: Facts On File, 1972.

Sinclair, Upton. *Boston: A Documentary Novel.* Cambridge, MA: Robert Bentley, 1978.

Bruno Richard Hauptmann Trial: 1935

Defendant: Bruno Richard Hauptmann
Crime Charged: Murder
Chief Defense Lawyer: Edward J. Reilly
Chief Prosecutor: David T. Wilentz
Judge: Thomas W. Trenchard
Place: Flemington, New Jersey
Dates of Trial: January 2–February 13, 1935
Verdict: Guilty
Sentence: Death by electrocution

SIGNIFICANCE: The use of scientific crime methods and the circus-like atmosphere of the trial made the Lindbergh baby kidnapping trial a landmark in American history. Because of the popularity of the father of the murder victim, probably no case has ever attracted greater worldwide attention.

Charles A. Lindbergh became the greatest hero of modern times in May 1927, when he made the first solo trans-Atlantic airplane flight. After Lindbergh's twenty-month-old son was kidnapped and murdered in 1932, the 1935 trial of Bruno Richard Hauptmann became, as the important social critic H. L. Mencken said, "the biggest story since the Resurrection."

In 1929, Lindbergh married Anne Morrow, daughter of the U.S. ambassador to Mexico. Their son, Charles Jr., was born June 22, 1930. Hoping to escape from the crowds that followed them everywhere, the Lindberghs moved into a new home in remote Hopewell, New Jersey. There,

Courtroom   Drama

on the evening of March 1, 1932, Charles Jr. was kidnapped from his nursery. His body was found May 12 in the woods, two miles from the Lindbergh home.

Discovered through Ransom Money

More than two years later, in September 1934, a man named Bruno Hauptmann used a $10 gold certificate to buy gasoline. By this time, gold certificates (bills backed by government-owned gold) were rare. The station attendant was suspicious of Hauptmann, and he took down Hauptmann's license number. The attendant then took the $10 gold certificate to the bank, where it was identified as part of the $50,000 ransom Lindbergh had paid his baby's kidnapper. Hauptmann was arrested.

Hauptmann was a German immigrant who had a record of petty (minor) crimes in his native land. He lived in the Bronx, a borough of New York City, with his wife and son (who in 1934 was the same age as the Lindbergh baby). The family occupied the rented second story of a house, where they also had the use of a garage. Behind the boards of this garage police found $14,590 in bills that had been part of the ransom payment. Written on the inside of Hauptmann's bedroom closet was the address and telephone number of Dr. John F. Condon. Condon was a seventy-one-year-old retired schoolteacher who also lived in the Bronx. He had earlier volunteered to be a go-between for Lindbergh when the aviator, unaware that his son was dead, was negotiating with the kidnapper about the ransom money. Condon had met the supposed kidnapper while Lindbergh was still within earshot. Later, at Hauptmann's trial, Lindbergh would identify Hauptmann as the kidnapper by testifying, "[Hauptmann's] is the voice I heard that night."

The Trial As Public Spectacle

The trial became one of the great news stories of the century. To cope with the demands of the press, the telephone company put together the largest telephone system ever created for a single event. It was large enough to serve a city of one million. Thousands of sightseers, 700 reporters, and hundreds of radio and telephone technicians came to Flemington, New Jersey, where the trial was held. Peddlers sold models of the ladder the kidnapper used to climb into the Lindbergh baby's nursery, fake locks of "the baby's hair," and photographs of the Lindberghs—supposedly autographed by them.

OPPOSITE PAGE

Crowds line the streets trying to gain entrance to the trial of Bruno Richard Hauptmann.

MURDER

On Sundays, tourists walked through the courtroom, posed for photographs in the judge's chair, carved initials in his bench, and tried to steal the witness chair. On Sunday, January 6, 1935, the crowd of curious sightseers numbered 60,000. The next weekend, the local Rotary Club, a group dedicated to public service, took charge of protecting the courthouse before souvenir hunters dismantled it.

Everything Matches

The thirty-eight-year-old New Jersey attorney general, David T. Wilentz, vowed that the state would prove that Hauptmann received the ransom money. He also would show that Hauptmann had kidnapped and murdered the Lindbergh baby and written the ransom notes. Wilentz produced forty examples of Hauptmann's handwriting and fifteen ransom notes that Lindbergh had received. The head of the New Jersey State Police was Colonel H. Norman Schwarzkopf (whose son would later act as commanding general of U.S. troops in the 1991 Persian Gulf War.) He testified that Hauptmann had willingly supplied samples of his handwriting. Schwarzkopf also testified that the unusual Germanic spellings found in the ransom notes and in the writing samples were Hauptmann's own, not a reflection of police dictation.

Eight handwriting experts took the stand. Two had testified at more than fifty trials. Another had helped to convict the infamous mobster Al Capone. Still another had been a key witness in a suit challenging the validity of the will of movie star Rudolph Valentino. Using enlargements, these experts pointed out similarities between words and letters in the ransom notes and in Hauptmann's handwriting. When their testimony ended after five days, Wilentz gloated about the victory he had gained for the state thanks to scientific investigation.

Even more damaging to Hauptmann was evidence concerning the ladder found alongside the Lindbergh driveway. Arthur Koehler, a wood technologist at the U.S. Department of Agriculture, told the jury how he had examined the ladder with a microscope. He determined that it was made of North Carolina pine. Using the marks made in the wood as it was finished, he traced the ladder to mills in South Carolina. The mills had sold their wood to a Bronx lumber company where Hauptmann had purchased some in December 1931. One of the suspect ladder's rails was unique: it had nail holes that matched four holes in the beams of Hauptmann's attic.

Shoebox On the Shelf

Hauptmann's defense attorney, Edward J. Reilly, had tried hundreds of murder cases. He was one of New York's most famous trial lawyers. *The*

New York Journal had hired him. It had also made a deal with Anna Hauptmann. If she would give the paper the exclusive right to publish her story, the paper would pay for her husband's lawyer.

To explain how he came to have the ransom money, Hauptmann testified that he had invested in a business with Isidor Fisch. In December 1933, Fisch had gone home to Germany, where he had died of tuberculosis in March 1934. Hauptmann said that Fisch had left behind a number of belongings, including a shoebox that Hauptmann had stored on the top shelf of a kitchen broom closet.

After rain leaked into the closet, Hauptmann found the shoebox. Inside it were $40,000 in gold certificates. In his garage, Hauptmann divided the money into piles, wrapped it up, and hid it. Because Fisch had owed him $7,500, he began spending some of the gold certificates.

Reilly called Mrs. Hauptmann to the witness stand to verify her husband's story. Under cross-examination, she revealed that although she hung her apron in the broom closet every day and kept her grocery coupons in a tin box on the shelf, she had never seen the shoebox there. Later, other witnesses testified that Fisch could not have been at the scene of the crime. Further, he did not even have money for his medical treatment when he was dying in Germany.

Reilly had boasted that he would call eight handwriting experts. But he came up with only one, who was discredited during cross-examination. Then Reilly brought in a witness who claimed to have seen Fisch in New York City on the night of the crime. The witness said that Fisch was with a woman who carried a two-year-old blond child. The woman was supposedly Violet Sharpe, a maid in the Morrow home. Like all servants in the Morrow and Lindbergh households, Sharpe had been questioned closely after the kidnapping. She committed suicide after her interrogation. Unfortunately for Reilly, this testimony was undermined by the fact that the person who gave it was a professional witness who had been paid to testify in dozens of trials.

Another defense witness claimed to have seen Fisch coming out of the cemetery where the ransom money was left. Prosecutor Wilentz made this witness admit that he had been previously convicted of a crime. Still another witness, who testified that he had seen Fisch with a shoebox, admitted under cross-examination that he had been in and out of mental institutions five times. To counter the evidence about the ladder, Reilly called on a general contractor who was an expert on wood. After the prosecutor attacked this witness's expertise, the judge allowed him to testify only as a "practical lumberman."

When the trial ended, no reliable witness had placed Hauptmann at the scene of the crime. His fingerprints were not found on the ladder, or in the nursery, or on the ransom notes. Still, the circumstantial evidence connecting Hauptmann to the crime was strong. He had the ransom money, experts said that he had made the ladder, and still other experts said that he had written the ransom notes.

Governor Gets Into the Act

When the jury found Hauptmann guilty of murder in the first degree, the crowds inside and outside the courtroom cheered. Hauptmann was given the death sentence. Execution was set for the week of March 18. Over the next year, however, Hauptmann's attorneys managed to postpone his execution by filing appeals.

New Jersey's governor, Harold G. Hoffman, secretly visited Hauptmann in jail and told the prisoner he was not convinced that he was guilty. Hoffman went on to say that he did not believe Hauptmann could have committed the crime by himself. In mid-January 1936, New Jersey's Court of Pardons turned down Hauptmann's request for a pardon. The governor, however, gave him thirty additional days to appeal this decision. The Court of Pardons once again rejected Hauptmann's request. By law, the governor could not grant a condemned prisoner a second stay of execution. On April 3, 1936, at 8:44 P.M., Hauptmann was electrocuted.

The Aftermath

The evidence and the testimony that led to Hauptmann's execution has been constantly re-examined. More than one examiner has criticized the investigation of the kidnapping and murder and declared that Hauptmann was an innocent man who had been framed.

In 1982, then eighty-two-year-old Anna Hauptmann sued the State of New Jersey, various former police officials, the owner of the *New York Journal,* and David T. Wilentz for wrongfully killing her husband. She claimed that newly found documents proved that government agents had manufactured some of the evidence used to convict Bruno Hauptmann. In 1983, the U.S. Supreme Court refused her request that the federal judge considering her case be disqualified. The next year, the judge dismissed her claim.

In 1985, 23,000 pages of police documents concerning the case were found in a garage that had been owned by former governor Hoffman, who

LUCKY LINDY

Charles Lindbergh was one of the great heroes of the era between World War I and World War II. Ironically, he was not actually the first to fly across the Atlantic. In 1919, two Englishmen had flown from Newfoundland to Ireland. However, their route was far shorter than Lindbergh's. Also, Lindbergh was the first to make a solo trans-Atlantic flight. His plane, *The Spirit of St. Louis,* had been specially designed to carry enough gas to allow him to make the 3,600-mile flight, which began on May 20, 1927, in Long Island. On this famous trip, Lindbergh carried only a few sandwiches and a quart of water. When he arrived in Paris thirty-three hours after takeoff, he was an international hero. His nickname became "Lucky Lindy." Partly because of Lindbergh's celebrity, the kidnapping case led to Congress passing a law that made kidnapping across state lines a federal crime. Later, Lindbergh became a supporter of German dictator Adolf Hitler and joined the "America First" movement to keep the United States out of World War II. He made many anti-Jewish remarks, and in 1938, he received a medal from Hermann Goering, Hitler's air minister. Nevertheless, during World War II, Lindbergh flew combat missions in the Pacific and after the war, he became a consultant to the Defense Department.

had died. Anna Hauptmann claimed that these documents, along with 30,000 pages of FBI files not used in the trial, proved the government had acted in bad faith. Again she appealed to the Supreme Court. The court let its previous ruling against her stand. In 1990, New Jersey Governor Jim Florio refused her appeal for a meeting intended to clear Bruno Hauptmann's name.

In October 1991, Mrs. Hauptmann, then ninety-two years old, called a news conference to plead for the case to be reopened. "From the day he was arrested, he was framed, always framed," she said. By that time, interest in the case had faded. Bruno Hauptmann's case seemed, to most of the public, to have been settled at last.

MURDER

Suggestions for Further Reading

Behn, Noel. *Lindberg: The Crime.* New York: Onyx, 1995.

Fisher, Jim. *The Lindbergh Case.* New Brunswick, NJ: Rutgers University Press, 1987.

Kennedy, Ludovic. *The Airman and the Carpenter.* New York: Viking, 1985.

Kennedy, Lodovic. *Crime of the Century: The Lindbergh Kidnapping and the Framing of Richard Hauptmann.* New York: Penguin Books, 1996.

King, Wayne. "Defiant Widow Seeks to Reopen Lindbergh Case." *The New York Times* (October 5, 1991): 24.

"Lindbergh Kidnapping's Final Victim." *U.S. News & World Report* (November 4, 1985): 11.

Rein, Richard K. "Anna Hauptmann Sues a State to Absolve Her Husband of 'The Crime of the Century.'" *People* (September 6, 1982): 34–35.

Scaduto, Anthony. *Scapegoat: The Lonesome Death of Bruno Richard Hauptmann.* New York: G. P. Putnam's Sons, 1976.

Samuel Sheppard Trials: 1954 and 1966

Defendant: Samuel Sheppard

Crime Charged: Murder

Chief Defense Lawyers: First trial: William J. Corrigan, William Corrigan Jr., Fred Garmone, and Arthur E. Petersilge; second trial: F. Lee Bailey

Chief Prosecutors: First trial: Saul S. Danaceau, John J. Mahon, and Thomas J. Parrino; second trial: John Corrigan

Judges: First trial: Edward C. Blythin; second trial: Francis J. Talty

Place: Cleveland, Ohio

Dates of Trials: October 18–December 21, 1954; October 24–November 16, 1966

Verdict: First trial: guilty, second-degree murder; second trial: not guilty

Sentence: First trial: life imprisonment

SIGNIFICANCE: In this, the most sensational American murder case of the 1950s, bias (unfair influence) connected with harmful media publicity deprived the defendant of his constitutional rights—including the right to a fair trial.

Balancing the news media's First Amendment right to free speech against a defendant's right to a fair trial has never been easy. In covering the Sam Sheppard trial, Cleveland's major newspapers ignored the defendant's rights altogether. The offenses they committed at a local level, popular radio columnist Walter Winchell committed nationally. Nearly everyone in

C o u r t r o o m   D r a m a

GOSSIP COLUMNISTS

The journalists who helped to make the Sheppard trial "a Roman circus"—Walter Winchell and Dorothy Kilgallen—were part of the new breed of "gossip columnists" that flourished in the 1920s. Gossip columnists were just what the name suggests: journalists who reported on gossip about famous personalities, as well as covering sensational trials like the Sheppard case. In Hollywood, Hedda Hopper and Louella Parsons were the most famous gossip columnists. Nationwide, however, Walter Winchell was one of the most influential journalists in America from the 1920s through the 1950s. Millions used to listen to his radio show, which began "Good evening, Mr. and Mrs. America," and which always ended, "This is Mrs. Winchell's little boy, Walter."

America believed Sheppard was guilty before even a word of testimony was heard. Certainly, his story sounded unlikely, but that alone did not prove Sheppard was guilty.

Sheppard's Wife Brutally Slain

This amazing story began on July 3, 1954. Samuel Sheppard, a well-to-do thirty-year-old doctor, and his pregnant wife, Marilyn, invited their neighbors, the Ahearns, over for drinks at the Sheppard home on the shores of Lake Erie. While the others watched TV, Sheppard dozed on the couch. Just after midnight the Ahearns left. Sam Sheppard remained sleeping on the couch while Marilyn Sheppard went to bed.

Sometime later, according to his version of events, Sheppard heard a loud moan or scream. He rushed upstairs to the bedroom and saw "a white form" standing beside the bed. Then, he said, everything went black. When he came to, Sheppard realized he had been clubbed on the neck. He stumbled across to the bed where his wife lay motionless. A sudden noise sent him racing downstairs. By the rear door he spotted "a man with bushy hair." He chased the intruder onto the beach and tackled him from behind. During the struggle Sheppard blacked out again. This time when he came to, he was partially immersed in the waters of Lake Erie. Groggily, he staggered back to the house and phoned for help.

OPPOSITE PAGE

Sam Sheppard at his trial on October 18, 1954. He was charged with the murder of his wife, Marilyn, on July 4th of that same year.

MURDER

Police found Marilyn Sheppard's half-nude body lying in a pool of blood. Downstairs, a writing desk had been looted and the contents of Sheppard's medical bag lay spread across the floor. It appeared that someone had come to rob the house and ended up killing Marilyn Sheppard.

Meanwhile, Sam Sheppard's two brothers whisked him away to the hospital they owned. It was this departure, more than anything else, that caused the press to treat Sheppard so harshly. Newspaper editors, eager to increase the number of their readers, claimed that the wealthy "Sheppard Boys" had drawn together to protect a member of their family.

The discovery at the house of a canvas bag, containing Sheppard's wristwatch, key chain and key, and a fraternity ring, caused some to speculate that he had faked a robbery to conceal the murder. When it was revealed that he was involved with another woman, official suspicion about Sheppard's innocence increased. Urged on by an increasingly hostile Cleveland press, police arrested Sheppard and charged him with murder.

The Carnival Begins

The state of Ohio opened its case against Sheppard on Monday, October 18. Judge Edward Blythin set the tone for the trial early. He would be up for reelection the following November. In order to increase his popularity with the press, he gave handwritten passes to the trial to such notable reporters as Dorothy Kilgallen and Bob Considine. He even provided them with their own special table at which to sit. Blythin presided over a court that was in an uproar, what *The New York Times* would later describe as "a Roman circus."

Prosecutor John Mahon made the most of what was a very weak case. Without any direct evidence against the defendant, other than that he was in the house when Marilyn Sheppard was killed, Mahon emphasized the possible flaws in Sam Sheppard's story. Why was there no sand in his hair when he claimed to have been stretched out on the beach? Where was the T-shirt that he had been wearing? Had bloodstains received during the attack forced him to destroy it? Also, why would a burglar first take the belongings found in the canvas bag and then throw them away? Besides which, said Mahon, "Police . . . could find no evidence that anyone had broken in." For a motive, Mahon pointed to Sheppard's affair with Susan Hayes, a lab technician at the family hospital, as reason enough for Sheppard to want to be rid of his wife.

Initially, the lack of a murder weapon posed problems for the prosecution. However, Cuyahoga County coroner Samuel R. Gerber got around this difficulty by telling the court that a bloody imprint found on the pillow beneath Marilyn Sheppard's head was made by a "two-blade surgical instrument with teeth on the end of each blade." He said it was probably the missing weapon. For some reason, the defense attorneys did not question this vague statement, a failure that would ruin their client's chances of acquittal.

Morals, not Murder

Hayes testified about her romantic relationship with Sheppard: "He said he loved his wife very much but not as a wife. He was thinking of divorce." Other than showing that Sheppard was unfaithful, Hayes' testimony proved nothing. Still, the damage had been done. Sheppard wound up being tried more for his morals (sense of right and wrong) than for any crime.

Probably the most effective prosecution witness was Judge Blythin. His dislike of the defendant was plain. Early in the trial he had remarked to Kilgallen: "Sheppard is as guilty as hell," and throughout the proceedings he made things as difficult as possible for the defense. Such an attitude on the bench ensured that Sheppard had no chance of receiving a fair trial. His own appearance on the witness stand made little difference. He performed well, but not well enough to overcome the hostile atmosphere in court.

Jury discussions lasted four days and resulted in a guilty verdict for second-degree murder. (A rumor that some jurors were unwilling to commit Sheppard to the electric chair and might therefore acquit him had forced Judge Blythin to offer them the possibility of a second-degree murder conviction.) Blythin pronounced sentence: "It is now the judgment of this court that you be taken to the Ohio Penitentiary, there to remain for the rest of your natural life."

A Second Chance

In November 1961, twenty-nine-year-old attorney F. Lee Bailey took up Sheppard's cause. He filed a stream of legal papers on Sheppard's behalf, every one of which was rejected. In March 1964, however, by chance Bailey attended a dinner party. Among the guests was Kilgallen, and she happened to repeat the off-the-record remark Judge Blythin made to her during Sheppard's trial. Bailey listened intently. If he could show that the judge had been biased, this would be grounds for a new trial.

Four months later a judge ordered Sheppard freed on bail, saying that the carnival conditions surrounding his trial "fell far below the minimum requirements for due process."

MURDER

SAM REESE SHEPPARD

Sam Reese Sheppard, son of accused murderer Sam Sheppard and murder victim Marilyn Sheppard, has continued to investigate his mother's murder, believing that justice was not served by his father's conviction. In 1995, nearly forty years after his mother's death, he co-authored *Mockery of Justice: The True Story of the Sheppard Murder Case,* with attorney and investigative reporter Cynthia L. Cooper. In 1997, in response to his efforts, the process of exhuming Sheppard's body to compare DNA samples to blood left at the crime scene got underway. Reese Sheppard still campaigns against the death penalty and works with groups such as Murder Victim Families for Reconciliation, Amnesty International, and the National Coalition to Abolish the Death Penalty.

The following year Bailey argued Sheppard's case before the U.S. Supreme Court. He claimed that Blythin had displayed prejudice and that the trial had been conducted in such a way that Sheppard's right to a fair trial had been violated. The court agreed. On June 6, 1965, the justices handed down their decision setting aside Sheppard's 1954 conviction because Judge Blythin "did not fulfill his duty to protect Sheppard from inherently prejudicial publicity which saturated the county."

Ohio tried Sheppard again. Media interest remained high, but this time it was kept in check when the trial opened October 24, 1966, before Judge Francis J. Talty. Prosecutor John Corrigan led witnesses through essentially the same stories that they had told over a decade earlier, but they now faced a defense attorney who was working at the peak of his powers. Bailey managed to overcome all their testimony, particularly that of coroner Samuel Gerber. Referring to the "surgical instrument" that might have served as a murder weapon, Gerber announced that he had spent the last twelve years looking for just such an item "all over the United States."

"Please tell us what you found?" asked Bailey.

Sadly, Gerber shook his head: "I didn't find one."

On December 16, 1966, the jury took less than twelve hours to return a verdict of not guilty: Sam Sheppard's ordeal was over. However, Sheppard had only a few years of freedom; he died in 1970.

Suggestions for Further Reading

Bailey, F. Lee with Harvey Aronson. *The Defense Never Rests.* New York: Stein and Day, 1971.

Cooper, Cynthia L. with Sam Reese Sheppard. *Mockery of Justice: The True Story of the Sheppard Murder Case.* Boston: Northeastern University Press, 1995.

Gaute, J. H. H. and Robin Odell. *The Murderers' Who's Who.* London: W. H. Allen, 1989.

Pollack, Jack Harrison. *Dr. Sam—An American Tragedy.* Chicago: Regnery, 1972.

Sheppard, Sam. *Endure And Conquer.* Cleveland: World, 1966.

Sheppard, Stephen with Paul Holmes. *My Brother's Keeper.* New York: David McKay, 1964.

Angela Davis Trial: 1972

Defendant: Angela Y. Davis

Crimes Charged: Murder, kidnapping, conspiracy

Chief Defense Lawyers: Leo Branton Jr., Margaret Burnham, Howard Moore Jr., Sheldon Otis, and Dorris Brin Walker

Chief Prosecutor: Albert Harris

Judge: Richard E. Arnason

Place: San Jose, California

Dates of Trial: February 28–June 4, 1972

Verdict: Not guilty

SIGNIFICANCE: An unusual mix of murder, race, and politics made this trial memorable.

At 10:45 A.M. on August 7, 1970, a gunman interrupted the Marin County trial of San Quentin inmate James McClain, who was facing a charge of attempted murder. The gunman, Jonathan Jackson, one of the so-called "Soledad Brothers," handed weapons to McClain and two other men in the courtroom, Ruchell Magee and William Christmas. Together, they took Judge Harold Haley, prosecutor Gary Thomas, and three women jurors hostage, then tried to escape in a van. When guards opened fire, Haley, Jackson, McClain, and Christmas were killed. Thomas and Magee were seriously injured.

Suspicion that the plot was connected to the Soledad Brothers—three radical black Soledad Prison inmates—increased when Angela Davis suddenly disappeared. Davis, a supporter of the Soledad Brothers, had recently been fired from her job as a professor at the University of California at Los Angeles because of her Communist sympathies. She was finally found in New York on October 13. After she was sent back to California, she was formally charged with murder, conspiracy, and kidnapping. The prosecutors wanted to prove that Davis had arranged the escape attempt in order to exchange hostages for the freedom of her boyfriend, George Jackson, the older brother of Jonathan Jackson.

Trial Opens

The task of selecting a jury began before Judge Richard E. Arnason on February 28, 1972. The racial and political aspects of the case made jury selection an especially difficult task, but eventually an all-white jury was chosen, and prosecutor Albert Harris was able to make his opening address. He outlined four elements necessary to establish guilt using circumstantial evidence (when there is nothing directly connecting the accused with the crime). The elements were motive, means, opportunity, and consciousness of guilt. "The evidence will show," he said, "that her [Davis's] basic motive was not to free political prisoners, but to free the one prisoner that she loved." The means came on August 5, 1970, when, in the company of Jonathan Jackson, "she purchased the shotgun that was used in the commission of the crime." Harris believed that the days leading up to the crime, many of which Davis spent with Jonathan Jackson, provided an opportunity to commit the crime. Finally, Davis's consciousness of guilt was proven by the fact that just hours after the shooting, she boarded a flight and went into hiding.

Davis Ridicules Case

Although she had an impressive team of attorneys, Davis chose to make the opening remarks to the jury herself. Wisely, she said little about her political beliefs. She focused instead on the flaws in the prosecution's case. These were that she had bought the shotgun openly, using her own name, and, more importantly, that the Marin shooting seemed to have had nothing to do with George Jackson. "The evidence will show that there's absolutely no credible proof of what the precise purpose of [the events of] August 7 was," she said.

This argument was answered by a prosecution witness, news photographer James Kean. He had taken several photographs of the shooting incident and now testified to hearing McClain say at the time, "Tell them we want the Soledad Brothers released by twelve o'clock."

Chief defense attorney Leo Branton cross-examined Kean: "This remark that was made about freeing the Soledad Brothers—it was the last thing that was said just as the group got on the elevator . . . is that a fact?"

"Yes. That's right."

"You never heard Jonathan Jackson say anything about free the Soledad Brothers, did you?"

"No, I did not."

"You didn't hear anybody say it other than McClain and it was the last thing he said as he headed down the elevator; is that right?"

"Yes."

"As though it were a parting gesture, is that correct?"

"That's right."

Branton must have been satisfied with this testimony. His satisfaction must have increased when Deputy Sheriff Theodore Hughes testified that he had heard some of the escaped convicts shout clearly, "Free our brothers at Folsom, free all our brothers."Again, there was no mention of Soledad Prison.

The testimony of Gary Thomas, the prosecution's star witness, was more difficult to dismiss. Permanently paralyzed by his bullet wound, he was brought into court in a wheelchair. The key part of his testimony was his statement that he had seen up close Magee shoot Judge Haley with the shotgun.

Branton had the difficult task of attempting to prove that Thomas's memory might have been clouded by the trauma he had suffered. "Isn't it a fact, sir, that the first fusillade [rapid fire] of shots that came into the van killed both Jonathan Jackson and McClain, and that you thereupon grabbed the gun that McClain was holding . . . and that you turned around and began firing into the back of the van . . . and that you hit Christmas and you hit Magee, and you possibly even hit Judge Haley?"

Thomas angrily denied this assertion, and Branton had to back down. He made little headway with Thomas, except getting the witness to agree that at no time did he hear anyone mention the Soledad Brothers.

Mysterious Telephone Number Surfaces

Prosecutor Harris next turned his attention to a piece of paper found on the body of Jonathan Jackson. On it was written a number that was assigned to a public telephone at San Francisco International Airport. Har-

Angela Davis Trial: 1972

OPPOSITE PAGE

Angela Davis is escorted by two FBI agents after her arrest in October 1970.

MURDER

THE FIRST AFRICAN AMERICAN WOMAN JUDGE IN MASSACHUSETTS

Angela Davis's lawyer, Margaret Burnham, went on to have a distinguished legal career. Davis was actually Burnham's first client after she had graduated from the University of Pennsylvania Law School. She later defended a prisoner charged with assault in the 1971 riots at Attica Prison in New York State. When the Communist Party tried to get on the ballot for the 1976 presidential elections, Burnham represented it. Then, on August 12, 1977, she was sworn in as an associate justice of the Boston Municipal Court, the first African American woman judge ever to serve in Massachusetts. Burnham was appointed by then-Governor Michael Dukakis. She chose a symbolic site for her swearing-in ceremony: the Harriet Tubman Community Center in the heart of Roxbury, a poor African American community. About her appointment, Burnham said, "I don't have any illusions that I can make *tremendous* changes in the character of justice by taking this particular seat. But I see it as *one* way to extend the struggle for human rights."

ris contended that this piece of evidence clearly showed that Jonathan Jackson intended to telephone Angela Davis at the airport. Further, when Davis did not receive the call she panicked and took the next flight to Los Angeles.

All of this sounded fine but did not hold up. First of all, Branton pointed out that the telephone was in the airport's South Terminal, near the Western Airlines counter. Why, he asked, had nobody seen Davis waiting by the phone? And why had she left the counter for Western Airlines—which offered flights every hour to Los Angeles—and walked over to the Central Terminal to catch a flight on Pacific Southwest Airlines? It did not make sense.

In one last desperate effort to save their case, the prosecutors fought to introduce into evidence an eighteen-page "diary" that Davis had kept.

While the diary clearly showed the love that Davis felt for George Jackson, it did not provide any evidence to support the charges against her.

Such a poor prosecution hardly called for much of a response. Branton called just twelve witnesses to support his assertion that Angela Davis was entirely innocent. The case went to the jurors on June 2, 1972. They came back two days later with not-guilty verdicts on all three charges.

But for Angela Davis it was not much of a victory. Six months before she faced her accusers, George Jackson had himself been shot to death in an alleged prison break.

Before the trial many people, including some on her own defense team, doubted Davis had a good chance of receiving a fair hearing from an all-white jury. That the jurors were able to separate politics and race from the essential facts of the case said a great deal about their individual honor and helped to make this trial one of the legal system's finer moments.

Suggestions for Further Reading

Aptheker, Bettina. *The Morning Breaks.* New York: International, 1975.

Davis, Angela. *Angela Davis.* New York: International, 1988.

Major, Reginald. *Justice in the Round.* New York: Third Press, 1973.

Mitchell, Charlene. *The Fight to Free Angela Davis.* New York: Outlook, 1972.

Timothy, Mary. *Jury Woman.* San Francisco: Glide, 1975.

Guildford Four Trial:
1975

Defendants: Patrick Armstrong, Gerard Conlon, Paul Hill, and Carole Richardson

Crimes Charged: Murder and conspiracy to cause explosions

Chief Defense Lawyers: John Leonard, Q.C. (Queen's Counsel), Arthur Mildon, Q.C., Eric Myers, Q.C., Gordon Ward, and Lord Basil Wigoder, Q.C.

Chief Prosecutors: Sir Michael Havers, Q.C., and Michael Hill, Q.C.

Judge: Sir John Donaldson

Place: London, England

Dates of Trial: September 16–October 22, 1975

Verdicts: Guilty

Sentences: Life imprisonment

SIGNIFICANCE: When the Irish Republican Army bombed three pubs (bars), killing seven people, the British people were outraged. Police were determined to produce quick arrests to calm the public and press. This case is a tragic example of how the overly intense investigation of terrorist activities led to a failure of justice.

During 1974, Irish Republican Army (IRA) threats to bring terrorism to the British mainland became a reality. The bloodshed peaked on October 5, when bombs exploded at two pubs popular with soldiers in Guildford, Surrey: the Seven Stars and the Horse and Groom. Five people, including four army recruits, were killed. A month later, on November 7, a second bomb thrown through the window of the Kings Arms pub in Woolwich, South London, killed two customers. On each occasion, in addition to the deaths they caused, the bombs injured many. Before the month was over, Parliament had passed the Prevention of Terrorism Act. Its most important section gave police the power to arrest with warrants individuals they reasonably suspected of being involved in terrorism.

Arrests Made

The first person arrested under this act was Paul Hill, age twenty, who had been born in Belfast, Northern Ireland, but was living in a run-down house in Kilburn, North London. Officially Hill's name first came to police attention from an informant's tip. However, they already suspected Hill of involvement in the abduction and murder of an ex-soldier, Brian Shaw, a crime for which he was later convicted. However Hill came to be detained by police, what is certain is that, while in custody, he signed a statement admitting responsibility for the Guildford and Woolwich bombings. He also named Gerard Conlon, twenty, as a co-conspirator (someone who helps commit a crime). The next day, Conlon was arrested at his home in Belfast. Further interrogation of these two led to more arrests, among them those of Patrick Armstrong, twenty-four, and his seventeen-year-old English girlfriend, Carole Richardson.

It appeared to be an easy case. When asked to plead, each defendant answered "Not Guilty," except for Hill, who declared, "I refuse to take part in this. Your justice stinks!" Hill's refusal to plead guilty or innocent—a tactic often used by IRA prisoners—made matters worse for his co-defendants. For the men, the sole defense was that the "confessions" had been made under pressure. This meant police threatened them or their families.

Strong Defense for Richardson

Carole Richardson was on far firmer legal ground. In late December 1974, a friend, Frank Johnson, had gone to police. He told them that, on October 5, he and Richardson had been watching a band together in south London at the time of the Guildford explosion. The band checked their records and confirmed the date, and there were even photographs of Richardson taken in the band's dressing room to confirm that she was there. According to Johnson, this information did not please the police, and he was repeatedly beaten until he took his story back. However, on the witness stand he stood by what he had originally said. Eric Myers, Q.C., Richard-

After spending fifteen years in prison, a court finally found the Guildford Four innocent of terrorism. Pictured below is Gerard Conlon, clenching his fist in victory.

son's lawyer, told the jury that the police had not "breathed a word" of Johnson's statement to the defense, adding, "This was straight out of the dirty tricks department."

Chief prosecutor Sir Michael Havers, Q.C., chose to ignore the most significant part of Johnson's testimony—that he had met Richardson in London at 6:30 P.M. Instead he concentrated on showing that Richardson had time to place the bomb in Guildford at 7:00 P.M. and get to the concert fifty minutes later. A police car, he announced, had managed to make this thirty-mile trip through South London's busy streets in a remarkable forty-eight minutes.

Detective Inspector Timothy Blake then took the stand. Conlon's lawyer, Lord Basil Wigoder, Q.C., accused him of physically abusing Conlon during questioning. Blake responded that he had not even set eyes upon Conlon until after he had been interrogated. Wigoder then asked Blake to roll up his sleeves. During the course of his beating, Conlon had seen tattoos on Blake's arms and was able to describe them clearly; now the court was able to see just how correct Conlon's description had been. Asked how Conlon could have come by such personal details, Blake

weakly suggested that Conlon might have seen him in his shirt sleeves at the police station.

As one of the main interviewing officers, Detective Sergeant Anthony Jermey denied defense claims that Hill had been threatened while in custody by a police officer with a gun. He was less sure, though, when Wigoder asked about the way the various confessions had been obtained. Jermey had produced twenty pages of confessions and the record of Conlon's interrogation; all of it was incriminating (showed proof of involvement in the crime) and none of it mentioned police brutality. Wigoder asked Jermey when he wrote these notes.

"Seven hours later," said Jermey. When Wigoder remarked that he had an excellent memory, the officer explained how a good memory was a requirement for good police work. At this point Wigoder inquired: "What was the first question I put to you in the witness box?" Jermey's mind appeared to go blank. He had just claimed to be able to recall a thirteen-hour interrogation word for word seven hours after it ended, yet he could not now repeat a question put to him just minutes earlier.

When it came time to testify, Hill kept his self-assured attitude, refusing to answer questions or responding sarcastically. When Conlon's turn came, he had to deal with accusations from Havers that he had deliberately inserted mistakes into his confession in order to "pull the wool" over the jury's eyes.

"I have no need to pull the wool over the jury's eyes," Conlon protested, "I am telling the truth."

"Did you enjoy leading the gang which blew up these people in Guildford?"

"I'd never been to Guildford till the police took me there. If they'd told me to put down the Pope's name as one of the bombers, I would have done it. I'd have put down anybody's name to save my Ma!" He was referring to police threats to hurt his family.

In summing up, Justice John Donaldson boiled the trial down to a single issue, telling the jury that they had to decide whom to believe—police officers with many years of distinguished service, or the defendants.

On October 22, 1975, the jury made it clear which version of events they favored. The verdict was guilty. In passing sentences of life imprisonment on all four defendants, the judge sounded as if he were sorry that the death penalty was no longer available. However, he did recommend that Hill should only be released "on grounds of old age or infirmity." This made Hill's the longest sentence ever handed down in a British court.

MURDER

Captured IRA Militants Claim Responsibility

As the case of the Guildford Four faded from the headlines, its place was taken by yet another trial arising from recent IRA terrorism. On January 24, 1977, four Irishmen arrested after a siege (attack) on Balcombe Street in London stepped into court. All of the defendants were admitted terrorists who refused to plead innocent or guilty because their indictments (charges of illegal acts) failed to include the bombings for which the Guildford Four had been convicted. On behalf of his fellow defendants, Joseph O'Connell admitted carrying out both bombings. He proved his claim by mentioning that he had spoken to a soldier at the Guildford pub about late-night bus schedules just before the bomb had exploded. This incident, related by the soldier at the time of the investigation, had never been made public.

Because of these developments, an appeal (legal request for new trial or reversal of conviction) was filed on behalf of the Guildford Four. On October 10, 1977, their hearing for a new trial began. All of the Balcombe Street defendants—Joseph O'Connell, Harry Duggan, Eddie Butler, and Brendan Dowd—gave evidence, freely admitting their terrorist activities and claiming they did not know anything about Hill and the others. At this hearing, Havers, once again the chief prosecution lawyer, was forced to admit that O'Connell, Duggan, and Butler had indeed been responsible for the Guildford bombing, yet he insisted that Hill had helped them. Despite the fresh evidence, the court preferred to rely on the confessions the Guildford defendants had signed, probably under great stress. On October 29, Lord Justice Roskill said: "We are all of the clear opinion that there are no possible grounds for doubting the justice of any of these four convictions or for ordering new trials."

A large number of people believed that O'Connell, a hardened terrorist destined to spend the rest of his life behind bars, had nothing to lose by admitting to the Guildford and Woolwich bombings. In any event, he succeeded in causing the British government great embarrassment.

Doubts About Statements

Others preferred to debate the justness or unjustness of the Guildford Four convictions. Those voicing concern about the convictions included two men at the top of the judicial system, Lord Patrick Devlin and George Scarman. As far back as the 1950s, Devlin, a distinguished trial judge, had expressed doubts about the truth of certain confessions and statements that had allegedly been given to police officers. Years of sitting on the bench listen-

THE IRISH REPUBLICAN ARMY

The Guildford Four were convicted in part because of strong British feeling against the Irish Republican Army (IRA). Originally, the IRA was organized by Michael Collins, a young Irish leader who had participated in the 1916 Easter Rebellion in Dublin. The rebellion was the first modern military attempt by the Irish to win national independence from Great Britain. However, the British suppressed the rebellion and struck back by executing many of its leaders. Collins and his colleagues fought back by forming a military group for the defense of Ireland. The IRA became the military wing of a political party that worked for Irish independence called the Sinn Fein (shin-FAYN). In 1922, southern Ireland was granted partial independence, but Northern Ireland remained under British rule. This the IRA could not accept, and it continued to agitate against the British. In 1969, the group split: the "official" majority opposed violence, while the "provisional" (temporary) wing believed that the British could be defeated only through terrorist actions.

ing to supposedly word-for-word accounts had taught Devlin something. There were often great differences between the speech patterns in the confessions and those of the accused individuals who appeared before him.

Such support kept the Guildford Four case in the public eye, and finally led to a request for an independent panel of police officers to examine all of the evidence. Exposed at last to fair examination, the prosecution's case collapsed. Investigators found draft notes that clearly proved that police officers had lied in saying that statements made by the accused had been written down as they were spoken. Investigators also found that genuine statements had been either deliberately withheld or changed.

Convictions Overturned

On October 19, 1989, a court under Lord Chief Justice Geoffrey Lane threw out the convictions of all four defendants. All were then released from prison.

MURDER

The latest chapter in this tragedy came on April 20, 1993. Three police officers connected with the investigation, Vernon Attwell, John Donaldson, and Thomas Style, went on trial, charged with conspiring to distort the course of justice. In effect, their hearing became a retrial of the Guildford Four. Defense lawyers successfully argued, however, that although the police might not have followed proper procedures, the men who were originally convicted were still guilty. On May 19, 1993, each officer was acquitted.

Suggestions for Further Reading

Bennett, Ronan. *Double Jeopardy.* London: Penguin, 1993.

Conlon, Gerry. *Proved Innocent.* London: Penguin, 1991.

Hill, Paul and Ronan Bennett. *Stolen Years.* London: Doubleday, 1990.

Maguire, Anne. *Miscarriage of Justice.* Boulder, CO: Roberts Rinehart, 1994.

McKee, Grant and Ros Franey. *Time Bomb.* London: Bloomsbury, 1988.

Woffinden, Bob. *Miscarriages of Justice.* London: Hodder & Stoughton, 1987.

Baader-Meinhof Trial: 1975–1977

Defendants: Andreas Baader, Ulrike Meinhof, Gudrun Ensslin, and Jan-Carl Raspe

Crimes Charged: Murder, attempted murder, robbery, the forming of a criminal association

Defense Lawyers: Marie-Luise Becker, Peter Grigat, Hans Heinz Heldmann, Dieter Konig, Manfred Kunzel, Karl-Heinz Linke, Arndt Muller, Rupert von Plottnitz, Helmut Riedel, Otto Schily, Dieter Schnabel, Eberhard Schwarz, and Gerd Temming

Prosecutors: Siegfried Buback, Werner Widera, Heinrich Wunder, and Peter Zeis

Judges: Theodor Prinzing and Eberhard Foth

Place: Stammheim, West Germany

Dates: May 21, 1975–April 21, 1977

Verdicts: Guilty

Sentences: Life imprisonment

SIGNIFICANCE: The notorious Baader-Meinhof gang injured, rather than advanced, its cause. During the trial, the defendants' disorderly behavior caused a change in the Code of Criminal Procedure. Trials thereafter could go forward without the defendants present. The trial also brought about a law that gave officials the power to end communication between unruly prisoners and their lawyers, other prisoners, or the outside world. Finally, the trial led to the assassination of West Germany's federal prosecutor general.

MURDER

The German terrorist group, the Baader-Meinhof Gang, began among students in West Germany. They believed that the private property system (capitalism) was unjust. Its young people, who grew up in comfort, drew inspiration from Ulrike Meinhof, a radical writer.

In 1968, a court convicted Andreas Baader and his girlfriend, Gudrun Ensslin, of firebombing two Frankfurt department stores. However, their jailers later released them as lawyers appealed their case. When the court rejected these appeals, they went into hiding to avoid jail. In February 1970, they met Meinhof. Their mutual interests in left-wing causes and such drugs as LSD soon bound them together.

Courthouse guards stand watch outside while accused group leaders from the Baader-Meinhof gang began their first day of trial on May 21, 1975.

Guerrilla Training

Baader and Ensslin established a Berlin headquarters for their followers. The group robbed banks, stole cars, and took over the apartments of their supporters. They traveled to Jordan for intensive training in guerrilla warfare and terrorist tactics. Back in Germany, they formed an organization known as the Red Army Faction, or RAF.

Authorities soon realized that the RAF had taken the law into its own hands. It was heavily armed and did not stop at arson and bombing. After American military forces mined harbors in North Vietnam in May 1972, terrorist bombings began in Germany. At the Fifth U.S. Army Corps officer's dining room in Frankfurt, one person was killed and thirteen were injured.

The RAF declared responsibility, saying, "West Germany will no longer be a safe hinterland for the strategists of extermination in Vietnam." Also in May, a pipe bomb injured five police officers in Augsburg. Sixty cars were blown up in Munich. The wife of a federal judge was severely injured in Karlsruhe. Seventeen people were injured in Hamburg. Finally, in the dining hall of the U.S. Army in Heidelberg, five American soldiers were injured and three were killed.

Leaders Seized

On June 1, 1972, the West German Federal Border Police went to a garage in Frankfurt where they had found large amounts of explosives. Amid tear gas and gunfire they captured Baader, Jan-Carl Raspe, and Holger Meins. A police sharpshooter wounded Baader in the thigh. A week later, police arrested Ensslin in a Hamburg dress shop after a sales clerk noticed a pistol in her jacket. Next, acting on a tip, police found Meinhof in an apartment in Hanover.

Imprisoned for nearly three years awaiting trial, the group undertook a hunger strike. They insisted they would eat only if guards released them from solitary confinement (being kept alone in a prison cell). Holger Meins died of starvation.

The trial opened on May 21, 1975, in a fortress-like building constructed specifically for the event. Barbed wire covered the area around it. Mounted police patrolled nearby. Steel netting covered the roof to catch any dropped explosives, even though aircraft were banned from the airspace over the building.

"Shut Up, Linke!"

Some 200 spectators were witnesses to the confusion that surrounded the trial. The defendants protested the use of courtroom microphones, interrupted constantly, and refused to sit down. Baader repeatedly told his court-appointed lawyer, "Shut up, Linke!" Ensslin ordered defense counsel Manfred Kunzel not to speak for her. The loud chaos soon included shouts from the audience. The judges frequently ordered the four defendants removed from the courtroom. The defense lawyers argued that their clients were physically unfit to stand trial. All suffered from such low blood pressure and loss of weight that their powers of concentration diminished. The defense lawyers finally walked out in protest when the judges allowed the trial to continue.

The next day, Baader and Raspe called their attorneys an obscene name, and the four were again expelled. Brought back one by one (Meinhof was carried in, her hands and feet held by four officers), they repeated their insulting language. They yelled "Fascist," and called the presiding judge an "old swine."

At last, after twenty-six days, Federal General Prosecutor Siegfried Buback was able to present the charge against Baader, Ensslin, Meinhof, and Raspe:

> . . . that maliciously and by methods constituting danger to the public they did on two occasions murder in all four persons, and on other occasions attempted to murder at least fifty-four other persons;
>
> . . . that they did employ explosive materials . . . endangering life and limb and causing danger to other objects of particular value . . . and they did form an association with the object of committing criminal offenses.

The defendants were not present. They were in their cells, which guards described as masses of cluttered, rotting food, cigarette butts, ashes, books, files, and newspaper clippings.

In the Absence of the Defendants

On the trial's fortieth day, the Code of Criminal Procedure, which governed how criminal trials took place, was changed. A trial could now continue in the absence of defendants if the judge ruled that they were themselves responsible for their absence. Noting that the prosecution had promised to present 997 witnesses, including 80 experts on various aspects of the evidence, Judge Theodor Prinzing ordered the proceedings to continue.

The defense lawyers charged bias. Meinhof pleaded, "The prisoner kept in isolation has only one possible way of showing that his conduct has changed, and that's betrayal. When you're in isolation, either you silence a prisoner, by which I mean he dies, or you get him to talk. And that means confession and betrayal."

On January 13, 1976, the defendants acknowledged they were members of a guerrilla group and claimed "political responsibility" for the bombings, while not admitting criminal responsibility. In February, March, and April, with the defendants usually absent, witnesses presented evidence on the bombings in the cities of Heidelberg, Augsburg, Munich, and Hamburg.

Prison guards reported bitter conflicts between Meinhof and the others, especially Ensslin. Meanwhile, defense lawyers tried to call several prominent witnesses, including former U.S. President Richard M. Nixon, former U.S. Secretary of Defense Melvin Laird, and former German Chancellor Willy Brandt. The defense wanted to determine whether using force against military establishments of the United States on West German territory was justified. Their request was denied.

"The Last Act of Rebellion"

On May 9, guards found Meinhof hanging from the grating of the window of her cell. She had made a rope by tearing prison towels into strips and tying them together. She left no note. Months earlier she had written, "Suicide is the last act of rebellion." The defense team then asked that the trial be adjourned. This request, too, was denied, as spectators cried, "Prinzing, murderer!" and "The suicide's a lie!"

The defense proposed to call five American witnesses to testify that the I. G. Farben building in Frankfurt had been a center of U.S. operations during the Vietnam War. "The Vietnam war is not the subject of this trial," ruled Judge Prinzing in refusing to admit the witnesses.

Witness Klaus Junschke, another gang member, calling Judge Prinzing "you Fascist," leapt from the witness box and grappled with a jurist. Both fell to the floor as Junschke shouted, "For Ulrike, you swine!"

Raspe, ordered to leave the courtroom after continued disruptions, had to be forcibly expelled. Baader and prison guards exchanged blows. Ensslin, when not screaming at her guards, was permitted to play her violin in her cell.

On December 8, 1976, the court ordered that from then on, for reasons of security, defense lawyers had to be searched at the checkpoint set up before the courtroom. A search of the prisoners' cells had revealed the presence of drugs as well as a toaster and a camera. Three weeks later, the defense brought its eighty-fifth charge of bias against Judge Prinzing. This time it was upheld by the judge's colleagues, and he was replaced by Judge Eberhard Foth.

Prosecutor Assassinated

Three court-appointed lawyers protested that conversations with their clients were bugged (electronic devices were used to eavesdrop on conversations). When the trial continued, the lawyers walked out in protest. On the morning of April 7, 1977, Federal Prosecutor General Siegfried Buback and his driver were assassinated on their way to court. A letter to the German Press Agency said "the Ulrike Meinhof Commando" took responsibility.

The trial ended on April 21, 1977. One week later, Judge Foth handed down the verdict. Baader, Ensslin, and Raspe were each guilty of three murders connected to six attempted murders, one further murder in connection with one attempted murder, and twenty-seven other attempted murders in connection with bomb attacks. They were also guilty of having formed a criminal association. All received life imprisonment.

A high-security block was built on Stammheim Prison's seventh floor by prisoner laborers. There, ten additional gang members, awaiting trial or already convicted of RAF terrorism, joined their leaders in "the safest prison in the world."

On September 5, 1977, Hanns Martin Schleyer, president of the Employers' Association, was kidnapped. His driver and three police officers were killed. A ransom note demanded the release of Baader, Ensslin, Raspe, and other gang members, and their free passage to "a country of their choice" in exchange for Schleyer's life. A Europe-wide manhunt for the kidnappers and their victim began. Over the next forty-four days, more ransom notes arrived, along with audiotapes and letters from Schleyer that reported on his health and mental condition. German authorities considered how they could negotiate with the kidnappers. On September 20, the parliament passed a special law that permitted the justice ministers to cut off all contact among the prisoners or between the prisoners and their lawyers or with the outside world. Baader, Ensslin, and Raspe threatened suicide.

Jet Hijacked

A Lufthansa Airlines jet bound from Palma de Mallorca in Spain to Frankfurt, carrying eighty-six passengers, was hijacked and flown to

ARMY BASES AND VIETNAM

The Baader-Meinhof gang portrayed its actions as a protest against the United States' involvement in the Vietnam War. At the same time, under its right of occupation after World War II, the United States was allowed to place its military bases in Germany. One of these was the base in Frankfurt where terrorist bombings began in May 1972. During the 1970s, under its North Atlantic Treaty Organization (NATO) agreements, many European countries hosted U.S. bases. Many also faced protests against U.S. involvement in Vietnam, as well as opposition to U.S. nuclear policy.

Rome on October 13. There, the hijackers' leader announced that Schleyer's life depended upon the release of the RAF prisoners as well as the release of two Palestinians imprisoned in Turkey and $15 million in ransom. The plane's passengers were held as hostages. Refueled, the plane was flown to Bahrain in the Persian Gulf, then to Dubai in the United Arab Emirates.

Meantime, German authorities worked to arrange for the delivery of the ransom money, and Baader, Raspe, and Ensslin filled out written questionnaires on where they would like to be sent if they were freed. In a radio interview, the Dubai defense minister praised the Lufthansa captain for giving information in code on the number of hijackers aboard. The hijackers heard the broadcast, executed the pilot, and ordered the copilot to take off for Aden, Yemen, another Persian Gulf state. Refueled there, the plane was flown to the Mogadishu airport in Somalia in northern Africa. There, German commandos who had followed the hijacked plane's zigzag course stormed aboard, killing three of the four hijackers and wounding one. All of the hostages were rescued.

That night in Stammheim Prison, Baader and Raspe each committed suicide with a pistol, and Ensslin hanged herself. Searches of the cells revealed that hiding places for guns, radios, and other illegal items had been built into the walls when the prisoner laborers constructed them.

Two days later, the body of Schleyer was found with three bullets in the head. Police caught his six kidnappers, who received life sentences.

MURDER

Suggestions for Further Reading

Aust, Stefan. *The Baader-Meinhof Group: The Inside Story of a Phenomenon.* Translated by Anthea Bell. London: The Bodley Head, 1985.

Becker, Jillian. *Hitler's Children: The Story of the Baader-Meinhof Terrorist Gang.* Philadelphia and New York: Lippincott, 1977.

Carr, Gordon. *The Angry Brigade.* London: Victor Gollancz, 1975.

Wright, Joanne. *Terrorist Propaganda: The Red Army Faction and the Provisional IRA, 1968–86.* New York: St. Martin's Press, 1991.

Stephen Biko Inquest: 1977

Presiding Magistrate: Martinhus Prins

Chief Lawyers for Biko Family: Sidney Kentridge and Ernest Wentzel

Chief Lawyers for State/Police: Klaus von Lieres and Retief van Rooyen

Place: Pretoria, South Africa

Date of Inquest: November 14–30, 1977

Verdict: Accidental death

SIGNIFICANCE: All the horrors of apartheid were uncovered in this single case.

For most of the twentieth century South Africa was a divided nation. Through a brutal system of racial separation known as apartheid (a-PART-hade), the ruling Nationalist Party ran the country as two separate systems. On the one side was the privileged white minority—rich and all-powerful. On the other were the millions of deprived "non-whites" that made up the overwhelming majority of the country, who endured lives of harsh repression and economic hardship.

While countries all over the world condemned South Africa, the seeds of ultimate change were sown from within the country by a few courageous voices. One of the most forceful and well-spoken of these belonged to Stephen Biko.

Biko was born in King William's Town, a black suburb of Cape Town, and grew up with the miseries of apartheid. Highly political, in the

MURDER

late 1960s he founded the Black Consciousness Movement, and in so doing made himself a marked man. Three times he was taken into custody, twice briefly and once for 101 days. His fourth and final imprisonment began on August 18, 1977, when he was stopped by the Security Police in the Eastern Cape Province and charged with breaking a restriction order that confined him to his own township.

Three weeks later he was hustled into room 619 of the Sanlam Building in Port Elizabeth, handcuffed, placed in leg irons, tortured, and beaten. Eventually, he lapsed into a coma from which he never recovered. On September 13, 1977, Stephen Biko died. He was just thirty-one years old.

At first, the officials blamed his death on the after-effects of a hunger strike. They then changed their story to say he had struck his head against a wall during a struggle while being questioned. Finally, after the conflicting stories had gone to absurd lengths, the government reluctantly agreed to an inquest (legal investigation) to determine if there had been wrongdoing on the part of police.

It was held at the Old Synagogue in Pretoria, and began on November 14, 1977. Despite a large media presence representing countries from all over the world, officials decided to conduct as much of the in-

The body of Stephen Biko lies in a mortuary in King Williams Town, South Africa. This picture was taken shortly after his death in September 1977.

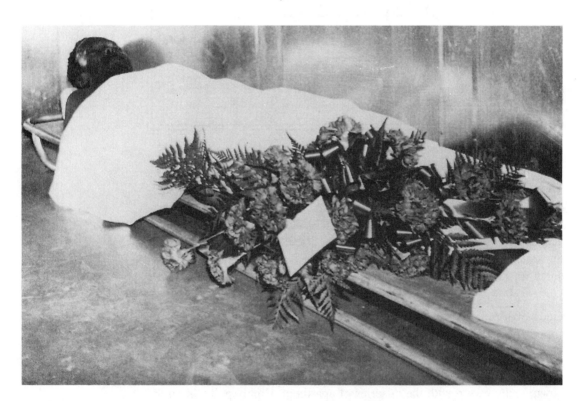

quest as possible in Afrikaans, the language of the ruling white Nationalists. This, combined with the court's poor sound level, often made it difficult to follow the testimony, which began with an autopsy report by Chief State Pathologist Dr. J. D. Loubser, who found that Biko had died of "extensive brain injury."

The Interrogation Begins

The Transvaal's Deputy Attorney General, Klaus von Lieres, led the officer in charge of Biko's interrogation, Major Harold Snyman of the Security Police, through his evidence. Snyman said the interrogation began at 10:30 A.M. and lasted until 6 P.M. During that time, he said, Biko was "extremely aggressive" and very uncooperative about answering questions concerning his political activities.

Sidney Kentridge, chief counsel for the Biko family, wanted to know "what method of persuasion did you use to make an unwilling witness talk to you?"

Snyman denied that he and other officers had beaten Biko, declaring such actions were necessary because they had unlimited time to get the information required. This explanation sounded fine until Kentridge pointed out that for Biko, a man used to prison cells, threats of incarceration would be meaningless.

Under Kentridge's persistent questioning, Snyman described how, after Biko's leg irons and handcuffs were removed, he went "berserk" and tried to attack Warrant Officer Johann Beneke. Snyman said he and Captain Daantjie Siebert went to Beneke's assistance and tried to restrain Biko, who was "clearly beside himself with fury." Several tables were knocked over in the scuffle. Snyman said the amount of violence used against Biko to get him under control was "reasonable, and only as much as was necessary to pin him down on the floor and handcuff him." Next morning Snyman visited Biko again. The shackled man, who had a "wild expression" in his eyes, and a visible swelling on his upper lip, still refused to answer questions and would not take any water. The following day Biko slipped into a coma. He was taken to hospital but failed to respond to treatment and died.

"How did you feel when you heard that Mr. Biko had died?" asked Kentridge.

"I felt bad about it," said Snyman. "He was worth more to us alive than dead."

"Were you surprised he had died?"

"I was surprised. We did not think there was so much wrong with him."

Snyman was followed to the stand by the other members of the interrogation team, all of whom repeated basically the same story as their commanding officer. None of this seemed to make sense alongside the photographs taken of Biko after his death, however, which showed vicious bruising around the wrists and ankles, where the shackles had cut into his skin.

In his final speech, after delivering a bitter attack on those doctors who had attended Biko in hospital, Kentridge asked the court to find that Biko had met his death from "a criminal assault upon him by one or more of the eight members of the Security Police in whose custody he was . . . on September 6th and 7th, 1977."

Answering for the police, Retief van Rooyen dismissed all talk of a cover-up as "sounding just like [mystery writer] Agatha Christie."

On November 30, 1977, Magistrate Martinhus Prins announced his decision. In his opinion, "on the available evidence the death cannot be attributed to any act or omission amounting to a criminal offense on the part of any person."

Mandela's Freedom

With those few words, Prins must have thought he had left the death of Stephen Biko to history. However, history never stands still, and with Nelson Mandela's release from prison in 1990 came the clearest indication yet that white-dominated South Africa was nearing its end. Mandela's election to the presidency shortly afterward raised hopes that something would be done to make up for the wrongs of the past, and ultimately led to the establishment of the Truth and Reconciliation Commission. Under the chairmanship of Archbishop Desmond Tutu, the commissions's task was to confront, expose, and, in most cases, forgive the past, in particular the worst excesses of the ruling Nationalists.

Then, on January 28, 1997, came the bombshell news that five of the officers who interviewed Biko had applied to the Truth Commission for amnesty (forgiveness for offenses). In their application, Snyman, Siebert, Beneke, and two other men—Lieutenant-Colonel Gideon Niewoudt, then a detective sergeant, and Warrant Officer Ruben Marx—all claimed that they were ordered to treat Biko "robustly" but that his death was an accident.

Their confessions sparked off demands, especially from the Black Consciousness Movement, that they should be punished. This was un-

A DISPUTE OVER LANGUAGE

One part of the Biko trial that angered many people was the government's decision to conduct most of the trial in Afrikaans, the language of the ruling Nationalists. Afrikaans came from Dutch, the language of the first permanent European settlers, who populated the Dutch East Indian Company station set up in South Africa in 1652. By 1795, the British had come to rival the Dutch as European settlers, and the two groups struggled over the right to dominate South Africa throughout the nineteenth century, ending in the British victory in the Boer War in 1902. The British established the Union of South Africa in 1910, and in 1931 the British colony achieved its independence. Throughout this time, however, Afrikaans-speaking settlers continued to live and work in South Africa. They were important figures in the Nationalist Party, which established apartheid when it came to power after World War II. The British, by contrast, were associated with more liberal ideas towards black South Africans. Moreover, English was seen as a language connecting South Africa and its people to the world, whereas Afrikaans represented the isolation of the apartheid government. Many political struggles, including riots at Soweto, concerned whether the country's schools should teach black children in Afrikaans or in English.

likely to happen. Without the protection of amnesty, which expired May 1997, the guilty would never have come forward to set the record straight. As for all those who complained that too many people were "getting away with it," President Mandela had this to say: "You can't build a united nation on the basis of revenge."

In 1987 the events surrounding the death of Stephen Biko were dramatized in the movie *Cry Freedom,* starring Denzel Washington and Kevin Kline.

—*Colin Evans*

Suggestions for Further Readings

Attenborough, Richard. *Richard Attenborough's Cry Freedom: A Pictorial Record.* New York: Random House, 1987.

MURDER

Briley, John. *Cry Freedom.* London: Penguin, 1987.

Lewis, Anthony. "Painful Truth." *The New York Times* (February 7, 1997): A33.

Woods, Donald. "Requiem for a Heavyweight." *Newsweek* (February 10, 1997): 43.

Red Brigades Trial:
1982–1983

Defendants: Mario Moretti, Prospero Gallinari, sixty-one others

Crimes Charged: The murder of Aldo Moro and his five bodyguards, eleven additional murders, related terrorist crimes

Chief Defense Lawyers: Various

Chief Prosecutor: Nicolo Amato

Judge: Severino Santiapichi

Place: Rome, Italy

Dates of Trial: April 14, 1982–January 24, 1983

Verdicts: Thirty-two: life imprisonment; twenty-seven: lesser sentences; four: acquitted.

SIGNIFICANCE: The arrest, imprisonment, trial, and conviction of sixty-three terrorists broke the power of the Red Brigades, a terrorist organization that nearly paralyzed Italian political life from 1976 to 1980.

Someone asked Red Brigade leader Mario Moretti what he expected from his trial on charges of killing the former Italian prime minister Aldo Moro. "The Moro trial has already taken place," Moretti said, turning away from the questioner. "It was held four years ago, by us."

That "trial" ended in the execution of Moro, the leader of Italy's Christian Democratic Party and the organizer of the party's historic 1978 alliance (partnership) with the Communist Party of Italy. Moro hoped to increase his party's popularity with a partnership with the Communists.

For their part, the Communists, who had never played an important role in the Italian government, the alliance offered a chance to share power.

The alliance drew intense opposition. Rightists (those with conservative political opinions) viewed any dealings with Communists as associating with the forces of Satan. Leftists (those with liberal political opinions) accused the Communist leader, Sergio Berlinguer, of selling out to middle-class politicians to advance his own career. Nevertheless, Moro and Berlinguer forged ahead. By March 1978, the alliance seemed certain to hold.

Former Prime Minister Kidnapped

The Italian Army State Police crowd the Red Brigades into vans after the first day of their trial.

On March 16, 1978, Moro was traveling to a session of parliament in Rome to celebrate the agreement when the Red Brigades struck. A new government, one that included Communists, was to be sworn in that day. Moro never reached the palace. In a carefully planned ambush near the Christian Democratic Party's headquarters and Moro's apartment, a commando squad opened fire on Moro's car. They killed his five bodyguards,

seized Moro—who was unharmed—and whisked him away to a terrorist hideout. There began the fifty-five-day ordeal that Moretti named the "people's court trial" of Aldo Moro.

The Red Brigades grew out of the radical student movement of the late 1960s. With Communist leaders Karl Marx, Vladimir Lenin, and Mao Zedong as revolutionary guides, the extreme tip of the left wing turned increasingly to violence. By the early 1970s, the Red Brigades had become a terrorist organization, calling for "revolutionary violence" against such officials as police officers, magistrate judges, and executives. Aldo Moro, his captors charged, had been "for twenty years the supreme manager of power in Italy."

Moro Murdered

An intense manhunt failed to uncover the Red Brigades' hideout. There the movement's political thinkers tormented the former prime minister. Moro apparently responded with dignity. Told he was being prosecuted in "the name of the people," he responded that the party he headed had received twelve million votes in the last election. He issued pleas through his captors to the Italian government and to Pope Paul VI to bargain in good faith for his release.

The government of Prime Minister Giulio Andreotti, with the support of Berlinguer's Communists, refused to consider the Red Brigades' demand of thirteen jailed terrorists for Moro. For this, Moro's wife Eleonora would later accuse the Italian government and the United States of being responsible for her husband's death. Moro's captors allowed him to write a last letter home. Then the shots rang out. On May 9, 1978, the police found Moro's bullet-riddled body in the trunk of a car parked near the Christian Democratic headquarters.

The authorities launched another manhunt. Police hauled in suspects, questioned and released them. Finally, in 1982, the kidnapping of an American general in Italy by the Red Brigades led to a big break in the case. Italian police raided the house in which General James Dozier was being held, freed him unharmed, and arrested a number of his kidnappers. Mario Moretti's plumbing sprang a leak, creating a second big break. Tenants on the floor below spotted a water stain on the ceiling and called the fire department. One thing led to another, and the police captured both evidence and the mastermind of the Moro killing.

Many Tried and Convicted

Legal action opened in mid-April 1982 to a burst of gunfire. Terrorists shot at security guards surrounding the trial location, the Olympic Sports Center in Rome. Three men were wounded; in the end, 1,500 troops and police were assigned to protect the sports center. Inside, the sixty-three defendants—twenty-three charged in connection to Moro's death, the others with various other murders, kidnappings, and lesser crimes—were held in six white cages. They were not handcuffed; they were allowed cigarettes. They could even chat with reporters and other observers (some of the defendants threatened those who had written unfavorably about them with violence).

The prosecution presented Moretti, a short, stocky twenty-six-year-old, as the leader of the Moro assassination plot. Prospero Gallinari, thirty-three years old, was Moro's jailer and executioner. The government accused Gallinari of killing his captive with a pistol shot, followed by a burst from an automatic weapon. Antonio Savasta and Patrizio Peci testified against their codefendants in exchange for lighter sentences. The judge, Severino Santiapichi, questioned Savasta closely, but Savasta resisted these attempts to make him give up his commitment to his political beliefs and manner of expressing them. "You have to respect my human dignity," Savasta shouted. "You have to understand that inside the Red Brigades there is difficult debate, much indecision. You should show there's not only scorn for us."

The trial continued well into the autumn. The presentation of dozens of witnesses and tens of thousands of pages of documents met with loud complaints from the defendants in their cages. Another five Red Brigade suspects followed the example of Savasta and Peci, rejecting terrorism, yet refusing to give evidence against any of the other defendants. Moretti stood by his beliefs. "You are trying to wipe out five years of armed struggle, but you will not succeed," he told the court. Moro's widow and children sat through many of the sessions, as did the families of the five slain bodyguards and the other victims.

Italy's top government officials testified towards the end of September. Prime Minister Andreotti said the government regarded the attack on Moro as the possible beginning of widespread revolt (uprising against the government). For that reason, the authorities decided against any form of truce (temporary pause in warfare). "In the first moments we had no idea whether the Moro kidnapping was an isolated incident or part of a nationwide armed revolution." Handing over thirteen experienced revolutionary leaders, he suggested, would have been stupid.

Bettino Craxi, the Socialist leader, took the witness stand on September 28. His party, he testified, established private links to the Red Brigades for the purpose of winning Moro's release. However, the Socialists, too, refused to go along with the terrorists' demands for the freedom of the thirteen jailed terrorists, and so the Craxi talks broke down.

The Christmas and New Year's holidays came and went. Finally, in early January, Judge Santiapichi sent the case to the jury of eleven men and one woman. After a week, the jurors announced their verdicts. Santiapichi handed down the sentences on January 24, 1983. Altogether, thirty-two Red Brigade terrorists, among them Moretti and Gallinari, received life imprisonment. (There is no death penalty in Italy.) Other defendants were given sentences ranging from four months to thirty years. Four were acquitted (found not guilty). Four other defendants, including a senior Red Brigade leader convicted in the Dozier kidnapping, remained a wanted criminal in 1983. They had been convicted despite their absence, as permitted under Italian law.

Some of the defendants looked grim, even stunned, others joked and lit up cigarettes, a few climbed the bars of the white cages to wave at friends or family members in the back of the courtroom.

Moro's Bitter Last Words Discovered

The government said that the verdicts were a substantial blow to the Red Brigades terror organization, and they were. "I remember, almost five years ago, a feeling of impotence (helplessness)," Virginio Rognoni, the interior minister, said afterward. "It seemed impossible to think that one day those responsible for the massacre would be in front of the judges."

Red Brigade attacks continued for several more years, but the organization's back had indeed been broken. The Moro case remained in the news, however. In 1990, the authorities announced that a group of workmen in a former Red Brigades apartment in Milan had found some letters Moro had written during his captivity. In them, Moro had harsh words for Andreotti and other senior government officials; Andreotti, he wrote, "moved at ease with his colleagues from the CIA." However, there were touching as well as bitter words in the doomed man's last communications. "Norina," he wrote his wife, "you can imagine the choir of angels that will conduct me from earth to heaven." And finally: "I have been killed three times—through insufficient protection, through refusal to negotiate, through inconclusive politics."

In 1996, the government finally convicted Moro's second killer, Germano Maccari. He received a life sentence for the crime.

MURDER

MULTI-PARTY GOVERNMENT

Italy has a multi-party (more than one party) form of government. The Italian Communists and the Christian Democrats were the two strongest parties in Italy during the 1980s. However, the Christian Democrats worked together with other political groups to exclude the Communists. In the Italian multi-party system, it is common for different political parties to share power and divide up governmental posts between them.

Suggestions for Further Reading

Drake, Richard. *The Aldo Moro Murder Case.* Cambridge, MA: Harvard University Press, 1996.

Haberman, Clyde. "Italy Sees Hidden Hand Reviving Moro Case." *The New York Times* (October 21, 1990): A6.

Katz, Robert. *Days of Wrath: The Ordeal of Aldo Moro.* Garden City, NY: Doubleday, 1980.

O'Grady, Desmond. "The Trial of the Red Brigades." *Commonweal* (July 16, 1982): 389–91.

Argentina's "Dirty War" Trial: 1985

Defendants: Jorge Videla, Emilio Massera, Orlando Agosti, Roberto Viola, Armando Lambruschini, Leopoldo Galtieri, Jorge Anaya, Omar Graffigna, and Basilio Lami Dozo

Crimes Charged: Murder, kidnapping, illegal detention, torture, robbery, use of false identification to conduct illegal searches

Chief Defense Lawyers: Twenty-two defense attorneys

Chief Prosecutors: Julio Strassera and Luis Moreno Ocampo

Judges: Six-member Federal Court of Appeals, presiding judge León Arslanian

Place: Buenos Aires, Argentina

Dates of Trial: April 22–December 9, 1985

Verdicts: Guilty (Videla, Massera, Viola, Agosti, and Lambruschini); not guilty (Galtieri, Anaya, Graffigna, and Lami Dozo)

Sentences: Life imprisonment (Videla and Massera); seventeen years' imprisonment (Viola); eight years' imprisonment (Lambruschini); four and a half years' imprisonment (Agosti).

SIGNIFICANCE: The trial of military officers responsible for the "dirty war," in which thousands of innocent civilians died, was Argentina's first major step in restoring democracy after years of dictatorship and political violence. It was also the first public trial of military dictators in Latin American history.

MURDER

On March 24, 1976, the military overthrew (forced from power) the government of President Isabel Perón in Argentina. Many hoped that the new government would strengthen the country and end violence. Between 1976 and 1979, however, this need for order became a national nightmare.

The new government—led by Army Lieutenant General Jorge Videla, Navy Admiral Emilio Massera, and Air Force Brigadier General Orlando Agosti—dismissed the nation's congress, got rid of elected officials, and banned all political activity. The new government was secretive about its goals. The leaders and their allies within the military agreed that Argentina needed social change if "Western, Christian values" were to survive there. They decided that everyone suspected of opposing the new government would have to die. The name of this policy was "the Process of National Reorganization." It soon came to be known by a name the government gave itself—"the dirty war."

The Terror Begins

The terror began quietly. Argentines were slow to recognize an enormous increase in arrests. Security forces kidnapped blue collar workers, professionals, students, journalists, nuns, teachers, psychiatrists, union members, and thousands of others. They tortured and murdered most. Some were buried in secret mass graves. Many more were thrown out of aircraft flying over the ocean, often while they were still alive.

The terror soon became great. Many Argentines would not openly speak of friends or relatives taken away by soldiers for fear that they too might be taken away. From 1976 to 1979, between 9,000 and 30,000 men, women, and children vanished. They were known as "the disappeared."

Courts rejected legal requests from worried family members that their loved ones either be freed or formally charged with crimes. Authorities reasoned that the police had no record of those named in these requests. Therefore, no charges against them existed. This made such requests meaningless. Suddenly those who made the requests were missing. Police sped up the deaths of prisoners named in them.

News of the Argentine government's secret war on its own people continued to leak out of the country. Other countries criticized Argentina but the dirty war continued well into 1979. In 1982, Argentina lost a war to England over control of the Falkland Islands, off Argentina's Atlantic coast, and the military leaders resigned in disgrace, clearing the way for free public elections. Before giving up control, though, the military passed a law pardoning anyone who had ever been involved in the dirty war.

Military Leaders Face Prosecution

Upon taking office on December 10, 1983, President Rául Alfonsín ordered the nine military leaders who held power between March 1976 and June 1982 to face trial. Also charged was the Buenos Aires police chief, General Ramón Camps. The pardon the military leaders had given themselves was canceled.

In spite of Alfonsín's pre-election promise to investigate the dirty war, prosecution went slowly. The Supreme Council of the Armed Forces, formed at Alfonsín's request and made up of retired military officers, was originally supposed to try the accused officers. After eight months of hearings, the council announced that it was having difficulty reaching a verdict. The council stated that the defendants could only be held "indirectly responsible" for the actions of those who actually carried out the crimes.

However, Alfonsín had also asked the National Commission on Disappeared Persons (CONADEP) to investigate the "disappearances." Its report arrived in September 1984, the same month the military council declined to charge the officers. CONADEP's 50,000-page report, "Never Again," revealed the dirty war as a well-organized plan for acts of cruelty approved by the military rulers. Testimony of witnesses described hundreds of cases of kidnapping, robbery, rape, murder, and secret burial. The report documented 8,921 "disappearances," and concluded that lives of thousands more had probably been lost in this "national tragedy." The investigation also named 1,300 military and police officers who had been involved in the terror, but their names were not made public.

Authority to try the cases was taken away from the military council and given to the Federal Court of Appeals. The cases of several hundred accused junior officers remained before the military council, but the officers responsible for authorizing the terror would now face a public court.

None of the military leaders were personally charged with crimes relating to the "disappeared." However, the leaders were held responsible for the crimes committed by those who carried out their orders. Six defendants—generals Jorge Videla, Roberto Viola, and Leopoldo Galtieri; admirals Emilio Massera and Armando Lambruschini; and Brigadier General Orlando Agosti—were charged with murder, kidnapping, torture, robbery, and making illegal searches with false identification. General Omar Graffigna faced the same charges, except homicide (murder). Admirals Jorge Anaya and Basilio Lami Dozo were charged with kidnapping and using false documents.

MURDER

Testimony Recounts Horrors

The trial began on April 22, 1985, with hundreds of spectators packing the courtroom of the Palace of Justice. Six public judges would decide the fate of the accused.

The CONADEP report's list of horrors was repeated in testimony that lasted for four months. Prosecutor Julio Strassera called over 1,000 witnesses. Over 700 individual cases were described. One mother who had been arrested for searching for her disappeared child spoke of hearing her daughter's screams through jail walls. Asked if she had anything more to say at the close of her testimony, her reply echoed the heartache of thousands: "I want to know if my daughter is alive or dead."

Prosecutors argued that as supreme rulers of the country, the nine commanders were not simply following orders by allowing cruel acts to take place. Evidence proved there was a pattern of crimes against humanity of which the commanders must have been aware.

The prosecution's final statement lasted for five days. When prosecutor Julio Strassera ended by crying *"Nunca mas!"*—"Never again!"— the hundreds of spectators crammed into the court began clapping.

While prosecutors called over 1,000 witnesses, the defense called fewer than 30. Defense lawyers argued that the military leaders could not be held responsible for any wrongs committed by junior officers or the police. The defense also said that the dirty war was a part of the government's earlier war with rebels.

The accused chose not to sit in court during testimony describing the crimes committed during their rule. When they appeared during the lawyers' final statements, none of them showed sorrow for their acts. They felt that they were on trial because their political enemies were out to get them.

Questions Remain

Although the law allowed prosecutors to seek the death penalty, they asked for life sentences for the military commanders. Long prison terms were requested for the other defendants.

The verdicts were announced on December 9, 1985. Videla and Massera were found guilty and sentenced to life in prison. Viola received a seven-year prison term and Lambruschini eight years. The Argentine air force was found to have been less involved in the terror than the army

REMEMBERING THE "DISAPPEARED"

Despite the brutal cover-up of the "dirty war," the Argentine people did organize protests. Women would bring pictures of "disappeared" family members to vigils, demonstrating that they remembered the loved ones they had lost, and demanding that the world remember, as well. The rock star Sting was so moved by these protests that he commemorated them in his song, *They Dance Alone.*

and navy. Instead of life imprisonment, the air force commander during the first military government, Agosti, received a sentence of four and a half years. Those who took his place in the second military government, Graffigna and Lami Dozo, were found not guilty. So were Galtieri and Anaya, who commanded the army and navy during the third military government, after the worst violence was past. All of those convicted were kicked out of the military.

Both prosecutors and defense attorneys were unhappy with the verdicts and sentences. Both sides appealed, without success. Human rights groups believed the sentences were too soft. Supporters of the military were equally angered by the verdicts. Still, many Argentines saw the guilty verdicts as a hopeful sign that the justice system might finally be free of government control.

The trial did not end questions about the dirty war. Several more high-ranking officers were convicted in later trials. President Alfonsín remained under pressure to pardon the men or, at least, to end the prosecution of hundreds of accused murderers and torturers still serving in Argentina's powerful military. Hoping to put the dirty war behind him, Alfonsín agreed to laws that stopped further prosecutions. The next president, Carlos Menem, continued to silence the right wing by granting pardons for 100 defendants still facing prosecution. On December 29, 1990, President Menem pardoned and freed Videla, Massera, and all other convicted officers still in jail.

Menem stated that five years he had spent in illegal detention during the dirty war gave him the right to "close a sad and black period of

MURDER

national history." Yet thousands of Argentines paraded to protest the unpopular pardons, proving that the dirty war was an open wound that would not soon heal.

Suggestions for Further Reading

Chavez, Lydia. "In Argentine Court, Tales of Horror and Heroism." *The New York Times* (May 28, 1985): 2.

Nunca Más: The Report of the Argentine National Commission on the Disappeared. New York: Farrar, Strauss, Giroux, 1986.

Rudolph, James D., ed. *Argentina: A Country Study.* Washington, D.C.: The American University, 1986.

Simpson, James and Jana Bennett. *The Disappeared and the Mothers of the Plaza.* New York: St. Martin's Press, 1985.

Timerman, Jacobo. *Prisoner without a Name, Cell without a Number.* New York: Alfred A. Knopf, 1981.

The Sharpeville Six Trial: 1985

Defendants: Mojalefa "Ja-Ja" Sefatsa, Reid Mokoena, Oupa Diniso, Theresa Ramashamola, Christiaan Mokubung, Gideon Mokone, Duma Khumalo, and Francis Mokhesi

Crimes Charged: Murder of Jacob Dlamini; a subversion charge of "acting with a common purpose unlawfully . . . [to influence the government . . . and/or to intimidate, demoralize, or persuade members of the public to do or not do something]"; other charges of malicious damage to property; arson

Chief Defense Lawyers: Jack Unterhalter, Ismail Hussain, and Prakash Diar

Chief Prosecutor: Eben Jordaan

Judges: Acting Justice Wessel Johannes Human, Assessors Dr. D. W. R. Herzog and I. L. Grindlay-Ferris

Place: Pretoria, South Africa

Dates of Trial: September 23–December 13, 1985

Verdicts: Guilty of murder (Sefatsa, Mokoena, Diniso, Ramashamola, Khumalo, and Mokhesi); guilty of public violence (Mokubung and Mokone); guilty of subversion (all)

Sentences: Sefatsa, Mokoena, Diniso, Ramashamola, Khumalo, Mokhesi: death by hanging on murder count (death sentences later changed to imprisonment); Mokubung, Mokone: five years' imprisonment on count of public violence; all defendants: eight years' imprisonment on count of subversion

SIGNIFICANCE: Judges and police ignored basic human rights in this case. This was common in South Africa, when the races were legally separated by the system of apartheid (a-PART-hade).

MURDER

Sharpeville is a black township of 6,000 small brick houses in the Johannesburg region of South Africa. It first came to world attention as the site of a 1960 massacre of sixty-nine blacks by white police officers. On September 3, 1984, widespread protests erupted against recent increases in public service fees. One local black leader died and police arrested eight local blacks. Police singled out people almost randomly as scapegoats for the violence committed by mobs. Courts gave them the death sentence for an act in which they played either a very minor role or possibly no role at all. The case of the Sharpeville Six (named after six of the eight defendants condemned to death) became well-known internationally.

The 1984 Incident

It started with the 1982 Black Local Authorities Act. Under this law, the white government shifted responsibility for local government to elected black councils. At the same time, they withheld proper funding for road maintenance and construction, trash removal, sewerage, electrification, and basic services. To close the financial gap, the councils raised service fees. Violence erupted, often directed at the black officials, many of whom were seen as corrupt servants of the white rulers.

In Sharpeville, Jacob Dlamini, a deputy mayor, became the focus of mob anger. On the night of September 2, stones shattered all the windows of his house. The next morning, several hundred protesters gathered to march to the township administrative offices to picket against rent increases. They carried placards (signs), sang, shouted slogans, and along the way forced onlookers to join them by threatening injury and damage to their houses. As the protesters neared Dlamini's house, they paused to throw stones. Police chased away the crowd with tear gas and rubber bullets, and asked Dlamini to leave with them because it was not safe to stay. Because of emergencies elsewhere, however, the police had to leave. A mob of some 100 shortly regrouped to stone the house some more. Dlamini shot a gun from inside and injured at least one person. Enraged, the mob tossed gasoline bombs at the house, setting it on fire. As Dlamini ran out, one or more persons struggled with him and took away his gun. They threw stones and knocked him down. Then they pushed his car into the street, overturned, and burned it. More horribly, the crowd dragged the unconscious Dlamini into the street and set him on fire. He was dead when the police returned at 9:00 that morning.

Two months passed before police took any action. They then arrested eight suspects. The police first came for Mojalefa "Ja-Ja" Sefatsa, a twenty-nine-year-old fruit seller. He insisted that at the time of the murder he had been away at his aunt's house. However, different testimony by Mrs. Dlamini and her neighbor, Jantjie Mabuti, placed him at the scene. Mabuti also placed five others at the scene. He said that Theresa Ramashamola, a twenty-four-year-old cook, had slapped a woman who had objected to the burning of Dlamini. Ramashamola said that she had been forced to join the march, had been hit in the head by a police rubber bullet, sought treatment, and then went home. Police tortured both Ramashamola and Sefatsa during interrogation.

Mabuti also testified that both Christiaan Mokubung and Gideon Mokone were in the mob tossing stones at the house. Mokone, in fact, had been injured by the bullet from Dlamini's gun, and then carried away for treatment at the hospital. Crowds had forced both to join the march. Mokubung had fled when the police broke up the crowd. Neither was present when the mob regrouped. Mabuti also placed at the scene Duma Khumalo, a twenty-six-year-old teacher-trainee. Mabuti said Khumalo had handed out gasoline bombs. Khumalo's story was that he had been forced to join the march. He admitted that he had witnessed the stoning of the house. (He was in fact related to Dlamini and said he had no anger against him.) However, he then carried a friend injured by a rubber bullet to a nearby house for treatment and later took him home. Therefore, he had not been present when the mob continued its attack.

Mabuti also accused Francis Mokhesi, a twenty-eight-year-old professional soccer player, of taking the lead in making gasoline bombs and of helping to push the car into the street. Arrested seven months after the murder, Mokhesi had as his alibi a week-long ankle injury that had sidelined him from soccer. Another witness, Joseph Manete, also accused Khumalo and Mokhesi. (In 1988, Manete would confess in a newspaper interview that he had given false testimony when pressured by police.)

Of the remaining two defendants, Reid Mokoena, a twenty-one-year-old unskilled laborer, had been arrested by the police and tortured into signing a false confession that he had thrown a stone at the house. He claimed that he had been forced to join the march, had been tear-gassed, and after washing his face at a nearby house had returned home. He had never reached Dlamini's house.

The final defendant, Oupa Diniso, a twenty-nine-year-old factory inspector, was arrested merely for possession of what the police claimed was Dlamini's gun. He had spent the day of the riot at a church and at home. The next day he came across three young boys arguing over a gun they had found. For reasons of safety, he said, he took the gun away from the boys and took it home. The state claimed that he had taken the gun from Dlamini.

MURDER

The Trial

Police arrested and held the suspects under the Internal Security Act. They kept seven in solitary confinement for over nine months before the trial. In court for the first time on April 25, 1985, they finally learned the charges against them: they were responsible for the actions of the mob. The state claimed that the defendants had intended to make the government give up its plan to give local authority to black leaders. It claimed they had caused those black authorities in office to resign and to have service fee increases canceled. The attorney general prevented the court from granting the defendants bail. In effect, this had become a political trial that could become a model for future trials of rioters.

The state brought seventy-two-year-old Wessel Johannes Human out of retirement to act as judge, even though most of his experience had been as a lawyer. The prosecution presented six state eyewitnesses. Of these, three gave evidence that did not relate to any of the defendants. Mrs. Dlamini implicated Sefatsa, Manete falsely implicated Khumalo and Mokhesi, and Mabuti—the key state witness—implicated all except Mokoena and Diniso. Defense cross-examination revealed serious problems with Mabuti's detailed story. Despite defense witness testimony supporting the alibis of the accused, the judge refused to accept this testimony. Instead he chose to accept that of Mabuti. Neither did the judge accept medical testimony pointing to the use of electric shock torture to make Mokoena talk. That the judge had already made up his mind in advance was suggested by his questioning of Mokoena:

Judge: But those people who told you . . . to walk with them, we know now . . . that these people were not on the way to the municipal offices, they were on the way to Dlamini's house in order to burn it down and to burn him to death. . . . Did they not say to you, look, we have to go to Dlamini's house now, and set it on fire and kill him?

Mokoena: No.

The Verdict and Sentences

In his verdict, the judge rejected evidence raising reasonable doubt or favoring the accused. Apparently to set an example for other violent protesters, he disregarded other factors, such as the effects of mob psychology, that might help to clear the defendants. Whereas a jury might well have considered the total situation, he simply found the defendants guilty. He condemned six to death and the two others to lengthy prison terms.

FROM SOWETO TO SHARPEVILLE

The 1984 incident at Sharpeville reminded many of a previous incident at Soweto in 1976. Whereas Sharpeville was the name of a single township, Soweto was the name for a group of townships about ten miles southwest of South Africa's capital, Johannesburg. The incident at Soweto began as a black student protest against the use of the Afrikaans language in the schools. (Afrikaans is a language that developed from the Dutch, spoken by the original European settlers of the region.) The students claimed that they should learn their native languages and English instead of Afrikaans, which is a language spoken only in South Africa, and only by a portion of the whites who lived there. The student protest was met with severe racial violence, and the riots that followed spread to other black urban centers. Many people at the time saw both Soweto and Sharpeville as symbols of police violence as well as signs of black resistance.

In the end, it was international publicity and pressure that embarrassed the president of South Africa, P. W. Botha, on November 23, 1988, into commuting the death sentences of the Sharpeville Six to 18, 20, and 25 years' imprisonment. This move did not, however, wipe out the original injustice of their conviction. The trial was, according to one foreign journalist, an exercise in "judicial terrorism."

An attempt was eventually made to right this wrong when the South African government began to reform itself. Christiaan Mokubung and Gideon Mokone—who had been found guilty only of public violence—were released on December 10, 1990. Oupa Diniso and Duma Khumalo were released on July 10, 1991. Theresa Ramashamola and Reid Mokoena were released (on parole) on December 13, 1991. Mojalefa Sefatsa and Francis Mokhesi were released on September 26, 1992.

Suggestions for Further Reading

Diar, Prakash. *The Sharpeville Six.* Toronto: McClellan & Stewart, Inc., 1990.

MURDER

Phillips, Norman. *The Tragedy of Apartheid: A Journalist's Experiences in the South African Riots.* New York: David McKay, 1960.

Reeves, Ambrose. *Shooting at Sharpeville: The Agony of South Africa.* Boston: Houghton Mifflin, 1961.

Smith, William E. "Black Rage, White Fist." *Time* (August 5, 1985): 24–32.

Jean-Bédel Bokassa Trial: 1986–1987

Defendant: Jean-Bédel Bokassa

Crimes Charged: Murder, cannibalism, embezzlement of state funds, illegal use of property, assault and battery

Chief Defense Lawyers: François Gibault and Francis Szpiner

Chief Prosecutor: Gabriel-Faustin M'Boudou

Judge: Presiding Judge Edouard Franck

Place: Bangui, Central African Republic

Dates of Trial: December 15, 1986–June 12, 1987

Verdict: Guilty

Sentence: Death, commuted to life imprisonment

SIGNIFICANCE: The prosecution of Bokassa for crimes committed during his notorious reign was the first fair trial by jury of a head of state in the history of post-colonial Africa.

Many dictators have been brought to justice for mistreating the people they rule. In 1986, however, Jean-Bédel Bokassa became the first tyrant to be prosecuted for eating his subjects.

Bokassa was the army chief of staff in the Central African Republic, a former French colony. In 1966, he led a successful effort to overthrow the government of his cousin, David Dacko. A decade after taking control, Bokassa imitated his hero Napoleon Bonaparte, the nineteenth-century French emperor, by declaring himself emperor of the Central African Republic. He marked the beginning of his reign with a lavish coronation that cost $25 million. This was a fantastic sum of money for his poor African country to spend.

Bokassa's Crimes

This extravagant show was soon surpassed by Bokassa's greed and cruelty. When he took for himself the choicest gems in the Central African Republic's diamond mines, he nearly drove the country into bankruptcy. He executed hundreds of politicians he imagined to be his enemies, and he had foreign journalists who criticized his actions beaten and jailed.

Bokassa's treatment of his subjects was even more vicious. He celebrated Mother's Day 1971 by hanging all those imprisoned for crimes against women. People whispered that those who crossed him were sometimes fed to the crocodiles and lions he kept in cages on the palace grounds. Some said that Bokassa himself ate the flesh of those he had killed.

Jean-Bédel Bokassa in 1979 during a trip to Paris. In 1987, a court found Bokassa guilty of murder, along with other crimes, and sentenced him to life in prison.

None of the Central African Republic's neighbors confronted Bokassa when they heard of his crimes. France, which hoped to keep its access to the country's diamond mines, also turned a blind eye. In April 1979, however, Bokassa personally participated in the slaughter of more than 100 schoolchildren. This proved too much for the rest of the world to ignore. On September 20, while Bokassa was visiting the northern African country of Libya, French paratroopers landed in the Central African Republic and restored David Dacko to power.

Bokassa went into exile (leaving one's country, not to return). First he went to Abidjan, the capital of the Ivory Coast, on the west coast of

Africa. Then he went to Paris, where he gained entry using the French passport he had earned fighting with France during World War II. Although many French citizens protested his presence, Bokassa stayed in the country for the next seven years, living off his French military pension. When that proved to be too little money, he sold the rights to his memoirs. One of the claims he made in the resulting book was that he had shared women in the Central African Republic with French President Valery Giscard d'Estaing when he visited Bokassa there. This claim resulted in French courts ordering that all 8,000 copies of Bokassa's books be destroyed. Bokassa also claimed that he had given Giscard d'Estaing $250,000 worth of diamonds in 1973. The French president's bid for re-election the next year failed, largely because of this claim.

The Emperor Returns to Face Trial

On October 23, 1986, Bokassa flew back to the Central African Republic. Incredibly, he expected his former subjects to welcome his return. Instead, he was arrested as soon as he stepped off the plane. Fifteen charges were filed against him, including murder, stealing state funds, and acquiring human flesh for purposes of cannibalism. In 1980, he had been convicted on these same charges in his absence and sentenced to death. However, now that he was back in the country, the law required the government to try him in person and give him a defense lawyer.

Prosecutors considered holding the trial in the capital's sports stadium, which had been the site of Bokassa's coronation. They decided against it, however, thinking that this plan might result in chaos. Instead, the trial opened on December 15, 1986, in the chambers of the Palace of Justice. Bokassa had two French lawyers. Judge Edouard Franck presided over a jury of six and a panel of three judges. This was the first time since foreign powers had left Africa that the continent saw a fair trial by jury of a head of state. For the first time the public had access to the trial.

Those who did not attend in person were able to follow the trial over the radio. All over the country, people listened to testimony about the cruelty they had experienced under Bokassa's government and the relatives they had lost. His victims ranged from political enemies to the newborn son of a palace guard who had been executed after trying to assassinate Bokassa. A nurse testified that the guard's pregnant widow told her Bokassa had threatened to kill her child if it was a boy. When the boy was born, Bokassa had the newborn killed by giving an injection of poison.

Bokassa also faced charges for the two crimes that led to his downfall. In January 1979, he had ordered all students wear expensive uniforms

MURDER

made in a factory owned by one of his wives. When a group of school-children protested, Bokassa ordered soldiers to fire on them. Several were killed. And when some elementary school children threw rocks at his car three months later, Bokassa ordered 180 children arrested and put in jail. That night the emperor went to the prison, where he smashed the skulls of half a dozen children with his walking stick. He ordered his soldiers to kill the others. Only 27 children survived.

Bokassa denied all the charges against him. Instead, he blamed others in his government. "I'm not a saint," he told the court. "I'm just a man like everyone else." As the evidence against him mounted, however, Bokassa lost his temper. "The aggravating thing about all this is that it's Bokassa, Bokassa, Bokassa. I have enough crimes leveled against me without you blaming me for all the murders of the last twenty-one years!"

Testimony about Cannibalism

Cannibalism was certainly the most sensational charge leveled against Bokassa, but it was not the most serious one. Laws forbidding cannibalism in the Central African Republic classified all acts connected with eating human flesh as minor crimes. When Andre Kolingba seized power from David Dacko in 1981, Kolingba pardoned all those guilty of misdemeanors that had been committed during Dacko's administration. Bokassa could not, therefore, be punished for cannibalism, even if he were found guilty.

Former president Dacko testified that he had seen photographs of cut-up bodies hanging in the cold storage room of Bokassa's palace in 1979. Bokassa's chef also testified that he had cooked human flesh and served it to Bokassa. The court did not examine rumors that Bokassa had served human flesh to President Giscard and other visiting foreign leaders.

On June 12, 1987, Bokassa was found guilty. The court found that although many murder charges had been brought against him, the evidence was strong in only about twenty cases. Regardless of the number, the result was the same. Bokassa cried quietly as he was sentenced to death. His lawyers appealed the sentence on grounds that the nation's constitution allowed only a former head of state to be charged with treason. The supreme court rejected this appeal.

On February 29, 1988, President Kolingba abolished (canceled) the death penalty in the Central African Republic. Bokassa was then ordered to spend the rest of his life in solitary confinement.

A REPUBLIC IN CENTRAL AFRICA

The Central African Republic rests on a savanna-covered plateau, with tropical forests to the south and a semidesert area to the east. Although the country has many rivers, only the Ubangi can be navigated by commercial vessels. The major economic activity of the nation is agriculture, with about 90 percent of the population engaged in subsistence farming. The country also produces cotton and coffee for export, as well as diamonds and timber. Despite the rich natural resources of the Central African Republic, the country remains extremely poor, with no railroads and few paved roads. The country is populated by the Mandjia-Baya, the Banda, the Mbaka, and the Zandhe peoples. Although French is the official national language—a legacy of colonial days—Sangho is the language most widely spoken. More than half of the people of the Central African Republic practice traditional *animist* religions (religions that believe that spirits inhabit and animate the natural world); most of the rest of the country's people follow Christianity.

Suggestions for Further Reading

Harmon, Jeff B. "His Former Majesty, Bokassa." *Harper's* (May 1980): 34–39.

Shoumatoff, Robert. *African Madness.* New York: Alfred A. Knopf, 1988.

"Trying the 'Butcher of Bangui.'" *Newsweek* (December 29, 1986): 27.

O. J. Simpson Trial: 1995

Defendant: Orenthal James Simpson
Crime Charged: Murder
Chief Defense Lawyer: Johnnie L. Cochran Jr.
Chief Prosecutor: Marcia Clark
Judge: Lance A. Ito
Place: Los Angeles, California
Dates of Trial: January 24–October 2, 1995
Verdict: Not guilty

SIGNIFICANCE: With its mixture of race and celebrity, the trial of sports hero O. J. Simpson attracted enough public attention to be called the "trial of the century." The racially divided reaction to the verdict in the case indicated how deep a gulf still separated black and white in America in the 1990s.

For many people, the murder trial of football hero and actor O. J. Simpson was "the trial of the century." The case began around midnight on June 12, 1994. Neighbors of Simpson's ex-wife, Nicole Brown Simpson, heard her dog whimpering and barking. The dog led some of these neighbors to the bodies of Nicole and Ronald L. Goldman, one of Nicole's friends. The bodies lay on the walkway outside Nicole's home in the Brentwood section of Los Angeles, California.

Police Detectives Investigate Murders

Before dawn, Detectives Philip Vannater and Tom Lange of the Los Angeles Police Department (LAPD) were investigating the crime. The de-

FOOTBALL HERO

When O. J. Simpson was first suspected of the murders of Nicole Brown Simpson and Ronald L. Goldman, the nation was shocked. Simpson had achieved widespread fame and admiration for his achievements as a football player. As a running back for the University of Southern California, he won the 1968 Heisman Trophy for the best college player of the year. From 1969 to 1977, Simpson played with the Buffalo Bills, and from 1978 to 1979 he played with the San Francisco 49ers. In his twenty-year career, his record of 11,236 yards gained rushing was second only to that of Jim Brown. Simpson ranked first in season records for most yards gained (2,003 in 1973) and for most touchdowns (twenty-three in 1975). After his football career ended, Simpson became a sportscaster, a movie actor, and a spokesperson for Hertz car rentals.

tectives were ordered to notify O. J. Simpson of his ex-wife's death and to arrange care for the Simpsons' two young children. After the children were taken from Nicole's home to police headquarters, the detectives went to Simpson's estate. They took with them Detective Mark Fuhrman. Fuhrman had been called to the estate ten years earlier to answer a distress call placed by a bruised and battered Nicole. Up until that time, most people thought that the Simpsons had the perfect interracial marriage: Simpson was African American, Nicole was white.

At Simpson's house, no one answered the bell outside the walled estate. While the detectives were waiting to get in, Fuhrman examined a Ford Bronco parked in the street near the estate's rear gate. He noticed what appeared to be bloodstains on the door of the car. Vannater then ordered Fuhrman to climb over the wall and let him and Lange inside. When no one answered the front door of the house, the detectives went to the guest house. Let in by Simpson family friend Brian "Kato" Kaelin, the detectives also found that Simpson's adult daughter, Arnelle, lived in the guest complex. She told them that her father had taken a late night flight to Chicago. Detective Ronald Phillips telephoned Simpson there to give him the news.

Kaelin told the other detectives that around 10:40 P.M. he had heard loud thumps outside the wall of his room. Fuhrman went outside to investigate a narrow passage between this wall and a chain-link fence. There he found a black leather glove that seemed to be bloody. It matched another glove the LAPD had found at the murder scene. The detectives also saw what appeared to be drops of blood on the driveway, on the path to the front door of the main house, and in the entryway of the house.

When Simpson returned the next day, Los Angeles police questioned him for three hours. They noticed that he had a cut on his left hand, which was bandaged and swollen. They also obtained a blood sample from him. When they declared Simpson their prime suspect and prepared to arrest him, however, he was gone.

The mug shot of O. J. Simpson, taken June 17, 1994, soon after he surrendered to police at his Brentwood estate in Los Angeles, California. The District Attorney charged him with two counts of murder in connection with the killings of his ex-wife, Nicole, and her friend, Ronald Goldman.

The "Chase"

That evening, networks broadcast the strange sight of police cars following a white Ford Bronco as it drove slowly along the Los Angeles freeways. Inside were O. J. Simpson's friend, Al Cowlings, and O. J. himself—reportedly holding a gun to his own head. After ninety minutes, the

Bronco returned to Simpson's estate, where Simpson was arrested. On Monday, June 20, a Los Angeles County grand jury charged him with murder. He was jailed without bail.

The news media coverage was intense. As television provided live coverage of every aspect of the case, thousands of people flocked to Simpson's estate to stare.

On July 29, Simpson appeared in court to be formally charged. He was accompanied by Robert L. Shapiro, a well-known white California lawyer, and Johnnie Cochran, who would soon become America's most famous African American trial attorney.

The state was represented by Deputy District Attorney Marcia Clark, who had not lost a murder case in ten years. She was also an expert on using circumstantial evidence and DNA (a molecule that appears in all living cells but is different in each individual) to prove guilt. She was assisted by Deputy District Attorney Christopher Darden, an African American prosecutor who had much experience trying murder cases.

**O. J.
Simpson
Trial: 1995**

*O. J. Simpson and
the "Dream Team"
defense attorneys
(left to right):
Robert Shapiro,
Johnnie Cochran,
and Simpson.*

MURDER

The Trial Begins

Toward the end of 1994, Judge Lance A. Ito seated twelve jurors and twelve alternate jurors. The majority of these jurors were African American and female. The trial itself opened on January 24, 1995. Clark told the jury that the prosecution would present evidence of "a trail of blood where there should be no blood." It led from the path outside Nicole Brown Simpson's home to a pair of socks found in Simpson's bedroom. Darden added a description of Simpson's years of abusing his wife, both physically and mentally. Cochran opened by telling the jury that the defense would present more than a dozen witnesses that the prosecutors did not know existed. Clark responded that this tactic amounted to "trial by ambush."

Judge Lance A. Ito presided over the Simpson murder trial, which opened on January 24, 1995.

The Prosecution Presents Its Case

The prosecutors first presented evidence of Simpson's past abuse of Nicole. Then they turned to the night of the murders. They carefully laid out the details of how the bodies had been discovered. Then the defense team went on the attack, claiming that the LAPD had mismanaged the entire murder investigation. The prosecution's theory was that a jealous Simpson had set out to kill his ex-wife, but ended up murdering two people when Ron Goldman unexpectedly appeared on the scene. The defense team responded with a theory of its own: that Nicole was murdered by drug dealers. When the prosecutors put Detective Fuhrman on the witness stand, however, he gave testimony that pointed strongly at Simpson as the murderer.

Experts on gloves were called to testify that the bloody gloves found at the murder scene and at Simpson's estate belonged to the defendant. Shoe experts testified that bloody shoe prints found at the murder scene had been made by shoes that belonged to Simpson. Still other experts testified about DNA evidence that strongly indicated Simpson was the murderer. As the trial went on for months, one juror after another was excused from the case and replaced by an alternate juror. On July 6, 1995, after 24 weeks during which it had presented 58 witnesses and 488 exhibits, the prosecution rested its case.

The Defense and the "Race Card"

At this point in the trial, the defense changed tactics. The first indication of this change came on July 12. Robert Heidstra, a witness for the defense, testified that at 10:40 P.M. on the night of the murders, he had been walking his dog past Nicole's home. As he passed, he heard two people arguing. He said they sounded to him like a younger white woman and an older black man. Cochran erupted. "You can't tell by someone's voice when they're black. That's racist, and I resent it."

The defense continued to present other evidence. Witnesses testified to such things as Simpson's arthritis, which they said was so disabling as to prevent him from carrying out the murders. Others testified that there had been no blood on the Bronco. Still others testified that the blood evidence that pointed to Simpson as the murderer had been contaminated.

None of these arguments was especially convincing. Then the defense delivered a bombshell. A North Carolina screenwriter, Laura Hart McKinny, revealed that she had sixteen hours of taped interviews with Detective Fuhrman. She had made these tapes years before as part of her research for a project. On the tapes, Fuhrman admitted to having in the past done such illegal things as arresting people without just cause and destroying evidence. Most telling of all, he repeatedly referred to African Americans—whom he clearly disliked—as "niggers."

Fuhrman's use of the "N word" made him guilty of perjury (lying under oath). Earlier in the trial, he had told defense attorneys under cross examination that he never referred to blacks in such a way. Simpson's attorneys had been trying to demonstrate that their client was framed by the LAPD because he was a rich, successful black man. Now, their task was easier. It appeared to many that the blood evidence had not just been mishandled, it had been tampered with. And Fuhrman, who had found the

MURDER

THE VERDICT—HOW THE PUBLIC FELT

In a *Newsweek* survey published in their February 17, 1997 issue, results showed that 82 percent of black Americans felt that O. J. Simpson should keep custody of his children. Only 44 percent of white citizens polled felt that he should keep custody. From *all* people questioned in this survey, 70 percent felt that Simpson would never be able to resume his part as a public figure, and 53 percent felt that they would refuse to buy a product he endorsed.

telltale bloody gloves, now seemed to be a lying racist who could easily have planted this crucial evidence.

By the time the attorneys delivered their closing arguments, nearly all of the original jurors had been replaced by alternates. Three-quarters of the jury was now African American. Cochran repeatedly referred to Simpson's failed attempt to try on the bloody gloves (the prosecution argued that as the blood dried, the leather gloves shrank): "If it doesn't fit, you must acquit."

After the trial was over, Shapiro, who had had a falling out with Cochran, said that the defense team had played "the race card" from the bottom of the deck. The claim of racism, Shapiro implied, was a dirty trick.

Less than four hours after the jury began its deliberations, it returned with a verdict. On October 2, 1995, the jury declared O. J. Simpson not guilty of either murder. Americans, who had followed the case for over a year, were divided into two camps, largely along racial lines. Whites for the most part believed that Simpson had gotten away with murder. Most African Americans, however, were elated that Simpson had beaten what they saw as an unfair judicial system. The split between blacks and whites over the case of O. J. Simpson was symbolic of the state of race relations in America in the 1990s.

Suggestions for Further Reading

Clark, Marcia with Theresa Carpenter. *Without a Doubt.* New York: Viking, Penguin, 1997.

Cochran, Johnnie. *Journey to Justice.* New York: Ballantine, 1996.

Timothy McVeigh Trial: 1997

Defendant: Timothy McVeigh

Crimes Charged: Murder, conspiracy to cause an explosion

Chief Defense Lawyers: Stephen Jones, Richard H. Burr III, Jeralynn Merritt, Robert Nigh Jr., and Cheryl Ramsey

Chief Prosecutors: Joseph Hartzler, Patrick Ryan, and Beth Wilkinson

Judge: Richard Matsch

Place: Denver, Colorado

Dates of Trial: March 31–June 2, 1997

Verdict: Guilty

Sentence: Death

SIGNIFICANCE: The mindless horror of the 1995 Oklahoma City bombing guaranteed that this would be one of the most important trials in American history.

At 9:02 A.M. on April 19, 1995, a rental truck packed with 4,000 pounds of explosives blew up outside the Alfred P. Murrah government building in Oklahoma City, Oklahoma. The bomb killed 168 people and injured hundreds more. This was the worst terrorist attack ever committed on U.S. soil.

Just seventy-eight minutes after the explosion investigators got a break. Some eighty miles north of Oklahoma City, State Trooper Charles Hanger stopped a car because it had no license plate. He found that the driver, a twenty-seven-year-old ex-soldier named Timothy McVeigh, had a 9-millimeter pistol. Hanger took McVeigh into custody. Forty-eight

MURDER

hours later McVeigh became a suspect in the Oklahoma City bombing. Officers matched his looks to a sketch of the man who had rented the truck used in the explosion.

That same day Terry Nichols, an old army buddy of McVeigh, surrendered to authorities near his home in Kansas. Newspapers had linked him to the bombing. A search of Nichols' house revealed enough evidence to charge both McVeigh and Nichols with the Oklahoma City bombing.

Trial judge Richard Matsch ordered that the two defendants face trial separately. He next granted a change of venue (the location of the trial)

Two U.S. Marshals escort Timothy McVeigh to the Federal Courthouse in Oklahoma City on January 31, 1996, to discuss a change of venue for McVeigh's trial. The government charged him and co-defendant Terry Nichols in the April 19, 1995, bombing of the Alfred P. Murrah Federal Building that killed 168 people.

to Denver. It was here, amid scenes of high security, that McVeigh went on trial for his life on March 31, 1997. Despite the mass murder in Oklahoma City, he faced just eight federal counts of murder and three charges of criminal conspiracy.

"Hate-Filled Mastermind"

After three weeks of jury selection, Joseph Hartzler opened for the prosecution. He depicted McVeigh as the "hate-filled" mastermind of the bombing. He said he was a man consumed by hatred for the federal government. He claimed McVeigh's murderous intentions were revealed in a file found on his sister's computer. The file threatened that "blood will flow in the streets." McVeigh's rage was fueled mainly by the 1993 Waco, Texas, siege that left seventy-five members of the Branch Davidian cult dead after a standoff with agents from the Bureau of Alcohol, Tobacco, and Firearms. In McVeigh's opinion the cult members had been victims of governmental oppression. Significantly, said Hartzler, the Oklahoma City Bombing had occurred two years to the day after Waco.

Defense counsel Stephen Jones responded dramatically. In a solemn voice he intoned the names of all 168 victims of the Murrah Building attack, saying "It is to our generation what the bombing of Pearl Harbor was to our parents." While conceding that McVeigh harbored strong feelings of mistrust toward the U.S. government, Jones argued a total absence of proof to suggest that his client had acted on that rage.

An early prosecution witness, Helena Garrett, brought an intensely human dimension to the grim proceedings. She recalled dropping off her sixteen-month-old baby at a day care center in the Murrah Building that morning. Then came the explosion. "I didn't see Tevin outside . . . I was screaming 'My baby's in there'. . . . Then they started bringing out the babies."

Several days would pass before she learned for sure that her son was dead. Because of the horrible injuries she was not allowed to see the whole body. "I kissed his feet and his hands," she told a tearful courtroom. "I couldn't go any higher."

The star prosecution witnesses would be Michael Fortier and Lori Fortier, long-time friends of McVeigh, who had been the best man at their wedding. First to testify was Lori Fortier. She described regular visits from McVeigh before the explosion during which he outlined plans to blow up the Murrah Building. He once pulled soup cans from the kitchen cupboard to illustrate how he would arrange barrels of explosive material in a truck.

She also claimed to have helped fake the driver's license in the name Robert Kling that prosecutors alleged was used by McVeigh to rent the Ryder truck that carried the deadly bomb. When she heard about the bombing her immediate reaction was that McVeigh had carried out his threat.

Jones was merciless on cross-examination. "You would agree with me that if your testimony is accurate, all you had to do to prevent the death of these 168 people was to pick up the telephone?"

"Yes," Fortier replied.

"And you did not do that, did you?"

"No, I did not."

"And as a result of your failure to pick it up, 168 people died?"

"Yes."

Lori Fortier admitted that she had received protection from prosecution in exchange for the truth. Then she admitted that she and her husband had lied to friends, family and the Federal Bureau of Investigation (FBI) about their friendship with McVeigh. "At the time we were lying about everything to everyone," she said.

The first flaw in the government's case came when Eric McGown, an employee at a Kansas motel supposedly used by McVeigh, testified that he saw McVeigh with the truck on Easter Sunday, 1995. This was one day before the date the government charged he had rented it. This helped the defense claim that more than one Ryder truck—and a widespread conspiracy—was involved in the bombing.

Michael Fortier proved a key witness for the government. He said McVeigh had revealed his murderous plans in letters, phone calls, and face-to-face talks between September 1994 and early April 1995. In December 1994, he and McVeigh had visited Terry Nichols in Kansas. Driving east on I-40 through New Mexico, McVeigh had pointed to a Ryder truck. He said he planned to rent one and convert it into a deadly truck bomb. Later, in Oklahoma City, they had slowly cruised past the Murrah Building's glass-fronted north side. McVeigh had asked Fortier if he thought a Ryder truck would fit into the loading zone at the north entrance, right where the Ryder truck ultimately exploded. Fortier had agreed that it would.

According to Fortier, McVeigh vowed to stay with the bomb-laden truck until it exploded. He would even drive it through the doors of the Murrah Building if necessary. McVeigh was not worried about the inevitable loss of life, said Fortier, calling the federal employees who worked there "storm troopers" who were "guilty by association."

THE DEATH PENALTY

On June 3, 1997, the Denver jury found Timothy McVeigh guilty on all charges. However, they still had to decide whether or not he should be executed for his offenses. Within a week of the announcement of the verdict, *Time* magazine conducted a poll (survey), asking "Do you think Timothy McVeigh should receive the death penalty?" Of all people surveyed, 78 percent said that he should receive the death penalty, while 17 percent said he should not. On July 13, 1997, Denver jurors decided that Timothy McVeigh should be put to death.

Like his wife, Michael Fortier admitted doing nothing to warn of the plot, excusing his silence on grounds that he had known McVeigh for a long time.

In a blistering cross-examination, Jones made the link between Michael Fortier's testimony and any punishment he might subsequently receive to a "sword of Damocles" hanging over the former hardware clerk's head. "They [the government] haven't made that sentencing decision yet," Jones said. "You are hoping that they feel you cooperated 100 percent. . . . It would not be to your advantage to say Tim is innocent."

"No," Fortier said, "because that would be a lie." Even so, the witness admitted that he had bragged to friends about making a million dollars off the case.

Key Evidence?

Toward the end of its case, the prosecution team sprang a surprise. It introduced a key, supposedly from the Ryder rental truck and found in the alley where McVeigh parked his getaway car. However, defense attorney Cheryl Ramsey got FBI agent Louis Hupp to admit that McVeigh's fingerprints were not on it. They were not found in any of the motels where McVeigh supposedly stayed in the weeks before the bombing, or on the rental agreement for the Ryder truck.

MURDER

Prints were found, however, on a receipt for 1,000 pounds of ammonium nitrate fertilizer. Lawmen discovered this in Terry Nichols' home. This fertilizer, said FBI agent Steven Burmeister, loaded into barrels of fuel oil, formed the heart of the Oklahoma City bomb. Burmeister found traces of this fertilizer embedded in a piece of the Ryder truck found at the scene. He also identified traces of a chemical used in blasting caps on the blue jeans and two T-shirts McVeigh wore that day.

The defense argued that someone else, not McVeigh, had driven the truck to the building and set off the bomb that day. Mild support for this theory came from Oklahoma state medical examiner Fred Jordan, who testified that one human limb was unmatched to any body identified in the blast. "We have one left leg which we don't know where it belongs," Jordan said, raising the possibility that the bomber had been killed in the explosion.

A big shock came with the testimony of Daina Bradley. Since the tragedy this witness, who lost three family members in the explosion and was herself grievously injured, had consistently told investigators the same story. She had seen a single, olive-skinned man get out of the truck and walk quickly away. Now, on the stand, she claimed there was a second, lighter-skinned male, although she could not be sure that this was McVeigh.

After this setback the defense regained some ground by attacking the FBI's handling of trace evidence. FBI forensic scientist Frederic Whitehurst, a highly vocal critic of his employers, said he could not be sure that ammonium nitrate was the basis of the bomb. British explosives expert Dr. John Lloyd agreed that FBI procedures for processing evidence were "not satisfactory."

To conclude what was a surprisingly brief defense, attorney Jones played a tape of Michael Fortier joking to his brother about all the media attention he had received. "Talk about a career! I can spin a fable," Fortier was heard to say. "I can talk all day!"

In his instructions to the jury, Judge Matsch cautioned them to "disregard anything you have heard, seen, or read outside this courtroom," and to return a verdict solely based on the evidence presented.

On June 2, 1997, after four days of deliberation, the jury convicted Timothy McVeigh of all charges. At the penalty phase of the trial the jury sentenced him to death. While McVeigh prepared his appeal, Nichols awaited trial for his alleged involvement in the bombing.

—Colin Evans

Suggestions for Further Reading:

Annin, Peter. "Selling Out a Soulmate." *Newsweek* (November 25, 1996): 34.

Hackworth, David and Peter Annin. "The Suspect Speaks Out." *Newsweek* (July 3, 1995): 23.

Padilla, Lana. *By Blood Betrayed: My Life With Terry Nichols and Timothy McVeigh.* New York: Harper Paperbacks, 1995.

Ross, Ryan. "A McVeigh Acquittal?" *The National Law Journal* (March 24, 1997): 1.

Stickney, Brandon M. *"All American Monster:" The Unauthorized Biography of Timothy McVeigh.* New York: Prometheus Books, 1996.

Toobin, Jeffrey. "Victim Power." *The New Yorker* (March 24, 1997): 40–43.